Readings in

STATE & LOCAL PUBLIC FINANCE

Readings in

STATE & LOCAL PUBLIC FINANCE

Edited by Dick Netzer and
Matthew P. Drennan

Copyright © Dick Netzer and Matthew P. Drennan, 1997

First published 1997

2 4 6 8 10 9 7 5 3 1

Blackwell Publishers Ltd
108 Cowley Road
Oxford OX4 1JF
UK

Blackwell Publishers Inc
238 Main Street
Cambridge, Massachusetts 02142,
USA

All rights reserved. Except for the quotation of short passages for the purposes of criticism and review, no part of this publication may be reproduced, stored in a retrieval system, or transmitted, in any form or by any means, electronic, mechanical, photocopying, recording or otherwise, without the prior permission of the publisher.

Except in the United States of America, this book is sold subject to the condition that it shall not, by way of trade or otherwise, be lent, resold, hired out, or otherwise circulated without the publisher's prior consent in any form of binding or cover other than that in which it is published and without a similar condition including this condition being imposed on the subsequent purchaser.

Library of Congress Cataloging-in-Publication Data
Netzer, Dick
    Readings in state and local public finance / Dick Netzer and Matthew P. Drennan.
    p.   cm.
    Includes index.
    ISBN 1-55786-713-5 (alk. paper)
    1. Finance, Public – United States – States.   2. Local finance – United
States.   3. State-local relations – United States.   4. Intergovernmental fiscal
relations – United States.   I. Drennan, Matthew P., 1937-•• . II. Title.
HJ275.N379   1997
336.73 – dc20

                                                                96-16614
                                                                CIP

British Library Cataloging in Publication Data

A CIP catalogue record for this book is available from the British Library.

Commissioning Editor: Rolf Janke
Desk Editor: Linda Auld
Production Manager/Controller: Rhona Richard
Text Designer: Lisa Parker

Typeset in 10 on 12 pt Plantin
by Best-set Typesetter Ltd, Hong Kong
Printed in Great Britain by Hartnolls, Bodmin, Ltd.

This book is printed on acid-free paper.

Contents

List of Contributors

William J. Baumol, Department of Economics, New York University, and Professor Emeritus, Princeton University.

James M. Buchanan, University Professor, Virginia Polytechnic Institute and State University, Blacksburg, Virginia.

Paul N. Courant, Department of Economics, University of Michigan, Ann Arbor, Michigan.

Matthew P. Drennan, Department of City and Regional Planning, Cornell University, Ithaca, New York.

Edward N. Gramlich, Department of Economics, University of Michigan, Ann Arbor, Michigan.

James Heilbrun, Department of Economics, Fordham University, The Bronx, New York.

Helen F. Ladd, Sanford Institute of Public Policy, Duke University, Durham, North Carolina.

Charles E. McLure, Jr, The Hoover Institution, Stanford University, Stanford, California.

Peter M. Mieszkowski, Department of Economics, Rice University, Houston, Texas.

John L. Mikesell, School of Public and Environmental Affairs, Indiana University, Bloomington, Indiana.

Richard A. Musgrave and Peggy B. Musgrave, Department of Economics, University of California, Santa Cruz.

Dick Netzer, Wagner Graduate School of Public Service, New York University.

James M. Poterba, Department of Economics, Massachusetts Institute of Technology, Cambridge, Massachusetts.

Robert D. Reischauer, The Brookings Institution, Washington, DC.

Andrew Reschovsky, LaFollette Institute of Public Affairs, University of Wisconsin, Madison, Wisconsin.

Daniel L. Rubinfeld, Department of Economics, University of California, Berkeley.

John J. Siegfried, Department of Economics, Vanderbilt University, Nashville, Tennessee.

Adam Smith (1723–90), Scottish philosopher and economist, author of *Inquiry into the Nature and Causes of the Wealth of Nations* (1776).

Paul A. Smith, Department of Economics, Vanderbilt University, Nashville, Tennessee.

Wilbur Thompson, Professor Emeritus, Wayne State University, Detroit, Michigan.

Charles M. Tiebout, Professor of Economics, University of Washington, at his death in 1965.

John Yinger, Department of Economics, Syracuse University, Syracuse, New York.

Dennis Zimmerman, Congressional Research Service, Library of Congress, Washington, DC.

George R. Zodrow, Department of Economics, Rice University, Houston, Texas.

Preface

Any textbook on the economics of public finance that is aimed at an American audience – unless it is resolutely and entirely theoretical – will devote a good deal of its space to state and local government public finance. After all, the real world to which the study of public finance is to be applied is one in which there is a lot of state and local finance. State and local governments in the United States raise about 45 percent of total public sector revenues, and both their revenue and expenditure practices and institutional arrangements are extremely diverse, across and even within states. So, to give little or no attention to state and local finance is ignore much of what American students see around them, and much of the reason why most are studying public finance – to understand the policy applications.

Moreover, the study of state and local finance provides a logical basis for attention to issues of public economics that are not at the core of the study of central government finance. One is fiscal federalism, the nature and extent of fiscal decision-making by sub-national governments and the fiscal relations among the levels of government, a public finance topic that has received systematic scrutiny from American and Canadian economists throughout this century, but from few others until recent years. Another such set of issues concerns fiscal instruments that are of considerable intellectual importance, but little used by central governments, notably the property tax and user charges.

The increasing openness of national economies to the world economy has called into question the traditional closed-economy assumptions used in the analysis of central government finances, in particular the presumption that cross-national tax differentials have little or no impact on the location of economic activity. However, in the study of state and local finance, the open-economy case has been, correctly, the standard one for many years. It is accepted that fiscal differentials affect the location of economic activity – the trick is to measure the effects – and that location patterns in turn can affect fiscal variables. No systematic treatment of state and local finance will fail to deal with this set of issues.

The two authors have taught public finance and urban economics to graduate students in urban planning, public policy and public management for some years. We each teach a course in state and local public finance. Until a few years ago, there was no textbook for such a course that was remotely satisfactory. In 1988, the first edition of Ronald C. Fisher's *State and Local Public Finance* was published by Scott Foresman, and a revised edition by Irwin in 1995. This book of readings is designed to accompany Fisher's excellent book, and its organization roughly follows that of the first edition of the Fisher book.

Naturally, the chapters in this book reflect our own teaching experience and preferences and the backgrounds of our students. While a few were undergraduate economics majors, most had minimal undergraduate exposure to economics in general and public finance in particular. All take a masters-level course in microeconomics and many take a masters-level course in public economics or public finance as well, before enrolling in our state and local public finance courses. Few are mathematically sophisticated, but none should be innumerate by this stage, or unable to decipher the limited math in these selections.

We think that the readings will be useful and accessible to masters-level students in economics *per se* and (with suitable course preparation) other fields as well. But the principal target audience, other than our own students, consists of undergraduates who are economics majors or who are in public-policy concentrations.

Any book of readings is intended, by its compilers, to replace the packets of journal articles and book chapters – "instant readers" – manufactured at your campus reprographics shop at the beginning of each term, and promptly discarded at the term's end. We hope this book will be more convenient, coherent and longer-lasting, as well as fair to the original authors, to whom we are most grateful.

Matthew Drennan
Dick Netzer

Acknowledgments

The authors and publishers wish to thank the copyright holders for permission to reprint the following copyrighted articles.

1   James M. Buchanan, "Public Finance and Public Choice," *National Tax Journal*, 28 (December 1975), pp. 383–94. Copyright 1975 by National Tax Association. Reprinted by permission.

2   Charles M. Tiebout, "A Pure Theory of Local Expenditures," *Journal of Political Economy*, 64 (February 1956), pp. 416–24. Reprinted by permission of The University of Chicago Press.

3   Richard A. Musgrave and Peggy B. Musgrave, "Principles of Multiunit Finance" from *Public Finance in Theory and Practice*, pp. 445–56. Copyright 1989. Reprinted by permission of McGraw-Hill, Inc.

4   James M. Buchanan, "Who Should Distribute What in a Federal System?" from *Redistribution Through Public Choice*, edited by Hochman and Peterson, pp. 22–42. New York: Columbia University Press. Copyright 1974 by James M. Buchanan. Reprinted by permission of the author.

5   Edward M. Gramlich, "The Economics of Fiscal Federalism and Its Reform" from *The Changing Face of Fiscal Federalism*, edited by Swartz and Peck, pp. 152–74. Copyright 1990. Reprinted by permission of M. E. Sharpe, Inc., Armonk, NY.

6   Adam Smith, "Of Taxes," from *The Wealth of Nations*, (1776), pp. 777–79 in Modern Library Edition, 1937.

7   Peter M. Mieszkowski, "Tax Incidence Theory: The Effects of Taxes on the Distribution of Income," *Journal of Economic Literature*, 7 (1969), pp. 1103–124. Reprinted by permission of American Economic Association.

8   George R. Zodrow and Peter Mieszkowski, "The Incidence of the Property Tax: The Benefit Views Versus the New View," from *Local Provision of Public Services*, edited by George R. Zodrow, pp. 109–29. Copyright 1983 by Academic Press, Inc. Reprinted by permission of the authors and Academic Press, Inc.

9   James Heilbrun, "Who Bears the Burden of the Property Tax?" *The Proceedings of the Academy of Political Science*, 35 (1983), pp. 57–71. Reprinted by permission of the author and The Academy of Political Science.

10   Dick Netzer, "Property Taxes: Their Past, Present, and Future Place in Government Finance" from *Urban Finance Under Siege*, pp. 51–78. Copyright 1993. Reprinted by permission of M. E. Sharpe, Inc., Armonk, NY.

11   James M. Poterba, "Lifetime Incidence and the Distributional Burden of Excise Taxes," *American Economic Review Papers and Proceedings*, 79 (May 1989), pp. 325–30. Reprinted by permission of the author and American Economic Association.

12   John J. Siegfried and Paul A. Smith, "The Distributional Effects of a Sales Tax on Services," *National Tax Journal*, 44 (1991), pp. 41–53. Copyright 1991 by National Tax Association. Reprinted by permission.

13   John L. Mikesell, "Fiscal Effects of Differences in Sales Tax Coverage: Revenue Elasticity, Stability and Reliance." *The Proceedings of the Eighty-Fourth Annual Conference*, edited by National Tax Association and Tax Institute of America, pp. 50–7. Copyright 1991 by National Tax Association. Reprinted by permission.

14   Charles E. McLure, Jr., "The State Corporate Income Tax: Lambs in Wolves' Clothing" from *The Economics of Taxation*, edited by Aaron and Boskin, pp. 327–96. Reprinted by permission of the authors, editors, and The Brookings Institution, publisher.

15   Dick Netzer, "Differences in Reliance on User Charges by American State and Local Governments," *Public Finance Quarterly*, 20 (1992), pp. 499–511. Reprinted by permission of Sage Publications, Inc.

16   Paul N. Courant and Daniel L. Rubinfeld, "Tax Reform: Implications for the State-Local Public Sector," *Journal of Economic Perspectives*, 1 (Summer 1987), pp. 87–100. Reprinted by permission of the authors and American Economic Association.

17   Dennis Zimmerman, *The Private Use of Tax-Exempt Bonds*, pp. 83–111. Copyright 1991. Reprinted by permission of The Urban Institute Press.

18   Dick Netzer, "State Tax Policy and Economic Development: What

should Governors Do When Economists Tell Them Nothing Works?" *New York Affairs*, 9 (1986), pp. 19–36. Reprinted by permission of the author.

19   William Baumol, "Macroeconomics of Unbalanced Growth: The Anatomy of Urban Crisis," *American Economic Review*, LVII:3 (1967). Reprinted by permission of the author and American Economic Association.

20   Wilbur Thompson, "The City as a Distorted Price System," *Psychology Today*. Copyright 1968 by Sussex Publishers, Inc. Reprinted with permission of *Psychology Today* Magazine.

21   Matthew P. Drennan, "The Present and Future Fiscal Problems of the Two New Yorks: What Happened This Time," *Public Budgeting and Finance*, 14:2 (Summer 1994). Reprinted by permission of Transaction Publishers.

22   Helen F. Ladd, "Big City Finances in the New Era of Fiscal Federalism," from *The Changing Face of Fiscal Federalism*, edited by Swartz and Peck, pp. 107–37. Copyright 1990. Reprinted by permission of M. E. Sharpe, Inc., Armonk, NY.

23   Andrew Reschovsky, "Are City Fiscal Crises on the Horizon?" from *Urban Finance Under Siege*, pp. 107–37. Copyright 1993. Reprinted by permission of M. E. Sharpe, Inc., Armonk, NY.

24   Robert D. Reischauer, "The Rise and Fall of National Urban Policy: The Fiscal Dimension" from *The Future of National Urban Policy*, edited by M. Kaplan and F. James, pp. 225–34. Copyright 1990. Reprinted by permission of Duke University Press.

25   John Yinger and Helen F. Ladd, "The Determinants of State Assistance to Central Cities," *National Tax Journal*, 42:4, pp. 413–28. Copyright 1989 by National Tax Association. Reprinted by permission.

26   Dick Netzer, "National Assistance to Urban Areas in the United States" from *Urban Change in the United States and Western Europe*, edited by A. Summers, P. Cheshire, and L. Senn, pp. 465–91. Copyright 1993. Reprinted by permission of The Urban Institute Press.

Part I
Public Choice and Fiscal Federalism

Introduction to Part I

Every sub-field of a discipline has an intellectual justification for its existence. In the case of state and local public finance, a federal system with three tiers of government, all of which have taxing and spending power, provides the justification. For public finance, one central question is: in a market economy, what is the role of the public sector? For the sub-field of state and local public finance, the central question is: in a national market economy, what are the roles of each of the three levels of government? That question is prior to others and it is the question addressed by fiscal federalism.

That sorting out of roles among levels of government requires economic criteria, and the criteria are efficiency and equity. A unique characteristic of state and local public finance is that considerations of efficiency and equity in taxing and spending by governments inexorably lead into spatial or geographic economic issues. Taxes imposed by subnational governments can have location effects on firms and households which have efficiency implications. Expenditures by sub-national governments may produce benefits which "spill over" into other jurisdictions, thus raising issues of efficiency and equity. So state and local public finance is necessarily linked with regional and urban economics, in which questions of household and firm location in space are central. It is no coincidence that many of the economists whose state or local public finance writings are included in this collection are also urban or regional economists.

Another characteristic which distinguishes state and local finance from public finance is that the cast of economic actors is not one government and many firms and households but rather many governments, some overlapping, plus many firms and households. Quite naturally then the theory of public choice is used to analyze the actions of governments as rational optimizers subject to constraints. So the other theme in Part I is public choice.

There are five pieces in Part I. The two by Buchanan are explicitly about public choice. The article by Tiebout predates the intellectual ascendance of public choice theory but it is a remarkable piece of analysis in which the local government actors behave as public choice theorists would have them behave. Tiebout introduces the idea of competition among local governments and he was probably the first to do so. As with most truly great ideas, it seems obvious once it is stated. The theoretical piece by Musgrave and Musgrave answers the central question of state and local public finance posed above, namely in a three-tiered system of government how should the functions of the public sector be sorted out among the different levels of government? The Gramlich article actually shows how the functions of government are distributed in dollar terms among federal, state, and local governments in the United States.

Introduction to Chapter 1

In this article Buchanan traces the transformation of public finance theory after World War II. Leaving aside the Keynsian macroeconomic theory, there were initially two strains of public finance theory: positive and normative. Positive theory focused on the issues of tax shifting and tax incidence in a partial equilibrium analysis in order to evaluate the efficiency effects of a tax. Normative theory focused upon independently derived "principles of taxation" which included the principles of vertical equity and horizontal equity as normative yardsticks for evaluating the equity of any tax. From a modern perspective, both of those strains seem peculiarly narrow. They only focus on the tax or revenue side of public finance, ignoring the expenditure side and the public choices about tax levels, tax instruments, expenditure levels and expenditure allocation. Buchanan and other public choice theorists argued that politicians and bureaucrats do not select tax instruments, tax rates, expenditure levels and expenditure allocations independently. They are jointly determined in a complex and messy process. Public choice theory unravels the complexity through an application of microeconomic concepts of self-interest and maximizing behavior of consumers and producers to the agents in the public sector. Before public choice theory, the naive sub-text of much public finance writing was: if politicians would only listen to us, they would understand the efficiency loss of this tax (positive analysis), or the inequity of that tax (normative analysis), and then do the right thing. But doing the right thing implies the selfless and earnest pursuit of the public interest by public officials, which is quite different from the assumed behavior of *homo economicus*.

Buchanan's article traces the path of public finance theory as it was profoundly changed, for the better, by its collision with public choice theory. Rather than wreckage, what has emerged, he argues, is "public economics," a much broader field. Buchanan was awarded the Nobel Memorial prize in economics in 1986 for his contributions in public choice theory.

Public Finance and Public Choice

James M. Buchanan*

Abstract

Public finance has undergone major transformation since World War II. This paper surveys this transformation, particularly from a public-choice perspective. Post-Marshallian public finance had two major gaps: the expenditure side of the fiscal account, and the public decision-making process. Both of these gaps have been partially filled, although much discussion of policy continues to take place in a now-outmoded setting. Social security financing is used as an illustration of the separate methodologies.

"Public finance," as a quasi-independent subdiscipline in the American academic setting, has been substantially transformed in the thirty years after the ending of World War II, although heritages of the earlier tradition remain, and notably as these affect practical political discussion. From its relatively minor role as one among many fields of applied microeconomic theory – akin to industrial organization, agricultural economics, or labor economics – public finance emerged to become "public economics," which, at least conceptually, is on all fours with "private economics," or, more familiarly, the economics of the private sector. If relative weights are assigned in accordance with relative shares in GNP, "public economics" promises, for better or for worse, to grow still more important in decades ahead.

My purpose in this survey paper is to discuss this transformation of "public finance" from a public choice perspective, one that reflects my own methodological presuppositions. I shall not include reference to the "theory of fiscal policy," which bloomed brightly in the early post-Keynesian environment only to fade somewhat in the face of political

* Center for Study of Public Choice, Virginia Polytechnic Institute and State University. I am indebted to my colleague, Gordon Tullock, for helpful comments.

realities. The macroeconomic policy emphasis derived from Keynes is a causal element in the relative growth of the governmental sector and, as such, one source for the increasing attention to "public economics." But there is no direct relationship between this emphasis and the fundamental paradigm shift that is the primary subject of my treatment in this paper.

Post-Marshallian Public Finance

I can commence by describing the content of "public finance" in post-Marshallian economics, as limited to English-language discourse. Positive analysis was restricted almost exclusively to theories of tax shifting and incidence. And, indeed, as Marshall himself explicitly recognized,[1] the theory of tax shifting becomes almost the ideal instrument for applying the principles of competitive price theory. Comparative statics offered a plausible predictive framework for analyzing tax alternatives. Within limits, and for certain simple forms, the economist could confidently predict the effects of a tax on the behavior of persons and firms in the private economy, and, through this, on the aggregate effects on such variables as relative prices, outputs, profits, and industry structure in particular sectors. For this strictly positive analysis, which could also yield empirically-refutable propositions, the economist had no reason to inquire about the political purpose of taxation, no reason to introduce external evaluation of alternative tax instruments.[2] This subarea of public finance, which is essentially applied price theory, has continued to be developed through more sophisticated technical analysis which has now moved beyond the Marshallian partial-equilibrium framework to general-equilibrium settings, including extensions to open economies. No basic paradigm shift has occurred here, but this subarea has necessarily been relegated to a relatively less important role in the larger theory of "public economics" which has emerged.

Alongside this post-Marshallian positive theory of taxation, there existed what I may label as the post-Pigovian normative "theory" of taxation. This unfortunate and somewhat confused discussion stemmed vaguely from the utilitarian philosophical tradition and had as its purpose the derivation of normative "principles" for taxation. The most sophisticated of these, developed most fully by Pigou,[3] was that of "equimarginal sacrifice," which was based on a simplistic application of the calculus in a context of assumed interpersonal utility comparability. This normative discussion was much less rigorous intellectually than the positive analysis of tax incidence, and, indeed, the normative treatment of taxation among English-language economists was almost a half-century out of phase from the more sophisticated discussion on the European continent. The normative "principles" of taxation that were seriously discussed may seem bizarre when viewed in a modern post-Wicksellian or public-choice paradigm. But these "principles" assume continuing practical importance as soon as we recognize that observed institutions of taxation find their intellectual origins in these norms, which also, to a large extent, inform modern political criticisms of tax structures, along with continuing calls for tax reform. For example, the most vocal modern advocates for reform, notably Joseph Pechman and Stanley Surrey, base their arguments on presupposed norms for the distribution of tax shares, norms which are derived independently.

There are two related, but quite distinct, gaps in the normative public finance of the post-Marshallian, post-Pigovian tradition. There is, first, the long-continued, and methodologically inadmissible, neglect of the expenditure side of the fiscal account. The necessary interdependence between the two sides of the public-sector budget must be incorporated into any analysis, even if the purpose is to lay down ideal standards drawn from some external scale of evaluation. Secondly, there is the neglect or oversight of the collective decision structure itself. The shift in paradigm which has occurred involves the incorporation of both these elements.

The European Theory of the Public Economy

Following the central contributions of the early 1870s, the economic theory of markets assumed a unified structure. The simultaneous operation of productive input and final product markets accomplished evaluative allocative, and distributive functions. The European attempts to extend this aesthetically satisfying logic structure to "explain" the operation of a public as well as a private sector now seem to represent predicted increments in scientific progress. The puzzle in intellectual history does not concern these efforts; the puzzle lies in the long-continued failure of English-language economists to make comparable extensions of their basic framework or to acknowledge an interest in the continental efforts.

As early as the 1880s, Mazzola, Pantaleoni, Sax, and De Viti De Marco made rudimentary efforts to analyze the public economy within an exchange framework. Sax and Mazzola discussed the demand side of public goods by identifying collective as distinct from private wants. Pantaleoni extended the marginal calculus to apply to the legislator who makes choices for both sides of the budget. De Viti De Marco explicitly constructed a model in which the consumers and the suppliers-producers of public goods make up the same community of persons.[4]

The most sophisticated contribution was made by Knut Wicksell in 1896.[5] He explicitly identified the fundamental methodological error in the then-orthodox approach, and he combined positive criticism with normative suggestions for reform. Wicksell recognized the necessity of bridging the two sides of the fiscal account, and he noted the indeterminacy of any proposed normative principles that were limited to tax-side considerations. More importantly, Wicksell admonished economists for their failure to recognize the elementary fact that collective or public-sector decisions emerge from a political process rather than from the mind of some benevolent despot. His suggestions for reform were concentrated on the institutional structure for fiscal decision-making, on the institutions of "public choice." The unanimity rule was presented as the normative benchmark for efficiency in public-sector decisions, and a clear distinction was made between those situations where genuine gains-from-trade might emerge and those which involve zero-sum transfers. Despite the essentially normative setting for Wicksell's reform suggestions, the groundwork was laid for subsequent positive analysis of political decision structures.

Subsequent to these early contributions, work was carried forward, notably in Sweden and in Italy. Erik Lindahl's attempt to examine more closely the relationship between standard efficiency norms and the political bargaining process offered a halfway house between Wicksell's seminal effort and modern analyses of public finance in democratic process.[6] Lindahl's proposed solution, the set of so-called Lindahl tax-prices, or Lindahl equilibrium, has come to occupy the attention of several sophisticated analysts who have attempted to extend the modern theory of general competitive equilibrium to include the public sector.[7]

The Italian tradition, following the early work by Pantaleoni and De Viti De Marco, was characterized by an emphasis on the necessary political assumptions required for either a positive or normative theory of the public economy. The Italians devoted much more attention to the implications of nondemocratic political structures for the emergence and viability of fiscal institutions, on both the tax and the expenditure sides, than did their continental conterparts. These aspects, in particular, become helpful in the analysis of the supply institutions of the public economy, an analysis that remains in its formative stages. Apart from these substantive contributions, Barone and Einaudi, in particular, were sharply critical of the naive utilitarian framework of the English-language normative discussion of tax principles.

The Transitional Setting

The substantial transformation in American public finance did not spring full blown from some rediscovery of the European theory of the public economy, although it might legitimately be claimed that this theory, appropriately modernized, was sufficiently complete to have allowed for this as an alternative intellectual scenario. The transformation emerged slowly and in bits and pieces, influenced by several sources other than the strict analysis of the continental scholars. Precedence in presenting the central ideas of what he called the "voluntary exchange" theory of the public economy belongs to R. A. Musgrave who, in his first paper, offered a highly critical evaluation.[8] However, Musgrave's analysis was not such as to attract independent and complementary attention to the body of work discussed. And Howard Bowen, in his original and much-neglected 1943 paper, showed no signs of having been influenced by the European analysis.[9] Bowen's paper combined two elements that were to be more fully developed later as separate strands of analysis, the theory of demand for public goods and the theory of voting. Although flawed by minor analytical errors, Bowen's paper was perhaps neglected because it was too much in advance of the analytical mind-set of its time. My own efforts, in my first substantive paper in 1949, one that was also largely neglected, were concentrated in a methodological critique of the post-Pigovian normative framework. In this, I was influenced almost exclusively by a fortuitous discovery of Wicksell's basic work.[10]

Developments of note came rapidly during the 1950s and 1960s. These may be discussed initially in terms of their independent emergence, with little or no direct interconnection one with another and with the corpus of public finance theory. In what follows, I shall discuss briefly four lines of inquiry or analysis: (1) the theory of demand for public goods; (2) the theory of voting; (3) the theory of constitutions; and (4) the theory of supply of public goods. In each of these, I shall attempt to distinguish positive and normative elements of analysis. After these strands are separately examined, I shall try to integrate these as they relate to modern public finance theory. Finally, I shall use a single example to demonstrate how the modern public-choice paradigm in public finance differs from the post-Marshallian, post-Pigovian paradigm which, although conceptually flawed, continues to inform some policy discussion.

The Theory of Demand for Public Goods

As previously noted, there were two gaping holes in the pre-World War II normative analysis of taxation, a neglect of the expenditure side of the fisc and a neglect of the collective decision process. Modern public finance theory incorporates both of these elements, but they remain conceptually distinct and they were, to an extent, independently developed. An internally consistent set of principles for efficiency in the public economy may be elaborated with no attention to the political decision process. This was the framework for Paul A. Samuelson's seminal paper in 1954,[11] in which he laid down the necessary marginal conditions for allocative efficiency in the provision of public or collective goods to a defined community of persons. Samuelson extended the accepted norms of theoretical welfare economics from the private to the public sector of the economy, using individual evaluations as the building blocks. Perhaps his primary contribution lay in his rigorous definition of a "collective consumption" good, embodying both complete nonexclusion and complete efficiency from joint consumption, the two acknowledged attributes of "publicness." Early criticisms of the polarity features of Samuelson's classification were, in my view, misplaced because this initial step seemed essential before the further elaboration of taxonomic detail could take place.

The Samuelson mathematical formulation of the conditions for public sector efficiency did not contain a comparable normative theory of the distribution of tax shares. Income-effect feedbacks of tax-shares on individual evaluations of collective-consumption goods were incorporated in the analysis, but the tax-share distribution itself was arbitrarily selected by resort to a social welfare function. This normative construction is quite different from that which is required for the definition of the allocative conditions for efficiency. Within Samuelson's conceptual framework, resort to the social welfare function for tax-share distribution was an implication of his unwillingness to close the model in a manner analogous to the exchange process of the private sector. He did not conceive the fiscal process as one of "exchange," even at the level of abstraction that the formal statement of the necessary marginal conditions for efficiency required.

Nonetheless, the Samuelson analysis can readily be interpreted positively, which necessarily implies an exchange framework. In this case, the necessary marginal conditions for allocative efficiency become conditions that must be satisfied for an equilibrium solution to the complex "trades" that the political or collective choice process embody. One such solution is the Lindahl equilibrium, which meets the basic Samuelson requirements, although it is arbitrarily restricted in its distribution of tax shares inframarginally. The more general Wicksellian approach makes no attempt to specify particulars of an equilibrium. Instead this approach concentrates on the institutions for "trading," and implicitly defines efficiency to be present when all gains-from-trade are exhausted. In a setting of zero transactions costs, including bargaining costs, unanimous agreement will be possible on both marginal tax-share distribution and on the quantity of public goods to be purchased, although the position of agreement will not be unique and its characteristics will depend strictly on the path of adjustment.[12]

The Theory of Voting

The Wicksellian paradigm for fiscal exchange, ideally operative under a decision rule of unanimity without prior constraints on tax-share distribution, places the "public economy," methodologically, on all fours with the "private economy." The importance of this Wicksellian benchmark or starting point for the developments that have followed cannot be overestimated. But the world is not characterized by zero transactions costs, and these loom especially large when many persons must agree on single outcomes. The two-party dimensionality of private-goods training, especially as constrained by the presence of numerous alternatives on both sides of exchange, allows the costs of reaching agreement to be minimized, and, because of this, to be largely neglected in analysis. No such neglect is possible for the complex trading process that politics embodies. Necessary departures from the idealized models become much more apparent, and enter analysis even at the level of institutional design. Wicksell himself recognized, in his discussion of qualified majorities, that the ideal political constitution could not embody a strict unanimity rule, even for the legislative assembly. And, of course, historical experience in democratic politics includes a wide variety of voting and decision rules-institutions, only a few of which approximate the unanimity-rule benchmark.

Once the ideal is abandoned, as necessary for the operation of political decision structures in accordance with more inclusive efficiency norms, what rules for collective choice should be chosen? Before this question can be addressed at all, there must be positive analysis of alternative voting rules and institutions. From a current vantage point, in 1975, it seems almost incredible that American public-finance economists completely ignored analysis of voting rules prior to World War II, even though they must have recognized that fiscal outcomes were related directly to the political structure. Aside from the paper by Bowen, noted above, there was no discussion of voting rules prior to the seminal contributions of Duncan Black and Kenneth Arrow, in the late 1940s and 1950s.[13]

Black's earlier efforts had been strictly within the post-Marshallian tradition of incidence analysis.[14] His reading of the Italian works was an acknowledged source of his shift of emphasis to an analysis of voting rules. Black's major work was largely confined to an analysis of majority rule as a means of reaching decisions in collectivities. In his analysis, which included the discovery of precursory work by Borda, Condorcet, and most notably, Lewis Carroll, Black noted the possibility of the majority cycle, but his emphasis was placed on the workability of majority rule rather than the reverse. This emphasis led him to examine restrictions on preference domains that might produce unique majority solutions. He discovered that if all individual preferences could be arrayed over alternatives so as to appear as single-peaked, the majority-rule outcome will always be that which meets the preferences of the median voter in the group. This median-voter construction was to emerge as an important tool in the public-choice theory of the 1960s, and especially in public-finance applications. Single-peakedness in preferences becomes a plausible assumption for many fiscal decision variables.

Kenneth Arrow's work exerted far more influence on economic theory generally than did the closely-related work of Duncan Black. However, the specific effects on public-finance theory are less direct. Arrow placed his analysis squarely in the social welfare function discussion that had emerged from theoretical welfare economics, and he demonstrated that there existed no collective decision rule for amalgamating individual preference orderings into a consistent social or collective ordering. This rigorous generalization of the cyclical-majority phenomenon, along with Arrow's emphasis on the impossibility of generating a social ordering meeting plausible criteria, had the effect of putting the analysis of collective decision rules directly on the research agenda of modern economists. Faced with results that they did not welcome, and with their somewhat naive political presuppositions exposed, economists were slowly forced to acknowledge that social welfare functions do not exist. Only two alternatives remained open. They might become public-choice analysts and examine the operation of alternative decision rules, no one of which is ideal. Or, they might revert to the normative post-Pigovian stance which requires the explicit introduction of private and personal value standards that bear little or no relationship to the decision-determining institutions of the real world.

The Theory of Constitutions (Voting Rules)

Once positive analysis of the operation of alternative voting rules was placed on the agenda, along with the Wicksellian recognition that no nonunanimity rule could guarantee efficiency in the narrow sense, the way was open for the development of a theory of constitutions, based on an analysis of the choice among a set of less-than-ideal institutions for generating collective outcomes. This was the setting for *The Calculus of Consent*, which I jointly authored with Gordon Tullock, and which was published in 1962.[15] This work carried forward the analysis of alternative decision rules, with emphasis on the political external diseconomies inherent in any less-than-unanimity rule and on the prospects for vote trading as a means of mitigating the results of differential preference intensities. Our central purpose was, however, that of analyzing the choice among collective decision rules, and of deriving criteria for "optimality" at this constitutional level. Our procedure was to shift backwards, to the level of choice among rules, the Wicksellian unanimity or general consensus criterion. The transactions costs barrier to general agreement may be fully acknowledged at the stage of reaching collective decision on specific fiscal (tax and spending) variables. But this need not imply that persons cannot agree generally on the rules or institutions under which subsequent decisions will be made, whether these be majority rule or otherwise. To the extent that individuals' future preference positions are uncertain and unpredictable under subsequent operation of the rules to be chosen, they may be led to agree on the basis of general criteria that are unrelated to economic position.[16]

Our analysis was positive in the conceptual sense, and we made few suggestions for institutional reform. Nonetheless, our discussion was admittedly informed by a vision or model of constitutional process that embodied individualistic norms. This vision was, in its turn, used to "explain" features of existing political structures, features which might, with comparable methodological legitimacy, be "explained" with alternative normative models. Our analysis of constitutions was not sufficiently complete to allow us to discriminate among widely varying explanations for the emergence and existence of observed political institutions.

The Theory of Supply of Public Goods

This gap in our analysis of the choice among constitutional rules stemmed, in part, from our neglect of the supply side of the public-goods exchange process. The theory of demand for public goods, the theory of voting, and the theory of voting rules – each of these lines of inquiry initially embodied the implicit assumption that individual demands for public goods, once these could be articulated and combined through some collective-choice process, would be efficiently and automatically met. It was as if the alternatives for public choice were assumed to be available independently from some external source; there was no problem concerning the behavior of the suppliers or producers. Governments are, however, staffed by persons who make up only a subset of the community, and any full analysis of fiscal exchange must allow for differences between the behavior of persons in producing-supplying roles and in consuming-demanding roles.

Precursors of supply-side analysis can, of course, be found in the Italian theory of public finance in the nondemocratic or monopolistic state. Models of this political structure were developed in some detail, models in which some ruling group or class collects taxes from the masses who are ruled and utilizes the proceeds to its own maximum advantage. But attention was also paid to the feedback or reaction effects on the behavior of those who were exploited. At the turn of this century, Puviani developed the interesting and still-relevant concept of "fiscal illusion," which he applied to both the tax and the spending side of the fiscal account.[17] However, aside from my own summary of some of these elements, which I did not sufficiently stress, there was no direct linkage between the monopolistic-state analysis of the Italians and the emergence of the modern theory of public-goods supply.

American scholars have operated within a continuing presupposition that their own political institutions remain basically democratic. Even within this structure, however, the demanders and the suppliers of public services must occupy differing economic roles, and the interests of the two groups need not coincide. The seminal American contribution toward the ultimate development of a theory of public-goods supply was made by Anthony Downs. In his book, *An Economic Theory of Democracy*, published in 1957, Downs presented a model of political party competition analogous to the competition among firms in an industry, with vote-maximization serving as the analogue to profit maximization.[18] The predictive power of Downs' model was sharply criticized by William Riker, who introduced a game-theoretic framework to suggest that political parties, even when treated as monolithic decision-taking entities, will seek to organize winning coalitions of minimal size rather than to maximize vote totals.[19] For purposes of this survey, however, the central contribution of these efforts lay not in the explanatory potential of the models themselves but rather in the fundamentally different setting offered for viewing the activities of governments. Once governments came to be viewed as collectivities of persons who were themselves maximizers – whether these persons be party organizers, political representatives, elected officials, judges, or bureaucrats – the emerging paradigm involving the passively-efficient supply response to public-goods demanders was dramatically changed in course.

The Downs-Riker models of interparty competition, which have been carried forward and elaborated in more sophisticated forms by other scholars, were paralleled by the development of a theory of bureaucratic behavior, both at the level of the individual member of the hierarchy and that of the agency or bureau itself. Gordon Tullock introduced the maximizing bureaucrat, who responds to his own career incentives like everyone else, and analyzed the implications of this behavioral model for the control problem faced by those at the top of the hierarchy.[20] Even on the extreme assumption that the agency head desires to meet the demands for public goods efficiently, Tullock's analysis suggests that this objective could not be met in organizations requiring personal services.[21]

William Niskanen boldly challenged the orthodox conception of bureaucracy by modeling separate bureaus as budget-maximizing units.[22] The implication of his polar model is that bureaus, acting as monopoly suppliers of public services, and possessing an ability to control the elected political leaders through a complex and interested committee structure in the legislature, fully drain off the potential taxpayers' surplus that might be possible from public-goods provision. Once again, it is not the particular predictive power of Niskanen's analysis that is relevant for our purposes; what is relevant is the contrasting setting within which the operations of agencies and bureaus may be examined.

The theory of public-goods supply has not been fully developed, and efforts to integrate this theory, as it exists, with the theory of demand, including the theory of voting and voting rules, have only commenced.[23]

The Expanded Domain for Positive Analysis

In the four preceding sections of this paper, I have briefly summarized four main lines of inquiry or analysis that have combined to form the still-emerging subdiscipline of "public choice."[24] My purpose has not been that of describing the substantive content of these separate but closely related bodies of analysis; this would have required further treatment of the specific modern contributions in each area.[25] My purpose has been the more restricted one of sketching with a broad brush the separated strands of public choice theory in order to suggest how these have combined to effect the transformation in public finance theory during the decades after World War II.

Methodologically, the central element in this transformation is the dramatic expansion in the scope or domain for positive economic analysis. The subject matter of public finance has shifted outward; the economist now has before him many more questions than his counterpart faced a half-century ago. This expansion in the set of opportunities for applying the economists' tools, both conceptual and empirical, may be discussed in terms of specific categories.

(1)   The Effects of Alternative Fiscal Institutions, Existing and Potential, on the Behavior of Persons and Groups in the Private Economy. As I have noted earlier, this is the only domain for positive economic analysis in post-Marshallian public finance. The results of the public-choice transformation have been to remove this still-important avenue for investigation from its place of exclusive dominance and to put it alongside other significant and equally legitimate applications of economic theory. This does not, of course, suggest that the theory of shifting and incidence, with expenditures added to taxes, has been reduced in absolute importance. The hard questions in incidence theory have not all been resolved, and these will, and should, continue to command the attention of economists.

(2)   The Effects of Alternative Fiscal Institutions, Existing and Potential, on the Behavior of Persons and Groups in the Public Economy, in Public Choice. In a relative sense, however, traditional incidence theory must be reduced in significance because other questions beckon. If the effects of a designated fiscal institution, say a specific excise tax, on the behavior of persons in private markets may be analyzed, what is to deter the intellectually curious and competent economist from examining the effects of this tax on the behavior of persons in "public markets"? If persons pay for public goods through such a tax, might they not be predicted to "purchase" differing quantities than they would do under alternative taxing schemes? Once such questions are raised, the need for answers along with the opportunities for research seem self-evident. An implicit assumption of invariance in fiscal choice over widely divergent institutional structures will simply not stand up to scrutiny.

The whole set of questions raised here stem from the "publicness" of the goods as these are demanded and consumed and as these are supplied through political or governmental institutions. Individuals do not pay "prices" for partitionable units of these goods. They pay "taxes," which are coercively imposed upon them through a political process, and this coercion is, in turn, made necessary by the "free rider" motivation inherent in general collective action. Few persons will voluntarily pay taxes if they expect to receive the benefits of generally-available public goods. But what quantity will persons, when they act collectively in public-choice capacities – as voters, actual or potential, as members of pressure groups, as elected politicians, as government employees – choose to provide and to finance? This choice depends on the bridge that is constructed between the benefits or spending side of the account and the costs or taxing side. Differing fiscal institutions influence the weighing of accounts. What are the implications for budgetary size if taxes are spread more generally than benefits? And vice versa? Quite apart from the "true" distribution of tax shares and benefit shares, the "perceived" distribution matters. Fiscal perception becomes an important and relevant area for positive analysis. By necessity, "fiscal psychology" merges with fiscal economics. The research potential for positive analysis seems almost unlimited, and relatively little has been done.[26]

(3)   The Effects of Alternative Political or Collective-Choice Institutions, Existing or Potential, on the Behavior of Persons and Groups in the Public Economy, in Public Choice. A closely related, but somewhat different agenda for positive analysis and one that is more central to what might be called "public-choice theory," as such, involves the choice-making institutions themselves, as these may be predicted to generate fiscal outcomes. This is the public-finance application of the theory of voting, summarized above.

What budget characteristics can be predicted to emerge under simple majority rule? What differences in size and composition might emerge when general-fund budgeting is compared with separate-purpose budgeting, with earmarked tax revenues? What differences in the willingness to issue public debt can be predicted when the effective voting franchise is expanded from local property owners to all members of the local electorate? What will be the comparative levels of public outlay on, say, education, when these services are provided through a set of monopoly school districts and through the market response to educational vouchers provided directly to families? What are the effects of school-district consolidation on budget size? What are the effects of franchising bureaucrats on the level and growth of public spending?

These are only a few of the questions that have been, and are being, asked by those who approach public finance from the general public-choice paradigm. As these sample questions suggest, the domain for positive analysis here includes institutional analysis at a level where explanatory hypotheses are derived deductively from extract models, and also at a level where these hypotheses are tested empirically.[27]

(4)   Analysis of the Behavior of Persons and Groups in the Collective Constitutional Choice Among Fiscal Institutions. This area for positive analysis is the direct public-finance application of the theory of constitutions, previously summarized. As they may be historically observed, certain fiscal institutions take on quasi-permanent or constitutional characteristics. For example, basic changes in the tax code are discussed as if these are expected to endure over a sequence of periods. Neither taxes nor spending programs are chosen *carte blanche* at the onset of each budgetary period. Indeed one of the primary difficulties in reducing the explosive rate of increase in federal outlays in the 1970s is alleged to be the high proportion of uncontrollable spending in the budget. Once the quasi-permanence of institutions is recognized, the analysis of fiscal choices is modified. Differing criteria for choice must be invoked, criteria which may be less directly identified with self-interest of persons and groups. The models which are designed to derive hypotheses become different in this context.

I shall not attempt to suggest research opportunities that exist in this extension of positive analysis, one that is perhaps less fully developed than the others. My point of emphasis in this listing is to indicate that at least three areas of actual and potential positive analysis now exist over and beyond the severely limited post-Marshallian field of shifting and incidence.

The Modified Domain for Normative Discussion

The domain for positive analysis in public finance has been greatly expanded. But what about the domain for normative discourse? So long as the economist proffers his advice as if some benevolent despot is listening to him, he may be much more willing to devote his efforts to persuasion based ultimately on his own personal, private scale of values, even if the argument is couched in quasi-philosophical terms. Despite Wicksell's clearly stated admonitions in 1896, this remains the setting for much of the normative discourse in public finance, even in 1975. If the public-choice paradigm is accepted, however, the assumption of the benevolent despot cannot accompany normative advice, even at the subconscious level. The economist must recognize that collective outcomes emerge from a complex political process in which there are many participants. Almost by necessity, he will be less willing to devote time and effort to persuasion here, even though his own personal convictions about ideal outcomes may be equally as strong as in the despotic paradigm. It should come as no surprise, therefore, that modern public finance is less characterized by normative advice concerning the "best tax" program and more concerned about predicting the effects of alternatives.

The public-choice paradigm does, however, allow for a parallel expansion in the normative realm of discourse. Once it is recognized that fiscal decisions emerge from a complex collective choice process, the economist may concentrate his normative advice on "improvements" in the process itself. He may, for example, say that direct taxation is preferred to indirect taxation, not because direct taxation is likely to be more or less progressive, but simply because direct taxation leads to a more rational choice calculus among voters and their representatives than indirect taxation. Similarly, he may suggest that withholding, as an institution, tends to reduce the rationality of the choice process because it tends to make the taxpayer somewhat less conscious of his costs. These are admittedly normative suggestions that emerge from a paradigm of the political world, one that embodies the democratic-individualistic standard that persons should get what they want so long as each person counts for one. This seems a more secure normative base than that which lays down criteria for choosing among separate persons and groups, in which one man must somehow count for more than another. These comments may, however, reflect my own personal normative biases and I shall not pursue them further in this survey.[28]

An Example: The Provision and Financing of Social Security

I shall conclude this paper by a brief discussion of a single example, one that is of current importance. I shall demonstrate that the transformation in public finance produced by the public-choice paradigm allows different and additional questions to be asked. In the process, policy discussion must be improved, independently of this or that economist's preferred set of norms.

Consider, first, the application of the post-Marshallian theory of shifting and incidence, along with the post-Pigovian norms for taxation. The social security system is financed by payroll taxes, and the shifting and incidence of these, both the employees' and the employers' shares, are proper subjects for inquiry. These taxes are, when viewed in isolation, "regressive," and this characteristic leads the post-Pigovian to denounce it on normative grounds.

Strictly speaking, this is all that public finance might have contributed to the policy discussion in the methodological mind-set prior to World War II. Straightforward extension of analysis to the other side of the budget, quite apart from the public-choice extension, would have allowed positive analysis of the effects of public pension commitments on the rate of private saving in the economy.[29] Similarly, the effects of the public pensions on retirement behavior might be analyzed. The normative strictures arising from the regressivity of the payroll tax might also have been tempered somewhat by the extension of simple incidence analysis to the benefits side, where progressive elements are significant.

The public-choice paradigm draws direct attention to the bridge between the tax and the spending side of the account. As noted earlier, this bridge is influenced by perception, and even within the confines of payroll-tax analysis, the effects of the structural features on voter-politician attitudes become important. In the first place, the public-choice analyst would note the earmarking features of the financing; payroll taxes are earmarked for the social security trust fund account. This fact, in itself, strongly suggests that these taxes are viewed differently from other general-fund revenue sources. Secondly, the public-choice theorist would suggest that the withholding feature of the employee share makes payroll taxes less influential on behavior than orthodox incidence analysis might imply. More importantly, he would suggest that the employers' share of payroll taxes, even if ultimately paid by the workers, may not directly influence the attitude of workers. The suppliers of pensions, the authorities of the social security administration, may have been privately quite rational in their early arguments for making this employee-employer tax separation.

The public-choice theorist would try to predict the effects of a proposed shift of the financing of social security, in whole or in part, from earmarked payroll taxes to the sources of general-fund financing, notably to personal and corporate income taxation. Rudimentary analysis would suggest that the direct linkage between tax and benefit sides would be severed by such a change, and that both sets of institutions would be subjected to wholly different political criteria. Could pensions be kept related to earnings (and contributions) under such a change? Could a means test for benefits be avoided? Even if the existing structure does not reflect the operation of genuine "insurance" principles, taxpayer-voters, and their political representatives, may acquiesce in its continuance so long as the intergeneration transfer process which the system seems to embody is plausibly acceptable. Young workers who enter the system may not worry when they are told that the present value of tax obligations exceeds manyfold the present value of future pension benefits provided that they continue to expect that future legislatures will insure a reasonable rate of return on their total contributions. Such continuing support may depend, however, on maintaining the separation of the system from the government's general fiscal account and also on insuring that severe limits are imposed on departures from earnings-related benefits.

The public-choice economist, to the extent that he is willing to make suggestions for reform, seems more likely to suggest institutional adjustments designed to insure against the "political bankruptcy" of the system than he is to suggest that the payroll taxes be made more progressive. Whether the discussion takes the form of positive analysis or normative statement, the public-choice economist looks on the fiscal process as a complex exchange, which must involve two sides of the account simultaneously. Those who pay the ultimate costs of public goods need not, of course, be identical with those who enjoy the ultimate benefits. But, in democracies, the intersection between these two sets must be large, especially when the budgets are considered in composite totals and over a sequence of time periods. Regardless of political structure, the proportion of the community's membership that shares in genuine "fiscal surplus" is related inversely to the size and coercive power of the government's police force.

Notes

1   "... there is scarcely any economic principle which cannot be aptly illustrated by a discussion of the shifting of the effects of some tax. ..." Alfred Marshall, *Principles of Economics*, 8th Ed. (London: Macmillan, 1930), p. 413.

2   Beginning attempts were made to extend an analogous positive analysis to the expenditure side of the fiscal ledger (see for example, Earl Rolph, "A Theory of Excise Subsidies," *American Economic Review*, 42 (September 1952), 515–27). But, as noted, the predominant emphasis was, and remains, on taxation.

3   A. C. Pigou, *A Study in Public Finance* (London: Macmillan, 1928).

4   For a brief summary discussion of the early continental contributions, see Richard A. Musgrave, *The Theory of Public Finance* (New York: McGraw-Hill, 1959), pages 68–80. For a more extended discussion which is, however, concentrated largely on the Italian contributions, see my, *Fiscal Theory and Political Economy* (Chapel Hill: University of North Carolina Press, 1960), pp. 24–74. For translations of most of the important contributions here, see *Classics in the Theory of Public Finance*, ed. by R. A. Musgrave and A. T. Peacock (London: Macmillan, 1958).

5   Knut Wicksell, *Finanztheoretische Untersuchungen* (Jena: Gustav Fischer, 1896). Major portions of this are translated and included in *Classics in the Theory of Public Finance, op. cit.*

6   Erik Lindahl, *Die Gerechtigkeit der Besteuerung* (Lund, 1919), A central portion of this has been translated and is included in *Classics in the Theory of Public Finance, op. cit.*

7   See, for example, Duncan Foley, "Lindahl's Solution and the Core of an Economy With Public Goods," *Econometrica*, 38 (January 1970), 66–72; T. Bergstrom, "A Scandinavian Consensus Solution for Efficient Income Distribution Among Nonmalevolent Consumers," *Journal of Economic Theory*, 4 (December 1970), 383–98; D. J. Roberts, "The Lindahl Solution for Economies With Public Goods," *Journal of Public Economics*, 3 (February 1974), 23–42.

8   R. A. Musgrave, "The Voluntary Exchange Theory of Public Economy," *Quarterly Journal of Economics*, 53 (February 1938), 213–37.

9   Howard R. Bowen, "The Interpretation of Voting in the Allocation of Resources," *Quarterly Journal of Economics*, 58 (November 1943), 27–48.

10   See, my, "The Pure Theory of Government Finance: A Suggested Approach," *Journal of Political Economy*, LVII (December 1949), 496–505, reprinted in my *Fiscal Theory and Political Economy*, *op. cit.*, pp. 8–23.

   I may add here an autobiographical note concerning this discovery that will be familiar to my students and former colleagues but which may deserve wider dissemination. In the summer of 1948, having finished my dissertation and fresh from having passed the German-language requirement, I spent some weeks wandering about the stacks in Harper Memorial Library at the University of Chicago. By chance, I picked up Wicksell's *Finanztheoretische Untersuchungen*, a book that had never been assigned or even so much as mentioned in my graduate courses, and, as I later ascertained, one of the very few copies in the United States. Quite literally, this book was responsible directly for the paradigm shift that I experienced.

11   Paul A. Samuelson, "The Pure Theory of Public Expenditure," *Review of Economics and Statistics*, XXXVI (November 1954), 387–9.

12   My book, *The Demand and Supply of Public Goods* (Chicago: Rand McNally, 1968), develops public-goods theory in the Wicksellian framework. The book's title is somewhat misleading; the analysis is almost exclusively devoted to the demand side; the supply side is neglected.

13   Their first papers appeared in 1948 and 1950, respectively. See, Duncan Black, "On the Rationale of Group Decision Making," *Journal of Political Economy*, LVI (February 1948), 23–34; Kenneth Arrow, "A Difficulty in the Concept of Social Welfare," *Journal of Political Economy*, LVIII (August 1950), 328–46.

   These were followed by their full-length works. See Kenneth J. Arrow, *Social Choice and Individual Values* (New York: Wiley, 1951); Duncan Black, *The Theory of Committees and Elections* (Cambridge: Cambridge University Press, 1958).

14   Duncan Black, *The Incidence of Income Taxes* (London: Macmillan, 1939).

15   James M. Buchanan and Gordon Tullock, *The Calculus of Consent* (Ann Arbor: University of Michigan Press, 1962).

16   The setting for our analysis has an obvious affinity to that which is used by John Rawls in his derivation of the principles of justice, a setting that has been made familiar since the publication of Rawls' treatise [John Rawls, *A Theory of Justice* (Cambridge: Harvard University Press, 1971)]. Although

our approach was independently developed, Rawls had employed the "veil of ignorance" in earlier papers in the 1950s. Other scholars have used essentially similar devices as a means of moving from the individual's short-term interest to what may be called, in one sense, the "public interest."

17   "For a summary discussion of Puviani's contribution, along with a treatment of fiscal illusion more generally, see my, *Public Finance in Democratic Process* (Chapel Hill: University of North Carolina Press, 1967), Chapter 10. An English translation of Puviani's basic work will be published in 1976, under the supervision of my colleague, Charles Goetz.

18.   Anthony Downs, *An Economic Theory of Democracy* (New York: Harper, 1957).

19   William H. Riker, *The Theory of Political Coalitions* (New Haven: Yale University Press, 1962).

20   Gordon Tullock, *The Politics of Bureaucracy* (Washington: Public Affairs Press, 1965).

21   Tullock's analysis of the bureaucrat represents perhaps the closest that public-choice analysis comes to a parallel, but quite different, development in modern economic theory, that which has been called the theory of property rights. The latter work of Alchian, McKean, Demsetz, Pejovich, and others, has been concentrated on predicting the effects of differing reward-penalty structures, as defined in terms of rights to property, on individual behavior. For a summary, see, Eirik Furubotn and Svetozar Pejovich, "Property Rights and Economic Theory: A Survey of Recent Literature," *Journal of Economic Literature*, X (December 1972), 1137–62.

22   William Niskanen, *Bureaucracy and Representative Government* (Chicago: Aldine, 1971).

23   Two introductory attempts should be noted: Albert Breton, *The Economic Theory of Representative Government* (Chicago: Aldine, 1974); and Randall Bartlett, *Economic Foundations of Political Power* (New York: Free Press, 1973).

24   Because of space limits, I have not included a fifth line of analysis, that of locational public choice, or "voting with the feet," which has exerted a significant influence on public finance theory, especially as applied to local governments and to the interrelations among levels of government. The seminal paper which stimulated much of this analysis was that by Charles Tiebout, "The Pure Theory of Local Expenditure," *Journal of Political Economy*, LXIV (October 1956), 416–24.

25   For a more extensive survey paper which does have this as its objective, see, Dennis Mueller, "Public Choice: A Survey," *Journal of Economic Literature* (forthcoming).

26   My own book, *Public Finance in Democratic Process* (1967), *op. cit.*, is largely a call for such research, along with a summary of some initial efforts, and the provision of a suggested research agenda.

27   Some of the early applications are contained in the separate studies included in the volume, *Theory of Public Choice*, edited by James M. Buchanan and Robert Tollison (Ann Arbor: University of Michigan Press, 1972). For a

textbook in public economics that consistently employs a fiscal choice paradigm, see Richard E. Wagner, *The Public Economy* (Chicago: Markham, 1973).

28   My methodological views are developed in several of my books, some of which have been noted. In my most recent book, I try to examine some of the problems that emerge in trying to define "an individual," including the preliminary distribution of rights. See, my, *The Limits of Liberty: Between Anarchy and Leviathan* (Chicago: University of Chicago Press, 1975).

29   Cf. Martin Feldstein, "Social Security, Induced Retirement, and Aggregate Capital Accumulation," *Journal of Political Economy*, 82 (September/October, 1974), 905–26.

Introduction to Chapter 2

In a famous article published in 1954 ("The Pure Theory of Public Expenditures") the economist Paul Samuelson demonstrated that the production of public goods is necessarily inefficient because consumers have an incentive to conceal their true preferences. That follows from the nature of public goods as nonexclusive and nonexhaustive. Tiebout does not dispute that argument for public goods provided by the federal government. But for local public goods such as police and fire protection, streets, schools, and parks, there are as many different providers as there are local governments in a metropolitan area. Tiebout develops a model in which rational households reveal their preferences for local public goods by their choice of residence in a community. Each community offers a different bundle of local public goods and taxes and so selection of a community reflects optimizing behavior by households with respect to their demand for local public goods. The Tiebout hypothesis, as it has been named, spun off a cottage industry of empirical studies which have mostly supported his theory. The Tiebout article may well be the most cited work in all of the local public-finance literature.

2

A Pure Theory of Local Expenditures*

Charles M. Tiebout[1]

One of the most important recent developments in the area of "applied economic theory" has been the work of Musgrave and Samuelson in public finance theory.[2] The two writers agree on what is probably the major point under investigation, namely, that no "market type" solution exists to determine the level of expenditures on public goods. Seemingly, we are faced with the problem of having a rather large portion of our national income allocated in a "nonoptimal" way when compared with the private sector.

This discussion will show that the Musgrave-Samuelson analysis, which is valid for federal expenditures, need not apply to local expenditures. The plan of the discussion is first to restate the assumptions made by Musgrave and Samuelson and the central problems with which they deal. After looking at a key difference between the federal versus local cases, I shall present a simple model. This model yields a solution for the level of expenditures for local public goods which reflects the preferences of the population more adequately than they can be reflected at the national level. The assumptions of the model will then be relaxed to see what implications are involved. Finally, policy considerations will be discussed.

The Theoretical Issue

Samuelson has defined public goods as "*collective consumption goods (X_n + 1, . . . , X_n + n) which all enjoy in common in the sense that each individual's consumption of such a good leads to no subtraction from*

* Reprinted from *Journal of Political Economy*, Vol. 64 (October, 1956), by permission of The University of Chicago Press. Copyright 1956 by The University of Chicago.

any other individual's consumption of that good, so that $X_n + j = X_n^i + j$ simultaneously for each and every ith individual and each collective good."[3] While definitions are a matter of choice, it is worth noting that "consumption" has a much broader meaning here than in the usual sense of the term. Not only does it imply that the act of consumption by one person does not dimish the opportunities for consumption by another but it also allows this consumption to be in another form. For example, while the residents of a new government housing project are made better off, benefits also accrue to other residents of the community in the form of the external economies of slum clearance.[4] Thus many goods that appear to lack the attributes of public goods may properly be considered public if consumption is defined to include these external economies.[5]

A definition alternative to Samuelson's might be simply that a public good is one which should be produced, but for which there is no feasible method of charging the consumers. This is less elegant, but has the advantage that it allows for the objections of Enke and Margolis.[6] This definition, unfortunately, does not remove any of the problems faced by Musgrave and Samuelson.

The core problem with which both Musgrave and Samuelson deal concerns the mechanism by which consumer-voters register their preferences for public goods. The consumer is, in a sense, surrounded by a government whose objective it is to ascertain his wants for public goods and tax him accordingly. To use Alchian's term, the government's revenue-expenditure pattern for goods and services is expected to "adapt to" consumers' preferences.[7] Both Musgrave and Samuelson have shown that, in the vertically additive nature of voluntary demand curves, this problem has only a conceptual solution. If all consumer-voters could somehow be forced to reveal their true preferences for public goods, then the amount of such goods to be produced and the appropriate benefits tax could be determined.[8] As things now stand, there is no mechanism to force the consumer-voter to state his true preferences; in fact, the "rational" consumer will understate his preferences and hope to enjoy the goods while avoiding the tax.

The current method of solving this problem operates, unsatisfactorily, through the political mechanism. The expenditure wants of a "typical voter" are somehow pictured. This objective on the expenditure side is then combined with an ability-to-pay principle on the revenue side, giving us our current budget. Yet in terms of a satisfactory theory of public finance, it would be desirable (1) to force the voter to reveal his preferences; (2) to be able to satisfy them in the same sense that a private goods market does; and (3) to tax him accordingly. The question arises whether there is any set of social institutions by which this goal can be approximated.

Local Expenditures

Musgrave and Samuelson implicitly assume that expenditures are handled at the central government level. However, the provision of such governmental services as police and fire protection, education, hospitals, and courts does not necessarily involve federal activity.[9] Many of these goods are provided by local governments. It is worthwhile to look briefly at the magnitude of these expenditures.[10]

Historically, local expenditures have exceeded those of the federal government. The thirties were the first peacetime years in which federal expenditures began to pull away from local expenditures. Even during the fiscal year 1954, federal expenditures on *goods and services exclusive of defense* amounted only to some 15 billions of dollars, while local expenditures during this same period amounted to some 17 billions of dollars. There is no need to quibble over which comparisons are relevant. The important point is that the often-neglected local expenditures are significant and, when viewed in terms of expenditures on goods and services only, take on even more significance. Hence an important question arises whether at this level of government any mechanism operates to insure that expenditures on these public goods approximate the proper level.

Consider for a moment the case of the city resident about to move to the suburbs. What variables will influence his choice of a municipality? If he has children, a high level of expenditures on schools may be important. Another person may prefer a community with a municipal golf course. The availability and quality of such facilities and services as beaches, parks, police protection, roads, and parking facilities will enter into the decision-making process. Of course, non-economic variables will also be considered, but this is of no concern at this point.

The consumer-voter may be viewed as picking that community which best satisfies his preference pattern for public goods. This is a major difference between central and local provision of public goods. At the central level the preferences of the consumer-voter are given, and the government tries to adjust to the pattern of these preferences, whereas at the local level various governments have their revenue and expenditure patterns more or less set.[11] Given these revenue and expenditure patterns, the consumer-voter moves to that community whose local government best satisfies his set of preferences. The greater the number of communities and the greater the variance among them, the closer the consumer will come to fully realizing his preference position.[12]

A Local Government Model

The implications of the preceding argument may be shown by postulating an extreme model. Here the following assumptions are made:

1   Consumer-voters are fully mobile and will move to that community where their preference patterns, which are set, are best satisfied.

2   Consumer-voters are assumed to have full knowledge of differences among revenue and expenditure patterns and to react to these differences.

3   There are a large number of communities in which the consumer-voters may choose to live.

4   Restrictions due to employment opportunities are not considered. It may be assumed that all persons are living on dividend income.

5   The public services supplied exhibit no external economies or diseconomies between communities.

Assumptions 6 and 7 to follow are less familiar and require brief explanations:

6   For every pattern of community services set by, say, a city manager who follows the preferences of the older residents of the community, there is an optimal community size. This optimum is defined in terms of the number of residents for which this bundle of services can be produced at the lowest average cost. This, of course, is closely analogous to the low point of a firm's average cost curve. Such a cost function implies that some factor or resource is fixed. If this were not so, there would be no logical reason to limit community size, given the preference patterns. In the same sense that the average cost curve has a minimum for one firm but can be reproduced by another there is seemingly no reason why a duplicate community cannot exist. The assumption that some factor is fixed explains why it is not possible for the community in question to double its size by growth. The factor may be the limited land area of a suburban community, combined with a set of zoning laws against apartment buildings. It may be the local beach, whose capacity is limited. Anything of this nature will provide a restraint.

In order to see how this restraint works, let us consider the beach problem. Suppose the preference patterns of the community are such that the optimum size population is 13,000. Within this set of preferences there is a certain demand per family for beach space. This demand is such that at 13,000 population a 500-yard beach is required. If the actual length of the beach is, say, 600 yards, then it is not possible to realize this preference pattern with twice the optimum population, since there would be too little beach space by 400 yards.

The assumption of a fixed factor is necessary, as will be shown later, in order to get a determinate number of communities. It also has the advantage of introducing a realistic restraint into the model.

7   The last assumption is that communities below the optimum size seek to attract new residents to lower average costs. Those above optimum size do just the opposite. Those at an optimum try to keep their populations constant.

This assumption needs to be amplified. Clearly, communities below the optimum size, through chambers of commerce or other agencies, seek to attract new residents. This is best exemplified by the housing developments in some suburban areas, such as Park Forest in the Chicago area and Levittown in the New York area, which need to reach an optimum size. The same is true of communities that try to attract manufacturing industries by setting up certain facilities and getting an optimum number of firms to move into the industrially zoned area.

The case of the city that is too large and tries to get rid of residents is more difficult to imagine. No alderman in his right political mind would ever admit that the city is too big. Nevertheless, economic forces are at work to push people out of it. Every resident who moves to the suburbs to find better schools, more parks, and so forth, is reacting, in part, against the pattern the city has to offer.

The case of the community which is at the optimum size and tries to remain so is not hard to visualize. Again proper zoning laws, implicit agreements among realtors, and the like are sufficient to keep the population stable.

Except when this system is in equilibrium, there will be a subset of consumer-voters who are discontented with the patterns of their community. Another set will be satisfied. Given the assumption about mobility and the other assumptions listed previously, movement will take place out of the communities of greater than optimal size into the communities of less than optimal size. The consumer-voter moves to the community that satisfies his preference pattern.

The act of moving or failing to move is crucial. Moving or failing to move replaces the usual market test of willingness to buy a good and reveals the consumer-voter's demand for public goods. Thus each locality has a revenue and expenditure pattern that reflects the desires of its residents. The next step is to see what this implies for the allocation of public goods at the local level.

Each city manager now has a certain demand for n local public goods. In supplying these goods, he and $m - 1$ other city managers may be considered as going to a national market and bidding for the appropriate units of service of each kind: so many units of police for the ith community; twice that number for the *j*th community; and so on. The demand on the public goods market for each of the *n* commodities will be the sum of the demands of the *m* communities. In the limit, as shown in a less realistic model to be developed later, this total demand will approximate the demand that represents the true preferences of the consumer-voters – that is, the demand they would reveal, if they were forced, somehow, to state their true preferences.[13] In this model there is no attempt on the part of local governments to "adapt to" the preferences of consumer-voters. Instead, those local governments that attract the optimum number of residents may be viewed as being "adopted by" the economic system.[14]

A Comparison Model

It is interesting to contrast the results of the preceding model with those of an even more severe model in order to see how these results differ from the normal market result. It is convenient to look at this severe model by developing its private-market counterpart. First assume that there are no public goods, only private ones. The preferences for these goods can be expressed as one of *n* patterns. Let a law be passed that all persons living in any one of the communities shall spend their money in the particular pattern described for that community by law. Given our earlier assumptions 1 through 5, it follows that, if the consumers move to the community whose law happens to fit their preference pattern, they will be at their optimum. The *n* communities, in turn, will then send their buyers to markets to purchase the goods for the consumer-voters in their community. Since this is simply a lumping together of all similar tastes for the purpose of making joint purchases, the allocation of resources will be the same as it would be if normal market forces operated. This conceptual experiment is the equivalent of substituting the city manager for the broker or middleman.

Now turn the argument around and consider only public goods. Assume with Musgrave that the costs of additional services are constant.[15] Further, assume that a doubling of the population means doubling the amount of services required. Let the number of communities be infinite and let each announce a different pattern of expenditures on public goods. Define an empty community as one that fails to satisfy anybody's preference pattern. Given these assumptions, including the earlier assumptions 1 through 5, the consumer-voters will move to that community which *exactly* satisfies their preferences. This must be true, since a one-person community is allowed. The sum of the demands of the *n* communities reflects the demand for local public services. In this model the demand is exactly the same as it would be if it were determined by normal market forces.

However, this severe model does not make much sense. The number of communities is indeterminate. There is no reason why the number of communities will not be equal to the population, since each voter can find the one that exactly fits his preferences. Unless some sociological variable is introduced, this may reduce the solution of the problem of allocating public goods to the trite one of making each person his own municipal government. Hence this model is not even a first approximation of reality. It is presented to show the assumptions needed in a model of local government expenditures, which yields the same optimal allocation that a private market would.

The Local Government Model Re-examined

The first model, described by the first five assumptions together with assumptions 6 and 7, falls short of this optimum. An example will serve to show why this is the case.

Let us return to the community with the 500-yard beach. By assumption, its optimum population was set at 13,000, given its preference patterns. Suppose that some people in addition to the optimal 13,000 would choose this community if it were available. Since they cannot move into this area, they must accept the next best substitute.[16] If a perfect substitute is found, no problem exists. If one is not found, then the failure to reach the optimal preference position and the substitution of a lower position becomes a matter of degree. In so far as there are a number of communities with similar revenue and expenditure patterns, the solution will approximate the ideal "market" solution.

Two related points need to be mentioned to show the allocative results of this model: (1) changes in the costs of one of the public services will cause changes in the quantity produced; (2) the costs of moving from community to community should be recognized. Both points can be illustrated in one example.

Suppose lifeguards throughout the country organize and succeed in raising their wages. Total taxes in communities with beaches will rise. Now residents who are largely indifferent to beaches will be forced to make a decision. Is the saving of this added tax worth the cost of moving to a community with little or no beach? Obviously, this decision depends on many factors, among which the availability of and proximity to a suitable substitute community is important. If enough people leave communities with beaches and move to communities without beaches, the total amount of lifeguard services used will fall. These models then, unlike their private-market counterpart, have mobility as a cost of registering demand. The higher this cost, *ceteris paribus*, the less optimal the allocation of resources.

This distinction should not be blown out of proportion. Actually, the cost of registering demand comes through the introduction of space into the economy. Yet space affects the allocation not only of resources supplied by local governments but of those supplied by the private market as well. Every time available resources or production techniques change, a new location becomes optimal for the firm. Indeed, the very concept of the shopping trip shows that the consumer does pay a cost to register his demand for private goods. In fact, Koopmans has stated that the nature of the assignment problem is such that in a space economy with transport costs there is *no* general equilibrium solution as set by market forces.[17]

Thus the problems stated by this model are not unique; they have their counterpart in the private market. We are maximizing within the framework of the resources available. If production functions show constant returns to scale with generally diminishing factor returns, and if indifference curves are regularly convex, an optimal solution is possible. On the production side it is assumed that communities are forced to keep production costs at a minimum either through the efficiency of city managers or through competition from other communities.[18] Given this, on the demand side we may note with Samuelson that "each individual, in seeking as a competitive buyer to get to the highest level of indifference subject to given prices and *tax*, would be led as if by an Invisible Hand to the grand solution of the social maximum position."[19] Just as the consumer may be visualized as walking to a private market place to buy his goods, the prices of which are set, we place him in the position of walking to a community where the prices (taxes) of community services are set. Both trips take the consumer to market. There is no way in which the consumer can avoid revealing his preferences in a spatial economy. Spatial mobility provides the local public-goods counterpart to the private market's shopping trip.

External Economies and Mobility

Relaxing assumption 5 has some interesting implications. There are obvious external economies and diseconomies between communities. My community is better off if its neighbor sprays trees to prevent Dutch elm disease. On the other hand, my community is worse off if the neighboring community has inadequate law enforcement.

In cases in which the external economies and diseconomies are of sufficient importance, some form of integration may be indicated.[20] Not all aspects of law enforcement are adequately handled at the local level. The function of the sheriff, state police, and the FBI – as contrasted with the local police – may be cited as resulting from a need for integration. In real life the diseconomies are minimized in so far as communities reflecting the same socioeconomic preferences are contiguous. Suburban agglomerations such as Westchester, the North Shore, and the Main Line are, in part, evidence of these external economies and diseconomies.

Assumptions 1 and 2 should be checked against reality. Consumer-voters do not have perfect knowledge and set preferences, nor are they perfectly mobile. The question is how do people actually react in choosing a community. There has been very little empirical study of the motivations of people in choosing a community. Such studies as have been undertaken seem to indicate a surprising awareness of differing revenue and expenditure patterns.[21] The general disdain with which proposals to integrate municipalities are met seems to reflect, in part, the fear that local revenue-expenditure patterns will be lost as communities are merged into a metropolitan area.

Policy Implications

The preceding analysis has policy implications for municipal integration, provision for mobility, and set local revenue and expenditure patterns. These implications are worth brief consideration.

On the usual economic welfare grounds, municipal integration is justified only if more of any service is forthcoming at the same total cost and without reduction of any other service. A general reduction of costs along with a reduction in one or more of the services provided cannot be justified on economic grounds unless the social welfare function is known. For example, those who argue for a metropolitan police force instead of local police cannot prove their case on purely economic grounds.[22] If one of the communities were to receive less police protection after integration than it received before, integration could be objected to as a violation of consumers' choice.

Policies that promote residential mobility and increase the knowledge of the consumer-voter will improve the allocation of government expenditures in the same sense that mobility among jobs and knowledge relevant to the location of industry and labor improve the allocation of private resources.

Finally, we may raise the normative question whether local government *should*, to the extent possible, have a fixed revenue-expenditure pattern. In a large, dynamic metropolis this may be impossible. Perhaps it could more appropriately be considered by rural and suburban communities.

Conclusion

It is useful in closing to restate the problem as Samuelson sees it:

> *However, no decentralized pricing system can serve to determine optimally these levels of collective consumption.* Other kinds of "voting" or "signaling" would have to be tried. . . . Of course utopian voting and signaling schemes can be imagined. . . . The failure of market catallactics in no way denies the following truth: given sufficient knowledge the optimal decisions can always be found by scanning over all the attainable states of the world and selecting the one which according to the postulated ethical welfare function is best. The solution "exists"; the problem is how to "find" it.[23]

It is the contention of this article that, for a substantial portion of collective or public goods, this problem *does have* a conceptual solution. If consumer-voters are fully mobile, the appropriate local governments, whose revenue-expenditure patterns are set, are adopted by the consumer-voters. While the solution may not be perfect because of institutional rigidities, this does not invalidate its importance. The solution, like a general equilibrium solution for a private spatial economy, is the best that can be obtained given preferences and resource endowments.

Those who are tempted to compare this model with the competitive private model may be disappointed. Those who compare the reality described by this model with the reality of the competitive model – given the degree of monopoly, friction, and so forth – *may* find that local government represents a sector where the allocation of public goods (as a reflection of the preferences of the population) need not take a back seat to the private sector.

Notes

1   I am grateful for the comments of my colleagues Karl de Schweinitz, Robert Eisner, and Robert Strotz, and those of Martin Bailey, of The University of Chicago.
2   Richard A. Musgrave, "The Voluntary Exchange Theory of Public Economy," *Quarterly Journal of Economics*, LII (February, 1939), 213–17;

"A Multiple Theory of the Budget," paper read at the Econometric Society annual meeting (December, 1955); and his forthcoming book, *The Theory of Public Economy*; Paul A. Samuelson, "The Pure Theory of Public Expenditures," *Review of Economics and Statistics*, XXXVI, No. 4 (November, 1954), 387–9, and "Diagrammatic Exposition of a Pure Theory of Public Expenditures," *ibid.*, XXXVII, No. 4 (November, 1955), 350–6.

3   "The Pure Theory . . . ," *op. cit.*, p. 387.

4   Samuelson allows for this when he states that "one man's circus may be another man's poison," referring, of course, to public goods ("Diagrammatic Exposition . . . ," *op. cit.*, p. 351).

5   There seems to be a problem connected with the external-economies aspect of public goods. Surely a radio broadcast, like national defense, has the attribute that A's enjoyment leaves B no worse off; yet this does not imply that broadcasting should, in a normative sense, be a public good (the arbitrary manner in which the level of radio programs is determined aside). The difference between defense and broadcasting is subtle but important. In both cases there is a problem of determining the optimal level of outputs and the corresponding level of benefits taxes. In the broadcasting case, however, A may be quite willing to pay more taxes than B, even if both have the same "ability to pay" (assuming that the benefits are determinate). Defense is another question. Here A is not content that B should pay less. A makes the *social judgment* that B's preference *should* be the same. A's preference, expressed as an annual defense expenditure such as $42.7 billion and representing the majority view, thus determines the level of defense. Here the A's may feel that the B's *should pay* the same amount of benefits tax.

   If it is argued that this case is typical of public goods, then, once the level is somehow set, the voluntary exchange approach and the benefit theory associated with it do not make sense. If the preceding analysis is correct, we are now back in the area of equity in terms of ability to pay.

6   They argue that, for most of the goods supplied by governments, increased use by some consumer-voters leaves less available for other consumer-voters. Crowded highways and schools, as contrasted with national defense, may be cited as examples (see Stephen Enke, "More on the Misuse of Mathematics in Economics: A Rejoinder," *Review of Economics and Statistics*, XXXVII [May, 1955], 131–3; and Julius Margolis, "A Comment on the Pure Theory of Public Expenditure," *Review of Economics and Statistics*, XXXVII [November, 1955], 247–9).

7   Armen A. Alchian, "Uncertainty, Evolution and Economic Theory," *Journal of Political Economy*, LVIII (June, 1950), 211–21.

8   The term "benefits tax" is used in contrast, to the concept of taxation based on the "ability to pay," which really reduces to a notion that there is some "proper" distribution of income. Conceptually, this issue is separate from the problem of providing public goods and services (see Musgrave, "A Multiple Theory . . . ," *op. cit.*).

9   The discussion that follows applies to local governments. It will be apparent as the argument proceeds that it also applies, with less force, to state governments.

10 A question does arise as to just what are the proper expenditures to consider. Following Musgrave, I shall consider only expenditures on goods or services (his Branch I expenditures). Thus interest on the federal debt is not included. At the local level interest payments might be included, since they are considered payments for services currently used, such as those provided by roads and schools.

11 This is an assumption about reality. In the extreme model that follows the patterns are assumed to be absolutely fixed.

12 This is also true of many non-economic variables. Not only is the consumer-voter concerned with economic patterns, but he desires, for example, to associate with "nice" people. Again, the greater the number of communities, the closer he will come to satisfying his total preference function, which includes non-economic variables.

13 The word "approximate" is used in recognition of the limitations of this model, and the more severe model to be developed shortly, with respect to the cost of mobility. This issue will be discussed later.

14 See Alchian, *op. cit.*

15 Musgrave, "Voluntary Exchange . . . ," *op. cit.*

16 In the constant cost model with an infinite number of communities this problem does not arise, since the number of beaches can be doubled or a person can find another community that is a duplicate of his now filled first choice.

17 Tjalling Koopmans, "Mathematical Groundwork of Economic Optimization Theories," paper read at the annual meeting of the Econometric Society (December, 1954).

18 In this model and in reality, the city manager or elected official who is not able to keep his costs (taxes) low compared with those of similar communities will find himself out of a job. As an institutional observation, it may well be that city managers are under greater pressure to minimize costs than their private-market counterparts – firm managers. This follows from (1) the reluctance of the public to pay taxes and, what may be more important, (2) the fact that the costs of competitors – other communities – are a matter of public record and may easily be compared.

19 "The Pure Theory . . . ," *op. cit.*, p. 388. (Italics mine.)

20 I am grateful to Stanley Long and Donald Markwalder for suggesting this point.

21 See Wendell Bell, "Familism and Suburbanization: One Test of the Choice Hypothesis," a paper read at the annual meeting of the American Sociological Society, Washington, D.C., August, 1955. Forthcoming in *Rural Sociology*, December, 1956.

22 For example, in Cook County – the Chicago area – Sheriff Joseph Lohman argues for such a metropolitan police force.

23 "The Pure Theory . . . ," *op. cit.*, pp. 388–9.

Introduction to Chapter 3

This piece is a short chapter from the most widely used and long-lived textbook of public finance, now in its sixth edition. Public-finance and public-economics texts usually begin by stating that the three functions of government in the economy are allocation, distribution, and stabilization. In this chapter the authors lay out the economic principles for sorting out which level of government is most appropriate for which function from the perspective of economic efficiency. There is limited discussion of the distribution and stabilization functions because the economic arguments for assigning them solely to the central government are so simple, clear and compelling. The allocation function, however, has a varying spatial dimension tied to the nature of the good or service provided and its cost of production. If the benefits are local in their extent, then financing the benefits should be through local taxes and user charges. So the analysis of how the allocation function is sorted out among levels of government then leads into an analysis of appropriate tax instruments for different levels of government. The principles laid out in this chapter from Musgrave and Musgrave are central to the economics of state and local public finance. All of the articles in this book explicitly or implicitly invoke those principles, with the notable exception of chapter 4.

3

Principles of Multiunit Finance*

Richard A. Musgrave and Peggy B. Musgrave

So far, our discussion has been largely in terms of a fiscal system with a single level of government only. We must now allow for the fact that fiscal operations are typically carried out by many units of government or jurisdictions. In the United States, this multiple unit system includes the federal government, fifty state governments, the District of Columbia, and some 80,000 local jurisdictions. Canada, Australia, and West Germany are further illustrations of a three-tier arrangement, whereas the United Kingdom, Switzerland, and Holland operate with two tiers only – central and local. This multiunit fiscal structure, as it prevails in any particular country, reflects the historical forces of nation-making, wars, and geography. Typically, modern nations have not been formed as a free association of individuals but have emerged by a combination of pre-existing sovereign jurisdictions which then join into national units. In so doing, member jurisdictions (such as the colonies and then states in the United States) may retain certain fiscal prerogatives while surrendering others, thereby joining in a compact which determines the fiscal aspects of the federation.

Political history thus tells much in explaining the structure of fiscal arrangements in any one country, but not all. There are also good economic reasons why certain fiscal functions should be operated on a more centralized level while others should be decentralized. Historical influences aside, we may consider what spatial fiscal structuring would

* Reader's Guide: The principles of multiunit finance which are considered in this chapter may be viewed as an extension of our discussion of social goods. The problem is first dealt with in a setting where the spatial location of fiscal functions is determined by considerations of economic efficiency only. Based on the feature of spatial benefit limitation, this leads to important findings regarding the structure of the allocation function.

be desirable if the arrangement could be determined on the grounds of economic considerations only. Taking each of the three major functions – allocation, distribution, and stabilization – we will begin with this efficient setting as our basic model. In the following chapter [chapter 28 in the original book] we consider how the nature of fiscal arrangements changes in the context of a federation, thereby permitting us to place the current discussion of a "new federalism" into focus.

3.1   Spatial Dimension of Allocation Function

To focus on economic efficiency in the provision for public services, we assume that a group of people, having landed on a new planet, consider what spatial fiscal arrangements should be made. We also suppose that individuals will permit their location choices to be determined by fiscal considerations. The question is whether social goods and services should be provided on a centralized or a decentralized basis. If the latter, what spatial arrangement of fiscal organization is most efficient in rendering such public services? To begin with and to link up with our earlier discussion of the theory of social goods, we will assume that all publicly provided goods and services are pure social goods, i.e., they conform with the characteristic of nonrival consumption. Let us then ask why the efficient provision of such goods might call for a multiunit system of government.

Benefit regions

The crucial feature which was noted already in our discussion of social goods is that of spatial limitation of benefit incidence. Some social goods are such that the incidence of their benefits is nationwide (e.g., national defense, space exploration, cancer research, the Supreme Court) while others are geographically limited (e.g., a local fire engine or streetlight). Therefore, the members of the "group" who share in the benefits are limited to the residents of a particular geographic region.

Allocation theory as applied to the public sector has led us to the conclusion that public services should be provided and their costs shared in line with the preferences of the residents of the relevant benefit region. Moreover, given the fact that a political process is needed to secure preference revelation, it follows that particular services should be voted on and paid for by the residents of this region. In other words, services which are nationwide in their benefit incidence (such as national defense) should be provided for nationally, services with local benefits (e.g., streetlights) should be provided for by local units, still others (such as highways) should be provided for on a regional basis. Given the spatial characteristics of social goods, there is thus an a priori case for multiple jurisdictions. Each jurisdiction should provide services the benefits of which accrue within its boundaries, and it should use only such sources of finance as will internalize the costs. The spatially limited nature of benefit incidence thus calls for a fiscal structure composed of multiple service units, each covering a different-sized region within which the supply of a particular service is determined and financed. Even though some services call for nationwide, others for statewide, and still others for metropolitan-area-wide or local units, the argument so far does not call for an ordering of "higher-level" and "lower-level" governments. Rather, we are faced with coordinate units covering regions of different sizes.

Optimal fiscal community

The theory of multiunit finance must provide an answer to the question of what constitutes the optimum number of fiscal communities and the number of people within each community. To deal with this complex problem, we begin with a simple model which allows for one public service only, the benefit incidence of which is limited to all within a given geographical area but vanishes beyond it.[1] To simplify, we also assume that consumers have identical tastes and incomes, so that they agree on the desirability of social-goods provision. The crux of the problem is that the cost to each consumer will be less the larger the number of consumers who partake of the benefits. Since we postulate a pure social good so that the quality of service received per person is not affected by the number of participants, it follows that the efficient solution calls for all consumers to congregate in the same benefit area. The presence of savings from cost sharing due to large numbers leads to a single benefit area and, in fact, to a unitary structure of fiscal provision. There are, however, other considerations which may pull in an opposite direction, toward a multiunit solution. One must allow for the fact that people may dislike crowding. Even the number of angels that can dance on the head of a pin is limited. Thus the design of optimal community size must strike a balance between the advantage of sharing in the cost of a given level of public services and the disadvantages of crowding. To bring out the nature of the problem, we begin with two simplifying assumptions, i.e., that people are similar in their preferences and income and that public services are pure social goods, subject only to spatial limitation of benefits.[2]

Optimal community size   The first step, involving the choice of *optimum size for a given service level*, is shown in figure 3.1. We assume that a given

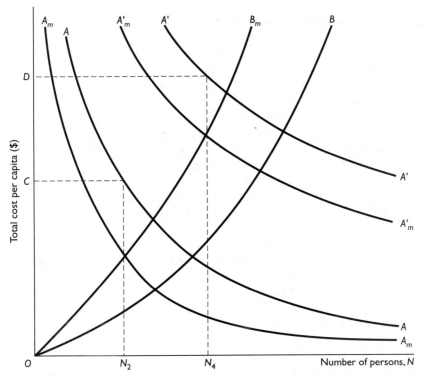

Figure 3.1 Choice of optimum size for given service level. (*AA* curve: per capita service cost or Z/N; A_mA_m curve: marginal savings in per capita service cost; *OB* curve: per capita crowding cost; OB_m curve: marginal per capita crowding cost.)

level of social goods is provided, the total cost of which (the cost to the group as a whole) equals Z dollars. Let us suppose further that each member pays a price equal to the marginal benefit received, which (given equal tastes and incomes) means that the cost is split equally among them. The AA curve then shows the per capita service cost (measured on the vertical axis) for various community sizes (measured on the horizontal axis). This cost decreases as numbers N increase. Since the total cost remains equal to Z throughout, the curve AA is a rectangular hyperbola with per capita cost equal to Z/N. It reflects a form of "decreasing per capita cost" with increasing numbers of consumers in the group.[3] The A_mA_m curve, which is derived from the AA curve, shows the marginal saving of (or reduction in) per capita service cost that results as the group number is increased.[4] If this were all there was to be considered, the optimal group size would be such as to include the entire community.

The community would be expanded so long as A_mA_m were positive (i.e., AA were downward-sloping), no matter how large the group became.

The situation changes if the cost of crowding is allowed for. Let OB trace the per capita cost or disutility of crowding for various sizes of the group while OB_m shows the marginal per capita crowding cost. The optimal size of the community will then be given by ON_2, where OB_m is equated with A_mA_m, calling for N_2 members in this case. The community will be expanded in numbers so long as the extra per capita savings from cost sharing with a larger group exceeds the incremental per capita costs of crowding. Beyond this point, further expansion of the group would reduce total welfare and is therefore not undertaken. Various governmental units of size ON_2 will thus be established with per capita costs for each unit set at OC. With a total population P and given total service cost Z in each community, there will be P/N_2 jurisdictions with per capita costs of Z/N_2.

Such is the solution for a service level with total cost Z, but we can readily see from figure 3.2 what happens if the service level increases. The AA and A_mA_m curves shift up and the optimum size of the group increases. Thus, for a higher service level involving cost Z', the per capita service cost curve rises to $A'A'$ and the marginal curve to $A'_mA'_m$, with the optimal group size increasing to ON_4 at a per capita service cost of OD and with the group enlarged to N_4 members.[5]

Optimal service level   We now turn to the second step, which is to determine the optimal service level for any given group size. This is shown in figure 3.2, where various service levels are measured along the horizontal axis and per capita unit service cost on the vertical. DD is an individual's demand schedule for the service, and since tastes and income levels are identical for all, it is representative for all members of the community. S_1S_1 is the cost schedule for the service showing cost to the community as a whole. The unit cost of the facility is here shown to rise with the service level, the slope of S_1S_1, depending on the nature of the facility and its production function (see Economies of scale section below). S_2S_2 is the supply schedule which presents itself to the individual if the community contains N_2 members, S_4S_4 reflects the supply schedule in an N_4-member community, and so forth. The vertical level of S_2S_2 is one-half of S_1S_1, that of S_4S_4 is one-quarter of S_1S_1, and so on. Given a tax structure which divides total cost equally, all face the same SS schedule. Since the same quantity is available to each member of the community, the service level purchased by various sizes of community will be determined at the intersection of the DD curve with the supply curve pertaining to the particular community size. Thus, the service level purchased

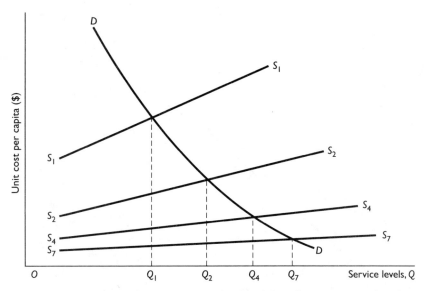

Figure 3.2 Choice of optimum service level for given community size.

with N_1 members will be that corresponding to the intersection of $S_1 S_1$ with DD, namely, OQ_1; the level purchased by N_2 members will be OQ_2 and the level desired by an N_4-member community will be OQ_4, as shown on the diagram.[6]

Optimal structure   In the final step, the two considerations are combined in figure 3.3, with community size N measured on the horizontal axis and service levels Q on the vertical axis. Returning to figure 3.1, we find that a service level involving a total cost Z calls for a community size N_2, that a higher level involving cost Z' calls for size N_4, and so forth. This relationship is traced in line NN of figure 3.3, which shows the optimal community size at each service level (measured in quantity terms), that corresponds to the various cost levels (Z, Z', etc.) of figure 3.1. Turning to figure 3.2, we find that community size N_1 calls for service level Q_1; size N_2 calls for Q_2, and so forth. This relationship is traced in line QQ of figure 3.3, showing the optimum service levels for various community sizes. The overall optimal solution is at E, where the two lines intersect, the optimal service level being Q_7 and the optimal group size N_7.

Extensions of model

The model of efficient design thus calls for multiple fiscal units differing in size and regional scope. Some will be nationwide (such as the provi-

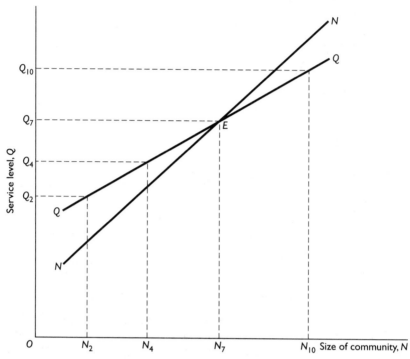

Figure 3.3 Combination of optimum size and service level. (*NN* line: optimal community size at various service levels; *QQ* line: optimal service level at various community sizes.)

sion for defense) while others will be quite local (such as the provision for streetlights). Now a number of complications must be allowed for.

Difference in taste   If we assume all tastes to be the same, local fiscal units will be similar; but tastes differ. Since people differ in their preferences for public services, the efficient solution will call for people with similar tastes to be grouped together. Thus, the system will contain multiple units, some similar and some different with regard to both size and composition of the public sector. At the same time, splitting up into smaller units will be at a cost. As the number of people in any one jurisdiction is reduced, some of the advantage from larger numbers (in terms of reduced per capita cost) is lost. Nevertheless, provision for local goods through a multiple system of differentiated fiscal units will remain more efficient than a uniform pattern of central provision.

Differences in income   The resulting structures of fiscal units will differ also because people have different incomes. Preferences with regard to social goods will differ by income groups. Demand will be more income-elastic for some services than for others. As a result, residents are more likely to be satisfied with the budget vote if their income varies little from the average for the community. Because of this, people with equal income will want to join in the same community.

But note also that the price (or taxes) which people are willing to pay for a given supply of social goods will be higher if their incomes are larger. As a result, the cost of social goods to me will be less if my neighbors have higher incomes and hence are willing to carry a larger share of the cost. This situation creates a further tendency for the wealthy to congregate. But it also induces the poor to follow the wealthy, and the wealthy to exclude the poor via zoning.

Congested goods   Up to this point, we have viewed the problem of multiple jurisdictions in terms of pure social goods, i.e., goods the consumption of which is truly nonrival, though limited to the residents of a geographic area. We must now allow for the important fact that local goods are frequently – or even typically – not of this type. Consider a fire station, a school of given size, a network of city streets, or a sewage disposal plant. They are all goods provided by the municipal government yet they do not meet the precise criterion of "nonrival" consumption. The addition of one extra consumer (at least after a certain point is reached) will dilute the quality of service obtained from the given size of operation by the old set of consumers. In other words, there arises a congestion cost to previous users.

Returning to figure 3.1, we may depict this cost in the same way as was done previously for crowding costs. Thus, the OB_m curve may now be interpreted as plotting the marginal cost arising from quality deterioration as additional numbers are added to the group.[7] For any given service level, the problem is again one of balancing the gain from reduced per capita cost as numbers are increased, against the additional crowding. Thus, members will be added to the group until the marginal cost of quality deterioration equals the marginal saving in the form of reduced tax cost (per capita).

Economies of scale   With a given facility size, adding to the number of users may reduce the quality of service per user, which is the just-examined problem of congestion. But provision of public services may also be subject to technical economies of scale. Provision of a given service quality (and degree of congestion) for a community of 100,000 may cost, say, $1,000,000, while similar provision for a community of 200,000 may cost $1,800,000. Per capita cost in the smaller community is then $100 while for the larger community it is only $90. Sewer construction, fire protection, sanitary facilities, and many other services may be analyzed in these terms, so that technical economies of scale (as distinct from spreading a given cost over more people) must also be considered in determining optimal community size.

Benefit overlap and arbitration   So far we have assumed that the benefit of a particular public service is confined to just the specified space over which the providing jurisdiction extends. Actually, benefits may not be uniformly distributed within any one space, and benefits from services provided by one particular jurisdiction may spill over into another jurisdiction. For the providing jurisdiction, this constitutes an externality which it will not take into account. Like all externalities, this results in inefficient provision and calls for correction. Such correction may result from cooperation on a bilateral basis. Thus, two jurisdictions adjoining the same lake may agree to maintain water quality. Or the spillover may involve many jurisdictions, e.g., educational services in a particular school district may generate general benefits via migration. It may then be necessary to internalize such externalities through a central system of grants designed to affect the action of particular jurisdictions. This will call for matching grants attached to those particular outlays which generate benefits outside the jurisdiction, with the matching rate depending on the fraction of benefits which are external.

Voting by feet

The preceding discussion has shown what the efficient solution would be like. As with our earlier discussion of social goods, defining the solution is only half the battle. The other is to consider how the solution may be reached. We concluded that a process of majority voting is needed to gain preference revelation, even though this can only yield a second-best solution. We now find that there may be another way, namely, "voting by feet." If we stipulate that each community is to defray its own cost of public services, individuals will find it in their interest to choose such communities as will suit their particular preferences.[8] Those who like sports will want to reside with others who are willing to contribute to playgrounds. Those who like music will join with others who will participate in building a concert hall, and so forth. Each community will do its own thing and preferences will be satisfied.[9] Of course, this mechanism will function only to the extent that fiscal considerations are a decisive factor in location choice, as distinct from job opportunities and housing, which makes the voting by feet hypothesis somewhat unrealistic, except in a setting where people work in the inner city and may choose among suburbs for residence. It is less applicable where location is determined by job and other considerations.

3.2   Tax-structure Design

As shown in Section 3.1, the logic of arranging fiscal structures in line with benefit regions is to enable people to "buy" and enjoy such levels and mixes of public services as suit their preferences. It is thus an inherent feature of the basic system – and especially its contribution to preference revelation via "voting by feet" – that the members of each benefit region or jurisdiction should pay for the services which that jurisdiction provides. This logic calls for an area-wide ("national," if you wish) tax for the finance of area-wide services and local (regionally limited) taxes for the finance of services provided by local jurisdictions. We may thus conclude what taxes are appropriate for what fiscal units or "levels" of government.

The central or national jurisdiction may conveniently use a broad-based income tax since all people (independent of location) benefit and hence should contribute. The choice of tax instruments to be used by local jurisdictions in turn should conform to the rule that each jurisdiction pay for its own benefits. Thus, jurisdiction A should charge members of jurisdiction B only to the extent that services provided by A are enjoyed by members of B. Such a rule becomes a problem because the various jurisdictions do not exist in isolation but trade with each other. Implementation of the rule is automatic if we assume that the entire revenue structure of jurisdiction A consists of strictly benefit charges. To the extent that jurisdiction A taxes income (including income earned by members of B) such taxation will merely recoup the input of A's public services into the earnings process; and to the extent that products are taxed at the point of origin (including those exported to B) such taxes will only charge for the input of intermediate public services rendered by A. Both income and products are thus taxed appropriately by the jurisdiction where production occurs. In addition, taxation of residents in A (including visiting members of B) is appropriate as a charge for public consumer goods which the jurisdiction provides.

Application of the benefit rule on an interjurisdictional basis has the further advantage that decentralized finance will not interfere with trade or the location of production within the national region. This follows since benefit taxation – requiring as it does a balance of tax burdens and benefit gains – neutralizes the impact of fiscal operations on location choice. If levels of taxation differ by jurisdiction, so will the level of services and benefits. The model of benefit taxation therefore bypasses the problem of distortion in location, a problem which arises once taxes are imposed on a nonbenefit basis across jurisdictions.

The assumption of universal benefit taxation takes care of the problem neatly. If each individual pays in line with his or her benefits received, it follows that the benefit rule applies across jurisdictions as well. The latter still holds if each jurisdiction taxes its residents on an ability-to-pay basis, provided that the burden stops within the jurisdiction and is not exported. This may, however, prove to be an unrealistic assumption. Such is the case especially for small benefit regions, but also applies at the international level, an aspect to be considered further later on.

3.3   Spatial Aspects of Distribution Function

We now turn to the distribution function. As before, we begin with its implementation in a setting unencumbered by the prerogatives which member jurisdictions in a federation may retain. Economic analysis suggests that provision for social goods proceed through a multijurisdictional setting, with national goods provided centrally and local goods provided on a decentralized basis. Can a similar multiunit case be made for the distribution function? At first this would seem to be the case. Just as the allocation model pointed to a decentralized system to permit variety in the provision for spatially limited social goods, so decentralization might serve to accommodate different tastes regarding income equality or inequality.[10] Those favoring a high degree of redistribution might favor locating in jurisdiction A, while those opposing it might locate in B. Jurisdiction A might then impose a progressive income tax and transfer system, while B would only use benefit or even head taxes for the finance of public services.

The analogy is tempting but it breaks down in an important respect. As long as there exists ready mobility between jurisdictions, the following population shifts would result. High-income people who oppose redistribution would move to B, while high-income people favoring redistribution and low-income people would flock to A. High-income proponents now find that the entire burden is placed upon them. Moreover, the achievable degree of equalization would be small, because most low-income people would flock to A. The redistribution process thus breaks down unless the scheme covers individuals across A and B, i.e., the distribution function is carried out at the national or central level.

Such at least is the case unless mobility is checked by nonfiscal factors such as job location, or unless A's border controls prohibit (or zoning devices deter) the immigration of low- and the out-migration of high-income people. But as such restrictions are introduced we leave the spirit of the unitary model and move to the other extreme of noncooperating sovereign jurisdictions.

3.4   Spatial Aspects of Stabilization Function

It remains to note that responsibility for stabilization policy cannot be left to local or regional fiscal units but must be conducted in a central fashion. Local fiscal units will be ineffective in dealing with unemployment or inflation, because markets are interrelated so that leakages result. Such will clearly be the case within the national unit where subunits share in an open market and resources and capital can flow freely. However, it also becomes increasingly the case across nations, thus calling for international coordination of macro policies.

In all, we find that economic analysis points to a clear-cut case for decentralized provision of many public services, but for national or central policy with regard to problems of distribution and with regard to the conduct of stabilization policy.

3.5   Summary

In this chapter we have inquired how the allocation, distribution, and stabilization functions of budget policy should be divided among units of government. Beginning with the allocation function in the basic model, we concluded the following:

1   Since the benefit incidence of various social goods is subject to spatial limitation, each service should be decided upon and paid for within the confines of the jurisdiction in which the benefits accrue.

2   This principle of benefit region leads to the concept of optimal community size.

3   With pure social goods, it would be desirable to have the number of residents as large as possible, thus reducing per capita cost. However, the cost of crowding enters to limit the optimal community size.

4   The roles of congestion and of economies of scale also enter into the determination of optimal community size.

5   Allowing for differences in tastes, we concluded that people with similar tastes for social goods will join the same jurisdiction.

6   This mechanism, via voting by feet, becomes a mechanism of preference revelation.

7   The impact of differences in income on location choice was considered.

8   Benefit spillovers involve externalities which call for correction.

9   The case for decentralization in the provision of local services is linked to the proposition that the cost should be borne in the jurisdiction in which the benefits are reaped.

10   Item 9 calls for the use of nationwide taxes in the finance of national services, and for the finance of local services through taxes the burden of which accrues within the benefiting jurisdiction.

     Turning to the assignment of the distribution function, we concluded that:

11   Although preferences regarding distribution differ, the distribution function must be performed largely at the central level.

     Regarding the placement of the stabilization function, we concluded that:

12   The stabilization function must be central because of leakages at the local level.

Notes

1 Instead of assuming that benefits are uniformly distributed within a specific area, it may also be postulated that the intensity of benefits tapers off as one moves away from the location of the service facility. Such would be the situation, for instance, with the quality of television reception. Residents would have a tendency to move toward the center, a tendency which would be restrained only by dislike of crowding.

2 The less technically inclined reader may wish to bypass this section, based on James M. Buchanan, "An Economic Theory of Clubs," *Economica*, February 1965.

3 The curve is similar in form to that of decreasing average fixed cost with increasing output as drawn in the usual cost-curve diagram for the individual firm.

4 Mathematically, $A_m A_m$, the marginal saving in per capita service cost, is equal to

$$\frac{d(Z/N)}{dN} = \frac{Z}{N^2}$$

i.e., the negative of the slope of the AA curve.

5   Two features of this presentation should be noted: (1) up to a certain community size, crowding costs may be negative, i.e., additional numbers may be considered a gain (e.g., from increased social contacts) rather than a disutility; (2) since we are here dealing with a pure social good, we assume the OB curve to be independent of the service level. If the "congestion phenomenon" is allowed for (i.e., a decline in service quality with rising numbers), the OB curve will swivel down to the right as service levels are increased. In this case, the increase in group size when moving from level Z to level Z' will be greater than that shown in figure 3.1.

6   Alternatively, the same solution might be obtained by taking S_1S_1 to reflect the supply schedule for the group and by picking its intersection with successive vertical additions of demand schedules as the size of the group is increased.

7   As noted before, an increase in service level now not only raises the AA or per capita service cost curve in figure 3.1, it swings the OB or congestion cost curve to the right. See Note 5. A composite OB curve may be constructed which allows for both crowding and congestion costs.

8   It is interesting to observe that this is another respect in which the social-goods and private-goods cases differ. With regard to social goods, since costs are shared, it is in a person's interest to associate with others whose tastes are similar. The opposite tends to hold for private goods, where a person with unusual tastes (provided that production is subject to increasing costs) will benefit from lower (relative) prices.

9   The proposition that optimal local budget patterns will result from location choices of individuals was first developed in Charles M. Tiebout, "A Pure Theory of Local Government Expenditures," *Journal of Political Economy*, October 1956.

10   See Mark V. Pauly, "Income Redistribution as a Local Public Good," *Journal of Public Economics*, February 1973.

Further Readings

Buchanan, James M.: "An Economic Theory of Clubs," *Economica*, February 1965.

Elazar, Daniel J.: "Federalism," *International Encyclopedia of Social Sciences*, New York: Macmillan, 1968, vol. 5, p. 360.

Tiebout, Charles M.: "A Pure Theory of Local Expenditures," *Journal of Political Economy*, October 1956.

Introduction to Chapter 4

This article is an assault upon one of the principles of multiunit finance set forth in the Musgrave and Musgrave article, namely the principle that only the federal or central government should assume the distribution function. Buchanan employs both utility theory and the Tiebout hypothesis. He argues that in a world with trade of private goods, the set of possible outcomes for the distribution of welfare may not all be Pareto optimal because the restrictive assumptions of the model are not always met. But because of the wide range of effective alternatives to any trade, namely many buyers and sellers, the possible welfare outcomes will lie within a narrow band close to and including the Pareto optimal outcomes. By introducing local public goods into the analysis, the welfare boundary is pushed outward because participants are made better off by the availability of such goods. Drawing upon the Tiebout hypothesis, Buchanan argues that again the possible set of welfare outcomes will be a narrow band along the Pareto optimal set because large numbers of local governments provide effective alternatives to any trade. That is, competition among local governments, the providers of local public goods, constrains them from moving far from the Pareto optimal frontier. Buchanan then introduces national public goods into the analysis and the welfare boundary is pushed further out. But now the range of possible outcomes becomes quite wide, including outcomes which make some worse off than they were in a world with no national public goods. The reason for that result, he argues, is that there are no effective alternatives to the central government as provider of national public goods. Its behavior is not constrained by competition as is the behavior of local governments. Into this structure Buchanan then introduces redistribution of income as a good, a novel idea. The result is that this economic analysis does not proscribe income redistribution by subnational governments. If voters demand some form of income redistribution at any level of government, then the governments should supply it.

4

Who Should Distribute What in a Federal System?

James M. Buchanan

It is frequently asserted that redistribution, as a governmental function, can be properly assigned only to the central or national government.[1] The remaining half of this assertion implies that allocative functions can, by contrast, be performed by local governmental units if the appropriately defined "publicness" ranges are spatially limited and if interjurisdictional spillovers are not significant. I want to examine this "principle" of modern public finance theory in some detail and in some depth.

It is difficult to separate positive and normative strands in the orthodox discussion of this principle. If redistribution is interpreted exclusively in terms of coercively-imposed transfers of income and wealth from some persons to others, discussion concerning the possibility of carrying out this activity at various levels of government reduces to a single positive proposition. The ability of any person, agency, or governmental unit to coerce another depends on the range of alternatives open to the one to be coerced. If an individual has available to him multiple options that offer substantially the same utility prospects, no other person exerts much power over him. In the limit, the perfectly competitive market minimizes man's power over man or, conversely, maximizes man's freedom from coercion by other men. It should be evident that the power of any government to extract income and wealth coercively from a person is related inversely to the locational alternatives that are available to that person. For this reason alone, a local governmental unit in a national economy is severely limited in its strictly zero-sum redistributive activity. It is constrained by the ability of individuals to shift among alternative locationally separated jurisdictions, and this constraining influence operates even when the existence of relevant and sometimes significant decision thresholds is acknowledged. Since persons do not have comparable abilities to shift readily across national boundaries, the power of a central or national government to enforce imposed redistribution policies is clearly greater than that possessed by local authorities.

If this is all there is to the "principle" that the redistributive function must be performed centrally, extended discussion would hardly seem to be warranted. In what follows I assume that those who advance the principle have something more than this in mind, and especially that attention is not exclusively focused on the strictly zero-sum redistributive activities of governments. In Section 4.1, I discuss the sharing of gains-from-trade from the provision of collective consumption of public goods at the various governmental levels. In Section 4.2 the related but analytically separate category that is commonly called "Pareto optimal redistribution" is examined. In this setting income-wealth redistribution is itself treated as a public good. In Section 4.3 the Pareto optimality approach is extended to apply to the whole set of institutions or processes that generate specific distributional outcomes. As will become evident, the discussion in this section is most closely related to the explicitly normative or value-laden treatment that is accorded distribution by many scholars. In both Sections 4.2 and 4.3 an attempt is made to restrict discussion to those aspects of the analysis that bear directly on the functional location of redistribution in a hierarchical governmental system, that is, in a federal polity.

4.1   Distribution of Gains-from-trade

Gains-from-trade in private goods

Modern economic theory is somewhat misleading in its distributive implications. Given an initial set of individual resource endowments, including capacities or skills, this theory implies that there is a uniquely determinate position on the utility-possibility frontier that tends to be produced through the operation of the market process. The final distribution of the gross gains-from-trade seems to be determined independently of the path or process through which it is reached. In one sense this suggests first the solving of the simultaneous equations of the whole complex system and second the inference from solution to that unique set of initial endowments that might have been required to generate it. This has always seemed to me to turn things around. The market process tends to generate an equilibrium, but the location of this equilibrium on the "social utility surface," that is, its distributional characteristics, depends on the path through which it is approached. It seems unreal to postulate the perfect recontracting that is required to produce a one-for-one correspondence between an initial set of endowments and a final distribution of utility or welfare among individuals. Any plausibly realistic model must allow exchange to be made, and implemented, before equilibrium is finally, if ever, attained. Trading at prices that are different from those that might characterize the potentially attainable final general equilibrium solution must be allowed to take place. Once this is done, however, the path toward the utility-possibility frontier delineates the set of positions attainable on the frontier.[2]

Markets do not work perfectly, and there are numerous constraints on the freedom of trading among individuals and groups. If we drop the formalism of modern general-equilibrium theory, we can discuss the market process within any given set of externally imposed constraints. It becomes meaningful to talk about the characteristics of the equilibrium that will tend to emerge within the set of institutional limits postulated, and we can utilize the concept of a feasible or attainable utility-possibility frontier, the location of which will be dependent on such limits.

I can illustrate this point geometrically and in such a way as to introduce the central elements of this paper. Figure 4.1 is drawn in a two-man utility space. I want to use this two-man construction, however, both here and later, to depict situations faced by individuals in many-person settings. Hence, to each person in the construction, the "other person" is conceived to be the whole environment that he confronts, including the behavior of many other persons, an environment that he considers to be beyond his own power of control or influence, at least in any direct sense.

In a Hobbesian world, where life is indeed "nasty, brutish, and short," and where neither property rights nor trade exists, the utility positions attained by the two persons, A and B, are shown at E in figure 4.1. This position depicts reaction-curve equilibrium in the savage and anarchistic "society." The distribution of utility, which reflects the instrumental distribution of real goods, depends strictly on the relative abilities of persons to survive and prosper in the hostile environment of potential conflict.

Once property rights are defined and legally protected, market-type exchanges become possible, and these allow dramatic gains to be secured by all parties. Modern microeconomic theory implies that movement takes place along a unique price vector, which could be indirectly represented in figure 4.1 by the heavily dotted line extending from E to point F, a position on a utility-possibility frontier under the institutional structure that allows voluntary exchange. As noted above, the one-to-one relationship between E and F exists only in a regime of perfect recontracting, which requires, in its turn, the presence of a large

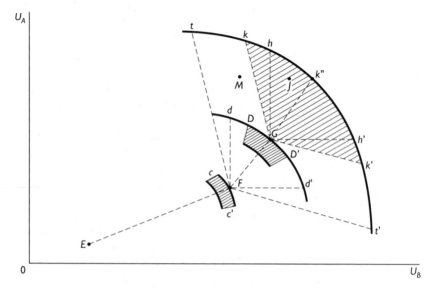

Figure 4.1 Gains from trade with property rights and public goods.

number of traders on both sides of all markets, along with an absence of all barriers to the consummation of trade. If we drop any of these requirements, the one-to-one correspondence vanishes and the initial position, *E*, along with a practically workable market order may produce a position along or near a finite and narrowly defined segment of a frontier. The shaded area between and below the points *c* and *c'* depicts this set of positions. Regardless of the particulars of the institutional process, we can think of the market or exchange system as insuring that one position in this set will be attained.

It is important to understand the basic reason for the relatively narrow limits within which the final distribution of the gains-from-trade is bounded. These limits are a direct consequence of the ability of single traders to select among alternatives. In the extreme and formal model each trader is a pure price taker in all markets. There is no room for bargaining, as such, despite the presence of mutual gains in each two-party contract. We need not impose the severe restrictions of the formal model, however, to confine the utility or welfare distribution within relatively narrow limits, as shown.

Gains-from-trade in local public goods

We may now introduce localized collective-consumption or public goods and services. Suppose that the existing technology along with existing individual preference functions makes possible the efficient joint consumption of certain goods and services that are spatially limited and that are nonexcludable among beneficiaries. Local governmental units emerge to finance and to provide these goods and services. We assume, as before, that the central government exists only to enforce property rights, to insure against fraudulent contracts, and to guarantee freedom of resource flows throughout the national economy.

If there are efficiency gains to be secured from the provision and consumption of such localized public goods, the utility-possibility frontier is shifted outward from that which is attainable in the setting that allows only for the provision of purely private goods.[3] In figure 4.1 the introduction of these goods allows positions to the northeast of the set bounded by c and c' to be attained.

How are the gains-from-trade in localized public goods to be distributed? If we assume that private-goods equilibrium is attained at F, any position within the inclusive limits defined by F, d, and d', would reflect mutual gains, or in the many-person setting, gains to all parties. In a regime of spatially competitive governments, however, we should predict that the range of attainable utility or welfare distributions would be considerably more confined than the set indicated. The reason is identical with that shown to impose bounds on the distributions of the gains from private-goods trade. If there are alternative sellers and buyers, the power of any one to impose terms of trade on market participants is restricted. This principle applies directly to the competition among local governmental units. Consider a single local government that provides a public good to its citizens. Can this unit extract from an individual citizen-taxpayer-beneficiary all the fiscal surplus that the enjoyment of this public good represents? It can do so only if and to the extent that he has no alternatives available to him, if there are no better "deals" in other locations, taking into account the costs of making a move. But it seems clear that the prospects of "voting with the feet" that individuals face in a regime of spatially competitive local governments in a federal system insure results that are broadly comparable in kind to the operation of effectively competitive markets.

This process of adjustment involves both distributional and efficiency dimensions. The distribution of the gross gains-from-trade in local public goods is restricted. At the same time these gains tend to be fully exploited, insuring that the equilibrium finally attained will fall along or near the utility-possibility frontier itself rather than inside it. The results are comparable in kind to those produced by workably competitive markets, but this is not to suggest that either the distributional or the efficiency constraints are nearly so confining as those that open-ended market adjustment tends to guarantee. The Tiebout adjustment mechanism does not offer a wholly satisfactory analogue to market competition, despite its directional effects.[4]

For purposes of illustration in figure 4.1, the provision of local public goods through a regime of spatially competitive local governmental units tends to narrow the set of attainable outcomes to the shaded area between and below the segment DD'. As drawn, this set is not so narrowly confined as that shown to be attainable from trade in purely private goods, although outcomes are still restricted to a subset of those positions that exhibit nothing more than mutual gains to all parties.

It is important to emphasize that these results do not depend in any way on the collective decision-making rules in local governments. These rules may range all the way from Wicksellian unanimity or quasi-unanimity, through the direct democracy of the New England town, the representative democracy of a city council, to the effective dictatorship of Boss Crump. Within any specific jurisdiction, the rule or institutions for reaching local fiscal decisions and the levy of taxes, along with the selection of the size and mix of the expenditure budget, will determine the final distributive outcomes, although these will rarely be unique. Conceptually, we can think of the distributional position attained by an individual, say A, as ranging over the whole set of possibilities represented by the shaded area between and below D and D' as this person shifts from one local jurisdiction to another and/or as the decision rules vary. If A should be dictator, a position at or near D might be secured, and if B replaces him, A might find himself at D'. But the point to be stressed here is that, regardless of the decision rules, the migrational or locational alternatives that are potentially available to all citizens in the federalism insure that the distributional set of outcomes attainable within any single local unit is narrowly bounded.

Gains-from-trade in national public goods

Assume that a position, shown by G in figure 4.1, is attained through the operation of market competition in supplying private goods and through spatially competitive local governments in supplying localized public goods. But we now assume further that there remain new welfare or efficiency gains to be exploited through the allocation of some resources to the production-provision of collective-consumption goods that are not confined geographically, at least not within the boundaries of the national government's jurisdiction. For purposes of analysis, we assume that neither local governments nor market institutions will devote resources to the provision of such goods.[5] Furthermore, we assume that all collective-consumption goods and services fall into one or the other of the two distinct categories examined here, the strictly local or the strictly national.[6] The effect of introducing the existence of national public goods is to shift the utility-possibility frontier outward.

If the central or national government in the federalism accepts the responsibility for organizing the provision of these goods, how will the gross gains-from-trade be distributed, and how efficient will the production-provision be? There is a major difference between this and the two earlier models examined, a difference in kind and one that should be immediately apparent. Since there are no competing "sellers" of the national public goods, there are no effective constraints on the range of distributional outcomes that are comparable to those demonstrated to be present both under private-goods market process and under localized public-goods provision through local governments. Alternatives always exist, and these will define the extremes of potential distributive outcomes. The individual can migrate across international boundaries and he can join others in revolutionary uprising against the national government. In the United States in the 1970s, however, these can scarcely be considered effective alternatives, and especially for individuals who are "representative" members of the national citizenry. And such extreme limits surely will not confine the distributional outcomes even within the set of positions that dominate the initial or no-trade position (G in figure 4.1) in the standard sense. There is no external constraint that insures against central government distributions of gains-from-trade that fall outside the set of positions that exhibit gains to all parties, that is, outside the area bounded by h, h', and G. One, some, or even many persons in the economy could be made worse off with than without central-government provision of national public goods.

It seems plausible, however, to postulate some broad limits on central-government or federal-government fiscal power. Constitutional restrictions do exist, despite Supreme Court confusion between constitutional order and "social justice." Elements of a fiscal constitution remain in being, and these prevent arbitrary and discriminatory exercise of the taxing power by the federal government. Although the extension to the spending side of the budget is not symmetrical, there are also some legal limitations on overt discrimination in the allocation of governmental benefits. Within existing constitutional constraints, and so long as the model is restricted to one where the central government supplies and finances only genuinely national public goods and services, as reasonably classified, we can talk meaningfully about some bounded set of distributional outcomes. In terms of our illustration in figure 4.1, we postulate that such constraints will insure outcomes within the shaded area defined by G, k, and k'. Note that this allows for some positions outside the set that dominates G for all persons in the group (the set Ghh') but that these nonintersecting positions are restricted in range. In the real world, of course, there are no necessary restrictions of the sort depicted in the construction.

The broader range of possible outcomes here than in the two earlier models is apparent, but a second feature should also be noted. In both earlier models the existence of effective alternatives serves to insure not only the limited range of distributional possibilities but also the approximate achievement of the utility-possibility frontier. That is to say, alternatives also generate pressures toward efficiency. The absence of effective alternatives to national public-goods provision eliminates such pressures. There is no force tending to push the system to positions along or near the kk' boundaries, and final positions well within the shaded area seem equally if not more likely to emerge.[7] The implications of the analysis for the relative efficiencies of local and central government are clear. It is directly predictable that central or national government will be less efficient than local units.[8]

In order to bound the set at all, we have found it necessary to resort to constitutional-legal constraints, a step that was not required in the discussion of local governmental provision of public goods. Within the set, as now bounded, the position actually attained will depend on the particular operation of the decision-making process at the central-government level. Since the set is relatively more inclusive, and by a wide margin, than the comparable one in the earlier or local-government model, the analysis suggests that the structure of collective decision-making rules is much more important in central-government or federal-government affairs, more important for individual participants, than in local-government matters or in the market. The reason, of course, is, again the relative absence of effective alternatives. Without alternatives, the individual is a necessary party to the outcome collectively selected even if he, personally, remains strongly opposed or is even harmed in the process.[9] At the central-government level, alternatives remain, at best, potential. In working democracies significant departures by governments from outcomes desired by majorities or even by intense minorities will, of course, provide incentives to nonincumbent parties and politicians to offer more efficient and more preferred alternatives.

The construction of figure 4.1 allows us to depict the distributional consequences of a transfer of local government functions to the central government. Suppose that local units are abolished and that the central government assumes the responsibility for providing localized public goods throughout the area of what becomes a unitary political system. The range of possible outcomes, under the same constitutional-legal constraints, is expanded to the area bounded by F, t, and t' in figure 4.1. Clearly, opportunities now exist for sharing the total gains from "public-goods trade" that were not present under the genuinely federal system. The central government may now, under certain decision-making processes, produce an outcome such as that shown at M, which lies wholly outside the set that was previously attainable. Furthermore, this position becomes attainable under the same rules. Note, also, that the new position, M, might lie farther inside the utility-possibility locus than J, which we may assume to have been the position attained under the federal organization. This reflects the reduced pressure toward efficiency in the structure characterized by less effective alternatives for individual choice.

The effects of shifting the dividing line between local and central government are clear. Centralization tends to widen the set of possible distributional outcomes and, simultaneously, to reduce the institutional pressures for efficiency in public-goods provision. In the analysis to this point we have assumed that there is a clear-cut distinction between localized and central public goods and services, that the efficient jointness-nonexcludability ranges are sharply delineated. As we know, however, these ranges are nearly always fuzzy, and intergovernmental spillovers exist for almost all localized public goods. The argument for central-government takeover often hinges on the relative significance of these spillover effects. Centralization allows for the internalization of the intergovernmental externalities that these spillovers represent; this, considered in isolation, can increase overall efficiency in public-goods supply. Against this must be placed the offsetting efficiency drain that centralization makes possible through its elimination of effective alternatives. The accompanying widening of the range of distributional possibilities may or may not be considered a desirable attribute in its own right.

As indicated earlier, to place any plausible restrictions on the set of outcomes produced by central-government action we found it necessary to resort to constitutional-legal constraints. In this context, and as the construction of figure 4.1 suggests, central-government takeover of local functions becomes equivalent to a relaxation of such constitutional limits. The elementary point developed in this and preceding paragraphs should not be excessively belabored. Perhaps it is obvious to everyone that the amount of redistribution of welfare that the federal government can accomplish under a budget of, say 50 billion dollars is significantly less than that which becomes possible with a budget of 250 billion dollars. Even with extreme progressivity in rate structure, with the general tax base, and with accompanying redistributive elements in spending patterns, the distributional possibilities in the former case may fall far short of those in the latter, even if, in shifting to the larger budget, the tax base is seriously eroded, the rate structure is made less progressive, and if the pattern of spending becomes, in itself, somewhat less redistributive.

4.2   Pareto Optimal Redistribution

In the discussion of Section 4.1, individual utility functions were implicitly assumed not to contain arguments for either the income-wealth characteristics of others (flows or stocks) or for their specific commodity and service characteristics (flows or stocks). If this assumption is dropped, and interdependence among persons in any or in all of these respects is introduced, redistribution may emerge as a specifically chosen objective in an idealized voluntaristic choice process. In the terminology of welfare economics, redistribution may involve Pareto shifts to the Pareto-welfare surface. This surface may be unattainable without redistributional activity. And this activity may be, but need not be, over and above the results forthcoming from the sharing of the gross gains-from-trade in private and in orthodox public goods and services.

Redistribution as a private good

I shall use a threefold classification and examine redistribution as (1) a purely private good, (2) a local public good, and (3) a national public good. If interpersonal interdependence exists, itself an empirical question, the form of this interdependence must be empirically ascertained since these alternative descriptive categories embody differing implications.

If an individual secures utility from the act of making income transfers to other persons but secures no utility from increases in the income or wealth levels of others apart from his own act of giving, or secures no utility from others' acts of giving, redistribution becomes analogous to the consumption of a purely divisible or private good.[10] There are no "public" properties; neither nonexcludability nor joint-consumption efficiency is present. We should observe this sort of redistribution to take place in the wholly voluntary sector. In the constuction of figure 4.1 this purely private redistribution would be embodied in the attainment of the market equilibrium somewhere in the set bounded by c and c'.

Redistribution as a local public good[11]

Our emphasis now shifts to those situations where individual utility functions include arguments for the income-wealth characteristics of others, as such, but where these "others" are residents of spatially defined local communities or jurisdictions. Individuals are wholly uninterested in the incomes of those beyond the confines of the local community. Furthermore, we assume that, for those potential transfer recipients within the local jurisdictions, specific identification is either not possible or not relevant for choice. That is to say, potential taxpayers in the local community are interested in the income level of the "local poor," but they make no identification of the members of this group, as such.[12]

Initially, we may examine a submodel in which taxpayers in the separate localities are immobile; they do not shift among communities in response to differential fiscal pressures. The potential welfare recipients are, by contrast, assumed to be fully mobile as among localities, and they respond directly to the level of welfare payments or income transfers.[13] If we ignore costs of migration, one condition for equilibrium in this model is that the transfer payments per person be equal in all localities. The potential recipients will distribute themselves among the communities to insure that this condition is fulfilled. The system of interaction between welfare or transfer recipients on the one hand and local taxpayers on the other generates an equilibrium that is Pareto optimal, despite the interdependence between the level of "bad" in a given community and the community's own efforts at eliminating this.

The interaction becomes more complex when we allow a Tiebout-like adjustment among potential taxpayers to accompany the migrational adjustments of welfare recipients. The equilibrium that will be produced retains Pareto optimality characteristics, however, since persons will tend to locate themselves among the spatially competitive local governments in accordance with their own preferences for redistributive activity. Although the migrational adjustments of potential recipients insure that transfers per person are equal in all localities, the net transfers away from taxpayers may differ among separate communities, with the trade-off being made in terms of the number of recipients.

In the geometry of figure 4.1 local-government action in providing income-wealth redistribution that can be classified as a strictly local public good becomes no different from the action involved in supplying any other local public good. The utility-possibility frontier is shifted outward, and the equilibrium will tend to fall in the area bounded by D and D', as before.

Redistribution as a national public good

If individual utility functions include arguments for the income-wealth positions of other persons throughout the national economy without spatial distinctions, local governments find themselves in what appears to be the familiar public-good dilemma. Since the single unit cannot exclude others from the benefit of its own action, investment in the activity of redistribution will be suboptimal. There are, however, differences between this and the standard public-good case. To an extent, redistribution, as an activity that generates utility, is divisible. The local community that carries out redistribution transfers income to specific local residents; it cannot, by the nature of the production process here, generate benefits that spill over equally to all persons in the nation. Hence, despite the assumed national scope of the utility interdependence that motivates the activity, the "production divisibility" restores at least elements of excludability. Local communities find themselves in a reciprocal-externalities interaction. This suggests that the suboptimality in result will be less than that indicated to be present in the pure public-good interaction and may, under some conditions, vanish.[14]

If a case for federal-government or national-government redistributive activity is to be based on the grounds of strict utility interdependence, evidence should be available to indicate that the sociocultural environment is such that the effective limits are, indeed, those determined by national boundaries rather than those more limited in space on the one hand and those more extensive on the other.

4.3 "Constitutional" Redistribution

Those who have advanced the "principle" that the redistribution function must be performed at the central-government level in a federal system need not accept either of the models developed above. In rejecting such models many scholars have, however, been too quick to resort to externally derived ethical norms. This step tends to remove the discussion from the realm of scientific discourse with predictable results.

To a partial extent the analysis of redistribution can be shifted to another plane, and without explicit value commitment, by examining what I have called "constitutional" redistribution.[15] This approach begins with the empirically valid proposition that explicit distributions of income are not, in fact, objects of choice for collectivities at any level. The relevant choices to be made are those among rules or institutions that, in turn, operate to generate probability distributions of distributive outcomes or allocations. At the stage of genuine "constitutional" choice, it is not appropriate to include the standard arguments in individual utility functions, nor is it at all appropriate to introduce explicit utility interdependence in the sense discussed in the preceding section. Conceptually at least, individuals engaged in "constitutional" choice remain uncertain about their own income-wealth positions in subsequent periods during which the rules to be adopted will remain in force.[16]

To clarify the argument here, it will be useful to compare and contrast allocation and distribution. At the "constitutional" stage market institutions may be chosen along with a decision to enforce contracts made under these institutions. Resources will be allocated, and it becomes meaningful to discuss the process under the "constitutional" rule that insures that these market institutions will remain in being. In the allocative process final products will be distributed in accordance with the rules. To this extent, distribution accompanies allocation. But the distributive pattern that accompanies market process, the distribution of the gross gains-from-trade, may not embody characteristics that are fully acceptable at the "constitutional" level of decision. The "game" may not seem "fair," quite independently of identification of particular recipients during specific market periods. If this is generally accepted, attempts may emerge, at the "constitutional" level, to introduce what we may call redistributive institutions, which are aimed to modify the distributive outcomes of market process.

This elementary logical derivation is not substantially changed when we allow for public-sector allocation, either at the central-government or local-government level. Constitutionally, a set of institutions may be established that determines the appropriate functions for the market, for local government, and for central government. Operating within these limits, the separate units allocate resources and distribute final goods and services. Over and beyond this pattern of results, however, explicitly redistributive institutions may also be constitutionally introduced.

The advantage of the "constitutional" approach is that it allows for a conceptual derivation of redistributive institutions in terms of Wicksellian efficiency, without resort to explicit value norms. Once redistributive institutions are constitutionally adopted, and as these operate, the actual redistribution that they produce must be zero-sum. Hence, at this stage, it becomes conceptually impossible to derive the unanimous support required for Wicksellian efficiency without introducing the utility interdependence of the type discussed in Section 4.2.

Whether or not such explicitly redistributive institutions will emerge constitutionally, for any of the several reasons that might be adduced,[17] is an empirical question. Also, even if these do emerge the criteria for efficiency may or may not be satisfied. These questions are not directly relevant to my purpose in this paper. The "principle" that redistribution must be performed at the central-government level may be restated as follows: If redistributive institutions or rules are to be selected at the "constitutional" level, these can be enforced only by the authority of the central or national government because of the zero-sum characteristics of the actual redistributions attempted during subsequent periods of application of these rules.

We may use an elementary example to demonstrate the validity of the principle as interpreted. For expositional simplicity only, assume that no public goods exist, and that the market has been constitutionally selected as the allocating process over a well-defined national economy, which includes local-government as well as central-governmental jurisdiction. Suppose that those persons living within a geographically defined subarea of the national economy should decide, again at some constitutional stage of deliberation, to modify the market-determined distributive pattern toward greater equality. Such rules are put into being for the single subarea government. As the rules are applied, however, individuals who are subjected to net taxes will find it advantageous to shift to other local jurisdictions, and potential recipients of net transfers will find it advantageous to shift into the redistributive jurisdiction. The Tiebout adjustment, by both groups, will make accomplishment of the intended distributive results impossible for the local community. This analysis is relevant even if it is acknowledged that those very persons who might have supported the imposition of the redistributive rules at the constitutional stage will themselves shift location when these rules come into operation. Effective enforcement of redistributive rules or institutions that are aimed at modifying the distributive outcomes in the market, or in the combined market-public sector process, must be carried out by the governmental jurisdiction that is itself coincident with the market in the geographical area.

There is, of course, nothing inconsistent in the combined presence of redistributive institutions, in the constitutional sense, and Pareto-optimal transfers, as chosen in the operational working of political process. A "constitutional" decision may be made to finance a major portion of central-government budgets with a progressive income tax, quite independently of and in advance of knowledge about the public-good mixes that describe such budgets. As these budgetary-mix choices are made, however, one of the components may well be the transfers of income designed for poverty relief.

As the analysis of Section 4.1 demonstrated, there is more range of variation in the distribution of the gross gains-from-trade in the central government's provision of public goods and services than there is in the distribution of such gains from the provision of goods either through the market or through local governments. When this is recognized, and if a sizable central-government sector exists, the institutionalization of redistribution may be limited largely if not wholly to tax-side constraints on central-government fiscal structure. If a "fiscal constitution" is designed to insure a substantial role for progressive taxation, regardless of the demand pattern for publicly supplied goods, marginally or inframarginally, the final distribution of welfare may be constrained to fall within specific limits. (In figure 4.1 such constitutional restriction may insure that the final distributional outcome falls between, say, the rays terminating at k and k''.) The institutionalization of redistribution in this manner will, necessarily, distort the in-sector allocative process of the central government. The satisfaction of the necessary marginal conditions for optimality in the provision of goods and services becomes more difficult and, in practical reality, may become impossible. These allocative inefficiencies may be offset against the distributional "efficiencies" that progression in the fiscal structure is predicted to generate.

4.4 Conclusions

Methodologically, this paper contains one tautological proposition and two sets of predictive hypotheses in political economy. The proposition states, quite straightforwardly, that zero-sum transfers, defined in utility dimensions, are limited by the extent of individual alternatives. The first set of hypotheses concerns the existence and the importance of utility interdependence as among specifically definable persons and groups, within the context of an operative political process. Individuals are observed to perform private charities, to join voluntary groups with charitable objectives, and to support redistributive transfers at local, central, and international governmental levels. The overall division of distributional responsibility among these separate institutional structures that might be required to meet Pareto criteria for optimality can be determined only empirically. The second set of hypotheses concerns the existence, actual or potential, of consensus among individuals on the establishment and maintenance, constitutionally, of rules of fiscal structure that embody income-wealth redistribution.

It is important to emphasize that nowhere in the discussion has it been necessary to introduce external ethical norms, either my own or those arbitrarily derived from some fanciful "social welfare function." In this sense, I have not answered the "should" question posed in the paper's title. Indirectly, my answer is: *The redistribution that "should" be performed at various levels of government is that which individuals, acting through their collective entities, local and central, expressly prefer.* Idealized outcomes that reflect some "true" amalgamation of individuals' preferences are not, of course, possible to attain. Political outcomes emerge from the workings of institutions, themselves imperfect, that exhibit stochastic variety and, on occasion, internal inconsistency. This makes the task of the political economist especially difficult; he cannot "read" the genuine preferences of individuals from the revealed political outcomes that he observes. The empirical testing of the hypotheses derivable from either of the two analytical models requires sophisticated and highly imaginative research. The potential for the central government to effect zero-sum transfers, derivable from no plausible model of consensus, and reflecting the will of a dominant political coalition, breaks any direct connection between observed governmental behavior and the Pareto conditions for efficiency, at the operational or constitutional level. Within certain carefully drawn limits, this obstacle could be handled in the simpler of the two models, that of straightforward Pareto-optimal transfers. For genuine constitutional choice, however, observed opposition to the actual operation of redistributive institutions cannot, in itself, provide evidence of an absence of "efficiency" in the more comprehensive choice of social institutions.

Despite such problems, the discussion of what we may call the "political economy of redistribution" has been substantially advanced in recent years.[18] There is no cause for retreat into obscurantist ethics, which does little more than embroil us, one with another, over just whose personal set of values "should" be selected by that nonexistent yet subservient elite through which too many of us seek in unconscious willingness to subvert ordinary democratic process.

Notes

James M. Buchanan is University Professor of Economics and General Director, Center for Public Choice, at Virginia Polytechnic Institute and State University. He is indebted to his colleague, Charles Goetz, for helpful comments.

1   For a statement to this effect, see R. A. Musgrave, "Economics of Fiscal Federalism," *Nebraska Journal of Economics and Business* (Autumn, 1971), p. 10.

2   For a sophisticated critique of modern general-equilibrium theory that expresses much of my own, and largely intuitive, dissatisfaction, see Maurice Allais, "Les théories de l'équilibre économique général et de l'efficacité maximale," *Revue d'Économie Politique* (May, 1971), pp. 331–409.

3   For purposes of discussion here, I assume that local public goods will not be provided through ordinary market processes. This is not a realistic assumption. In the absence of local government, entrepreneurs would find it

profitable to organize arrangements through which local public goods would be provided, even those that are nonexcludable. In some circumstances, and especially where tie-in arrangements can be introduced that effectively reinstate excludability, market organization may prove even more efficient than local governmental units. In other circumstances, where exclusion cannot be introduced even indirectly, market arrangements may emerge, but these may remain seriously inefficient in supplying the local collective goods.

4   The now-classic paper here is Charles M. Tiebout, "A Pure Theory of Local Expenditures," *Journal of Political Economy* (October, 1956), pp. 416–24. For a critical assessment of the Tiebout adjustment process, under its most favorable assumptions, and in terms of efficiency-optimality criteria, see James M. Buchanan and Charles J. Goetz, "Efficiency Limits to Fiscal Mobility," *Public Economics* (April, 1972), pp. 25–44.

5   As noted with reference to the market supply of local public goods, this is an unrealistic assumption. It is made here only for the purpose of simplifying the exposition.

6   Much the same applies here as in the preceding footnote, although genuine problems emerge when we allow for the existence of public goods whose efficiency jointness-nonexcludability ranges are geographically limited but not sufficiently to allow for effective competition among spatially defined collective bodies.

7   William Niskanen has presented plausible arguments to the effect that central-government bureaus, possessing monopoly powers in the provision of particular public goods and services, "sell" these services, in effect, at all-or-none terms to "buyers," that is, to legislatures. In this case, all the fiscal surplus is squeezed out as bureaucratic waste, at least in the limit, and net gains-from-trade vanish. In terms of our model, the Niskanen hypothesis suggests that, with many central-government goods, the actually attainable utility-possibility frontier does not extend beyond G. See William A. Niskanen, *Bureaucracy and Representative Government* (Chicago: Aldine, 1971).

8   This prediction may seem bizarre in the face of popular mythology about local-government corruption. Local governments have their own equivalents of Bobby Baker and the Rayburn Building, but governments at this level cannot, by the nature of their situations, have their own Tulsa ship canals, Florida barge canals, maritime and farm subsidies, HEW bureaucracy, F-111 airplanes, or, even, their own Vietnam wars.

9   In the market, the individual need not be at all interested in the "decision rules." In fact, these are rarely discussed. He does not "vote" on the prices that he confronts in the marketplace. He has no need to do so because his protection is provided, ideally and conceptually, in the presence of alternative sellers and buyers. The individual in a local government may vote, directly or indirectly, on tax and budget matters, but the possible increments or decrements to his utility that such choices can produce are confined in value by his migrational prospects. The basic difference be-

tween the importance of decision rules at the central-government and local-government levels seems to have been wholly ignored in the Supreme Court reapportionment decisions, which were apparently based on bad economics as well as naive political science.

10   This motivation may, of course, be mixed with others. For a discussion that emphasizes this aspect, see Thomas Ireland, "Charity Budgeting," in Thomas Ireland and David B. Johnson, *The Economics of Charity* (Blacksburg: Center for Study of Public Choice, 1971).

11   This subject has recently been discussed in some detail by Mark Pauly. My discussion is confined to only a few of the models that he develops. At certain points, however, my results diverge from those suggested by Pauly. See Mark V. Pauly, "Redistribution as a Local Public Good," paper presented at COUPE meeting, Cambridge, October 1971.

12   In this model the making of income transfers becomes analogous to the removal of a "bad" rather than the purchase of a "good." In some respects, these two acts are behaviorally equivalent, but here it seems useful to make a conceptual separation between them.

13   This model seems realistic because nonfiscal elements may well dominate the fiscal in taxpayer locational decisions.

14   The "distribution of redistribution" among separate local units may be nonoptimal while at the same time the total amount of redistribution may be larger than that which would be generated under fully centralized redistribution by the central government. For a discussion of the general model, see James M. Buchanan and Milton Z. Kafoglis, "A Note on Public-Goods Supply," *American Economic Review* (June, 1963).

15   In more general terms, the shift to "constitutional" levels of choice or decision making, and especially when collective alternatives are involved, allows many of the standard tools of welfare economics to be used in what would otherwise seem value-laden territory. On this, see my, "The Relevance of Pareto Optimality," *Journal of Conflict Resolution* (December, 1962), pp. 341–54, and also James M. Buchanan and Gordon Tullock, *The Calculus of Consent* (Ann Arbor: University of Michigan Press, 1962).

16   The similarity between this approach and that of John Rawls should be apparent. See John Rawls, *A Theory of Justice* (Cambridge, Mass.: Harvard University Press, 1971).

17   I have, in earlier works, discussed some of these. See Buchanan and Tullock, *The Calculus of Consent*, and also my *Public Finance in Democatic Process* (Chapel Hill: University of North Carolina Press, 1967). For further discussion, see Richard E. Wagner, *The Fiscal Organization of American Federalism* (Chicago: Markham, 1971), pp. 4–6. Also, see paper 9, by Mitchell Polinsky, in this book.

18   For a paper that summarizes much of this discussion, see Harold M. Hochman. "Individual Preferences and Distributional Adjustment," presented at the New Orleans meeting of the American Economic Association, December, 1971.

Introduction to Chapter 5

Gramlich lays out the normative ideal for fiscal federalism which reflects the "broad concensus" of public-finance economists. It embodies the principles of the Musgrave and Musgrave article, chapter 3. He does not consider the stabilization function since it is not an issue in fiscal federalism. However, he adds an additional function of government in a market system, the provision of social insurance. Specific expenditure programs which most analysts would group together under the distribution function (social security, Medicare, disability insurance and unemployment insurance) Gramlich labels as the provision of social insurance.

Gramlich examines expenditures by broad program and tax revenues by type of tax instrument for the three levels of government in the United States to determine whether and to what extent the actual divisions of functions and their financing through taxes conforms with the normative ideal. A number of problems with the existing system of fiscal federalism are identified, problems which create efficiency losses or inequitable outcomes or both. He performs a very careful analysis of categorical grants. The article ends with suggested reforms of the present system of fiscal federalism, reforms which most public finance economists would endorse in their broad thrust toward greater efficiency and greater equity.

5

The Economics of Fiscal Federalism and Its Reform

Edward M. Gramlich

The United States has always had one of the best-developed systems of fiscal federalism in the world. The fifty states have a large degree of autonomy from the national government: there are 75,000 local governments and special taxing districts that have a large degree of autonomy from both the national government and their state government. More than 3 percent of GNP is devoted to grants and tax expenditures paid by the national government for the benefit of states and localities, and another 3 percent devoted to grants paid by states to localities. State government direct (nongrant) spending accounts for 6 percent of GNP and local government spending for another 8 percent.

It should not be surprising that various aspects of this extensive system of fiscal relations have been examined thoroughly and often. Pages of several leading journals have been full of articles about federalism for decades. While it is impossible to distill an exact consensus out of this extensive literature, there is a broad consensus on a few important features concerning how a system of fiscal relationships between governments should be organized. In this paper I summarize that consensus, and then attempt the more interesting job of comparing the existing US system to this normative ideal. The two match up surprisingly well, but as might be expected, there are still discrepancies – discrepancies that are a good place to look in designing policy reform proposals.

Divisions of Responsibility: A Normative Model

The paper begins by comparing actual divisions of responsibility among governments for spending programs with the responsibilities that might be predicted by normative theoretical considerations. I divide spending into programs that are done for collective consumption motives, those that redistribute income, and those that provide social insurance. For each, the actual division of responsibility is compared to the theoretical ideal. Then I repeat the exercise on the tax side of the budget and for intergovernmental grants and tax subsidies. The instances turned up by this tour, where the present system does not conform well to the theoretical ideal, inspire a few suggested reforms to remedy the defects. Each of the suggested reforms should improve economic efficiency and equity, and the whole package together would make a sizable dent in the federal budget deficit.

Spending

The logic behind any division of functional responsibilities among governments follows directly from the logic that rationalizes government intervention in a market economy in the first place. Governments are collective organizations that can do certain things more efficiently than private individuals: protect rights, enforce laws and contracts, provide public goods, alter the distribution of income, and provide insurance against privately uninsurable risks. The last three in particular have been the focus of economists in their writing about government intervention in market economies, and I now extend the same logic to deal with federalism questions.

Public goods

The public goods rationale for intervening in a market economy is that certain goods have the physical property that it is difficult or costly to exclude consumers from consumption. Examples are lighthouses, defense goods, public parks, and streets, all of which provide benefits to those who do not pay for the good along with benefits to those who do pay. Given this physical property, it is difficult or costly for the provider of these goods to sell services to pay for them; and difficult or impossible for any one consumer to charge others for the external benefits yielded by her or his own consumption. Hence when people consume such goods individually, there will be suboptimal consumption levels because the individual consumers will not take into account the benefits of all others who consume automatically by virtue of the individual's consumption. The remedy is to provide the goods collectively, working out some political arrangements to vote on and pay for the goods jointly.

This reasoning is normally used to justify public intervention in a market economy, but it also provides a good platform from which to think about the division of functional responsibilities among governments. Beginning with any one individual, the advantage of organizing collectively, or adding individuals to the decision-making unit, is that others reap external benefits from the consumption activity. Hence the group gets closer to the social optimum level of consumption if more individuals are brought into the collective decision-making unit: the external benefits of consumption by one party are made internal.

On the other side, the disadvantage of adding people to the collective process is that at some point strong differences in tastes are likely to emerge. At some point the external benefits for a particular consumption item begin to decrease. Since the relatively unwilling consumers are forced to pay some share of the cost of the good, they will not obtain their desired amount unless they are taxed according to their marginal willingness to pay, a difficult requirement in the real world. This leads to rising distortionary costs as people are added to the decision-making unit.

While it may be difficult to apply in practice, this reasoning leads to a proposition about the optimally sized jurisdiction for the provision of any public good. A jurisdiction has reached this optimal size when the marginal advantage of adding people and reducing externalities equals the marginal disadvantage of adding people and increasing distortionary losses from taste differences.[1] If there is a public good that makes nobody outside the city better off – a public park in an area inaccessible to outsiders – the good should be provided by the city, because there are no externalities to be internalized in adding others to the political unit, but there is still a rising distortionary cost. If on the other hand there is a good from which all individuals in the country benefit, such as national defense and foreign aid, the good should be provided by the national government because there is a gain from internalizing the externalities, and minimal cost in forcing various consumers to consume the same amount.

Income distribution

A second problem requiring public intervention in a market economy involves the distribution of income. A market economy distributes income according to the marginal product of labor and capital owned, yielding what could be wide extremes in income between rich and poor. Public taxes and transfers are necessary to limit this variance in outcomes.

There is a federalism dimension to income distribution as well. If the jurisdiction for which redistribution is being carried out is a small one, rich people who would be taxed have an easy escape – they can leave the community. By contrast, poor people have an incentive to enter the community to gain from the redistribution, hence raising the number of poor people and the cost of redistribution for the remaining taxpayers. It follows that redistribution over a wide area such as a nation, where both emigration and immigration are quite costly, is more efficient than redistribution over a narrow area where emigration and immigration are relatively cheap.[2]

Social insurance

A third rationale for government intervention in the private market involves social insurance. People desire many types of insurance against social risks: insurance against old age poverty, catastrophic medical disability, long term unemployment. Since the costs of providing this type of insurance could be large, are quite uncertain, are realized in the long run, and are heavily concentrated in particular geographic areas, private insurers have been reluctant to provide it. Backed up by the ultimate power to tax, governments have provided this insurance, often forcing private citizens to join the scheme and contribute to costs.

Although social insurance schemes could in principle be provided by any level of government, many of the risk-pooling considerations that argue for them in the first place argue for national schemes. Most social insurance schemes work over the life cycle – workers pay in when working, and receive benefits when they are retired, in need of medical care, unemployed, or disabled. The United States is a country with a great degree of mobility across state borders, and many claimants on the social insurance fund will be living in a different state when time comes to collect benefits. It would not be impossible to work out a system of state payments to keep track of people moving from state to state, but it is generally cheaper just to assign people a national social security number and finance national benefits for people wherever they are. National trust funds for social insurance programs are neither inevitable nor unavoidable, but they are probably more efficient than state trust funds when the population is mobile.

Actual Budgets

Although the propositions outlined in the previous section are vague and often hard to apply, the actual division of responsibilities for spending programs among governments conforms reasonably well to the theoretical standards. Table 5.1 gives a breakdown of what is called direct spending at various levels of government for 1985. Direct spending is

Table 5.1 Direct expenditures of various levels of government, 1985

Item	Type	Amount in billions of current dollars	Percent of GNP
National		754.7	18.8
National defense	P	259.0	6.5
Social Security	S	166.8	4.2
Medicare	S	72.0	1.8
Agricultural subsidies	R	29.8	0.7
Veterans' benefits	P	28.8	0.7
Disability insurance	S	26.3	0.7
Welfare (food stamps)	R	21.9	0.5
Unemployment insurance	S	15.9	0.4
Foreign aid	P	14.3	0.4
Other		119.9	3.0
State		236.3	5.9
Higher education	P	41.0	1.0
Medical care (Medicaid)	R	40.5	1.0
Highways	P	26.4	0.7
Health and hospitals	P	25.2	0.6
Welfare	R	23.3	0.6
Other		79.9	2.0
Local		310.6	7.7
Elementary, secondary education	P	142.0	3.5
Police and fire	P	32.3	0.8
Health and hospitals	P	26.9	0.7
Welfare	R	17.5	0.4
Highways	P	16.9	0.4
Sewage and sanitation	P	9.5	0.2
Other		65.5	1.6

Source: David J. Levin and Donald C. Peters, "Receipts and Expenditures of State Governments and of Local Governments: Revised and Updated Estimates, 1983–6," *Survey of Current Business* 67 (November 87), 29–35.

total spending less interest payments less grants to other governments. Interest payments are excluded because they merely reflect the fiscal history of the respective governments; grants, so that the government actually running the program gets credit for it, even if the spending is partly financed by a grant from some other government. The table also designates whether each type of spending program is fundamentally a public goods program (P), a redistribution program (R), or a social insurance program (S). For these purposes education is considered a public good, even though there are certain ways in which education does not satisfy the requirements of being a public good (more consumers can use a bridge without much cost; the same cannot be said of a classroom or a college).

The table shows that relatively few public goods are operated by the national government. The only ones are those with a clear national span of benefits such as national defense, foreign aid, and veterans' benefits, which are properly thought of as an adjunct to national defense – and all social insurance programs are operated by the national government. The public goods programs operated by state governments – highways and health and hospitals – are those that must be planned regionally and in effect have a geographic span of benefits that exceeds local areas. The remaining public goods are operated locally.

But two aspects of the actual division of spending responsibility are harder to justify from a normative point of view. First, the redistribution programs at all levels of government are mixed in a way that no one could justify very convincingly. Some – agricultural subsidies and food stamps – are financed and operated at the national level; some – welfare and Medicaid – are partly financed by federal grants but actually run by states or localities. One of the reform proposals I will make below involves sorting these welfare responsibilities out more cleanly.

The second area where the actual responsibility is hard to justify involves higher education. Higher education is mainly financed by grants or tuition reductions from state governments to students. It is not clear why the subsidy should be a grant, and the donor the state government. Students recapture a reasonable share of their education expenses in the form of higher postgraduate incomes, and it is not clear why taxpayers at large should provide grants, as opposed to loans. Moreover, it is not clear why these taxpayers should be at the state level, as opposed to some other level of government. These questions lead to a proposal for an alternative approach to the financing of higher education. Under this alternative, students would receive loans for their education, to be repaid later either on a present value basis or on an income related basis. With this latter arrangement, many of the advantages of having national trust funds would come into play, and it would be logical to move this credit-type subsidy for higher education up to the national level.

Taxation

On the tax side, the lessons are much the same as on the spending side. Taxes with a high redistributional content – those that take from the rich and give to the poor – should generally be imposed over a large jurisdiction from which emigration and immigration are costly. If not, the rich can leave and go to where they are not taxed so heavily. Taxes imposed by localities should look more like benefit charges, where the consumers that actually benefit from the public goods pay the cost. This insures a close correspondence of actual and desired spending for citizens of local governments. And social insurance fees should be assessed at the same level of government as the trust fund that finances their benefits.

The actual distribution of taxes in 1985 by the three levels of government is shown in table 5.2. In line with the theoretical prediction, income and corporate taxes are relied on much more heavily by the national government. The income taxes that are imposed at the state level are generally of the flat-rate variety, generally not entailing much redistribution. There are some state corporate taxes, but since not all states impose such taxes, firms tend to flee high corporate tax states, and the corporate tax rates in those states that still have such taxes seem destined to remain at very low levels.

Table 5.2 Taxes of various levels of government, 1985

Item	Amount in billions of current dollars	Percent of GNP
National	788.7	19.7
Income	339.3	8.5
Corporate	58.5	1.5
Social insurance	310.9	7.8
Excise	34.6	0.9
Customs	12.2	0.3
Other	33.2	0.8
State	283.5	7.1
Income	66.1	1.6
Corporate	18.9	0.5
Social insurance	32.0	0.8
Sales	109.0	2.7
Other	57.5	1.4
Local	196.4	4.9
Social insurance	10.1	0.3
Sales	21.9	0.5
Property	103.4	2.6
Other	61.0	1.5

Source: See table 5.1.

Sales taxes, which entail very little redistribution, and property taxes, which are probably the closest to benefit charges, are not used at all at the national level, but only at the state and local level. Social insurance charges for the national trust fund benefits – for old age pensions, Medicare, disability, and unemployment – are imposed entirely at the national level. The small social insurance fees at the state and local level are for pension plans for the employees of these governments, which naturally would be operated by the governments for which the employees worked.

Grants and subsidies

The role of grants and subsidies in a federal system is to take care of those instances where jurisdictions and spending responsibilities cannot be perfectly matched. Even if a public service is provided by the optimally sized jurisdiction, there will be some benefit spillovers – some benefits realized by outsiders. These present a rationale for categorical grants from the national government to states and localities. Even if there is a national income redistribution plan, there will be some regional income differences and these could lead to differential abilities to support public services. They present a rationale for noncategorical assistance from the national government to states and localities.

Categorical grants

The basic rationale for categorical grants is benefit spillovers. Suppose that a jurisdiction's public spending generates some benefits to those living outside the jurisdiction. Just as individuals underconsume public goods when others benefit but do not pay, so also the jurisdiction will underconsume public goods unless the externalities can be internalized. One way of internalizing these externalities is for those outside the jurisdiction to bribe those inside to consume more.[3] But if there are lots of spending programs with externalities affecting lots of governments, the requisite system of bribes may be quite costly to work out. Further, there is no theoretical reason why the bargains among governments will ultimately be made: the various parties may simply hold out for better deals. In the end it is probably simpler for the national government just to provide price subsidies to encourage greater consumption of whatever public service it is that generates the externalities. These price subsidies, rebates of a certain share of the cost of certain public expenditures, are known as categorical grants.

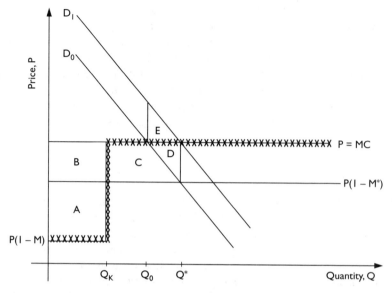

Figure 5.1 The inefficiency of categorical grants.

Notes: M is actual matching rate, M* is efficient rate yielding Q*.
xxxx is effective price schedule.
Converting inefficient to efficient grants yields the following gains and losses:
Federal taxpayers gain area (A – C – D)
State citizens gain area (C – A)
Outsiders gain area (D + E)
Net gain is area E

To see how the system works, refer to figure 5.1. Suppose the demand for a public service within a community is given by D_0 and the total demand including externalities is given by D_1. If the community faces a price, say equal to the marginal cost, of P, it will consume at quantity Q_0. The social optimum level of consumption including the externalities is Q^*. This level of consumption can be achieved by what is known as an open-ended categorical grant equal to m^* of the cost of this public service. The subsidy lowers the price to $P(1 - m^*)$, the community goes to Q^*, and everybody lives happily ever after.

The national government has an extensive system of categorical grants, shown in table 5.3 as $42.3 billion in 1987, 1 percent of GNP. About half of these grants are in areas where there would seem to be benefit spillovers, particularly transportation and sewage treatment. But even for these grants, the correspondence between the actual system and the theoretical ideal breaks down for two reasons:

Table 5.3 Limited federal categorical grants, 1987

Type	Amount in billions of current dollars	Matching rate (%)
Highways	12.3	83
Compensatory education	3.1	100
Employment and training	2.9	94
Sewage treatment	2.6	55
Mass transit	2.0	80
Human services	1.9	83
Public housing	1.9	100
Unemployment trust fund	1.6	100
Food donations	1.4	100
Rehabilitation services	1.3	83
Handicapped	1.2	99
Vocational education	1.0	58
Airports	0.9	80
Others	8.2	not calculated
Total	42.3	81

Source: Unpublished Office of Management and Budget data.

- The grant matching ratios, shown in the right column, are very high, much higher than would be rationalized by benefit spillovers.

- Perhaps because of this, the grants are not open-ended.

The upshot of these two drawbacks can be seen from figure 5.1. The ideal price structure from an efficiency standpoint is a price line that is flat at $P(1 - m^\star)$. The actual price line features highly favorable national matching provisions out to the grant limit amount, Q_K, but then no more matching. The price line reverts to P, the community consumes Q_0, and we have the ironic result that because the matching rate was too favorable, the amount had to be limited, and the limited categorical grant does not encourage any added spending.

Were grants made efficient by switching to the flat price line at $P(1 - m^\star)$, national taxpayers would gain area $(A - C - D)$. State citizens would gain area $(C - A)$ and outsiders would gain area $(E + D)$. The net gain of all together, known as the Kaldor-Hicks gain, is area E, that reflects the present-day loss of the underconsumption. Converting grants in this way thus improves economic efficiency, and it will reduce the federal budget deficit if area $(A - C - D)$ is positive. I propose, below, to convert grants in this manner.

Noncategorical grants

The rationale for categorical grants is based on the properties of the public good or service – whether there are external benefits. The rationale for noncategorical grants, given to augment the spendable resources of the recipient community without regard for what the community does with the grants, is based on the properties of the recipient government. If this government presides over a poor jurisdiction, with below-average income that can be taxed to provide public goods, its "tax price" for public services is higher than average and it will have subpar consumption levels of the public service. This would present no particular problem unless the public service in question were something like education. In that case the local financing of the public service in effect perpetuates the income disparity: poor communities have high tax prices for education, they stay poor, their tax price stays high, and so forth. Half of the federal grants shown in table 5.3 – those for compensatory education, employment and training, human services, handicapped and vocational education – have this rationale. Even more significant are what are known as "power equalization" grants from state governments to local governments. These power equalization grants in effect try to equalize education spending across states by differential price reductions. Approximately 2 percent of GNP is devoted to education grants from states to localities, though it is hard to know how much equalization of tax prices is implicit in these grants without much more detailed analysis. The recently killed federal general revenue sharing program could also be rationalized along these lines, though the distribution of funds in that program was not particularly focused on poor districts.

There would be grounds for a policy reform in this area, but the case is a good deal weaker than in other areas because the states are already assuming responsibility for district power equalization. Any new federal initiatives, along the lines of upgraded compensatory education programs, risk causing reductions in such programs at the state level, and hence merely transferring resources from federal to state taxpayers. Moreover, it is hard to work out the details of the program because there are such wide differences in functional responsibilities and tax prices across states. In Hawaii, for example, the state government runs the schools – how would the national government work out a grant that treats Honolulu and some equally sized city with responsibility for its own schools even handedly? For this reason no federal power equalization scheme will be suggested below, though a case for it could certainly be made.

Tax subsidies

There are two main tax subsidies that flow from the federal government to states and localities:

- State and local income and property taxes are now deductible on the federal income tax, permitting some state taxpayers to recover some of their state and local taxes.

- State and local interest is now tax exempt, permitting state and local taxpayers to borrow at subsidized rates.

Tax deductibility might seem to be an ideal way to give a slight open-ended price subsidy to state or local governments for all their public services, not unlike the ideal matching program shown in figure 5.1. Letting t stand for the marginal federal income tax rate faced by a voter who itemizes deductions, deductibility effectively lowers the price of public services from P to $P(1 - t)$ for this voter, probably pretty close to $P(1 - m^\star)$ for most public services. But we should recognize three factors that complicate this neat solution to the externalities problem:

- Tax rates are progressive, so rich voters get a bigger tax-induced subsidy than poor voters.

- Since most low income taxpayers do not itemize deductions, they get no subsidy at all.

- The fact that state or local public goods are provided at the sale level throughout the jurisdiction makes it particularly hard to tell who will benefit from the tax deduction.

The situation is described in figure 5.2. Demand functions for local public services without externalities are shown for a typical rich itemizer (D_I) and a typical poor nonitemizer (D_N). The rich itemizer has a higher demand for public services but also faces a higher tax price because of his greater taxable income or property. For simplicity I assume these two differences are exactly offsetting, so both voters prefer quantity Q_0 without tax deductibility. Tax deductibility lowers the tax price of public services for the rich itemizer but not the poor nonitemizer.

If nonitemizers have a voting majority, as in the low-income community shown in the left panel, public spending will not change and tax deductibility is only a transfer from all federal taxpayers to rich itemizers. If itemizers have a voting majority, in the high-income community shown in the right panel, deductibility raises spending but is economi-

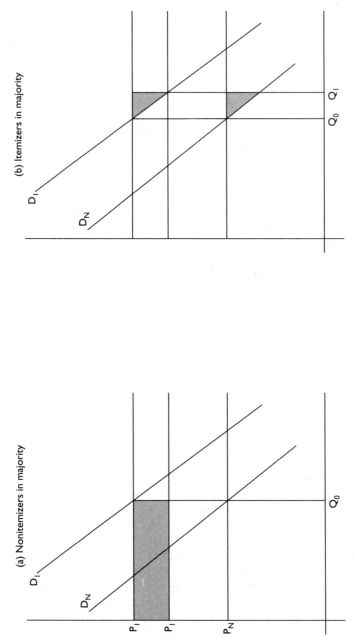

Figure 5.2 The inefficiency of tax deductibility.

(a) Deductibility does not change public spending, but only transfers shaded area to high income itemizers.

(b) Deductibility raises public spending to Q_i and generates upper shaded triangle efficiency loss for each itemizer and lower shaded triangle efficiency loss for each nonitemizer.

cally inefficient. The marginal valuation of public services is less than federal taxpayer cost for the rich, and less than local taxpayer cost for the poor. The subsidy does not look good either way. It subsidizes public spending in the rich but not the poor community – just the opposite of a power equalization grant.

One would, of course, want to study the matter more deeply because there could be all manner of combinations of voting majorities, initial desired spending levels, externalities, and patterns of price reductions. On a previous occasion I did try to work this all out, for a sample of Michigan voters with the tightening provisions implicit in the Tax Reform Act of 1986 (TRA) and with the assumption of full elimination of tax deductibility.[4] The results are shown in table 5.4. A partial elimination of tax deductibility, as was experienced under the TRA through the reduction in numbers of itemizers and the removal of the sales tax deduction, would be predicted to reduce public spending slightly in the high-income suburbs of Detroit and not at all elsewhere in the state. A full elimination would reduce public spending by up to 10 percent in

Table 5.4 Desired local government spending under different tax deductibility provisions[a]

Place	Decrease				Increase			
	>10	6–9	1–5	No change	1–5	6–9	>10	Sum
				1980 Tax Law[b]				
Detroit	7	5	2	*87*	3	27	18	149
Suburbs	20	16	9	*229*	3	30	25	332
Other	54	42	40	*428*	3	61	61	689
Total	81	63	51	*744*	9	118	104	1,170
				TRA of 1986[b]				
Detroit	23	6	15	*56*	8	26	15	149
Suburbs	65	26	*81*	100	21	27	12	332
Other	118	58	126	*265*	21	64	37	689
Total	206	90	222	*421*	50	117	64	1,170
				Full elimination[b]				
Detroit	37	14	6	*54*	4	21	13	149
Suburbs	165	*32*	14	93	3	17	8	332
Other	234	86	*47*	250	5	37	30	689
Total	436	132	*67*	397	12	75	51	1,170

[a] Number of voters desiring specified changes in local spending and taxes, Michigan, 1978.

[b] Median voter class in italics.

Source: Edward M. Gramlich, "Federalism and Federal Deficit Reduction," *National Tax Journal* 40 (September 1987), 299–313.

those high-income suburbs of Detroit, slightly throughout the rest of the state, but not at all in the low-income city of Detroit. With these more detailed calculations, the subsidy still looks like perverse power equalization, and still transfers tax to high-income itemizers wherever they live. An obvious reform proposal is simply to eliminate income and property tax deductibility on the federal income tax.

The impact of the interest exemption is harder to predict because of what is known as the tax arbitrage problem. If state and local interest is not taxable, the state and local bond rate(s) will be bid down until marginal investors are indifferent between buying a taxable bond and earning $r(1 - t)$ and buying a nontaxable bond and earning $s = r(1 - t)$, where r is the market interest rate. It might seem that this reduction in the cost-of-capital would stimulate state and local borrowing and construction, and indeed it might to some extent. But in this era of sharp bond traders, there is another more likely impact. What is to stop local governments from borrowing at s, investing at r, pocketing the difference, and not changing capital construction at all? The Treasury has rules to limit this particular form of arbitrage, but other forms are possible, and exist in the real world.[5] The possibility of tax arbitrage makes it both inefficient and inequitable to open up differences in borrowing and lending rates such as is done by the tax exemption, and another obvious reform proposal is to eliminate the federal tax exemption of state and local interest.

Reform Proposals

This review of the present fiscal system has been motivated by a search for aspects that are inefficient and/or inequitable because they violate some basic canons of the theory of federalism. There are a number of aspects that fall into this category, which suggests several interesting policy changes. I now detail these suggestions in my own personal preference ordering, giving the rationale and, in table 5.5, the likely improvement in the federal budget deficit in 1990 from making the change. That table also documents the source of any numbers that are used.

Convert categorical grants

The present matching grants do not achieve their goal of increasing spending in particular areas because the price subsidy is too generous on inframarginal units and not generous enough on marginal units. Roughly half of the grants listed in table 5.3, those for transportation and sewage,

Table 5.5 Bold fiscal reform plan, fiscal year 1990

Policy change	Federal deficit reduction (in billions of dollars)
Convert categorical grants	$5[a]
Eliminate tax deductibility	26[b]
Tax state and local interest	13[c]
Convert welfare grants	−9[d]
Net impact	$35

[a] Author's calculation.
[b] Congressional Budget Office, *Reducing the Deficit: Spending as Revenue Options* (March 1988) Option Rev. -15, p. 322.
[c] Edward M. Gramlich, "Federalism and Federal Deficit Reduction," *National Tax Journal* 40 (September 1987), 299–313.
[d] Edward M. Gramlich, "Cooperation and Competition in Public Welfare Policies," *Journal of Policy Analysis and Management* 6, no. 3 (Spring 1987), 417–31.

could be converted to open-ended matching form with a price subsidy of about 0.3, roughly the level suggested by the pattern of internal and external benefits.[6] The federal budget saving would be about $5 billion in 1990, state citizens would lose a small amount, but there would be an economic efficiency gain of about $1 billion from the change.

While reductions in federal matching shares would seem to be logical policy changes in the face of pressures to reduce federal spending, there have as yet been very few such reductions. Most actual and proposed cuts are simply cuts in the amounts of grant-funded spending or consolidations of grants, both of which can be seen from figure 5.1 to generate no improvements in economic efficiency. But there have been two recent movements in the direction of my proposal. The Omnibus Water Bill of 1986, for rivers, harbors, and other "pork barrel" type projects, requires state and local cost matching on new projects for the first time. The two Clean Water Acts passed in the 1980s have also reduced federal matching shares from 75 percent to a much lower figure by converting grants to a subsidized loan revolving fund.

Eliminate tax deductibility

The present deductibility of income and property taxes on the federal income tax is both inefficient and inequitable. It is inefficient because it subsidizes public spending unduly in some high-income communities. It is inequitable because it only goes to high-income taxpayers, whether they live in high- or low-income communities. The federal budget saving from completely eliminating deductibility would be enormous, $26 billion in 1990.

While a full elimination of tax deductibility has often been proposed, and was even included in the Treasury Department's initial tax reform proposal in 1985, steps in this direction so far have been very timid. State gasoline taxes were made nondeductible in the energy crisis of 1978 and sales taxes in the TRA of 1986. As was mentioned above, the cost of deductibility was further reduced in the TRA by the reduction in numbers of itemizers and the reduction in marginal income tax rates. Beyond this, there are various schemes to do part of the job: only let taxes be deducted at the bottom bracket rate, only let a share of taxes be deducted, only permit deduction of taxes in excess of some share of income. Any of these would be desirable changes, but the best change of all would be to eliminate tax deductibility altogether.

Tax interest

The exclusion of state and local interest from federal taxable income drives down state and local bond rates. It might stimulate some capital construction, but its more likely effect is to open up arbitrage opportunities for state and local governments – they can borrow tax exempt and buy taxable bonds. The Internal Revenue Service does have rules against arbitrage, but there are lots of pairs of rates (r, $r(1 - t)$, and s) that can be paired against each other and it is virtually impossible to police all forms of arbitrage. A good principle of tax administration is to keep arbitrage opportunities as low as possible, hence keeping the burden on the administrative enforcers as light as possible. This can be done by the simple expedient of taxing state and local interest, raising $13 billion in the process.

As with the other measures suggested, there have been some recent movements in this direction. By lowering marginal tax rates, the TRA reduced rate spreads on many forms of arbitrage. Moreover, the TRA contained some direct quantitative limits on arbitrage, limiting the amount of private-purpose bonds that could qualify for the interest exemption.

Convert AFDC grants

One could make a strong case that the main welfare programs, Aid to Families with Dependent Children (AFDC) and Medicaid, should be straightforward national redistribution programs, just as is the federal personal income tax. Operating them at the state level, as is done now, leads to wide variations in state benefits and to unduly low average levels of benefits to the extent that state legislators are worried about the threat of migration (high benefits may attract welfare recipients to the state). These impacts are reduced by federal matching grants – which in this area are open-ended, with federal matching shares that range between 78 percent for low-income states and 50 percent for high-income states – and by the evening out that results from the national food stamps program. But benefit levels still vary widely across states, being roughly twice as high in high-benefit states as in low-benefit states.

It would be hard to revamp this system without a fundamental change, but there is a simpler way. There are efficiency reasons for having states bear some of the cost of Medicaid, in order to have an incentive to police costs. This program could be left as is. But there is no obvious sense in having states bear some of the cost of very low AFDC benefit levels. A simple reform would be to base federal matching shares not on state income, as now, but on benefit levels themselves. Federal matching ratios could be quite generous in those states that pay very low welfare benefits, just to bring these benefits up to decent levels. They could be quite strict, or indeed there could be no matching at all, in high-benefit states. Such a scheme would greatly reduce disparities in AFDC benefits around the country because it lowers the price most where the most reduction is needed.

To make a specific proposal, suppose federal matching shares for AFDC were raised to 100 percent for combined AFDC–food stamp benefits up to 60 percent of the poverty line; to 75 percent for benefits up to 80 percent of the poverty line; and to 50 percent up to the poverty line. Such a plan would raise living standards among welfare recipients by more than $3 billion in 1990, switch about $6 billion in welfare costs from states to the federal government, and cost the federal government about $9 billion in 1990.

For the first three policy reform proposals suggested, one can discern some recent movement in the direction of the proposal. In the case of AFDC, however, the drift is away from my proposal. The AFDC program actually had matching provisions along the lines I am proposing in its early days, from its first passage in the 1930s to the late 1960s. When the Medicaid program was added in the late 1960s, states were given the option of using the old kinked matching grant schedule or switching over to their Medicaid formula, which made matching rates constant for all benefit levels, at a rate determined by state relative income. In a sense, my proposal does nothing more than return to the old formulas for determining AFDC matching shares.

Higher education loans

At present, state governments pay large tuition subsidies to students to attend state supported universities. This scheme is arguably inefficient, both in subsidizing an activity where students probably can recapture most of their investment costs in subsequent income gains, and in distorting student college choices. It is also arguably inequitable, in that many low income taxpayers who do not benefit or have not benefited from higher education or higher education subsidies, subsidize the education of the middle and upper classes.

It is difficult to convert the subsidy to a loan program if it remains at the state level. The problem with states running life-cycle-type social insurance programs in this country is that interstate mobility is very high, necessitating complex tracking schemes. If states made higher education loans instead of grants, they would either have to collect on the graduate's income tax, in whatever state the graduate moves to, or on the graduate's loan. Experience with student loan repayment is already discouraging, and it would presumably become even more so if the university (to which the graduate might have some allegiance) is supplanted by some faraway state as the creditor.

The only way states can run nonsubsidy higher education plans is by a prepayment plan, examples of which are being studied in several states. In these, parents pay into a trust fund when children are very young and the savings accumulate into tuition credits when the child is ready for college. These credits will almost certainly be differential, implying distortion of choice, and there could be an incentive for the state to regulate the pricing and other policies of the university to make sure that prepaying parents' tuition credits can in fact pay the cost of higher education at the designated provider. Interstate mobility as the children are growing up could also present problems. These schemes are just now being adopted and perhaps will work well, but there are several potential inefficiencies.

If not the states, the national government. The national government can run an intertemporal trust fund, and a higher education loan program would be one such. The loans could in principle be repaid on either a debt- or an income-contingent basis: the issues here are complex and controversial, but they do not involve the federalism dimension. The only federalism point is that the national government seems best situated to conduct the type of higher education support program that seems most rational from an efficiency and equity standpoint.

In terms of details, one such plan, for loans ultimately supported by income-contingent payroll tax payments into a social insurance trust fund, was actually proposed by Michael Dukakis in the 1988 presidential campaign.[7] Were such a plan to be adopted, present federal subsidies to higher education running about $4 billion a year could either be dropped or devoted to grants to low income students. Beyond this, the true incremental budget cost of such a plan should be zero.

The latter claim concerns an important issue in budgetary accounting. On a cash basis, a postpayment plan would certainly entail budget outlays now and repayments later. But as the Congressional Budget Office has often argued, the cash budget is a very poor way to represent the government's financial position in the case of loans. These generally involve simple asset transfers, which leave both income and net worth unchanged for both the government and the private sector. In such cases a better representation can be gotten by recording the true subsidy, in a present value sense, whenever the government makes any credit transaction with the private sector. Were such accounting to be adopted for any nonsubsidized postpayment plan, the proper outlay entry would be zero, precisely what is entered in the federal deficit reduction in table 5.5.

Summary

The US system of fiscal federalism relationships conforms to the theoretical ideal reasonably well. With a few outstanding exceptions, public goods are by and large run by the governments that preside over their benefit area and social insurance funds are generally run at the national level. Taxes are redistributive at the national level and based more closely on benefits at the local level, as also conforms to the logic of federalism.

The outstanding exceptions concern income redistribution programs and higher education support, both of which seem inappropriately lodged at the state level. A programmatic remedy for the first anomaly is to alter the structure of welfare grants to lessen interstate benefit differences. Such a change would leave program operation at the state level but alter price incentives to narrow interstate differences in benefits and migration incentives. A programmatic remedy for the second anomaly is some form of a national loan program supported by a national trust fund.

There are other inefficiencies not involving the division of responsibilities but rather the structure of grants and tax incentives that benefit state and local citizens. The grant inefficiencies can be dealt with by reducing federal matching ratios but making grants open-ended. The tax inefficiencies can be dealt with by continuing the spirit of the TRA, under which tax preferences are eliminated so that marginal tax rates are kept as low as possible.

Were a package of such changes made, the federal deficit could be reduced by as much as $35 billion in 1990, 0.6 percent of GNP anticipated for that time or 20 percent of the deficit anticipated for that time. The reduction is not enormous, but not trivial either, and all the measures suggested improve both efficiency and equity.

Notes

1 The principle is described and defended by Wallace E. Oates, *Fiscal Federalism* (New York: Harcourt, Brace, Jovanovich, Inc., 1972), chapter 2.
2 This issue is discussed in more detail in Edward M. Gramlich, "Reforming US Fiscal Federalism Arrangements," in John M. Quigley and Daniel L. Rubinfeld, eds., 34–69, *American Domestic Priorities: An Economic Appraisal* (Berkeley: University of California Press, 1985).
3 This remedy was suggested by Ronald Coase, "The Problem of Social Cost," *Journal of Law and Economics* (October 1960).
4 Edward M. Gramlich, "Federalism and Federal Deficit Reduction," *National Tax Journal* 40 (September 1987), 299–313.
5 See Roger H. Gordon and Joel Slemrod, "An Empirical Examination of Municipal Financial Policy," in Harvey S. Rosen, ed., 53–78, *Studies in State and Local Public Finance* (Chicago: The University of Chicago Press, 1986).
6 Gramlich, "Federalism and Federal Deficit Reduction," pp. 299–313.
7 The details are similar to that studied by Robert D. Reischauer, "HELP: A Student Loan Program for the Twenty-first Century," in Lawrence E. Gladieux, ed., *Radical Reform or Incremental Change? Student Loan Policy Alternatives for the Federal Government* (New York: The College Board, 1988).

Part II

Revenues for State and Local Governments

Introduction to Part II

The chapters in this part of the book are about state and local government tax structure decisions, in theory and in practice.

What makes one revenue instrument better than others, or one specific feature of a revenue instrument better than other features? Of course, the revenue instrument should be capable of yielding the revenue that is expected from it, at the time the decision to use it, or to use another instrument, is made. Of course, the instrument should be amenable to administration that is relatively cheap; collection costs should not consume a substantial share of the revenue collected. But these points almost go without saying.

In everyday political discourse and to ordinary people, "fairness" in the distribution of the tax burden among the members of the political community surely is the most important criterion, as it has been for centuries. The main point of Magna Carta in 1215 was the King's pledge not to extract taxes from his subjects except "according to law;" the immediate issue precipitating the American Revolution in 1775 was the unfairness of "taxation without representation;" and many historians consider that the immediate cause of the French Revolution in 1789 was heavy and unfair taxation that ordinary people increasingly refused to pay. There are various definitions of what is fair in taxation. In recent generations in Western countries, fairness has come to be measured by how the tax burden is distributed with respect to the income of households: people with like incomes should be taxed alike ("horizontal equity") and people with unequal incomes should be taxed differentially in some relation to their incomes ("vertical equity"). It is seldom easy to ascertain the economic "incidence" of taxes (who *really* bears them). There are both theoretical and measurement problems, not all of which have been solved by economists.

The second major criterion in evaluating taxes is the economic consequences of alternative revenue instruments – what economists refer to as
the "efficiency effects." Both public officials and economists worry about
this. The public-policy objective is or should be to minimize distortions
in economic decision-making. At the state and local level, the most
important issue is how differences in the level of taxation among state
and local government affect the location decisions of firms and
households.

The chapters in Part II explore the theory of incidence and major
types of revenue instruments used by state and local governments, with
some emphasis on their incidence – property tax, consumption taxes in
the form of sales and excise taxes, the state corporate income tax and
charges for the use of public services.

Another group of chapters focus on how *state-local* fiscal decisions are
much affected by provisions of *federal* tax law, such as deductibility of
state-local taxes on federal income tax returns. Two chapters in Part II
consider the effects on state and local fiscal decisions of the most important change in federal tax law in many years, the Tax Reform Act of
1986.

The last chapter in Part II deals with the effects of state and local tax
policy on the state or local economy.

Introduction to Chapter 6

Adam Smith in 1776 laid out what he called "the maxims of taxes in general," in a passage that sounds remarkably modern, for the simple reason that, in democratic countries, Smith's principles are subscribed to by virtually everyone who has thought even briefly about taxation. Taxes ought to be fairly distributed, meaning in relation to individuals' ability to pay taxes; they ought not to damage the economy that provides the wherewithal for paying taxes; and they ought to be precisely specified and collected in a reasonable manner. The devil being in the details, there are endless arguments about what these principles mean in a given situation, but the principles are accepted. Adam Smith wrote about them as clearly as anyone ever has.

6

Of Taxes

Adam Smith

The private revenue of individuals, it has been shewn in the first book of this Inquiry, arises ultimately from three different sources; Rent, Profit, and Wages. Every tax must finally be paid from some one or other of those three different sorts of revenue, or from all of them indifferently. I shall endeavour to give the best account I can, first, of those taxes which, it is intended, should fall upon rent; secondly, of those which, it is intended, should fall upon profit; thirdly, of those which, it is intended, should fall upon wages; and, fourthly, of those which, it is intended, should fall indifferently upon all those three different sources of private revenue. The particular consideration of each of these four different sorts of taxes will divide the second part of the present chapter into four articles, three of which will require several other subdivisions. Many of those taxes, it will appear from the following review, are not finally paid from the fund, or source of revenue, upon which it was intended they should fall.

Before I enter upon the examination of particular taxes, it is necessary to premise the four following maxims with regard to taxes in general.

1   The subjects of every state ought to contribute towards the support of the government, as nearly as possible, in proportion to their respective abilities; that is, in proportion to the revenue which they respectively enjoy under the protection of the state. The expence of government to the individuals of a great nation, is like the expence of management to the joint tenants of a great estate, who are all obliged to contribute in proportion to their respective interests in the estate. In the observation or neglect of this maxim consists, what is called the equality or inequality of taxation. Every tax, it must be observed once for all, which falls finally upon one only of the three sorts of revenue above

mentioned, is necessarily unequal, in so far as it does not affect the other two. In the following examination of different taxes I shall seldom take much further notice of this sort of inequality, but shall, in most cases, confine my observations to that inequality which is occasioned by a particular tax falling unequally even upon that particular sort of private revenue which is affected by it.

2 The tax which each individual is bound to pay ought to be certain, and not arbitrary. The time of payment, the manner of payment, the quantity to be paid, ought all to be clear and plain to the contributor, and to every other person. Where it is otherwise, every person subject to the tax is put more or less in the power of the tax-gatherer, who can either aggravate the tax upon any obnoxious contributor, or extort, by the terror of such aggravation, some present or perquisite to himself. The uncertainty of taxation encourages the insolence and favours the corruption of an order of men who are naturally unpopular, even where they are neither insolent nor corrupt. The certainty of what each individual ought to pay is, in taxation, a matter of so great importance, that a very considerable degree of inequality, it appears, I believe, from the experience of all nations, is not near so great an evil as a very small degree of uncertainty.

3 Every tax ought to be levied at the time, or in the manner, in which it is most likely to be convenient for the contributor to pay it. A tax upon the rent of land or of houses, payable at the same term at which such rents are usually paid, is levied at the time when it is most likely to be convenient for the contributor to pay; or, when he is most likely to have wherewithal to pay. Taxes upon such consumable goods as are articles of luxury, are all finally paid by the consumer, and generally in a manner that is very convenient for him. He pays them by little and little, as he has occasion to buy the goods. As he is at liberty too, either to buy, or not to buy, as he pleases, it must be his own fault if he ever suffers any considerable inconveniency from such taxes.

4 Every tax ought to be so contrived as both to take out and to keep out of the pockets of the people as little as possible, over and above what it brings into the public treasury of the state. A tax may either take out or keep out of the pockets of the people a great deal more than it brings into the public treasury, in the four following ways. First, the levying of it may require a great number of officers, whose salaries may eat up the greater part of the produce of the tax, and whose perquisites may impose another additional tax upon the people. Secondly, it may obstruct the industry of the people, and discourage them from applying to certain branches of business which might give maintenance and employment to great multitudes. While it obliges the people to pay, it may thus dimin-

ish, or perhaps destroy, some of the funds which might enable them more easily to do so. Thirdly, by the forfeitures and other penalties which those unfortunate individuals incur who attempt unsuccessfully to evade the tax, it may frequently ruin them, and thereby put an end to the benefit which the community might have received from the employment of their capitals. An injudicious tax offers a great temptation to smuggling. But the penalties of smuggling must rise in proportion to the temptation. The law, contrary to all the ordinary principles of justice, first creates the temptation, and then punishes those who yield to it; and it commonly enhances the punishment too in proportion to the very circumstance which ought certainly to alleviate it, the temptation to commit the crime. Fourthly, by subjecting the people to the frequent visits and the odious examination of the tax-gatherers, it may expose them to much unnecessary trouble, vexation, and oppression; and though vexation is not, strictly speaking, expence, it is certainly equivalent to the expence at which every man would be willing to redeem himself from it. It is in some one or other of these four different ways that taxes are frequently so much more burdensome to the people than they are beneficial to the sovereign.

The evident justice and utility of the foregoing maxims have recommended them more or less to the attention of all nations. All nations have endeavoured, to the best of their judgment, to render their taxes as equal as they could contrive; as certain, as convenient to the contributor, both in the time and in the mode of payment, and in proportion to the revenue which they brought to the prince, as little burdensome to the people. A review of some of the principal taxes which have taken place in different ages and countries will show, that the endeavours of all nations have not in this respect been equally successful.

Introduction to Chapter 7

Peter Mieszkowski's 1969 article remains, for economists, the definitive summary of the economics of fairness in taxation, that is, the theory of how taxes affect the distribution of income within a country. Three aspects of the article are especially noteworthy. First, although much of the theory is not controversial, there are two major taxes about whose incidence there has been real dispute, the corporation income tax and the property tax. This article explains the controversies, places them in perspective and reviews the empirical evidence with respect to the corporation income. Mieszkowski's views on the incidence of the property tax are now widely accepted, and have been almost from the day this article was published.

Second, attention is paid to the spatial dimension of incidence, how taxes affect location of people and activities, which before this article was not considered part of incidence theory. Third, the effects of taxation on saving and growth also are treated, not just a world with fixed amounts of capital and labor.

7

Tax Incidence Theory: The Effects of Taxes on the Distribution of Income

Peter Mieszkowski

I am indebted to Arnold C. Harberger, W. D. Nordhaus, and Alan R. Prest for comments on, and corrections of, an earlier draft of this paper.

Associated with tax policy are a number of interrelated effects. Taxes have a direct impact on the level of effective demand and employment. Taxes affect work incentives, the amount of saving and the level and pattern of investment. Some taxes distort the allocation of resources and lead to inefficiencies. Finally, the level and structure of taxes determine the level of disposable income, and the *distribution* of after-tax income among different groups.

The analysis of tax incidence is the investigation of the distributive effects of taxes. In a general way incidence theory is applied distribution theory in which the focus is on how various tax regimes affect factor returns and commodity prices. The distributive impacts of some taxes are fairly straightforward, while the effects of others are quite complex. For example, the burden of a proportional income tax, that is imposed on all income, is proportional to a household's share in national income. On the other hand, taxes that do not apply to all types of income, or to all commodities, change relative commodity prices, influence factor use in particular industries and change the production structure of the economy. A full analysis of the incidence of taxes that produce such effects requires a general equilibrium approach which accounts, as fully as possible, for tax-induced changes in commodity and factor prices.

Modern general equilibrium incidence theory is based on the marginal productivity theory of distribution that assumes firms choose factor proportion so as to minimize costs, and set commodity prices at profit maximizing levels. A large part of this review is devoted to incidence theory built on these neoclassical assumptions. Initially a set of simplifying assumptions is made: (1) that commodity and factor markets are perfectly competitive; (2) that there is no foreign trade; (3) that factors of production are perfectly mobile (shiftable) between different industries; and (4) that the *total* supplies of all factors are in perfectly inelastic supply to the economy as a whole. Then, whenever possible, the assumptions will be relaxed. We shall review the literature on dynamic incidence which allows for longer-run effects of tax policy through changes in the level of capital formation, and will also consider the effects of imperfect mobility of factors and the introduction of foreign trade.

The second major section of this review will examine the effects of market imperfections and the implications of non-maximizing behavior. Central to this part of the discussion is the econometric work on the shifting of the corporate profits tax. This quantitative work is an indirect test of the fundamental question of whether concentrated industries, in the aggregate, maximize profits.

Neoclassical Incidence Theory

Marginal productivity distribution theory postulates that in each industry there are a number of possible technologies and that cost-minimizing firms choose production techniques on the basis of relative factor costs (prices). In a constant-returns-to scale, perfectly competitive economy prices will be equal to average costs and factors of production will receive the value of their marginal products.

In contrast with Austrian capital theory that viewed capital as goods in process, modern distribution theory emphasizes capital as durable producers' goods, such as plant and equipment. There are, of course, many types of capital goods of varying durability and the annual rentals, or quasi-rents, on different types of capital will not be the same. Despite the diversity of capital, well-functioning capital markets will, in the absence of differential risk, establish a single rate of return on real capital (the rate of interest) which would equate the present value of the rentals (gross profits) on a particular asset to its cost of production.

The result, i.e., factor returns are determined by real agents such as technology and material or resource endowments of the economy, has straightforward, simple implications for the burden (incidence) of general taxes, imposed at the same rate on all commodities, or on particular types of factor income. For if the *total* supply of each factor is fixed, full employment of all factors is automatically achieved through wage and price flexibility, and if government spends the tax proceeds in such a way as to leave relative factor prices unchanged by an increase in the government budget, the real burden of a general tax will fall on its legal tax base.

For a general sales or excise tax which taxes final commodities and which taxes capital goods as well as consumption goods, the tax base is gross national product (GNP). On the assumption that government expenditures are distributionally neutral, the decrease in the real income of each household, resulting from the imposition of such a tax, is proportional to its share in GNP. The base of a proportional income tax that allows for the depreciation of capital is net national product (NNP) so the incidence of this tax is a household's share in value-added. The burden of a general profits (wage) tax falls fully on profits (wages). Also, if capital is homogenous, a general property (wealth) tax is equivalent to a tax on profits. Similarly, it does not matter in the case of payroll taxes whether the legal liability of the tax is imposed on employees or on employers. The burden of general payroll taxes falls fully on wage-earners.

All these results follow from the condition that factors receive the value of their marginal products, and general taxes in no way affect the absolute or relative marginal productivities of the factors. For a given set of commodity prices the before-tax incomes of factors will not be affected by general factor taxes. General sales taxes can "get into" the price structure in one of two ways. When there is an accommodating monetary policy, commodity prices will increase by the amount of the tax, or at constant commodity prices factors will have to accept a proportional decrease in their monetary earnings in order to remain fully employed. Regardless of the direction of the adjustment, the incidence of a general sales tax is (depreciation aside) equivalent to that of a proportional income tax.

The view that incidence is a matter of relative price changes and *real* income changes was established primarily by R. A. Musgrave [50. 1953; 51. 1959, pp. 205–31, 379–82]. This point and other aspects of incidence methodology were developed by Musgrave in response to the stimulating contributions of E. R. Rolph [66. 1952; 67. 1952; 68. 1953; 69. 1953; 70. 1954]. Rolph, following the lead of H. G. Brown [7. 1939] argued that the traditional view, that excise taxes are shifted to consumers, is fallacious and that the burden of the tax must be borne by factor owners in proportion to their incomes. Rolph placed great stress on the backward shifting of indirect taxes, not only for general excise taxes but also for partial excises.

While it is generally accepted that Musgrave's emphasis on relative rather than absolute prices is correct, the important question is whether an excise tax on capital goods is equivalent to a tax on savings. For if it be so, a general excise tax, including in its base capital goods, is equivalent to a proportional income tax. On the other hand, an excise tax system that taxes only consumption goods increases the prices of consumption goods relative to capital goods and is more burdensome to consumers, relative to an income tax of equal yield.

As a tax on newly produced capital goods will not change the rentals (yield) on capital, and as the price of capital goods is increased by a tax on them, a larger amount of current consumption has to be given up for the same amount of future consumption. This conclusion accords with the results presented by Musgrave [51. 1959, pp. 378–9].

J. F. Due [16. 1963] originally took the quite general position that a general sales or production tax is borne in relation to consumption spending. Due also concluded [17. 1965] that a value-added tax of the income type was equivalent to a general consumption tax.

More recently, however. Due [18. 1968, pp. 207–15] restricted these earlier results to imperfectly competitive economies and agreed that in a competitive situation a tax on capital goods is equivalent to a profits tax on new capital.

In addition to reopening discussion on the incidence of general excises, Rolph questioned the conventional methodology of incidence theory investigation. He went so far as to deny that there is a burden associated with taxes and attributed changes in the real income of the private sector to changes in the level of public expenditures. Rolph's approach to incidence analyzed the distributive effects of a tax increase or decrease, while holding expenditure levels fixed. This approach has not been generally adopted as there is general agreement that the distributive effects of tax policy should be studied with reference to full utilization of resources. J. M. Buchanan [8. 1960, p. 142] makes the fundamental point that Rolph's procedure is illogical as it assumes as constant, things which, by the very nature of the analysis, must vary.

There are two complementary approaches to incidence, the first, called "balanced-budget" or "expenditure-incidence," varies taxes and expenditures simultaneously on the condition that full employment is maintained. The second approach is differential incidence in which real expenditures are held constant, and the effect of substituting one type of tax finance for another type is analyzed. The expenditure-incidence approach has the advantage that it calculates the absolute decrease in real income resulting from the imposition of a particular tax, rather than being limited to analysis of income changes resulting from changes in tax regimes. Also, in qualitative analysis it is always possible to abstract from the possible effects of the pattern of government expenditures on relative factor prices by assuming the expenditure pattern to be distributionally neutral. In practice, however, the differences between the two approaches is minor as most results on differential incidence can easily be translated into absolute burdens by using the proportional income tax as a "reference point." Here too, it is almost inevitable that the differential approach will be used in one way or other, for one of the basic aims of incidence analysis is to establish equivalence between different tax systems and to determine the real income of various groups for different tax regimes.

A recent example of differential incidence analysis has been the study of value-added taxes. C. S. Shoup [74. 1955] argued that a value-added tax of the income type (IVA) under which the depreciation of capital is excluded from the tax base, is equivalent to a proportional income tax. Shoup also concludes that a value-added of the consumption tax (CVA), which taxes gross value added minus material purchases and gross investment, is equivalent to a proportional consumption tax, or a sales tax on consumption goods. Rolph [71. 1964] reached the same conclusions. W. H. Oakland [56. 1967] while concurring with Shoup's results for IVA and noting the equality of the tax bases of CVA and a consumption tax, argues that the two taxes are not equivalent in their incidence. Oakland's definition of equivalence requires that a given amount of real revenue be raised and that real, after-tax disposable income be the same. While this definition of equivalence is quite conventional, Shoup [76. 1968] has shown that the fallacy in Oakland's analysis is that his concept of disposable income uses only the price of consumption goods as a deflator. This view makes the size of the consumption tax and the deflator depend on the division of output between consumption and investment.[1]

Professor Shoup in another recent contribution [75. 1969, pp. 267–9] argues that *quite generally* a tax on wages is equivalent to a consumption tax. This result is correct when there are only two classes in society, workers and capitalists, and workers consume all of their income and capitalists save all their profit income. Similarly, if an individual inherits no capital, consumes all his accumulated capital during retirement, and makes his savings independent of the return on capital, he will be indifferent between a wage tax and a consumption tax. In fact, in this simplest of life-cycle models, wage taxes, apart from considerations of timing, will also be equivalent to wealth or profits taxes.

Apart from these special cases, Shoup's demonstration that the bases of a consumption tax and a wage tax are equal, or nearly so, ignores considerable differences in the wealth and income positions of different groups. Even if, *in the aggregate*, consumption is equal to wages, this position says very little about the varying consumption behavior of specific groups or individuals. Nevertheless, Shoup's attempt to compare the differential incidence of a wage tax and a consumption tax may well break new ground in incidence analysis. His provocative result raises the possibility that quite different types of taxes may have very similar effects on individual households when viewed from a life-cycle perspective.

The existence of monopoly power makes the incidence of a general profits tax one of the most controversial areas of tax analysis. However, it is generally agreed that in a competitive economy with a fixed capital stock the burden of a general profits tax falls fully on profits. What is not widely understood is that a general property or wealth tax imposed at the same rate on all income producing wealth has more or less the same economic effects as a general profits tax. To be sure, a comprehensive property tax is not strictly equivalent to a profits tax because required rates of return on different investments vary according to differences in risk. But apart from this complication, and monopoly elements, the equivalence should be obvious; the market value of capital is equal to the capitalized value of future profits.

This is not a novel argument and it dates back at least to the work of H. G. Brown [6. 1924, pp. 178–212]. More recently J. M. Buchanan [9. 1965, pp. 491–7] likened the property tax to a tax on wealth, and L. Rosenberg [72. 1963] and A. C. Harberger [26. 1966] in analyzing the efficiency aspects of profits taxation treat property taxes as taxes on profits. Nevertheless, their view of the property tax remains the minority position. D. Netzer [53. 1966; 54. 1968; 55. 1968], the recognized voice on the property tax, treats this tax on the whole as of the regressive excise variety and pays special attention to the effects of the tax on housing prices. The US Department of Commerce in its GNP accounts lumps property taxes with sales and excise taxes in the category of indirect taxes.

The tradition that the part of the property tax on improvements (reproducible capital) is shifted to consumers and the burden of the tax on land falls on landlords goes back to the work of A. Marshall [42. 1897], W. G. Pierson [60. 1902], F. Y. Edgeworth [19. 1925] and H. A. Simon [77. 1943]. Although these writers were analyzing the effects on residential real estate their results were applied in quantitative work by R. A. Musgrave et al. [49. 1951], G. A. Bishop [4. 1961] and W. I. Gillespie [20. 1965], to property taxes on industrial and commercial property as well as to residential real estate.

If the property tax were a general, flat-rate tax imposed by the Federal government, the conventional view on the property tax could not be accepted for any economy where firms maximize profits. Yet even though the tax is used primarily by thousands of local governments, and despite the fact that tax rates, coverage, and appraisal practices vary considerably among jurisdictions, this writer finds it difficult to justify the excise tax perception of the property tax. Most localities tax a broad segment of capital holdings and the aggregative data presented by Netzer [53. 1966, tables 2.4, 2.6, and 2.7] suggest that for the country as a whole, the effective property tax for broad industry groups is remarkably similar. While there are, undoubtedly, numerous complicated excise tax effects resulting from differing tax rates in the many communities, and varying effective property taxes on finer industry classifications, I suggest that drastic reorientation is needed in work on the incidence of the property tax. Surely the starting point must be that property taxes are taxes on income producing wealth that may lead to changes in relative commodity prices and shifts of capital and population between communities. If local governments imposed a morass of wage and salary taxes, varying in their effective rates between communities, industries, and occupations, would these taxes be classified as excises? From my standpoint, it seems rather doubtful.

The Incidence of Partial Commodity and Factor Taxes

The excise tax effects of property taxes result from the tax induced changes in relative commodity prices. If capital is taxed at a differentially higher rate in a particular industry, the relative prices of commodities produced by this industry will increase. Moreover, as the cost of the taxed factor to that industry will increase, other factors of production will be substituted for it. The taxed factor will, therefore, be released from the taxed industry for two distinct reasons: first, because the output of the taxed industry is decreased by the tax, and second, because of the effect of factor substitution. The final change in relative factor prices will depend, in part, on the characteristics of the untaxed industries absorbing the factors released from the taxed industry.

In situations where both commodity prices and factor prices change, incidence should be studied in terms of the expenditure purpose of income (consumption patterns) and in terms of the sources of income. However, if each group spends the same proportion of its income on the taxed and untaxed commodities, it is possible to disregard the spending side and to concentrate only on factor price changes. This is the approach followed by A. C. Harberger [25. 1962] in his analysis of the incidence of the corporate profits tax. Harberger treats this tax as a partial profits tax on corporate earnings and assumes that in equilibrium the *after-tax* rates of return will be equal in the corporate and noncorporate sectors. Consequently, any tax on corporate bodies would induce a flow of capital from the corporate into the noncorporate sector. Harberger measures all prices in terms of the price of labor, P_L (the wage rate). His analysis is carried out for small changes in the tax rate so that the general equilibrium system is differentiated with respect to T_{xK}; the corporate tax is expressed as a per-unit tax in sector x. The tax yield is approximated by the expression $T_{xK}Kx$, where Kx is the amount of corporate capital.

To analyze the distribution of the tax yield, it is necessary to solve for the change in the *after-tax* rate return on capital, dp_K, relative to the price of labor. National income, measured in terms of the price of labor, is equal to $p_KK + P_LL +$ taxes, where K and L are the total amounts of capital and labor, respectively. When the relative prices of labor and capital remain unchanged after the imposition of a tax, that is, $dp_K = 0$, national income, measured in terms of the wage rate, will increase by the amount of the tax proceeds. As the relative prices of labor and capital are unchanged, their relative shares in national income remain the same, so in its distributive effects the tax would be equivalent to a proportional income tax. In general, the relative prices of labor and capital will change after the imposition of a corporate tax. If the fall in the after-tax rate of return on all capital is equal to the tax proceeds, *i.e.*, $-dp_KK = T_{xK}Kx$, capital bears the full burden of the tax, because the share of labor in *total* national income is unaffected by the imposition of the tax.

Harberger derives a general expression for the change in the after-tax return on capital in a two-sector, two-factor model commonly used in the theory of international trade. Even for the simplest of general equilibrium systems, the general expression for the changes in factor prices is fairly complex and a wide range of results are possible. To estimate incidence Harberger carried out a numerical analysis of his model where he used factor price information to estimate factor proportions and factor shares. Using a fairly wide range of assumptions for the elasticities of substitution between labor and capital in the two sectors, Harberger concluded empirically that capital probably bears most of the burden of the corporate tax in the United States.

P. M. Mieszkowski [48. 1967], using Harberger's model to analyze the incidence of other partial taxes in both sectors, emphasizes the differential incidence of various taxes. In the first part of his analysis, where he follows Harberger by assuming identical spending functions for different groups, Mieszkowski distinguishes between two general effects: the *output effect* and the *factor substitution effect*. The size of the output effect depends on the elasticity of substitution in demand and on the relative factor intensities of the two industries.

The output effect relates to the tax induced changes in the output structure of the economy. Judging the situation solely on the basis of the output effect it will always be to capital's advantage to encourage taxes on the labor intensive sector. The factor substitution arises only when a partial factor tax is imposed in one of the two sectors; the untaxed factor will be substituted for the taxed factor and this factor substitution acts to depress the relative price of the taxed factor. Capital will always be better off with a tax on labor in one of the two sectors than with an equal yield commodity tax in the same sector. The worst tax, from capital's point of view is, of course, a tax on profits. When the elasticity of substitution is zero in a particular sector, the three partial taxes on that sector are equivalent to each other. Another equivalence is between a commodity tax and partial factor taxes in the same industry imposed at the same rate on labor and capital. This result serves to demonstrate the rather artifical distinction between direct and indirect taxes and illustrates the excise tax effects of partial factor taxes.

The results of the differential incidence of taxes imposed in different sectors are much less clear cut. The differential incidence of the two commodity taxes depends only on the relative factor intensities of the two industries. Factor taxes, on the other hand, also depend on the different degrees of substitutability between factors in the two sectors. Capital may be better off under a tax on capital in the capital intensive sector (if the elasticity of substitution is relatively small in that sector) than under a capital tax in the labor intensive industry.

The introduction of variations in spending patterns among different groups further complicates matters. P. Wells [85. 1955] H. G. Johnson [29. 1956], and A. Williams [86. 1963, pp. 210–35] attempt to combine uses (demand for goods and services) and the sources (of income) sides of incidence by means of geometrical analysis. The first algebraic approach to the problem is a neglected contribution of J. E. Meade [46. 1955, pp. 34-46].

On the production side, Meade's model is the standard neoclassical two-sector model. Meade distinguishes between two groups, workers and capitalists, and derives sufficient conditions under which a small increase in an excise tax in one sector accompanied by a small decrease in an excise tax in the other sector will increase social welfare. Government expenditures are held fixed in real terms. In one important respect Meade's analysis is quite general as taxes exist in the system before any tax change is made. His analysis introduces excess burden considerations; one of Meade's conditions for an improvement in social welfare is that the tax substitution shifts demand to the commodity for which there existed the larger excess of marginal social value over marginal social cost. Meade's use of a social welfare function also introduces normative distributional weights for the two groups.

Mieszkowski [48. 1967] disregards excess burdens and analyzes the differential incidence of a wide range of taxes from the position of capitalists. He takes the first-order change in real income, dR, resulting from the imposition of a tax as equal to

$$dR = pxdX_K + pydY_K$$

where px and py are the original prices of the two commodities X and Y respectively; and dX_K and dY_K are the change in the consumption of X and Y by capitalists, respectively.

As is well known from index number theory, this kind of measure, by using original prices, overstates the loss in real income.

The introduction of separate demand functions for different groups broaches a demand condition that depends on the spending propensities of different groups on particular commodities. If relative factor prices are fixed, i.e., $dp_K = 0$, a tax of any type on commodity X will decrease the real income of capitalists more than would an equal-yield tax on Y, if capitalists spend a larger proportion of their income on X than do workers, the converse also holds. When relative factor prices change, the results on differential incidence are unambiguous only if the factor-intensity (output) effect, the demand effect, and the factor substitution effect operate in the "same direction." For example, the substitution of a tax on labor in X for a tax on capital in Y will be certain to increase the real income of capital if X is labor intensive relative to Y and if capitalists spend a higher proportion of their income on Y than workers do.

It is fairly clear that qualitative analysis of general equilibrium models can only modestly narrow the range of outcomes on incidence. Yet the complexities involved in doing empirical research with such models should not serve as a basis for the readoption of more primitive methods of analysis. The work of H. G. Brown [6. 1924, pp. 178–212] suggests a numerical example which serves to illustrate the pitfalls of over-emphasizing a single dimension of incidence problems.

Brown took exception to the view that a property (profits) tax on residential real estate is shifted to the consumer and argued that a tax on housing would shift capital out of housing and would be a tax on capital in the economy as a whole. Brown also pointed out that the small size of a taxed sector is not a sufficient reason for ignoring general equilibrium adjustments.

In our example, we assume an economy consisting of three groups, A, B, C. A property tax is imposed on apartment dwellings, a service consumed only by group A. Group C owns all of the capital, and originally 1 percent of the total capital stock is used as apartment buildings. No labor is used in the production of the residential services in apartment buildings. By choosing the value of other parameters appropriately, we can obtain the result that the total level of after-tax profits in the economy will fall by the amount of the tax proceeds.[2] As only 1 percent of the capital is originally employed in the taxed sector, this proposal means that the after-tax rate of return on *all* capital will fall by 1 percent of its original value. It would appear that Brown might very well be correct. The owners of capital (group C) appear to bear the full burden of the property tax as wages have not changed and total profits have fallen by the amount of the tax.

On the other hand, the consumers of apartment building services (group A) have also suffered a loss in real income. The change in the price of the taxed commodity is equal to $f_K(dp_K + T_X)$ as f_K (the share of capital in the taxed industry) is equal to 1, and since dp_K is very small relative to T_X the price of X will rise by approximately the amount of the tax. Paradoxically, it appears that the real incomes of both the consumers of the taxed product and the owners of capital fall by the amount of the tax proceeds. What has happened is that in addition to providing government revenue, the tax, by decreasing the price of capital, transfers purchasing power to group B, the group that does not consume any of the taxed product and does not own any capital. If the tax proceeds are 200 and Group A earns 1 percent of total income and spends one quarter of their income on housing, and the shares in total income by groups B and C are 0.69 and 0.30 respectively, then the change in real income is -198 for A, $+138$ for B, and -140 for C. Group C loses 200 units of income in its capitalist role and gains 60 units in its consumers' role.

Interregional Incidence

Two interrelated extensions of the general equilibrium approach to incidence are: (1) to drop the assumption of perfect factor mobility between industries and; (2) to introduce trade between countries. The two extensions are closely connected because the standard model of international trade is a two-country, two-commodity model where both countries produce the two commodities and labor and capital are perfectly immobile. The Harberger model may also be interpreted as a two-country trade model where both countries are completely specialized in the production of one commodity and factors may, or may not, be mobile between countries.

The importance of interregional or international incidence results from the growing interest in fiscal federalism in the United States and in the European Common Market. It may be in the self interest of a community (a city, state, or nation) to export as much of the tax burden as possible. Also, the "urban crisis" in America and elsewhere has stimulated interest in the effects of local taxes, especially their effects on residential choice and industrial location.

Despite the importance of these issues there are few published papers dealing specifically with interregional incidence. Beyond the contributions of H. E. Brazer [5. 1961] R. H. Parks [59. 1961] and C. E. McLure [43. 1964] there is only the related literature on international trade. Although the trade literature has developed models which could be used to analyze incidence, it has, in fact, ignored incidence, with the important exception of the famous contribution of W. Stolper and P. A. Samuelson [82. 1941] on the distributive effects of tariffs; instead it has concentrated on questions of efficiency and on the real income of a country as a whole. In what follows I shall rely primarily on unpublished material and attempt to sketch the models that have been used, and could be used, to study interregional incidence.

Again, it is convenient to begin with the standard trade model where both capital and labor are perfectly immobile. As in a closed economy, general taxes such as a proportional income tax, a production tax, or a general sales tax are equivalent in effect and the burden of each is proportional to the citizens' contribution of national income in any country imposing the taxes. The burden of partial commodity taxes, partial factor taxes, and taxes on trade, for a small country that has no effect on the world terms of trade, falls fully on the country imposing the tax. The analysis of these taxes is made easier under the condition that world prices are fixed. The introduction of variable terms of trade introduces a complicated dimension that might be used by a country to "export" some of its tax burden. Also, in this case, a partial production tax is not equivalent to a partial consumption tax. One of the interesting possibilities of this analysis is the comparison of the effects on income distribution of taxes on trade, with the distributive effects of other partial taxes.[3]

In two unpublished articles C. L. McLure [44. 1968; 45. 1969] has analyzed models of incidence in which one of the two factors is perfectly mobile between two countries and the other factor is perfectly immobile. Both countries are perfectly specialized in the production of one commodity. When labor is immobile a wage tax in one of the two countries will be borne fully by the workers subject to tax. McLure shows that a commodity tax is really a combination of a tax on labor and a tax on capital. As capital is perfectly mobile, it will flow out of the taxing country and this capital outflow will decrease the wage rate there, while increasing (decreasing) the wage (profit) rate in the non-taxing country.

A high elasticity of demand for the taxed commodity and a high elasticity of substitution in the taxing country works against labor in the taxing country, and in its favor in the non-taxing country, while a low elasticity of substitution in the non-taxing country reduces the burden on labor in the taxing country. These results, derived by McLure, form only a small part of his analysis and are clearly interpretable. The main weakness of his analysis is the assumption of perfect specialization.

A number of models developed in the international trade literature by M. C. Kemp [30. 1966] and R. W. Jones [28. 1967] can be used to extend incidence analysis to situations in which capital is perfectly mobile and at least one of the two countries is incompletely specialized. Also, J. S. Chipman [10. 1968] has shown that when technologies differ between countries, perfect capital mobility will not necessarily lead to specialization as there will be positive production of each commodity in both countries.

A variation that should be useful in the study of the incidence of local taxes is a three factor model where one of the two (or three) commodities is not traded between communities. Such goods might be housing or other local services. The importance of the third factor, land, is suggested in an article by R. L. Richman [65. 1967] in which he argues that a property tax on improvements is shifted fully onto the owners of land. If a property tax is imposed at a higher rate in a particular city and is not translated into a higher level of public services, and if labor (the population) is also perfectly mobile, then, indeed, land which is perfectly immobile must bear the full burden of such a differential tax. What is crucial to this result is the assumption that labor is perfectly mobile. If labor is perfectly immobile, or imperfectly mobile, part of the property tax on improvements will fall on the residents.

Let us clarify this point by considering the situation where the residents of a city are perfectly immobile and all the capital used in the city is imported. There is one native good in the community, housing services, which is heavily capital intensive. Originally the share of capital in this industry is 0.80 and the share of land rents is 0.20. All of the residents in the community work in an export industry (guns) and use their wages and land rents to purchase housing services and imports (golf clubs). Capital is perfectly mobile, and will receive the rate of return that is determined by national conditions. The prices of exports and imports are also given to the community. If the community taxes capital in both sectors wages and land rents have to fall in the export industry in order for that industry to remain competitive. The exact change in the relative prices of the two immobile factors, labor and land, is a complicated general equilibrium problem that depends, as in previous problems, on relative factor intensities of the two industries, the partial elasticities of substitution between pairs of the three factors, and between pairs of products – all of which bear on the final division of resources between home goods and exports, which pay for imports. For purposes of illustration, we shall assume that wages and land rents fall in proportion to their original shares in the export industry, which we specify as 0.70 and 0.10 respectively. If the tax is \$5.00 per unit of capital, the price of labor falls by \$0.87 and the price of land by \$0.13. The price of housing goes up by (approximately) the tax multiplied by the share of capital in that industry.

For this very special case the results accord, at least in part, with conventional wisdom – the price of housing services goes up substantially as the result of the tax on improvements. Also, the part of the tax on industrial activity is shifted backward onto immobile factors of production, a possibility that has been emphasized by Rolph. Perhaps a complete analysis will someday show that everyone has been partially right and everyone has been partially wrong.

Dynamic Incidence

To this point we have discussed work which assumes that total supplies of labor and capital are fixed. The analysis of the growth effects of tax policy, or "dynamic incidence," is primarily an investigation of the effects of tax policy on the level of savings and growth. There is no single well-defined approach to dynamic incidence. Some investigators have studied long run factor shares, others the per-capita wage rate, and still others the effect of taxes on the rate of return on capital in the long run. The variations in approach stem from the fact that in the long run taxes not only have an effect on the distribution of income, but may also have a pronounced effect on the size of the total income.

D. Dosser [14. 1961], who made one of the first contributions on dynamic incidence, suggested that a tax system could be progressive with respect to absolute income at a given point in time yet will be regressive at some later point in time if the rate of change of income differs significantly between groups. Dosser's concept of dynamic regression or progression refers to whether groups or types of income that are growing relatively quickly were taxed at relatively higher rates.

Dosser's article and the discussion that followed in A. D. Bain [2. 1963], A. R. Prest [63. 1963] and Dosser [15. 1963] raised the question whether tax liabilities should be based at least in part on rate of growth of income, rather than just on absolute levels, and whether certain types of tax systems had good automatic redistributive features.

I find it difficult to justify a differential rate of tax on the "old" rich relative to the "new" rich (incentives aside), and the whole notion of dynamic incidence, as used by Dosser, seems rather empty unless it refers to the quite general question of the role of tax policy in modifying long run factors that influence income inequality.

A different, more specific, approach to dynamic incidence, or long shifting, is contained in a series of articles by Marian Krzyzaniak [34. 1966; 36. 1967; 38. 1968]. Using a one sector and a two sector neoclassical growth model, Krzyzaniak numerically analyzed the long run effects of a corporate profits tax on factor shares, rates of return on capital, total profit income and total wage income. A key assumption is that savings out of profits are substantially higher than out of wages, so that the profits tax would have a significant effect on capital formation in absolute and in differential (when substituted for a wage tax) terms. Krzyzaniak reaches two principal conclusions: first, that the decrease in capital formation will lead to a significant increase in the before-tax rate of return on capital, and second, that the long run indirect effects of a profits tax may be very substantial. He finds [36. 1967, p. 487] for a particular set of production and growth parameters, the long run global tax burden to be 2.7 times the tax revenues and that workers bear 44 percent of the total burden. In other words if the government imposes a small tax and collects $1.00 in revenue, at some point in the future total output, because of the decrease in capital formation, will be $1.70 less at that point in time than it would have been in the absence of the tax and total wages will fall by $1.20. Krzyzaniak although expressing surprise at the size of the growth effects, does not draw any concrete policy implications from his findings. There is the danger that the inference might be asserted that the profits tax should be lowered because of growth effects and even that it is to the long run advantage of labor to accept lower taxes on profits and higher taxes on wages. There are good reasons for being wary of such inferences. First, we can question the assumed substantial difference in the rate of savings out of profits and wages. But even if this difference is granted the growth effects of a tax should be considered in differential terms rather than in terms of what happens when a profits tax is imposed. The differential effect on savings may be the same as the absolute effect if savings out of wages are negligible, but the effect on after-tax wages will be quite different. P. M. Mieszkowski [47. 1963], using a model and numerical estimates very similar to those of Krzyzaniak, found that if a small decrease in the profits tax is accompanied by an equal yield increase in a wage tax, it takes a very long time (between 50 to 60 years) for the after-tax real wage rate to rise above the level it would have been under higher profits taxation. Thus, disregarding the lower level of after-tax wages in the intervening period, it will take an indefinite period for labor to reap the benefits of higher capital formation. These results are consistent with the Krzyzaniak findings where he observes that the effects of a tax change on any individual worker's welfare take an extremely long period to work themselves out. It seems safe to say that a decrease in the profits taxes or in taxes on high income groups in general, if accompanied by an increase in taxes on low income groups, will decrease the absolute level of income of the poor for a very long period of time, if not permanently. If we are to have faster growth with equity, the additional saving should come through budget surpluses and not through changes in tax structure.

A significant impact of profit tax on growth and rates of return does not depend on the assumption that savings must stem from profits. P. A. Diamond [13. 1967] found that for an economy of identical individuals who save in their working life and dissave during retirement, the substitution of a profits tax for a lump sum tax will increase the gross rate of return on capital and may even increase the net rate of return, depending on the nature of the technology.

One of the basic shortcomings of the distributive aspects of neoclassical growth models is that they are highly aggregative and limited to two highly artificial groups, workers and capitalists. In a paper on the theory of distribution of wealth, J. E. Stiglitz [81. 1967] takes the first steps towards breaking out of this narrow classification. Stiglitz' basic objective is to determine, on the basis of specific assumptions about reproduction, inheritance, and savings behavior, whether in a neoclassical growth model the distribution of wealth will become more or less equal among groups. He concludes that in the long run, the distribution may well tend towards equality; he is also concerned with the effects of various taxes on the speed of equalization. He assumes that taxes collected are distributed equally among citizens. For any given government revenue, he finds that wealth taxes are equivalent to profit taxes and dominate proportional income taxes in their effect on the speed of equalization. Progressive income taxes have a greater equalization effect than proportional income taxes. Stiglitz elsewhere [80. 1966] studies the long run effects of various taxes on the dispersion of income as measured by the Gini coefficient. Clear-cut results of this type of work will ultimately depend on empirical research, but the research should relate the results on profit rates and wage rates derived through an aggregative growth model to a much more satisfactory measure of income inequality.

Monopoly Elements and Incidence

The introduction of monopoly elements does not necessarily lead to a drastic revision of the results on incidence derived from competitive models. If monopolies maximize profit and/or if the markups used by concentrated industries are independent of the corporate profits tax, the competitive results remain more or less unchanged.

A profit-maximizing monopoly (or oligopoly where industry profits are maximized) is a firm that recognizes it has monopoly power, and attempts to maximize the value of the firm. There will be two types of profits in monopoly situations, the competitive, or required, rate of return that stock holders could earn in the competitive sectors of the economy, and monopoly profits. By not undertaking investments yielding less than the required rate of return the firm will maximize monopoly profits. Monopoly profits will be capitalized in the market value of the company's stock. As is well known, the imposition of a profit tax will not affect any of the conditions that determine profit maximizing prices and output so the burden of a general profits tax falls fully on profits. All of the results on general taxes discussed for our competitive model remain unchanged except that a property tax is not equivalent to a profits tax as monopoly profits do not get into the tax base. Since relative commodity prices will not change with a general tax, a proportional income tax, imposed on income gross of depreciation, will be equivalent to a general sales tax, on final goods and services under monopoly. Also, if the degree of monopoly is relatively not greater in the capital goods sector, an excise tax on capital goods will increase the relative price of the goods and will decrease the real return on savings. The presence of monopoly elements does, however, complicate the analysis of partial excise and partial factor taxes. In the competitive model when the taxed industries have the same factor intensities the incidence of an excise tax will depend on the levels of spending by different groups on the taxed good. In the presence of monopoly rents, monopoly profits will fall (rise) when the partial excises are imposed on the monopoly (competitive) sectors as the output of the taxed industries will fall.

Harberger [25. 1962] was the first formally to introduce monopoly into a general equilibrium incidence model by assuming that in the monopoloid industry a constant markup over normal costs exists.

$$p_x = \left(f_K p_K + f_L p_L \right)\left(1 + M \right)$$

where f_K, f_L are the shares of capital and labor respectively, p_K is the competitive (required) rate of return on capital, p_L is the wage rate and M is the markup. The basic difference between the markup model where M is constant and profit maximizing monopoly is that the implicit markup for the latter will vary with shifts in demand and cost.[4] The constant markup model is an intermediate case between profit maximizing monoply and non-profit maximizing situation in which the markup varies freely. The constant markup if it is applied to taxes will increase the relative price of these commodities relative to what they would be under competition or profit maximizing monopoly for the imposition of partial taxes. General taxes will not change the price of factors, so even for the constant markup model the results on general taxes are the same as under competition. In short, the basic complication introduced by monopoly elements when markups are constant or monopoly profits are maximized is that partial taxes by affecting the output mix of the economy will change the level of monopoly rents. Otherwise, the competitive results persist.

A variety of reasons have been put forth as to why firms will not maximize short run profits and will increase markup and before-tax profits in response to taxes, especially profits taxes. The explanations range from fear of anti-trust action, the belief that unions will increase their wage demands if profits are raised to profit maximizing levels, to the idea put forth by R. G. Penner [61. 1967] that managers are uncertain about final sales prices and, being risk-averters, will set output below the level equating marginal expected (mean) revenue to marginal cost.

The most formal model, where firms do not maximize profits, is the theory of managerial capitalism of W. J. Baumol [3. 1967] and R. Marris [41. 1964]. According to these writers the salary of a manager is more closely related to sales (size) than profitability and they will pursue expansion at the expense of profits subject to a minimum profit constraint. To be more specific, we can assume that firms strive to achieve a 10 percent after-tax rate of return to keep stockholders happy. All firms in the economy have considerable monopoly power and profits could be much higher than 10 percent, but in their emphasis on sales, firms in the aggregate price their products below profit-maximizing levels. If a profit tax of 50 percent is imposed, managers, in order to maintain dividends and/or to preserve the level of retained earnings for expansion, increase prices relative to costs and partially or fully shift the corporate tax. This result is at sharp variance with the results derived for profit-maximizing behavior and the conflict between the two theories should ideally be resolved by empirical work.

Econometric Studies of Incidence

A number of studies, including those by E. H. Lerner and E. S. Hendrikson [40. 1956], J. C. Clendenin [11. 1956], B. K. Ratchford and P. B. Han [64. 1957] and M. A. Adelman [1. 1957] attempted to draw empirical conclusions about the incidence of the corporate profits tax by analyzing the relationship between tax rates and factor shares or rates of return. While these studies are suggestive, they were all defective in that they did not control for factors, other than taxes, that affect rates of return or factor shares.

The first systematic attempt to isolate the effects of the corporate profits tax on rates of return was the study for American manufacturing by Marian Krzyzaniak and R. A. Musgrave [32. 1963] (K-M henceforth). Their results were quite startling as they found that an increase in tax liabilities of $1.00 per unit of capital, will increase before-tax profits to $1.35. The corporate profits tax in manufacturing is shifted by more than 100 percent. These results, a measure of short run shifting for a fixed capital stock, have far reaching implications for tax policy, and for price and distribution theory. The price theorist who has based his work on the equality between marginal cost and marginal revenue is asked to believe that corporations can increase profits at will or, at the very least, that in the absence of the 50 percent tax on corporate profits, corporate profits in manufacturing would be lower than they are at present even after the 50 percent tax has been paid.

Furthermore, the high levels of shifting are not restricted to the United States. Using the K-M model, R. W. Roskomp [73. 1965] and B. G. Spencer [79. 1969] found the corporate tax to be shifted by 100 percent for West Germany and Canada, respectively.

The K-M contribution has been severely criticized by Richard Goode [21. 1966], R. E. Slitor [78. 1966], J. G. Cragg, A. C. Harberger and P. M. Mieszkowski [12. 1967] (C-H-M, henceforth), and by R. J. Gordon [22. 1967; 23. 1968].

The basic criticism made by all these writers is that the K-M model significantly overstates the degree of shifting *because it is incorrectly specified*. The variables included by K-M to reflect non-tax variables do not adequately capture the cyclical swings that were so pronounced during their sample period. The sample period begins in 1935 when the unemployment rate was 20 percent and the corporate profits tax was 14 percent and ends in 1959 when the unemployment rate was 5.5 percent and the corporate profits tax was 52 percent. In the intervening years there are the war years 1941–42 and 1950–52 (1943 through 1947 is excluded) characterized by very high degrees of capacity utilization and by very high corporate taxes.

In short, levels of effective demand and taxes were highly correlated during K-M's sample period and if, as C-H-M have shown, a variable that is omitted from the regression is positively related with the before-tax rate of return *and* the tax variable the causal influence of the tax variable will be overestimated. All of the critics believe that the non-tax variables used by K-M have little *a priori* justification, and do not resemble the variables, such as sales or output, which are used to explain profits in numerous econometric models. In addition to taxes K-M explain before-tax profits in year t, by the increase in consumption as a percentage of GNP in year t-1, the ratio of inventories to sales in year t-1, and the ratio of net tax accruals (other than corporate taxes) to GNP in year t. The consumption variable is peculiar and its influence seems to depend on the nature of past business cycles as its sign cannot be determined, *a priori*, if the fraction of consumption decreases in booms and increases in recessions. The ratio of inventories to sales, which K-M lag one period, makes sense only if it is on a current period basis. The finding that the influence of other taxes is negative and is statistically significant adds little to the credibility of the model, nor does the finding that the influence of government expenditure on the before-tax rate of return is negative. Furthermore, when K-M use the budget surplus to capture the influence of government, the only variable that is statistically significant is the corporate tax variable. Similarly, when K-M take first differences of their standard model, their estimate of shifting remains unchanged, but all the other variables become statistically insignificant.

Gordon [23. 1968, pp. 1366–7] has extended the period of fit of the K-M model back from their initial year, 1935, to 1924. This causes the consumption variable to change sign and the inventory variable to border on insignificance. Gordon also demonstrates that the K-M model fails to predict the fall in profits between 1929 and 1932 and the boom in profits in the middle 1960s. Both periods were characterized by constant tax rates.

A more direct attempt at demonstrating the inadequacy of the K-M model was made by Goode, Slitor and C-H-M who added cyclical variables to the K-M regressions. Goode and Slitor added the ratio of actual to potential GNP, while C-H-M used the employment rate as an additional pressure variable. As predicted, the addition of a pressure variable decreased the estimate of shifting, but it remained very high at about 100 percent. When C-H-M also added a dummy variable for the mobilization and war years 1941, 1942, 1950, 1951, and 1952, the estimate of shifting drops to 60 percent and the tax variable is not statistically different from zero. Even more striking is the regression presented by C-H-M when profits are explained by the employment rate and the war dummy; both are positive and significant, and the tax rate is statistically insignificant and has a negative sign.

K-M in their reply [37. 1968] to C-H-M object to the use of the war dummy and attempt to re-establish their position by excluding the mobilization and war years. Using only peace years they estimate the degree of shifting to be over 100 percent.

Although the introduction of a war variable is somewhat arbitrary, especially as many of the really significant tax changes occurred during the war years, these "negative" exercises tend to confirm the sensitivity of the K-M model to changes in specification and/or sample period.

The only clue provided by K-M for their original specification of the profits equation is contained in their reply [35. 1966] to Goode and Slitor where they object to the use of unlagged pressure variables that are endogenous on the grounds that the inclusion of such variables leads to biased and inconsistent results. While C-H-W have shown that the resulting bias in the estimate of shifting is upward, not downward, it appears that statistical considerations dictated K-M's use of lagged variables, and lead to a model that is not very plausible.

Gordon's comments [22. 1967] on the K-M model are only a minor part of his contribution to the incidence literature. He used a model based on a mark-up theory of pricing, namely that firms apply a markup over variable costs such as wages and materials cost. The test of shifting in this model is, essentially, a test of whether the markup is set, in the absence of corporate taxes, at its profit maximizing level. Reduced to its bare essentials Gordon's estimating equation is

$$Z_t = \alpha_1 \frac{C_t}{\left(1 - vt\right)}$$

where Z_t and C_t are before-tax profits and costs respectively, normalized by the amount of capital or total revenue; α_1 is the markup parameter, t is the tax rate, and v is the shifting parameter. The interpretation of this parameter is as follows. In the absence of taxes there will be a relation between costs and profits as determined by the markup parameter. For example, if profits are one-third of variable cost, α_1 is equal to 0.33. If a 50 percent corporate tax is imposed, profits will remain unchanged if there is no shifting of the tax so that v will be equal to zero. If the tax is fully shifted, before-tax profits will double and the markup parameter is "blown up" by the denominator, $i.e.$, v will be equal to 1 and $\alpha_1/0.5$ will be equal to 0.66.

Gordon's complete equation contains a full capacity variable that accounts for fixed costs which are independent of the level of output in the short run and variables reflecting rates of change of prices and output, which are designed to pick up swings in inventory profits and the reaction of profits to cyclical movements.

The last two variables were introduced in an *ad hoc* fashion. Yet Gordon has shown [23. 1968, p. 1362] their inclusion merely decreases the goodness of fit and does not affect the estimate of shifting. Gordon's estimates of the shifting parameter for *total* United States manufacturing are all small (around 0.2) and not statistically different from zero. His estimates of shifting for various two digit manufacturing industries are quite varied, being negative for some industries and close to 100 percent for industries such as rubber products and chemicals.

One problem with Gordon's results is that they are biased toward zero, for due to data limitations, he used revenue (price) information rather than data on variable costs. Although the effects of taxes may be reflected in the price, the resulting bias is tolerable. The size of the bias depends on the relation between normal profits and variable cost; when the normal markup is one-third, shifting of 100 percent will be estimated to be 75 percent. When the normal markup is one-eighth, full shifting would be estimated as 90 percent because of the use of price data.

A completely different approach to the estimation of shifting, based on cross-section data, is found in the work of R. W. Kilpatrick [31. 1965] for the United States and R. J. Lévesgue [39. 1967] for Canada. They assume that the degree of shifting in an industry is positively related to the degree of concentration in that industry. Zero shifting is assumed for industries with a zero concentration index. On this basis, shifting is measured by regressing the change in industry profits on the concentration index, and other variables between two time periods, between which there was a significant change in tax rates. Both studies conclude that the degree of shifting in manufacturing is somewhere in the order of 100 percent. The accuracy of these estimates depends, of course, on the isolation of nontax influence. Lévesgue's results for Canada are suspect on this score, since in his regressions, changes in industry profits seem to depend primarily upon the degree of industry concentration. While Kilpatrick's work is more successful, he himself shows that in the pre-Korea years (his base period) profits and concentration were positively related for pairs of years for which there was no change in corporate tax.

Gordon [22. 1967, p. 752] has questioned Kilpatrick's assumption that before-tax profits will remain unchanged for industries with zero concentration. Gordon's own work suggests that the degree of shifting is negative for these industries and he concludes that even if some industries shift the tax, the shift of resources to the more competitive manufacturing sector will decrease prices and rate of return in these industries so that the degree of shifting in manufacturing as a whole will be very small.

One of Gordon's explanations for the difference between his results and those of Krzyzaniak and Musgrave is that he used costs per unit of capital as an explanation variable and K-M failed to account for changes in the productivity of capital over time.

A much more explicit account of long run factors is the production function approach developed by C. A. Hall, Jr. [24. 1964]. Although Hall's untimely death prevented him from completing his work on the effects of the corporation income tax, he deserves much credit for pioneering an estimating procedure that has firm theoretical foundations and directly accounts for changes in the productivity of capital on the rate of return.

Hall's estimates of the incidence of the corporate profits tax in American manufacturing are based on two steps. He first estimates the rate of neutral (assuming disembodied) technological progress at each point in time by relating changes in output to changes in factor inputs weighed by their marginal productivities (factor shares). Hall notes that the observed factor shares may be distorted by a shifting of the profits tax, and calculates three sets of estimates of technical change. One set is based on the assumption of zero shifting, a second on the assumption that the tax is shifted fully to consumers, and the third that the tax is shifted back onto labor in the form of lower wages. Hall then uses the three sets of estimates for technological change to adjust the output series and fits two production functions, one a Cobb-Douglas and the other a linear production function. For both functional forms the goodness of fit turns out to be best for the zero shifting assumption and Hall concluded that the tax was not shifted in manufacturing.

Musgrave [52. 1964] criticized this conclusion on the grounds that the coefficients of determination, the R^2s, were not sufficiently different to allow any firm conclusion about shifting. For example, in the Cobb-Douglas case, the R^2 for the zero shifting assumption was 0.9722 and for full sales shifting it was 0.9455. The small differences in the R^2s according to Musgrave was too thin a margin of victory to base a firm conclusion about shifting.[5]

Hall's approach has been extended by Joan L. Turek [83. 1970]. Turek assumes a constant elasticity production function of American manufacturing, and that the degree of monopoly, apart from the possible effects of taxes, was constant during her sample period. On these assumptions she derives an estimating equation for the ratio of factor shares using a tax rate variable, time to represent a constant rate of technological progress, a capital to labor ratio, and two cyclical variables as explanatory variables. The point estimate of shifting when the basic statutory tax rate is used as the tax variable was about 12 percent. However, the standard error of the estimated tax coefficient is about three times the size of the coefficient. This means that the point estimate may be highly unreliable because of sampling error. Turek concluded, nevertheless, on the basis of likelihood ratio tests, that it is 2 times more likely that the true value is zero, given the actual estimate of 0.12 and the high standard error of the estimate, than that the true value of the shifting parameter is 50 percent. On the same basis, Turek concluded that the "odds" are 100 to 1 in favor of zero shifting relative to 100 percent shifting. In other words, the policy maker can be moderately confident (the odds are 2 to 1) that the degree shifting is low rather than 50 percent, and he can be highly confident that the tax is not fully shifted.

Though his is not an econometric study, Harberger's [25. 1962] general equilibrium analysis has important bearing on the interpretation on results discussed above. We have noted Gordon's conclusion that for some industries, because of general equilibrium adjustment within manufacturing, the degree of shifting is negative, and for those industries negative and positive shifting will cancel out. Actually, as noted by Cragg, Harberger, and Mieszkowski [12. 1967, p. 819], one should expect to find an increase in the before-tax rate of return of the corporate sector because of the reallocation of capital from the corporate to the noncorporate sector. In fact, once this adjustment is complete, the K-M measure would show 50 percent shifting even though capital actually bears the full burden of the tax. What needs to be emphasized is that even if it can be established, without a shadow of doubt, that large segments of the corporate sector fully shift the corporate tax in the sense of K-M, the burden of the corporate tax may well fall on capital taken as a whole. It is easy to show, by extending the Harberger approach, that if concentrated industries make investments on the basis of a target rate of return criterion, the sharp decrease in the use of capital in these industries can drive down the rate of return in the competitive sectors of the economy to an extent that the return on all capital falls by considerably more than the yield of the corporate profits tax.

Concluding Remarks

Even in a long review some topics are inadequately treated. For example, I have not discussed the empirical studies on the allocation of tax burden by income class. I do not doubt the value of such studies, but these studies merely utilize existing theory of incidence, and in large measure, the well-known criticisms of such work by A. R. Prest [62. 1955] question the underlying theory on which the quantitative allocations are based.

Certain complications that bear on the incidence of the corporate income tax such as the fact that the tax applies only to equity capital and the preferential treatment of capital gains have also been omitted in the discussion. While the aggregative results are probably little affected by these factors, differences in debt-equity ratio in so varied a sector undoubtedly means that a tax on equity will have complicated differential price effects within the corporate sector.

One important recent development in incidence analysis has been the increased use of general equilibrium techniques. However, there is the danger that unless the difficult task of estimating these models is undertaken, we will merely end up with a set of very general qualitative statements. The use of econometric analysis, while it has not definitely settled anything, is a big advance. In addition to the estimates of corporate shifting, the econometric studies by L. L. Orr [58. 1968], J. D. Heinberg and W. E. Oates [27. 1970], and Oates [57] on the incidence and capitalization of property taxes and J. Weitenberg's [84. 1969] estimates of the incidence of social security taxes represent long overdue developments of this type of approach to the analysis of tax incidence.

Notes

1   The following heuristic argument shows that the flat rate consumption tax is equivalent, in all respects, to a value-added tax of the consumption type. A firm is faced with two sets of separable decisions: (1) profit-maximizing short-run production and pricing decisions made for a fixed capital stock; (2) investments made by the firm for existing owners of capital, and new savers. Gross investment decreases the firm's tax liability under CVA but the firm will not invest unless it is instructed to do so, directly or indirectly, by the stockholders. Just as for a consumption tax, the individual has full discretion, if the firm acts in his best interests, to determine the size of his tax bill by changing the amount he consumes. The deduction of gross investment, under CVA, from the tax base, is a rebate of the tax imposed on capital goods so that the net effect of this tax is to tax consumption.

2   We have assumed that the elasticity of substitution between labor and capital in the taxed industry is zero, that the ratio of capital in the taxed industry to capital in the untaxed industry is .01, and that no labor is employed in the taxed industry. Under these assumptions the general expression for the changes in the price of capital, relative to the price of labor, which is the numeraire, derived by Harberger [25. 1962, p. 227] reduces to

$dp_K = \dfrac{.01ET_x}{.01E(g_k - 1) - S_y}$ where E is the elasticity of demand for X. T_x is the

tax on capital in X expressed as a per-unit tax. g_k is the share of capital in the untaxed sector and S_y is the elasticity of substitution in the taxed industry.

We assume $E = S_y = -.5$ and $g_k = .25$ to obtain the result that $dp_K = -.01\ T_x$. As only 1 percent of total capital is subject to tax, total after-tax profits fall by the amount of the tax proceeds.

3   Work along these lines is being carried out by Maria Schmundt of the University of Western Ontario. What is especially interesting about her research is that she also studies models that allow for the mobility of capital in situations in which both countries are not completely specialized.

4   A fixed markup is fully consistent with profit maximization, if costs are constant and if the elasticity of demand, as seen by the monopolist, is constant.

5   As the value of the dependent variable is changed by a change in the shifting assumption, the R^2 criterion is incorrect and Hall should have based his conclusions on the sum-of-squared residuals. Also, as Musgrave suggests [52. 1964, p. 301] Hall should have attempted to maximize the goodness of fit by investigating values of shifting between zero and one. However, Musgrave's comments [52. 1964, p. 300] are misleading, for although the R^2 criterion may be correct (we can't tell without examining the sum-of-squared residuals) the test of whether a change in specification affects the goodness of fit relates *not* to R^2 but to $1 - R^2$. And the change in shifting assumption had a dramatic effect on the latter statistic.

References

1.   Adelman, M. A. "The Corporate Income Tax in the Long Run." *J. Polit. Econ.*, April 1957, *65*, 151–7.

2.   Bain, A. D. "Tax Incidence and Growth: A Comment," *Econ. J.*, September 1963, *73*, 533–5.

3.   Baumol, W. J. *Business Behavior, Value and Growth.* Rev. ed., New York: Harcourt, Brace, and World, 1967.

4.   Bishop, G. A. "The Tax Burden by Income Class, 1958," *Nat. Tax J.*, March 1961, *14*, 41–58.

5.   Brazer, H. E. "The Value of Industrial Property as a Subject of Taxation," *Can. Pub. Administration*, June 1961, *4*, 137–47.

6.   Brown, H. G. *The Economics of Taxation.* New York: Holt, 1924.

7.   ——. "The Incidence of a General Output or a General Sales Tax," *J. Polit. Econ.*, April 1939, *47*, 254–62.

8.   Buchanan, J. M. "The Methodology of Incidence Theory: A Critical Review of Some Recent Contributions," in *Fiscal Theory and Political Economy*, Chapel Hill, 1960.

9.   ——. *The Public Finances.* Rev. ed., Homewood, Ill.: Irwin, 1965.

10. Chipman, J. S. "International Trade with Capital Mobility: A Substitution Theorem," Mimeographed paper, 1968.

11. Clendenin, J. C. "Effect of Corporate Income Taxes on Corporate Earnings," *Taxes*, June 1956, *34*.

12. Cragg, J. G., Harberger, A. C., and Mieszkowski, P. "Empirical Evidence

on the Incidence of the Corporation Income tax," *J. Polit. Econ.*, Dec. 1967, *75*, 811–21.

13. Dlamond, P. A. "Incidence of an Interest Income Tax," M.I.T. Working Paper 5, Oct. 1967.

14. Dosser, D. "Tax Incidence and Growth," *Economic Journal*, Sept. 1961, *71*, 572–91.

15. ——. "Incidence and Growth Further Considered," *Econ. J.* Sept. 1963, *73*, 547–53.

16. Due, J. F. "Sales Taxation and the Consumer," *Amer. Econ. Rev.*, Dec. 1963, *53*, 1078–84.

17. ——. "The Value Added Tax," *West. Econ. J.*, Spring 1965, *3*, 165–71.

18. ——. *Government Finance: Economics of the Public Sectors*, Fourth ed., Homewood, Ill.: Irwin 1968.

19. Edgeworth, F. Y. *Papers Relating to Political Economy*. New York: B. Franklin, 1925.

20. Gillespie, W. I. "Effects of Public Expenditures on the Distribution of Income," in *Essays in Fiscal Federalism*, R. A. Musgrave (ed.), Washington, 1965.

21. Goode, R. "Rates of Return, Incomes Shares and Corporate Tax Incidence," in M. Krzyzaniak, 1966.

22. Gordon, R. J. "The Incidence of the Corporation Income Tax in U.S. Manufacturing 1925–62," *Amer. Econ. Rev.*, Sept. 1967, *57*, 731–58.

23. ——. "Incidence of the Corporation Tax in U.S. Manufacturing: Reply," *Amer. Econ. Rev.*, Dec. 1968, *58*, 1360–7.

24. Hall, C. A. Jr., "Direct Shifting of the Corporation Income Tax in Manufacturing," *Amer. Econ. Rev., Papers and Proceedings*, May 1964, *54*, 258–71.

25. Harberger, A. C. "The Incidence of the Corporate Income Tax," *J. Polit. Econ.*, June 1962, *70*, 215–40.

26. ——. "Efficiency Effects of Taxes on Income From Capital," in M. Krzyzaniak, 1966.

27. Heinberg, J. D. and Oates, W. E. "The Incidence of Differential Property Taxes on Urban Housing: A Comment and some Further Evidence," *Nat. Tax J.*, March 1970, 23, 2, 92–8.

28. Jones, R. W. "International Capital Movements and the Theory of Tariffs and Trade," *Quart. J. Econ.*, Feb. 1967, *81*, 1–38.

29. Johnson, H. G. "General Equilibrium Analysis of Excise Taxes: Comment," *Amer. Econ. Rev.*, March 1956, *46*, 151–6.

30. Kemp, M. C. "The Gain from International Trade and Investment: A Neo-Heckscher-Ohlin Approach," *Amer. Econ. Rev.*, September 1966, *56*, 788–809.

31. Kilpatrick, R. W., "The Short-Run Forward Shifting of the Corporation Income Tax," *Yale Economic Essays*, Fall 1965, *5*, 355–420.

32. Krzyzaniak, M. and Musgrave, R. A. *The Shifting of the Corporation Income Tax*. Baltimore: Johns Hopkins, 1963.

33. Krzyzaniak, M., ed. *Effects of Corporation Income Tax*, Detroit, 1966.

34. ——. "Effects of Profits Taxes: Deduced from Neoclassical Growth Models," in M. Krzyzaniak, 1966.

35. Krzyzaniak, M. and Musgrave, R. A. "Discussion," in M. Krzyzaniak, 1966.

36. Krzyzaniak, M. "Long-Run Burden of a General Tax on Profits in a Neoclassical World" *Public Finance*, 1967, *22*, 473–91.

37. —— and Musgrave, R. A. "Corporate Tax Shifting Rejoinders," Harvard Institute of Economic Research, Discussion Paper No. 31, May 1968.

38. Krzyzaniak, M. "The Burden of a Differential Tax on Profits in a Neoclassical World," *Publ. Finance*, 1968, *23*(4), 447–73.

39. Lévesgue, R. J. "The Shifting of the Corporate Income Tax in the Short Run," *Studies of the Royal Commission on Taxation*, No. 18, Ottawa, 1967.

40. Lerner, E. M. and Hendriksen, E. S. "Federal Taxes on Corporate Income and the Rate of Return on Investment in Manufacturing, 1927 to 1952," *National Tax Journal*, Sept. 1956, *9*, 193–202.

41. Marris, R. *The Economic Theory of Managerial Capitalism*. New York: Free Press-Macmillan, 1964.

42. Marshall, A. *Reply to the Questionnaire of the Royal Commission on Local Taxation, 1897*. Quoted by C. F. Bickerdike, "Taxation of Site Values," *Economic Journal*, No. 12, 1902, 472–84.

43. McLure, C. E., Jr., "Commodity Tax Incidence in Open Economies," *Nat. Tax J.*, June 1964, *17*, 187–204.

44. ——. "The Theory of Tax Incidence with Imperfect Factor Mobility," Mimeographed paper, 1968.

45. ——. "The Inter-Regional Incidence of General Regional Taxes," *Publ. Finance*, 1969, *24*(3), pp. 457–84.

46. Meade, J. E. *The Theory of International Economic Policy*, Vol. 2, *Trade and Welfare Mathematical Supplement*. New York: Oxford University Press, 1955.

47. Mieszkowski, P. M. "General Equilibrium Models of Tax Incidence," unpublished doctoral dissertation, Johns Hopkins University, 1963.

48. ——. "On the Theory of Tax Incidence," *Journal of Political Economy*, June 1967, *75*, 250–62.

49. Musgrave, R. A. et al., "Distribution of Tax Payments by Income Groups: A Case Study for 1948," *Nat. Tax J.*, March 1951, *4*, 1–53.

50. Musgrave, R. A. "On Incidence," *J. Polit. Econ.*, Aug. 1953, *61*, 306–23.

51. ——. *The Theory of Public Finance*. New York: McGraw-Hill, 1959.

52. ——. "Discussion," *American Economic Review Papers and Proceedings*, May 1964, *54*, 300–2.

53. Netzer, R. *Economics of the Property Tax*. Washington: Brookings, 1966.

54. ——. "Taxation: Property Taxes," in *International Encyclopedia of Social Sciences*, New York, Vol. 15, 1968, 545–50.

55. ——. "Impact of the Property Tax: Its Economic Implications for Urban Problems," *J.E.C. Print.*, 90th Congress, Washington, 1968.

56. Oakland, W. H. "The Theory of the Value-Added Tax: I A Comparison of Tax Bases," *Nat. Tax J.*, June 1967, *20*, 119–36.

57. Oates, W. E. "The Effects of Property Taxes and Local Public Spending on Property Values: An Empirical Study of Tax Capitalization and the Tiebout Hypothesis," *J. Polit. Econ.*, forthcoming.

58. Orr, L. L. "The Incidence of Differential Property Taxes on Urban Housing," *Nat. Tax J.*, Sept. 1968, *21*, 253–65.

59. Parks, R. H. "Theory of Tax Incidence: International Aspects," *Nat. Tax J.*, June 1961, *14*, 190–7.

60. Pierson, N. G. *Principles of Economics*. Vol. I, New York: McMillan, 1902.

61. Penner, R. G. "Uncertainty and the Short-Run Shifting of the Corporation Tax," *Oxford Econ. Pap.*, March 1967, *19*, 99–110.

62. Prest, A. R. "Statistical Calculations of Tax Burden," *Economica*, August 1955, *22*, 234–45.

63. ——. "Observations on Dynamic Incidence," *Econ. J.*, Sept. 1963, *73*, 535–46.

64. Ratchford, B. U. and Han, P. B. "The Burden of the Corporate Income Tax," *Nat. Tax J.*, December 1957, *10*, 310–24.

65. Richman, R. L. "The Incidence of Urban Real Estate Taxes Under Conditions of Static and Dynamic Equilibrium," *Land Econ.*, May 1967, *43*, 172–80.

66. Rolph, E. R. "A Proposed Revision of Excise-Tax Theory," *J. of Polit. Econ.*, April 1952, *60*, 102–17.

67. ——. "A Theory of Excise Subsidies," *Amer. Econ. Rev.*, Sept. 1952, *42*, 515–27.

68. ——. "The Distribution of Government Burdens and Benefits: Discussion," *Amer. Econ. Rev.*, May 1953, *43*, 537–43.

69. ——. "A Theory of Excise Subsidies: Reply," *Amer. Econ. Rev.*, Dec. 1953, *43*, 895–8.

70. ——. *The Theory of Fiscal Economics*. New York: Ronald Press, 1954.

71. ——. "The Economic Effects of a Federal Value Added Tax," in Committee on Ways and Means, *Excise Tax Compendium–Compendium of Papers on Excise Tax Structure*, Washington, 1964.

72. Rosenberg, L. G. "Total Income from Capital by Non-Financial Industry Group, Average 1953–59," unpublished doctoral dissertation, University of Chicago, 1963. To be published in *The Taxation of Income from Capital*, A. C. Harberger and M. J. Bailey, eds.

73. Roskamp, K. W. "The Shifting of Taxes on Business Income: The Case of West German Corporations," *Nat. Tax J.*, Sept. 1965, *18*, 247–57.

74. Shoup, C. S. "Theory and Background of the Value-Added Tax," *Proceedings* of the National Tax Association, Oct. 1955, 6–19.

75. ——. *Public Finance*, Chicago: Aldine, 1969.

76. ——. "Consumption Tax, and Wages Type and Consumption Type of Value-Added Tax," *Nat. Tax J.*, June 1968, *21*, 153–61.

77. Simon, H. A. "The Incidence of a Tax on Urban Real Property," *Quart. J. Econ.*, May 1943, *57*, 398–420.

78. Slitor, R. E. "Corporate Tax Incidence: Economic Adjustments to Differentials Under a Two-Tier Tax Structure," in M. Krzyzaniak, 1966.

79. Spencer, B. G. "The Shifting of the Corporation Income Tax in Canada," *Can. J. Econ.*, Feb. 1969, *2*, 21–34.

80. Stiglitz, J. E. "The Distribution of Income and Wealth Among Individuals," unpublished paper presented at the meetings of The Econometric Society, Dec. 1966.

81. ——. "Distribution of Income and Wealth Among Individuals," Cowles Foundation Discussion Paper No. 238, Nov. 1967.

82. Stolper, W. F. and Samuelson, P. A. "Protection and Real Wages," *Rev. Econ. Stud.*, Nov. 1941, *9*, 58–73.

83. Turek, J. L. "Short Run Shifting of the Corporate Income Tax in Manufacturing," *Yale Econ. Essays* Spring 1970, *1*, 127–48.

84. Weitenberg, J. "The Incidence of Social Security Taxes," *Public Finance*, 1969, *24*, 2, 193–208.

85. Wells, P. "A General Equilibrium Analysis of Excise Taxes," *Amer. Econ. Rev.*, June 1955, *45*, 345–59.

86. Williams, A. *Public Finance and Budgetary Policy*. New York: Humanities Press, 1963.

Introduction to Chapter 8

We turn now to one of those controversial taxes, the property tax. Alfred Marshall, who for decades just before and after 1900 was the most prominent British economist and a frequent adviser to government, pointed out that local taxes could be "beneficial" in the sense of paying for services that taxpayers would be entirely willing to pay for if they were available in private markets, or "onerous" in the sense that taxpayers gain nothing from the expenditure of the taxes they pay. Of course, most local taxes are likely to be mixed in this sense.

Zodrow and Mieszkowski, in this article, never refer explicitly to Marshall's distinction between "beneficial" and "onerous" local property taxes, but the article is about the consequences of that distinction, in modern language and reflecting developments in economic theory in recent decades. If real-world American local government finance is more or less like that described by Tiebout in 1956 (see chapter 2, above), then local property taxes are benefit taxes, freely chosen by residents and businesses in their choice of where to live, and very much like charges for the use of public services.

If not, then a significant element of the local property tax is "onerous," such as school taxes paid by people who do not have children in the public schools. On a nationwide basis, the property tax will be borne by owners of capital, and will be progressive in incidence. But the differential rates and coverage of local property taxes will result in migration of people and capital, and the incidence of the tax differentials locally will be quite different.

The article is not an empirical study, but an evaluation of the plausibility of the assumptions needed to support each of the two sides of the argument.

8

The Incidence of the Property Tax: The Benefit View Versus the New View[1]

George R. Zodrow and Peter Mieszkowski

8.1 Introduction

Two conflicting views of the incidence of the property tax are prominent in the public finance literature; these views have starkly contrasting implications for the allocative and distributive effects of the tax. The first is the "benefit view" which integrates the local property tax in a Tiebout (1956) framework of perfect consumer mobility and competition among local governments. This approach was pioneered by Hamilton (1975, 1976) who showed how a system of residential property taxes, coupled with either strict zoning ordinances which ensure homogeneous housing or perfect capitalization of property tax differences in house values, is equivalent to a set of non-distortionary user charges. Fischel (1975) and White (1975) extended this approach to property taxes on industrial capital in models where firms are highly mobile between communities and, again with the appropriate zoning ordinances, industrial property tax payments are equivalent to fees for public services.

In contrast, the proponents of a second view, due to the work of Thomson (1965), Mieszkowski (1972), and Aaron (1975), argue that, in general, capital owners bear the burden of the property tax, and thus the system of local property taxes is a progressive tax on capital rather than a benefit tax. This "new view" of the property tax takes into account the taxation of both residential and non-residential capital, but is developed independently of any considerations of benefits received from local public expenditures or of zoning. More generally, the new view is based on the general equilibrium incidence model developed by Harberger (1962) for the analysis of national taxes; this approach does not take into account consumer or firm mobility among local jurisdictions offering different expenditure and tax packages. Instead, local property taxes are taken as given and the differential incidence of a national system of local property taxes, relative to a proportional income tax, is determined following what is now fairly conventional methodology (see McLure, 1975).

In this paper, we examine the theoretical approaches which lead to such drastically different results regarding the allocative and distributive effects of the property tax. We focus on two critical differences between the two approaches. First, we consider the importance of zoning (or perfect capitalization) in obtaining the benefit view results. Mobility and interjurisdictional competition, in combination with the appropriate residential and non-residential zoning ordinances, ensure that households and firms are stratified according to demands for public services and located in jurisdictions where tax payments equal public services demanded – or production externalities generated – at the margin. (As stressed by Hamilton, perfect capitalization achieves the same result in models where residential zoning does not result in homogeneous housing consumption.) Thus, the distortionary effect of property taxation on capital allocation across jurisdictions, which is one of the critical elements in the derivation of the new view, is eliminated. To illustrate this point, we show that the benefit view result regarding the incidence of the residential property tax can be obtained in a Harberger-type model (which otherwise generates the new view result) simply by imposing the appropriate zoning constraint on housing consumption.

Second, we consider the implications for the new view of the Tiebout-type interjurisdictional competition stressed by proponents of the benefit view. The new view implies that the property tax is non-benefit tax on capital owners; we inquire whether such exploitation of capital owners can occur once interjurisdictional competition is taken into account. Our approach is to construct a Cournot-Nash model of interjurisdictional competition where each government sets its property tax rate to maximize the welfare of its residents, assuming that all other jurisdictions hold their tax rates fixed. Our model does not allow for production-augmenting effects of local expenditures, as capital is assumed to receive no benefits from local services; capital can be compensated for higher property taxes only by a higher before-tax rate of return. Under these circumstances, as long as each local government has a head tax at its disposal, the optimal tax rate on mobile capital is zero; the competitive equilibrium is not characterized by non-benefit taxation of capital. However, if each government, for statutory, political or other reasons, can finance local public services only through the property tax, the new view result obtains even in a perfectly competitive environment (as the number of local jurisdictions in the economy gets very large). Thus, as long as local governments are constrained to use property tax finance, interjurisdictional competition does not eliminate the exploitation of capital implied by the new view; also, since each government believes the property tax will drive mobile capital out of its jurisdiction, there is a tendency for local governments to provide an inefficiently low level of public services. However, this equilibrium is unstable in the sense that each community can increase the welfare of its residents by reducing its property tax rate and imposing a head tax, as long as all other communities hold their tax rates constant. Thus, to get the new view result within a competitive framework, local governments must be acting myopically or must, for some reason, be prevented from switching from property tax to head tax finance of local services.

We conclude that our analysis suggests that the new view is a viable alternative to the benefit tax explanation of the effects of the property tax; that is, the new view of the property tax has relevance even in a world characterized by interjurisdictional competition, as long as the competition does not extend to the use of head taxes rather than property taxes to finance local public services. Under these circumstances, the property tax has a non-benefit component so that allocative efficiency is impaired and, since this non-benefit component is borne by the owners of capital, the property tax is progressive in comparison to a benefit tax.

8.2   Zoning, Capitalization and the Allocative Effects of the Property Tax

The essential idea underlying the benefit view of the property tax is that perfectly mobile households and firms can move to the community with the public service package that best meets their needs and pay for these services through the local property tax. Since the property tax is effectively a user charge for local public services,[2] the use of the property tax causes no distortions; thus, the resulting equilibrium is allocatively efficient.

A variety of mechanisms can convert the property tax into a user charge. Hamilton (1975) shows that the residential property tax is a benefit tax when consumers are perfectly mobile and residential communities are zoned so that housing is homogeneous; in equilibrium, tastes for public services as well as property tax payments are identical for all households who reside in the community. Hamilton (1976) also shows that perfect capitalization of residential property taxes and services into house values yields the same result in communities with nonhomogeneous housing. In both cases, all the households who reside in a community are homogeneous with respect to their demand for local public services.[3] Fischel (1975) and White (1975) demonstrate that the nonresidential property tax is a benefit tax when firms are perfectly mobile and communities enact the appropriate nonresidential zoning restrictions; public services are treated as another factor of production and the product of the local tax rate and a firm's taxable property equals its public service consumption. In all these cases, households or firms are appropriately stratified so that, at the margin, property tax payments equal local public services received and the resulting equilibrium is allocatively efficient.

Note that the critical element in these analyses is sorting according to demands for public services. Similar results could be obtained for wage or output taxes, as long as the appropriate "zoning" restrictions could be devised and implemented. Thus, in contrast to the new view result that the property tax is a much more progressive tax than a wage tax, the benefit view implies that the substitution of a wage tax for a property tax would, in the long run, have virtually no effect on the distribution of income. Zoning requirements would change and, in some cases, households and firms would have to relocate in order to match property tax payments to benefits received. The benefit view implies that the choice of tax instrument at the local level is largely irrelevant; with the appropriate zoning ordinances, all tax systems are equivalent to a system of non-distortionary fees for public services.[4]

Thus, one of the key differences between the theoretical analyses yielding the benefit and new views is that in the former case, allocative efficiency is ensured through a variety of zoning or capitalization mechanisms so that the property tax is a non-distorting benefit tax at the margin, while in the latter case, the property tax distorts the capital allocation. This misallocation plays a central role in the Harberger-type differential incidence models which yield the new view result.

To illustrate this point, we consider the incidence of a residential property tax within the context of a Harberger-type model. Our objective is to construct a simple model which demonstrates that without restrictions on the amount of housing consumed, the incidence of a residential property tax is completely on capital and land, as households whose income is solely from wages bear none of the burden of the residential property tax. In contrast, when the amount of housing consumption is restricted by the appropriate zoning ordinances, the residential property tax becomes a lump-sum tax on housing consumption. The burden of the tax is proportional to the amount of housing consumed which, within the context of our model, converts the residential property tax to a benefit tax (as in Hamilton, 1975).

Since we wish to focus on the "average" burden of the tax stressed by
Mieszkowski (1972), we consider an economy with a fixed national
capital stock and a fixed number of identical local jurisdictions. We
assume that each jurisdiction simultaneously uses a residential property
tax to finance an increase in publicly provided local services.[5] Each of the
representative local jurisdictions in the model is described by the following system of fourteen equations.

Equation 8.1 shows that a composite good (X) is produced using a
Cobb-Douglas production function with capital (K_X), land (V_X) and all
the local labor supply (L), while equation 8.2 indicates that housing (H)
is produced using a Cobb-Douglas production function with capital
(K_H) and land (V_H):

$$X = K_X^a V_X^b L^c, \quad a+b+c+1 \tag{8.1}$$

$$H = K_H^d V_H^e, \quad d+e=1 \tag{8.2}$$

Equations 8.3–8.5 are the profit-maximizing factor demands; r, s, and w
are the net returns to capital, land and labor (capital and land can be
used in the production of either the composite good or housing and thus
earn the same net return in both uses):

$$K_X = L(a/c)(w/r) \tag{8.3}$$

$$V_X = L(b/c)(w/s) \tag{8.4}$$

$$K_H = V_H(d/e)(s/r) \tag{8.5}$$

Equations 8.6 and 8.7 indicate that the fixed stocks of capital (K) and
land (V) are fully employed in production of one of the two goods:

$$K = K_X + K_H \tag{8.6}$$

$$V = V_X + V_H \tag{8.7}$$

Equations 8.8 and 8.9 are the marginal product pricing equations implied by the assumptions of constant returns to scale production functions and perfectly competitive markets, where q is the price of housing
(the composite good is the numeraire with a unitary price $p = 1$) and T
is the ad valorem rate of property taxation of the rental values of the
capital and land used in the production of residential housing:

$$X = wL + rK_X + sV_X \tag{8.8}$$

$$qH = (1+T)(rK_H + sV_H) \tag{8.9}$$

Government services are treated as "publicly provided private goods."[6] These services are financed in one of two ways. First, the government sells a total of G_1 of the numeraire composite good to its residents, assessing them a user charge of one dollar per unit; in this case, the government is merely a non-profit intermediary which costlessly "transforms" the composite good into public services and sells them to the public. Second, the government provides a total of G_2 of the composite good to its residents, financing the purchase with revenues from the residential property tax; each resident receives G_2/n public services, where n is the population. The case where all public services are financed by user charges ($G_2 = 0$) results in an efficient allocation of resources and serves as a benchmark in the analysis. Thus, equation 8.10 indicates that all of the composite good is either purchased as a private consumption good (C), sold by the government as public services but financed through user charges (G_1), or provided by the government as public services financed by the residential property tax (G_2). Equation 8.11 indicates that the government budget for purchases of G_2 must be balanced:

$$X = C + G_1 + G_2 \tag{8.10}$$

$$G_2 = T(rK_H + sV_H) \tag{8.11}$$

Finally, equations 8.12–8.14 are the consumer demand equations. All consumers are assumed to maximize a Cobb-Douglas utility function defined over private consumption of the composite good, housing and public services (G_1 and G_2 are perfect substitutes), and all factors are assumed to be locally-owned. Thus, the aggregate consumption demands given in equations 8.12–8.14 can be derived from the maximization of an aggregate Cobb-Douglas utility function

$$U = C^\alpha H^\beta (G_1 + G_2)^\gamma, \quad \alpha + \beta + \gamma = 1,$$

subject to the aggregate income constraint

$$Y = rK + sV + wL = C + G_1 + qH$$

We assume that all individuals in a jurisdiction have the same income so that each individual receives the same public service level regardless of the choice of tax instrument; thus, any redistribution which occurs in the model results from the tax side, rather than the expenditure side, of the local government budget:

$$C = \alpha\left(Y + G_2\right) \tag{8.12}$$

$$qH = \beta\left(Y + G_2\right) \tag{8.13}$$

$$G_1 + G_2 = \gamma\left(Y + G_2\right) \tag{8.14}$$

Also, in order to focus on the incidence of the property tax in terms of the functional distribution of income, we assume that no individual receives more than one type of factor income; U^K, U^V, and U^L denote the aggregate utilities of capital owners, landowners and labor.

The economy is assumed to be in a zero-tax, undistorted initial equilibrium where all government services are financed by user charges. This assumption implies that the imposition of a residential property tax does not change the level of aggregate utility in the economy.[7]

The incidence of an increase in the residential property tax is analyzed by totally differentiating equations 8.1–8.14 and solving for the changes in the endogenous variables. This procedure yields the factor real-locations caused by the substitution of property tax finance for user charge finance in the model

$$\hat{K}_X = \left(K_H/K\right)\left(1 \hat{+} T\right) \tag{8.15}$$

$$\hat{K}_H = -\left(K_X/K\right)\left(1 \hat{+} T\right) \tag{8.16}$$

$$\hat{V}_X = \left(V_H/V\right)\left(1 \hat{+} T\right) \tag{8.17}$$

$$\hat{V}_H = -\left(V_X/V\right)\left(1 \hat{+} T\right) \tag{8.18}$$

where the circumflex indicates logarithmic differentiation; thus, the housing sector shrinks and the composite good sector expands as a result of the residential property tax.

It is straightforward to show that property owners bear the burden of the property tax in this variant of the Harberger model. The utility change experienced by each income group, net of the increase in publicly-provided services which is shared equally by all residents, is

$$dU^i/\lambda - dG_2/n = dY^i - H^i dq, \quad i = K, \ V, \ L, \tag{8.19}$$

where λ is the common marginal utility of income and Y^i and H^i are the incomes and housing consumption of each income group. Revenues from the residential property tax can be separated into a capital component $R_K = TrK_H$ and a land component $R_V = TsV_H$. Solving for the net utility change for each group of factor owners yields the incidence results

$$\left(dU^K/\lambda - dG_2/n\right)/Y^K = -\left(K_H/K\right)\left(1 \hat{+} T\right) = -dR_K/Y^K \tag{8.20}$$

$$\left(dU^V/\lambda - dG_2/n\right)/Y^V = -\left(V_H/V\right)\left(1 \hat{+} T\right) = -dR_V/Y^V \tag{8.21}$$

$$\left(dU^L/\lambda - dG_2/n\right)/Y^L = 0 \tag{8.22}$$

Thus, capital owners bear the capital component of the residential property tax burden, land owners bear the land component, and labor bears none of the tax. That is, labor benefits from its share of the publicly provided services, but the real income of wage-earners is unchanged by the imposition of the residential property tax (independently of how much of the tax-financed G_2 is distributed to this income group). This new view type result – all capital and land-owners bear the burden of a residential property tax – obtains because labor receives the publicly provided services G_2 by residing in the jurisdiction but reduces its housing consumption in response to the residential property tax. The effect of the resulting factor reallocation is a reduction in the returns to property owners sufficiently large that they bear the entire burden of the tax.

This result is straightforward in the case of Cobb-Douglas utility and production functions. With more general functional forms, the strong result that labor bears none of the burden of the residential property tax does not obtain. Nevertheless, the general tendency for capital and land to bear a disproportionate share of the burden remains. The residential property tax leads to a shrinkage of the housing sector and the shift of capital and land into the composite good sector increases the relative return to labor.

This new view type result hinges on the assumption that there are no zoning constraints on housing consumption. Suppose instead that the local governments require residents to purchase the quantity of housing which maximizes their utility. Since the initial zero-tax equilibrium is Pareto efficient, this is equivalent to imposing the requirement that $\hat{H} = 0$ as the property tax is increased. In this case, an increase in the residential property tax rate has no effect on factor allocation or on factor prices, while housing prices increase by the full amount of the tax,

$$\hat{q} = \left(1 \hat{+} T\right), \tag{8.23}$$

households bear the full burden of the property tax financed increase in publicly provided services in proportion to their consumption of housing, which is proportional to income.

Thus, with the appropriate zoning constraint, the model yields the benefit view – consumers of local public services bear the full burden of the residential property tax which finances them. With no excess burden effects, the changes in the levels of utility resulting from the imposition of the residential property tax are all zero.

Finally, note that in the model above, in keeping with the benefit view literature (e.g., Hamilton, 1975), housing consumption is constrained by the zoning ordinances. It is straightforward to show that the benefit view result does not obtain if instead the amount of land used for housing is fixed (e.g., minimum lot zoning) at the value of V_H in the zero-tax equilibrium. Solving the same system of equations subject to the constraint that $\hat{V}_H = 0$ yields the results that capital owners bear the capital component of the residential property tax, while residential land owners bear the land component; the latter result obtains because the zoning constraint prevents a reallocation of land to production of the composite good. Thus, labor and non-residential land owners receive the benefits of publicly provided local services without bearing any burden of the residential property tax when residential land, rather than housing consumption, is subject to a zoning constraint.

8.3 Interjurisdictional Competition and the New View of the Property Tax

The results in the previous section provide a set of conditions under which a new view result obtains – capital owners bear the full burden of the capital component of a residential property tax. Under these conditions, capital owners are "exploited" in the sense that they pay more in property taxes than they consume in services. The benefit view result regarding the incidence of the residential property tax is obtained within the Harberger framework only when the demand for housing is constrained so that the factor reallocations which lead to the new view type result are ruled out. However, if we modified our model to consider the simultaneous taxation of non-residential and residential capital stressed by Mieszkowski (1972) in the derivation of the new view, constraining housing consumption would not be sufficient to yield the benefit view result; since capital is taxed at the same rate in both production sectors, the exploitation result does not obtain due to a reallocation of capital between sectors. Instead, exploitation occurs because the application of the Harberger fixed national capital stock model to the analysis of a system of local property taxes implies that all local governments simultaneously use the property tax so that capital can not escape the tax – not surprisingly, these assumptions lead to the new view result.

However, the application of the Harberger model to the analysis of a national system of local property taxes is somewhat tenuous because it does not properly take into account either the independence of local governments in setting their own property tax rates or the constraints local governments operate under due to the interjurisdictional competition stressed by proponents of the benefit view. By emphasizing the effects of the average rate of property taxation in the nation, the approach poses the question in the context of a simultaneous increase or decrease of the tax by all governments. This "experiment" is suggestive of collusive behavior among local governments, although the mechanism by which this collusion occurs is not specified.

In this section, we present a model that should put the new view on somewhat firmer footing. First, we demonstrate that interjurisdictional competition is inconsistent with non-benefit taxation of mobile capital as argued by proponents of the benefit view, as long as local governments can raise revenues through lump sum taxes. However, if local governments are constrained, for statutory, political or any other reasons, to finance local public services only through property taxes on capital, the new view result obtains. That is, even with perfect competition among jurisdictions, capital owners bear the full burden of the property tax. Moreover, we show that property tax finance leads to an inefficiently low level of local public service provision.

Again, our model is a simple one. To focus on the question of possible non-benefit taxation of capital, we assume that non-residential production uses no local services and generates no externalities. According to the benefit view, non-residential capital should not be taxed. Our approach, following Epple and Zelenitz (1981), is an application of standard industrial organization theory to a model of a national economy with a fixed number (N) of identical local jurisdictions. That is, we determine the level of property taxation chosen by each local government under the assumption that all other local governments hold their property tax rates fixed; perfect competition among local jurisdictions in this Cournot-Nash setting is modeled as the case where the number of jurisdictions becomes very large.

Consider a perfectly competitive economy with a fixed national capital stock where each of the N jurisdictions has a fixed land supply $V = 1$. Equations 8.24–8.27 describe a representative jurisdiction i ($i = 1$, ... N). Output X_i is produced in each jurisdiction with capital (K_i) and land using a strictly concave, constant returns production function

$$X_i = F(K_i), \quad F' > 0, \quad F'' < 0, \tag{8.24}$$

where the fixed land argument is suppressed. Marginal product pricing ensures

$$r(1 + T_i) = F'(K_i) \tag{8.25}$$

where r is the net return to capital which is assumed to be perfectly mobile among the N jurisdictions, T_i is the *ad valorem* property tax rate on capital rental values in jurisdiction i, and output is the numeraire. It will be convenient to define $\tau_i = T_i/(1 + T_i)$ as the tax rate expressed as a percentage of the gross rental payment to capital. The return to land-owners is the residual after capital payments

$$s_i = X_i - r(1 + T_i)K_i, \tag{8.26}$$

where s_i is the net return to landowners in jurisdiction i and land is not subject to the property tax. Local government services (G_i) are again treated as publicly provided private goods and are modeled as public purchases of output which are financed either with the property tax on capital or with a head tax with total revenue H_i:

$$G_i = T_i r K_i + H_i \tag{8.27}$$

Local services, as well as the head tax, are shared equally by local landowners; the ownership of all land in the jurisdiction is equally divided among these local landowners, who have no other source of income. Note that in this model the head tax is equivalent to a land value tax. The model is closed by imposing the fixed national capital stock constraint:

$$K = \sum_{i=1}^{N} K_i \qquad (8.28)$$

Since the local government in each jurisdiction acts on the assumption that all other jurisdictions will not respond to changes in its property tax rate, the effect on the net return to capital expected by a representative jurisdiction j when it increases its property tax rate is obtained by differentiating equation 8.25 and substituting into the result of differentiating equation 8.28 for $dT_i = 0$, $i \neq j$:

$$\hat{r} = -\varepsilon_{rj}\left(1 \hat{+} T_j\right), \qquad (8.29)$$

where

$$\varepsilon_{rj} = \frac{\left(1+T_j\right)\big/ F''\left(K_j\right)}{\sum_i \left(1+T_i\right)\big/ F''\left(K_i\right)} > 0$$

In the Nash equilibrium, when all N jurisdictions behave identically, $\varepsilon_{rj} = 1/N$; as N gets large, ε_{rj} approaches zero, indicating that any individual jurisdiction cannot affect the national rate of return to capital.

The capital supply elasticity with respect to increases in T_j is obtained by substituting from equation 8.29 into the result of differentiating equation 8.25:

$$\hat{K}_j = -\varepsilon_{Kj}\left(1 \hat{+} T_j\right), \qquad (8.30)$$

where

$$\varepsilon_{Kj} = -\frac{r\left(1+T_j\right)}{F''\left(K_j\right)} \frac{\left(1-\varepsilon_{rj}\right)}{K_j} > 0$$

The effect of an increase in property taxes on land prices in the jurisdiction is obtained by substituting from equations 8.25 and 8.30 and from the result of differentiating equation 8. 24 into the result of differentiating equation 8.26:

$$\hat{s}_j = -\left(\theta_{Kj}/\theta_{Vj}\right)\left(1-\varepsilon_{rj}\right)\left(1 \hat{+} T_j\right), \qquad (8.31)$$

where θ_{Kj} and θ_{Vj} are the capital and land shares in production costs in jurisdiction j. Substituting from equations 8.29 and 8.30 into the result of differentiating equation 8.27 yields the differential equation for the government budget constraint:

$$\hat{G}_j = \phi_{Tj}\left[1/\tau_j - \left(\varepsilon_{Kj} + \varepsilon_{rj}\right)\right]\left(1 \hat{+} T_j\right) + \phi_{Hj}\hat{H}_j, \tag{8.32}$$

where ϕ_{Tj} and ϕ_{Hj} are the shares of government services financed by property taxes and by head taxes. The revenue-maximizing tax rate for each jurisdiction is thus the inverse of the sum of its capital supply and interest rate elasticities.

The equilibrium for the economy can be calculated once the objective function for each local government is specified. Since we are concerned with the hypothesis of exploitation of capital owners, we adopt the assumption most conducive to such exploitation – local governments act to maximize the welfare of resident landowners. Local residents are assumed to have an identical utility function which is homogeneous of degree one in net income and government services, so the government maximizes the welfare of local resident landowners by choosing H_j and T_j to maximize the same utility function defined over aggregate resident landowner income (Y_j) and government services:

$$U_j\left[Y_j\left(H_j, T_j\right), \ G_j\left(H_j, T_j\right)\right],$$

where

$$Y_j = s_j - H_j;$$

differentiating and substituting from equation 8.31 yields:

$$\hat{Y}_j = -\frac{s_j}{Y_j}\frac{\theta_{Kj}}{\theta_{Vj}}\left(1 - \varepsilon_{rj}\right)\left(1 \hat{+} T_j\right) - \frac{H_j}{Y_j}\hat{H}_j \tag{8.33}$$

The first order conditions for the local government optimization problem[8] indicate that, at the optimum, the marginal rate of substitution between public and private goods (m_j) should be one

$$m_j = \left(\partial U_j/\partial Y_j\right)/\left(\partial U_j/\partial G_j\right) = 1, \tag{8.34}$$

and that the optimal tax rate is implicitly defined by

$$\tau_j = \varepsilon_{rj} / \left(\varepsilon_{Kj} + \varepsilon_{rj} \right) \tag{8.35}$$

The optimal tax rate thus depends on the extent of interjurisdictional competition in the economy as we have obtained a typical Cournot-Nash result – the extent of appropriation of capital rents varies from none ($\tau_j = 0$) to total ($\tau_j = 1$) as the nature of interjurisdictional competition varies from perfect competition ($\varepsilon_{rj} = 0$) to pure monopoly ($\varepsilon_{rj} = 1$, $\varepsilon_{Kj} = 0$).

Although the oligopoly model ($\varepsilon_{rj} > 0$) may have some relevance if local jurisdictions view the metropolitan capital stock as fixed and the number of competing suburban jurisdictions is relatively small, our principal result is that in a competitive environment the optimal tax on mobile capital is zero; only head taxes (or land value taxes in our model) will be used to finance local expenditures. The explanation for this result is quite straightforward. As the number of communities becomes large, a single community acting in isolation must take the after-tax rate of return as given; any tax on capital increases the supply price of capital by the amount of tax. However, a tax on capital also distorts the allocation of capital and results in an excess burden – by restricting the use of capital, a capital tax lowers output and decreases land rents. Landlords, or more generally the owners of fixed factors, recognize they will bear the burden of a head tax. However, since they are unable to exploit capital through non-benefit taxation in any case, the head (benefit) tax is preferred to distortionary tax on the mobile factor.

Our model thus suggests that the interjurisdictional competition stressed by proponents of the benefit view (as well as by Tiebout) does imply that the property tax will be used only as a benefit tax. However, the model can easily be altered to yield the new view result. Suppose that for statutory, political or other reasons, local governments can raise revenues to finance local public services only through a property tax on capital; there are no head taxes. In this case, even with perfect competition among local jurisdictions, each local government will engage in non-benefit of taxation and the new view result obtains.

Our model is unchanged except that head taxes are constrained to be zero so that the only control variable available to each local government is its property tax rate. In this case, the first order condition for each local government yields the following implicit expression for the optimal tax rate:

$$\tau_j = \left(1 - m_j \right) / \varepsilon_{Kj} \tag{8.36}$$

The interpretation of this condition is straightforward. At the optimum, the marginal rate of substitution must equal the slope of the perceived "production possibilities frontier" for the representative jurisdiction. The latter, which is obtained by combining equations 8.32 and 8.33 when $H_j = \varepsilon_{rj} = 0$ to yield

$$-dG_j \big/ dY_j = 1 - \tau_j \varepsilon_{Kj},$$

is equal to one at the zero-tax (and zero-service) equilibrium. As long as $m_j < 1$ at the zero tax equilibrium and the production possibilities frontier is concave for tax rates below the revenue-maximizing level, the optimal property tax rate must be positive; we assume these plausible conditions hold for the balance of the discussion.

Thus, when local public services can be financed only through the property tax, the optimal tax is positive, increasing as m_j falls (preferences for public services are strong) and as ε_{Kj} falls (the capital out-migration expected by each local jurisdiction in response to property taxation falls). Since all jurisdictions act identically and the national capital stock is fixed, we obtain the new view result that capital bears the entire burden of the property tax. Moreover, there is a tendency toward underconsumption of public services – $m_j = 1$ at any income level with head tax finance while $m_j < 1$ with property tax finance as local governments reduced services to mitigate the effects of the expected reduction in capital supply, output, and land rents induced by property taxation. However, the net effect on the level of government services (relative to the head tax case) is theoretically ambiguous since in the competitive Nash equilibrium landowners effectively have another source of income with which to purchase public services – expropriated capital rents.

Thus, interjurisdictional competition cannot eliminate the exploitation of capital implied by the new view if the property tax is the sole source of local revenue. However, note that the Nash equilibrium described above can be unstable in the sense that any single jurisdiction has an incentive to impose a head tax and reduce its reliance on the property tax. Suppose that a single jurisdiction, again assuming that all other jurisdictions hold their tax rates fixed, introduces a head tax and reduces its property tax, holding service levels constant. Local resident landowners will benefit from this substitution if

$$dY_j = ds_j - dH_j > 0$$

Substituting from equations 8.31 and 8.32 when $dG_j = 0$ and evaluating at $H_j = 0$, $\tau_j = (1 - m_j)/\varepsilon_{Kj}$ shows that this condition is satisfied:

$$dY_j = rK_j\left(1 + T_j\right)\left(1 - m_j\right)\left[-\left(1 \hat{+} T_j\right)\right] > 0$$

The substitution of a non-distorting head tax for a distorting capital tax is desirable for the same reason that property taxes were not used when the head tax was available. Each community, taking the tax rate of all the other communities as given, attempts to obtain an advantage relative to other communities by attracting more capital. The loss in tax revenues resulting from the decrease in taxes on mobile capital is offset dollar for dollar by a decrease in the cost of capital, which in turn induces increases in the local capital stock, output, and land rents.

In general, equations 8.35 and 8.36 are non-linear expressions and cannot be solved explicitly for the optimal property tax rates under the head tax and property tax regimes. However, explicit solutions are straightforward for the case of Cobb-Douglas functional forms, and for illustrative purposes are presented below for the perfectly competitive case ($\varepsilon_{rj} = 0$).

Suppose that the utility and production functions in the model are given by:

$$U_i = Y_j^{\alpha}G_i^{\beta}, \quad \alpha + \beta = 1$$

$$X_i = K_i^{a}V^b = K_i^{a}, \quad a + b = 1$$

In this case, we can solve for

$$r = aK^{-b}\left[\sum\left(1 + T_i\right)^{-1/b}\right]^b$$
$$K_i = \left[r\left(1 + T_i\right)/a\right]^{-1/b}$$
$$\varepsilon_{Kj} = \theta_{Vj}^{-1} - 1/b$$

The optimal tax rate is zero under the head tax regime and is given by

$$\tau_j = b\left[1 - ab/\left(\beta + \alpha a\right)\right]$$

when the head tax is not available. Equilibrium values for the endogonous variables (when $K = N$) are given in table 8.1 where the parameter ψ is defined as

$$\psi = a/(a + \beta b) = 1/(1 + T_j), \quad 0 < \psi < 1$$

Note that when only the property tax on capital can be utilized to raise local revenues, we obtain the new view result – capital bears the entire burden of the property tax as the after-tax rate of return falls by the average rate of tax relative to the head tax case. Note also that the level of government spending is lower with the property tax than it is under the head tax. Thus, in the Cobb-Douglas case, the distortionary effect of the property tax at any income level – local governments cut back on services to avoid expected reductions in the capital stock, output, and land rents – dominates the income effect associated with the expropriation of capital rents. Finally, note that it is quite possible that the utility of landowners will be higher under the property tax system than under the head tax system even though the level of services is reduced. To see this, note that resident landowner net income is higher in the property tax case than in the head tax case; land rents are the same under the two tax regimes, but under the tax system part of these rents are used to finance public services, whereas in the property tax system all land rents are spent on private goods and expropriated capital rents finance public services. Substituting from table 8.1 yields the result that

$$U_P/U_H \gtreqless 1 \text{ as } \alpha^{-\alpha}\psi^\beta \gtreqless 1,$$

Table 8.1 Endogeneous variable values for a representative jurisdiction for the two models of interjurisdictional competition

Endogenous variable	Property tax and head tax available	Only property tax available
τ_j	0	$\beta b/(\beta + \alpha a)$
H_j	βb	0
G_j	βb	$\psi \beta b$
Y_j	αb	b
s_j	b	b
$r(1 + T_j)$	a	a
r	d	ψa

where U_P and U_H are the utility levels of landowners in the representative jurisdiction under the property tax and head tax systems. Although not always the case, landowners' utility is higher under the property tax regime for most plausible parameter values. For example, if 10 percent of income is devoted to local public services in the undistorted head-tax equilibrium ($\beta = 0.1$), $U_P/U_H > 1$ as long as the capital share in gross production costs is greater than 6 percent ($a > 0.06$).

8.4   General Evaluation and Conclusions

Property taxation of capital has not disappeared – the property tax has not been replaced by a system of neutral land value or local head taxes as suggested by the model of competition we have developed. What are we to make of the persistence of property taxes? One explanation is the benefit view of the property tax. The model above makes no provision for benefits associated with capital taxes. Capital is taxed for the benefit of the immobile factors of production (land and possibly labor) and receives no benefits in return. The benefit view suggests that the model we have developed is incorrect in that interjurisdictional competition, when accompanied by the appropriate zoning restrictions, transforms a set of apparently distorting capital levies into neutral user charges or benefit levies.

Although the internal logic of this argument is unassailable, its grounding in fact is open to question. In particular, the complex pattern of strict zoning ordinances which is required to convert the industrial property tax into a payment for public services received seems to be a rather severe requirement.

An alternative explanation of the persistence of property taxes is that local governments choose not to substitute head taxes or land value taxes for property taxes, even though our results at the end of section 8.3 suggest that it would appear to be in their interests to do so. This may occur for at least three reasons. First, due to legal or political constraints, local governments may simply not be able to make the substitution. Second, local governments may engage in a plausible type of collusion to expropriate rents from capital owners. Our Nash equilibrium with the property tax occurs in a model where jurisdictions compete with respect to tax rates, but the competition does not extend to eliminating the property tax as the source of local revenue; our results suggest that this type of collusion is likely to be profitable in the sense that it benefits all landowners, and the traditional use of the property tax as "the" local tax instrument provides a ready vehicle for this type of collusion. Third, local governments may be fully aware of the implications of perfect capital mobility in the long run, but they may have a shorter time perspective in choosing their tax instruments; since capital is highly durable in the short run, current revenue losses from lower capital taxes may outweigh the long run benefits or higher land rents from the perspective of local government officials. The general point is again that the assumptions which imply the elimination of non-benefit taxation of mobile capital are severe and somewhat unrealistic.

Are local property taxes benefit taxes? They may be – but we remain skeptical. Instead, it seems plausible that there is a non-benefit component to the property taxation of capital which is borne primarily by the owners of capital as predicted by the new view of the property tax.

Notes

1   Research support from the National Science Foundation (Grant SES82-09210) is gratefully acknowledged. We have benefited from the comments of Joseph Stiglitz and John Wilson.
2   The non-residential property tax can also be viewed as a payment for externalities generated; see Fischel (1975) and White (1975).
3   See the article by Hamilton for further elaboration.
4   See Mieszkowski (1976) for further elaboration.
5   Thus, we are conducting a "balanced budget incidence" analysis rather than a "differential incidence" analysis; see Musgrave and Musgrave (1980).
6   For a justification of this treatment of local public goods, see the article by Hamilton.
7   At a zero-tax initial equilibrium, excess burden effects are of the second order and thus do not appear in differential incidence expressions; see Ballentine and Eris (1975) and Vandendorpe and Friedlaender (1976).
8   Our optimal tax formulas are special cases of the results presented by Arnott and Grieson (1981) in their comprehensive treatment of this local government optimal taxation problem.

References

Aaron, H. J., 1975. *Who Pays the Property Tax?* Washington, D.C.: Brookings Institution.
Arnott, R. and R. E. Grieson, 1981. "Optimal Fiscal Policy for a State or Local Government," *Journal of Urban Economics* 9:23–48.
Ballentine, J. G. and I. Eris, 1975. "On the General Equilibrium Analysis of Tax Incidence," *Journal of Political Economy* 83:633–44.
Epple, D. and A. Zelenitz, 1981. "The Implications of Competition Among Jurisdictions: Does Tiebout Need Politics?", *Journal of Political Economy*, 89:1197–217.
Fischel, W. A., 1975. "Fiscal and Environmental Considerations in the Location

of Firms in Suburban Communities," in E. S. Mills and W. E. Oates (eds.), *Fiscal Zoning and Land Use Controls.* Lexington, Mass.: Lexington Books.

Hamilton, B. W., 1975. "Zoning and Property Taxation in a System of Local Governments," *Urban Studies* 12:205–11.

Hamilton, B. W., 1976. "Capitalization of Intrajurisdictional Differences in Local Tax Prices," *American Economic Review* 66:743–753.

Harberger, A. C., 1962. "The Incidence of the Corporate Income Tax," *Journal of Political Economy* 70:215–40.

McLure, C. E., Jr., 1975. "General Equilibrium Incidence Analysis: The Harberger Model After Ten Years," *Journal of Public Economics* 4:125–61.

Mieszkowski, P. M., 1972. "The Property Tax: An Excise Tax or a Profits Tax?" *Journal of Public Economics* 1:73–96.

Mieszkowski, P. M., 1976. "The Distributive Effects of Local Taxes: Some Extensions," in R. E. Grieson (ed.), *Public and Urban Economics: Essays in Honor of William S. Vickery.* Lexington, Mass.: Lexington Books.

Mills, E. S., 1979. "Economic Analysis of Urban Land-Use Controls," in P. Mieszkowski and M. Straszheim (eds.), *Current Issues in Urban Economics.* Baltimore: Johns Hopkins University Press.

Musgrave, R. A. and P. B. Musgrave, 1980. *Public Finance in Theory and Practice.* New York: McGraw-Hill.

Thomson, P., 1965. "The Property Tax and the Rate of Interest," in G. C. S. Benson, S. Benson, H. McClelland, and P. Thomson, *The American Property Tax.* Claremont, Cal.: The Lincoln School of Public Finance.

Tiebout, C. M., 1956. "A Pure Theory of Local Expenditures," *Journal of Political Economy* 64:416–24.

Vandendorpe, A. L. and A. F. Friedlaender, 1976. "Differential Incidence in the Presence of Initial Distorting Taxes," *Journal of Public Economics* 6:205–29.

White, M. J., 1975. "Firm Location in a Zoned Metropolitan Area," in E. S. Mills and W. E. Oates (eds.), *Fiscal Zoning and Land Use Controls.* Lexington, Mass.: Lexington Books.

Introduction to Chapter 9

The preceding chapter should leave the reader with the conviction that the question of the incidence of the property tax is so complicated in theory that there is no hope of being able to draw policy-relevant conclusions about this important question. In this chapter, Heilbrun's clear and deliberate exposition makes matters considerably less complex. He shows how the "capital-tax" and the "excise-tax" aspects of the tax can be reconciled; his figure is a superb simplification of the relation. Heilbrun also shows clearly how real-world phenomena like non-uniform property assessment practices and differences in the income elasticity of the demand for housing by income level affect findings on incidence.

9

Who Bears the Burden of the Property Tax?

James Heilbrun

Unfortunately, there is no short answer to the question "Who bears the burden of the property tax?" The reason lies in the complex nature of the institution itself. Consider the following complications. First, the tax applies to property in all its variety of forms, and there is every reason to believe that the tax on land has a different incidence from the tax on housing, which in turn has a different incidence from the tax on commercial or industrial property. Second, the tax is a local one. Although it is levied everywhere, the rate of taxation varies across jurisdictions. This variation has consequences that would not occur under a uniform national tax. Third, the tax, at least in the United States, is levied on an administratively determined tax base, namely assessed value. Its incidence within a locality therefore depends importantly on how the assessment function is carried out. No other tax varies along so many significant dimensions.

The incidence of any tax is said to be on those persons who bear its burden. At the outset one must distinguish between legal incidence and economic incidence. For example, the city of Boston levies a tax of so many dollars per hundred on the assessed value of real property and sends each property owner an appropriate bill. The legal incidence is on the owner, who is required to remit payment. But if, after the tax is imposed, property owners can raise the rent they charge to occupants, they will have shifted some or all of the burden "forward" to users of property. Or, if imposition of the tax leads eventually to lower wages or lower land prices in Boston, then some or all of the burden will have been shifted "backward" to suppliers of those inputs. Since some form of shifting is highly probable in the case of the property tax, it is obvious that one cannot "observe" its economic incidence simply by seeing who remits payments. Instead, one must rely on insights provided by tax incidence theory.

In the case of the property tax, the task of incidence theory is, first, to explain how the burden of the tax is divided among such functional economic classes as landowners, building owners, tenants, owners of capital, and workers and then to deduce what the incidence of the tax on those functional groups implies about its distribution by income class among the population as a whole. For example, if the tax falls entirely on landowners, then its distribution across income classes will depend on how landownership is distributed. If landownership is concentrated in the middle- and upper-income classes, then the incidence of the tax will tend to be progressive with respect to income.

Incidence of the Tax on Land Value

Although the property tax in the United States is commonly levied on the assessed value of land and improvements combined, the tax on land is conventionally analyzed separately from the tax on improvements, since the two parts of the tax have quite different effects. It is the standard view among economists that, unlike a tax on improvements, a tax on the market value of unimproved land cannot be shifted by the owner to any other party. It is also generally agreed that tax shifting in itself causes economic waste, for a tax can only be shifted if some economic agent adjusts behavior to bring it about, and such adjustments distort prices and prevent the market system from operating as efficiently as it otherwise could. Since the land value tax cannot be shifted, however, it creates no economic inefficiency. To use technical terminology, it is perfectly "neutral" in that it does not disturb an otherwise desirable allocation of resources. This characteristic sets it apart from all other major levies and explains why many economists have long regarded it as a particularly attractive tax.

Why can no tax on unimproved land value be shifted? The reason is that the tax will not cause landowners to alter their behavior in any way. When land value – the base to be taxed – is correctly defined, it is independent of the particular use to which the land is devoted. In that case, the amount of tax to be paid does not vary with the owner's choice among uses and therefore will not influence that choice. Whatever use would be most profitable in the absence of such a tax will remain so when the tax is levied. For example, a tax on land value will not induce owners to withdraw land from use in order to avoid the tax, because the same tax will be payable whether the land lies vacant or is developed. Hence supply will not be reduced by the tax, and if supply is not reduced the price of land will not rise and no part of the tax will be shifted to users.

The above result follows as long as land value is defined for purposes of taxation as the market value that the land would have if it were sold cleared of improvements. Under some other definitions, such as the value of land in its current use, the tax would affect owners' choices among types of development and would therefore not be completely neutral. This conclusion points again to the impact that assessment practices can have on the economic consequences of property taxation.

Capitalization of the Land Value Tax

The argument up to this point has been that the incidence of a tax on land value is entirely on landowners. However, that conclusion must now be qualified by noting that it rests on those who own land at the time the tax is introduced or its rate increased but not on subsequent owners. It is reasonable to assume that investors in land, as in other assets, allow for the anticipated level of taxes when deciding how much to bid for land. Consequently, anyone who buys subsequent to a tax increase pays a price that takes the higher tax into account and therefore "buys free of tax." Owners at the time the tax rate is increased therefore cannot escape its burden by selling, because the sales price will fall by the capitalized amount of the tax increase.

Heavy taxes on land value have sometimes been advocated on grounds of equity as well as on those of neutrality. Since the days of Henry George it has been generally agreed that the value of unimproved land (often enormously high in built-up areas) is created not by the efforts of the individual landowner but by the growth and development of the community as a whole. The landowner is usually only a passive beneficiary. If that is so, society would be justified in recapturing through heavy taxation of land the increase in value that would otherwise go to owners. This argument, however, overlooks the fact that land frequently changes hands. Today's owners may have paid the current market price (or even more) for their holdings, so that any "unearned increment" passed irrecoverably into the hands of those from whom they bought. Therefore, attempting to recapture land value from present owners would likely be inequitable. On the other hand, a heavy tax on future gains in land value (beyond those resulting simply from general price inflation) could not be opposed on those grounds.

The Tax on Improvements

By far the greater part of property-tax revenue comes not from the tax on land but from the levy on improvements – including housing, commercial and industrial structures. The analysis of the incidence of that part of the tax underwent radical change during the 1970s. A "new view" of property-tax incidence emerged, based on the work of Peter Mieszkowski, who had built on an earlier analysis of the corporation income tax by Arnold C. Harberger.[1] The "old view," which predominated before the 1970s, had held that in the long run the portion of the tax falling on improvements would largely be shifted forward from property owners to users of property or their customers. For example, store owners would pass the tax on to their customers, as they would any other cost of doing business, while owners of rented housing would be able to shift the tax to their tenants in the form of higher rents.

The logic behind the old view can best be explained by looking at the case of rental housing in a particular city. Assume that initially there is no property tax in Boston, for example. The rent obtainable by owners is determined in the market by the supply and demand for housing. Owners will expand the stock of housing in Boston by new investment as long as the net rate of return on housing exceeds the going rate (adjusted for risk, of course) on other investments nationwide. It follows that in the long run the net return on rental-housing investment in Boston will tend to equal the net return obtainable on investment in general, and the level of rents in Boston will be just sufficient to generate that net return. If Boston imposes a property tax, owners will not immediately be able to raise rents to cover the additional cost, since neither supply nor demand will have changed. Initially, they will have to bear the burden of the tax themselves. Therefore, the net return to local rental housing will fall below the going rate of return on capital in general. In the long run, however, if population or income in Boston rises the demand for housing will increase. Rents will gradually rise and, with them, the net return on housing investment. When rents have risen enough to bring the net return back to the level obtainable on capital in general, investment in the expansion of Boston's housing stock will resume. At that point the rent per unit of housing will have risen just enough to cover the property tax per unit, and the tax will have been fully shifted from owners to tenants. The identical argument would apply, of course, in the case where one assumes not the introduction of a new property tax but simply an increase in the tax rate.

Such, briefly, is the old view of the property tax. In each jurisdiction, rents will rise to cover the cost of the tax, so that in the long run investors in housing will receive (as they must if they are to maintain their investment) a net return equal to the nationwide going rate of return on capital. High-tax towns will tend to have higher rents than low-tax towns. In either case, tenants, as consumers of the services produced by the property, will bear the tax burden.

The New View

The new view of the property tax reaches a quite different conclusion. According to this view, much of the burden of the tax on improvements remains with owners of capital in the form of a lower net return instead of being shifted to users of property in the form of higher rents or prices. The error of the old view arose from trying to generalize about the effects of the tax from an argument that examined only one jurisdiction at a time. If only one jurisdiction is assumed to levy the tax, it is plausible to argue, as the old view did, that the tax will not affect the nationwide going rate of return on capital. But if – as we know to be the case – all jurisdictions levy the tax, it cannot be assumed that the going rate of return will be unaffected. Indeed, to generalize from the case of the single jurisdiction is an example of the fallacy of composition. Proponents of the new view point out that the tax on improvements is essentially a nationwide tax on capital. When the tax is examined in that perspective, its incidence will depend on the characteristics of supply and demand for capital nationally rather than in a single market.

It was argued above that a tax on land value cannot be shifted by landowners to tenants or consumers of the services of land because the tax does not affect the amount of land supplied and therefore cannot affect its price. Proponents of the new view have reached a similar conclusion with respect to the tax on improvements. In their view, the historical evidence indicates that the rate of saving in the United States is insensitive to variations in the net return to capital. But if the rate of saving is not affected by the rate of return to capital, then the stock (or supply) of capital will not be reduced by a general tax on capital. The price charged for the use of capital will not increase to cover the cost of the tax, and the tax will not be shifted.

That the rate of saving should not vary directly with the rate of return to capital may seem counterintuitive. Nevertheless, that is what both Harberger and Mieszkowski concluded from the evidence available to them. As Mieszkowski showed, it follows, more or less directly, that a uniform nationwide property tax on improvements cannot be shifted by the owners to tenants or users of property. Thus, if the property tax were levied at the same rate everywhere, the principal result according to the new view would be a reduction in the real rate of return to capital. For example, if the rate of return had been 6 percent before the tax was levied, and a tax rate of 2 percent were imposed, the net return to capital would fall to 4 percent, while the gross cost of using capital (that is, its price) would remain unchanged at 6 percent, of which 4 percent would remain with owners and 2 percent would go to the tax collector. This is just the opposite of the old view, according to which the gross price of capital would eventually rise to 8 percent, so that the burden of tax would be passed on to users of capital, leaving the net return to capital owners unimpaired.

"Global" Effects and "Excise" Effects

Mieszkowski recognized, of course, that the property tax in the United States is not a uniform nationwide levy but rather a system of local taxes levied at geographically varying rates. He dealt with this complication by distinguishing between "global" effects, which result from the impact of the system as a whole, and "excise" effects, which result from the variation among local rates.[2]

Because capital is highly mobile within a national economy, it is reasonable to assume that differences in the rate of the property tax among jurisdictions will cause capital to flow from high- to low-tax areas. A hypothetical example is illustrated in figure 9.1.

Assume that before any property tax is imposed the rate of return to capital in all localities is 6 percent, as shown in the left-hand column of figure 9.1. Property taxes are then imposed at three different local rates: 3 percent in high-tax towns, 2 percent in towns taxing at the national average rate, and 1 percent in low-tax areas. The immediate effect in all areas is to reduce the rate of return to owners of local property by the amount of the tax. This result is shown in column 2. It follows necessarily from the fact that the supply of improvements in each locality does not change in the short run, and owners therefore cannot raise the price charged for the use of property or for its products in order to shift the tax.

Capital markets, however, are not in equilibrium in the situation depicted in column 2, since net rates of return are higher where tax rates are lower. Owners of capital, seeking the highest available returns, now move their resources from high- to low-tax towns. This reduces the supply of capital in high-tax areas, causing the net return in those areas to rise, and increases its supply in low-tax areas, causing the net return there to fall. Presumably, migration of capital continues until net returns

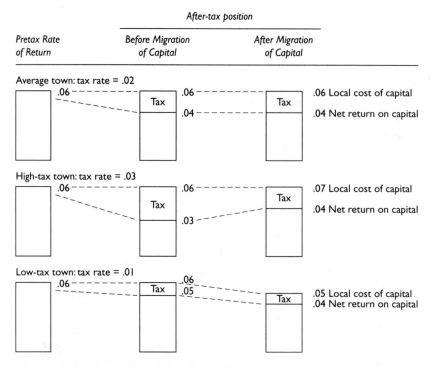

Figure 9.1 "Global" and "excise" effects of the property tax.

in all areas are equal. This long-run equilibrium is shown in column 3. However, although net returns are now equal everywhere, the gross cost of capital services, which equals the net return plus the tax, is now higher where taxes are higher. The tax can be thought of as a wedge between the net return to owners, which is everywhere equal, and the gross cost of capital, equivalent to the price paid for capital services by local users, which is higher, the higher the local tax rate.

Figure 9.1 illustrates both the "global" and "excise" effects of the property tax. The global effect is the long-run decline in the net return to capital that occurs as a result of imposing property taxes at varying local rates. It is the difference between the net return of 6 percent in column 1 and 4 percent in column 3. This 2 percent decline, it should be noted, is equal to the average rate of tax in the nation as a whole.

If all towns levied the tax at the same rate, or if the tax were a uniform national levy, there would be only a global effect. However, since local tax rates are not equal, there are also excise effects. These are shown by the differences in the local gross cost of capital, after the capital market has fully adjusted to local taxes, as shown in column 3.

According to the old view, the property tax on improvements was, in the long run, passed forward to tenants or users of property, leaving the rate of return to capital unimpaired. The new view comes to a radically different conclusion: the rate of return to capital is reduced by approximately the nationwide average rate of property tax. That is the substance of the global effect. It is only the excise effect that can be shifted by capital owners to other agents in the economy; for example, to tenants in rental housing units or to customers of department stores.

The reader should be reminded that since excise effects are measured as the difference between the local property-tax rate and the national average, they impose positive burdens in some places and negative burdens (i.e., positive advantages) in others. Where excise effects are positive, taxpayers will attempt to shift the burden to others in a process that will be discussed below. However, where the excise burden is negative, taxpayers will be forced by competition to share the benefits of below average tax rates with customers or suppliers, or both, in a process that is the mirror image of the one to be discussed here.

With some exceptions, adherents of the old view had emphasized forward shifting of the property tax. The new view differs in stressing that the excise effects of the tax are likely to cause "backward" shifting to land and labor (if labor is not fully mobile) as well as, or instead of, forward shifting to tenants or customers, Some of these possibilities will be discussed briefly below.

Owner-occupied Housing

The owner-occupant stands in a double relation to housing. He or she is both the owner who produces housing services and the tenant who consumes them. According to the new view, the global effect of the tax does not raise the cost of housing but, rather, reduces the return to capital. In the role of owner, the owner-occupant cannot escape that part of the burden. If the local tax rate exceeds the national average, however, there is also a positive excise effect. This will increase the local cost of capital and, therefore, of housing services. As the tenant consuming such services, the owner-occupant would also bear that burden. If that were the whole story, it would be clear that the owner-occupant cannot shift any part of the tax. However, the possibility that higher taxes will be capitalized into lower land values must be taken into account. Higher taxes on improvements will reduce the demand for building sites and will therefore lead to lower prices for land that will, in part, offset the higher cost of local capital. This will not help owner-occupants in possession of sites at the time the tax is raised, since it is their land that falls in value, but subsequent home buyers will benefit.

Industrial and Commercial Property

Again, the global effect of the tax is not shiftable: businesses that own property bear the burden of the global effect in their capacity as owners of capital. Excise effects, however, may be shifted both forward and backward. But since the tax is a local one, it is important to distinguish carefully between firms that sell only in the local market and those that export products or services to other communities. The former typically have little competition from outside the jurisdiction and consequently would be able, in the long run, to pass at least part of the excise effect of high taxes forward to local customers in the form of higher prices.

Firms that export to the national market face a different situation. They must compete with producers who may pay lower taxes in other towns. In that case, they could not shift the excise effect forward to customers. One would expect such firms, in the long run, to locate away from high-tax jurisdictions. There is one exception, however: if the high-tax town has locational advantages for a given firm's production, the firm could, so to speak, pay the higher taxes out of its locational advantages without becoming either noncompetitive or less than normally profitable. (This, of course, explains why cities may be tempted to assess very heavily the property of established local industries for which they believe they have special locational advantages.) Finally, backward shifting to landowners may help to offset the excise effect of high local taxes for both local market and national market firms, but with the same caveat regarding current owners that pertains for owner-occupied housing.

Is the Property Tax Regressive or Progressive?

What does the preceding analysis imply about the incidence of the property tax by income class? Let us dispose of the tax on land first, since it is the least controversial element. It is almost universally agreed among economists that a tax on unimproved land value is borne by landowners in proportion to the value of their holdings. Since landownership is on average distributed progressively with respect to income, that portion of the tax is a progressive one.

Concerning the tax on improvements, there are many more complications and much less agreement. No tax is beloved, but the levy on property for many years had a poor reputation, even among taxes, because generations of economists, relying on the old view of its incidence, pronounced it seriously regressive. As already explained, proponents of the old view usually concluded that the tax on rental housing would, in the long run, be passed forward to tenants, in the form of higher rent; the tax on owner-occupied housing would be borne by owners in their capacity as consumers of housing service; the tax on business property would be largely passed forward to customers in the form of higher prices. Housing expenditures were thought to be highly regressive to income and other consumption outlays moderately so. Hence a tax that impinged on households in proportion to such outlays would be distinctly regressive.

Proponents of the new view, on the other hand, have concluded that the tax on improvements is highly progressive. The global effect falls unambiguously on owners of capital. Income from capital is distributed progressively with respect to total income. Ergo, that part of the tax is highly progressive. But what about excise effects? From a national perspective these conveniently cancel out: it is plausible to argue that the burdens borne by those in high-tax towns are offset by the gains of those in low-tax communities, so that the net impact of excise effects by income class can be ignored.

Table 9.1 illustrates these conclusions with estimates of the actual incidence of the tax in 1970, employing alternately the assumptions of the old view in the first column and the new view in the second. (In both cases, the tax on land is assumed to be borne entirely by landowners.) The difference between the two estimates is striking: according to the old view, those in the lowest income class pay 9.0 percent of their income in property tax, while those in the highest pay only 0.8 percent; according to the new view, the burden on the lowest class is only 3.8 percent, while the highest income group pays 10.9 percent.

It should be pointed out that the version of the new view presented here, in which the global effect is completely unshiftable by owners of capital, depends on the strong assumption that saving, and hence the supply of capital, is completely unresponsive to changes in the rate of return. The relation between saving and the rate of return is best summarized by a measure known as the interest elasticity of saving, defined as the ratio of a percentage change in saving to the percentage change in the rate of return that brings it about. If saving is completely unresponsive to changes in the rate of return, as assumed by Mieszkowski in first presenting the new view, then the value of the interest elasticity is zero.

The actual value of this elasticity, however, must be settled by empirical investigation. The question has received far less attention than it

Table 9.1 Alternative estimates of property tax incidence, 1970

Income class	Tax as a percentage of income	
	Old view	New view
$0–3,000	9.0	3.8
3–5,000	6.2	3.6
5–10,000	4.5	2.9
10–15,000	3.8	2.4
15–20,000	3.5	2.5
20–25,000	3.1	2.4
25–30,000	3.1	2.9
30–50,000	3.2	4.1
50–100,000	3.7	6.8
100–500,000	3.6	8.7
500–1,000,000	1.6	10.3
1,000,000 and over	0.8	10.9
All classes	3.7	3.4

Assumptions:

Old view: tax on improvements borne in proportion to housing expenditures and consumption.

New view: tax on improvements borne in proportion to income from capital.

Tax on land: in both old and new views. borne by landlords.

Source: Joseph A. Pechman, *Federal Tax Policy*, 3d ed. (Washington, D.C.: The Brookings Institution, 1977), p. 262.

deserves, and for many years the available evidence has been regarded as inconclusive. In 1978, a study by Michael J. Boskin concluded that the interest elasticity of saving is substantial; he offered a series of estimates ranging from 0.2 to 0.6.[3] Should other studies confirm a value in that range, then the conclusion that no part of the global effect of the property tax can be shifted is incorrect. If the interest elasticity is positive, the property tax discourages capital formation, reduces the stock of improvements, and raises their price. Consumers of the services produced by real property would, in the long run, share the tax burden with owners of capital.

Since the empirical question "What is the true value of the interest elasticity of saving?" has not been resolved, a large element of uncertainty remains in the analysis of property-tax incidence. Unfortunately, it is not helpful to say that its incidence probably falls somewhere between the two extremes shown in table 9.1.

The Local versus the National Perspective

It is important to recognize that answers to questions about the property tax will vary radically, depending on the point of view from which they are asked. For example, the most frequently heard question may be: "Is the property tax regressive or progressive?" From the national point of view the answer depends on the global effect of the tax, since positive and negative excise effects probably cancel out at the national scale. If one believes that the global effect cannot be shifted, then its burden clearly rests on owners of capital and the tax is markedly progressive with respect to income. Many will think that desirable.

From the local point of view the situation is entirely different. For any decision that will be made locally, the global effect is of no consequence. It would be a mistake for local voters to support an increase in property-tax rates because they had heard that the tax was progressive. Increasing the local tax rate will have no perceptible impact on the (progressive) global effect. Instead, it will increase the excise effect, which depends on the difference between the local tax rate and the national average. The most direct and most important result will be to raise the cost of capital locally relative to its cost elsewhere. (See figure 9.1.) Much of the burden of this increase will probably be passed forward to consumers of housing services and other local goods in a pattern that may well be regressive to income. To the extent that the burden is not shiftable by business, the increased cost of capital would also make the locality less attractive to regional or national market businesses, thus reducing private employment and weakening the local tax base. None of that could be thought desirable.

Thus a paradox emerges: if one prefers progressive taxes, then from a national point of view the property tax can look quite attractive. Yet the tax is not a national but a local one, and raising the local tax rate above the national average is likely to have undesirable consequences.

Further Complications: Variation in Assessment Practices and Tax Rates

The incidence estimates in table 9.1 are based on aggregate data for households in the United States. They have been constructed by taking the observed total of property-tax payments for the United States and distributing it across income classes in proportion to whatever allocator economic theory suggests is appropriate. Under the old view, the tax burden is distributed in proportion to housing expenditures and general consumption, under the new view in proportion to income from capital. Unfortunately, this method of estimating incidence systematically conceals effects that might show up in a study of individual taxpayers or jurisdictions. Some of these will now be developed for the case of owner-occupied housing.

The relationship between tax payments on housing and the income of an owner-occupant taxpayer can be analyzed into two components by means of the following equation (an analogous argument applies to renters):

$$T/Y = T/MV \cdot MV/Y$$

On the left-hand side is the ratio of property-tax payments (T) to household income (Y). The tax is progressive if this ratio *rises* as income rises, regressive if it *falls* as income rises, and proportional if it is constant over all income classes.

Algebraically, T/Y equals the product of the two ratios on the right-hand side. The first of these is the ratio of tax payments to the market value of the owner-occupant's house (MV). This ratio is a measure of the "effective property-tax rate." Two sources of variation in this ratio are of interest because they may systematically affect the value of T/Y. First of all, state law usually requires that within a given jurisdiction all properties be assessed at the same ratio to full market value, i.e., that the "assessment ratio" be constant for all properties. If that were done, the value of T/MV would also be the same for all local taxpayers. However, numerous studies have turned up systematic local variation in the assessment ratio, so that one cannot assume that T/MV will be uniform within any jurisdiction. Second, the ratio T/MV may vary systematically across jurisdictions, because the effective property-tax rate, which it measures, is higher in some types of communities than in others. These two sources of variation in T/MV will now be analyzed.

First, consider tax incidence within the single jurisdiction. Assume for simplicity that the ratio MV/Y is constant across all income groups. If the locality applies a single assessment ratio to all properties, the T/MV will also be equal for all owners. In that case, T/Y will also be constant: the tax will be proportional to income. Starting from this case, one can easily see the potential impact of variation in the assessment ratio. For example, if the ratio is higher for low-income than for high-income families, then T/Y will also be higher for low-income families and the tax will be regressive instead of proportional.

In separate studies of data for the city of Boston, both Robert F. Engle and David E. Black found a strongly inverse relationship between the assessment ratio and house values.[4] This intrajurisdictional bias in assessment practice means that the property tax could be quite regressive in practice even when it would be proportional or progressive if assessment ratios were uniform. Engle showed that the bias resulted from the failure to adjust assessments as market values changed: in neighborhoods where market value was rising rapidly the ratio fell relative to its level in neighborhoods where values rose more slowly. Since the latter were primarily poor neighborhoods, the result was a tax system biased against the poor. Keith R. Ihlanfeldt's 1982 study of Atlanta and Philadelphia confirmed the presence of assessment bias in those two central cities.[5] Ihlanfeldt stratified each housing market into low-, middle-, and upper-income segments and found that regressive assessment occurred mostly within the first two groups.

The three studies cited here, and many others, show that assessments in the United States are subject both to large random error and to important systematic bias. Both lead to intrajurisdictional inequities that better administration could substantially reduce.

Of course, the term "better administration" makes the problem of assessment bias sound apolitical, as if it were simply an accident of sloppy practice when, in fact, it usually has deep political roots. For example, a study of the property tax in New York City directed by Dick Netzer found that in 1979 the assessment ratio for one- and two-family houses was only 24.6 percent, whereas it was 59.3 percent for all other residential property.[6] One- and two-family units in New York are occupied by the substantial middle class, while the poor are concentrated largely in the "other," or rental, sector. Thus assessment bias clearly works against the poor. Yet when the state legislature, under court order, was forced to deal with the problem of unequal assessments, the political power of New York City's minority of homeowners was so great that instead of requiring equalized assessment of housing in the city, the legislators adopted a law that virtually legalized the existing unequal pattern.

The ratio of property-tax payment to house value varies between as well as within jurisdictions in ways that may be correlated with household income and so affect the nationwide incidence of the property tax. For example, Henry J. Aaron noted that for the 356 United States cities with a population above 50,000 in 1971, there is a significant positive correlation between the effective property tax rate and average per capita income: tax rates are higher in cities where incomes are higher.[7] Such a finding suggests that the property tax is less regressive, or more progressive than is indicated by estimates of the type presented in table 9.1, which do not reflect the influence of local variations in tax rates.

This line of reasoning, however, raises serious problems. If property tax rates differ between jurisdictions, then local expenditures, which confer benefits on local taxpayers, may also differ in the same direction. Higher tax rates may be deliberately employed in some localities to provide the citizenry with a richer mixture of public services. In that case, the equity implications of a higher ratio of tax payments to income become unclear. No such problem arises in connection with intrajurisdictional studies, such as the studies of assessment ratios cited above, since it is a tenable assumption that expenditure benefits do not vary systematically with tax payments within a single jurisdiction. For that reason, some analysts would argue that the local tax jurisdiction is the most appropriate area in which to measure the incidence of the property tax.

Permanent Income versus Current Income

A final question to be discussed is the appropriate concept of income for use in estimating the incidence of the property tax. The relationship between house value and household income is best summarized by the income elasticity of demand for housing, which can be defined as the percentage change in the value of housing per family divided by the percentage change in family income with which it is associated. If the value of this elasticity is unity, then the ratio MV/Y in the equation presented in the previous section will remain constant as income increases, because its numerator and denominator will change by the same percentage. If the elasticity has a value less than one, the ratio will fall; and if the elasticity is greater than one, it will rise as income rises. It is well established that the value obtained for this elasticity in empirical estimates depends on the income concept employed. If current annual income is the measure used, the income elasticity of housing demand always has a value well below one, and the ratio MV/Y falls as income rises. In that case, and if T/MV were independent of income, as would be the case in the absence of assessment bias, the left-hand term, T/Y, would also fall as income rises, and the tax on owner-occupants would be regressive to income.

In recent years, however, a number of economists, led by Aaron, have argued that the appropriate concept to use is "permanent income" – which can be measured by a household's average income over a number of years – rather than current income.[8] Using permanent income, the income elasticity of housing demand is usually found to have a higher value. In that case, the ratio MV/Y may be constant or even increase as income rises, and the tax on owner-occupied housing accordingly will be either proportional or progressive. (The incidence estimates presented in table 9.1 were calculated with respect to current income, which undoubtedly contributes to the regressivity of the pattern shown for the old view.)

Clearly, incidence studies of the property tax depend heavily on the choice of an income concept and the associated value of the income elasticity of housing demand. In the early 1960s, estimates using permanent income usually showed a value greater than one, suggesting progressive incidence for the property tax, even under the old view. More recent estimates put its value close to unity for owner-occupants, indicating proportional incidence, and somewhat lower for tenants, indicating mild regressivity. However, the range of estimated values remains wide enough to introduce considerable uncertainty into the resulting conclusions on incidence.

Ihlanfeldt's 1982 study adds yet another dimension. He found, for Philadelphia and Atlanta, that the elasticity of house value with respect to permanent income is very low for low-income owners but close to or above unity for middle- and upper-income groups.[9] This finding would indicate that the incidence of the property tax on home-owners approaches a U-shape: highly regressive over a range of low incomes but becoming much less regressive or even mildly progressive over a middle and upper range. The pattern of demand for housing that underlies these results might be explained as follows. There is a minimum quantity of housing that even those at the lowest income levels require: as income rises, housing demand at first increases only slightly but, further up the scale, rises more rapidly. "Better quality" housing then has almost the character of a luxury good.

Conclusion

The question of property tax incidence has received a good deal of attention from economists ever since the late nineteenth century. The 1960s and 1970s were especially fruitful decades for research. This brief essay necessarily omits some aspects of the problem as well as much detail even of those portions that it covers. Nevertheless, the essay has indicated how complex the institution and its effects are, and has pointed out several important issues that remain unsettled. It is therefore appropriate to close by saying that the question "Who bears the burden of the property tax?" is not yet fully resolved.

References

1   Peter Mieszkowski, "The Property Tax: An Excise or a Profits Tax?" *Journal of Public Economics 1* (April 1972): 73–96; Arnold C. Harberger, "The Incidence of the Corporation Income Tax," *Journal of Political Economy, 70* (June 1962): 215–40.

2   Mieszkowski, *op. cit.*, pp. 74–81.

3   Michael Boskin, "Taxation, Savings, and the Rate of Interest," *Journal of Political Economy, 86*, no. 2, pt. 2 (April 1978): S3–S27.

4   Robert F. Engle, "De Facto Discrimination in Residential Assessments: Boston," *National Tax Journal 28* (Summer 1975): 445–51; David E. Black, "Property Tax Incidence: The Excise-Tax Effect and Assessment Practices," *National Tax Journal, 30* (December 1977): 429–34.

5   Keith R. Ihlanfeldt, "Property Tax Incidence on Owner-Occupied Housing: Evidence from the Annual Housing Survey," *National Tax Journal, 35* (March 1982): 89–97.

6   New York University Graduate School of Public Administration, *Real Property Tax Policy for New York City* (New York, 1980), pp. 1–11.

7   Henry J. Aaron, *Who Pays The Property Tax?* (Washington, D.C.: The Brookings Institution, 1975), p. 46.

8   Aran, *op. cit.*, pp. 27–32.

9   Ihlanfeldt, *op. cit.*, p. 94.

Introduction to Chapter 10

The importance of the property tax in the finances of American local governments has declined radically in this century. The decline occurred in two spurts, in the 1930s and 1940s and then again between 1965 and 1980. Advisory Commission on Intergovernmental Relations surveys regularly report the property tax to be the most unpopular of the major taxes, in part no doubt because it is widely perceived to be regressive in incidence, but for other reasons as well. Repeatedly, the tax has been the target of efforts, often successful, to impose state-wide caps on the level of local property taxes. The question this article addresses is whether yet more drastic decline in the role of the tax is to be expected, given this unpopularity.

The method is to examine past trends and reasons for them as a basis for prediction. The article emphasizes the importance of shrinkage in the coverage of the tax, as well as rate limitations, and the consequences of that shrinkage. A final point is the question of whether a large further reduction in the role of the tax is on balance desirable, relative to conceivable alternatives.

10

Property Taxes: Their Past, Present, and Future Place in Government Finance

Dick Netzer

The role of the property tax in local government finance has diminished drastically over the past sixty years. Just before the Great Depression of the 1930s, the property tax provided about two-thirds of all the revenue of American local governments, compared to about one-fourth today (see table 10.1). However, that decline has not been continuous. The change in the role of the property tax occurred in two stages, the forties and the seventies, two episodes distinctly different from the long periods of stability in the relative role of the property tax that occurred before and after each of these two periods. Since roughly 1980, we have been in one of those periods of stability, possibly even in a period in which there may be a small reversal of the long decline. This is surprising because, simultaneously, the legal base of the property tax has continued to narrow, limitations on property tax rates and levies have spread, and abatements and exemptions for economic development purposes have spread even more. Thus, the absence of a decline in the property tax implies an increase in the burdens on that part of the nation's tangible wealth not excluded from the base or protected from the full rigors of the tax. But because every aspect of the property tax is highly varied geographically, the national statistics hide considerable variation among and within regions, that is, from state to state.

The main goal of this chapter is to consider whether the property tax is likely to enter a new period of shrinkage in relative importance, or the reverse, and the implications of both trends – implications for the distribution of the tax burdens, the distribution of people and economic activity within and among regions, and the financing of public services.

Table 10.1 The property tax and local government revenue, selected years 1902–89

| | Property tax revenue as percent of – | | | |
	Personal income	Total local government revenue	All own-source revenue	Total tax revenue
1902	N.A.	68.3	72.7	88.6
1927	N.A.	68.8	76.1	97.3
1932	8.4	67.2	77.3	97.3
1940	5.4	54.0	72.0	92.7
1946	2.7	49.5	63.9	91.9
1950	3.1	43.7	60.3	88.2
1955	3.3	42.7	58.0	86.9
1960	3.9	42.3	58.0	87.4
1965	4.0	40.8	57.0	86.9
1966	4.0	40.2	57.6	87.4
1967	3.9	39.0	56.7	86.6
1968	3.8	38.2	56.1	86.1
1969	3.9	37.5	55.8	85.4
1970	4.0	37.0	55.3	84.9
1971	4.1	36.4	55.2	84.6
1972	4.3	36.2	55.3	83.7
1973	4.0	34.0	54.0	82.9
1974	3.9	32.4	52.4	82.2
1975	3.8	31.3	51.1	81.6
1976	3.8	30.8	50.5	81.2
1977	3.8	30.7	50.4	80.5
1978	3.5	29.9	49.1	79.7
1979	3.1	26.6	44.7	77.5
1980	2.9	25.4	42.1	75.9
1981	2.9	25.0	40.8	76.0
1982	3.0	25.0	39.7	76.1
1983	3.0	25.4	39.3	76.0
1984	3.0	25.3	38.7	75.0
1985	3.0	24.8	37.7	74.2
1986	3.1	24.7	37.3	74.0
1987	3.1	24.7	37.0	73.6
1988	3.1	25.7	38.3	74.1
1989	3.1	25.8	38.4	74.3

Source: US Census Bureau, Government Finance diskettes, 1989.

Also, do the likely trends suggest another period of tax revolts and new limitations? Before those prospective issues can be addressed, we need to consider the past and present, however.

The Past and Present Role of the Tax

The most important long-term effect of the Great Depression on American fiscal federalism was a profound and permanent change in the role of the federal government in American society, from an essentially peripheral financer of civilian public expenditure to its present central role. However, that took years to implement fully, and in the short run, the federal role in dollar terms remained modest in the 1930s and 1940s. What did change sharply in response to the collapse in property values and incomes and the severity of social problems during the Depression, was the role of the state governments. The first protracted decline in the role of the property tax shown in table 10.1 – during the 1930s and 1940s – was almost entirely a result of major increases in state government aid for important local government functions, notably education, welfare, health, and highways, financed by state government taxes on income, sales, and highway users.

In the first fifteen or so years after 1950, the relative role of the property tax changed little, as property values and effective property tax rates rose about as fast as local government expenditure. But the subsequent fifteen years – after 1965 – witnessed another sharp decline. This decline was largely attributable to relatively increased state and federal aid to local governments, but in addition, the property tax lost ground to both local nonproperty taxes and, more significantly, to increased reliance on nontax revenues, especially user charges.

In the 1980s, as table 10.1 shows, the property tax did not decline as a share of total local government revenue and declined very little relative to local nonproperty taxes, although the importance of user charges has continued to rise somewhat vis-à-vis the property tax.

In summary, the historic decline in the role of the property tax mostly reflects the decision, within the fifty state-local fiscal systems, to replace local property taxes with state (and, to a much lesser extent, local) nonproperty taxes, which is both a tax policy and a fiscal federalism decision. Figure 10.1 shows the declines and plateaus in property taxes as a percent of total state-local tax collections. The other variables have been federal aid direct to local governments and nontax revenues. There was fairly steady relative growth in local nonproperty taxes until recently (see the last column of table 10.1), but they continue to be only slightly more than one-fourth of local tax revenue.

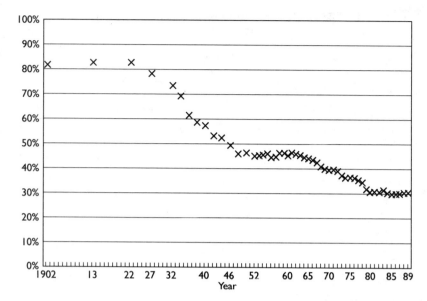

Figure 10.1 Property tax revenue as percent of total state-local tax revenue.

Source: US Census Bureau.

So far, the discussion has dealt only with aggregates for all local governments. Table 10.2 identifies the role of the property tax in the finances of different types of units of local government over the last decade.[1] It is clear that the recent relative stability in the role of the property tax is largely attributable to school finance. The property tax role continued to shrink for county governments and for city governments, especially the larger cities. The municipal governments of the nation's larger cities now obtain more revenue from local nonproperty taxes than from the property tax, with the exception of a few that operate their own dependent school systems.

Regional disparities

Table 10.3 indicates the geographic disparities in the role of the property tax as of 1989.[2] There are significant regional differences: the Northeast and Midwest rely more on the property tax than the South and West. But there are substantial intra-regional differences, including major disparities between adjacent states: Oregon and Washington, Mississippi and Alabama, New Jersey and Pennsylvania, Michigan and Ohio, Missouri and Kansas and Iowa, Virginia and North Carolina, Montana and

Table 10.2 Role of the property tax in local government revenue, by type of governmental unit, 1979 and 1989

	(Property tax revenue as percent of revenue aggregate shown)		
	All general revenue	General revenue from own sources	Tax revenue
All local governments			
1978–79	29.5	53.3	77.5
1988–89	29.3	46.7	74.3
County governments			
1978–79	26.0	49.7	77.1
1988–89	27.9	43.7	72.9
Independent school districts			
1978–79	37.0	81.2	96.7
1988–89	36.2	79.3	97.5
53 largest cities			
1978–79	20.1	35.0	48.4
1988–89	19.9	28.9	42.5
45 largest cities without dependent schools			
1978–79	17.3	28.1	42.9
1988–89	18.7	24.0	40.9
Large cities with dependent schools: New York City			
1978–79	22.2	40.4	51.6
1988–89	20.2	32.1	41.3
7 other cities			
1978–79	23.2	45.1	55.9
1988–89	23.0	38.8	52.0
All smaller cities			
1978–79	25.6	39.9	63.5
1988–89	25.1	33.5	59.4

Source: US Census Bureau, Governmental Finances and City Government Finances for 1978–79 and 1988–89.

Table 10.3 Regional and intra-regional differences in the role of the property tax in state–local
tax systems, 1989

*(Property tax revenue as percent of total tax revenue of
state and local governments combined)*

US mean	30.4
Northeast	32.1
New England	37.4
Connecticut	40.1
Massachusetts	32.3
Maine	34.1
New Hampshire	65.7
Rhode Island	38.7
Vermont	39.4
Middle Atlantic	32.3
New Jersey	43.4
New York	30.5
Pennsylvania	27.0
Midwest	33.0
East North Central	33.7
Illinois	35.2
Indiana	30.3
Michigan	38.4
Ohio	28.1
Wisconsin	35.2
West North Central	31.2
Iowa	35.5
Kansas	35.9
Minnesota	30.5
Missouri	21.8
North Dakota	29.9
Nebraska	41.5
South Dakota	41.1
South	27.4
South Atlantic	27.4
District of Columbia	31.7
Delaware	13.7
Florida	33.5
Georgia	27.2
Maryland	24.7
North Carolina	20.4
South Carolina	24.5
Virginia	29.4

Table 10.3 *Continued*

(Property tax revenue as percent of total tax revenue of state and local governments combined)

West Virginia	17.9
East South Central	18.6
Alabama	11.9
Kentucky	16.4
Mississippi	24.6
Tennessee	22.6
West South Central	31.8
Arkansas	17.7
Louisiana	17.0
Oklahoma	18.1
Texas	39.2
West	27.9
Mountain	30.6
Arizona	32.6
Colorado	35.5
Idaho	27.6
Montana	43.6
New Mexico	11.6
Nevada	21.5
Utah	29.1
Wyoming	43.2
Pacific	27.2
Alaska	32.1
California	26.0
Hawaii	13.9
Oregon	44.0
Washington	28.4

Source: US Census Bureau, Government Finance diskettes, 1989.

Idaho, all combinations of states that do not differ enormously from one another *except* in regard to their tax systems. There are no obvious explanations for these differences between adjacent states in the choice among fiscal institutions.[3]

Changes in the Tax Base

In practice, the American property tax never was what it was supposed to be in law and in theory in the mid-nineteenth century: a general tax on the current value of all privately owned wealth. It was too easy to avoid entirely the taxation of some important types of assets and to undervalue drastically other types of assets. By the late nineteenth century, states had begun to narrow the reach of the tax to reduce the inequities associated with the resulting poor enforcement. In the early part of this century, further tax base narrowing was connected with the adoption of new forms of state taxation, which substituted for various components of the property tax in different states, including: the state corporate income tax for property taxes on business tangible personal property in Delaware, Pennsylvania, and New York; various state business taxes for property taxes on intangible personal property in the great majority of the states; state motor vehicle registration taxes for property taxes on motor vehicles in about half the states; state gross receipts taxes on utilities for property taxes on specific types of utilities in several states.

Economic adversity had strong effects on the coverage of the property tax. The agricultural depression of the 1920s led to the adoption of classification systems in Minnesota and Montana, providing for much reduced taxes on agricultural and homeowner residential property. This foreshadowed the more widespread adoption of restrictions in the 1930s, including large "homestead exemptions" in several states (in some cases, like Louisiana, coming close to excluding almost all owner-occupied nonfarm houses from the tax rolls), exemption of some or all agricultural personal property and household personal property in numerous states, and the adoption of property tax rate limits that truly were binding (rather than empty gestures) in a few states, notably Ohio and West Virginia. In the quarter century after 1940, the institutional structure of the property tax changed little, but during the past two decades the pace of structural change has been rapid.

Recent tax base narrowing

One change has been the removal of ever more nonreal property, that is, property other than land and buildings, from the tax base, what is known as personal property in the law. Thirty years ago, virtually all personal property was exempt from tax in four states and motor vehicles in about half the states, but farm and nonfarm business inventories and equipment were taxable, with a few exceptions, in forty-six of the states. By 1989, personal property was entirely exempt in nine states; agricultural personal property was entirely exempt in ten other states and nearly exempt in several more; business inventories were generally taxable in fewer than ten states; and there were widespread exemptions of various types of business equipment, especially manufacturing machinery, in a good many states (*1987 Census of Governments*; Netzer 1966, chapter 6). State actions to exempt business personal property have been especially common in the late 1970s and 1980s.

Not surprisingly, the personal property share of the tax base declined from more than 17 percent of the tax base in 1956 to about 10 percent in 1986. This was in the face of a significantly more rapid increase in the market value of business equipment than of business structures during the same period (US Department of Commerce 1987; Musgrave 1990). Had the property tax coverage of personal property remained unchanged, the personal property share of the property tax base would have increased, not declined.

In all but one of the states (Wisconsin),[4] the state governments have removed a substantial portion of the value of agricultural and other open-space land from the property tax rolls by providing that such land be taxed at its value in the current use, rather than at its market value. Except in wholly nonurban states, the actual economic value in the current uses often is far below the market value for alternative uses; in practice, farmland tends to be drastically underassessed even on a current-use basis, so that agricultural land is a very small component of the tax base even in Cornbelt states, for example, about one-eighth of total assessed value in Indiana. The formal provisions for preferential assessment of farmland almost all date from the mid-1960s. Consequently, property listed on the tax rolls as acreage and farms declined from about 10 percent of all assessment rolls in 1956 to about 6 percent in 1986 (Netzer 1966; 1987 Census of Governments).

Until recently, nearly all states had formal requirements for uniformity of treatment of the property that is on the tax rolls (although systematic differences in assessment levels by type of property have been endemic), but by now fifteen states and the District of Columbia have what is known in the trade as "classification" systems, that is, formal provisions for dividing taxable property into use classes and either assessing the different classes at different percentages of market value or applying different tax rates to the assessed value of the property. Without exception, these systems tax owner-occupied residential property at the lowest effective rates; usually, farm property is equally favored (this is in addition to current-use valuation); and business property is taxed at the highest rates, often with utility property taxed at even higher rates than ordinary businesses (*1987 Census of Governments*, Appendix A and B; US Advisory Commission 1990, table 38). In some states, the formal differentials among the classes are small; in others, the differences are very large, as much as a ratio of 5:1 for major classes in New York.[5] Formal classification narrows the tax base in the sense of limiting local governments' ability to fully tax the low-rated types of property, which is not to say that local government officials have been opponents of classification systems.

As noted earlier, owner-occupied residential property received favorable treatment in a number of states more than fifty years ago, in the form of "homestead exemptions," usually by exempting the first thousand dollars of assessed value from tax. If the ratio of assessed to market value for homeowner property is low and the exemption large, the homestead exemption can remove a large fraction of this property from the tax rolls, as has been the case in Louisiana for many years.[6] Homestead exemptions have spread to forty-six states and the District of Columbia. In eighteen of these states, the exemption (in Indiana, it takes the form of a credit) is available to all property owners. In the others, it is restricted to the elderly, the disabled, veterans, and households with low incomes or low house values. In most of the first group of eighteen states, the exemption is larger for one or more of these presumably disadvantaged groups.

Another widespread form of property tax relief for residential property takes the form of rebates or credits against income taxes, based on property tax payments, provided by the state government. In thirty-two states and the District of Columbia, there are state-financed "circuit-breakers" – the amount of the relief is a function both of income and of the relation of the property tax payment to income. In some states, the program applies only to the elderly; where it applies to all ages, it is (like the homestead exemption) usually more generous for the elderly. Some of the all-age programs are very costly: in 1988 Michigan's circuit-breaker payments, for example, were equal to about 10 percent of total property tax revenue and close to 20 percent of the revenue from taxes on residential property (US Advisory Commission 1990, table 36; *1987 Census of Governments*, tables 1 and 4). Paradoxically, the circuit-breaker may act to limit the narrowing of the property tax base – the greater the extent that residential property tax bills are in effect paid from state funds, the less the pressure from homeowners for reducing the taxable value of their property.

An increasing number of states have authorized or directed local governments to provide property tax reductions to foster local economic development, typically in the form of time-limited exemption of some or all new investment in business structures and/or equipment (sometimes called abatements because of the supposedly temporary nature of the exemptions).[7] Because the abatements and exemptions take such different forms, there are no national data on the extent of these incentives in the aggregate. However, in a good many cities, especially large cities in the Northeast and Midwest, almost all major nonresidential building projects in the late 1970s and 1980s had some degree of property tax incentive before the project was launched. Of course, in some of these cities, because of the traditional discriminatory practices, the effective rates on newly built commercial structures would have made any investment unprofitable, in the absence of tax breaks.

Another structural change affecting the tax base has been almost entirely involuntary. Around the beginning of this century, state and local governments made a 180-degree turn in their policies toward public utilities and railroads: They had been willing captives of railroad and utility moguls in respect to both regulation and taxation, and they became, in the wake of the progressive movement, exploiters, especially in property taxation. For decades, railroads and utilities were subject to property taxes that were dramatically higher than those on ordinary businesses; sometimes this was explicitly provided by law, but more often it was the result of a combination of formal provision and informal administrative discretion. First, it was generally believed that this was a sure-fire way of exporting part of local tax burdens to residents of other places; and, second, it was also believed that the price elasticity of the local demand for the services produced by these industries was so low that the utilities were neutral and convenient intermediaries in the tax collection process. It should have been obvious decades ago that both propositions were nonsense, but it took ages for that to be understood by economists; some decision-makers still subscribe to the old nonsense.

Thirty years ago, railroads, other major transportation carriers (i.e., airlines, pipelines, and interstate motor carriers), and public utilities accounted for about 13 percent of total property tax revenues; their property tax payments amounted to 6.3 percent of national income originating in the sector, compared to less than 2 percent for other nonfarm business sectors (Netzer 1966). But this has been changing, and rapidly. Economic changes have removed some major segments of the capital stock of this sector from the property tax base: The railroad network has shrunk, especially in those parts of the country where the railroads had been the most overtaxed (the Northeast, in general), and a large amount of telecommunications equipment is now owned by customers rather than telephone companies and is either exempt from property taxation entirely or taxed at the lower effective rates characteristic of ordinary businesses. In addition, federal legislation enacted beginning in 1976 now prohibits states from discriminatorily taxing interstate railroads, airlines, and motor carriers, and state tribunals have become less reluctant to intervene against discriminatory taxation of energy and telecommunications utilities.

By the time of the 1987 census of governments, transportation and public utility property accounted for only about 5 percent of the total assessed value of property subject to tax, compared to about 9 percent thirty years earlier. This was mostly a consequence of tax policy, for the value of structures and equipment owned by this sector declined far less as a share of the total value of privately owned structures and equipment over the same years, from 18.5 percent to 14.6 percent. Moreover, most of that relative decline occurred early in the period, when there were few property tax structural changes (Department of Commerce 1987, 1989 tape).[8]

Effects of changes on tax base composition

The structural changes that effectively narrowed the tax base had contradictory results from the standpoint of the before-and-after composition of the tax base. Progressively exempting more business personal property, restricting the taxation of farmland, reluctantly changing the property tax treatment of transportation and public utility companies, and offering all sorts of economic development incentives can reduce the nonresidential share of the tax base. But classification and homestead exemptions will reduce the residential share: the shares of both sectors cannot be reduced simultaneously.

What has been happening, in reality? Residential real property accounted for about 40 percent of taxable property values in 1956, and a slightly larger percentage of property tax revenue (Netzer 1966, chapter 2). Similar calculations for 1966, 1979, and 1981 show a persistent rise in the residential percentage. The *1987 Census of Governments* shows that in 1986 the residential percentage of taxable property values was just over 50, a large increase over the entire period. In part, this does reflect underlying economic trends: The national wealth statistics show that the value of residential structures has been rising somewhat more rapidly than that of private nonresidential structures.

On the other hand, the value of business equipment (equal to that of business structures since about 1980) has been rising substantially more rapidly than the value of either residential or business structures – about 40 percent more rapidly since 1956 and with an even greater disparity in more recent years (US Department of Commerce 1987; Musgrave 1990). The shrinking scope of the taxation of business personal property may be the culprit in the decline in the nonresidential share of the tax base (also, transportation and utilities own a good deal more equipment than structures). But changes in land values also may be a significant explanatory variable. Land is surely a larger share of the total value of residential real property than of business real property. Therefore, if land values rose more rapidly than structure values, which probably is the case, the residential share would have risen, with a constant structure of the property tax. In sum, we really don't know the net contribution of the structural changes in those changes that have occurred in the composition of the tax base.

Ceilings on tax rates and tax levies

Strictly speaking, the adoption of state restrictions on the overall level of local property taxes is not a structural change that narrows the scope of the tax base, but property tax limitations usually are meant to reduce the ability of local governments to exploit whatever tax base is defined by law – they *are*, effectively, reductions in the tax base. Constitutional limits on local property tax rates go back more than a century, but, with few exceptions, they were readily circumvented. In the past two decades, however, many states have adopted limitations that really bind. One type of effective limitation is setting a ceiling on the amount by which local governments can increase their property tax levies – the total amount they intend to collect from the tax – in any one year, either a prescribed percentage-point increase or a limitation keyed to some external economic indicator. The ceiling cannot be circumvented by increases in the property tax rolls, as was the case for most of the older types of ceilings on property tax rates. Limitations in this form were adopted explicitly to prevent local governments from exploiting reassessments that tracked rising market values, especially in inflationary periods. Thus, such limitations are found mostly in states in which local assessments do a reasonable job of tracking market values, like Minnesota and New Jersey.

Inflation plus good assessment practice (or reforms that promised to improve assessment practices) led, by the late 1970s, to a second form of effective limitation, setting a low ceiling on effective property tax rates, perhaps well below the rates that exist at the time the ceiling is adopted, as in the case of Proposition 13 in California in 1978 and Proposition $2\frac{1}{2}$ in Massachusetts in 1980. In the California case, there is also a drastic limit on increases in the taxable value of properties that do not change ownership, in effect immunizing an increasing share of the value of real property from taxation over time. There have been other types of limitations adopted in the 1970s and 1980s as well, including restrictions on the rate at which assessments can be increased (regardless of market values) in states where local politics tends to focus on nominal tax rates.

Structural change in places with economic distress

It can be argued that most of the important structural changes in the property tax during the 1970s and 1980s were political responses to rapid growth and inflation in prosperous states and parts of states, which tended to produce rapid increases in taxable property values, thus making it easy for officials to satisfy the demands for public services associated with rapid growth by increasing property tax revenues without increasing published tax rates. This enraged both those whose current incomes had kept pace with growth and inflation and those whose current incomes had not but who had substantial unrealized capital gains on their real property. But the narrowing of the tax base and limitations on tax rates and levies also affected places in which economic and population decline, not growth, was the rule. Economic trends had spectacular effects on the market value of real property, the bulk of the property tax base, effects that tended to be exacerbated in the case of declining cities by the changes in the structure of the property tax.

This is shown in table 10.4 for most of the large central cities of the country, divided in the table into Frostbelt and Sunbelt cities, for the 1966–81 period. The table covers all the cities for which the requisite *Census of Governments* data are available; it stops in 1981 because the *1987 Census of Governments* contains no data on market value, only assessed value. The first column shows the effects of economic change alone; property values in constant dollars decreased sharply in a good many of the Frostbelt cities and increased sharply in most of the Sunbelt cities, and the percentage changes were a good deal larger than those in per capita income. The second column shows the changes in the taxable property tax base (excluding changes that were solely a result of differences in assessment administration practices). In all of the Frostbelt cities in the table for which data are available, the taxable property tax base declined in real terms, except for Indianapolis, which had a small increase. If we had data for 1991, it is probable that we would note that the declines in the taxable property tax base had been reversed in some, but not all, northeastern cities, but had continued in most of the midwestern cities. So, it should be no surprise that fiscal crisis has become a more or less permanent state of affairs for a good many large cities, with huge shrinkage in the property tax base and little hope of rescue from the outside in the form of major increases in state and federal aid.

Journalists will see the dramatic numbers in table 10.4 in terms of physically devastated neighborhoods, the acres of abandonment in residential areas of Detroit, the legendary South Bronx, and boarded-up stores and older office buildings in central business districts. In fact, Detroit aside, physical abandonment was largely a phenomenon of the 1966–76 period, with a fair amount of subsidized rebuilding since then. However, much of the new investment did not go onto the property tax rolls because of various exemptions and abatements. The economist's explanation for the severity of the decline in the property tax base in Frostbelt cities (and the corresponding rapidity of the increase in Sunbelt cities) lies in the magnified effect of decline and expansion on land values, which have been close to zero, or even negative, in large sections of the Detroits. Even in the Frostbelt cities that were prosperous in the 1980s, land values in constant dollars seldom rose significantly in large parts of those cities outside the central business district and most desirable gentrified residential areas.

Table 10.4 Percent change in property values, in constant dollars, large "Frostbelt" and "Sunbelt" cities, 1966–81[a]

City	Percent change in market value of real property[b]	Percent change in taxable property value base[c]	Exhibit: Percent change in personal income in constant dollars[d]
Detroit	−64.3	−66.4	[−16.9]
Cleveland	−47.9	N.A.	[−8.3]
St. Louis	−34.9	−40.5	−26.0
Newark	−34.3	−39.0	[−9.7]
Buffalo	−25.8	−24.0	[−2.3]
Pittsburgh	−17.0	−17.0	[5.5]
New York	−8.6	−9.7	−11.6
Milwaukee	−3.4	−15.2	[−0.5]
Cincinnati	−3.1	N.A.	[6.2]
Philadelphia	−1.3	−1.3	−11.3
Boston	−0.1	−0.4	−4.9
Baltimore	4.5	−16.0	−13.8
Toledo	8.9	N.A.	[6.6]
Minneapolis	9.1	−4.1	[23.5]
Indianapolis	14.1	3.8	[4.6]
Chicago	21.0	−12.2	[−0.8]
Columbus	45.7	N.A.	[27.3]
New Orleans	17.3	−6.9	5.5
Atlanta	54.3	18.7	[18.0]
Jacksonville	56.3	71.7	37.7
Oklahoma City	57.8	53.4	[58.4]
Nashville	83.4	62.2	28.0
Portland	93.9	101.7	[67.0]

Table 10.4 *Continued*

City	Percent change in market value of real property[b]	Percent change in taxable property value base[c]	Exhibit: Percent change in personal income in constant dollars[d]
Baton Rouge	102.9	20.1	82.0
Denver	113.4	77.0	22.7
Tulsa	120.4	118.7	[65.9]
Albuquerque	132.4	132.2	[66.6]
Memphis	145.1	46.0	[35.5]
Honolulu	151.6	153.7	51.2
Charlotte	191.5	191.8	[44.5]
Phoenix	397.3	326.8	[123.3]

[a] The Frostbelt cities in the top half of the table include seventeen of the nineteen cities in the Northeast and Midwest with a 1980 population of 300,000 or more. The Sunbelt cities include fourteen of the thirty cities in the South and West with a 1980 population of 300,000 or more. The excluded cities are: (a) cities for which the requisite data are not available (usually because assessed value data are published in the *Census of Governments* only for whole counties, true for all cities in Texas); (b) all cities in California, because of the effect of Proposition 13 on assessed values; and (c) Washington, D.C.

[b] Based on data from Volume 2 of the *Census of Governments* for 1967 and 1982. Market value estimates are based on the gross assessed value of locally assessed real property divided by the weighted average ratio of assessed values to actual prices of a sample of properties sold, for "ordinary real estate" in 1966 and for "measurable sales of all use categories" in 1981. The percentage change in market value so estimated was divided by the change in the implicit price deflator for state and local governments between 1966 and 1981, from the National Income and Product Accounts. Because there are partial exemptions of certain types of property in some of the cities, these estimates are not precise measures of the change in the constant dollar market value of real property actually subject to tax.

[c] These estimates take into account changes in provisions for partial exemptions, as well as changes in the coverage of other components of the property tax, notably locally assessed "personal" property (largely business machinery, inventories, and motor vehicles, with major variations in coverage among the states) and property (mostly public utility and mining property) assessed by state government agencies. In essence, such changes are treated as exogenous to the city government, while changes in the way in which real property is assessed by local assessing officers are treated as endogenous. The figures in this column indicate how the tax base would have changed if local assessment practices in 1981 were similar to those in 1966, but with the actual changes in market value of real property, exemptions, and coverage of the property tax. The deflator described in note b was applied here. The *1982 Census of Governments* does not provide data on assessed values of personal and state-assessed property below the county level for Ohio; no estimates can be made for Ohio cities.

[d] Personal income estimates in current dollars, from the Bureau of Economic Analysis, US Department of Commerce, deflated as described in note b. Personal income data are available only for counties and for cities that are co-extensive with counties or are independent of counties. The figures in brackets are for entire counties that include suburban territory as well as the city; because population suburbanized during this period, the bracketed figures in most cases understate the declines in real income or overstate the increases actually experienced in the central city itself.

Efficiency and Equity Effects of the Changing Property Tax

One cannot discuss the effects of the property tax without specifying the theoretical basis from which the discussion proceeds, that is, who bears the burden of changes in property taxes. Usually, such discussions are cast in terms of the supposed conflict between the "New View" and the "Traditional View" of the incidence of the tax. That conflict is not a real one, in general and in the specific context of this chapter. In the shortest of short terms, the burden (benefit) from an increase (decrease) in the property tax on a specific asset almost always will be borne by the owner of that asset. In the longest of long terms, when equilibrium has finally been achieved, the burden (benefit) in the main will be diffused among all owners of capital in the form of a reduced rate of return on all types of capital in all locations, that is, in proportion to the amount of capital that each household owns.

In between, in the long period that is truly relevant for policy – and when the policy issue at hand is whether to increase (decrease) the property tax in a particular place, or to narrow or broaden its coverage, or to grant new types of economic development incentives or remove old ones – the burden is borne by or the benefit accrued to the owners of the least mobile factors of production in the places where and in the economic sectors for which the tax changes are being made or contemplated. So reducing the property taxes on business property by exempting inventories from personal property taxation, a popular action in the last two decades, will most benefit owners of in-state businesses whose goods and services compete least with the output of firms in other states (like most retailers and producers of consumer services), the least skilled (and therefore least mobile) employees of those businesses, the owners of the land and structures occupied by those businesses, and the purchasers of their goods and services who themselves are not especially mobile geographically. The reverse is true for business property tax increases, in both cases framing the issue as increases or decreases relative to the actions that other states are taking at the same time.

The fact that the ultimate burden or benefit from a property tax change in one state or city accrues to immobile local factors of production and immobile local households does not mean that everyone else is indifferent to the economic processes through which these effects are realized over time. Immobile factors and households benefit from tax reductions as capital is attracted to the city or state and employment, income, sales, and asset values rise. As with economic growth triggered by any other cause, there are a few losers from the process, but mostly winners – and the enterprises and people who are attracted to the area are likely to see themselves as winners, even if we economists do not.

A similar situation exists with regard to changes in property tax on residential property in a state or city. Because the structures and, especially, the land are less mobile than their occupants, the burden or benefit accrues mainly to the owners of the land and structures. For owner-occupied housing, there is, of course, no distinction between the two economic roles. For renter-occupied housing, some of the burden or benefit will accrue to tenants, because some of them are quite immobile geographically – but many are not, over time.

These probable outcomes suggest that reduced reliance on the property tax is likely to be a popular course of action, in the future as it has been in the past. Is this a good thing, compared to the conceivable alternatives, which are higher local government expenditures or other types of local government revenue? What is right and wrong about a tax that has become one largely on the value of housing, public utility property, commercial and industrial structures built before the era of generous tax incentives for new investment, and – in some states – motor vehicles?

(1)   Equity: A reduced role for the property tax in a given city or state will have mixed income distribution effects, assuming that the reductions are across the board. Relatively low-income people will benefit as immobile workers in local establishments, immobile consumers, and immobile tenants. But relatively high-income people also will benefit as landowners, newspaper proprietors and owners of television stations, managers and shareholders of local utilities, and so on. The best evidence on the income-elasticity of demand for owner-occupied housing suggests that it is fairly low, so reductions in local taxes on owner-occupied housing should benefit low-income homeowners disproportionately.

(2)   Another consideration in actual decision making, and one that has been held to be a virtue in regard to the "fiscal health" of cities by some economists (Ladd and Yinger 1989), is the extent to which the tax burden can be exported. Superficially, given that business property is ordinarily a large component of the tax base in central cities, it appears that the property tax should be the preferred revenue instrument on this score. However, as my analysis of incidence above suggests, I am skeptical about the exportability of the business property tax except in the very long run. Therefore, a reduction in the use of this tax in one city

should not make its tax burden less exportable in any significant way. As Ladd and Yinger suggest, the local tax that may be the most exportable of all is a city earnings tax on nonresident commuters, whose status as earners in the city is likely to be a relatively immobile one.

(3)   The other side of that coin is the effect of the level of the property tax on new investment in that city, obviously of special concern to cities that are not in good economic health. If the burdens and benefits of property tax differentials (or increases/decreases) are not very exportable, that means that local people and enterprises will gain from tax reductions. The mechanism by which they benefit is the inflow of capital, that is, economic development. Indeed, it may not matter much whether the taxes are reduced on a targeted basis or across the board, from the standpoint of economic development over time. Because the property tax is one that is measured by the value of capital, its reduction should be more beneficial to local economic growth than reductions in local sales and income taxes.[9] On the other hand, a considerable portion of the tax base consists of the value of land itself; reducing taxes on land values has no effect other than to make the present owners of that land richer.

(4)   It does seem likely that lower property taxes would have positive effects on the quality of the housing stock, in particular the rental housing stock. However, the price effects in this sector are likely to be more important than the quality effects because at the lower end of the rental housing market both the price and the income elasticity of demand for quality appears to be very low.

(5)   Stability of the tax base: The data in table 10.4 suggest that the market value of taxable property may be an exceedingly unsafe tax base for very poor cities, far more so than alternative tax bases, like income. Stability aside, there is real question about the adequacy of a property tax largely on housing in very poor cities, the value of which may be lower relatively than personal incomes. A few years ago, in connection with school finance litigation in New Jersey, I calculated the value of residential property in a number of the poorest cities in the state, which had lost much of their business tax base over the years.[10] In Camden, New Jersey, the mean value per housing unit in 1981 was about $6,000, less than a tenth of the statewide average!

(6)   The property tax has a very long history of being inexpensively but very poorly administered, because of the difficulty of valuing real property and both discovering and valuing personal property, and because of populist opposition to effective administration even when technically

feasible. The narrowing of the tax base, along with technological improvements, has made the tax far less difficult to administer, provided money is spent to do so (like for auditing business personal property tax returns, which is a startlingly uncommon practice), so that it really is no longer correct to praise reduced reliance on the property tax as substituting inherently easy-to-administer taxes for an inherently difficult-to-administer tax.[11]

(7) Frequently, the property tax has been denounced from the standpoint of the disparities in the taxable capacity of local jurisdictions. But this, of course, is true of any local tax. If public services are to be financed largely from local revenues, there will be interjurisdictional disparities.

Most urban economists agree on what would be the best of all possible revenue systems for cities: taxes on the value of land to finance public goods and the external benefits from publicly provided private goods and marginal-cost-based user charges for everything else. But of course, the property tax we do have is not a land value tax. Nonetheless, the theoretical prescription tells us something about the conceptual advantages and disadvantages of the actual real-world property tax vis-à-vis actual real-world alternatives. The fact that land value is an important component of the property tax base is, as the above discussion makes clear, a major factor in the evaluation of the tax. The inclusion of land makes the tax better in most respects, and, therefore, makes the case for less reliance on it weaker on both equity and efficiency grounds. On the other hand, the property tax is an exceedingly inept user charge, and therefore should be replaced, for the financing of private goods, by properly designed user charges, as economists never tire of saying.

Future Prospects

There is no reason to expect that, in the foreseeable future, the property tax will be displaced in local finance by a substantial increase in the role of federal and state aid to local governments, as occurred in the 1930s and again in the 1960s and 1970s. No doubt, in some states, there will be major reforms in school finance, leading to more state financing of the schools. Also, reforms in the health-care finance system may marginally reduce local government spending for hospitals, in some places. But even these important policy shifts will not amount to a major shift in intergovernmental fiscal relations in this country.

The rapid decline in the importance of the property tax from the mid-1960s to the late 1970s was not solely caused by the changes in the intergovernmental fiscal system during those years. In addition, there was the widespread perception, right or wrong, that the property tax is inequitable, along several dimensions, relative to plausible alternatives. It is not obvious that this remains the dominant perception or is seen as a particularly urgent policy concern. Perhaps as important in explaining the major role of voter- and legislature-generated property tax ceilings and caps – on rates, assessments, and levies, sometimes done indirectly via classification schemes – in the decline of the property tax was the rapidity of the increases in the value of owner-occupied housing, especially in places where assessments did track market values reasonably well (and also in places where there were threats that assessments might do so in the near future). House values rose rapidly because of inflation in general and the existence of negative real mortgage interest rates; both are conditions that are unlikely to return soon. If house prices do not increase rapidly, a new wave of Proposition 13s is most unlikely.

On the other hand, huge declines in housing values can lead, as they did in the Great Depression, to strong reactions against the property tax (in the 1930s, Florida voters nearly approved a referendum proposal to abolish the tax entirely) if assessed values do not decline commensurately. But there is no reason to expect that scenario to be played out on a national basis.

Conceivably, however, there could be new rounds of the experience depicted in table 10.4, collapsing property values in major Frostbelt cities. However, it is implausible to assume that the 1989–92 difficulties in real estate markets, notably the high vacancies in commercial property and the sharp decline in sales and prices in the upper part of the residential market, represent some fundamental change, and that we should expect perpetual low values, even perpetually declining values in constant dollars as our future, in a large number of cities. It is true that, in the worst of cases – as in the table 10.4 worst cases – substantial declines in the property tax base in real terms will aggravate difficult social and fiscal problems, with large increases in central city tax rates on any property that remains taxable and massive capital losses. But that need not be the universal experience even of Frostbelt cities, any more than it was in the late 1960s and 1970s.

Thus, circumstances that will lead to wholesale replacement of the property tax do not seem likely, in the near-to-intermediate future. Nor *should* the property tax be replaced wholesale in the light of its relative strengths and weaknesses.

Conclusion

Just over thirty-five years ago, a public finance economist who is now largely unknown but who then was regarded as one of the most perceptive analysts and practitioners in the field, George W. Mitchell, forecast that in twenty years, "the property tax will . . . have become an all-but-forgotten relic of an earlier fiscal age" (Mitchell 1956, 494), that is, it would renew its decline as a source of local government revenue.[12] The decline did start once more a few years later, but stopped. About a decade ago, I revisited the Mitchell forecast and concluded that during the 1980s some decline but not much was likely. That is also my forecast for the 1990s. For good and bad reasons, decision-makers (including the voters in occasional referenda) will chip away at the coverage of the tax, offer more incentives and preferences, cap rates and levies, and increase the use of local nonproperty taxes and user charges. But without major changes in fiscal federalism in the shape of shifting financing responsibilities for local public services to the higher levels of government, the overall role of the property tax will change little.

Notes

1   "General revenue" rather than total revenue is used in table 10.2 because the data by type of local government are readily available only for general revenue. The main difference is that general revenue excludes water, electric power, gas, and transit utility revenue.

2   The denominator of the measure used is total state-local tax revenue in order to avoid distortions due solely to decisions concerning the locus of the administrative responsibility for functions that are largely financed by the state governments.

3   The diversity in fiscal institutions within the American system of fiscal federalism in general is not easy to explain: In a related paper, I tried to explain interstate differences in reliance on user charges without much success (Netzer, 1991).

4   In Wisconsin, the "State legislature has elected to provide owners of farmland subject to agricultural use restrictions with income tax credits and refunds rather than use-based assessments" (*1987 Census of Governments*, Appendix C).

5   There are even larger differentials among classes of personal property in some states, but the classes with the very low rates are small ones. The large differential for New York is the combined result of a number of formally discriminating provisions, rather than a single explicit provision; however, it is obvious to this observer that the legislature has been entirely aware of the combined effect from the time the classification system was enacted in 1981.

6   As of 1986, the gross assessed value of single-family houses (rented or owner-occupied) in that state was $4,858 million. The total amount of the homestead exemptions was $4,040 million (*1987 Census of Governments*, tables 2 and 4). Some single-family houses were rented, not owner-occupied, so it is likely that the exemption removed more than 90 percent of the gross assessed value of single-family owner-occupied houses from taxation.

7   Substantively, this was not entirely a new thing. Extralegal informal drastic underassessment of industrial property had been the rule in most medium-sized and small cities in the United States for decades, especially in regions that early on were aggressive competitors for industry (the South in general) and in places where the dominant local industries had been declining. But few large cities had been participants in this until recently, and the conversion of the practice from informal to formal surely increased its impact in other places.

8   This last set of calculations ignores land values, which is part of the reason why the Department of Commerce wealth data do not match the tax roll data even approximately.

9   An exception may be the reduction of taxes on selected business inputs like utility services (or some other business purchases covered by the general sales tax), which could be strategic for the industries that are closest to the margin with respect to choosing whether or not to locate in that city (e.g., telecommunications services for financial services companies).

10   The case was *Abbot v. Burke*, decided by the New Jersey Supreme Court in favor of the plaintiffs, who were residents of a number of the state's poor cities.

11   Besides, one substitute for the property tax, more reliance on user charges, involves revenue instruments that are indeed difficult to administer.

12   Mitchell at that time was the vice president in charge of research at the Federal Reserve Bank of Chicago. A student of Frank Knight, Henry Simons, and Simeon Leland at the University of Chicago, he had been director of research for the Illinois Tax Commission (and a member of the commission), director of studies for Congressional committees, and Illinois finance director during the administration of Adlai Stevenson. In 1961, he became President Kennedy's first appointee to the Federal Reserve Board and later became vice chairman of the board. He retired in 1975.

References

Ladd, Helen F. and Yinger, John. 1989. *America's Ailing Cities*. Baltimore: Johns Hopkins University Press.

Mitchell, George W. 1956. "Is This Where We Came In?" In *Proceedings of the Forty-Ninth Annual Conference on Taxation*, National Tax Association.

Musgrave, John C. 1990. "Fixed Reproducible Tangible Wealth in the United States, 1982–89." *Survey of Current Business (September):* 99–106.

Netzer, Dick. 1966. *Economics of the Property Tax*. Washington, D.C.: The Brookings Institution.

Netzer, Dick. 1991. "Differences in Reliance on User Charges by American State and Local Governments." Paper presented at the annual research conference of the Committee on Taxation, Resources and Economic Development, Cambridge, Massachusetts. The conference papers are to be published in a special issue of the *Public Finance Quarterly* in 1992.

US Advisory Commission on Intergovernmental Relations. 1990. *Significant Features of Fiscal Federalism*, Volume 1, *Budget Processes and Tax Systems*.

US Department of Commerce, Bureau of the Census. 1989. *1987 Census of Governments*. Volume 2, *Taxable Property Values*. Washington, D.C.: Government Printing Office.

US Department of Commerce, Bureau of Economic Analysis. 1987. *Fixed Reproducible Tangible Wealth in the United States, 1925–85*. Washington, D.C.: Government Printing Office.

US Department of Commerce, Bureau of Economic Analysis. 1989. *National Wealth Tape*. Computer tape sold through Atlanta office of BEA.

Introduction to Chapter 11

With this chapter we turn to taxes on consumption, in the aggregate the most important source of revenue for American state governments. Sales and excise taxes do conform well to three of Adam Smith's "maxims of taxation." For the most part, they are relatively easy to collect and to comply with and often – in the US – imposed at rates that cause minimal economic damage. But they do have one major problem: they are considered by most people to be very regressive and therefore considered by some people to be unfair.

But are they regressive? In one sense, consumption taxes generically must be regressive with respect to income, because the ratio of saving to income rises, and the ratio of consumption spending to income falls, as income rises. This aspect of regressivity does not seem to bother the electorate much in regard to broad-based consumption taxes, like the sales tax.

This is not the case for the most important of selective excises, those on gasoline, liquor and tobacco. American tax rates are very low by international standards, in part because the taxes are perceived to be highly regressive. Poterba in this article examines the incidence of these taxes, using the perspective of long term fairness: that is, incidence of the taxes over a lifetime.

11

Lifetime Incidence and the Distributional Burden of Excise Taxes

James M. Poterba*

Although theoretical papers have noted the potentially important distinction between annual and lifetime tax burdens, with one exception the lifetime perspective is absent in empirical studies of tax incidence.[1] Calculations based on annual income may provide particularly unreliable guidance on a central tax policy issue of the early 1990s: the incidence of excise taxes. Conventional wisdom holds that these taxes are regressive, falling most heavily on the poorest households. This has long been one of the central objections to proposals for raising excise taxes. Nevertheless, the evidence for this view may depend critically on the time horizon in incidence studies. Joseph Pechman writes:

> . . . whether regressivity of [sales and excise] taxes with respect to income would remain for accounting periods longer than one year is not known. It seems clear, however, that the regressivity shown at the lowest income levels on the basis of annual figures would be moderated, if not completely eliminated, over the longer period. [p. 51]

There is relatively little systematic evidence, however, evaluating this conjecture.[2]

* Department of Economics, MIT, Cambridge, MA 02139. I am grateful to Thomas Moehrle and Frank Sammartino for providing me with data from the Consumer Expenditure Survey, to David Cutler for research assistance, and to Roger Gordon, Joseph Pechman, Nancy Rose, and Lawrence Summers for helpful discussions. This research was supported by a grant from the National Science Foundation and is part of the NBER Program in Taxation.

The present paper begins by documenting the unsurprising proposition that household income measured over long horizons is less variable than annual household income. This implies that low-income households in one year have some chance of being higher-income households in other years. Thus, even if the share of income consumed by lowest-income groups is higher than that for higher-income groups, excise taxes or taxes on consumption more generally may be less regressive than calculations based on annual income suggest. Section 11.2 explores the differences between the annual and lifetime incidence by considering the incidence of excise taxes on gasoline, alcohol, and tobacco. It shows that expenditure on these items as a share of total consumption is much more equally distributed than expenditure as a share of annual income. If households base their spending plans on their expected lifetime income, then consumption provides a more accurate measure of lifetime resources than does annual income. From a longer-horizon perspective, these taxes are therefore much less regressive than is usually thought.

11.1   Do Lifetime and Annual Incidence Differ?

Many studies provide detailed information on the tax burdens facing households at different points in the annual income distribution. If households stay at the same position in the income distribution over long periods of time, then these calculations provide reasonable indications of longer-term tax burdens as well. Data on income dynamics, however, suggest a surprising degree of instability in the annual income distribution.

Table 11.1 presents data on movements up and down the income distribution by individuals in the *Panel Study of Income Dynamics (PSID)*. The entries are transition probabilities relating an individual's location in the distribution in 1971 to the same individual's position in 1978. A randomly chosen individual had a 41 percent chance of being in the same income quintile in these two years. The chance that an individual in the lowest-income quintile in 1971 would be there again in 1978 was 0.54, significantly higher than the one-in-three chance that an individual near the middle of the income distribution would remain in the same quintile.

Transition data may overstate the true incidence of mobility since survey data on household income are subject to measurement error. The magnitude of the overstatement may be small, however. John Bound and Alan Krueger (1988) find that only 15 percent of the cross-sectional variation in reported income in the *Current Population Survey* is due to noise. Duncan and Daniel Hill (1985) report similarly encouraging

Table 11.1 Family income mobility over a seven-year interval

1971 Income Quintile	Probability of 1978 Income Quintile:				
	1	2	3	4	5
1	.54	.20	.13	.10	.03
2	.20	.31	.27	.14	.08
3	.09	.19	.30	.30	.13
4	.04	.10	.19	.34	.34
5	.04	.07	.11	.21	.58

Notes: Income quintile 1 refers to the lowest-income quintile. This table is drawn from Greg Duncan and James Morgan (1981, table 1.1).

results for the *PSID*. Both studies also find important positive correlation between the measurement errors for earnings in adjacent years (.43 in Duncan and Hill), undermining the common claim that much of the year-to-year variation in reported earnings is due to measurement error.

Substantial instability in the income distribution is confirmed by evidence from other studies using other data sets. Frank Hanna (1948), analyzing Wisconsin income data from the 1929 to 1935 period, finds markedly less inequality in the distribution of total income over the period than in the distribution of annual income. Paul Taubman (1977) examines mobility in the NBER-Thorndike/Hagen data set that reports earnings in 1969 and 1955 for a sample of 4,600 men aged 18–26 in 1943. This homogeneous sample controls for lifecycle variation in earnings, but Taubman nevertheless finds that an individual's chance of falling in the same earnings decile in 1955 and 1969 is only 22 percent. Lee Lillard (1977) uses the same data and estimates the Gini coefficient for annual income to be .28, significantly larger than the estimate of .19 for the present value of lifetime earnings.[3]

Since studies using annual income data find that the burden of the US tax system is roughly proportional to income except at the top and bottom of the income distribution, mobility into and out of these parts of the income distribution has the largest effect on incidence studies. Martha Hill's (1981) study of the *PSID* sample finds that one-third of the individuals who were in poverty had not been in poverty the previous year. Taubman's results show less mobility: 39 percent of individuals in the lowest-earning decile in 1955, as well as 44 percent of those in the highest decile, were in the same decile again in 1969.

Even modest mobility is sufficient to alter basic incidence results, particularly regarding excise taxes. Davies et al. find that the average burden of Canadian sales and excise taxes for the lowest-income decile falls from 27 percent when annual income is the benchmark to 15 percent with lifetime incidence (the average across all groups is 13 percent). For the highest-income decile, the excise tax burden rises from 8.5 percent with annual incidence to 12 percent with lifetime incidence. For the progressive corporate income tax, lifetime incidence reduces the burden on top decile households from 10 to 5 percent and raises the burden on the lowest decile from 1 to 2 percent.

Focusing on lifetime incidence introduces two considerations that annual incidence calculations omit. First, lifetime incidence incorporates predictable lifecycle patterns in earnings, asset accumulation, and consumption, yielding more sensible inferences with respect to the distribution of tax burdens. For example, consider the gasoline excise tax burden on two city-dwelling households with no current gasoline expenditures, one a young couple and the other two elderly pensioners. While the annual incidence framework might imply identical burdens on the two households, the lifetime approach correctly imputes a higher burden to the younger couple because they are likely to move to the suburbs and become substantial gasoline consumers in future years.

Second, lifetime incidence averages over many years, reducing the importance of variation in annual earnings due to unemployment or changes in family status. In practice this effect is more important than the lifecycle effect in estimating the distribution of excise tax burdens. For many low-income households, current income provides an unreliable indication of lifetime economic status. Pechman attempts to correct for this problem in measuring tax burdens on the lowest-income decile. His reported tax burdens for the lowest decile (first through tenth percentiles) are based on households in the *sixth* through tenth percentiles.

11.2 Excise Tax Increases from the Lifetime Incidence Perspective

The current policy debate surrounding excise taxes on gasoline, tobacco, and alcohol provides an excellent illustration of the differences between annual and lifetime incidence measures. Table 11.2 presents the share of gasoline, tobacco, and alcohol expenditures in annual income (excluding in-kind transfers) and in annual consumption for households at various points in the income and expenditure distribution. Provided households adhere to the basic tenets of the lifecycle-permanent income hypothesis by setting consumption in relation to lifetime resources rather than

Table 11.2 Income and expenditure shares of gasoline, alcohol, and tobacco spending, 1984

Quintile	Gasoline	Alcohol	Tobacco
Income: percent of income before taxes			
1	15.0	4.6	4.6
2	7.0	1.9	2.0
3	5.3	1.4	1.3
4	4.3	1.1	0.9
5	2.8	0.9	0.5
Expenditure: percent of total current expenditures			
1	6.0	1.6	2.2
2	7.2	1.7	2.0
3	7.1	1.8	1.7
4	6.6	1.6	1.3
5	3.9	1.2	0.7

Source: US Department of Labor, BLS *Consumer Expenditure Survey Results from 1984* (1986), and unpublished tabulations. In each case quintile 1 refers to the lowest quintile. Current expenditures equal total expenditures less pension, retirement, and Social Security contributions.

current income, total expenditure provides a better measure of long-term household well-being than annual income.

I follow Pechman in assuming that excise taxes are fully reflected in consumer prices. The distribution of expenditures across households therefore determines the incidence of the tax. The burden on low-income or low-consumption households would be reduced if the analysis recognized the indexed nature of most transfer payments, which provide increased income in response to tax-induced price changes.

The results in the upper panel of table 11.2 show expenditures on each good as a share of pre-tax income and support the general view that excise taxes are regressive. Low-income households spend a much higher fraction of their income on these commodities than do higher-income households. For both gasoline (col. 1) and alcohol (col. 3), expenditures as a fraction of income are more than five times larger for the bottom quintile of the income distribution than for the top quintile. Tobacco tax burdens are even more uneven: the income shares differ by a factor of ten. These results reflect a ratio of total expenditures to income excluding in-kind benefits of well above unity for low-income households.

The statistics are based on quintile averages and conceal important horizontal inequities in the consumption of these goods. Sammartino (1987) reports that only 52 percent of families with before-tax incomes of less than $5,000 in 1985 purchased gasoline, compared with more than 99 percent of families with incomes of more than $20,000. Gasoline expenditures are therefore well above 15 percent of annual income for some low-income households. Similar issues arise on a smaller scale for alcohol and tobacco purchases.

A completely different pattern emerges when total current expenditures, rather than annual income, are used to calibrate the incidence of taxes on these commodities. These data are reported in the lower panel of table 11.2, with households again divided into quintiles but now using total expenditures as a basis for classification. For the lowest consumption quintile, gasoline and motor oil expenditures account for 6.0 percent of total outlays, slightly less than the shares for the three middle quintiles of the consumption distribution. For the highest quintile, the expenditure share for gasoline declines to 3.9 percent. The divergence across different parts of the consumption distribution is much smaller, however, than the variation in spending as a share of income. Alcohol expenditures display a similar compression, varying only between 1.2 and 1.8 percent of total spending across different groups. For tobacco, however, even using the consumption metric, the excise tax appears regressive: the expenditure share of the least-well-off quintile is three times that for the highest expenditure class.[4]

The striking difference between the distributional burdens that emerge from incidence calculations in the annual and lifetime frameworks could be due either to lifecycle variation in the consumption-to-income ratio (C/Y), or to short-run fluctuations in annual income, table 11.3 addresses the relative importance of these two factors by presenting the consumption-income ratio and the fraction of expenditures devoted to different taxed commodities by age group. While there is some evidence of a lifecycle pattern in consumption-to-income ratios, with young households exhibiting higher average propensities to consume than older ones, the variation in C/Y across age groups is much smaller than the variation across income groups in table 11.2. The share of total expenditures devoted to gasoline, alcohol, and tobacco is also quite stable across age groups. Although the elderly consume less of each of these commodities than do younger households, there is very little variation in the budget shares of these goods for households headed by individuals between the ages of 25 and 74.

The small variation in expenditure shares across age groups is

Table 11.3 Lifecycle patterns in the expenditure shares

Age Group	Percentage of current expenditures for			Current expenditures/ pre-tax income
	(1)	(2)	(3)	
<25	6.2	1.2	3.0	.99
25–34	5.1	1.1	1.7	.80
35–44	5.0	1.1	1.3	.79
45–54	5.7	1.2	1.3	.81
55–64	5.4	1.2	1.3	.74
65–74	5.0	1.1	1.1	.91
75+	3.2	0.6	0.8	.89

Note: Col. 1 denotes Gasoline and Motor Oil; Col. 2 is Alcoholic Beverages; Col. 3 is Tobacco.
Source: US Department of Labor (1986, table 3).

matched by limited dispersion within age groups.[5] Table 11.4 disaggregates households by age and consumption quintile and shows little variation in the age-specific shares of expenditure devoted to gasoline, alcohol, and tobacco. This is particularly evident for the lowest four-fifths of the expenditure distribution. Tobacco expenditures are an exception to this rule: even using the consumption basis for incidence, tobacco taxes appear to be regressive since the expenditure share is approximately three times as large for those in the bottom consumption quintile as for those in the top quintile. In every age group, the share of expenditures devoted to tobacco declines with household status. The effects are weaker for both alcohol and gasoline. For alcohol, especially among younger age groups, the least-well-off may devote twice as much of their total budget to alcohol as their better-off counterparts. The expenditure share for gasoline varies less. For each of these commodities, however, the variation in expenditure shares is smaller than the variation in expenditure to income ratios suggested by table 11.2. The results may also understate the burden on top-quintile consumers, since they tend to be making transitory purchases of durable goods, and therefore overstate regressivity.

The differences between incidence calculated from income and from consumption have implications beyond the analysis of excise taxation. A recurrent issue in the tax base debate is the regressivity of consumption taxes, due to the higher expenditure-income ratio at low-income levels.

Table 11.4 Age-specific expenditure shares, 1985[a]

| | Expenditure quintile | | | | |
Age group	1	2	3	4	5
Expenditure share for gasoline					
<25	7.1	7.1	7.0	6.4	2.3
25–34	8.2	7.0	7.3	6.0	3.3
35–44	6.3	8.0	6.5	6.8	4.0
45–54	4.8	8.9	8.3	7.4	4.3
55–64	7.0	8.3	6.7	5.5	4.0
>65	5.2	4.8	5.8	5.2	2.6
Expenditure share for alcohol					
<25	3.9	3.4	2.2	2.9	0.8
25–34	2.0	2.1	2.3	1.9	1.4
35–44	1.6	2.0	1.6	1.5	1.0
45–54	1.2	1.0	1.3	1.6	1.2
55–64	1.2	1.6	1.7	1.7	1.0
>65	0.4	1.2	1.2	1.2	1.0
Expenditure share for tobacco					
<25	1.6	1.3	1.9	1.1	0.5
25–34	2.2	2.3	1.7	1.1	0.6
35–44	4.2	2.0	1.7	1.4	0.7
45–54	4.3	2.8	2.1	1.6	0.8
55–64	2.9	2.2	1.8	1.6	0.5
>65	1.2	1.5	1.1	0.9	0.3

[a] Shown in percent.

Source: Author's calculations based on 1985 Consumer Expenditure Interview Survey, first-quarter data. Expenditures are defined as in CES and include some contributions to retirement programs. In each case quintile 1 denotes the lowest-expenditure quintile.

Classifying households by consumption rather than income, however, eliminates the apparent disparity. The ratio of expenditures to before-tax, in-kind exclusive income for households in the lowest-income quintile in the 1984 Consumer Expenditure Survey is 3.17. For households in higher quintiles, the ratios are 1.3, 0.98, 0.84, and 0.69, respectively. When classified by consumption quintiles, however, the ratios are quite different. From lowest-consumption quintile to highest, they are 0.79, 0.82, 0.80, 0.82, and 1.05. These calculations suggest the need for further study on the lifetime burden of consumption taxes.

11.3   New Directions for Incidence Research

Failure to distinguish between lifetime and annual incidence overstates the degree of inequality in tax burdens between groups, suggesting that progressive taxes are more progressive and regressive taxes more regressive than a lifetime analysis would suggest. The illustrative calculations presented here suggest that for studying the incidence of excise taxes, these biases may be substantial.

These findings suggest three research directions. First, stochastic models of the income distribution need to be linked with more traditional incidence approaches. The rapid advance in computing power in the last decade makes it possible to envision general equilibrium models of tax incidence where random elements of household income are explicitly simulated. Second, further research is needed on the inequality of lifetime and annual incomes. The increasing availability of longitudinal data, such as the fourteen-year match of the *Panel Survey of Income Dynamics* and the recently released IRS taxpayer panel, facilitates such work. Finally, the lifetime incidence approach with its emphasis on mobility draws attention to classes of households with a conspicuous *lack* of mobility. Retired individuals, for example, may not experience the same variation in income flows that younger households face. For the elderly, the burden of some excise taxes may therefore be greater than for other households with similar consumption, although Kasten and Sammartino (1988) suggest this is not the case for the gasoline, tobacco, and alcohol excises. Additional research is needed to identify low-mobility groups and measure their tax burdens.

Notes

1   The general equilibrium incidence model of Charles Ballard et al. (1985), as well the tax burden calculations of Joseph Pechman (1985), allocate households to categories based on annual income. The study that does consider lifetime issues (James Davies et al., 1984), finds that the choice of time interval has important effects on the estimated distribution of Canadian taxes. Theoretical treatments of lifetime tax issues include David Levhari and Eytan Sheshinski (1972) and E. John Driffill and Harvey Rosen (1983).

2   Two recent papers (Frank Sammartino, 1988, and Richard Kasten and Sammartino, 1988) recognize the potential importance of this annual income bias. They compare expenditures on particular commodities to total expenditures, and examine the incidence of taxes on a number of products not discussed in this paper.

3   Comparisons of the inequality in lifetime and annual earnings hinge critically on the assumed persistence of the component of individual earnings that

cannot be explained by observable individual attributes. Roger Gordon (1984) finds very little difference between the interpersonal distribution of human wealth and annual earnings, presumably because of differences in his stochastic specification. A detailed discussion of individual wage histories and their random components is found in the Report of the Consultant Panel on Social Security . . . (1976), which reports an autocorrelation coefficient of approximately .50 for an individual's wages at the beginning and end of a decade, after correcting for economywide growth trends.

4   Edgar Browning and William Johnson (1979) also note that expenditure shares on these goods do not vary a great deal, but they stratify households by income rather than expenditures in making these comparisons.

5   Stratifying within age groups based on before-tax income yields the same pattern of high C/Y ratios at low incomes and low values at high incomes, that was observed in the entire population.

References

Ballard, Charles, et al., *A General Equilibrium Model for Tax Policy Evaluation*, Chicago: University of Chicago Press, 1985.

Browning, Edgar K. and Johnson, William R., *The Distribution of the Tax Burden*, Washington: American Enterprise Institute, 1979.

Bound, John and Krueger, Alan, "The Extent of Measurement Error in Longitudinal Earnings Data: Do Two Wrongs Make a Right?," working paper, Princeton University Industrial Relations Section, 1988.

Davies, James, St. Hilaire, France and Whalley, John. "Some Calculations of Lifetime Tax Incidence," *American Economic Review*, September 1984, *74*, 633–49.

Driffill, E. John and Rosen, Harvey S., "Taxation and Excess Burden: A Life Cycle Perspective," *International Economic Review*, October 1983, *24*, 671–83.

Duncan, Greg J. and Hill, Daniel, "An Investigation of the Extent and Consequences of Measurement Error in Labor Economic Survey Data," *Journal of Labor Economics*, October 1985, *3*, 508–32.

—— and Morgan, James N., "Persistence and Change in Economic Status and the Role of Changing Family Composition," in Martha S. Hill et al., eds., *Five Thousand American Families: Patterns of Economic Progress*, Vol. IX, Ann Arbor: ISR, University of Michigan, 1981.

Gordon, Roger H., *Differences in Earnings and Ability*, New York: Garland, 1984.

Hanna, Frank A., "The Accounting Period and the Distribution of Income," in his (et al.), eds., *Analysis of Wisconsin Income*, NBER *Studies in Income and Wealth*, No. 9, University Microfilms, 1948.

Hill, Martha S., "Some Dynamic Aspects of Poverty," in her (et al.), eds., *Five Thousand American Families: Patterns of Economic Progress*, Vol. IX, Ann Arbor: ISR, University of Michigan, 1981.

Kasten, Richard, and Sammartino, Frank, "The Distribution of Possible Federal

Excise Tax Increases," unpublished paper, Congressional Budget Office, 1988.

Levhari, David and Sheshinski, Eytan, "Lifetime Excess Burden of a Tax," *Journal of Political Economy*, February 1972, *80*, 139–47.

Lillard, Lee A., "Inequality: Earnings vs. Human Wealth." *American Economic Review*, March 1977, *67*, 42–53.

Pechman, Joseph A., *Who Paid the Taxes, 1966–1985*, Washington: Brookings Institution, 1985.

Sammartino, Frank, "The Distributional Effects of an Increase in Selected Federal Excise Taxes," Working Paper, Congressional Budget Office Staff. January 1987.

Taubman, Paul J., "Schooling, Ability, Nonpecuniary Rewards, Socioeconomic Background, and the Lifetime Distribution of Earnings," in F. Thomas Juster, ed., *The Distribution of Economic Well-Being*, Cambridge: Ballinger Publishing, 1977, 419–500.

Consultant Panel on Social Security, *Report of the Consultant Panel on Social Security to the Congressional Research Service*, Washington: USGPO, August 1976.

US Department of Labor, Bureau of Labor Statistics, *Consumer Expenditure Survey Results from 1984*, Washington: USGPO, June 1986.

Introduction to Chapter 12

The typical state and local sales tax base in the US includes a broad range of consumer purchases at retail and business purchases of many types of inputs, or intermediate goods and services. Generally, only a limited range of consumer and business services are subject to tax. There are frequent proposals in the states to increase sales tax revenue by expanding the tax base to include more services, instead of increasing the tax rate on the existing tax base.

This article is an examination of the effect on the incidence of a state sales tax of a major expansion in the coverage of services, especially services to businesses. The article develops a method of analyzing empirically that part of the sales tax that is collected from sales to businesses rather than final consumers (it is estimated that, in the average state, about 40 percent of sales tax revenue comes from business purchases). Then the authors apply that method to Florida's 1987 experiment, in which a 5 percent sales tax was imposed on many types of services. They conclude that the tax on services was marginally less regressive than the alternative, an increase in the rate of the existing sales tax.

12

The Distributional Effects of a
Sales Tax on Services**

John J. Siegfried* and Paul A. Smith*

Abstract

The short-lived 1987 sales tax on services in Florida is used to illustrate the distributional effect of a sales tax levied on both intermediate and final consumption products. The ultimate burden of a sales tax on intermediate products is traced to final consumers through input-output relationships. The main effect of accounting for the burden of taxes levied on intermediate products is to move the overall distributional effect of a sales tax more toward proportionality, because the wide variety of uses for most intermediate products spreads the impact of a tax on them throughout the economy so that it affects consumers with different incomes proportionately. Florida's temporary 5 percent sales tax on services was slightly less regressive than the 1 percent boost in the general sales tax on commodities that replaced it.

12.1 Introduction

Since Mississippi enacted the first general state sales tax in the US in 1932, sales taxes have become a staple of state and local finance, growing from 11 percent of revenues raised by state and local governments in 1932 to 26 percent by fiscal year 1987–88.[1] Today, 45 of the 50 states levy a general sales tax, the exceptions being Alaska, Delaware, Montana, New Hampshire, and Oregon (Commerce Clearing House, 1990).

Unrelenting fiscal pressure leads states periodically to seek additional

* Vanderbilt University, Nashville, TN 37235.

** David Sjoquist, Malcolm Getz, Eleanor Craig, William Fox, John Due, the editor, and 3 anonymous referees provided helpful comments on an earlier version of this paper. Roger Blair helped us obtain the relevant portions of the Florida tax code. James Francis of the Tax Research division of the Florida Department of Revenue provided essential unpublished data. Alison Roberts contributed research assistance.

tax revenues. Four considerations usually dominate political debates about how to augment revenues: (1) the effectiveness of alternative revenue sources, i.e. how much money can be raised; (2) compliance, or whether tax avoidance or tax evasion will prevent the state from collecting the potential revenue; (3) the effect on attracting new business to the state; and (4) who will ultimately bear the burden of the additional taxes. A fifth consideration, the effect of tax increases on incentives (and economic efficiency), is also sometimes important, although perhaps less so for broad-based taxes that do not dramatically alter *relative* prices.

Because of its revenue potential, the sales tax has been an appealing vehicle to relieve fiscal pressure. As its use has spread, however, opportunities to expand sales tax revenues have diminished. Sales tax revenues can be increased by either increasing the tax rate or expanding the tax base, i.e., expanding the transactions to which the tax rate applies. In October 1989, 27 states had sales tax rates of at least five percent; 11 states had a basic sales tax rate of six percent or more, with Connecticut levying the highest general sales tax rate of eight percent (Advisory Commission on Intergovernmental Relations, 1990). Furthermore, local governments also sometimes levy a general sales tax. People in some US cities now face sales tax rates approaching ten percent Residents of Chicago, Huntsville and Mobile, Alabama, and New Orleans all pay at least a nine percent general sales tax.[2] Taxpayer resistance to sales tax rates approaching double digits encourages fiscal authorities to seek means other than rate hikes to generate additional revenues from the sales tax. This has led a number of states to propose, and some to enact, legislation expanding the tax base to which the sales tax rate applies (in effect, to reduce exemptions from the tax base).

There are three obvious options for expanding the most common tax base, which consists of retail sales of non-essential consumer goods (Due and Mikesell, 1983). First, the base might be broadened to include *essential* consumer goods. Food for home consumption, for example, is included in the sales tax base of 19 of the 45 states with a general sales tax (Advisory Commission on Intergovernmental Relations, 1990). Second, the base might be expanded to include consumer *services* (both essential and/or nonessential), e.g., cable television, rental services, and lawn care services, as was done in the states of Minnesota and Texas in 1987 (Boucher, 1988) and as Florida attempted in 1987. Third, the base might be expanded to include *intermediate* goods and/or services transactions, as the states of New Mexico, Hawaii, and South Dakota have done for a long time (W. Hellerstein, 1988; Boucher, 1988) and as the state of Florida did for services from July 1 to December 31, 1987 (W. Hellerstein, 1988; Boucher, 1988).[3]

The short-lived 1987 ad valorem tax on selected service transactions in Florida expanded the tax base in two directions. First, it brought a substantial share of the service sector within the purview of Florida's general sales tax. Second, it covered both services sold to consumers for final personal consumption and services sold to businesses for intermediate use. The Florida legislature was concerned not only with the revenue potential of a sales tax expanded to cover services, but also with the incidence and fairness of the tax (W. Hellerstein, 1988). Providing accurate distributional information on which to judge fairness is our focus in this article.

12.2   Measuring Distributional Effects of a Sales Tax

The distributional effects of ad valorem sales and excise taxes are commonly determined by comparing the relative effect of a tax increase on families of different income levels. Sometimes family consumption expenditure or a variant thereof is used as the basis of comparison (Davies, 1970; Ghazanfar, 1975), but income is the most commonly used measure of "ability to pay." If the tax rise causes a greater percentage increase in total expenditures relative to income for a low income family than for a high income family, the tax increase is regressive. If, on the other hand, the tax rise causes a greater percentage increase in total expenditures relative to income for a high income family than for a low income family, the tax increase is progressive.

Such distribution studies[4] are frequently based on data from the *Consumer Expenditure Survey* (CES), which is undertaken periodically by the Bureau of Labor Statistics to update the expenditure weights in the consumer price index. This detailed study of the purchases of about 20,000 US households enables the analyst to determine who – rich or poor consumers – purchases different goods and services. First, the CES data are reorganized on the basis of product. Then, the relative share of each product in total income is computed for consumers of different income levels. This forms the basis for deducing who bears a greater relative burden of the tax.

Studies of the burden of a sales tax conducted as we describe above are entirely appropriate for a tax that applies only to final sales made to ultimate consumers (i.e., a consumption tax). The burden of a state sales tax which applies only to the *retail* sale of commodities to *final consumers* can be captured directly from *Consumer Expenditure Survey* data. The burden of a sales tax on goods or services that are used in further production or for resale, however, is entirely overlooked by this methodology. If a sales tax is applied to *all* sales of some commodities or services, as was attempted in the 1987 Florida service tax, the distributional effect will depend not only on the income and expenditure pattern of those consumers who purchase the commodity or service for final personal consumption, *but also* on the pattern of intermediate uses to which the commodity or service is put and the income and expenditure pattern of the consumers who ultimately purchase the value of the intermediate products (and the sales tax thereon) embedded in other final consumption goods and services.

Early attempts to account for the distributional impact of the sales tax burden imposed through coverage of business transactions included the crude efforts of Daniel Morgan (1964) and Jeffrey Schaefer (1969), and a study by Daicoff and Glass (1979). Morgan used arbitrary pass-through proportions that varied among industries. No reasons for the various proportions were given and the industries specified were quite broad. Schaefer reports that he made "rough calculations" with "various assumptions about the incidence of sales taxes on transactions between firms and with different weights attributed to the tax yield from the business sector" (Schaefer, 1969, p. 517). He concluded that estimates of the burden of sales taxes would not be affected much by the incorporation of affected business transactions in the analysis. Daicoff and Glass (1979) apparently relied on the assumption that the ultimate burden of a tax on business transactions is divided between consumers of the businesses' products and other sources of income. The result of their assumption was that sales and use taxes were regressive throughout the income scale and members of the lowest income groups actually faced a sales and use tax rate in excess of the statutory rate, partly because of the burden shifted to them from businesses.

More recently, Raymond Ring (1989) noted that the burden of a sales tax depends on the degree to which it falls on intermediate goods or services. "If stockholders or employees bear the business share of a 'consumption tax,' the incidence is much different from that of a true consumption tax. Even if the business share is shifted onto consumers its incidence pattern differs from that of the share levied directly onto consumers" (Ring, 1989, p. 167). Ring estimated that about 40 percent of state sales and use taxes fall on intermediate goods and services. He claims that "the usual approach of treating the sales tax as exclusively a tax on consumers when allocating the tax burden among income classes will . . . overstate regressivity for states with relatively low consumers' share" (Ring, 1989, pp. 176–7).

In perhaps the most comprehensive attempt to evaluate the distributional pattern of the burden of state and local taxes, Donald Phares (1980, table A-1) found that the general sales tax was consistently regressive in 1976, taking a progressively smaller proportion of a family's income as income rises. His conclusion applies equally well to Florida (Phares, 1980, table A-1). Phares based his general sales tax burden estimates on the expenditures and income levels of consumers who purchased the taxable goods and services directly, ignoring the ultimate burden of taxes levied on goods and services which were purchased for use in subsequent production. Phares recognized the problem, however, when he analyzed the distributional effect of the specific tax on motor fuels. For the gasoline tax he assumed that one-third of the tax falls on businesses, which pass it on fully to their customers. Thus Phares allocated two-thirds of the gasoline tax on the basis of the pattern of gasoline purchases by consumers, and one-third of the gasoline tax on the basis of consumption in general (implicitly assuming that the ultimate burden of a tax on gasoline consumed for intermediate use is proportional to the value of final consumer goods and services, whether or not the intermediate goods actually require gasoline as an input).

In earlier research one of the present authors and two collaborators made sufficient estimates of distributional effects to assess the combined direct *and indirect* (i.e., through intermediate goods and services purchases) effects of an increase in the sales tax or an expansion of sales tax coverage as is represented by the recent Florida experience (McElroy, Siegfried and Sweeney, 1982). They evaluated the impact of a price change (i.e., tax change) on all goods and services, not just those purchased directly for personal consumption. This was accomplished by tracing the impact of a price change for intermediate goods (such as steel and glass) to the consumers who purchased the products (such as automobiles) which, in turn, employed those intermediate goods in production. To do this they used input-output analysis, tracing a price increase of an intermediate good or service through the sectoral interrelationships in the economy until it eventually could be attributed to an ultimate user of a final consumption product or service. With this procedure they were able, for example, to estimate the combined direct and indirect effects of a price or tax increase on the ultimate consumers of the value of such intermediate products as pulp, gypsum, bearings, and surgical instruments, as well as the direct effects of a price or tax increase on the ultimate consumers of direct consumption products such as bread, hats, beer, toys, and cigars.

Because the *Detailed Input-Output Structure of the US Economy* is assembled at a broader level of aggregation than the very detailed *Consumer Expenditure Survey*, such a distributional analysis must be done at the more aggregated level of product and service definition, approximately the "$3\frac{1}{2}$ digit S.I.C." level of aggregation that is used in the Department of Commerce's input-output tables. The input-output tables measure only current account transactions among industries (because input-output analysis does not measure the quantity of capital goods consumed in production). Consequently, the measures reported should be considered indicative of short-run, rather than long-run economic adjustments, since they do not reflect changes in plant and equipment.

Tracing the implications of a price change through the input-output structure of the economy requires a behavioral assumption about the structure and conduct of markets in which the various goods and services are bought and sold. For example, it is well known that an increase in marginal cost (e.g., from an ad valorem tax hike) will in the long run lead to a greater price increase in a constant cost competitive industry than in a comparable monopolized industry. Following tradition, we assumed that a one dollar increase in the average cost of production results in a one dollar increase in the price of a product. In other words, we adopted the assumption of full pass-through of a tax increase.[5] To the extent that some or all of a sales tax burden falls on the Ricardian rents that would have accrued to owners of businesses in competitive industries facing less than perfectly inelastic demand, or to the extent that part of the burden of a sales tax falls on owners of firms that enjoy some degree of market power, our assumption of complete pass-through of a sales tax to ultimate consumers will overstate the tax burden on those consumers. Some of the burden would have fallen on certain business owners. How that affects the distribution of the tax burden depends on how the incomes of those ownership claimants compare with the incomes of the ultimate consumers of the products made with the intermediate goods.[6] If business ownership claimants have, on average, higher incomes than the consumers of most services, if some of the burden of a sales tax on services lodges with them, and if the proportion falling on ownership claimants does not vary with the income level of final consumers, the actual distribution of the burden will be more progressive than we report. To the extent that ownership claimants bear a decreasing share of the burden of the tax as the income levels of final consumers rise (i.e., relatively more of the tax is passed on to the richer consumers) the actual distributional effect of the tax will be even more progressive.

The extent to which it is necessary to integrate input-output analysis with standard consumer expenditure analysis to evaluate the distributional effects of an ad valorem tax depends on the degree to which the tax affects intermediate use rather than personal consumption. For services, the distinction between intermediate use and personal consumption is frequently ambiguous, because by their very nature services are difficult to hold in inventory, ship, and resell independently of the original producer. How, for example, could one "retail" gall bladder surgery apart from the direct production of the service? Commodities, while often suffering from similar problems, are frequently provided through specialized distribution outlets to purchasers who use them as intermediate goods. Thus a sales tax on the personal consumption of commodities can be administered by enlisting the collection services of retail stores and prohibiting (however effectively) "wholesalers" from selling to anyone other than firms using the products as intermediate goods. Services cannot be segregated as easily into those purchased for intermediate production and those purchased for final personal consumption on the basis of the function of distribution outlets. While there remain serious problems in distinguishing intermediate from final consumption goods, and undoubtedly the sales of many final consumption goods are disguised as sales of intermediate goods to avoid taxation, the situation seems even worse for services.

For this reason, as well as the temptation of higher revenues, it is more likely that service taxes will be imposed on *all* sales – those for both intermediate use and final personal consumption. Some of the service industries that hold the greatest revenue potential (e.g., railroad and motor freight, utilities, communication, banking, insurance, real estate, advertising, business services, and professional services) produce most of their output for intermediate use. Thus, in order to enhance state revenues, a legislature may wish to tax intermediate use of the service even if it recognizes some of the inherent hazards of such a policy.[7] If there are exemptions from a service tax they are likely to be based on perceived "need" rather than stage of production, for example medical services, basic transportation, and day care services. Therefore, an accurate estimate of the distribution of the burden of a sales tax on services will often require the more sophisticated analysis employing input-output relationships described above.

The extent to which the more sophisticated input-output analysis is required to assemble reliable distributional information varies directly with the relative importance of intermediate use of each service subject to the tax. Table 12.1, based on data from the *Detailed Input-Output Structure of the US Economy: 1972,* reports the fraction of total industry output that is purchased for intermediate use in the transportation, utilities, finance, real estate, and services sectors. Thus, for example, one can see that none of the output of the beauty and barber shop industry goes to intermediate use, but all of insurance agents' (no one hires an insurance agent without buying insurance since such agents are "hired" only through the payment of commissions when insurance is actually purchased) and almost all advertising output is purchased for intermediate use.

Table 12.1 Intermediate use and personal consumption[a] of service industry production, US, 1972–3

Input output code	Name	Intermediate use ($ millions)	Personal consumption ($ millions)	Percentage that is intermediate
6501	Railroads	10,379.6	2,485.9	81
6502	Local transportation	2,388.3	4,157.9	36
6503	Motor freight	20,174.0	6,675.1	75
6504	Water transportation	4,119.9	1,027.8	80
6505	Air transportation	6,495.6	5,805.9	53
6506	Pipe lines	1,243.5	289.7	81
6507	Transport services	802.0	195.6	80
6600	Communication not broadcasting	13,208.1	12,878.7	51
6700	Broadcasting	4.2	0.0	100
6801	Electric services	17,120.3	12,220.2	58
6802	Gas production/distribution	13,821.5	6,555.0	68
6803	Water supply and sanitation	3,034.8	2,801.4	52
6901	Wholesale trade	48,396.6	38,162.8	56
6902	Retail trade	8,511.5	102,157.9	08
7001	Banking	10,652.1	12,373.9	46
7002	Credit agencies	2,072.0	3,604.5	37
7003	Security and commodity brokers	4,038.9	3,974.9	50
7004	Insurance carriers	8,262.8	19,081.5	30
7005	Insurance agents	10,304.1	0.0	100
7101	Owner occupied dwelling	0.0	76,687.8	00
7102	Real estate	57,837.3	31,977.3	64
7201	Hotels	2,949.7	4,699.2	39
7202	Personal and repair services	5,459.9	11,362.4	32
7203	Beauty and barber shops	0.0	4,309.8	00
7301	Miscellaneous business services	30,210.1	1,900.9	94
7302	Advertising	22,926.5	123.3	99
7303	Miscellaneous professional services	19,207.5	5,350.1	78
7400	Eating/drinking establishments	12,643.0	37,495.9	25
7500	Auto repair shops	10,289.8	13,779.7	43
7601	Motion pictures	2,279.1	1,671.5	58
7602	Amusements	1,811.6	6,997.5	21
7701	Doctors and dentists	147.5	21,675.7	01
7702	Hospitals	1.5	19,744.6	00
7703	Other medical	1,218.9	4,897.9	20
7704	Educational services	462.2	10,078.0	04
7705	Non-profit organizations	2,499.0	12,369.6	17
7706	Job training	225.0	386.3	37
7707	Child day care	0.0	660.1	00
7708	Residential care	0.0	574.8	00

[a] Total Intermediate Use and Personal Consumption differ from Total Final Demand due to accounts for inventory adjustment, domestic fixed investment, imports and exports, and various purchases by units of government.

Source: United States Department of Commerce, Bureau of Economic Analysis, *The Detailed Input-Output Structure of the US Economy: 1972*, table 1 – The Use of Commodities by Industry, pp. 9–178.

If the distribution of the burden of a tax on intermediate use services is similar to the distribution of the burden of a tax only on services that constitute direct personal consumption, then the true distributional effects of a tax on services purchased for both intermediate use and final consumption will not differ from estimates based only on services purchased for personal consumption. Or, if relatively few covered services are used for further production the true distribution of the burden of a service tax will not differ much from estimates based only on services purchases for personal consumption. The significance of this latter condition can be as sessed on the basis of information reported in table 12.1. The estimated distribution of the burden of sales taxed on the imputed rental value of owner-occupied housing, on beauty and barber shop services, on physician, hospital and dental services, on schools and colleges, on day care services, and on residential care services would be fairly accurate if based exclusively on personal consumption patterns because so little of those categories goes to intermediate use. On the other hand, accurate estimates of the distribution of the burden of sales taxes on railroad, truck, and water transportation services, on most business services, and on advertising would require an analysis of the income levels of the ultimate consumers of such intermediate use services.

The distribution of the burden of a sales tax applied to both intermediate use and final consumption of various services is shown in table 12.2. Full pass-through of the tax at all intermediate production stages is assumed. The table reports for an "average family" at each of six relative income levels the additional fraction of the family's income that would be paid in taxes if a ten percent sales tax were levied on *all* sales of the service. The estimates are based on the 1972–3 *Consumer Expenditure Survey* of the Bureau of Labor Statistics and the 1972 *Input-Output Tables* of the US, and apply to the nation as a whole. These were the latest data available when the precursory study was initiated. The income levels reported are for the 5, 20, 40, 60, 80, and 95 percentiles of the US distribution of income. Consumption patterns for each percentile were established on the basis of the actual purchases of CES sample families in a class including all families with incomes ten percent above or ten percent below the class level. For example, the consumption pattern for all families from the twentieth percentile income level was based on the actual purchases of the eighteenth through twenty-second percentile.

It is apparent from table 12.2 that the distributional effect of a tax on services used for both intermediate and final consumption purposes depends on which services are subject to taxation. Sales taxes on certain

Table 12.2 Burden at six representative income levels of a ten percent sales tax levied on both intermediate use and personal consumption of various services in the US, 1972

Input output code	Industry description	Percentage of income paid as tax for consumer units at stated percentile of income distribution[a]					
		5th percentile	20th percentile	40th percentile	60th percentile	80th percentile	95th percentile
6501	Railroads	0.0576	0.0497	0.0483	0.0453	0.0438	0.0385
6502	Local transportation	0.0378	0.0223	0.0184	0.0155	0.0156	0.0182
6503	Motor freight	0.1449	0.1188	0.1074	0.1004	0.0972	0.0842
6504	Water transportation	0.0270	0.0245	0.0218	0.0205	0.0198	0.0151
6505	Air transportation	0.0972	0.0706	0.0707	0.0645	0.0642	0.0837
6506	Pipe lines	0.0198	0.0180	0.0163	0.0149	0.0132	0.0099
6507	Transport services	0.0045	0.0036	0.0041	0.0037	0.0036	0.0036
6600	Communication not broadcasting	0.4977	0.3290	0.2754	0.2381	0.2076	0.1747
6700	Broadcasting	0.0000	0.0000	0.0000	0.0000	0.0000	0.0000
6801	Electric services	0.4995	0.3283	0.2686	0.2412	0.2124	0.1711
6802	Gas production/distribution	0.5085	0.2909	0.2054	0.1717	0.1440	0.1191
6803	Water supply and sanitation	0.1593	0.0965	0.0775	0.0701	0.0690	0.0572
6901	Wholesale trade	0.6120	0.5213	0.4821	0.4390	0.4080	0.3380
6902	Retail trade	0.8721	0.7618	0.7120	0.6603	0.6312	0.5517
7001	Banking	0.2790	0.2678	0.3556	0.4191	0.3810	0.3442
7002	Credit agencies	0.0567	0.0547	0.0755	0.0905	0.0822	0.0749
7003	Security and commodity brokers	0.0441	0.0382	0.0428	0.0453	0.0420	0.0390
7004	Insurance carriers	0.9135	0.7819	0.8004	0.7868	0.7680	0.7587
7005	Insurance agents	0.3375	0.2887	0.2958	0.2902	0.2832	0.2798

Table 12.2 *Continued*

Code	Description						
7102	Real estate (7101 plus 7102)	2.7981	2.2630	2.2168	1.8172	1.7628	1.2620
7201	Hotels	0.0234	0.0202	0.0218	0.0229	0.0306	0.0395
7202	Personal and repair services	0.1008	0.1123	0.0979	0.0930	0.0810	0.0707
7203	Beauty and barber shops	0.0378	0.0367	0.0299	0.0273	0.0234	0.0192
7301	Misc. business services	0.3519	0.2254	0.2128	0.2170	0.2076	0.2137
7302	Advertising	0.1845	0.1490	0.1414	0.1314	0.1248	0.1097
7303	Misc. professional services	0.1152	0.0936	0.0857	0.0806	0.0786	0.0697
7400	Eating/drinking establishments	0.1629	0.1404	0.1387	0.1345	0.1362	0.1378
7500	Auto repair shops	0.2178	0.2030	0.1986	0.1711	0.1614	0.1565
7601	Motion pictures	0.0108	0.0086	0.0082	0.0074	0.0078	0.0073
7602	Amusements	0.0819	0.1087	0.0789	0.0781	0.0846	0.0910
7701	Doctors and dentists	0.2268	0.1930	0.1720	0.1395	0.1362	0.1108
7702	Hospitals	0.1134	0.0655	0.0456	0.0304	0.0192	0.0140
7703	Other medical	0.0558	0.0425	0.0320	0.0260	0.0246	0.0182
7704	Educational services	0.0315	0.0468	0.0496	0.0589	0.0852	0.1234
7705	Non-profit organizations	0.3474	0.2110	0.1897	0.1835	0.1842	0.2116
7706	Job training	0.0009	0.0007	0.0007	0.0006	0.0006	0.0005
7707	Child day care	0.0000	0.0007	0.0014	0.0012	0.0006	0.0005
7708	Residential care	0.0072	0.0007	0.0020	0.0025	0.0018	0.0016

[a] The income levels for the 5, 20, 40, 60, 80, and 95 percentile for mid-1990, using the latest available data (for 1987) inflated by the GNP deflator to 1989 and inflated further by 6 percent from 1989 to 1990, are $4,660, $16,970, $29,470, $42,970, $62,120 and $101,320 respectively. If consumption patterns depend on relative rather than absolute income levels, these figures can be used to interpret the distribution of the burden of the tax in this table. The income levels for all except the fifth percentile are from US Bureau of the Census, Current Population Reports, Series P-60, No. 162, *Money Income of Households, Families, and Persons in the United States: 1987*, US Government Printing Office, Washington, D.C. 1989, table 12, p. 42. The fifth percentile income level is interpolated from data in table 2, p. 10 of the same volume. The GNP deflator is from *The Economic Report of the President*: February 1990, US Government Printing Office, Washington, D.C. 1989, table C-3, p. 298.

Source: Katherine Maddox McElroy, John J. Siegfried and George H. Sweeney, "The Incidence of Price Changes in the US Economy," *Review of Economics and Statistics*, Vol. 64, No. (May 1982), table 1, pp. 193–8.

services – for example, electric and gas utilities, and hospitals – are highly regressive. On the other hand, sales taxes on credit agencies, banking, hotels, and education services are progressive, the wealthy bearing a greater burden relative to their income than the poor.

Table 12.2 reveals that sales taxes on services sold largely for use in further production or for resale, e.g., railroad and motor freight transportation, wholesale trade, and advertising, are fairly close to proportional. This finding is analogous to the distributional effect of a tax on *commodities* used primarily in further production. Based on the same input-output methodology, for example, a sales tax on bearings, pulp, industrial chemicals or textiles is found to be almost proportional (McElroy, Siegfried and Sweeney, 1982, p. 199). The wide variety of uses for most intermediate goods diffuses the impact of a tax on them throughout the economy so that the burden is spread proportionally on consumers at all income levels. There is no reason to expect a different outcome for services.[8]

While a tax on services can certainly affect the progressivity of a sales tax system, to the extent that services purchased for intermediate use are taxed, the main effect will be to move the overall tax structure more toward proportionality. This implies that the legislative debate about the fairness of a sales tax on services is likely to be hotter than would be warranted if the leveling effect on distribution caused by the diffusion of the tax's impact throughout the economy via intermediate purchases were better understood.

12.3   Distributional Effects of the 1987 Florida Sales Tax on Services

To illustrate our proposed methodology for assessing distributional effects, we apply it to the sales tax on services that existed in Florida from July 1 through December 31, 1987. Before 1987, Florida's sales tax applied primarily to commodities, but also included a few services such as commercial rentals and admissions. Business purchases of capital goods were historically included in the tax base if those capital goods were not deemed to have been purchased for resale (Rockwood, Fresen and Francis, 1988, p. 161). Thus a precedent for the taxation of intermediate goods (and services) existed in the Florida sales tax structure prior to 1987. The "sale for resale" exemption was also adopted for the service tax. Thus purchases of automobile body work by an automobile mechanic would be exempt from the Florida service tax while law firms' purchases of courier services would not (W. Hellerstein, 1988). A Coopers and Lybrand study concluded that about 80 percent of the Florida service tax would be paid directly by business (Rockwood, Fresen and Francis, 1988). In contrast, Ring (1989, p. 171) estimated that 57 percent of the traditional Florida sales tax falls on business.

On April 23, 1987 the Governor of Florida signed the bill that extended Florida's five percent general sales tax to selected services. This brought numerous business services into the tax base, including advertising, legal, accounting, and construction services. Exemptions were limited mainly to medical and health services, educational and social services, services that employees provide for their employers (so that it was not a direct tax on labor services), occasional and isolated services (e.g., babysitting and periodic lawn work), agricultural services, local passenger transportation, religious services, and those services purchased for direct resale. The tax on business services had high revenue potential.

Unfortunately for the politicians in Florida, not only is a tax on business inputs likely to raise substantial tax revenue, it is also likely to raise concerted and effective opposition. Unlike the diffuse incidence of a tax on personal consumption, a tax on business inputs has a very substantial direct impact on a small number of politically astute and sophisticated taxpayers. Thus national advertisers, supported by the media and Florida lawyers, realtors, and homebuilders, unleashed a vigorous attack on the tax. The strong opposition to the tax from businesses in Florida suggests that our assumption of complete pass-through of the tax may be inaccurate. At the least it indicates that some Florida service businesses compete with rivals from other states. Eventually, on December 11, 1987, the service tax was repealed and replaced by an additional one percent levy on the sales tax base that existed prior to July 1, 1987. Thus was created a natural experiment in assessing the distributional effect of a sales tax.

The alternative to the expansion of the five percent tax rate base to include selected services in Florida is clearly an additional one percent levy on the old (mostly commodities) sales tax base. The alternative was revealed when the Florida legislature turned to the old sales tax base when it became evident that the service tax would not survive. How does the relative burden on low income families compare to the burden on high income families for the two taxes?

To answer this question we estimated the distributional effects of the burden of Florida's six-month service sales tax. First, we carefully identified the specific services to which the tax applied. This was a tedious process, since the exemptions are numerous and complex, and rarely apply cleanly to the input-output industry definitions used in our analysis. We subdivided the input-output industries into their component four-digit S.I.C. codes and examined the coverage of the Florida service tax to each code in turn, eventually reaching a conclusion about the extent to which the services in each code were covered by the tax.[9] We then aggregated the four-digit industries into the input-output categories (reported in tables 12.1, 12.2 and 12.3) and determined the fraction of each input-output category covered by the tax. This technique implicitly assumes that those services within an input-output industry which are covered by the tax are purchased in a similar pattern (with respect to family income) as those services within the same input-output industry which are not covered by the tax. The fraction of each input-output service category covered by the sales tax is reported in table 12.3.

The next step was to assess the quantity of each service *ultimately* purchased by consumers of various income levels and relate the implied effect on their expenditures to their relative income levels. To accomplish this we used the estimated effect of a price (tax) change on the expenditures of families at the 5, 20, 40, 60, 80 and 95 percentile income levels in the US in 1972–73 (McElroy, Siegfried, and Sweeney, 1982), related expenditures to income and aggregated the effect over all of the taxed service categories. This procedure assumes that Floridians' consumption patterns are well represented by the national average and have not changed appreciably since 1972–3.[10] Alternatively, our exercise can be interpreted as applying the 1987 Florida service tax structure to the whole nation in 1972–3 and evaluating the distribution of the burden.

The results of our analysis are revealed in the last row of table 12.3, where the increase in the ratio of expenditure to income caused by a 5 percent increase in price of covered services (i.e., the 5 percent sales tax on services) is reported for consumer units at selected points in the income distribution. According to our estimates, the Florida sales tax on services was generally regressive, but not much so beyond the twentieth percentile of the income distribution, and it was even progressive between the sixtieth and eightieth percentiles. The impact on a family at the twentieth percentile was only four percent more than the impact on a family at the eightieth percentile, basically a proportional tax. Whether a proportional tax is "fair" or not, is, of course, a separate question.

The five percent tax on services added approximately one-half of one percent of gross income to the tax burden of most Florida families. A family at the 40th percentile in the income distribution, for example, could have expected to pay 0.45 of one percent more of its income to the State of Florida as a consequence of the sales tax on services.

The effect of the sales tax on services can be compared with a boost to the sales tax on commodities using a State of Florida analysis of the distribution of the burden of the Florida tax structure for 1975 (Florida House of Representatives, 1978). That analysis was also based on

Table 12.3 Distribution of the burden of Florida's five percent sales tax on services[a]

I/O Codes	Industry	Share of industry output taxed in Florida[b]	Percentage of income paid as tax for consumer units at stated percentile of income distribution[c]						
			5th percentile	20th percentile	40th percentile	60th percentile	80th percentile	95th percentile
2601	Newspapers	100.0	0.0126	0.0068	0.0054	0.0047	0.0042	0.0039
2602	Periodicals	100.0	0.0036	0.0032	0.0031	0.0028	0.0030	0.0031
2603	Book publishing & printing	100.0	0.0140	0.0144	0.0139	0.0140	0.0138	0.0143
2604	Miscellaneous publishing	100.0	0.0014	0.0011	0.0010	0.0009	0.0009	0.0010
2605	Commercial printing	4.3	0.0007	0.0006	0.0006	0.0006	0.0006	0.0005
2608	Typesetting & photoengraving	51.6	0.0016	0.0015	0.0014	0.0014	0.0014	0.0013
6504	Water transportation	5.3	0.0007	0.0006	0.0006	0.0005	0.0005	0.0004
6700	Radio & TV broadcasting	100.0	0.0000	0.0000	0.0000	0.0000	0.0000	0.0000
7001	Banking	3.4	0.0047	0.0046	0.0060	0.0071	0.0065	0.0059
7003	Security & commodity brokers	21.0	0.0046	0.0040	0.0045	0.0048	0.0044	0.0041
7202	Personal & repair services (no auto/barber)	12.2	0.0062	0.0069	0.0060	0.0057	0.0050	0.0043
7301	Miscellaneous business services	66.6	0.1171	0.0750	0.0708	0.0722	0.0691	0.0711
7302	Advertising	86.5	0.0798	0.0645	0.0612	0.0568	0.0540	0.0475
7303	Miscellaneous professional services	72.9	0.0420	0.0341	0.0312	0.0294	0.0286	0.0254
7500	Auto repair & services	5.6	0.0062	0.0057	0.0056	0.0048	0.0046	0.0044

Table 12.3 Continued

I/O Codes	Industry	Share of industry output taxed in Florida[b]	Percentage of income paid as tax for consumer units at stated percentile of income distribution[c]					
			5th percentile	20th percentile	40th percentile	60th percentile	80th percentile	95th percentile
7602	Amusement & recreation services	34.1	0.0140	0.0185	0.0135	0.0133	0.0144	0.0155
1201	Maintenance & repair-residential	83.3	0.2230	0.1727	0.1521	0.1508	0.1979	0.1648
1202	Maintenance & repair-non-residential	83.3	0.0746	0.0543	0.0481	0.0436	0.0412	0.0360
6505	Air transportation	81.2	0.0395	0.0286	0.0287	0.0262	0.0261	0.0340
7002	Credit agencies	2.4	0.0007	0.0007	0.0009	0.0011	0.0010	0.0009
Total effect (vertical sum)			0.6469	0.4979	0.4547	0.4408	0.4772	0.4385

[a] Based on national 1972–3 consumption patterns and 1972 interindustry relationships.

[b] Includes only those service industries covered by Florida's 1987 service tax.

[c] The income levels for the 5, 20, 40, 60, 80, and 95 percentiles for mid-1990, using the latest available data (for 1987) inflated by the GNP deflator to 1989 and inflated further by 6 percent from 1989 to 1990, are $4,660, $16,970, $29,470, $42,970, $62,120 and $101,320 respectively. If consumption patterns depend on relative rather than absolute income levels, these figures can be used to interpret the distribution of the burden of the tax in this table. The income levels for all except the fifth percentile are from US Bureau of the Census, Current Population Reports, Series P-60, No. 162, *Money Income of Households, Families, and Persons in the United States; 1987*, US Government Printing Office, Washington, D.C. 1989, table 12, p. 42. The fifth percentile income level is interpolated from data in table 2, p. 10 of the same volume. The GNP deflator is from *The Economic Report of the President*: February 1990, US Government Printing Office, Washington, D.C. 1989, table C-3, p. 298.

Source: Katherine Maddox McElroy, John J. Siegfried and George H. Sweeney, "The Incidence of Price Changes in the US Economy," *Review of Economics and Statistics*, Vol. 64, No. 2 (May 1982), table 1, pp. 193–8.

Table 12.4 Comparison of the distribution of the burden of Florida's sales tax on commodities and 1987 sales tax on services

1972–73 Percentile	1972–73 Income levels	1972–73 Income level adjusted to 1975[a]	1975 Florida Tax burden study income classes	Burden[a] of 4% commodities sales tax	Burden of 4% commodities sales tax	Burden of 5% services sales tax	Burden of 1% increase in commodities sales tax
5	2,406	3,002	Under 3,000 3,000–4,999	0.0231 } 0.0203 }	0.0214	0.0065	0.0054
20	5,612	7,003	5,000–6,999 7,000–9,999	0.0210 } 0.0215 }	0.0212	0.0050	0.0053
40	9,300	11,606	10,000–11,999 12,000–14,999	0.0214 } 0.0201 }	0.0207	0.0046	0.0052
60 80	12,855 17,760	16,043 } 22,164 }	15,000–24,999	0.0183	0.0183	0.0046[c]	0.0046
95	27,836	35,741	Above 25,000	0.0141	0.0141	0.0044	0.0035

[a] 1972–3 income levels adjusted to 1975 on the basis of the average consumer price index (CPI) for 1972 and 1973 and the CPI for 1975 (*Economic Report of the President*, US Government Printing Office, Washington, D.C., 1989, table B-58, p. 373.
[b] Tax burden relative to gross income implied by the tax.
[c] Average of the burden of 60th percentile (0.0044) and 80th percentile (0.0048).

Sources: The Burden of Florida Taxes by Income Class: 1974–5 and table 12.3 of this paper.

consumption pattern data from the 1972–3 *Consumer Expenditure Survey*.[11] It did not trace the distributional effects of the tax on commodities purchased for *intermediate* use. The Florida sales tax on commodities was 4 percent in 1975, and increased to 5 percent in 1982.

Table 4 reports the comparison. Our study of the distribution of the burden of the 1987 sales tax on services and the earlier Florida Department of Revenue study of the distribution of the burden of the sales tax on the direct purchase of commodities are based on different income classes. By interpolating, however, we can make fairly direct comparisons between the two. The appropriate comparison is between a 5 percent sales tax levy on the services that were covered in 1987 and a 1 percent increase in the sales tax rate on the commodities taxed by Florida's traditional sales tax. Income class data for 1972–73 were inflated to 1975 on the basis of the consumer price index. Then, income classes used in the two studies (one of the service tax, the other of the commodities tax) were aggregated to roughly comparable levels. The results are reported in the final two columns of table 12.4 and reveal, as apparently anticipated by the Florida legislature, that the fiscal impact of a new 5 percent levy on those services actually covered by Florida's 1987 service tax is approximately equivalent to the fiscal impact of a one percent increase in Florida's traditional sales tax rate on commodities.

The distributional effect of the two sales tax alternatives is also roughly the same. Comparing the increased burden on a family at the fifth percentile in the income distribution with that of a family at the ninety-fifth percentile reveals that the sales tax on services is slightly less regressive than the sales tax on commodities. In both cases the lower income family pays about a fifth of a percent more of its income to meet the tax than does the higher income family (0.0065–0.0044 for the services tax, and 0.0054–0.0035 for the commodities tax). There is much less difference in the impact of the alternative taxes between families at the twentieth and eightieth percentiles. The service tax is slightly less regressive than the commodities tax,[12] but the difference is hardly noticeable. Repeal of the service tax and replacement of the foregone revenues with an additional one percent sales tax levy on commodities apparently shifted the tax burden in Florida slightly toward lower income families.

Notes

1   *Economic Report of the President* (United States Government Printing Office: Washington, D.C., 1990), table C-83, p. 391.

2   See Commerce Clearing House (1990, pp. 6021–812), and Advisory Commission on Intergovernmental Relations, 1990, table 27, pp. 78–80.

3   The sales tax has also been expanded recently to cover selected services in Minnesota, Texas, and Connecticut (Boucher, 1988; Carpenter and McFarlin, 1988). The Massachusetts legislature expanded sales tax coverage to some services in 1990, but as of early 1991, implementation of the legislation remained in doubt.

4   See, for example, Schaefer (1969), Ghazanfar (1975), Phares (1980), and Bohm and Craig (1988).

5   See, for example, Phares (1980, p. 30): "The general sales tax is assumed to be fully shifted forward to the consumer. This has become a standard assumption about this tax . . ." Aronson and Hilley (1986, p. 95) also assume full shifting of a general sales tax when they acknowledge the implications of tax liability for intermediate goods: "The tax on goods used in production is shifted forward and becomes a cost of the relevant consumer goods which, in turn, are taxed when sold at the retail level." Daicoff and Glass (1979), however, investigate alternative shifting assumptions for the sales tax.

6   This criticism of the pass-through assumption applies as well to distributional analyses of goods and services purchased directly for final consumption, which uniformly assume the tax is passed completely through (the single stage of production) to final consumers.

7   See, for example, Blair and Kaserman (1985, p. 285): "If an external (market) transaction is taxed or penalized more than an internal (integrated) transaction, there will be an obvious incentive for vertical integration." Also see Fox (1986, p. 387): "Still, other things equal, a high tax imposed directly on an industry, such as the sales tax on retail sales, can generally be expected to create the greatest disincentive for that industry to produce in a state."

8   It would be instructive to compare the distributional effects reported in table 2 with comparable estimates based only on final personal consumption of services. Unfortunately, such a straightforward comparison was not completed with the 1972 *Consumer Expenditure Survey* data and the cost to reconstruct the CES data into input-output industries would be prohibitive. An analysis of the distributional effects of the sales tax on selected services using direct purchases for personal consumption by families in 1984, however, has been done (Bohm and Craig, 1988). Some categories of services in the 1984 analysis are close to those in the 1972 study of the distributional effects of purchases for both intermediate use and final personal consumption. The comparable industries support our conclusion that including the effects of indirect purchases of services moves the overall burden of the tax towards proportionality.

9   The Florida legislation specified covered transactions by three- or four-digit S.I.C. codes. The Florida Department of Revenue supplied a table summarizing the percentage of each S.I.C. code that was covered under the tax. The McElroy, Siegfried, and Sweeney (1982) tables are based on US

Department of Commerce, Bureau of Economic Analysis input-output table codes. These codes are more aggregated than four-digit S.I.C. codes. The coverage data from Florida were converted to input-output codes via "Industry Classification of the 1972 Input-Output Tables" in *The Detailed Input-Output Structure of the US Economy: 1972.* This table also provided the S.I.C. codes for the non-taxed elements of each input-output code (if any). Whenever an input-output category contained both taxed and untaxed S.I.C. components (or components that were taxed at different rates), we used S.I.C. value of shipment weights to determine the average tax rate for the entire input-output category.

10 Florida's sales tax is actually a sales and use tax. Use of national data on the distributional effects of the burden of the tax implicitly accepts the premise that service exports out of and imports into Florida balance. And, of course, few Floridians (or consumers anywhere) purchased many compact discs, personal computers, or mini-vans in 1972.

11 The Florida study, however, used only households in the southern part of the United States.

12 Due and Friedlaender (1981, p. 425) predict that the distributional pattern of a sales tax would be less regressive if all services were taxed.

References

Advisory Commission on Intergovernmental Relations, *Significant Features of Fiscal Federalism*, Vol. 1, January 1990, M-169, Washington, D.C.

Aronson, J. Richard and John L. Hilley, *Financing State and Local Governments.* Washington, D.C.: The Brookings Institution, 1986.

Blair, Roger D. and David L. Kaserman, *Antitrust Economics.* Homewood, Ill.: Richard D. Irwin, Inc., 1985.

Bohm, Robert A. and Eleanor D. Craig, "Sales Tax Base Modification, Revenue Stability, and Equity," *Proceedings of the 80th Annual Conference of the National Tax Association – Tax Institute of America*, 1988, 167–74.

Boucher, Karen J., "Sales Tax on Services: The New Source of State Revenues," *Journal of State Taxation*, Fall 1988, Vol. 7, No. 3, 273–86.

Carpenter, Raymond P. and Monica M. McFarlin, "Sales and Use Taxation of Service Transactions in Georgia and Selected States After the Florida Experiment," *Journal of State Taxation*, Fall 1988, Vol. 7, No. 3, 221–42.

Commerce Clearing House, Inc., *State Tax Guide*, 1990.

Daicoff, Darwin and Robert Glass, "Who Pays Kansas Taxes?" *Kansas Business Review*, May, 1979, Vol. 2, No. 9, 1–11.

Davies, David G., "The Significance of Taxation of Services for the Pattern of Distribution of Tax Burden by Income Class," *Proceedings of the Sixty-Second Annual Conference of the National Tax Association – Tax Institute of America*, 1970, 138–46.

Due, John F. and John L. Mikesell, *Sales Taxation: State and Local Structure and Administration.* Baltimore: Johns Hopkins University Press, 1983.

Due, John F. and Ann F. Friedlaender, *Government Finance*, 7th edn. Homewood, Illinois: Richard D. Irwin, Inc. 1981.

Florida Department of Revenue, Division of Tax Research, unpublished table entitled "Fiscal Impact of Ch. 87-6, Laws of Florida."

Florida House of Representatives, Finance and Taxation Committee, *The Burden of Florida Taxes by Income Class: 1974–5*, June 9, 1978.

Fox, William F., "Tax Structure and the Location of Economic Activity Along State Borders," *National Tax Journal* December 1986, Vol. XXXIX, No. 4, 387–401.

Ghazanfar, S. M., "Equity Effects and Revenue Potential of Sales Taxation of Services: Some Empirical Findings," *Public Finance Quarterly*, April 1975, Vol. 3, No. 2, 163–89.

Hellerstein, Walter, "Florida's Sales Tax on Services," *National Tax Journal*, March 1988, Vol. XLI, No. 1, 2–18.

McElroy, Katherine Maddox, John J. Siegfried and George H. Sweeney, "The Incidence of Price Changes in the US Economy," *Review of Economics and Statistics*, May 1982, Vol. LXIV, No. 2, 191–203.

Morgan, Daniel C., Jr., *Retail Sales Tax*. Madison and Milwaukee: The University of Wisconsin Press, 1964.

Phares, Donald, *Who Pays State and Local Taxes?* Cambridge, Mass.: Oelgeschlager, Gunn and Hain, 1980.

Ring, Raymond J., Jr., "The Proportion of Consumers' and Producers' Goods in the General Sales Tax," *National Tax Journal*, June 1989, Vol. XLII, No. 2, 167–79.

Rockwood, Charles E., Edger A. Fresen and James Francis, "Broadening the Sales Tax Base to Include Services: The Florida Experience," *Proceedings of the 80th Annual Conference of the National Tax Association – Tax Institute of America*, 1988, 161–7.

Schaefer, Jeffrey M., "Sales Tax Regressivity Under Alternative Tax Bases and Income Concepts," *National Tax Journal*, December 1969, Vol. XXII, No. 4, 516–27.

United States Department of Commerce, Bureau of Economic Analysis, *The Detailed Input-Output Structure of the US Economy: 1972*.

Introduction to Chapter 13

As is true of almost everything about American state and local finance, the states differ considerably in what their sales taxes cover. This article briefly presents the facts on the variations in coverage, and analyzes the effects of these variations on the stability of sales tax revenue and on the responsiveness of sales tax revenue to economic growth in the state, two sides of the same coin, but both desirable outcomes.

13

Fiscal Effects of Differences in Sales Tax Coverage: Revenue Elasticity, Stability, and Reliance

John L. Mikesell

States collected almost $100 billion from their general sales taxes in fiscal 1990, more than they collected from any other tax.[1] That continues an unbroken record of reliance started after World War II. The first general sales taxes emerged in the 1930s when a few states adjusted their business occupation taxes by: (1) raising the rate on retailing gross receipts from fractions to one percent or more; and (2) excluding non-retail transactions from the base. They were driven to do so by the collapse of real property tax yields in the Great Depression. By fiscal 1948, general sales taxes produced more revenue than any other state tax, being levied by twenty-six states.[2] The success of the sales tax as a revenue producer undoubtedly was the engine for a more significant state role in the state-local fiscal relationship in the last forty-five years.

Sometime in the 1990s, and sooner rather than later, the individual income tax will replace the general sales tax as the most lucrative state tax. But replacing all those collections will not be possible – in fiscal 1990 states raised 34 percent of their tax revenue from general sales taxes – so the yield of such taxes will remain important. As the following sections argue, the structure of the sales tax is far from consistent across the states and these differences translate into considerable differences in fiscal performance of the taxes.

The Diversity of American Sales Tax Structures

The American sales taxes may be defined as "broad based taxes on most goods and a varying number of services" that apply to sales from retailers to consumers.[3] Some transactions are specifically exempt because of: (1) the nature of the seller or the buyer; (2) the use of the subject of the transaction; or (3) the nature of the subject of the transaction. The presumption of the taxes, as distinct from the selective excise, is one of taxation unless specifically exempt, however. Exemptions, particularly of items for resale, are by suspension of tax, often through presentation of certificates, not through after-the-fact credits used in value-added taxes. And the taxes are accompanied by use taxes, as an attempt to balance the tax on interstate transactions. They may be legally on the buyer or the seller and either on gross receipts or the accumulation of individual transactions; neither of these differences are critical, however.

Within this general outline, states have made many choices with regard to what transactions will be excluded or exempt, not to mention the choices made about what statutory rate will apply to the base, however defined. (State rates presently range from three to seven and one-quarter percent, a considerable range of choices actually selected, and about thirty states allow accompanying local taxes.) The wide range in the share of the state economy in the sales tax base reflects these choices about the base; table 13.1 arrays the states according to their implicit sales tax base as a percentage of gross state product, using 1986 data (the most recent gross state product data series readily available).[4] That index shows the extent to which the state has chosen broad or narrow coverage of its sales tax. The less inclusive the sales tax, the smaller will the base be in relation to state product.

The differences in coverage are striking. For instance, the median coverage of the fifteen broadest (52.9 percent) is sixty percent higher than the median for the fifteen narrowest (32.8 percent). The range from broadest to narrowest is obviously even more extreme. While differences in state economic structure contribute to levels of this index, choices made by the states in structuring their taxes play a critical role; although Georgia and New York, for instance, both levy a state sales and use tax,[5] they differ dramatically in their coverage of state economic activity of the taxes because they legally have different coverage.

Structuring a sales tax entails several choices that will make the tax relatively broad or narrow. Several important structural regularities appear when the fifteen broadest taxes are compared against the fifteen narrowest. The variations in legal structure of the taxes appear in tables 13.1 and 13.2.[6]

1   Food Exemption. All states exempt purchases made with food stamps, but twenty-seven states plus the District of Columbia generally exempt food purchased for at home consumption and Illinois taxes such purchases at a reduced statutory rate. Of the fifteen broad base states,

only five exempt such purchases; of the fifteen narrow base states, only two fully tax such purchases.

2   Clothing Exemption. Only six states remove clothing purchases (children's clothing only in one state); all fall in the group of fifteen narrow base states.

3   Producer Good Taxability. Only four of the broad base group do not fully tax producer purchase of machinery and equipment; of the narrow base group, eleven states do not tax such purchases.

4   Religious, Charitable, and Educational Organization Exemption. Only three of the broad base taxes provide exemption for purchases made by such organizations; only three of the narrow base taxes do not provide the exemption. (A number of states exempting purchases likewise exempt sales by those organizations, to the extent the transaction would have otherwise been taxable.)

5   Utility Services. States differ in the extent to which some or all traditional public utility services are taxable. Some states exclude because utilities do not fit within coverage they limit to tangible personal property. Others tax, but exempt certain purchases, sometimes for residential purchases, sometimes for industrial purchases, sometimes dependent on use made of the service. Other expand a narrow tax on tangible property purchases by specific extension to certain utilities. And some exempt under the sales tax but apply a separate utility tax (those taxes do not appear in sales collections). Table 13.2 broadly identifies those states which fully exempt or exclude electric, gas, water, and interstate telephone service from their standard sales tax base, distinguishing between residential and business purchases. For electric and gas purchases, the narrow base taxes are more likely to exempt residential purchases than are the broad base taxes (twelve states against eight states) and slightly more likely to exempt business purchases (five versus three). Differences in water taxability are similar (residential – thirteen narrow exempt, ten broad; business – ten narrow exempt, eight broad), but there is little difference in interstate telephone taxability.

6   Other Taxable Services. Four of the fifteen broad base states have broad or general coverage of services; only one of the narrow base states has such coverage.

To summarize, the broad base sales taxes have considerably greater scope of both personal and business purchases than do the narrower coverage taxes. That breadth is associated with several elements of coverage, and seems to emerge from considerable difference in philosophy about the sales tax. Indeed, the two groups of taxes in general

Table 13.1 Relative size of state sales tax base and critical elements of sales tax structure

State	Implicit sales tax base as % of gross State product 1986	Food exemption	Clothing exemption	Broad producer good exemption or exclusion (machinery, equipment)	Exemption for religious, charitable, and educational non-profit organizations
Hawaii	91.8%	No	No	No	No
New Mexico	74.3%	No	No	No	Yes
Florida	56.6%	Yes	No	No	Yes
Arkansas	55.1%	No	No	No	No
Arizona	54.8%	Yes	No	Yes	No
South Dakota	54.3%	No	No	No	No
Mississippi	54.0%	No	No	No	No
Georgia	52.9%	No	No	No	No
Wyoming	52.6%	No	No	No	No
Utah	50.3%	Yes	No	No	No
South Carolina	50.1%	No	No	Yes	No
Washington	47.2%	Yes	No	No	No
Oklahoma	46.7%	No	No	Yes	No
Tennessee	46.7%	No	No	Yes	Yes
Nevada	46.5%	Yes	No	No	No
North Carolina	45.7%	No	No	No (RR)	No
Idaho	45.6%	No	No	Yes	No
Maine	44.2%	Yes	No	Yes	No
Kansas	44.0%	No	No	Yes	No
Michigan	43.8%	Yes	No	Yes	Yes
Iowa	43.8%	Yes	No	Yes	No
Missouri	43.4%	No	No	No	Yes

Table 13.1 *Continued*

Colorado	41.5%	Yes	No	Yes	Yes
Texas	41.4%	Yes	No	No	Yes
North Dakota	41.2%	Yes	No	No	No
California	41.0%	Yes	No	No	No
Indiana	41.0%	Yes	No	Yes	Yes
Wisconsin	40.1%	Yes	No	Yes	Yes
Alabama	39.4%	No	No	No (RR)	No
Maryland	39.1%	Yes	No	Yes	Yes
Kentucky	39.1%	Yes	No	No	Yes
Virginia	38.2%	No	No	Yes	No
Louisiana	38.1%	Yes	No	No	No
Nebraska	37.5%	Yes	No	No	No
Vermont	36.0%	Yes	No	Yes	Yes
Ohio	36.0%	Yes	No	Yes	Yes
Minnesota	34.5%	Yes	Yes	No	Yes
New York	32.8%	Yes	No	Yes	Yes
Illinois	32.2%	Reduced rate	No	Yes	Yes
Rhode Island	31.9%	Yes	Yes	Yes	Yes
Connecticut	30.7%	Yes	Children's only	Yes	Yes
West Virginia	30.6%	No	No	Yes	Yes
Massachusetts	29.8%	Yes	Yes	Yes	Yes
Pennsylvania	29.4%	Yes	Yes	Yes	Yes
New Jersey	28.2%	Yes	Yes	Yes	Yes

RR: reduced rate.

Sources: US Bureau of Census, *State Tax Collections in 1986* (GF-86-1). Washington: US Government Printing Office, 1989; *Prentice Hall's Guide to Sales and Use Taxes*, 1989 Edition Paramus, N.J.: Prentice Hall, 1989; and John L. Mikesell "Sales Taxation of Nonprofit Organizations: Purchases and Sales." 1991 National Tax Association Sales Tax Symposium (New Orleans).

Table 13.2 Coverage of utility and other services under state sales taxes

State	Utilities fully exempt (or excluded) from general sales tax coverage							Telephone (intrastate)		Other service coverage
	Electric		Gas		Water					
	Residential	Business	Residential	Business	Residential	Business	Residential	Business		
Hawaii	Yes	Yes	Yes	Yes	Yes	Yes	Yes	Yes	B/G
New Mexico	No	No	No	No	No	No	No	No	B/G
Florida	Yes	No	Yes	No	Yes	Yes	No	No	S
Arkansas	No	No	No	No	No	No	No	No	S
Arizona	No	No	No	No	No	No	No	No	N
South Dakota	No	No	Yes	No	Yes	No	No	No	B/G
Mississippi	Yes	No	Yes	No	Yes	Yes	No	No	S
Georgia	No	No	No	No	Yes	No	No	No	N
Wyoming	No	No	No	No	No	Yes	No	No	S
Utah	No (RR)	No	No (RR)	No	Yes	Yes	No	No	S
South Carolina	Yes	No	Yes	No	Yes	Yes	No	No	N
Washington	Yes	Yes	Yes	Yes	Yes	Yes	Yes	Yes	B/G
Oklahoma	Yes	No	Yes	No	Yes	Yes	No	No	N
Tennessee	Yes	No	Yes	No	No	No	No	No	S
Nevada	Yes	Yes	Yes	Yes	Yes	Yes	Yes	Yes	N
North Carolina	No	No	No	No	Yes	Yes	No	No	N
Idaho	Yes	Yes	Yes	Yes	Yes	Yes	Yes	Yes	N
Maine	No	No	Yes	No	Yes	No	No	No	N
Kansas	Yes	No	Yes	No	Yes	No	No	No	S
Michigan	No	No	No	No	No	No	No	No	N
Iowa	No	No	No	No	No	No	No	No	B/G

Table 13.2 *Continued*

Missouri	Yes	No	Yes	No	Yes	No	No	N
Colorado	Yes	No	Yes	No	Yes	Yes	No	N
Texas	Yes	No	Yes	No	Yes	Yes	No	S
North Dakota	Yes	Yes	No	No	Yes	Yes	No	N
California	Yes	No	Yes	Yes	Yes	Yes	Yes	N
Indiana	No	No	No	No	No	No	No	N
Wisconsin	No	No	No	No	Yes	Yes	No	S
Alabama	Yes	Yes	Yes	Yes	Yes	Yes	Yes	N
Maryland	No	No	No	No	Yes	Yes	Yes	N
Kentucky	Yes	No	Yes	No	Yes	No	No	N
Virginia	Yes	Yes	Yes	Yes	Yes	Yes	Yes	N
Louisiana	No (RR)	No (RR)	No (RR)	No (RR)	No (RR)	No (RR)	No	S
Nebraska	No	No	No	No	No	No	No	N
Vermont	Yes	No	Yes	No	Yes	Yes	Yes	N
Ohio	Yes	Yes	Yes	Yes	Yes	Yes	No	S
Minnesota	No	No	No	No	Yes	No	No	N
New York	Yes	No	Yes	No	Yes	Yes	No	S
Illinois	Yes	Yes	Yes	Yes	Yes	Yes	Yes	S
Rhode Island	Yes	No	Yes	No	Yes	No	No	N
Connecticut	Yes	No	Yes	No	Yes	Yes	No	N
West Virginia	Yes	Yes	Yes	Yes	Yes	Yes	Yes	B/G
Massachusetts	Yes	No	Yes	No	Yes	No	No	N
Pennsylvania	Yes	No	Yes	No	Yes	Yes	No	S
New Jersey	Yes	Yes	Yes	Yes	Yes	Yes	No	S

RR: reduced rate.

Source: John L. Mikesell, "Sales Tax Coverage for Services – Policy for a Changing Economy," *Journal of State Taxation*, IX (Spring 1991).

originated in different fiscal eras: the mean age of the fifteen broadest taxes is fifty-two years, compared to thirty-six years for the fifteen narrowest taxes.[7] Their differences are almost great enough to consider the states to have different taxes.

While states sometimes radically revise their sales taxes, thus changing the scope fo their tax base, many states maintain consistent patterns for many years. An analysis of the implicit tax base relative to state personal income (a somewhat more accessible proxy for gross state product in long-time-period analysis) across the years since the last sales tax adoption, 1970 through 1990, shows seven states to have remained in the fifteen broadest coverage group (Arizona, Arkansas, Georgia, Hawaii, Mississippi, New Mexico, and Wyoming) and ten to have remained in the fifteen narrowest group (Connecticut, Massachusetts, Minnesota, New Jersey, New York, Ohio, Pennsylvania, Rhode Island, Virginia, and Maryland.)[8] These two categories of states form the basis for the further analysis.

Base Choice and Fiscal Behavior

At the simplest level, a broad base means that a given advertised tax rate will yield more revenue and that a change in that rate will have a larger revenue impact. That relationship, while presumably of little economic consequence, may have great political significance for governors, legislators, and voters; effective rates are significantly less obvious than the advertised rates applied to each taxed transcaction.

Table 13.3 compares the behavior of the broad and narrow base tax states in regard to statutory sales tax rates and sales tax reliance. These data show the narrow base taxes to levy higher statutory rates than do the broader base taxes. The mean of the narrow taxes is now slightly more than 25 percent higher than for the broad taxes. Throughout the last two decades, the states with narrower bases have had higher rates and the growth rate for these taxes has been considerably greater than for the broader taxes. In earlier years the broad base taxes levied higher rates, although this pattern may be importantly related to the year of initial adoption: only one of the broad base group does not date from the 1930s while only one of the narrow base taxes was not from the post-World War II period, Indeed, half of these narrow taxes were adopted in the 1960s.

The same table shows the states using broad base taxes to more heavily rely on the sales tax than do the states with a narrow base. This pattern has held for the last twenty years, although the relative difference is less in the latter part of the period than it was from 1972 through 1982. Mean reliance in the narrow base states is now about three-quarters of its

Table 13.3 Statutory rates and sales tax reliance in broad and narrow base states, 1970–91

	Mean statutory rate (January 1)			Mean sales tax reliance (fiscal year)			
Year	All	Broad	Narrow	Ratio of narrow to broad	All	Broad	Narrow	Ratio of narrow to broad
1970	3.527	3.571	3.800	1.06	0.319	0.377	0.268	0.71
1971	3.627	3.571	4.100	1.15	0.323	0.381	0.273	0.72
1972	3.727	3.571	4.450	1.25	0.321	0.393	0.269	0.68
1973	3.761	3.571	4.500	1.26	0.319	0.403	0.266	0.66
1974	3.772	3.571	4.450	1.25	0.330	0.414	0.272	0.66
1975	3.805	3.714	4.400	1.18	0.332	0.423	0.270	0.64
1976	3.872	3.714	4.700	1.27	0.331	0.417	0.273	0.65
1977	3.907	3.714	4.800	1.29	0.335	0.420	0.268	0.64
1978	3.932	3.714	4.900	1.32	0.339	0.421	0.277	0.66
1979	3.927	3.678	4.900	1.33	0.342	0.430	0.281	0.65
1980	3.925	3.678	4.900	1.33	0.342	0.430	0.280	0.65
1981	3.980	3.678	5.050	1.37	0.336	0.425	0.275	0.65
1982	4.102	3.642	5.150	1.41	0.335	0.410	0.274	0.68
1983	4.267	3.642	5.350	1.47	0.336	0.392	0.279	0.71
1984	4.500	4.107	5.350	1.30	0.345	0.400	0.289	0.72
1985	4.558	4.107	5.350	1.30	0.350	0.407	0.296	0.73
1986	4.566	4.107	5.350	1.30	0.354	0.409	0.304	0.74
1987	4.654	4.250	5.400	1.27	0.358	0.409	0.316	0.77
1988	4.779	4.250	5.400	1.27	0.354	0.395	0.307	0.78
1989	4.801	4.250	5.400	1.27	0.353	0.388	0.302	0.78
1990	4.865	4.392	5.450	1.24	0.355	0.399	0.301	0.754
1991	4.971	4.428	5.650	1.28	NA	NA	NA	NA

Sources: US Bureau of Census, *State Tax Collections* (various years) and Commerce Clearing House, State Tax Reporters.

level in broad base states. A broad base appears to be associated with greater state reliance on the sales tax, along with somewhat lower statutory rates.

Sales taxes differ in their income elasticity and stability, although it is expected that they will generally be less elastic than, say, a progressive income tax and less stable than, say, a property tax. State finances can be significantly influenced by changes in the sales tax base because those changes determine the revenue yield that will emerge without changing the statutory tax rate. Table 13.4 presents the tax base elasticities for the broad and narrow sales taxes from the first quarter of 1970 through the first quarter of 1991, allowing for differences in elasticity that may result

Table 13.4 Regression results: income elasticity and recession-influenced income elasticity (t-statistics in parentheses)

	Intercept	In income	In income* recession	R	D.W.
Broad					
Arizona	6.9196	0.8366	0.0040	0.973	–
Rho = 0.426	(24.8381)**	(30.3130)**	(1.1767)		
Arkansas	6.1014	0.9059	0.0009	0.992	–
Rho = 0.637	(23.4396)**	(33.8220)**	(0.5038)		
Georgia	6.5881	0.8689	0.0009	0.997	–
Rho = 0.800	(19.5380)**	(27.8807)**	(0.8094)		
Hawaii	4.8350	1.0970	0.0035	0.994	–
Rho = 0.310	(37.7405)**	(78.8490)**	(2.0371)*		
Mississippi	7.5113	0.7618	0.0045	0.989	–
Rho = 0.760	(17.6489)**	(17.5094)**	(2.4786)*		
New Mexico	6.2307	0.9206	0.0034	0.990	–
Rho = 0.879	(5.1078)**	(7.1076)**	(1.2531)		
Wyoming	6.0350	0.9295	0.0042	0.974	–
Rho = 0.803	(6.6848)**	(8.6416)**	(0.9243)		
Narrow					
Connecticut	3.7465	1.0708	−0.0035	0.961	1.826
	(14.9080)**	(44.9706)**	(−1.1415)		
Maryland	5.2649	0.9203	−0.0157	0.795	2.473
	(9.2289)**	(17.3498)**	(−2.3552)*		
Massachusetts	1.7813	1.2220	−0.0062	0.978	
Rho = 0.328	(5.2961)**	(40.1439)**	(−2.0060)*		
Minnesota	5.4807	0.9179	−0.0029	0.978	1.827
Rho = 0.328	(33.4428)**	(59.3247)**	(−1.5444)		
New Jersey	4.3275	0.9983	−0.0001	0.988	
Rho = 0.472	(16.5204)**	(43.3905)**	(−0.0662)		
New York	7.2329	0.7883	−0.0017	0.914	
Rho = 0.500	(10.7938)**	(14.3346)**	(−0.4725)		
Ohio	4.6435	0.9920	−0.0036	0.991	
Rho = 0.565	(16.7045)**	(41.1169)**	(−2.4653)*		
Pennsylvania	4.1971	1.0145	−0.0033	0.959	1.720
	(15.4695)**	(43.5308)**	(−1.4054)		
Rhode Island	5.3017	0.9135	−0.0015	0.983	
Rho = 0.747	(10.7029)**	(16.8827)**	(−0.5477)		
Virginia	6.3092	0.8397	−0.0007	0.994	
Rho = 0.708	(21.487)**	(31.1515)**	(−0.4521)		

* Significant at 0.05 level; ** Significant at 0.01 level.

during economic recession.[9] The statistics come from the regression equation

$$\ln B = \ln a + b \ln Y + c\left(\ln Y * R\right) + e$$

where B = the sales tax base, Y = state personal income, and $R = a$ dummy variable set to 1.0 during recession quarters and to 0.0 otherwise. When the Durbin-Watson test for autogression was unsatisfactory, the offending equation as reestimated using the Cochrane-Orcutt iterative technique; only the revised equation is reported in those instances. The recession-influenced variable adjusts the basic elasticity to suggest the extent to which the tax base to state personal income relationship, the link between taxable activity and the state economy, differs between expansion and recession.[10] The critical question for present purposes is the extent to which broad base and narrow base sales taxes perform differently.

The evidence suggests that the income elasticities vary widely within the two groups of state taxes. In each group, some taxes show relatively high elasticities while for others the elasticities are relatively low. Overall, however, the elasticities are generally higher for the narrow base taxes than for the broad base taxes. That is not especially remarkable. States may intentionally or accidentally exclude transactions that have lower income elasticities than those transections left in the base, thus bringing their elasticities above those of states with more inclusive bases. The narrow base states could also have removed transcations with higher elasticities, but they seem not to have done so.

The evidence also suggests that recessions influence the groups of taxes differently as well. For the broad base taxes, the sign of the interaction is always positive and significant at the five percent level or better in two states. That indicates that, in recession, the broad tax is better able to capture revenue from increased nominal personal income that in expansion periods. For the narrow base taxes, the sign is always negative and significant at the five percent level or better in three states. Thus, the recession worsens the base-to-nominal personal income relationship in recession. Overall, the broad taxes would give greater cyclical revenue cushioning during recessions than would the narrow base taxes.

Conclusion

American sales and use taxes show great variation from state to state in what transactions are exempt and what are taxed. At the extremes of coverage, the taxes have little in common save a transaction basis and resale exemptions. The differences are sufficient to guarantee that any single federal replacement, a value added tax for instance, would leave some states with revenue windfalls and others with great shortfalls.

In contrasting sales tax performance over the past two decades of the broad base taxes with the narrow base taxes, the evidence shows: (1) statutory rates to be higher and rising more rapidly for the narrow base taxes; (2) greater reliance on the sales tax in the broad base states; (3) wide range in income elasticities in both groups with generally higher elasticities for the narrower base taxes; and (4) less sensitivity to recessions in the broad based taxes.

Notes

1 US Bureau of Census, *State Government Tax Collections: 1990* (GF-90-1), Washington: US Government Printing Office, 1991.
2 US Bureau of Census, *Sources of State Tax Revenue* (Washington: US Government Printing Office), volumes from 1928 through 1948. The reported collection figure exceeds motor fuel excises a few years earlier, but it includes revenue from taxes in Delaware, Indiana, Washington, and West Virginia that would not be recognized as American retail sales taxes.
3 OECD, *Taxing Consumption*, p. 25.
4 Census data were adjusted to a consistent base sales tax yield by a) removing the yield from business and occupation taxes in Washington and West Virginia and from the Indiana gross income tax, b) adding the special auto, aircraft, or watercraft excise taxes which substitute for general sales tax coverage in some states (and associated rental taxes), c) removing yield from local collection charges, and d) subtracting non-standard rate revenue from the Hawaii tax. Yield was divided by the statutory rate to estimate the sales tax base for the years. The adjustments generally follow those developed in John F. Due and John L. Mikesell, *Sales Taxation* (Baltimore: Johns Hopkins University Press, 1983), pp. 6–9.
5 Georgia (*Code*, Title 48, Chapter 8, Sales and Use Taxes) and New York (*Consolidated Laws*, Chapter 60, Article 28, Sales and Compensating Use Tax).
6 These taxability distinctions are not finely made; for instance, special exemptions for new or expanded industry, seasonal residential utility exemptions, or exemption for special classes of non-profit organization purchases are not captured here. These and other exemptions are detailed in the sources given for the tables.
7 Due and Mikesell, *Sales Taxation*, p. 3.
8 All but Maryland fall into comparable groups when the base is compared to gross state product (table 1).

9   Quarterly sales tax data from US Bureau of Census, *Quarterly Tax Report* (various issues) and personal income data from *Survey of Current Business*.
10 Regressions which substituted the capacity utilization rate in manufacturing for the recession dummy exhibited similar results, although they are not reported here.

Introduction to Chapter 14

Nearly all states employ the corporate income tax, including some that emphatically reject personal income taxes, like Florida. During the 1960s and 1970s, the tax was a popular instrument of state government finance, and increases in effective tax rates were very widespread in that period, despite vigorous lobbying by business groups against the tax. McLure and other economists have suggested that the tax was popular because it was believed to be largely exported from the state imposing it, and progressive in incidence.

More recently, the states have been more circumspect in taxing corporate income, apparently in the belief that businesses are especially sensitive to this tax in their location decisions. In this article, McLure shows that both the earlier popularity and the more recent unpopularity were based on mistaken understanding of the economic character of the tax. McLure argues that, at the state level, the tax is not one on profits at all, but a combined property, sales and payroll tax that is not very progressive, probably mostly borne within the state itself and unlikely to be an important factor in most business location decisions.

14

The State Corporate Income Tax: Lambs in Wolves' Clothing

Charles E. McLure, Jr.

Corporation income taxes have accounted for roughly 8 percent of state tax revenues and some 4.5 percent of all state and local tax revenues over recent years.[1] Although they are clearly less important to state or local governments than to the federal government, where they have accounted for over 20 percent of tax collections, corporation income taxes are an important source of state revenue. Moreover, revenues from state corporate taxes have risen substantially faster over the past quarter-century than have those from the federal tax.[2]

The increased yield of the state corporation income taxes results in part from corporate growth. But some 60 percent of the increase in yield from 1975 to 1976 has been attributed to rate changes, extensions of the tax base, and administrative actions,[3] and there is little reason to believe that that period is atypical. Though there is no way such things can be known with certainty, it seems safe to surmise that part of the attractiveness of the state corporate income tax can be traced to the belief that the tax adds significantly to the progressivity of the state tax system.

In an earlier paper I asserted that state corporation income taxes levied on multistate firms have essentially the same effects as discriminatory state taxes on corporate payrolls, property, or sales (at origin or destination, as the case may be) if the profits of the firm are allocated among the states for tax purposes on the basis of formulas that include payrolls, property, or sales (at origin or destination).[4] This paper provides a more rigorous justification for this assertion, describes the circumstances under which (or the extent to which) it is accurate, and reviews the implications of this analysis for public policy toward state corporation income taxes – especially the need to replace the taxes with federal revenues.

I assume initially that the state corporation income tax applies only to economic profits. Later I modify this unrealistic assumption to recognize alternatively: (1) that the tax may apply as well to the normal return to equity capital; and (2) that a national corporate income tax may have no effect on the cost of capital at all. No explicit account is taken of the deductibility of state taxes in calculating federal income tax liabilities. But in general such deductibility should not affect the qualitative analysis, as the "federal offset" should roughly halve any effect that would otherwise occur.

In this analysis I take the point of view of one taxing state; taxes in other states are taken as given. I have not asked a different (and important) question: what is the effect of the system of corporation income taxes levied in the United States?[5] In this regard the analysis resembles Mieszkowski's analysis of the excise effects of the property tax.[6] Mieszkowski correctly notes that any local change in property taxes will primarily affect the real incomes of locally specific factors and consumers, and will have little effect on the return to capital; in contrast, a nationally uniform change in property tax will alter the returns of owners of capital and have few other important effects.[7] By the same token a change in any one state's corporation income tax can be expected to have the effects postulated here, even though in the aggregate, state corporation income taxes are indeed income taxes.[8]

Tax on Economic Profits

Suppose that a given multistate corporation has total economic profits, π, where $\pi = S - R - W$, and S is total sales, R is payments to owners of property (including the normal return to equity invested in the firm), and W is the firm's total wage bill. For convenience it is assumed that the firm has no other expenses.

Under a three-factor allocation formula that includes sales, payrolls, and property, state i would levy a tax on the basis of the firm's sales, use of property, and wage payments occurring in state i, respectively S_i, R_i, and W_i. Profits attributable to state i, π_i, are commonly computed as follows:

$$\pi_i = \left[(S_i/S) + (R_i/R) + (W_i/W)\right]\pi/3.^9$$

Letting t_i denote the tax rate and T_i the revenue yield of state i, one could also write

$$T_i = t_i\pi_i = t_i\left[(S_i/S) + (R_i/R) + (W_i/W)\right]\pi/3.$$

The state "profits" tax could also be characterized as being composed of three separate smaller taxes, each levied at one-third the statutory rate, on $\pi S_i/S$, $\pi R_i/R$, and $\pi W_i/W$. For simplicity I shall focus on T_{is}, the sales-related portion of the profits tax. In state i

$$T_{is} = t'_i \pi \left(S_i / S \right) = t'_i a\pi, \tag{14.1}$$

where t'_i is one-third the statutory corporate tax rate in state i and a is state i's share in the total sales of the firm. The object will be to compare explicitly the effects of the sales-related portion of the state corporate profits tax with the effects of both a true income tax and a simple gross receipts tax on corporate output, and by analogy, the payroll and property-related portions of the "profits" tax to a true income tax and to taxes levied directly on corporate payrolls and property.

The following simple exercise demonstrates clearly that state income taxes based on formula allocation are not truly taxes on income arising in the state. Assume that some exogenous event changes a firm's profits truly attributable to the taxing state but not its sales in either the taxing state or the rest of the nation. In such a case tax receipts from the sales-related portion of the "profits" tax change, not by the product of the tax rate and the change in the profits truly attributable to the taxing state, as under a true income tax, but by only the fraction S_i/S times that much.[10] Because of formula allocation the change in profits truly attributable to a given state is effectively divided among the states in proportion to sales, rather than entering solely and entirely the tax base of the state in which, by assumption, it actually occurs.[11]

In contrast, consider an increase in profits generated by cost savings, none of which was truly attributable to the taxing state. The state would tax its share of changes in the total national tax base regardless of whether profits truly attributable to the state change.[12]

It is also true that the sales-related portion of the profits tax is likely to affect corporate decisions in much the same way as a tax on corporate gross receipts in (from) the taxing state. As a preliminary step, recall that the result of traditional analysis is that a national tax on economic profits of the corporation has no effect on price and output decisions of a profit-maximizing firm. Either with or without the tax, a profit-maximizing firm expands sales until marginal cost equals marginal revenue.[13] This result does not hold for a state tax on corporate profits, as usually imposed.

To see this, I begin by differentiating the definition of profits, π, with respect to Q_i, the quantity of sales in state i, and setting the result equal to zero:

$$d\pi/dQ_i = dS/dQ_i - dR/dQ_i - dW/dQ_i = 0.$$

In the absence of a state income tax profits are maximized by setting marginal revenues resulting from sales in a given state equal to the marginal capital and labor costs associated with those sales. But this result does not hold when state i imposes a sales-related corporate profits tax. Subtracting equation 14.1 from profits, π, yields profits net of this part of the state corporation tax, π_n, where[14]

$$\pi_n = \pi - T_{is} = \pi\left(1 - t_i' S_i / S\right) = \left(S - R - W\right)\left(1 - at_i'\right). \tag{14.2}$$

Thus the sales-related part of the state corporation tax causes marginal revenue to exceed marginal cost at the sales level that maximizes profits.[15]

The nature of the sales-related portion of the state corporate tax appears most clearly if one assumes that the firm sells only a small fraction of its output in the taxing state but that the change in sales under analysis occurs principally in the taxing state. In that case a is approximately zero and dS/dS_i is near unity. In that event the deviation of marginal revenue from marginal cost at an output that maximizes profits is

$$dS/dQ_i - dR/dQ_i - dW/dQ_i \cong \left(t_i' \pi / S\right)\left(dS_i / dQ_i\right).[16] \tag{14.3}$$

From this it is easily seen that the divergence between marginal cost and marginal revenue arises from the sales-related portion of the corporation income tax.[17]

Equation 14.3 is quite similar to the expression showing the output at which profits would be maximized if the firm faced a tax levied on gross receipts at the rate t_s.[18] In that case net profits, π_n, are given by

$$\pi_n = S - R - W - t_s S_i. \tag{14.4}$$

Differentiating equation 14.4 with respect to Q_i and setting the result equal to zero yields

$$d\pi/dQ_i = dS/dQ_i - dR/dQ_i - dW/dQ_i - t_s dS_i/dQ_i = 0 \tag{14.5}$$

or

$$dS/dQ_i - dR/dQ_i - dW/dQ_i = (T_s/S_i)(dS_i/dQ_i).$$ (14.5a)

Comparison of equations 14.3 and 14.5a for a given revenue yield from the taxed firm shows that the divergence between marginal costs and revenues is almost identical in the two cases. Thus for a state constituting a small fraction of the national market for a firm's products, the sales-related portion of the state corporation income tax under a formula allocation rule is essentially equivalent to a simple gross receipts tax levied on the corporation's sales in that state, though at rates that differ between firms. Thus it is likely to have roughly the distributional effects of a tax levied on the firm's sales in the state and will not simply reduce profits by the amount of the tax as a general income tax does. Similar procedures would establish analogous results for the payroll and property-related portions of the state corporation income tax.

Because no state accounts for a zero fraction of the sales of a firm actually selling in the state, the corporate profits tax is not fully equivalent to a gross receipts tax. Table 14.1 shows the percentage of the sales-related part of the profits tax that is equivalent to a sales tax.[19] Except for very high tax rates the value of $(1 - a)/(1 - at_i')$ is very near the value of $(1 - a)$. Since state corporate tax rates in the United States typically fall within the range of 5–8 percent,[20] only the first two columns of table 14.1 are relevant. Unless firms operate predominantly within one state, most of the sales-related part of the profits tax is equivalent to a sales tax. While the equivalence is not total, it is quite strong for multistate corporations. Finally, to the extent that payrolls and property are more

Table 14.1 Proportion of the sales-related part of the state corporation income tax that is equivalent to a sales tax, for selected values of t_i' and S_i/S^a

Percent of corporate sales occurring in the taxing state, $a = S_i/S$	Values of t_i' (percent)		
	1	5	10
5	95.0	95.2	95.5
10	90.1	90.5	90.9
20	80.2	80.8	81.6
50	50.3	51.3	52.6
80	20.2	20.8	21.7

[a] The values in this table are calculated from the relation $[(1 - a)/(1 - at_i')]$. Data are rounded.

concentrated in a few states than are sales, the payroll and property-related portions of the state profits tax are more nearly true profits taxes than is the sales-related portion – but only for the states in which production is concentrated.

Modification of the Analysis

The results presented in the previous section apply strictly only to monopolistic firms and perhaps to firms operating in oligopolistic industries because in competitive industries there are no economic profits except as a transitory phenomenon. Moreover, it might be objected either: (1) that the results presented thus far depend on the unrealistic assumption that corporation income taxes are levied only on economic profits; or (2) that recent theoretical analyses suggest that corporate income taxes are basically lump-sum taxes and have no effect on the cost of capital or investment decisions. The remainder of this section demonstrates that the results presented above are generally valid and that these objections are misplaced.

Tax on accounting profits[21]

Define taxable corporate profits for a nationwide tax, π_t, to include the normal return to equity capital, N. Then $\pi_t = \pi + N = S - W - R + N$, and net economic profits, π_n, are shown as $\pi_n = (S - R - W)(1 - t) - tN$.

Differentiating this equation for net profits with respect to Q shows that profits are not maximized when marginal revenue equals marginal cost but at a lower level where marginal revenue exceeds marginal cost.[22] Thus

$$d\pi_n / dQ = \left(dS/dQ - dR/dQ - dW/dQ\right)(1 - t) - tdN/dQ = 0 \qquad (14.6)$$

or

$$dS/dQ - dR/dQ - dW/dQ = \left[t/(1-t)\right]dN/dQ. \qquad (14.6a)$$

If one differentiates the equation for net profits with respect to Q_i rather than with respect to Q, it is seen that there is no qualitative difference in the results:

$$dS/dQ_i - dR/dQ_i - dW/dQ_i = \left[t/(1-t)\right]dN/dQ_i. \qquad (14.6b)$$

The result is quite different if taxable profits are defined to include the normal return to capital but are apportioned among the states according to formula. Net profits, taking account of only the salesrelated portion of the profits tax in state i, are then

$$\pi_n = (S - R - W)\left[1 - t_i'S_i/S\right] - (t_i'S_i)N/S.$$

Differentiating this equation with respect to the quantity of sales in the taxing state and setting the result equal to zero yields the following:

$$d\pi_n./dQ_i = (dS/dQ_i - dR/dQ_i - dW/dQ_i)(1 - t'a)$$
$$- (t'\pi/S)\left[(dS_i/dQ_i) - a(dS/dQ_i)\right]$$
$$- t_i'\left[adN/dQ_i + (N/S)\{(dS_i/dQ_i) - a(dS/dQ_i)\}\right] = 0. \qquad (14.7)$$

As before, this can be rewritten for the special case of $dS = dS_i$, this time as follows:

$$dS/dQ_i - dR/dQ_i - dW/dQ_i = \left[t_i\pi_t(1 - a)/S(1 - t_i'a)\right]dS/dQ_i$$
$$+ \left[t_i'a/(1 - t_i'a)\right]dN/dQ_i. \qquad (14.7a)$$

The comparison of equation 14.7a with equation 14.6b shows that in the former there is an extra component in the divergence between marginal cost and marginal revenue due to the formula allocation of taxable profits, and that this extra term is analogous to the right side of the second equation in note 15. Moreover, the component corresponding to the divergence in equation 14.6b is now $[t_i'a/(1 - t_i'a)](dN/dQ_i)$ rather than simply $[t/(1 - t)](dN/dQ_i)$. This component vanishes for small values of a, the taxing state's share of the firm's total sales. As before, for small values of a (if S_i/S is small) the difference between marginal cost and marginal revenue approaches $(t_i'\pi_t dS_i/dQ_i)/S$, and the sales-related portion of the profits tax is merely a disguised gross receipts tax. Similar comments apply to the property and payroll-related portions of the tax on profits defined to include the normal return.

State taxes and the cost of capital

One of the important theoretical developments of recent years is the demonstration by Stiglitz that under certain conditions the corporation income tax would have no effect on marginal decisions.[23] This result occurs because in the presence of the corporate tax all marginal invest-ment is debt-financed and the optimal amount and nature of debt-financed investment is independent of the tax. Does this result carry over to state corporate income taxes and must the results developed so far in this paper be modified by the Stiglitz analysis?

These questions are most easily answered by considering the decision of a firm with national profits π_o and sales S_o, all attributable to no-tax states, which is considering whether or not to expand into a state with a corporate income tax levied at rate t_i. Suppose, following Stiglitz, that any required investment would be debt financed. The firm's total poten-tial base for state corporate income taxes is π_o, and its base for the sales-related portion of the tax $\pi_o/3$. If the firm sells S_i in the taxing state but does not increase its profits it incurs sales-related tax liability of $t_i\pi_o S_i/(S_o + S_i)3$. Thus the state tax is likely to affect marginal decisions on the location of economic activity, and the analysis presented in earlier parts of this paper is applicable in the Stiglitz world.

Tentative Thoughts on Incidence

Yet another way to see the similarity between the sales-related portion of the state corporation income tax and an ordinary sales tax in the case of $dS = dS_i$ and values of a near zero is to rewrite equations 14.3 and 14.5 as

$$MR_i\left(1 - \pi t_i'/S\right) = MC_i \tag{14.8}$$

and

$$MR_i\left(1 - t_s\right) = MC_i. \tag{14.9}$$

It is useful at this point to distinguish between sales-related profits taxes and sales taxes that are based on destination of sales and those based on origin of sales. In equations 14.8 and 14.9 the marginal costs (MC) and marginal revenues (MR) are marginal in the sense that they give the incremental costs and revenues of sales to state i for destination-based taxes. For origin-based taxes the incremental costs and revenues would relate to sales from state i.

One can expect reactions to the sales-related part of the profits tax that are similar to reactions to gross-receipts taxes. This is most clearly seen in the monopoly case. We begin with a destination-based tax. Figure 14.1 shows the marginal cost (MC_i), demand (D_i), marginal revenue (MR_i), and net marginal revenue (MR_i') of a monopolistic firm that sells a small proportion of its output in the taxing state. The difference between MR_i and MR_i' is due to the sales-related part of the corporate income tax. This tax affects the corporate decision on prices and output in much the same way an equal-yield sales tax does.[24] It reduces the marginal revenue curve as seen by the firm from MR_i to MR_i', where $MR_i' = (1 - t_i'\pi/S) \, MR_i$ (compared with $(1 - t_s) \, MR_i$ for the sales tax case) and results in a fall in the profit-maximizing output from Q_i to Q_i' and a rise in price from P_i to P_i'. Two points bear emphasis.[25]

First, in the case of a destination-based tax, it is useful to characterize

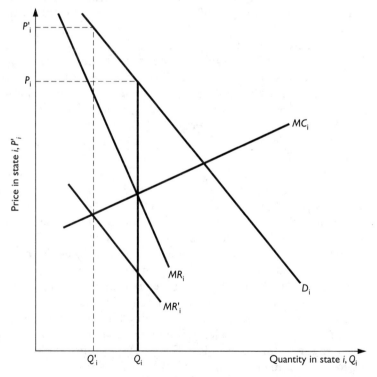

Figure 14.1 Effect of a sales-related profits tax on a monopoly.

the MC_i curve not merely as the marginal *production* cost of selling in the taxing state, but as the *opportunity* cost of doing so. For nationally marketed goods sold in a small state, the MC_i curve is likely to be quite flat, because the firm has the alternative of selling in other states. For that reason the sales tax equivalent of the corporation income tax will cause a maximum effect on price in the taxing state. The MC_i curve for "home goods" (those with primarily a local market) should have a greater slope than the MC_i curve for goods produced for national markets by multistate producers, so that more of the burden would be borne by factor owners. Because capital is mobile between states, land and immobile labor are likely to bear a substantial part of the tax. But in either of these cases the tax would be borne in part from economic profits.

Second, an origin-based tax is most usefully seen as a tax on production. By analogy with the argument presented above for destination-based taxes, the relevant marginal revenue curve for goods with national markets is quite flat, because the national market can be served from other states. As a result, the origin-based tax on nationally or regionally marketed goods would be borne in large part by immobile factors. On the other hand, for "home goods" substantially more forward shifting is to be expected.

It seems likely that results for oligopolistic industries will also be similar to those for a true gross receipts tax, though the analysis required to demonstrate it is not so clear-cut. Two considerations are relevant. First, for a given firm the tax falls somewhere in the spectrum between a true profits tax and a sales tax, depending on the firm's value of a. Second, for the interstate firm the effective sales tax rate depends on the firm's profitability in the nation as a whole. Because various firms have different values of a and different profit margins, and therefore different effective sales tax rates, the likely degree of shifting for a given industry is not clear, even if one ignores the usual complexities of market interaction that plague the analysis of incidence of taxes in oligopolistic industries. It seems reasonable to believe, however, that for destination-based taxes levied on national industries dominated by interstate firms, the high-profit firms selling relatively small fractions of their output in a given state are likely to hold a price umbrella over the less profitable firms and/or intrastate firms for whom the tax is more truly a profits tax. Thus it seems quite likely, especially for the smaller states, that this sales-related portion of the state profits tax is shifted in roughly the way one would expect a true state sales tax to be.[26] Oligopolistic interaction merely strengthens this supposition. For taxes on profits of oligopolistic firms producing primarily for local markets – firms that are likely to be basically intrastate firms – this conclusion of forward shifting is less certain; burden on profits seems somewhat more likely.

The arguments of the previous paragraph apply, strictly speaking, only to a state tax levied on economic profits. But there is little reason to believe that the result would be much different for a tax on accounting profits, except that burdens on capital are even less likely than if the tax were on economic profits.

Next, consider briefly the case of pure competition, for the destination-based tax on accounting profits. (In long-run equilibrium there would be no profits in the competitive case, and therefore no tax if economic profits were the tax base.) Though the analysis would again be tricky, it seems likely that the tax would be reflected in higher prices. By how much the price would rise, however, is unclear, as firms would pay different tax rates, and there is less presumption of price umbrella effects.[27]

Except for one important analytical difference, factor-related profits taxes and origin-based sales-related profits taxes are usefully considered together. As with any tax on the use of a factor, rather than on sales, the property and payroll-related portions of the corporate income tax are not easily portrayed using the partial equilibrium diagram of figure 14.1, except in the case of complete impossibility of factor substitution.[28] But in the cases of both monopoly and pure competition the property and payroll portions of the tax on economic or accounting profits are almost certainly borne, at least in part, by owners of immobile factors, land and perhaps labor, located in the taxing state.[29] The real analytical problems involve the oligopolistic sector. Here it seems quite possible that both origin-based sales-related profits taxes and the factor-related portions of state profits tax are shifted in part to consumers of taxed products throughout the nation via price umbrella effects rather than reflected in lower factor returns, especially if production is dominated by a few firms and geographically centered in the taxing state.[30]

Concluding Remarks: Implications for Policy

The analysis presented here has important implications for tax policy. But as in the case of Peter Mieszkowski's analysis of the incidence of the property tax, the implications depend on whether one takes the point of view of one state or the nation as a whole. Nonetheless, the most important implication of both points of view is that the corporation income tax is an unsatisfactory source of revenue for state governments and should be replaced by other forms of state or federal taxation.

State tax policy

The upshot of this analysis for state tax policy is clear. Economists have long recognized that state and local governments have little business engaging in redistributional taxation implemented through corporate income taxes and progressive personal income taxes because geographic mobility is likely to doom such efforts.[31] My analysis suggests that the prospects are even worse than usually supposed. Rather than being the potentially progressive tax that it appears to be, the state corporation income tax is actually levied, in effect, on two bases that would usually be agreed to lead directly to regressive taxation: sales and payrolls. Moreover, recent analysis of the incidence of the property tax suggests that the property-related portion is likely to be regressive as well.[32] Thus the state corporation income tax does not do what many would seem to intend it to do, and it works only very clumsily and possibly at considerable cost. Therefore, any single state would seem to be well advised at least to replace the corporation income tax with a tax levied directly on corporate sales, payrolls, and property (or whatever else happens to be in its present allocation formula). The only real changes would be: (1) the use of a standard rate of tax instead of one that depends on the firm's national profit performance; and (2) a considerable simplification of tax administration and compliance. Moreover, unless there is a clear reason for preferring to discriminate against the corporate form of organization, it would seem even better to levy the sales, payroll, and property tax on all economic activity, not just that in the corporate sector. Finally, the portions of the substitute tax based on payrolls, property, and sales at origin could probably be replaced by a more general source-based state tax, such as an origin principle value-added tax, and that on sales at destination could be replaced by a destination principle value-added tax or absorbed into the (perhaps newly enacted) state retail sales tax or personal income tax.[33] I submit that this kind of replacement of the corporation income tax would make economic and administrative sense for any state.

The national perspective

There are at least three good reasons why state governments should not employ corporation income taxes, in addition to the two already presented (that states have no business levying taxes such as this that are supposedly progressive and that the tax, as seen by any one state, is not really an income tax anyway).

First, even as a federal levy, the corporation income tax makes no sense, except as a withholding device. Second, it is generally logically impossible to tax accurately the corporate profits originating in any particular state of a multistate firm. Third, the locational allocation of resources is distorted by differentials in the corporate profits taxes levied in various states.

The first of these is beyond the scope of this paper and has been discussed elsewhere.[34] But the analysis of this paper is directly germane to the second and third.

Like overhead, neither economic nor accounting profits can be accurately allocated to any one state. That is the fundamental reason why it is necessary to employ such an arbitrary and unsatisfactory approach as formula apportionment to allocate the national profits of a firm among states. Nor is the use of separate accounting (the practice under which a firm's activities in each state are treated as constituting a separate business) much better. As experience with section 482 of the US Internal Revenue Code has demonstrated in the international sphere, joint costs and problems of transfer pricing render separate accounting as arbitrary as formula apportionment.[35] Because accurate state taxation of corporate income is often a logical impossibility, it seems best to abandon this tax as a source of state revenue.[36] One way to encourage this abandonment would be to disallow the deduction of state corporate income taxes in the calculation of income for federal tax purposes.

In discussions of state taxation of multistate corporations, relatively little has been said about the extent to which differential rates of profit taxation distort investment and other decisions, except in the context of specialized discussions of the effects of taxes and tax incentives on industrial location. This inattention contrasts markedly with the considerable attention focused on the consistency of various systems of international taxation with worldwide efficiency, that is, the neutral allocation of resources (primarily capital), among nations.[37]

It is usually thought to be necessary for the achievement of locational efficiency that the tax levied on a given amount of profit be invariant with regard to the geographic source of that profit.[38] In the present context – and inevitably where analysts are concerned with taxes levied in an open economy – one cannot generally identify the geographic source of profits, as noted above. But it seems reasonable to argue more generally that locational efficiency requires that the tax levied on a given amount of profit should be invariant with respect to where property is located.[39]

Naturally enough the property-related portion of the total corporate tax of the firm is invariant to the location of property only if the tax rate in all jurisdictions is the same (or if the firm earns no profits).[40] Formula apportionment is generally nonneutral (if profits are positive), as it tends to discourage investment in high-tax states.

Concern with locational efficiency of resource allocation thus suggests that states should not use formula-apportioned corporation income taxes, or at least that rates should be uniform across states.[41] If the tax continues to be used, this last conclusion has important ramifications for intergovernmental fiscal relations. First, it suggests that the Multistate Tax Commission (MTC), or something like it, should concern itself with rate differentials as well as with the definition of income and apportionment formulas.[42] This may be a large order indeed, since membership in the MTC is voluntary, and some member states do not currently levy corporation income taxes. Elimination of differentials would require either elimination of all state corporate taxes or, as a first step, the imposition of corporation income taxes in the states now abstaining from using this source of revenue. But I have argued above that this is an inferior form of state tax, regardless of whether it is appraised from the state or the national point of view. Thus any federal requirement that all states levy state corporate income taxes so that rates could be equalized is hardly a clear step forward. A more sensible approach would be to prohibit state use of this tax and make up the lost revenues through federal taxation and grants to the states.[43] A surcharge on the federal corporation income tax might be the obvious choice since it is more or less equivalent to a uniform state tax. But given the faults that an unintegrated corporation income tax has, even at the federal level, one might hope that a better source of revenue could be found.[44] Though this is not the place to go into that question, logical candidates might be a value-added tax, the personal income tax, or a progressive tax on personal expenditures.

Notes

This paper was originally written under a contract from the Office of Tax Analysis of the US Department of the Treasury. The author wishes to thank Michael Boskin, Gary Hufbauer, Peggy Musgrave, and Wayne Thirsk for comments on an earlier draft but not to implicate them or the Office of Tax Analysis in any errors or views expressed here. The paper has not been reviewed by the Board of Directors of the National Bureau of Economic Research.

1   See Advisory Commission on Intergovernmental Relations, *Significant Features of Fiscal Federalism*, vol. 2: *Revenue and Debt*, 1976–77 ed. (Government Printing Office, 1977), p. 10.

2   Ibid., p. 9.

3   Ibid., p. 52.

4   Charles E. McLure, Jr., "Revenue Sharing: Alternative to Rational Fiscal

Federalism?" *Public Policy*, vol. 19 (Summer 1971), p. 472. For a description of state practices in the field of corporation income taxation and recent efforts to gain uniformity, see Charles E. McLure, Jr., "State Income Taxation of Multi-State Corporations in the United States of America," in United Nations, *The Impact of Multinational Corporations on Development and on International Relations*, Technical Papers: Taxation (New York: United Nations, 1974), pp. 58–111. Whether all states use the same allocation formula and definition of income for tax purposes is largely immaterial for the argument made here, but it is convenient to assume uniformity. Finally, references to sales are to gross receipts rather than to retail sales to consumers.

5   For a further discussion of this approach, see Charles E. McLure, Jr., "The Interstate Exporting of State and Local Taxes: Estimates for 1962," *National Tax Journal*, vol. 20 (March 1967), especially pp. 51–2. State corporation income taxes perhaps constitute even less of a system than do local property taxes.

6   Peter Mieszkowski, "The Property Tax: An Excise or a Profits Tax," *Journal of Public Economics*, vol. 1 (April 1972), pp. 73–96.

7   For an elementary exposition of how these apparently conflicting results can be reconciled, see Charles E. McLure, Jr., "The 'New View' of the Property Tax: A Caveat," *National Tax Journal*, vol. 30 (March 1977), pp. 69–75.

8   Again, following Mieszkowski, one can use the analysis presented here for deviations from the average rate of state income taxation, the average being borne like a nationwide income tax.

9   The text relation is similar to the Massachusetts formula, which employs the capital stock rather than payments to capital in the property component. Little is lost and some simplification is gained by using the return to capital as the measure of property. If there are any rents resulting from such assets as patents and mineral deposits owned by the firm, they can be thought of as being included in π. No distinction is made between sales at origin and sales at destination since the mathematics does not require it. If the profits tax is based on a formula that includes sales at destination, the sales portion of the tax resembles a conventional destination principle sales tax. If the formula includes sales at origin, the resemblance is to a tax on sales at origin, or production.

10   Differentiating equation 14.1 with respect to $\bar{\pi}_i$, profits truly attributable to the taxing state, reveals that

$$dT_{is}/d\bar{\pi}_i = t_i'(d\pi/d\bar{\pi}_i)(S_i/S) = t_i'S_i/S.$$

This result might occur, for example, if the firm discovered mineral deposits in state i that increased profits but not sales in state i.

11   It should be noted that strictly speaking, the formulas given in footnotes 10 and 12, and therefore the statements in the text, are completely accurate only if the taxing state's share of the firm's total sales does not change when

profits change. Otherwise the sales allocation factor changes and an additional term, $t_i\pi d(S_i/S)d\bar{\pi}_i$, must be added to the right-hand side of the expression in note 10. (In the equation in note 12, $d\pi$ would replace $d\bar{\pi}_i$ in the additional term.) Of course, it is not possible for profits to increase with neither an increase in sales nor a decrease in labor or capital costs. Thus it is only approximately true that an increase in profits truly attributable to the taxing state (or to the rest of the nation) is allocated among the states in proportion to their shares in sales, payroll, and property.

12   Differentiating equation 14.1 with respect to π, the firm's total (national) profits yields

$$dT_{is}/d\pi = t_i'S_i/S.$$

13   Presuming that the slope of the marginal cost curve exceeds that of the marginal revenue curve.

14   This equation and the conditions for profit maximization are based on the assumption that there are no corporate taxes in other states, and they would be different if indeed other states levied corporate income taxes. But if one impounds other taxes in ceteris paribus, the *differences* in conditions for profit maximization with and without a corporate tax in state i are as indicated here. Alternatively, if one were examining a national system of state corporate income taxes, this analysis would be appropriate for differentials from the national average tax rate.

15   This conclusion can be shown formally by differentiating equation 14.2 with respect to Q_i and setting the result equal to zero:

$$d\pi_n/dQ_i = \left(dS/dQ_i - dR/dQ_i - dW/dQ_i\right)\left(1 - at_i'\right)$$
$$- t_i'\left(\pi/S\right)\left[\left(dS_i/dQ_i\right) - a\left(dS/dQ_i\right)\right] = 0.$$

Of course, dS/dS_i is determined by the interplay of supply conditions and characteristics of demand in the taxing state and elsewhere. But if an increase in sales to the taxing state also represents an increase in total sales rather than a reduction in sales in other states (that is, if $dS/dQ_i = dS_i/dQ_i$), algebraic manipulation of the expression above produces the following equation:

$$dS/dQ_i - dR/dQ_i - dW/dQ_i = \left[\left(1 - a\right)/\left(1 - at_i'\right)\right]\left(t_i'\pi/S\right)dS_i/dQ_i.$$

Of course, if the firm either has no profits ($\pi = 0$) or has sales only in the taxing state ($S_i = S$ and $a = 1$), marginal cost equals marginal revenue. But in the case that is of interest here, that of a profitable multistate corporation, marginal revenue exceeds marginal cost for the profit-maximizing firm. One is tempted to go on from this result to say that the tax reduces sales in the taxing state, increases the prices of goods sold there, and is passed on in part to consumers. That is more than need be said at this point, however, and more than can be said without a more detailed examination of conditions in the industry, including the market interaction of corporate firms of various degrees of profitability, unincorporated firms, and consumer demand. The point I want to make here is that the sales-related portion of the profits tax should affect corporate behavior in roughly the same way as a corporate sales tax levied at differential rates on different firms. The further repercussions of such a sales tax are discussed further below.

16   This equation is derived from the second equation in note 15 under the stated assumptions. As noted in equation 14.1, $t_i' \pi / S = T_{is}/S_i$.

17   Since a profits tax represents a different fraction of sales for various firms in a given state, the sales-related part of the corporate tax is not a uniform flat-rate sales tax. This point is considered further below.

18   For ease of comparison this sales tax rate is defined here as a percentage of the tax-inclusive price rather than of the tax-exclusive price, which is more common in the United States.

19   In particular, table 14.1 shows the proportion of a sales-related profits tax that results in a divergence between marginal costs and marginal revenues. Table 14.1 is based on $dS/dS_i = 1$. Adjustment for other cases is straightforward.

20   ACIR, *Significant Features of Fiscal Federalism.* pp. 219–22. Recall that t_i' is only one-third the statutory rate and is further reduced by federal deductibility. Higher values of t_i' would be relevant, however, if formula allocation were adopted in an international context.

21   The analysis presented here is essentially short run, abstracting from the intersectoral repercussions described by Arnold C. Harberger in "The Incidence of the Corporation Income Tax," *Journal of Political Economy*, vol. 70 (June 1962), pp. 215–40. The point is that the state corporation income tax will have effects more like those of a state tax on corporate sales, property, or payrolls than like those of a tax on corporate profits in the short run, and hence even if long-run general equilibrium interactions are taken into account.

22   The part of the tax levied on economic profits does not distort economic decisions, but the part levied on normal profits does. Suppose the tax were levied *only* on normal profits. Thus $\pi_n = (S - R - W) - tN$. Differentiating, the result is $dS/dQ - dR/dQ - dW/dQ = tdN/dQ$. The component dN/dQ can also be written as $(dN/dS)(dS/dQ)$, the product of the normal profit margin on marginal sales and marginal revenue. Employing $m = dN/dS$, equation 14.6a can be rewritten as

$$dS\big/dQ\big[1 - mt\big/(1-t)\big] = dR\big/dQ + dW\big/dQ.$$

The divergence between marginal cost and marginal revenue thus depends on the profit margin and the tax rate.

23   See Joseph E. Stiglitz, "Taxation, Corporate Financial Policy, and the Cost of Capital," *Journal of Public Economics*, vol. 2 (February 1973), pp. 1–34.

24   In order to draw figure 14.1 the operations attributable to sales in state *i* are treated as separable from those in other states, though they will generally not be separable.

25   The discussion that follows goes back to Charles E. McLure, Jr., "An Analysis of Regional Tax Incidence, with Estimation of Interstate Incidence of State and Local Taxes" (Ph.D. dissertation, Princeton University, 1965), pp. 79–86, but incorporates analysis from Mieszkowski, "The Property Tax," and McLure, "The 'New View' of the Property Tax."

26   If the apportionment formula employs sales at destination, the shifting would be to consumers. If it includes sales at origin, backward shifting to immobile factors, land and perhaps labor, is more likely.

27   Long-run competitive equilibrium, however, would seem to require that all firms have identical ratios of sales to accounting profits and equal fractions of their sales in given states.

28   For a further discussion of this problem, see Charles E. McLure, Jr., "General Equilibrium Incidence Analysis: The Harberger Model after Ten Years," *Journal of Public Economics*, vol. 4 (February 1975), pp. 125–61.

29   See also McLure, "The 'New View' of the Property Tax." For a discussion of this issue in a slightly different context, see Charles E. McLure, Jr., "The Relevance of the New View of the Incidence of the Property Tax in Less Developed Countries," in Roy W. Bahl, ed., *The Taxation of Urban Property in Less Developed Countries* (University of Wisconsin Press for the Committee on Taxation, Resources and Economic Development, 1979), pp. 51–76. To the extent that locational monopoly rents exist, the tax may be borne in part by owners of the firm (or other owners of the economic interest in the assets generating rents).

30   For the use of such an assumption, see McLure, "The Interstate Exporting of State and Local Taxes."

31   See, for example, Richard A. Musgrave, *The Theory of Public Finance* (McGraw-Hill, 1959), pp. 181–2; and Wallace E. Oates, "Theory of Public Finance in a Federal System." *Canadian Journal of Economics*, vol. 1 (February 1968), pp. 37–54.

32   Recall that I am dealing with the tax as seen from the vantage point of individual states, so it is "excise effects" that are relevant. As noted earlier, what is true for each state is not true for all states acting together. That is, if all states levied the same corporation income tax, corporate profits *would* be burdened (if the Harberger-type shifting to owners of noncorporate capital is ignored). But this is largely irrelevant to decisions made in any statehouse because any deviations from that uniform tax would have the effects described here.

33   One real problem with state personal income taxes is the difficulty of including corporate-source income, especially retained earnings. This is one possible justification for not taking the final step to replacing the state tax on sales at destination with a state personal income tax. On the other hand,

allowance can be made for family circumstances under the personal income tax, but this is difficult under the present corporate profits taxes and flat-rate payroll and property taxes. Similarly, retail sales taxes allow exemption of key items, which does not occur under state corporation income taxes. If the corporate and personal income taxes were integrated at the federal level, it would be substantially easier to obtain the information necessary to tax personal income at residence at the state level.

34   For a detailed discussion of the lack of rationale inherent in a separate tax on corporation income, see Charles E. McLure, Jr., "Integration of the Personal and Corporate Income Taxes: The Missing Element in Recent Tax Reform Proposals," *Harvard Law Review*, vol. 88 (January 1975), pp. 532–82. Administrative difficulties of integration and divided relief are the subject of Charles E. McLure, Jr., *Must Corporate Income Be Taxed Twice?* (Brookings Institution, 1979).

35   For discussions of problems of section 482 see, for example, M. L. Hamlin, "Correct Allocations under Section 482 Are Still Difficult Despite New Regs," *Journal of Taxation*, vol. 43 (December 30, 1975), pp. 358–63; and Lawrence C. Phillips, "The Current Status of the Application of Section 482 to Foreign Related Corporations," *Taxes*, vol. 48 (August 1970), pp. 472–8.

   In recent years there has been some interest in the use of formula apportionment to replace the separate accounting approach found in the tax treatment of multinational firms by national governments. As evidence of this, see United Nations *The Impact of Multinational Corporations*. For an expression of preference for formula apportionment in the international field, see Peggy B. Musgrave, "International Tax Base Division and the Multinational Corporation," *Public Finance*, vol. 27, no. 4 (1972), pp. 394–413. The present criticism of formula-apportioned income taxation should not be interpreted as a preference for separate accounting. Which of these approaches is a superior way of allocating the unallocable is beyond the scope of this paper.

36   The basic problem is jointness or indivisibility of the firm's operations, and the same principles that apply to public goods in the literature on fiscal federalism seem to apply here also. The allocation of responsibility for the provision of various public goods among levels of government should depend on the area over which benefits extend. Similarly taxation of the multistate firm should be imposed by the jurisdiction most nearly congruent with the area the firm's activities cover. If the decision units are smaller than optimal, problems arise. Among the problems are the locational effects discussed below.

37   This difference in emphasis almost certainly reflects the different principles on which state and national income taxes are based. State corporation income taxes are based essentially on a territorial principle. That is, states ostensibly attempt to tax only profits whose source lies within their borders, independently of the legal site of residence of the corporation or its owners. On the other hand, many nations (but not all of even the important

industrial nations) apply a worldwide principle under which all profits of resident firms are subject to profits tax, wherever earned.

Under the territorial or "source" principle the net return to investment (assuming the corporation income tax actually is levied on profits produced in a given area instead of through formula apportionment) depends on where capital is invested, unless effective tax rates are the same in all jurisdictions. Thus the territorial principle inherently interferes with worldwide or nationwide efficiency. By comparison, the achievement of worldwide efficiency is at least generally consistent with the worldwide or "residence" principle. Nations applying this approach, however, almost always also tax all profits originating within their borders. For an excellent background discussion of various methods of relieving the double taxation that results from overlapping taxes being levied on the same income, and other issues relevant to the material covered in this section, see Mitsuo Sato and Richard M. Bird, "International Aspects of the Taxation of Corporations and Shareholders," *International Monetary Fund Staff Papers*, vol. 22 (July 1975), pp. 384–455. I take as given continued state reliance on the territorial principle because corporate taxation at residence does not have the appeal in the interstate context that it has in the international sphere.

38 See, for example, Peggy B. Musgrave, *United States Taxation of Foreign Investment Income: Issues and Arguments* (Harvard Law School, International Tax Program, 1969).

39 Concern with locational effects on investment is most analogous to concern about equal taxation of profits, which is essentially a matter of the locational allocation of capital.

40 Of course, if tax rates are uniform, many systems of taxation are locationally neutral. In order to show that formula apportionment does not generally result in locational efficiency, I write the following expression for the property-related portion of the profits tax on a firm collected in state i and in all other states (lumped together as $j \neq i$):

$$T = \left[bt_i + (1-b)t_j \right]\pi$$

or

$$T = \left[t_j + b(t_i - t_j) \right]\pi,$$

where t_j is the weighted average of tax rates in all states other than i. Differentiating, with respect to b, the fraction of total property of the firm located in state i, the result is

$$dT/db = (t_i - t_j)\pi.$$

41   It is ironic, but natural, that the property-related portion of the state tax is both the culprit most responsible for adverse locational effects and perhaps that most natural choice as the best single apportionment factor in the Massachusetts formula.

42   For descriptions of the MTC and its activities, see McLure, "State Income Taxation of Multistate Corporations"; "Taxation of Multi-Jurisdictional Corporate Income: Lessons of the US Experience," in Wallace Oates, ed., *The Political Economy of Fiscal Federalism* (Lexington Books, 1977), pp. 241–59, and especially Eugene F. Corrigan, "Interstate Corporate Income Taxation: Recent Revolutions and a Modern Response," *Vanderbilt Law Review*, vol. 29 (March 1976), pp. 423–42.

43   This suggestion might seem to be inconsistent with my questioning of the role of unconditional grants in "Revenue Sharing: An Alternative to Rational Fiscal Federalism," pp. 474–6. But I argued there that state corporation income taxes have no place in a rational system of fiscal federalism, whereas unconditional grants may be more or less equivalent to broad-based general taxes, such as sales and personal income taxes, and therefore acceptable.

44   Moreover, if this tax were used, there might be a natural tendency to assume that grants to states should be based on corporate income originating in the states. But such an assumption would resurrect the insurmountable problems of income measurement that lead me to suggest that the states should not use the corporate income tax.

Introduction to Chapter 15

Charges paid by users for services and facilities provided by governments that are related to the nature and extent of the use by the individual user are highly regarded as a source of revenue by economists. When charges are properly designed, they are like the prices that confront buyers of goods and services sold in well-functioning markets: they contribute to efficiency in the allocation of resources.

User charges, sometimes well designed, more often not, have been significant in local government finance ever since municipalities began operating water-supply and electric-power utilities in the late 19th and early 20th centuries. They have grown in relative importance since the early 1970s and account for more than one-third of the revenue raised by local governments from their own sources.

This article attempts to answer the question of whether the growth reflects no more than the relative expansion in spending for functions traditionally financed in significant part by user charges, rather than by a shift in their pattern of financing particular functions. The second question addressed is why there is such wide variation among the states in the extent of reliance on user charges.

15

Differences in Reliance on User Charges by American State and Local Governments

Dick Netzer

Abstract

Reliance on user charges by American local governments has increased substantially since the early 1970s. Changes in the mix of expenditure are partly responsible, but the major cause has been increased user charge financing of specific functions. Differences in the mix of expenditure also partly explain the wide interstate differences in reliance on user charges, but a more important variable is personal income, negatively associated with user charge reliance. Another significant variable is the ability to export business taxes, which discourages user charges as would be expected.

In recent years, there has been considerable discussion in the popular press about a supposed major shift to reliance on user charges in local government finance in the United States in the face of fiscal difficulties that have been either external in origin – like reductions in federal aid and especially severe local or regional recessions – or self-imposed – like the adoption of caps on local property taxes by voters and state legislatures. Some academics have written about this as well, presumably because we like to see signs that, at long last, voters and legislatures are beginning to appreciate the economic sense of the change, that is, the rather obvious efficiency gains from moving from general tax financing to marginal cost pricing of the private goods aspects of local government expenditure.

Although the focus of this article is on persisting regional and state differences in reliance on user charges, it is useful to examine the nature of the changes over time as context. This is done in the first section of the article. Reliance on user charges by local governments has, in fact, increased considerably since the 1960s, but much of the increase took place in the 1970s rather than in the 1980s as the journalistic accounts would have it.

The second section deals with recent interstate differences and their possible explanation. Differences in the mix of expenditures – whether a state emphasizes functions for which user charges traditionally have been important – are a partial explanation. The other significant explanatory variables, with a negative influence on reliance on user charges, are the level of personal income – it is not obvious why this should be the case – and the relative extent to which business taxes can be exported.

Trends in Reliance on User Charges Over Time

It is unquestionably true that the importance of user charges in US state-local revenue systems has increased since the early 1970s, although the increase is rather less dramatic than most journalists and some academicians claim it to be. I employ two definitions of user charges, that is, a narrow and a broader combination of Census Bureau revenue categories.[1] The narrow definition includes "current charges" and utility revenue. The broad definition adds highway-user taxes, special assessments, and fines.

For all state and local governments combined, user charges narrowly defined changed little during the 1960s but increased from 18.5% of own-source general and utility revenue in 1972 to 22.1% in 1989 (see table 15.1). There was little change between 1972 and 1989 when the broad definition is employed, which is a consequence of the relative decline in state government highway-user tax revenue over the period.[2] However, for local governments by themselves, user charges – however

Table 15.1 Trends in reliance on user charge revenue, 1962–89 (user charge revenue as percentage of own source general and utility revenue)

	1962	1972	1982	1989
State and local governments combined				
Narrow definition[a]	18.9	18.5	21.8	22.1
Broad definition[b]	29.7	26.6	26.8	26.9
Local governments only				
Narrow definition	26.4	25.6	33.4	33.7
Broad definition	28.1	26.9	34.8	35.1

[a] "Narrow definition" is current charges and utility revenue.
[b] "Broad definition" adds highway-user taxes, special assessments, and fines, the latter mostly related to road and street use.
Source: Census Bureau Government Finance diskettes, 1989.

measured – clearly have increased in importance in recent years. User charges, defined either way, declined relatively during the 1960s and early 1970s and rose substantially from 1975 onward, with most of the increase occurring in the 1970s.

Various explanations can be offered for the increased reliance on user charges. The change could be a response to the reductions in federal aid over the past decade and also a response to the limitations on local property tax revenues imposed by state constitutional and statutory measures adopted beginning in the early 1970s; the timing of the second explanation is consistent with the timing of the increased reliance on user charges, but the timing of the first explanation is not. More sophisticated explanations include (a) the shift in the composition of local government expenditure away from services like K-12 education, for which user charges are not important, to services like the environmental services, for which user charges *are* important; (b) heightened interstate tax competition, which would encourage a shift toward financing mechanisms that appear to location decision makers to be tied to specific benefits; and (c) the decreased value of federal income tax deductibility caused by lower marginal income tax rates.

Formally, the increase in the overall reliance on user charges over time must be caused by some combination of three factors: declines in the share of total revenue provided by grants from external governments, shifts in the mix of expenditures toward or away from functions that traditionally are heavily financed by user charges, and increases in the extent to which specific functions are financed by user charges. Because the concern of this article is with choice by subnational government, the discussion here will focus on user charges relative to own-source revenue and expenditures net of the share financed by intergovernmental assistance. In this part of the article, the treatment is confined to local governments, which are the governments mainly responsible for the functions for which user charges traditionally have been of consequence, except for highways and higher education, mainly state responsibilities.

Table 15.2 presents data for 1972, 1982, and 1989 for 13 specific functions that have always had a good deal of user charge financing. There is a substantial private-goods aspect to all of these functions, which accounts for well over 80% of all local government user charge revenue. The table compares user charge revenue, broadly defined, to expenditure for the function, less federal and state aid received for that purpose.[3] For 9 of the 13 functions, the user charge percentage increased substantially from 1972 to 1989. The exceptions were the water supply and energy utilities, which were essentially self-financed (with few exceptions) at the beginning of the period, and transit, for which the user

Table 15.2 Changes in local government reliance on user charges for financing selected functions, 1962–89 (user charge revenue as percentage of expenditure less federal and state aid)

	1962	1972	1982	1989
All general and utility activities	25.8	24.8	34.5	34.1
Transportation activities				
Highways and parking	14.1	30.7	29.9	35.5
Transit	83.4	55.1	31.2	41.7
Air transportation	56.2	52.7	82.4	79.2
Water transportation	53.2	64.3	77.6	83.1
Energy and environmental activities				
Water supply	83.1	84.8	74.6	81.8
Electric power supply	103.2	86.3	78.1	93.7
Gas supply	107.8	107.9	104.1	103.1
Sewerage	40.3	45.2	56.0	76.2
Solid waste management	17.6	24.8	34.5	46.0
Parks and recreation	14.0	15.4	18.8	23.4
Natural resources	21.9	14.2	15.5	21.6
Selected other activities				
Hospitals	43.8	57.9	77.6	78.5
Housing and community development	32.6	52.4	63.4	63.3
Total for selected actvities	45.8	53.5	59.5	68.1
All other functions	9.6	7.7	10.6	9.0

Source: Calculated by the author from Census Bureau Government Finance diskettes, 1989, which contain data essentially identical with *Governmental Finances in 1989*.

charge percentage declined sharply from 1972 to 1982 but recovered partially between 1982 to 1989.[4]

The reasons for the increased reliance on user-charge financing varied among the other nine selected functions. The stereotypical explanation for increased reliance on user charges – imposing charges for services that previously had been entirely tax-financed and increasing the rates of existing charges that had been relatively minor revenue producers – appears to have been the basis for the increase for the four environmental services and probably for local government highway finance as well. For airports, water transportation (mainly terminal facilities), and housing and community development, the increase in reliance on user charges may be more apparent than real, related to the mix of spending between capital and current operations.[5] Finally, in the census classification sys-

Table 15.3 Explaining changes in local government reliance on user charges between 1972 and 1989 (user charge revenue as percentage of expenditure less federal and state aid)

		1989, *With expenditure mix for:*		
		1972	*1989*	*1972*
	Actual,	*and user charge percentages for:*		
	1989	*1989*	*1972*	*1972*
All functions	34.1	29.6	28.9	26.6
Selected activities (table 15.2)	68.1	64.4	57.6	53.5
All other functions	9.0	9.0	7.7	10.6

Source: Calculated by the author from Census Bureau Government Finance diskettes, 1989.

tem, all third-party reimbursements received by government hospitals, including Medicare payments, are current charges, so that increases in intergovernmental funding of hospital costs in those forms are recorded as increased reliance on user charges rather than as a substitution of external grants for local taxes.

The expenditure mix also was changing during these years. The selected functions that traditionally involved relatively more user charge financing increased, as a group, from 37% of total locally financed expenditure in 1972 to 43% in 1989. Spending for the energy and environmental activities increased relatively in this period, as did spending for airports and hospitals. Spending for the other selected functions declined relatively but only slightly so (except for housing).

Table 15.3 is an effort to sort out the two formal causes of the overall change in reliance on user charges between 1972 and 1989: the change in expenditure mix and the change in user charge shares for individual functions. User charge revenue in 1989 was 26.6% higher than it would have been had neither the expenditure mix nor the user charges percentages for individual functions changed from 1972. Apparently, the change in the user charge percentages was the weightier factor: It accounts for about 57% of the change in overall reliance on user charges.

Explaining Interstate Differences

A casual inspection of the data shows wide variations among the states in the ratio of user charge revenue to total revenue excluding federal aid (see table 15.4): the standard deviation of the ratio in 1989 was more than 25% of the mean value for the country and there was a 3:1 range in the state values. Most of the low values are in the Northeast and most of the highest ones in the South, but there are major differences between adjacent states. Compare, for example, Kentucky and Tennessee or Nebraska and Kansas. There is no obvious logical explanation for such differences, aside from a crude version of the Tiebout hypothesis: At some early point, when the population was much smaller, voters who preferred to finance local and state government public services from general taxes chose to settle on one side of the state boundary and those who preferred explicit general taxes settled on the other side, each becoming a magnet for future settlers with tastes similar to those of the voters already in place. This section examines some plausible explanatory factors, including expenditure mix, income levels, tax structure, tax base composition and the size of the state-local fisc.

The literature contains few efforts to explain systematically the differ-

Table 15.4 Regional differences in reliance on user charges, 1989 (ratio of user charge revenue to total own-source revenue)

Northeast		South (continued)	
New England	0.194	East South Central	0.399
CT	0.163	AL	0.396
MA	0.209	KY	0.274
ME	0.189	MS	0.386
NH	0.215	TN	0.486
RI	0.160	West South Central	0.297
VT	0.250	AR	0.300
Middle Atlantic	0.186	LA	0.271
NJ	0.171	OK	0.344
NY	0.184	TX	0.295
PA	0.203		
		West	
Midwest		Mountain	0.293
East North Central	0.242	AZ	0.297
IL	0.215	CO	0.305
IN	0.305	ID	0.292
MI	0.244	MT	0.219
OH	0.240	NM	0.239
WI	0.237	NV	0.292
West North Central	0.304	UT	0.368
IA	0.320	WY	0.237
KS	0.270	Pacific	0.272
MN	0.268	AK	0.151
MO	0.276	CA	0.267

Table 15.4 *Continued*

ND	0.331	HI	0.218
NE	0.472	OR	0.269
SD	0.264	WA	0.358
South			
South Atlantic	0.283		
DC	0.192		
DE	0.273		
FL	0.287		
GA	0.326		
MD	0.174		
NC	0.320		
SC	0.370		
VA	0.266		
WV	0.246		

Note: User charge revenue is the sum of current charges, utility revenue, and revenue from motor fuel and motor vehicle license taxes; detail on a state basis is not available for 1989 for other revenue items included in the "broad definition" of user charges. Total own-source revenue is own-source general revenue plus utility revenue.
Source: Census Bureau Government Finance diskettes, 1989.

ences among the states in their relative reliance on user charges instead of general taxes. In one of the few such efforts, Tannenwald (1990) found that expenditure mix and exportability of the state-local tax burden are important variables in explaining the relatively low use of user charges in the New England states.[6] Specifically, there is a high correlation between the percentage of total expenditure for public welfare and "collective services" and user charges as a share of total own-source revenue.[7] Also, the average net burden of a deductible tax dollar paid by households is relatively low in New England and federally deductible household taxes are a relatively large share of total household taxes, suggesting substitution of deductible taxes for user charges.

In this article, regression equations are estimated to explain differences among the states in aggregate state-local reliance on user charges in fiscal 1989, and using the same independent variables, reliance on user charges for three specific functions.[8] The variables are defined in the appendix.

Regression variables

The dependent variables are the ratios of user charge revenue to (a) total revenue from own sources and (b) expenditure less federal aid for highways, solid waste management, and transit, functions for which there is a good deal of interstate variation in reliance on user charges.[9] The independent variables describe fiscal institutions and economic characteristics.

Expenditure mix   Obviously, the proportion of total spending that is devoted to functions for which user charge financing is relatively important in nearly all states – and always has been must explain a good deal of the differences in user charge use. The variable is the combined expenditure for the functions identified in table 15.2 as a proportion of total expenditure, excluding electric, water-supply, and gas utilities (for which the interstate variation in the user charge percentage is trivial); the expected sign is, of course, positive.

Taste for public spending   Conceivably, the choice between taxes and user charges reflects households' attitudes toward the relative merits of public and private goods, if voters view spending that is user charge financed as being the equivalent of private goods and make Tiebout decisions about the state of residence. One variable is a measure of preferences for public spending that abstracts from the level of personal income per se: total expenditure financed from state-local sources divided by personal income. An alternative view of the taste for public spending is a simple index of personal income per capita. This derives from likelihood that the income elasticity of demand for state-local spending for "collective goods" is higher than the very low income elasticity of demand for utility and transportation services. The implication is that higher income should increase the willingness to pay general taxes more than the willingness to pay user charges. Thus the expected sign of both these variables is negative.

Taste for progressivity in state-local tax systems   There is considerable diversity in the degree of progressivity in state-local tax systems, and the relative position of individual states in this regard has been fairly consistent over they years. Why this should be is hardly self-evident, but if voters in a state do in fact have a taste for progressivity, then they would tend to prefer general taxes to user charges. Alternative measures of this taste are used here. The first is the ratio of revenue from state-local income taxes to federal individual income tax liability for the state's federal taxpayers. The second is the maximum marginal rate for the state's individual income tax. The sign of both coefficients should be negative.

Relative role of the state (vs. local) government   Because state governments generally might be more or less aggressive employers of user charges than might local governments, the relative importance of the two levels of government itself can influence the user charge versus general tax decision. The likely direction of the effect, however, is unclear: For example, user charge financing of highways at the state level is much greater than at the local level, whereas state-operated transit utilities have very high subsidy rates.

Potential for tax exporting   It is plausible that the higher the federal marginal tax rate confronting individual income taxpayers who itemize and the greater the percentage of taxpayers who do itemize, the more likely it is that the state will rely on general taxes rather than on user charges. The first variable dealing with this explanation is a fabricated measure that combines both aspects of deductibility.

But nonhousehold tax burdens also can be exported, especially by the natural resource producing states. The measure of this used here is a crude one: the ratio of gross state product to resident personal income. High ratios occur in states with extensive natural-resource-based production and, to a lesser extent, in states with substantial net in-commuting by residents of other states. The expected sign of both exporting variables is negative.[10]

Regression results

As table 15.5 shows, only three of the independent variables proved to be statistically significant in the all-functions equations: expenditure mix, personal income per capita and exporting of business taxes. The three had the right signs and, by themselves, explain about 60% of the interstate differences in reliance on user charges. Of the other independent variables, the signs of the coefficients were in the expected direction only for one of the two "taste for progressivity" variables.[11]

The per capita personal income variable is the most powerful, accounting for about half of the combined influence of the three significant variables (as measured by standardized regression coefficients). The expenditure mix variable accounts for roughly a third of the combined influence of the three variables, and the business tax exporting variable accounts for about one sixth.

Three functions – highways, solid waste management, and transit – were analyzed separately because financing policies for these functions differ considerably among the states. In some states, virtually all local

Table 15.5 Regression results (standard error in parentheses)

	Equations with the user charge percentage of own-source revenue (all functions) as the dependent variable				
	1	2	3	4	5
Constant	0.3596	0.3640	0.3712	0.3747	0.3146
Expenditure mix	0.4470*	0.4476*	0.4579*	0.4574**	0.5368*
	(0.1610)	(0.1553)	(0.1563)	(0.0153)	(0.1397)
Expenditure relative to personal income	0.0362				
	(0.1402)				
Personal income index	−0.0018*	−0.0019*	−0.0019	−0.0018*	−0.0017*
	(0.0004)	(0.0003)	(0.0004)	(0.0003)	(0.0002)
State-local income revenue relative to federal income tax liability	−0.0546	−0.0351			
	(0.0515)	(0.0386)			
Maximum marginal rate, state individual income tax	0.0012	−0.0002			
	(0.0021)	(0.0015)			
Relative role of state government	−0.0483	−0.0450	−0.0520	−0.0527	
	(0.0469)	(0.0440)	(0.0438)	(0.0426)	
Federal personal income tax deductibility index	0.0662	0.0767	0.0339		
	(0.0986)	(0.0951)	(0.0908)		
Exporting of business taxes	−0.0576***	−0.0528**	−0.0562**	−0.0560**	−0.0536**
	(0.0334)	(0.0218)	(0.0217)	(0.0213)	(0.0213)
R^2	0.6224	0.6191	0.6122	0.6109	0.5980

* $p < 0.001$; ** $p < 0.01$; *** $p < 0.05$.

highway spending, as well as state government spending, is financed from state highway-user revenues; in others, there is significant local financing of local highway spending, but in some of those cases, local governments employ their own highway-user taxes and charges importantly. There are wide differences in transit financing policies among the states, although the states with the lowest user charge ratios for the function tend to be those in which transit systems are small in size. Even greater variation is found with respect to user charge financing of solid waste management: The standard deviation for this dependent variable is about 70% of the mean.

The individual function regression equations are not very persuasive and are not displayed in table 15.5. The R^2s range from 0.49 for highways down to 0.28 for transit. In all of these equations, two variables that had no significance in the all-functions equations – expenditure as a percentage of personal income and one of the "taste for progressivity" variables – were significant, but the signs are contradictory.

On balance, these findings are not very satisfying and probably would not be even if some of the nonsignificant variables had had smaller standard errors. It is neither surprising nor particularly informative to discover that Alaskans prefer to exploit their natural resources in the form of severance taxes instead of paying user charges. The meaning of the per capita personal income variable can be interpreted in vaious ways – for example, it may in fact be the appropriate way to measure the influence of federal income tax deductibility of personal taxes – in addition to the perhaps fanciful way advanced earlier in this article. And the interesting issue with regard to expenditure mix is how the states came to differ in this measure, as opposed to the almost tautological statistical results shown here. The single "discovery" that appears clear from this exercise is that there is no relation between tax structure progressivity and reliance on user charges, which probably can be construed to mean that voters and legislators really do *not* see user charges as regressive to an objectionable extent.

Notes

1   The government finance data in this article are, unless otherwise specified, Census Bureau Governments Division data, almost all extracted from the Government Finance Series, 1989, diskettes provided by the Census Bureau. A few of the items are census data extracted from Advisory Commission on Intergovernmental Relations diskettes.

2   This, of course, results from the typical structure of these taxes, with the tax base measured in physical volume terms rather than ad valorem.

3   There are all sorts of data problems with these comparisons, including the

failure to distinguish between debt-financed capital expenditure and other expenditures, the failure to account for interest on debt incurred for the function (except for the four functions that the Census Bureau classes as utilities), and the lack of coincidence in timing of receipts and expenditures in the census system (in part due to differences in fiscal years between grantors and grantees). However, the alternative comparisons that are conceivable, given the nature of the data, are worse.

4   This is a function of trends in federal aid: Increased federal aid in the 1970s was associated with increased subsidy from local governments, whereas declining federal aid in the 1980s was offset only in part by increased locally financed subsidies.

5   In 1989, a much larger share of expenditure for these functions was for current operation (and debt service originating in past capital outlays) than was true in 1972 when capital outlays were relatively more important for these functions; capital outlays are financed by borrowing, so a change in the character of expenditure for these functions results in a measured increase in reliance on user charges.

6   Robert Tannenwald, "Taking Charge: Should New England Increase Its Reliance on User Charges?" in Federal Reserve Bank of Boston, *New England Economic Review*, January/February 1990. As the title of the article suggests, the focus is on the criteria for policy decisions rather than the more elementary question that this article addresses.

7   The results may be affected by aspects of the definitions of both the variables. Tannenwald included liquor store revenue in his definition of user charges but excluded highway-user taxes. Perhaps more important, his definition of "collective services" includes interest on general debt. However, the great bulk of outstanding state-local debt was issued for functions that have important private-goods aspects and are classified by Tannenwald as "mixed services."

8   In the time-series discussion, the focus has been on local governments. However, in cross-sectional analysis over the states, it is necessary to focus on combined state-local data because of the considerabe differences among the states in the allocation of functional and financial responsibilities.

9   There is virtually no difference between the regression results for the all-functions dependent variable with and without federal aid. Therefore, only the results for the ratio of user charges to total own-source revenue are presented here.

10 Time-hallowed practice in regression analysis would appear to call for the use of a dummy variable to capture otherwise unexplained regional differences in this situation, where the dependent variable in one region – the Northeast – is so much lower than it is in the other regions (see table 15.4). Regressions with a regional dummy were estimated. The dummy variable was not significant and its presence had almost no effect on the results.

11 The simple correlation coefficients among the independent variables were high only for expenditure relative to personal income and business tax

exporting and personal income per capita and the federal personal tax deductibility index. Conceivably, there might be a simultaneity problem in that the right-hand term is a revenue one and some of the left-hand terms are expenditure. However, all of the terms in question are defined either as mix (the dependent variable and the first independent variable) or as expenditure or revenue relative to something that is exogenous to this system. The significance of the expenditure mix variable in the allfunctions equations thus does provide more information than simply reflecting the fact that total expenditure equals total revenue.

Appendix

Definitions of Variables Used in Regression Equations

Dependent variables
  Equations for all functions combined: User charge revenue, broadly
  defined to include current charges, highway-user taxes, and transit
  utility revenue, divided by general revenue from own sources plus
  transit utility revenue

Independent variables
  Expenditure mix: Expenditure for functions for which user charges are
  traditionally relatively important (highways, hospitals, housing and
  community development, natural resources, parking, parks and recreation, sewerage, solid waste management, transit subsidies, and
  transit utilities) divided by total general expenditure plus transit utility
  expenditure

  Expenditure relative to personal income: Total expenditure less federal aid, 1988–9, divided by personal income, calendar 1988

  Index of personal income per capita, 1988, US = 100

  State-local income tax revenue relative to federal income tax liability:
  Revenue from state and local income taxes, 1988–9, divided by federal
  individual income tax liability of state residents for the tax year 1988[a]

  Maximum marginal rate, state individual income tax, 1988[b]

  Relative role of state government: State government own-source revenue divided by total own-source state-local government revenue

Federal personal income tax deductibility index: Percentage of federal individual income taxpayers itemizing for tax year 1985 multiplied by an index of the marginal rate for those itemizers[c]

Exporting of business taxes: Gross regional product divided by personal income[d]

[a] *Statistics of Income Bulletin,* Fall 1990.

[b] Advisory Commission on Intergovernmental Relations, *Significant Features of Fiscal Federalism,* Vol. 1: *1990,* table 19.

[c] Data prepared by Daniel Feenberg of NBER for Robert Tannenwald of the Federal Reserve Bank of Boston, shared by the latter with Howard Chernick and by Howard Chernick with me.

[d] Gross state product data from *Survey of Current Business,* May 1988.

Sources: Except where otherwise indicated, from 1989 Census Bureau Government Finance and 1989 Advisory Commission on Intergovernmental Relations diskettes.

Introduction to Chapter 16

The finances of state and local governments are affected by an array of actions of the Federal government in addition to the most obvious one, Federal grants. Historically, taxes paid to state and local governments have been deductible on Federal individual income tax returns and interest received by investors in state and local bonds and notes has been exempt from Federal income tax, both for individuals and for corporations. Since the 1960s, there have been proposals to eliminate or restrict these advantages, and restrictions have been enacted, culminating in the major changes of the landmark Tax Reform Act of 1986, which also reduced the top bracket rates of the income tax.

These changes in Federal tax rates and rules increase the net cost to the taxpayer of state and local tax payments and can lead to increases in the cost of state-local borrowing. The next two chapters address these questions, the first dealing with deductibility of state and local taxes and the second with both deductibility and the tax exemption of interest payments.

Conceivably, the strong political pressures for tax reduction at the state and local level may be based on voter perceptions that the net cost to them of state and local taxes is now considerably higher than it was prior to 1988, when the Tax Reform Act of 1986 became fully effective.

16

Tax Reform: Implications for the State-Local Public Sector

Paul N. Courant and Daniel L. Rubinfeld

The Tax Reform Act of 1986 should provide valuable information which will allow economists to distinguish among competing models of the determinants of state and local spending and taxes. This paper outlines the implications of current public finance theory and empirical work for the direction and (where possible) likely magnitudes of the effects of the tax bill after it is fully in effect in 1988. We analyze separately the effects of the bill on the level and distribution of state and local spending, and on the mix of revenue sources employed by state and local governments.

The effects of the tax reform in this area will be fairly small; we expect state and local spending to fall by between 0.9 percent and 1.9 percent, with the lower end of the range the more plausible. A reduction in the number of itemizers – taxpayers who will be unable to deduct their state and local income and property taxes – will account for about half of this change. The elimination of sales tax deductibility, which also makes citizens pay more for state and local government, accounts for slightly more than a third of the decrease in spending. Finally, reductions in marginal tax rates, which make the deductions for income and property taxes worth less to taxpayers who continue to itemize, accounts for the rest. Moreover, states will probably shift away from sales taxes toward deductible sources of revenue, thereby making the effect of the tax reform on state spending smaller still.

The conclusion that aggregate spending is unlikely to change very much does not imply that the Tax Reform Act is unimportant to the state and local public sector. The fiscal and economic circumstances of state and local governments vary enormously, and the federal tax reform

Paul N. Courant and Daniel L. Rubinfeld, "Tax Reform: Implications for the State-Local Public Sector," *Journal of Economic Perspectives*, *1* (Summer 1987), 87–100. Reprinted by permission of the authors and the publisher.

will therefore affect them very differently. Local governments with relatively large numbers of high income homeowners can be expected to reduce their expenditures substantially and to expand their reliance on user charges. The relative fiscal attractiveness of localities within metropolitan areas will be altered, leading to changes in population distribution and house values, and increasing the incentives for higher income households to segregate themselves from lower income households. From both an efficiency and an equity perspective, these effects on local governments are likely to be much more important than the aggregate effect on either state or local spending.

The Tax Reform Act has the immediate effect of changing state revenues; most states will enjoy an increase at current rates, while some will lose revenue. Over the longer run, apart from the obvious incentive to move away from the non-deductible sales tax to other deductible taxes, the effect of tax reform on the mix of revenue instruments is difficult to predict. The new tax bill also has major implications for bond financing: it limits the use of the tax-exempt bond instrument (since industrial development bonds have been cut back and regulations regarding the use of tax-exempt bonds generally have been tightened), and may also change the relative attractiveness of the instrument in financial markets.

The Effect of Tax Reform on Aggregate State and Local Expenditures

Voters' demands for state or local government spending can be modeled the way economists model demands for private goods – as functions of income, prices, and social, economic, and demographic variables that are proxies for voters' tastes. Based on the preferred spending levels of each voter, political processes determine the level and content of public spending. Unfortunately, viewing the problem in this way is not very helpful, since the data required to calculate the distribution of demands for public spending and to specify the political algorithm that determines spending would be expensive to obtain even if it were conceptually clear how to do so. An alternative that has been widely employed is to model the level of expenditure in a given jurisdiction as depending on the preferences of the "decisive voter" – a hypothetical individual whose voting behavior best explains the choices made by the electorate of the jurisdiction as a whole.

Decisive voter models pose both theoretical and empirical pitfalls; one must be especially wary of drawing welfare implications from demand functions for public spending that are estimated in this way. Yet, such models have done well in predicting the behavior of local governments, the area in which they have been used most. No one would claim that there is an identifiable "decisive voter," and even if there were, the identity of such a person would change in response to a change in the environment. But here, as in many other cases, it has proven useful to model as if such a person existed.

Models of Expenditure Determination

In one form of the model, the decisive voter is taken to be the "median voter," the voter with the median demand who, given prices and incomes, separates into equal-sized groups voters who want more and less spending. In most empirical work that employs the median voter model, the median voter is identified as the individual or household with the median income, although the conditions under which this assumption is warranted are quite restrictive. The median voter construct is an appealing one because the desired spending level of the median voter will defeat any other spending level in a majority rule referendum.[1] Richer forms of the decisive voter model take into account the fact that intensity of preferences and the structure of political institutions, rather than just a desire for "more" or "less" spending, generally affect spending outcomes. The "mean voter" model is perhaps the simplest of this class.

In the "mean voter" model it is assumed that voters are able to organize matters (presumably through political institutions) so that the intensity of preferences matters. Indeed, under the mean voter model it is assumed implicitly that all potential gains from trading income for votes are realized. (This assumption is not so farfetched when one considers the practice of "logrolling," in which proponents of one element of public spending form coalitions with those who favor another and vote to have both, and the fact that voter turnout is positively correlated with intensity of preference.) In the mean voter model, the entire distribution of tastes for public spending affects the outcome. It is conceptually difficult to choose a single measure of income and tax price that reflects the entire population distribution. In this paper, we choose the easy way out by using measures of mean income and mean price for the jurisdiction. A more sophisticated analysis would look for the characteristics of the mean voter, which may well differ from the mean characteristics of the jurisdiction.

Clearly, the difference between the median and mean voter models will be greatest when the distribution of preferred spending levels is most skewed. For example, where many voters prefer a small amount of spending and a few prefer a much larger amount, the median voter model will predict a lower level of spending than will the mean voter model.

In using either form of the decisive voter model to predict responses to the Tax Reform Act, we look at the effects of the Act on the income and tax price faced by the decisive voter. The tax price P can be interpreted as the cost to the taxpayer of a one dollar increase in tax-financed per capita public spending. This concept can be expressed by the formula

$$P = ns\left(1 - gt\right)$$

Where n is the population of the jurisdiction, s is the share of total taxes in the jurisdiction that the individual pays (it would equal the individual's taxable income divided by aggregate taxable income if all public spending in the jurisdiction were financed by a proportional income tax), t is the individual's federal marginal tax rate, and g is the proportion of state and local taxes that the individual may deduct from federal taxable income. The ns term weights individuals by how much tax they pay relative to the mean in their jurisdiction; ns will equal 1 if the individual pays an average amount of tax, 2 if he pays twice the average, and so on. The term in parentheses adjusts for what share of the individual's state and local tax payments are deductible. If the individual does not itemize, gt falls to zero and the tax price reduces to ns.

Of course, the same taxpayer will face different tax prices for state government and local government expenditures, provided that the individual accounts for different shares of the taxes paid in the two cases. Thus, any discussion that combines the tax price of state and local government, like the one that follows, involves a degree on averaging that masks much variation in the population.

Effects on State and Local Spending

The major effects of the Tax Reform Act on the tax price facing voters in states and localities are through a lower federal marginal tax rate t and the reduction in the deductibility of state and local taxes g, which falls both because sales taxes are no longer deductible and because many taxpayers, who currently itemize will no longer do so. To estimate the effect of the tax reform, then, first we estimate how the tax reform will affect the federal marginal tax rate of the decisive voter and the percentage of state and local taxes g that voter can deduct; then we calculate the percentage change in the tax price P of state and local spending; and finally use estimates of the price elasticity of demand for tax-financed state and local expenditure to calculate the change in expenditure demand. Fortunately, we can and do assume that the populations within jurisdictions (n) and each individual's share of state and local taxes paid (s) do not change.

In 1982, 40.8 percent of all taxpayers itemized deductions, and 81.8 percent of state and local taxes were deductible. The average marginal tax rate of itemizers was 0.284, ranging from 0.307 in the District of Columbia to 0.210 in Mississippi (Kenyon, 1985, p. 37). Those figures imply that the average level of P for tax-financed state and local spending was 0.905 in 1982. In fiscal year 1984 general sales taxes accounted for 23.5 percent of state and local tax revenue (US Bureau of the Census, 1985, p. 4). Assuming that this ratio still holds, making sales taxes non-deductible will reduce the deductible share g of state and local taxes paid by itemizers to 0.583. The federal tax rate facing the average itemizer will fall to about 25 percent under the Tax Reform Act, and the fraction of taxpayers itemizing will fall to about 0.26. Thus, the average level of P will rise in 1988 to 0.962 (that is, $1 - 0.26 \times 0.583 \times 0.25$), an increase of 6.3 percent over its 1982 levels.

Our reading of the current literature places the price elasticity of demand for state and local spending between −0.50 and −0.25, implying that increasing P by 6.3 percent will reduce tax-financed state and local spending by from 3.2 percent to 1.6 percent. The Tax Reform Act does not alter the taxpayer's cost of (and thus demand for) expenditure financed by user charges and federal grants. These latter two categories accounted for 41 percent of state and local general revenue in 1983–4, leaving 59 percent of state and local spending that was tax-financed.[2] Assuming that marginal changes in public spending are tax financed, our best estimate from the mean voter model is that total spending will fall by from 1.9 percent to 0.9 percent relative to what it would have been.[3]

The median voter model cannot be applied meaningfully to national averages. Since the median voter is not an itemizer, such a model would imply that changes in g and t for itemizers should have no effect on state and local spending. Some estimates of the effect of the Tax Reform Act on state and local spending have been made assuming that the median voter is the median itemizer. Such estimates imply reductions in spending that are many times larger than the ones we present here, but we do not believe the underlying assumption. We present mean voter estimates here because we believe that the appropriate version of the decisive voter model should represent an amalgam of the preferences of all influential interest groups in the jurisdiction. This view implies that expenditures will fall in jurisdictions with a substantial number of itemizers, whether or not the median voter is an itemizer, but they will not fall by as much as is predicted by models in which only itemizers matter.

The Effect of Tax Reform on Individual Communities

That the average effects on state and local spending will be fairly modest does not imply that they will be small in all cases. High income communities in which the median voter is an itemizer whose tax rate falls from 50 percent to 28 or 33 percent will experience large increases in the tax price facing the decisive voter. In the extreme case of a change from 50 percent to 28 percent (a very high income suburb) the tax price for local public services would rise by 44 percent, or enough to reduce expenditures on public schools by over 10 percent. Of course, this increase in tax price is an increase in the relative price of public education, and built into the elasticity estimates is some shift towards private education. Such substitution towards private spending is implicit in all of our estimated responses to increases in tax prices. Similarly, states that rely heavily on sales taxes will have much greater than average increases in the tax price of state expenditures, although not as high as 44 percent. On the other hand, local jurisdictions in which almost no one currently itemizes will experience smaller than average effects on spending.

Because the effects on tax price will vary greatly among jurisdictions, the change in federal rules should provide a natural experiment for distinguishing among models of expenditure determination. By examining household microdata within communities, it should be possible to discover which form of the decisive voter model predicts best. Ideally, such new studies of the determinants of state and local expenditure will also characterize the effects of the different types of rules (referendum, elected city council, and so on) under which public choices are made.

Mobility Effects and Capitalization

The preceding analysis implicitly assumes that voters will not relocate in response to changes in their state and local tax burdens. But in some cases the relative fiscal attractiveness of different locations will change appreciably, especially for high income residents of relatively high tax jurisdictions with lower tax jurisdictions nearby. What matters here is not so much relative changes in tax price as changes in the total tax bill paid; for high income itemizers, these can be quite large. The most important consequence of this change is that reductions in federal marginal tax rates may increase the pressures for economic segregation.

Deductibility tends to reduce the differences in tax prices and tax bills between locations that have different tax rates, since it reduces big tax bills in localities that generally pay high federal marginal rates more than it will reduce smaller tax bills in localities that pay lower federal marginal rates. This increased differential by itself is probably not sufficient incentive to move, given the transaction costs involved, but it surely is enough to alter the location choices of some households that are new to the area or that were planning to move within the area for other reasons. Thus, reducing the deductibility of local taxes will: (1) lead to some shift in population towards low-tax, low-spending jurisdictions; (2) lead to a reduction in the price of high income housing in high-tax, high-spending jurisdictions relative to the price of similar housing in low-tax jurisdictions, to compensate for the fact that less of a local property tax bill can be deducted; and (3) reduce spending more in high-tax jurisdictions that in low-tax ones (where spending may even rise) because of the effects that (1) and (2) will have on the property tax base.

Edward Gramlich (1985) points out that deductibility of local taxes currently serves as a bribe to higher-income households to live in high-tax, lower income communities, because much of their increased tax share is returned through the federal income tax. Gramlich thus argues that one unfortunate consequence of reducing federal marginal tax rates (indeed, in this view, the only unfortunate consequence) is that the reduction will tend to enhance the already powerful fiscal incentives for higher income households to segregate themselves from lower income households by living in high income, lower-tax jurisdictions. Gramlich argues that reductions in federal tax rates will tend to widen income differentials between Detroit and its suburbs. Similar incentives will exist between New York City and its suburbs, some of which are in low-tax states, making the fiscal differentials larger to begin with and more affected by the new federal tax rates. The same analysis should apply to large metropolitan areas throughout the country.

For these same reasons, tax reform will tend to increase business tax differentials across communities, too. Corporations will still be allowed to deduct all state and local taxes paid, but will face a marginal rate of 34 percent rather than 46 percent. If state and local fiscal policy is unchanged, the net differential between tax rates in different locations will increase by 0.12 (the change in the federal marginal rate) times the statutory differential; similarly, the differential in tax payments will rise by 12 percent of its previous value. The incentive for businesses to locate in lower-tax jurisdictions will be increased, and recent evidence indicates that business is somewhat responsive to such differentials.[4] Again, the implication is that tax reform will tend to reduce tax bases and expenditures in high-tax communities relative to low ones.

Public finance economists have long argued that redistributive activity is best undertaken at the federal level because if state and local governments engage in such behavior, lower income households will tend to migrate towards the "generous" jurisdiction and higher income households tend to migrate away. By making low-tax jurisdictions relatively more attractive to both households and businesses, the Tax Reform Act further reduces the ability of state and local governments to engage in redistributive activities. Were the federal government to establish a national system of income maintenance, this effect would not be a problem. Reducing the implicit federal subsidy to state and local spending would only enhance economic efficiency, partly because it would bring the relative prices of privately and publicly provided goods closer together. In the world we live in, where many of the largest (and highest tax) states and localities engage in greater than average levels of income redistribution, and where federal programs are very limited in their coverage, this poses a genuine problem. The incentives to migration set up by the Tax Reform Act will increase economic efficiency in the allocation of resources, but absent a nationwide program of income redistribution, they will also reduce the ability of more generous localities to implement their preferences for redistribution.

Effects on the Property Tax Base

The conclusion that the aggregate spending effects of the new tax bill are small, although the effects on some individual jurisdictions will be larger, must be tempered by the possibility that the value of the local property tax base may change. It is impossible to predict with any accuracy how important this possibility may be, but we can list some important considerations.

First, the cost of capital net of tax used for owner-occupied housing will tend to rise (especially so for the most expensive housing), because fewer individuals will be itemizing and those individuals who do will generally face lower marginal tax rates (so that the mortgage interest deduction and property tax deduction are worth less). Additionally, rental housing will receive much less favorable tax treatment, as the new law severely limits the extent to which "passive losses" in real estate (and other activities) can be used to offset other income, and also reduces the value of depreciation allowances for rental real estate. All other things equal, then, the value of the residential tax base should fall.

But all other things are not equal. From the perspective of the overall portfolio effects of the tax bill, owner-occupied housing continues to do well because other forms of capital investment are treated even less generously. (Under the Tax Reform Act, mortgage interest is the only kind of personal interest that remains deductible.) Commercial and industrial capital are also in the local property tax base. Since the effect of the tax bill will be to reduce the attractiveness of essentially all forms of domestic investment relative to investment abroad, the local property tax base may fall further still. On the other hand, if the decreased demand for capital lowers interest rates, the present discounted value of the net income stream that remains will go up, raising property values. And in any case, macroeconomic policy can be used to influence both the real interest rate and the fraction of wealth that is held in the form of government debt and not subject to property taxation, thus indirectly affecting the value of the property tax base in ways that may overwhelm the effects of the Tax Reform Act.

The overall effect of the tax reform act on the local property tax base is impossible to predict, but it is potentially important. Given the long-standing reliance of the local public sector on property taxes, major changes in the property tax base would cause major shifts in the mix of revenue instruments used by local government.

The Effect of Tax Reform on the Mix of Revenue Instruments

The income tax statutes in most states define state income liability as some function of federal taxable income or federal tax liability. Thus, unless and until offsetting actions are undertaken, the Tax Reform Act has the immediate effect of changing state (and in some cases local) income tax revenue. These effects will differ among states. The eight states that use federal taxable income – adjusted gross income less deductions and exemptions – as their income tax base will enjoy increased revenues at current tax rates because of the broadening of the federal tax base. Similarly, the seventeen states that use federal adjusted gross income and some but not all deductions and exemptions in defining taxable income all get substantial revenue increases at current rates, because federal adjusted gross income will rise and deductions will fall. The seven states that use federal adjusted gross income have smaller increases.[5] The effect will be similar but smaller in those states that have tied their corporate income taxes to the federal corporate income tax. However, the four states that piggy-back their income taxes directly on federal personal income tax collections will lose revenue, because they collect fixed shares of federal income tax revenue, which will fall as federal corporate taxes increase.

The response of states to these windfall revenue changes (mostly windfall gains) will be of some interest to political economists. The classic static equilibrium models of budget determination suggest an immediate adjustment of tax rates to offset the federal changes (except insofar as they affect the demand for state and local public services, as discussed above) while dynamic political and economic models predict a more gradual response; that is, states with positive windfalls will be able to improve their fiscal positions because of the lax reform while those with negative windfalls will have to "eat" some of their losses. In almost all states, however, these direct effects on state income tax receipts should be large enough to prompt a major political examination of state tax structures.

The dynamic responses of state and local governments to budgetary windfalls has been a subject of substantial debate. The empirical literature provides some evidence for a "flypaper effect," in which windfalls are spent publicly rather than returned to the citizenry as tax reduction ("money sticks where it hits") and theoretical treatments have approached the issue as well (for example, Courant, Gramlich and Rubinfeld, 1979). The Tax Reform Act of 1986 should provide a natural experiment to help resolve the question of the size and existence of the "flypaper effect."

Long-Run Effects on Revenue Sources

Tax reform will have a number of effects on the way that state and local governments raise revenue. First, state and local governments will almost surely move away from the sales tax and toward deductible taxes. In considering a repeal of all personal deductions for state and local taxes, Feldstein and Metcalf (1985) argued that state and local governments would shift toward business taxes, which would remain deductible. But given that income and property taxes remain deductible for households under the new tax bill, and given the tremendous competition among states and localities to foster a favorable "business climate," it seems likely that the shift will be toward income taxes at the state level and property taxes at the local level, but not toward business taxes at either level. States that currently rely most heavily on sales taxes may encounter pressure to shift to a value-added tax, which would act much like a sales tax but also be deductible by business. Since federal tax reform will result in a windfall increase in personal income taxes in most states, one obvious response would be to let at least some of the windfall stand and use the proceeds to reduce sales taxes.[6]

Second, the higher tax price associated with the use of deductible taxes encourages the recent trend towards an increased reliance on user charges, especially at the local level. This change appeals to those who view goods provided by the local public sector as essentially private in character, since user charges generally resemble prices more than property taxes do. In fact, one of the efficiency arguments against the deductibility of state and local taxes is that it leads to a bias against user charges even when the latter would be more efficient. Reducing federal tax rates reduces this bias.

Third, the Tax Reform Act has major implications for bond financing. It curtails severely the ability of local governments to issue industrial development bonds by limiting the volume of such issues to $50 per person (or $150 million per state, whichever is less), compared to $100 per person under previous law. It also makes interest on industrial development bonds subject to the alternative minimum tax in the personal income tax, reducing the value of such bonds as a tax shelter. These changes, in combination with an extremely complicated set of new regulations designed to prevent localities from using tax-exempt issues to invest in private financial instruments, will clearly reduce the incentives to issue tax-exempt bonds.

However, if the spread between tax exempt and taxable bonds rises, there may be a (partially) offsetting increase in the incentive to use tax-exempt bonds. On the face of it, the spread should fall because federal tax rates will fall, and being exempt from a lower tax rate has less value. However, the sharp curtailment of other kinds of tax shelters under the personal income tax – notably the curtailment of deductions for investing in IRAs and other supplemental retirement programs and the treatment of capital gains as ordinary income – makes municipal bonds more attractive to investors seeking tax-exempt financial instruments. Whether the portfolio effect (making bonds more attractive) outweighs the effect operating through changed tax rates is unclear. Given that the spread between tax-exempt and taxable issues has been low by historical standards in recent years, and this phenomenon is widely alleged to be due to the many other methods of tax-preferred saving available, we believe that municipals will become relatively more attractive and the yield spread will rise.

In any event, the municipal bond market aspects of tax reform should not have much effect on municipal spending in the aggregate. The new tax law sharply increases the restrictions on direct arbitrage, whereby governments issue tax-exempt debt and invest in private-sector financial instruments with the proceeds. But nothing in the new law prevents indirect arbitrage, issuing tax-exempt debt as a substitute for taxation.

This indirect arbitrage mechanism is especially attractive to low income communities with few itemizers and low personal tax rates, as it enables residents of such communities to "borrow" (by substituting the issuance of debt for tax levies) at the municipal bond rate and invest, privately, at the after-tax rate on private financial instruments. Even for the lowest income communities, however, the tax savings for residents is very small, suggesting that the effect on municipal spending would not be noticeable. This finding is controversial: the traditional view is that exempting municipal bonds from taxation stimulates capital spending. Again, the Tax Reform Act provides a natural experiment. If the yield spread (controlling for the portfolio effects) changes as a result of the tax bill, will the proportion of the public budget spent on physical capital improvements change? (If it does not, the implication is that the requirement that bond funds be used for "capital spending" does not bind.) Will be debt-financed proportion of the budget change? Will these changes be correlated with the income of the jurisdictions involved? The answers to these questions should help us to evaluate the role of tax-exempt bonds in financing the local public sector.

Evaluating the Tax Reform Act of 1986

By all accounts the broadening of the federal income tax base is a good idea as is the limitation on the use of industrial development bonds. The other limitations on bonds are probably also warranted, although anything that requires as many detailed regulations to implement as the "anti-arbitrage" provisions of the new bill is not likely to be very effective.

Evaluation of the elimination of sales tax deductibility must begin with an evaluation of deductibility in general. According to one popular view of state and local public economics, most state and local public expenditures (especially local) are essentially private in character, even if the goods are publicly provided. From this perspective, competition among communities allows citizens to "vote with their feet" for desired spending and tax pack ages, and mobility assures an efficient allocation of resources. Local taxes can be considered benefit taxes. In this view, deductibility creates inefficiencies by distorting spending choices and weakening the link between benefits received and taxes paid.

An alternative theoretical view holds that state and local government provide purely public goods. Tax payments for these goods are real reductions in disposable income, not tied to any particular benefits received, and should therefore be deducted from the federal tax base. In this view, full or partial deductibility of state and local taxes makes sense for reasons of equity. A more pragmatic "rough efficiency" argument that yields the same result is that deductibility encourages state and local spending, thus repaying state and local governments for positive spillovers that arise when public spending undertaken in one jurisdiction benefits residents of other jurisdictions. A weakness in this argument is that the value of deductibility depends on the federal marginal tax rates of the citizens of jurisdictions. It is hard to make an efficiency case, and probably impossible to make an equity case for a program that subsidizes (say) education more in high income suburbs than in lower income central cities, but that regressive pattern of subsidy is exactly what deductibility generates.

In general, we believe that state and local taxes should not be deducible; that is, the goods that they finance have a substantial private component. Where spillovers exist, direct matching grants from the federal government would be a better way of internalizing the externalities, because the matching rates could (in principle) be varied with magnitude of the spillover. In addition, deductibility imposes efficiency costs by making user charges less attractive. But this general argument against deductibility is much weaker as an argument against eliminating deductibility of only one tax, such as the sales tax. Governments will tend to substitute other sources of deductible revenue for the sales tax in the long run. To the extent that the sales tax belongs in the optimal tax mix, the result will be a distortion in the mix of state and local tax instruments, and official estimates of the federal revenue gain from eliminating deductibility of the sales tax will be too high.

Given the conclusion that deductibility in general is not good policy, it follows that lower marginal tax rates will enhance efficiency by reducing the federal subsidy to local and state spending. Those states that use federal taxable income (in whole or in part) as their tax base should also receive an efficiency gain because the same revenue can be collected at lower marginal rates. (Of course, such jurisdictions could have reformed their tax bases at any time, but the fact the federal government has done so greatly simplifies the task.) However, if local property tax bases do fall, then higher marginal tax rates would be required to maintain a given level of local government revenue.

While the efficiency aspects of the tax bill are somewhat appealing, the increased burden on high tax states and localities remains troubling. The biggest decreases in state and local public spending should occur in high tax states and localities, many of which allocate a relatively large share of their budgets towards redistributive programs. At the local level, the pattern will be mixed, with the richer communities losing more than the poorer communities initially, but with the real possibility that the fiscal incentive for the rich to leave higher-tax, lower income jurisdictions will impair the fiscal position of large central cities over time. Still, increasing federal tax rates with the goal of restoring the importance of deductibility is hardly the optimal policy response to this problem. We hope (without much confidence) that these effects of reducing deductibility may lead to reform of the intergovernmental grant and national income maintenance systems. If that were to happen, we could unambiguously favor the Tax Reform Act from the perspective of its effects on the state and local sectors.

Notes

Note: We are grateful to Henry Aaron, Edward M. Gramlich, Dephne R. Kenyon, Carl Shapiro, Joseph Stiglitz, and Timothy Taylor for helpful comments and discussions.

1   This conclusion requires the additional assumption that if a voter prefers spending level x to level y, the voter also (weakly) prefers y to any level farther from x than y, for all x and y. Preferences of this form are termed "single-peaked."

2   US Bureau of the Census, table 3, p. 4. We exclude utility, liquor store, and insurance trust revenue from general revenue.

3   These calculations ignore the increase in household disposable income arising from the Tax Reform Act.

4   See Wasylenko and McGuire (1985) for a review of the recent evidence.

5   The source of the data in this paragraph is "Governor's Weekly Bulletin," May 16, 1986, pp. 1–3.

6   We do not expect the shift away from sales taxes to take place rapidly. In many states specific portions of the sales tax revenues are earmarked to go to localities, school districts and the like. To obtain political agreement to shift away from sales taxes, it may be necessary to prevent harm to many of the beneficiaries of such existing rules, and that, in turn should require some revenue increase.

References

Bergstrom, Theodore C., Daniel L. Rubinfeld and Perry Shapiro, "Micro Based Estimates of Demand Functions for Local School Expenditures," *Econometrica*, September 1982, *50*, 1183–05.

Chernick, Howard and Andrew Reschovsky, "Federal Tax Reform and the Financing of State and Local Governments," *Journal of Policy Analysis and Management*, Summer 1986, *5*, 683–706.

Courant, Paul N., Edward M. Gramlich and Daniel L. Rubinfeld, "The Stimulative Effects of Intergovernmental Grants: or Why Money Sticks Where it Hits." In Mieszkowski, P. and W. Oakland, eds., *Fiscal Federalism and Grants-in-Aid*. The Urban Institute, 1979.

Feldstein, Martin and Gilbert Metcalf, "The Effect of Federal Tax Deductibility of State and Local Taxes and Spending." NBER Working Paper No. 1791. January 1986.

Gordon, Roger H. and Joel Slemrod, "An Empirical Examination of Municipal Financial Policy." In Rosen, Harvey S., ed., *Studies in State and Local Public Finance*, Chicago: University of Chicago Press, 1986, pp. 53–78.

Gramlich, Edward M., "The Deductibility of State and Local Taxes," *National Tax Journal*, December 1985, *38*, 447–466.

Gramlich, Edward M. and Daniel L. Rubinfeld, "Micro Estimates of Public Spending Demand Functions and Tests of the Tiebout and Median Voter Hypotheses, *Journal of Political Economy*, June 1982, 536–560.

Inman, Robert, "Markets, Government, and the 'New' Political Economy." In Auerbach. A. J. and M. Feldstein, eds., Handbook of Public Economics, vol. 2. North Holland, 1987.

Kenyon, Daphne A., "Federal Income Tax Deductibility of State and Local Taxes. To be published in US Treasury, Office of State and Local Finance, Federa State-Local Fiscal Retations: Report to the President and the Congress. Draftdated June 1985.

Netzer, Dick, "The Effect of Tax Simplification on State and Local Governments. In Aaron, Henry, et al., *Economic Consequences of Tax Simplification*. Boston, Federal Reserve Bank of Boston, 1985, pp. 222–51.

Tiebout, Charles, "A Pure Theory of Local Expenditures," *Journal of Political Economy*, 1956, *64*, 416–24.

US Bureau of the Census, *Government Finances in 1983–4*. Washington, D.C., GPO, October 1985.

Wasylenko, Michael and Theresa McGuire, "Jobs and Taxes: The Effect of Business Climate on States' Employment Growth Rates," *National Tax Journal*, *XXXVIII*, 4, 497–512.

Introduction to Chapter 17

This chapter is a chapter in a book that provides a thorough account of the history and rationale for Federal income tax exemption of interest payments on state and local government debt, and a comprehensive economic analysis of the case for and against the exemption. Like most public finance economists, Zimmerman is highly skeptical of the case for the exemption.

The exemption is a form of Federal aid, or subsidy, to state and local governments. In this selection, Zimmerman takes us through the rationale for Federal aid, discusses grants and state-local tax deductibility, but focuses on the interest tax exemption. Like other economists, he finds the exemption to be highly inefficient.

17

The Private Use of Tax-exempt Bonds

Dennis Zimmerman

Perhaps the policy area affected most by tax-exempt bond legislation is intergovernmental relations. The federal revenue loss from municipal bonds ($20.9 billion in 1989) amounted to 12 percent to total federal intergovernmental assistance; and an even more impressive 20 percent if grants-in-aid designated for pass-through to individuals (e.g., Medicaid and Family Assistance Program) are removed from the intergovernmental assistance base. In contrast, tax-exempt bonds are a minor part of the federal income tax. The revenue loss from these bonds amounted to about 4 percent of income tax revenue in 1989.

The tax-exempt bond legislation of the last 20 years is best understood and evaluated if placed in the context of what was a very dynamic intergovernmental policy. This chapter provides that context. First, the economic rationales for federal intergovernmental assistance are described. Although there is theoretical support and guidance for a federal responsibility to provide financial assistance to state and local governments, the implementation of that responsibility is sufficiently subjective to allow for a wide range in the level and breadth of federal financial support. Second, the chapter briefly reviews the last 30 years of federal financial assistance, indicating that the range of support has varied. Intergovernmental policy has evolved from a relatively broad view of federal domestic program responsibilities in the 1960s and 1970s to an increasingly narrower view of those responsibilities. This changing philosophy has been accompanied by reductions in federal funding for all types of intergovernmental assistance. The chapter closes with discussions of three other issues that appear periodically in the intergovernmental policy debate: the extent to which the federal government can control the budget cost of the different types of intergovernmental assistance; the relative merits of each type of assistance in promoting economic efficiency, minimizing administrative costs, and maximizing the state and local subsidy per dollar of federal revenue cost; and the justification for restricting intergovernmental assistance to one factor of production – in particular, to tax-exempt bonds for capital.

The Economic Case for Federal Support of State-local Services

As mentioned in the discussion of intergovernmental tax immunity, there are, or at least the federal government behaves as if there are, "good" and "bad" bonds. Although many claim that congressional disallowance of tax exemption for some activities represents ad hoc decisions motivated solely by federal revenue considerations, the last 20 years of federal efforts to define a public purpose or a private activity can be rationalized on the basis of public goods theory.

One hesitates to suggest that the political community in the nation's capital consciously incorporates the abstract theories of economists into their policy deliberations, but there is ample evidence that such abstractions occasionally seep by osmosis through the public policy membrane to make a small contribution to the decision-making process. For example, the tax-exempt bond legislation of the last 20 years seems a good illustration of Keynes's dictum: "The ideas of economists and political philosophers . . . are more powerful than is commonly understood. . . . Practical men, who believe themselves to be quite exempt from any intellectual influences, are usually the slaves of some defunct economist" (Keynes 1936).[1] The next section of the chapter cites instances when intergovernmental funding changes have been justified on the basis of the type of concepts presented in this section.

The intellectual parentage of federal efforts to limit use of tax-exempt bonds can be explained in two easy steps. First, one must understand the reasons why a state or local government intervenes in the operation of the private market and provides public services. Second, one must understand that federal financial support of this intervention requires that the benefits of the public services provided extend beyond the boundaries of the state or local government to federal taxpayers more generally.

The decision to intervene in private markets

A good that requires public provision is known as a pure public good and possesses two essential characteristics: (1) consumption cannot be denied to those unwilling to pay for the good (like national defense, which once provided can be consumed whether or not an individual pays for it); and (2) one person's consumption of the good does not prevent another person from using it (again, like national defense). If these characteristics are present, this pure public good cannot be provided at a profit, and the private sector has no incentive to produce an adequate amount of the good. The benefits from these goods are consumed collectively, or jointly.

Beyond producing pure public goods, there may be reasons for public intervention in the market for a good that is produced by the private sector. This is because the private sector may not produce the "correct" amount of the good at the "correct" price. There may be some costs (such as pollution from manufacturing activities) or benefits (such as good citizenship from education) associated with production of the good that are imposed on or enjoyed by society as a whole, and for which the decisions of private producers and consumers do not account. These external costs and benefits provide justification for some intervention by the public sector in the production and consumption decisions of the private sector. In effect, the "external" portion of the good's benefits or costs are consumed collectively, or jointly.

A special case of the private sector not producing the correct amount of a good is monopoly. By dint of being the sole producer of a good, either due to peculiar cost characteristics in an industry or coercive behavior, the monopolist maximizes its profits by producing less than the socially desirable amount of the good.[2] It is necessary for the public sector to regulate the monopolist's production to assure the socially desirable output.

One can conclude from this very brief discussion of the economic justification for public intervention in private markets that there exists a spectrum of, for want of a better word, "publicness." The public sector must decide how much of society's resources should be devoted to producing those goods all of whose benefits are consumed collectively; otherwise, the decision will be to produce none of them. In contrast, those goods, some of whose benefits are consumed collectively and some privately, will be produced by the private sector in some amount, but not necessarily in the socially desired quantities. In neither case does this mean the public sector must physically produce the good – it can contract with the private sector to produce the quantity agreed upon through the public decision-making process. It is this latter category of quasi-public goods that creates the difficult decisions about public intervention with tax-exempt bond financing.

The importance of spillovers

The decision about public sector intervention is further complicated in the context of the federal system of government in the United States. Since external costs and benefits exist with many privately produced goods and services, taxpayers in a state or a local region often judge public provision or financial support of private provision of a particular good to be justified. This does not, however, necessarily justify federal financial support for this state or local decision. In fact, from an economic perspective, federal support should only be provided to those state and local public services that are likely to be underprovided by state and local governments.

Such underprovision results from the spillover of benefits among jurisdictions. The sheer number of state and local political jurisdictions implies that any one jurisdiction is likely to have a geographic reach that fails to encompass all individuals and businesses who benefit from its public services. Thus, some of the collective consumption benefits spill over the border of a taxing jurisdiction, such as in the case of redistributive welfare programs, some educational services, or environmental projects. Collective consumption benefits from providing such goods exceed the benefits to taxpayers in the providing jurisdiction. Because many taxpayers are unlikely to be willing to pay for services received by nonresidents, it may be desirable for a higher level of government (which does receive tax payments from the spillover beneficiaries) to subsidize their consumption in order to induce state and local governments to provide the proper, that is, larger, amount.[3]

Thus, federal financial support of a state and local service is only justified if a portion of the benefits from state or local provision accrues to taxpayers who reside outside the state or local area providing the service.[4] If such spillovers do not exist, then federal financial support for state and local provision simply has the effect of redistributing income geographically, which may not be the intent of the subsidy.

In consequence, an economic case can be made for federal financial support of some state and local services and for the denial of such support to other state and local services. Some services make economic sense and are "good" because a federal interest is served. Others do not make economic sense and are "bad" because there is no justification for public provision of the service provided or because only local benefits are produced. Applying the reasoning to particular cases, however, raises a host of measurement problems that are addressed later in this book.

Intergovernmental Assistance: The Policy Record

Tax-exempt bonds are but one of several vehicles by which the federal government provides financial support to state and local governments. Grants-in-aid have long provided direct assistance both for current services and for particular types of public capital formation such as highways, mass transit facilities, water treatment plants, hospitals, and the like. Most major state and local taxes have also been deductible from federal taxable income. Deductibility provides indirect assistance to state and local governments: after-federal-tax incomes of taxpayers are increased and the after-federal-tax cost of a state and local tax dollar is decreased, both of which presumably make state and local taxpayers willing to pay additional state and local taxes. This section provides a brief overview of federal spending on the three types of aid and then discusses each one separately in more detail.

These three major types of federal assistance have been funded at very different levels. Table 17.1 provides data on federal government costs from 1980 to 1989. Grants-in-aid is by far the largest category of assistance. Grants-in-aid outlays rose from $91.5 billion in 1980 to an estimated $123.6 billion in 1989. The federal government exercises some control over the spending of grant monies, ranging from very specific purposes (categorical grants) to less specific purposes (block

Table 17.1 Cost of federal, financial assistance to state and local governments, by type of assistance. Current dollars: 1980–9 ($ billions)

Type of aid	1980	1985	1989	Percentage change, 1980–9	
				Nominal	Real[a]
Grants-in-aid	91.5	105.9	123.6	35.1	−9.4
General revenue sharing	6.8	4.6	0.0		
Tax-exempt bonds	7.7	18.2	20.9	171.7	82.5
Tax deductibility	20.5	32.2	27.7	35.2	−9.3
Tax-exempt bond share of total costs (%)	6.1	11.3	12.1		

[a] Real percentage changes are calculated using the deflator for "total outlays" that appears in Office of Management and Budget, "Deflators for 1990 Budget." Jan. 4, 1989.
Sources: Office of Management and Budget (1989); and Office of Management and Budget, *Special Analyses: Budget of the United States Government*, various years.

grants). General revenue sharing (GRS) is listed as a subcategory of grants-in-aid because the terms of its provision (for unspecified purposes) were very different from other grants-in-aid. GRS was the smallest type of assistance, and was eliminated during the decade. The foregone federal revenue from state and local tax deductibility was $20.5 billion in 1980, it rose above $32.2 billion in 1985, and declined to $27.7 billion after the Tax Reform Act of 1986 terminated sales tax deductibility, reduced tax rates, and lowered the proportion of taxpayers who itemize. The foregone revenue from tax-exempt bonds was $7.7 billion in 1980 and rose to $20.9 billion by 1989.

Several things are noteworthy in these data. First, the share of federal intergovernmental assistance costs attributable to tax-exempt bonds doubled over the decade, from 6.1 percent to 12.1 percent. Second, foregone revenues from municipal bonds grew by 171.7 percent during the decade, compared to 35 percent increases for grants-in-aid and tax deductibility. Third, when the substantial price increases that occurred during the decade are taken into account, bonds represent the only source of intergovernmental assistance that experienced positive real growth, a very substantial 82.5 percent. In contrast, grants-in-aid and deductibility both suffered negative real growth of 9.4 and 9.3 percent, respectively.

Tax-exempt bonds

State and local use of tax-exempt bonds grew rapidly from the mid 1960s through the first half of this decade. The first panel of figure 17.1 traces the growth in long-term tax-exempt bond volume from 1965 to 1987. Volume rose from $11.1 billion in 1965 to a peak of $204.3 billion in 1985, before falling to $98.7 billion by 1987. The annual growth rate between 1965 and 1985 was a remarkable 14.6 percent.

This rapid growth did not escape the attention of Congress or Treasury Department officials. Aside from the revenue loss, concern was expressed that an increasing proportion of this federal financial assistance was being used for conduit financing, in which a state or local governmental entity issued bonds and passed the proceeds through to businesses and individuals for their private use. Witness President Ronald Reagan's concern when presenting his tax reform proposal in 1985:

> Increasingly, however, State and local governments have used their tax-exempt financing privilege to obtain funds for use by nongovernmental persons. . . . The revenues lost as a result of tax-

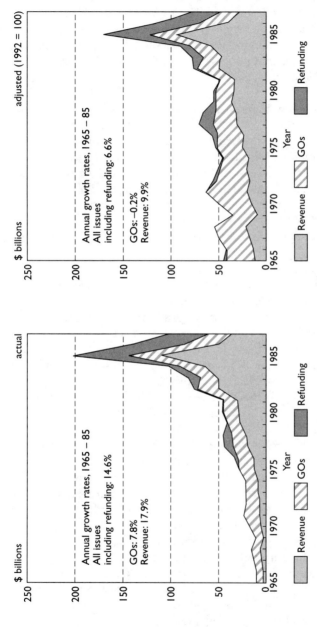

Figure 17.1 Long-term tax-exempt bond volume, 1965–87: actual and adjusted for inflation and state-local size.

Note: Revenue and general obligation (GO) bonds are net of refunding issues.

Source: The Bond Buyer (1988).

exempt nongovernmental bonds represent an indirect Federal subsidy program, based in the tax code, and thus significantly free of
the scrutiny that attaches to direct Federal expenditures. In many
cases, the issuer of nongovernmental bonds would not spend its
own revenues to support the activities that are Federally subsidized
through tax-exempt nongovernmental bonds. (Executive Office of
the President 1985, 283.)

Activities being financed included: student loans and mortgages for
owner-occupied and multifamily rental housing; facilities for sports
events, convention and trade show centers, airports, docks, wharves,
parking, sewage and solid waste disposal, utility services, air and water
pollution control, and industrial parks; and virtually any activity using a
bond issue of less than $1 million for the acquisition, construction, or
improvement of land or depreciable property.

Similar concerns were expressed by Congress when explaining the
reasons for adoption of the bond provisions of the Tax Reform Act of
1986:

Congress was concerned with the large and increasing volume of
tax-exempt bonds being issued under prior law. . . . Congress recognized the important cost savings that tax-exempt financing could
provide for State and local governments, in a period marked by
reductions in direct Federal expenditures for such purposes. To
the extent possible, Congress desired to restrict tax-exempt
financing for private activities without affecting the ability of State
and local governments to issue bonds for traditional governmental
purposes. (Joint Committee on Taxation 1987b, 1151.)

The growth of private-use bonds is difficult to document because data
on bond volume by private use was not collected until 1983. One way to
get a rough approximation is to divide bond volume between its general
obligation (GO) and revenue components. Almost all GO bonds are
issued to support what has come to be termed public purposes.[5] Almost
all bonds issued to finance what have come to be called private activities
are issued in the revenue bond form, although many activities considered
to satisfy public purposes are also financed with revenue bonds.[6]

The first panel of figure 17.1 also provides a rough idea of the growing
importance of revenue bonds, and thus to some extent of bonds issued
for private activities. Those bond issues (both GO and revenue) that
represent refundings of pre-existing bond issues (usually to take advantage of lower interest rates) are subtracted from total volume, and the
remaining bond volume used to finance new capital facilities is divided

between GOs and revenue bonds. These original-issue revenue bonds (the checkered area in figure 17.1) grew at an annual rate of 17.9 percent from 1965 to 1985, while original-issue GOs (the lined area in the figure) grew at a much more modest 7.8 percent rate. Thus, the type of bond (revenue) issued for private activities was growing much more rapidly than the type (GO) normally used to finance traditional public-purpose activities. It must, however, be reiterated that some activities considered to be public purpose are financed with revenue rather than GO bonds.

Of course, one would expect tax-exempt bond volume to grow in order to accommodate growth in the size of the state and local sector and the effect of inflation. For that reason, the second panel of figure 17.1 adjusts the bond volume data for the effects of inflation and population growth. These adjustments cut the annual growth rate of total volume by more than half, to a rate of 6.6 percent. Decomposing this growth rate by type of bond shows that revenue bonds grew in real terms at a 9.9 percent annual rate, whereas GOs actually had a very small negative growth rate over the 20-year period of −0.2 percent. Clearly, these data indicate that revenue bonds were responsible for the expanding municipal debt market. And private activities are invariably financed with revenue bonds.

An alternative and also less-than-precise view of the bond volume issued for selected private activities is available for a shorter time period, 1975 to 1986. The data in table 17.2 from 1975 to 1982 are from the Joint Committee on Taxation (1983). The private-activity volume data cover only seven private activities (but probably 90 percent of all private-activity bond volume): single-family housing, multifamily housing, veterans' housing, small-issue industrial development, private hospitals, student loans, and pollution control. These private activities accounted for an increasing share of total long-term bond volume, rising from 20.6 percent in 1975 to 53.6 percent in 1980. The data in table 17.2 from 1983 to 1986 come from Auten and Chung (1988) and are derived from reports filed with the Treasury Department for every private-activity bond issue. These data include all activities classified by the tax law as private. By 1984, private-activity bond share of new issue long-term bond volume was 72.7 percent.

Congress reacted to the growth of revenue bonds for private activities by imposing a series of limitations on the issuance of bonds for private activities beginning with the Revenue and Expenditure Control Act of 1968 and culminating in the Tax Reform Act of 1986. These limitations included attempts to define what constituted a private-activity bond that would be taxable (based upon governmental/nongovernmental use of the proceeds and the presence of trade or business property as security backing for the bonds); a string of exceptions that allowed private-

Table 17.2 Private-activity bond volume for selected private activities, as a percentage of total
bond volume. 1975–86 ($ billions)

	Private activity ($)	Share of total volume (%)
1975	6.2	20.6
1976	8.4	24.0
1977	13.1	27.9
1978	15.8	32.2
1979	24.6	51.1
1980	29.4	53.6
1981	27.4	48.5
1982	44.0	51.7
1983	49.9	71.0
1984	65.8	72.7
1985	99.4	67.9
1986	17.2	20.0

Sources: Data for 1975–82, from Joint Committee on Taxation
(1983): 1983–6 private-activity data from Auten and Chung
(1988): 1983–6 new issue volume for share calculation from
The Bond Buyer (1989). Joint Committee data do not include
data for such private activities as ports, airports, sports or
convention facilities, industrial parks, and the local furnishing
of electivity or gas. Auten and Chung data are comprehensive.

activity bonds issued for certain activities to remain tax exempt (refer
back to the list of private activities enumerated at the beginning of this
section); restrictions on arbitrage profits; and volume caps on those
private-activity bonds that were favored with continued tax exemption.

By 1986, private-activity bond volume had fallen to 20 percent. This
precipitous drop was attributable primarily to the acceleration of bond
issuance in 1985 in anticipation of forthcoming restrictions (the original
House bill was to be effective on December 31, 1985), and to some of
the provisions adopted in the Tax Reform Act of 1986, particularly the
volume cap. The revenue savings to the federal government from the
1986 act were estimated by the Joint Committee on Taxation to start at
a mere $78 million in 1988 and to grow to $716 million by 1991.

Grants-in-aid

The 1960s and 1970s saw the most extensive increases in federal assumption of domestic responsibilities since the depression years of the

1930s. As might be expected, this period was marked by substantial increases in the federal intergovernmental assistance devoted to implementing these responsibilities in a federal system of government. Grant outlays more than tripled during the 1960s, from \$7.1 billion in 1961 to \$24.1 billion in 1970; and almost quadrupled in the 1970s, to \$91.5 billion in 1980. A brief review of the earlier period is helpful to an understanding of current policy.[7]

Approximately 160 grant programs were authorized in 1962, and another 379 in 1966. They included what is today the largest grant program, Medicaid, which was enacted in 1966 as an addition to the entitlement programs created by the Social Security Act of 1935. The 1960s also witnessed the first funding for compensatory education of the disadvantaged. In the 1970s, large increases were made primarily in grants to local governments for economic development, local public works, public service employment, and antirecession fiscal assistance.

Efforts were made in the 1970s to simplify the grant structure by replacing numerous categorical grants (for specified programs) with a general revenue-sharing grant and six special revenue-sharing programs. The General Revenue Sharing (GRS) program and three of the special revenue-sharing programs (community development, comprehensive employment and training, and law enforcement assistance) were enacted as block grants. Nonetheless, authorization continued for many of the categorical programs that were supposed to be replaced by these block grants.

The Nixon administration's efforts to reduce expenditures included an attempt to impound funds for some categorical programs, primarily for wastewater treatment and highway construction grants. The Congressional Budget and Control Act of 1974, however, required the executive branch to ask Congress for permission to withhold appropriated funds. As a result, little progress was made in controlling grant outlays.

By 1979 both the Carter administration and Congress questioned the national benefit from the proliferation of grant programs. As a result, the first large cutbacks occurred that year: the elimination of the antirecession fiscal assistance and local public works programs; a reduction in wastewater treatment and public service employment grants; and discontinuance of the state portion of GRS and a refusal to adjust the nominal dollars in the local government portion of GRS for inflation.

At this point the Reagan administration rode in from the West with an agenda that included reassessment of federal reponsibility for a broad range of domestic programs. Its conceptual crystal ball revealed that the federal government was providing financial support for a host of services that either should be provided by state and local governments or stripped of public support and returned to the private sector. The administration's New Federalism plan of 1981 sought to implement this philosophy, proposing increased reliance on states, local governments, and the private sector for the financing of domestic programs.

Although much of this proposed realignment of responsibilities between the states and the federal government did not take place, the decade of the 1980s was marked by a reduction in grants-in-aid funding and a change in the structure of grants-in-aid. This reduction in grants-in-aid funding is best understood in the context of the entire US budget.

Total US budget outlays expanded from $590.9 billion in 1980 to $1137.0 billion in 1989, an increase of 92.4 percent. When corrected for inflation, this increase is reduced to 29.1 percent. The allocation of this growing public budget was unevenly distributed among the major budget functions listed in table 17.3. The most rapidly growing portion of the budget during this period was the "net interest" category. The burgeoning deficit caused inflation-adjusted net interest payments to grow by 111.7 percent. The other major budget categories that exhibited real growth over this period were "national defense/international affairs" (41.3 percent) and "direct payments for individuals" (27.8 percent).

In contrast to these three categories, outlays for the other two major budget functions decreased in real terms. "Grants to state and local governments" increased in current dollars from $91.5 billion in 1980 to $123.6 billion in 1989, while "all other federal outlays" increased over this period from $54.6 billion to $70.7 billion. When adjusted for inflation, these figures represent decreases of 9.4 percent for "grants to state and local governments" and 13.1 percent for "all other outlays."

A 9.4 percent reduction in real spending spread over a decade does not seem like a sea change in federal intergovenmental policy. But to appreciate fully the change in federal policy toward the state and local sector, the "grants to state and local governments" category must be broken down further. The Office of Management and Budget divides this category into two types: payments for state and local programs (labeled "for states" in the table), and payments for individuals (labeled "for individuals" in the table). This distinction emphasizes that some grants provide cash or in-kind benefits to identifiable individuals – through Medicaid and the Family Assistance Program, for example. Other grants provide funding for state and local programs that in a sense benefit all state and local taxpayers – such as highway construction and environmental cleanup programs or General Revenue Sharing.

The component of "grants to state and local governments" that is

Table 17.3 US Budget outlays by selected categories of expenditure: 1980–9. Current dollars ($ billions)

Category of spending	1980	1985	1989	Percentage change, 1980–9 Nominal %	Real[a] %
Total US budget outlays	590.9	946.3	1137.0	92.4	29.1
National defense/ international affairs	146.7	268.9	309.0	110.6	41.3
Direct payments for individuals	245.6	377.5	468.0	90.6	27.8
Interest (net)	52.5	129.4	165.7	215.6	111.7
Grants to state and local governments	91.5	105.9	123.6	35.1	–9.4
For individuals	31.9	48.1	66.5	108.5	39.9
For states	59.6	57.8	57.1	–4.2	–35.7
All other federal outlays	54.6	64.6	70.7	29.5	–13.1

[a] Real percentage increases are calculated using the deflator for "total outlays" in Office of Management and Budget. 1989. "Deflators for 1990 Budget." Jan. 4.
Source: Office of Management and Budget (1989).

channeled to individuals contains transfer-type (pro-poor) activities of the Federal government that are similar to the nongrants category in table 17.3 called "direct payments for individuals." The primary difference between the transfer-type activities included in the "grants to state and local governments" category and those in the "direct payments" category is that, for one reason or another, the degree of financial and administrative responsibility varies between the levels of government.[8]

These two categories have, in fact, fared reasonably well in the 1980s. Table 17.3 shows that the "for individuals" component of "grants to state and local governments" grew in constant dollars by 39.9 percent, compared to 27.8 percent for "direct payments for individuals." Thus, in a sense, the effort to evaluate changes in federal responsibility to provide financial support for state and local service provision should be based upon the "for states" component of the "grants to state and local governments" category in table 17.3.

This "for states" component in table 17.3 decreased in real terms by 35.7 percent. Clearly, the two grant components did not suffer uniformly during the 1980s. Those that represented the federal contribution for the needier members of society continued to grow in real terms. Those that represented federal payments for programs considered primarily to be state and local responsibilities experienced large negative real growth, a number whose magnitude suggests a serious redirection of intergovernmental policy.

Not only was the level of grants-in-aid reduced, but efforts were made to alter their structure.[9] Smaller categorical programs were merged into block grants. Direct payment of grant monies to local governments was largely eliminated, although some of the funding was rechanneled to the states. A federal commitment was made to provide a "safety net" (income maintenance and social services) and support for elementary and secondary education, but with increasing state participation. And transportation grants were increased while funds for other programs were reduced. As a result of all this activity, grant programs decreased from 534 in 1981 to 422 in 1987, with a corresponding increase in block grants from 4 to 13.[10] The Federal government seemed to be sweetening its reduced financial commitment with a greater willingness to allow state and local governments to utilize greater discretion in the allocation of grant monies.

State and local tax deductibility

The major state and local nonbusiness taxes for general purposes – income, general sales, excises, and real and personal property – were deductible from the federal income tax base upon its adoption in 1913.[11] Two categories of state and local taxpayer payments were not allowed to be deducted: user charges such as those for sewer and water services, as well as special fees for the use of facilities, such as recreational and cultural facilities; and special assessments for property improvements, such as construction of sidewalk and drainage systems. Only two changes were made to these arrangements prior to the 1980s. The Revenue Act of 1964 eliminated the deduction for motor vehicle operators' license fees and state and local excise taxes, other than on gasoline. The Revenue Act of 1978 eliminated the deductibility of the gasoline excise tax. These changes were justified on the basis of removing encouragement for consumption of socially undesirable products (primarily cigarettes and alcohol), simplifying the tax structure, or acknowledging the essential nature of the tax as a user charge (motor vehicle license fees and gasoline excise taxes).[12]

Thus, while tax-exempt bonds and grants-in-aid have been the center of attention at the intergovernmental party, dancing every dance as it were, the big three general-purpose state and local taxes remained wall-flowers until invited onto the dance floor in the mid-1980s. Just as the 1980s saw a decrease in grants-in-aid, so was the intergovernmental assistance provided through deductibility ultimately subjected to a cut-back. The Reagan tax reform proposal of May 1985 suggested elimination of the deduction for all state and local taxes.

> The deduction for State and local taxes may also be regarded as providing a subsidy to State and local governments, which are likely to find it somewhat easier to raise revenue because of the deduction. A general subsidy for spending by State and local governments can be justified only if the services which State and local governments provide have important spillover benefits to individuals in other communities. The existence of such benefits has not been documented. (Executive Office of the President 1985, 64.)

Elimination of all deductible taxes was expected to generate between $33 and $40 billion revenue each year from 1987 to 1990. After considerable debate, the Tax Reform Act of 1986 terminated the deduction only for nonbusiness general sales taxes. Elimination of the sales tax deduction was expected to generate between $4.5 and $5.0 billion revenue per year from 1988 through 1991.

Federal Budgetary Control of Intergovernmental Assistance

The discussion here of the economic rationale for intergovernmental assistance suggests that there is a priori justification for denying federal financial support for every dollar of public service provided by state and local governments, because many of these services provide minimal or no benefits to federal taxpayers. If this is the case, it is desirable to put the decision about the budgetary cost of the subsidy in the hands of the federal government.

Grants-in-aid

In this regard, financial support provided in the form of grants-in-aid is very different from the two tax subsidies. The major types of grants are specific (categorical), which facilitates federal conditions and control on state and local performance, and block, which increases the programmatic latitude of the recipients. More important for the purposes here, the grants may be open-ended or closed. If the federal government appropriates a given amount for a grant, and this amount determines the matching ratio of state-local funds, the grant is closed; the federal budgetary cost is fixed and controlled. If, however, the matching ratio is set and the federal contribution is determined by the amount of state and local spending, the grant is open-ended.[13]

Most federal grants have historically been closed, particularly those for the state and local programs portion of grants-in-aid (see table 17.3). The major exceptions have been the public assistance programs that have historically been open-ended, such as Medicaid and the Family Assistance Program that appear in the "for individuals" portion of grants-in-aid (see table 17.3). The uncertainty these open-ended grants impose on federal budget policy has been a source of considerable friction, and Congress has moved in recent years to control and cap these programs.

Tax-exempt bonds and tax deductibility

Tax-exempt bonds and state and local tax deductibility are, in effect, the equivalent of open-ended matching grants for the entire spectrum of state and local services. The federal government loses its ability to control its budget (defined as the sum of its direct expenditures and the tax revenues foregone from preferential treatment of some sources and uses of income). The federal government has attempted to deal with this problem for tax-exempt bonds by enacting a series of restrictive measures to control the types of services for which the exemption can be used and to cap the dollar volume of certain types of bonds that can be issued in any year. This suggests that it is possible, in principle, to tinker with the tax-exempt bond law and convert what amounts to an open-ended grant into a closed grant with budgetary control. The question remains, however, as to whether the Internal Revenue Service (IRS), whose primary responsibility is to collect revenue, is equipped to administer and enforce a host of laws and regulations whose purpose is to allocate scarce spending (the foregone revenue) among a plethora of claimants. This issue is discussed more fully.

Efficiency of Intergovernmental Assistance

The discussion to this point has focused on the cost of intergovernmental assistance to the federal government. Another issue appears in policy discussions of tax-exempt bonds – the contention that they are not a very efficient subsidy instrument. Care must be taken when using the term *efficient*, for it means different things to different people. To an economist, economic efficiency in this context means ensuring that intergovernmental assistance adjusts prices and marginal costs so that producers' and consumers' decisions allocate resources "efficiently." To a program manager, administrative efficiency means making certain that administrative costs are kept to a minimum. To others, *efficiency* may mean transfer efficiency, whereby a subsidy is structured so that the greatest possible share of federal costs go to the intended recipients. Each of these "efficiencies" is discussed in turn.

Economic efficiency

If the object of the federal government's intergovernmental assistance is correction of state and local underspending due to externalities and spillovers, spending is encouraged by lowering the cost of the under-provided services in proportion to the external benefits. Given these cost adjustments, economic efficiency is maximized by allowing state and local governments maximum flexibility to adjust to the change in relative prices by exercising their decentralized decision making.

The type of subsidy instrument should depend on how broadly based is the state and local underspending. If underspending is present in equal proportion across all types of state and local programs, then unconstrained assistance such as revenue sharing, tax deductibility, and tax-exempt bonds may be appropriate. The choice among them ought to be based upon such considerations as the magnitude of the underspending, which, if it is not great from the federal perspective, might suggest revenue sharing (which imposes a limit) rather than tax deductibility or tax-exempt bonds (which are open-ended commitments); and whether the underspending is focused on a particular factor of production, which, if capital is the underutilized factor, might suggest tax-exempt bonds or a capital-constrained revenue-sharing program (the likelihood of capital underspending is discussed later in this chapter). If the underspending is specific to one or two functions, then a categorical grant or tax-exempt financing restricted to the relevant function may be considered, but tax deductibility is out.

Administrative efficiency

When Congress creates intergovernmental assistance programs, it is establishing spending priorities in conformance with its own view of social objectives. Accomplishing these goals often requires fairly specific restrictions on how these dollars are to be spent and substantial administrative guidelines and reporting requirements to ensure compliance with federal objectives. The state and local perspective is different, stressing that needs and priorities vary greatly across the 50 states, and within the states across very different kinds of local governments. Restrictions and administrative guidelines reduce state and local officials' flexibility to take diverse needs into account when establishing spending priorities, and chew up dollars that could be spent on direct provision of public services.

Administrative costs are greatest for grants. Categorical aid, almost by definition, generally is accompanied by mandates to provide special services, reporting requirements to ensure compliance, and other provisions requiring minimum service levels or maintenance of effort. From the state and local perspective, categorical grants have high administrative costs. As for block grants, although claims have been made of an efficiency advantage (relative to categorical grants) of up to 25 percent, a more conservative figure offered by organizations representing the states is a block grant advantage relative to categorical grants of about 10 percent (Osbourn 1981). Additional but unspecified savings are generally ascribed to the even less restrictive General Revenue Sharing program (US General Accounting Office 1982).

Administrative costs for tax deductibility and tax-exempt bonds are a largely unexplored area, but are almost surely considerably lower per dollar of foregone federal revenue than for any type of grant. The Internal Revenue Service does not disaggregate its administrative and enforcement costs by individual provisions that appear on form 1040, such as the itemized deduction for state and local taxes. Withheld state and local taxes are recorded on wage earners' W-2 forms, and the 1040 is computer checked at a very low cost per return. Undoubtedly, the administrative costs for tax deductibility are very small per dollar of foregone federal revenue compared to any type of grant.

Information on tax-exempt interest income did not even appear on tax returns until 1987. The IRS has relied primarily on private bond counsel for voluntary compliance with the tax-exempt bond laws, and its small enforcement effort has been reactive to external information received about abusive bond deals. The administrative costs for tax-exempt bonds are also likely to be very low per dollar of foregone revenue compared to any type of grant.

Transfer efficiency

Tax-exempt bonds have long been plagued with the allegation that the federal government's revenue loss exceeds the reduction in state and local borrowing costs, thereby making bonds an inefficient method for transferring money from the federal to state and local governments. This is true, but its importance is overstated for two reasons. First, this "transfer inefficiency" was greatly reduced by the lowering of the marginal tax rate schedule that occurred in 1986. And, second, it is also true that grants-in-aid and state and local tax deductibility do not convert every dollar of grant or revenue loss into an increase in state and local budgets. This section begins by explaining the nature of this transfer inefficiency and its reduction that occurred in 1986.

A taxpayer with marginal tax rate t who can purchase a corporate (taxable) bond with an interest rate equal to r_c will earn an after-tax return equal to $r_c(1 - t)$. He or she will be indifferent between purchasing this corporate bond and a tax-exempt bond of equivalent risk yeilding r_m, where $r_m = r_c(1 - t)$. In effect, the taxpayer has traded the higher yield on the corporate bond for the absence of tax on the interest income on the municipal bond. This implicit tax is $t = (r_c - r_m)/r_c$. The taxable bond yield foregone by the taxpayer $(r_c - r_m)$ just equals the tax revenue foregone (tr_c) by the federal government on the taxable bond yield.

If the marginal tax rate that clears the municipal bond market and establishes the differential between taxable and tax-exempt bond yields is equal to t_m, any bond purchaser whose marginal tax rate exceeds t_m $(t_x > t_m)$ saves taxes on foregone taxable bond income $(t_x r_c)$ that exceed the value of the foregone taxable bond yield. The taxpayer earns a windfall, that is, he or she receives a higher yield on the municipal bond than was necessary to induce him or her to purchase the bond. What this means is that the federal revenue loss $(t_x r_c)$ is greater than the reduced borrowing costs of state and local governments $(r_c - r_m)$.

This can be seen by comparing the federal revenue loss and the reduction in state and local borrowing costs, where t_m is the market clearing tax rate, t_x is the average marginal tax rate of municipal bond-holders, and S is the stock of municipal debt:

$$t_x r_c S > t_m r_c S \tag{17.1}$$

The federal revenue loss is on the left-hand side of the equation – the stock of municipal debt times the interest income the taxpayer would have earned in a taxable bond times the average tax rate of municipal bondholders. The value of the tax subsidy to state and local governments is on the right-hand side of the equation, and is calculated in the same way except that the relevant tax rate is that which clears the municipal bond market.[14]

The transfer efficiency of tax-exempt bonds is calculated by dividing the reduction in state and local borrowing costs by the federal revenue loss, which reduces to the ratio of t_m/t_x. It is not difficult to obtain a ballpark estimate for this ratio. Prior to the 1986 tax reform, individual tax rates ranged to 0.5 and the corporate rate to 0.46. Assuming the average household marginal tax rate of municipal bondholders was 0.38, and the household and corporate shares of municipal debt were 0.517 and 0.483, respectively, a weighted average tax rate of municipal bondholders was 0.42. If the market clearing rate was 0.24 (see the yield ratios), the transfer efficiency of municipal bonds prior to the 1986 tax reform was 0.57.

The 1986 tax reform reduced and flattened the individual progressive rate structure and reduced the corporate tax rate, eliminated the deductibility of bank interest expense for most municipal bond purchases, and instituted an alternative minimum tax on all corporate tax-exempt interest income. All of these changes acted to reduce the differential between t_x and t_m (some by decreasing the share of municipal bonds held in corporate portfolios). As a result, the transfer efficiency of tax-exempt bonds increased to about 0.80.[15] Thus, although tax reform may have had an adverse impact on the supply of bonds and damaged state and local claims to intergovernmental immunity, it did succeed in making the bonds a more attractive intergovernmental subsidy alternative to grants-in-aid.

I turn now to the second issue, a demonstration that none of the available subsidy instruments succeeds in transferring anywhere close to 100 percent of the federal cost to increased state and local services. The transfer efficiency of grants depends in some sense on how one defines the issue. If the objective is to provide dollars to state and local decision makers, by definition every dollar of federal grants goes to state and local governments as fiscal assistance. In this sense the transfer efficiency of grants-in-aid is 1. But this approach seems unnecessarily mechanical and ignores any state and local responses to the receipt of the grant dollars. Taking a broader perspective, the objective can be viewed as the increase of state and local spending.

This latter perspective acknowledges that the recipient government has the option of using the grant funds for the intended purpose or substituting the funds for state and local tax effort and reducing its own tax levies. Government is viewed as nothing but a veil for state and local taxpayers, who ultimately decide how to divide the federal funds between private and public consumption (between tax relief/debt reduction and public expenditure increases). The tradeoff between these two options differs according to whether the structure of the grant program changes only taxpayer income (a grant not requiring matching funds) or also alters the relative prices of public and private consumption (a grant requiring matching funds).

An extensive literature investigates the extent to which state and local governments substitute grant dollars for their own tax effort. Excellent surveys of this literature have been done by Gramlich (1977), Inman (1979), and the US Department of the Treasury (1985). Gramlich breaks grants into three categories: open-ended matching grants that affect taxpayer incomes and prices; closed-ended matching grants that affect taxpayer incomes and prices; and closed-ended lump-sum grants that affect only taxpayer incomes. The lump-sum grants, of which GRS was the primary example, experience the greatest proportion of grant dollars used for state and local tax reduction. Surprisingly, the proportion of GRS dollars siphoned off for tax relief was not nearly so great as consumer theory suggested it should be. If one takes the income elasticity of demand for public goods to be approximately 10 percent, and if taxpayers perceive the monetary consequences of GRS clearly through the governmental veil, tax reduction should have been about $0.90 on the dollar. But empirical estimates of tax reduction's share ranged from about $0.60 to more than $0.90, implying that the increase in state and local spending ranged somewhere between $0.40 and less than $0.10 per dollar.[16] This text uses a mid-range estimate of 0.20 for the transfer efficiency of GRS – about $0.20 of a lump-sum grant dollar is spent on providing state and local services and $0.80 is spent on tax relief.

Studies of open and closed-ended matching grants indicate, on average, a smaller proportion of substitution for tax reduction, with the proportion depending on the presence of effort-maintenance provisions (restrictions that attempt to prohibit substitution of state and local tax reduction for spending). Although there is no generally accepted number for the spending response, its magnitude has declined as more and more studies have been completed. Gramlich's 1982 study suggested that categorical grants with an average matching rate of 20 percent generated additional state and local spending of $0.38.[17] In other words, on the average, $0.62 of every grant dollar appears as a reduction in state and local spending.

The deductibility of state and local nonbusiness taxes from the federal income tax base provides financial assistance to state and local taxpayers in a very different way than does grants-in-aid. Deductibility reduces the after-federal-tax price (cost) of state and local taxpayers' tax dollar and increases their after-federal-tax income. Both the lower price and higher income cause taxpayers to desire a higher level of state and local services, and to increase their willingness to pay higher state and local taxes. The extent of this increase in state and local taxes and spending depends upon the sensitivity of itemizers' demand for public services to these changes in their tax price and income, and on itemizers' success in making the political process reflect their changes in demand. Thus, just as every dollar of federal grants-in-aid does not appear as an increase in the state and local budget, the effect of the deductibility subsidy on state and local spending is also less than federal revenue loss figures for deductibility that appear in table 17.1.

Early estimates of the transfer efficiency of tax deductibility were made by Noto and Zimmerman (1983) and Kenyon (1984). Noto and Zimmerman used assumptions that tended to maximize the spending response: that the itemizer controlled the political decision on spending level; and that spending was responsive to price changes (a price elasticity of demand equal to -0.5). Using an early-1980s estimate of the itemizer's marginal tax rate of 0.34, deductibility reduced the price of a state and local tax dollar from $1.00 to $0.66, a 41 percent reduction in price. This implied a 20.5 percent increase on that portion of spending financed with deductible taxes. Thus, every dollar of state and local tax deductions cost the federal government $0.34 in revenue and raised state and local spending by $0.205. The transfer efficiency of tax deductibility was approximately 0.60; $0.40 of every dollar of federal revenue loss was not received by state and local governments. Thus, using very generous assumptions to maximize the state and local spending response, deductibility seems to fare well compared to grants-in-aid.

Deductibility's transfer efficiency worsened after the Tax Reform Act of 1986. Statutory tax rates were lowered, thereby lowering the price reduction on deductible taxes. And the percentage of taxpayers who itemize was reduced, thereby reducing the share of taxpayers who receive a price reduction. Both of these changes made taxpayers desire a lower level of public spending and taxation.[18] Incorporating these changes into the estimates reduces the transfer efficiency of deductibility.

This discussion assumes that itemizers' average marginal tax rate falls to 0.24, costing the federal government $0.24 for every dollar of deductible taxes. Now, however, relax the assumption that itemizers control the political process and allow nonitemizers to have an equal vote. If 60 percent of state and local taxpayers do not itemize (and have a tax price of 1.0 compared to 0.76 for itemizers), the weighted tax price for all taxpayers is 0.9. This implies a percentage price reduction of 10.0 percent, and an increase of spending financed with deductible taxes of 5.0 percent. Thus, every dollar of state and local tax deductions costs the federal government $0.24 in revenue and raises state and local spending by $0.05. The transfer efficiency of tax deductibility is approximately 0.21; $0.79 of every dollar of revenue loss is not received by state and local governments.

Comparable types of estimates have not been made for tax-exempt bonds. But surely the state and local sector's demand for capital formation is not perfectly elastic. Spending on capital formation is unlikely to have increased by the amount of the foregone federal tax revenue, and the 0.80 post-1986 tax-exempt bond transfer efficiency discussed earlier is obviously an overestimate. None of the subsidy instruments manages to translate every dollar of Federal cost into higher state and local public service spending.

A Capital Subsidy and Factor Price Distortion

Political acceptance that the economic justification (the spillover test) for federal subsidy of some state and local activities is satisfied is not equivalent to justification of subsidy provision via tax-exempt bonds. Although the focus of this book is not to question the tax exemption for municipal bonds (for which political support seems solid) but, rather, its use for certain activities (for which political support is sometimes weak), it is worth taking a moment to spell out the tenuous conceptual basis for this form of subsidy. In effect, the tax-exempt bond lowers the price of capital relative to the price of other factors of production such as labor and operating costs.[19] In public finance terms, the interest exemption appears to "distort" factor prices.

In the face of this distortion, can it make sense to provide financial support in the form of a capital subsidy for debt instruments? It might if capital services are underprovided relative to current services. One can muster several arguments for why state and local budgets might favor current services and underspend on capital formation, thereby rationalizing a subsidy such as tax-exempt bonds that alters the relative prices of state and local factors of production.

Electoral pressures: a bias for current spending?

The first possibility arises from the incentives facing state and local officials. These officials want to get reelected, and the electoral process may induce them to favor spending that produces immediate benefits to constituents. The only evidence of such a bias seems to be as a response to cyclical factors – many observers have noted that tightening of budgets tends to generate efforts to maintain current services in the short run by scrimping on capital replacement and maintenance (National Council on Public Works Improvement 1988). But a cyclical phenomenon such as this is not a basis for justifying a permanent structural subsidy for capital spending.

Does mobility create a preference for current services?

Second, citizens in a mobile society may be reluctant to spend on long-lived assets at the local level because they expect to move before these assets produce benefits. Although it is undeniably true that US society is extremely mobile, two other factors would have to occur for this to be an important factor. The time pattern of repayment on the bonds used to finance capital facilities would have to be accelerated relative to the time pattern of services provided by the capital facilities. This is certainly possible, as one indicator of a mismatch (but by no means a conclusive one) – bond maturity – is sometimes shorter than the actual productive life of the physical capital. But even if this were the case, citizens would have to be sufficiently sophisticated about the financial aspects of public capital formation to be aware of the mismatch.

Is there capital services illusion?

Third, citizens may simply be unaware of the contribution capital spending makes to their consumption of current services. Such a result implies that taxpayers suffer from some sort of fiscal illusion, that is, that they do not see the economic world clearly. The idea that people suffer from "money" illusion or "tax" illusion has a long history in the economics literature, so it is not outlandish to suggest that taxpayers may misperceive the relationship between capital spending in prior years and consumption of current services.[20]

Do capital services have more spillovers?

And fourth, it may be that some capital services have a larger spillover component than do current services, and are thus more likely to be underprovided. For example, access to such services as garbage collection and fire protection can be easily restricted to residents. But denying nonresidents access to such things as parks, libraries, and pollution abatement may entail prohibitively large transaction costs.

Any or all of these four factors could produce a tendency for the state and local sector to in effect use too high a discount rate when evaluating what some call infrastructure projects. If this were the case, a federal subsidy of capital goods acquired by state and local governments need not result in a misallocation of resources in every case, contrary to Treasury Secretary Andrew Mellon's argument in the 1920s.

Conclusions

A more restricted view of federal domestic program responsibilities has emerged over the last 10 years, a change that has been accompanied by reduced intergovernmental funding. This perspective on federal program responsibility is consistent with the economic justification for federal subsidy of state and local service provision. Federal subsidy is appropriate only when the service being provided generates collective benefits for federal taxpayers as well as for the state or local taxpayers in the jurisdiction providing the service. Since the tax-exempt bond subsidizes all state and local activities whether or not this criterion is satisfied, some federal control is suggested. The difficulty arises in trying to write legislation that applies this concept to particular activities.

The federal government has attempted to deal with the problem of budgetary control of tax-exempt bonds by enacting a series of restrictive measures to control the types of services for which the exemption can be used and to cap the dollar volume of bonds that can be issued in any given year. Thus, it is possible, in principle, to tinker with the tax-exempt bond law and convert what amounts to an open-ended grant into a closed grant with budgetary control. The question remains, however, whether the Internal Revenue Service, whose primary responsibility is to collect revenue, is equipped to administer and enforce laws whose purpose is equivalent to that of a direct spending program.

No form of intergovernmental assistance is clearly superior in terms of efficiency. When the objective is to stimulate all types of state and local spending, bonds have a role to play in promoting economic efficiency (ignoring their role in distorting factor prices), but are a poor second cousin to categorical grants when specific programs are to be targeted. Of course, bonds can be targeted to specific private activities, as the legislation in 1968 and the 1980s has increasingly done, but administrative costs probably will have to rise if they are to be well targeted. The tax subsidies probably entail lower administrative costs than grants, but undoubtedly achieve that by directing less of the subsidy to the desired groups. And none of the alternatives delivers a large share of the federal cost to increased state and local spending, although the tax-exempt bond share has improved due to the rate reductions enacted in 1986.

The case for subsidizing one factor of production, such as capital, depends upon whether that factor of production is underprovided relative to other factors. Several rationales can be summoned in support of such claims of underprovision of public capital, but evidence to support these rationales is scant: electoral pressures create a bias among officials for current spending; mobility creates a preference among taxpayers for current services; citizens underestimate the contribution capital services make to their welfare; and capital services have a larger spillover component than do current services.

Notes

1   Discussions of what constitutes a public purpose can be found as early as Adam Smith's *Wealth of Nations*. Some suggest that the formalization of modern public goods theory began with Paul Samuelson's 1954 article on the pure theory of public expenditures. The systematic application of public goods theory to the federal budget process can be found in public finance texts beginning with Richard Musgrave (1959). One of the early and thorough discussions of the spillover rationale for intergovernmental assistance is provided by Break (1967, 71–7).

2   In technical terms, the monopolist maximizes profits at the output where marginal revenue equals marginal cost rather than the output at which price equals marginal cost. The result is that consumers attach a greater value to their last unit of consumption from the monopoly producer (measured by the price they pay) than to their last unit of consumption from nonmonopoly producers (measured by the monopolist's marginal cost, that is, what the monopolist has to pay for the resources it hires away from other producers). Consumer welfare can, therefore, be increased by decreasing the output of (and shifting resources from) nonmonopoly producers whose production is valued by the consumer at the monopolist's marginal cost and increasing the output of (and shifting resources to) monopoly producers whose production is valued at the monopolist's price.

3   In fact, taxpayers are often likely to be unwilling to provide services to resident nontaxpayers, a situation worsened by the existence of fiscal disparities among jurisdictions. The per-person tax base varies substantially from state to state, requiring taxpayers in one state to make a greater tax effort (pay a higher tax price) than taxpayers in another state in order to provide equivalent public services. The desire to reduce this unequal tax-base wealth and its potential effect on the provision of basic services in different states is often cited as a "fiscal disparities" justification for federal subsidy of the state and local sector.

4   Although the Reagan revolution has questioned the legitimacy of most grants to state and local governments, the necessity for federal support of public assistance programs has been recognized. This is attributable to the fact that a much greater proportion of the collective consumption benefits from transfer programs spill over state and local political boundaries than is true for most other public services.

5　Major exceptions to this conclusion are veterans' housing bonds issued primarily in California, Oregon, and Texas, and some industrial development bonds issued by the state of Maine. The 1986 volume for veterans' housing bonds was $0.34 billion in California, $1.053 billion in Oregon, and $0.967 billion in Texas.

6　Some revenue bonds are actually retired from earmarked tax revenues, such as motor fuel taxes used to finance highway construction, or lease payments financed by annual appropriations, which are equivalent to interest and debt redemption payments for public buildings and jails constructed by state agencies and leased to the state.

7　A more detailed discussion of this background is available in Miller (1988).

8　For example, Food Stamp benefit levels are set and financed by the federal government, and the program is classified in the "direct payments for individuals" category. Aid to Families with Dependent Children benefit levels are set and partially financed with state funds, and the program is classified in the "grants to states" category. The federal share of benefit levels in 1987 ranged from 50 percent in 11 states to 78.5 percent in 1 state.

9　This discussion of structure is based upon Nathan et al. (1987) and Miller (1988). The Reagan administration proposed a 25 percent cut in these programs. Funding for the merged programs as approved by Congress averaged about 12 percent below the total for the prior year for all programs placed in the block. These cuts ranged from zero for the energy assistance block grant to a 34 percent cut in the cummunity services block grant.

10　An additional five proposals for block grants were defeated during this period. Even though block grants were replacing categoricals, the proportion of funds distributed through categorical programs continued to increase, accounting for 87 percent of total grants in 1988 compared to 79 percent in 1980. (See Advisory Commission on Intergovernmental Relations 1987, 1–2).

11　In the Income Tax Act of 1861, state and local taxes and federal taxes were the only deductions specifically allowed.

12　For more complete discussions of the history and rationales for deductibility, see Brazer (1959) and Noto and Zimmerman (1983).

13　Revenue sharing is not discussed here because it served a different function than did traditional grants-in-aid. General revenue sharing (GRS) was predicated on a belief that the federal government had an interest in seeing that standard state and local functions were provided at some base level, and that the federal government's tax-raising ability was superior to that of state and local governments. In other words, the motivation was not underprovision due to spillovers but, rather, to a mismatch between local needs and revenue-raising ability. (See Maxwell and Aronson 1977, 71.)

14　The state and local interest savings are $(r, r_m)S$, the difference between taxable and tax-exempt rates times the stock of debt. Referring back to the expression for the implicit tax rate, cross multiplication shows that $r_c - r_m = t_m r_c$.

15   This estimate uses household and corporate holding shares of 0.643 and 0.357, and assumes the average tax rate for households is 0.28 and the market clearing tax rate is 0.24.

16   The difference between the high estimates of the GRS impact on state and local spending and the estimate suggested by consumer theory was labeled the "flypaper effect," because it suggested that money sticks where it hits. See Oates (1979) and Courant, Gramlich, and Rubinfeld (1979). Gramlich's (1982) study of President Reagan's 1982 New Federalism proposal suggested a short-term increase in spending from unconstrained grants of $0.04 per dollar and a long-term response of $0.18.

17   Rymarowicz and Zimmerman (1988) suggested that both states and local governments behaved in the 1980s in a manner consistent with grant substitution by substituting their own tax effort for reduced grant dollars. From 1980 through 1986, in response to reduced grants-in-aid, the states' own-source revenue increase in excess of inflation was sufficient to reduce the federal contribution ratio by $9.21 per $100 of own-source revenue; the comparable ratio for local governments was $1.92 per $100 of own-source revenue.

18   The deductibility of sales taxes was also eliminated. This would also work to reduce the effect of deductibility on state and local spending but not necessarily on the transfer efficiency of the remaining deductible taxes. Rough estimates of the effect of these three tax reform changes on the level of state and local spending by state have been made by Kenyon (1988). The reduction in tax costs from deductibility was estimated to have raised state and local spending in 1982 an average of 3 percent above what it would otherwise have been. This increase in spending was expected to decline to about 1 percent in 1987. This suggests a small reduction in state and local spending from the Tax Reform Act of about 2 percent. In only two states (Utah and Colorado) was the decline estimated to be as high as 3 percent.

19   This is not literally true in all cases. If money is borrowed to pay for current expenses such as salaries and supplies, the price of these factors is also reduced. Generally, state and local statutes and regulations, as well as the risk avoidance behavior of investors, prevents such borrowing for noncaptial expenses. But the New York City fiscal crisis in the late 1970s illustrates the ability of elected officials to circumvent such hurdles when faced with difficult budgetary problems.

20   Money illusion suggests that people feel better off when their incomes rise, even though real income has not risen due to price increases. Tax illusion suggests people are not aware, due to such things as income tax withholding and indirect sales and excise taxes, of the share of their income being paid in taxes.

Introduction to Chapter 18

One of the most important criteria in practice in decisions on state and local tax policy is the economic development impact of the proposed action. If a tax increase is necessary, what is the least economically damaging form of the tax increase? If a tax reduction is feasible in budgetary terms (or even if it is not feasible), what is the most economically beneficial form of tax cut? Which tax, or specific feature of a tax, or tax rate, has the most severe impact on business decisions to invest in a given place, or continue in business in that place?

This concern is anything but new. However, it is inherently difficult to provide convincing evidence about the quantitative effect of a given change in tax policy on the local economy. This chapter examines the difficulties involved, and recounts the increasing conviction on the part of economists that taxes *do* matter. It also explores tax changes at the state level that are good for the national economy, as well as the individual state.

18

State Tax Policy and Economic Development: What Should Governors Do When Economists Tell Them That Nothing Works?

Dick Netzer

For at least thirty years, economists have been surveying the empirical evidence on the effects of state and local taxation on the location of economic activity within the United States and usually telling policymakers that state-local tax differentials are of no consequence.[1] For about as long, economists have been considering the question from a theoretical standpoint and concluding that there are indeed circumstances – and not far-fetched ones at that – in which state-local tax differentials should make a difference in the location of economic activity.[2] But most such analysts then qualify their findings with the unwelcome advice that the locational effects are to be deplored, rather than sought, for the effects are seen as cancelling one another, from the standpoint of national economic well-being: one state's gain is another's loss and, if the states compete for economic activity using the instruments of tax policy, we will all be worse off.

What do we really know about the effects of state tax policies on the location of economic activity?[3] Are there changes in state tax policies for the sake of economic development that are not beggar-thy-neighbor in effect but that, instead, can improve national economic well-being?

To telegraph the message: The answer to the first question is dismayingly inconclusive. It would be absurd for governors to act on the conviction that location is entirely indifferent to state-local taxes, but equally absurd for them to accept the proposition that there is usually a big bang for the buck. Ordinarily, it will cost a great deal in tax revenue to get strong economic effects and, in some circumstances, even a very costly tax change may have negligible effects (except perhaps in the very long run). But there are conditions in which strategic tax actions can have a strong impact. Those conditions relate to geography, a state's economic structure and the specific features of its tax system.

Second, there are indeed changes in state tax policies that will provide what economists call "efficiency gains," that is, improvements in the functioning of the national economy. The gains will not be spectacular in magnitude, but could be significant if the changes are widespread among the states, perhaps even large enough to offset the competitive losses that some states – those with lower taxes now, or with more economically-beneficent tax structures – might suffer as a result.

What We Know About Taxes and Location

The nature of the evidence

Why is it so hard to answer the seemingly straightforward question, "What are the effects of tax differentials on the location of economic activity?" To see why, we have to examine the nature of the empirical evidence. There are four main kinds of data that have been used to answer the question. The first, going back a good many years, consists of surveys of firms and business decision-makers in which the respondents are asked to rank, or assess the importance of, various factors in business location decisions, including state and local taxes. There have been surveys confined to firms that have moved recently and others covering both movers and non-movers; sometimes the respondents are asked not only about their own decision-making processes, but also their views as to how businesses in general view the various factors. Some surveys are very open-ended in asking about the factors, while others have a set list of factors to be evaluated.

The cynic would expect respondents to say that taxes are very important in location decisions: after all, if enough businesses report that, it might persuade politicians to go easy in taxing, thus benefiting even those firms that have no intention of moving, ever. In fact, only a minority of these surveys over the years have found respondents reporting that state-local taxes are an important factor in location decisions, and these are not the best done of the type. The best of the surveys seem to demonstrate that respondents, when prodded, will tell the interviewer that taxes are an important factor in business location decisions in general, but have not been so in their own cases, in which other considerations were decisive. This is hardly conclusive, and there is no reason to expect survey techniques to improve enough in time to make this a source of persuasive evidence on the question.

A second kind of evidence, also with a long history, is the use of tax rates or levels as the single variable to explain differences in growth rates among the states over time. So stated, the approach sounds too crude to be believed by anyone: we all know that taxes cannot possibly be the only factor to consider. Yet the argument continues to be advanced, although discredited years ago. For example, New Yorkers frequently hear this alleged syllogism: New York State's economy was doing badly before 1977 and state personal income tax rates were very high relative to those in other states; top bracket personal income tax rates were then cut substantially; the state's economy has done rather well since 1977; the tax cuts, therefore, are responsible for the economic recovery.

Most of the empirical evidence that economists consider acceptable is in the form of multiple-regression analysis. In the typical analysis, the variable to be explained is differences among the states in some measure of economic growth over a specified period. The analyst takes into account numerous possible explanatory variables, including measures of tax rates and/or tax burdens, but also including other things likely to affect growth rates, ranging from labor costs to climate. The procedure measures the quantitative effect of each of the explanatory variables, holding all others constant. With enough observations, statistically reliable results can be achieved.

Statistical reliability does not mean that the results will be clear-cut guides to policy decisions. Indeed, all too often the results for the tax variables are indeterminate ("not statistically significant") or implausible (as when a very high tax rate is associated with more, rather than less, economic growth). This is not surprising, for the multiple-regression technique tends not to give clear answers in situations like the one considered here. First of all, shifts in location by firms are relatively rare events, and the regression technique is not good at explaining the causes of rare events. (In a celebrated case thirty years ago, the statistical results of the field trials of the Salk vaccine, concerned with a rare disease, polio, "proved," implausibly, that the Salk vaccine did not work; the authorities rightly rejected those results.) Second, we know in advance that the tax variable must be a minor one in location decisions, compared to labor costs, transport costs, market access, access to raw materials and other similar variables, when comparing location choices among the states; the regression technique does a good job of quantifying the effects of explanatory variables that prima facie are important, but not of isolating the separate effects of minor factors.[4] Third, it is difficult to find satisfactory data to represent many of the other explanatory variables in the regression equations. Consider, for example, the difficulty of statistically specifying differences in climate among the fifty states; Where does one measure it within a state? How does one weigh humidity as compared to temperature? Is a warm winter more important than a cool summer? If some variables are improperly measured, then it is possible to have erroneous results for those variables that are easy to measure, and therefore are measured properly, like tax rates and tax burdens.

A fourth type of empirical inquiry on the effects of taxes on location is simulation analysis. The analyst develops a model of economic behavior, using data on how firms actually do behave in response to changes in various elements of cost and net returns; such data usually are derived quite indirectly, on the basis of more or less plausible hypotheses about production functions and the like. Then tax changes are introduced, and converted into changes in particular cost items (for example, a reduction in the rate of a gross receipts tax on utilities can be converted into a reduction in electric power rates) and/or into changes in profits (for example, for a change in the state corporate income tax). The result is an estimate of how economic activity will be changed if taxes change. Simulation studies do tend to yield clearcut results; the problem lies not in their lack of decisiveness, but in their lack of persuasiveness. They tell us what should happen, not what actually did happen.

What should happen

That, of course, is what theory – reasoning by deduction, rather than from empirical evidence – tells us. A full elaboration of the theoretical work economists have done on this subject is unnecessary; the basic notions are fairly simple. The first is that what counts for the location of economic activity are deviations from the national average tax burden for the particular type of tax, not the absolute tax burden in any particular place.[5] Second, tax differentials that reflect the costs of services that location decision-makers consider essential, but that are publicly provided in some places while privately purchased in other places, will not affect location. Third, if there are further tax differentials, they will have an effect only to the extent that the tax differentials overwhelm the unique nontax attributes – advantages and disadvantages – of each potential location for a firm or line of economic activity.

That third condition has important implications. For most economic activities that primarily serve local consumer markets, the advantage of a local site usually is overwhelming, so much so that even extraordinarily high taxes on these activities in one state will not induce moves to other states (except in cases of state-borderline metropolitan areas), or – what is the same thing – open the local market to penetration by outside suppliers that previously had found the market unpromising. This is especially true in the short run; over time, outside suppliers may find economical ways to break into local consumer markets if the outsiders have lower tax burdens. For example, one reason for the success of mail-order retailing is the avoidance of sales taxes (for mail-order firms without premises in a given state). The increase in sales tax rates by itself was not a sufficient condition for the change in consumer buying habits, but the tax factor bolstered others, including the decline in delivery costs in real terms (due to UPS), the development of the 800-number long-distance calling system and the universal use of credit cards.

So, in the long run, there can be locational effects even with regard to taxes on local consumer activities.[6] Meanwhile, there will be economic consequences from tax differentials with regard to activities serving broader regional and national markets. Almost always, those activities in one state are in competition with similar activities located in other states. If everything else is held constant – however unrealistic that proviso – and there are "excess' (in excess of the costs of essential services and of unique nontax attributes) tax differentials, those tax differentials must affect economic activity. Enterprises will leave the high-tax place or fail to start or expand there; employment will decline; wage and salary levels will decline; and/or local land values and returns from investments in real property will decline. The opposite will happen in the low-tax places. Given the assumptions, these things must happen, even if we cannot observe them through the background "noise" of continual change in all the other variables. The issue is not whether the theoretically prescribed effects happen at all, but how large they are – relative to the revenue amounts in question.

Simulation studies, for all their "iffiness," can place some quantitative dimensions on the likely effects. Two examples, both New York cases, illustrate the point. In 1980, my colleagues and I estimated the effects on private sector employment in New York City of moving to complete uniformity in property tax assessments, which would have involved an average business property tax reduction of close to 25 percent. We thought that this probably would have a significant positive effect on employment; the simulation model predicted no net change.[7] A year later, we did another simulation study, this one examining the economic consequences of a package of tax reforms designed to end the discriminatory taxation of telephone service in New York State, which would have involved a reduction in total state and local taxes paid by New York

Telephone Company of more than 50 percent. Our model predicted an increase in private sector employment in the state of at least 43,000.[8]

One other type of simulation study should be mentioned. Before one can estimate the economic effects of an existing tax differential or of a proposed tax change, it is necessary to know how taxpayers – firms and households – are actually impacted by the tax provision in question: for firms, just how much, relative to some standard measure like profits, is the tax differential or tax change worth? Given the complexity of some of the major state-local taxes, notably the corporate income tax, it is often far from self-evident what that initial impact of a tax provision is. Over the years, analysts have dealt with this question by simulating the tax bills of hypothetical firms (and, less often, hypothetical households) in various locations. Recently, a very ambitious simulation model has been constructed by James Papke of Purdue University and Leslie Papke, his daughter, of MIT, that can show the effect of highly specific and detailed tax law provisions on after-tax profits for firms with different characteristics at different locations. Their "AFTAX" model has been used in analyzing business tax provisions in Midwestern states and, recently, for an intensive analysis of New York State business taxes.[9]

The regression studies: a quick review

A generation ago, regression studies designed to measure the impact of state-local tax differentials on the location of economic activity almost always were done by academics on their own initiative. Elected officials knew, without formal study, either that tax differentials were terribly important (and therefore warranted the passage of an increasing array of special "incentive" features) or that tax differentials were of no consequence because the local economy was not vulnerable to such minor cost disadvantages (the dominant position in New York during the 1960s, for example). More recently, state governments themselves have been the initiators of such studies, in some abundance.

Those initiatives have produced both original empirical studies and comprehensive reviews of the work done by others. One widely cited such review was done by Roger Vaughan under the aegis of the Council of State Planning Agencies in 1979.[10] Within the last year, two state tax study commissions, one in Minnesota and the other in New York, have released reports that include very extensive reviews of the literature. The New York report[11] finds (p. 7) that:

> In large part, the studies that have been undertaken conclude that state and local taxes have little, if any, effect on industrial locational

decisions. This conclusion emerges both from studies that survey decisionmakers and from those which analyze actual locational decisions [usually, regression studies]. Moreover, the most recent studies reaffirm the body of research accumulated on this subject over the last three decades.[12]

The Minnesota report, by Michael Wasylenko (dated June 28, 1984), incorporates both original econometric work and a review of the literature substantially the same as that reviewed in the New York report. Although Wasylenko is highly critical of much of the theoretical literature, and therefore the regression analyses based on that theory (for example, there is almost uniform neglect of moving costs, uncertainty and information costs, as well as of the personal locational preferences of business location decision-makers), he assesses the results of prior work rather differently than is done in the New York report (p. 22):

There is some evidence in these studies that taxes and business climate in general influence manufacturing employment growth. The evidence is weak in that some research supports the view that taxes matter, but in other research there is little evidence to support this view. The more recent studies tend to find that taxes matter in regional location decisions. While these studies tend to use more variables to explain location choice and to use more sophisticated econometric techniques, they also look only at total manufacturing or at a very narrow set of industries. These focuses result in evidence that is not sufficient to draw general conclusions about whether taxes are important in employment growth. Taxes may matter for some industries but not for others and in examining aggregate manufacturing, the taxes (and other variables) on employment growth may appear to have no effect on location due to aggregation of industries and resulting bias.

Most of the empirical research has been on manufacturing rather than non-manufacturing industries, for some obvious reasons: first, manufacturing activity has been shifting among and within regions dramatically for several decades, and the shifts have left in their wake considerable economic distress in many places; second, most manufacturing is not for local markets and therefore should be more susceptible to location-affecting policy measures, and the states themselves usually focus on retention or attraction of manufacturing; and third, the factors affecting manufacturing location decisions are easier to quantify and the theory more elaborated. But other types of economic activity are increasingly important. Also, most of the research has concentrated on the analysis of taxes explicitly on business as such, but of course location could be influenced by the other taxes used at the state-local level, including sales, property and personal income taxes. There have been some studies over the years that have considered nonmanufacturing activities, alone or in addition to manufacturing, and also the other forms of taxation. Some of these have concluded that taxes can and do make large differences in location.

For example, an analysis of the economic effects of the New York City sales tax through 1964 (up to 1965, there was no sales tax at all any place else in the Standard Consolidated Area) showed that the tax caused substantial shifting of sales to other parts of the region, with a significant adverse effect on employment in retail trade.[13] A study of the economic effects of New York City's change in the form of business taxation, accompanied by an increase in effective rates, in 1966 showed that employment in manufacturing was severely impacted by the tax change, but other industries were not.[14] Another study, by the same principal author, Ronald Grieson, showed that increases in the Philadelphia city income tax had large negative effects on employment in both manufacturing and nonmanufacturing.[15] A very recent study by Michelle White used evidence from California experience after the passage of Proposition 13 in June 1978 to estimate the impact of the very large reductions in property taxes on business location. Because the reduction was large, virtually overnight and differed considerably among the counties, conditions were almost like those of a laboratory experiment, with other variables held constant. She found a significant positive effect of the cut for nonmanufacturing industries, but not for manufacturing.[16]

The econometric study by Wasylenko, in his 1984 report to the Minnesota Tax Study Commission mentioned earlier, is one of the few to deal explicitly with the effect of the personal income tax on the location of economic activity. This is not surprising, for it is very difficult to address the issue head-on in a formal model. Logically, differentially high state-local personal income tax burdens will not affect location if they are offset by lower burdens of other personal taxes with similar incidence or if they are offset by higher state-local services that upper-bracket income taxpayers value (like substantial state school aid to affluent suburban school districts). High personal income tax burdens will affect location in the following ways:

1   by affecting the residential choices of people who live largely on property income or taxable pension income;

2   by raising the salary demands of key managerial and professional people who are recruited in national markets and who tend to be mobile between firms and places;

3   by lowering the net after-tax personal incomes of those who make the decision on where to locate the firm or facility; or

4   through longer-term indirect effects of (1), (2) and (3) on total size of the resident population and its income and demand for goods and services.

It is difficult to model (2) and (3), and there are data problems for all of these factors that appear insurmountable. So the subject is mostly unexplored. What is surprising is that so many policymakers and analysts, who – after considering the inconclusive results of all those years of study of the economic effects of differentials in business taxes – are skeptical about the efficacy of business tax reductions or incentives, are quite willing to believe – on the basis of zero years of research on the economic effects of state personal income taxes (but many anecdotes) – that costly reductions in personal income taxes will make a major difference in a state's economy.

Wasylenko's study does not explicitly trace the effects of personal income tax differentials, but includes various tax rate variables along with a number of other variables as possible explanations of differences in employment growth between Minnesota and a number of other states. He finds that the decline in Minnesota's overall state-local tax burden during the 1970s was a significant contributor to the state's good economic performance, but that was partly offset by the negative effects of the relatively high state personal income tax rates.[17]

It should be noted that regression studies are inherently unsuited to analysis of highly detailed tax incentive features, because those features are likely to differ in their specifics among the states so much that each one is unique. Nor can this method be applied to types of taxes that are used in only a few places, or that are used in very different forms in different states. Instead, regression studies focus on overall tax burdens and on explicit tax rates for commonly used taxes. Therefore, it is conceivable that the special incentives or unusual tax instruments could have an effect on location even when taxes more generally do not, or vice versa. The simulation approach is suggestive, although hardly conclusive. Another approach is to calculate "break-even" points for tax incentives designed to elicit new investment (or employment): the fraction of investment for which the tax reduction is given that must be induced by the tax break, if the revenue loss is to be justified. (For any tax incentive, some of the new investment or employment that elicits the tax break would have occurred even in the absence of the tax break.) Often, the break-even point is so high that it is inconceivable that it can be reached.[18]

Intra-regional versus inter-regional

The reader will have noted that a good deal of the empirical work cited, and some of the theoretical work as well, deals with location within metropolitan areas, rather than inter-regional location. It is fairly obvious that tax differentials should have more impact within metropolitan areas than among regions, simply because the nontax factors affecting location (like labor and transportation costs) vary less within small areas. What relevance can the intra-metropolitan results have for state government tax policy decisions? For thirty states, the intra-regional results are significant because they are homes to the 30-odd metropolitan areas that genuinely straddle state lines.[19] In these cases, tax differentials between the two (or three) states can impact short-distance, rather than long-distance, locational choices. In addition, the smaller the state in area, the more likely it is that its non-tax aspects will be like those of its immediate neighbors, which means that the findings with regard to intra-metropolitan effects probably are applicable to the small states of the Northeast, whether or not there are urban areas that actually straddle the state lines. The intra-metropolitan effects also can be relevant to any state, to the extent that it feels constrained in state-level tax decisions by concern about reducing within-state fiscal disparities because of the locational effects of those disparities. To be more concrete, however much a state government may wish to reduce certain state taxes to encourage economic growth, it may feel unable to do so if the price is less than state aid to local governments. The most hard-pressed of those local governments would then probably have to raise their own taxes, damaging the local economies.

But here too, while theory suggests that intra-regional tax differentials that are not capitalized into land values will have discernible effects on intra-regional location decisions, the empirical findings are less than clearcut. Some studies, including some cited above, show tax differentials to have powerful effects, but not all do. One of the most ambitious of the recent efforts, done with heavy Federal funding (Schmenner, 1982), found evidence that taxes affect long-distance moves, but no evidence whatever of effects within the major metropolitan area studied.

Drawing conclusions

The flippant answer to the question of what we know about taxes and location is that we know tax differentials matter. We don't know how much they matter. It is, however, possible to be somewhat more helpful than that.

First, with regard to location choices among widely separated places (in contrast to the borderline metropolitan area situation): it is plausible, and there is some empirical evidence to support the proposition[20] that differentials in the aggregate state-local tax burden among the states can make a substantial difference in the economic outcome. The difficulty here is obvious: it is hard to reduce the overall tax burden in a given state quickly as a deliberate act of policy (except in unusual situations, like having the massive surplus California had acquired by June 1978). It can be reduced over time, by restraining expenditure growth when other states are not, or by containing expenditures during a period when the state's economy is doing especially well (the Minnesota case in the 1970s).

As for particular tax measures, the evidence seems clear that differentials in the general corporate income tax rate are not potent locational influences. As noted earlier, there is very little systematic evidence at all with respect to personal income tax rate differentials; if these differentials are in fact important, they can be reduced substantially only at great cost, because the high income tax states derive large shares of their tax revenue from the personal income tax.[21] That may be worth doing but it is very difficult, and will be especially difficult in the intergovernmental fiscal environment that exists now.

The evidence with regard to specific features of broad-based taxes and narrow-based taxes is that changes in them are likely to affect economic development favorably and to a measurable extent only if the tax change is large for the industries and firms benefiting. This is not the usual case for tax incentive features in corporate income tax laws, but can be true with regard to some programs providing deep cuts in local real estate taxes for particular commercial real estate developments and with regard to utility tax reforms. Here again, deep-subsidy tax incentives may be a good deal; the drawback is that there inevitably will be some undeserving recipients of the deep subsidies, and that can lead to the program's demise.

Turning to the borderline metropolitan area situation, the economic development impact of tax changes can be close to zero if the reductions in tax burden simply raise land values, which is often the case. But where there is no capitalization, the economic impact per dollar of tax change is likely to be much larger than in the case of inter-regional location decisions, which suggests that it is worth being more adventurous in offering tax incentives when the target area is geographically small, and in reducing tax disparities between the two states in which the urban area is located.

With regard to the different economic sectors, the evidence is fairly clear that it is hard to affect manufacturing location decisions by tax measures alone (and tax measures may add little to whatever other inducements are on offer), and the bigger the enterprise or facility, the harder it is to be effective via tax policy. Financial and other business services are increasingly footloose, but taxes are likely to matter for these sectors only selectively, for example, where taxes affect some other cost factor of great importance (like energy costs or rent) for that firm or industry. Also, there are some distinctive situations, like the taxation of banks in some states, where existing practices have resulted in large differentials that can easily trigger locational shifts by firms that histori- cally were thought to be immobile, but which are no longer captive. That is, the source of the tax differentials lies in a tradition of imposing selectively heavy taxes on particular sectors or inputs. The more general and neutral state and local tax measures and systems are, the less the likelihood that the financial and business service sectors will need special tax breaks to encourage their growth in a given state.

Some observers have argued that much of this discussion is beside the point in its focus on the dollar costs of tax differentials. The argument is that business decision-makers are swayed as much by the symbolism of tax levels and tax provisions as by their dollar costs. One interpretation of this argument is that the costs of accurate comparative information on the things that the public sector can vary and that do matter to business location decision-makers – including the actual liability for all state and local taxes combined in numerous different locations, as well as that vector of variables referred to by the term "business climate" – are so high that the conspicuous features of state tax laws, like nominal tax rates, are taken as proxies for what is of real concern. Thus, careful econometric studies in which the tax variable is some kind of effective tax rate or dollars of actual tax liability may show no significant coefficients, while some tax variable that is far too crude (or has no plausible theoreti- cal basis) for economists to put into their regression equations may very well have real effects on location, as a proxy for those real concerns.

The key question may be where the burden of proof lies in proposals to shape state tax policy to encourage economic development. Is it on those who propose to reduce taxes or provide special incentives to foster economic development? Should they be required to demonstrate the economic gains will be worth the revenue foregone? Or is the burden of proof on those who deny the efficacy of the proposed tax reductions? The former usually was the case a generation ago; the latter tends to be the case today; with the states now faced with picking up burdens formerly borne by the Federal government, perhaps the burden of proof should be shifted to the proposers of state tax rate reductions and the advocates of tax incentive provisions.[22]

Positive Sum-game State Tax Reforms

The empirical studies reviewed in the previous section are, with few exceptions, analyses of how the states (or local areas) fare economically compared to one another because of tax differentials. Although the results in fact may have wider implications, the usual interpretation is that the studies are measuring only the extent to which one state has gained from or lost to others. Tax competition among the states is real enough, but in concept, state tax policy can make additions to the national pie, as well as playing the zero-sum-game of moving the same total amount of economic activity from one state to another or, even worse, encouraging locational shifts that reduce the aggregate value of the nation's output. In fact, most state tax changes are likely to have a mixture of effects. Our concern at this point is how can the tax policies of individual states contribute to the national economic well-being, rather than detract from it?

Public finance theorists over the years have described imaginary taxes that have no effect whatever on economic decisions by firms and households. The theoretical construct requires the tax to be designed so that no individual action can affect tax liabilities (for example, a national head tax can be escaped only by emigration or death) or it requires implausibly restrictive assumptions about how the economy works (for example, a uniform national property tax applying to all forms of capital would have no effect on economic decisions if the aggregate amount saved is completely insensitive to the rate of return on savings. There is debate about this sensitivity, but no one really believes that it is zero). In the real world, all tax instruments impose what economists call efficiency losses, in that they cause some economic factors to alter some decisions that would be made otherwise in the absence of the tax in question, and the changed decisions must make someone worse off (assuming that each of the private parties were pursuing their own best interests prior to the imposition of the tax).[23] But some real-world tax instruments are worse than others.[24]

We have heard a great deal in recent years about supply-side economics, which is mainly concerned, at the policy level, with the effects of

Federal taxes on aggregate economic variables, in particular, real economic growth over time. State, as well as Federal, taxes can have macroeconomic supply-side effects – on the decision between work and leisure, between saving and consumption and between risk-taking and risk avoidance. For example, many state income taxes are coupled to the Federal income tax, so that when deductions for contributions to IRAS were permitted for the Federal taxes, they also were permitted for many state personal income taxes. That marginally increased whatever effect the Federal IRA provision had on the aggregate level of saving. But no individual state can rationally assume that any tax change it makes on its own to further national macroeconomic policy goals will have very much discernible impact on the economy of the state itself – the leakages are too large. For example, there is no reason for any state to believe that the IRA deduction provision will lead to any increase in investment within its own boundaries: the deduction is allowable for any qualified plan, no matter where the financial institution administering the plan invests the funds.

However, changes in an individual state's taxes can have microeconomic effects, for good or for bad, on both the national economy and on the state's economy. State taxes (like Federal taxes) can distort choices among production inputs and they can distort choices by households as consumers. The nation will be somewhat better off if a state were to reduce, for example, differentially high taxation of labor inputs, but the state itself will benefit because firms within the state now will be in a better competitive position than they were previously. Take, for example, the study of taxation of telephone service in New York cited earlier (in note 8), which simulated the economic effects of a large reduction in state and local taxes collected through the Bell operating company; the tax reductions involved treating the telephone company like an ordinary business for income and property tax purposes, instead of taxing it much more heavily than other businesses. About half of the predicted increase in demand for the company's service reflected an increase in private sector employment in the state, and a good deal of this might have been at the expense of other states. But the remainder reflected improvements in efficiency on the part of business customers, that is, the elimination of tax-induced inefficiency-causing excessive prices, and those improvements represent net gains – albeit small ones – for the national economy.

There is another class of positive-sum-game results that can stem from changes in tax policies by individual states. Although the effects of state-local tax differentials on the location of economic activity may not be large, there are some locational decisions that would be made otherwise, were it not for the distortions caused by the existing tax provisions.

When a state reduces a tax that repels economic activity, it makes itself better off, but also makes a small contribution to the national economy, a contribution that might be sufficient to offset the small losses incurred by all those other states that previously had gained from the first state's folly.

There is a tax policy principle to which most public finance economists subscribe implicit in the previous discussion: the more nearly uniform state taxes are – among the states and within a single state, among industries, production inputs and objects of household expenditure decisions – the fewer the distortions and the less the efficiency losses. Of course, as the earlier discussion of the limited and uncertain locational effects of tax differentials suggests, the economic gains to a high-tax state are not likely to be sufficient to persuade it to reduce its overall tax effort and the individual taxes it imposes to the levels imposed by the lowest-tax states. But that should not preclude a search for strategic tax reductions that are good for all of us, nor the quest for revisions in state tax laws that, holding revenue constant, produce fewer economic distortions.

Likely candidates for reform

Perhaps the most widespread of the various economically distorting features of existing state-local tax systems is the characteristic heavy taxation of railroads, other regulated transportation industries and public utilities (including telecommunications, as well as the energy utilities). The instruments of this differentially heavy taxation have been the long-standing and virtually universal practice of employing what amounts to a quite different system of property taxation than is applied to property owned by ordinary businesses and, in most states, the use of gross receipts, rather than net income, taxes. The reasons for these practices include the conviction that heavy taxation of railroads and other interstate transportation companies is a way of exporting part of the tax burden to people located outside a state's boundaries (in line with the ancient principle that the best of all possible taxes is one on foreigners living abroad), and the belief – only recently shown to be invalid – that the demand for utility services is utterly insensitive to the prices charged for such services, so that the utilities can be used, without any economic damage whatever, as tax-gathering conduits. The result is that, typically, utility services to consumers are taxed more heavily than most other forms of consumer expenditure (alcoholic beverages and cigarets aside) and utility services to businesses are taxed more heavily than most other business inputs.

Over the years, some portion of the competitive weakness of the railroads vis-a-vis other forms of transportation can be attributed to excessive state-local tax burdens.[25] The damage done by the excess taxation of non-transportation utilities is less dramatic. Examples include more diversion of telephone business from AT&T and regulated local telephone companies to competitors that are not taxed as utilities than would be warranted by price and quality considerations alone, and distortions of residential heating decisions from utility-provided – and therefore heavily taxed – natural gas to non-utility-provided – and therefore lightly taxed – fuel oil, notably in the Northeast. The solutions are to tax the utilities' property and income like that of other businesses, and use the regulatory process to assure that tax reductions are reflected in rates.

Another widespread practice is the inclusion in the base of the sales tax of many items that are not final purchases of goods and services by consumers, but purchases by businesses of goods and services that are intermediate to the process of production and distribution. In large part, this is done to simplify compliance by retailers and administration by the tax-collecting agency and to narrow the opportunities for evasion. It is easy enough to exclude from the base goods bought for resale (for example, by retailers from their wholesale suppliers) or goods that are physically embodied in the product that the purchaser of those goods makes; it is considerably more awkward to exempt a law firm's purchases of office supplies from the commercial stationer down the street. In the states with the fewest exemptions of intermediate business purchases, as much as one-fifth of sales tax collections may be derived from this source, rather than from consumer purchases. The economic distortions are relatively small, but real nonetheless, mostly in the form of encouraging what economists call "vertical integration," to avoid sales taxes on transactions among separate firms. For example, if building cleaning and maintenance services are subject to the sales tax, there is an inefficient inducement for companies to provide those services internally, rather than contract out for them. Legislatures often have been sensitive to this issue when manufacturing firms are involved and have provided special exemptions covering them. There has been much less sensitivity to the issue with regard to other sectors of the economy.[26] But of course the other sectors are the rapid growth ones, and therefore ought to be treated like manufacturing, if the extent of the distortion caused by this practice is not to grow.

Quite apart from the typical treatment of public utilities, the property tax is everywhere a highly non-uniform tax by legal provision, and the extent of non-uniformity is often exaggerated by assessment practices.

The ideal tax would apply uniformly to all forms of physical capital, but many forms of privately-owned physical capital are not included in the tax base – some forms excluded in nearly all states (consumer durable goods other than motor vehicles), some in a third or more of the states (motor vehicles, inventories, various types of non-real property used in farming) and some in a small number of states, including some large ones (business machinery and equipment in such states as New York, Pennsylvania and Illinois). Increasingly, types of real property are partly or wholly exempted from the tax and formal schemes of classification (involving taxing different types at different rates) rates have been adopted. Moreover, the one form of non-uniformity that most economists agree is justifiable – higher rates of tax on land than on improvements to the land – is not only rare, but is usually the reverse of what assessors and state tax laws produce – heavier taxation of improvements than land.

Reformers have urged uniformity in property taxation on state tax policy decision-makers for many decades, with a few temporary successes (for example, the relatively high degree of uniformity in California achieved before Proposition 13), but mostly with spectacular lack of persuasiveness. Nonetheless, this remains an area where reforms in an individual state can have positive effects, albeit small ones, on the national economy and – usually – stronger positive effects on the state's own economy.

The corporation income tax affords another opportunity for positive-sum-game reform. There is much debate about whether a corporate income tax makes as much sense as a national tax, given that the incidence and economic effects of a partial tax on profits is so hard to trace. At the state level, the corporate income tax is not a tax on profits at all, but instead a tax on payrolls, property and receipts (the proportion depending on the allocation formula the state uses for multistate corporations).[27] Depending on how "payrolls" and "property" are defined and measured, the tax can distort the choice between capital and labor inputs; it can distort locational choices; and it is highly uneven among industries and firms. Moreover, it probably is regressive with respect to income in incidence to boot, not the progressive tax many legislators believe it to be. If there must be taxation at the state level on a base that is some measure of business activity within that state, a far less distorting tax would be the value-added tax. At the national level, the value-added tax is essentially a tax on all consumption; at the state level, it is not, but instead is a rational substitute for the corporate income tax, one that like the other reforms suggested here is good for both the state making the change and the rest of the country.

Another, less conventional area for reform has to do with specific features of state taxes that discourage the use of labor and encourage the substitution of capital for labor. It s true that national economic growth requires the productivity advances that come in part from investment that substitutes capital for labor. However, the substitution that comes from calculation of what is inherently efficient is different from the substitution that comes from calculation of what is most advantageous from the standpoint of taxation. There is no reason to believe that the latter kind of substitution contributes to national economic growth. By now, many states have provisions in their corporate income and property tax laws explicitly designed to lower the after-tax cost of capital – even including provisions that are misleadingly labeled employment incentives.[28] Meanwhile, some states have arrangements for financing unemployment insurance, workmen's compensation and other social insurance programs that yield very high payroll tax rates for some firms and industries. In combination, these provisions must be generators of economically inefficient production choices.

Do economists really tell governors that nothing works in regard to the effect of tax policy on economic development? Sometimes it may seem so. But a careful reading of the evidence leads to a much more agnostic type of advice: there are indeed conditions in which tax policy changes that are not enormously costly can make a difference. Don't expect miracles, however. To get a big bang will take a lot of bucks, more often than not, and the scene is littered with examples of a lot of tax relief or reduction bucks producing no economic development bang at all (not unlike experience at the source of the metaphor, the US Department of Defense).

Meanwhile, there are plenty of opportunities for the states to reform their tax systems to do good for themselves while doing well for the nation. If the Federal government is indifferent to the economic well-being of the nation in its tax policy decisions, then the modest role that the states acting individually can perform is even more worth doing that it might have been some years ago, when interstate tax competition began to be a league sport rivalling the pirating of commercial football, baseball and basketball teams.

Notes

1   Perhaps the most frequently cited finding along these lines is in a 1961 article by John Due.
2   An elegant exposition is found in Brazer (1961).

3   "State tax policies" in this context include state government decisions on
     local government tax instruments and level of taxation. It would be absurd
     to ignore the $123.5 billion in local taxes (twelve months ending in June
     1984), about 63 percent of the state total of $197.0 billion, or to pretend
     that state governments have nothing to do with the taxes local governments
     within their borders use.
4   There have been a number of efforts to grapple with this problem by
     confining the analysis to industries that are thought to be less affected by the
     conventional major variables but those studies also have been inconclusive.
5   To my knowledge, the first study in which this was emphasized was in a
     paper by Wolfgang Stolper done for a state tax study in Michigan in 1958
     (*Michigan Tax Study*, 1958).
6   Moreover, in the long run, there can be secondary effects even if all taxes on
     local market activities are borne by local consumers: the higher consumer
     price level in an area may mean lower real income, and thus encourage net
     out-migration of people, with a lowering of demand for local-consumer-
     serving industries in the area.
7   See Gayer, with Miller, in *Real Property Tax Policy for New York City* (1980).
     This was a two-part analysis: the first part used data from a sample of firms
     to estimate the sensitivity of business activity in New York to space occu-
     pancy costs, with a special focus on industries that, on a priori grounds,
     should be especially sensitive to such costs; the indicated sensitivity is very
     low. The sensitivity coefficients were then used in simulations to estimate
     the employment effects of the approximately 25 percent reduction in aver-
     age business property tax payments resulting from full uniformity in assess-
     ments. The most plausible estimate of the net employment change is zero,
     taking into account the reduction in spendable income of New York City
     consumers associated with large increases in property taxes on housing; the
     maximum gross increase in employment, before the residential offset, is
     estimated at 0.6 percent of total private sector employment.
8   Netzer, Gayer and Miller (1981). The simulation model was one compo-
     nent of a larger study. The model traced the employment effects of the total
     package of tax reforms. The price effects of this, to business customers, are
     reduction (all data are as of 1979) of 6.0 percent, leading to a 1.26 percent
     increase in demand, which would be composed of:

     – business gained from non-utility competitors 0.23%
     – input substitution by customers, without expansion in
       the volume of activity 0.40%
     – expansion in business activity 0.64%

     The last figure implies an increase in private sector employment of upwards
     of 43,000 statewide, an increase of about 0.7 percent.
9   New York State Legislative Tax Study Commission (1984). The simulation
     study measures the differences in after-tax returns in various locations that

are caused by specific tax law features (coverage, definitions, credits and exemptions as well as nominal rates), holding all other locational determinants constant at all locations. A number of representative firms in each of seven different manufacturing industries are examined at fifteen locations, eight within New York State and one site in each of seven other states; in all, 693 comparisons are simulated under current tax provisions, and then the effects of possible changes are simulated. The report characterizes New York sites (outside New York City) as generally quite competitive, but also suggests – incorrectly, I believe – that the differences generally are small ones. In fact, in most comparisons, the range of after-tax returns is roughly from 8 to 13 percent, a large spread. The policy changes simulated are all connected with the corporate franchise (net income) tax: various credits (very small effects) and other changes with more consequential effects. For a comprehensive description of the AFTAX model, see Papke and Papke (1984), and for a very recent application of the model, see Papke (1985).

10   Vaughan concludes, firmly, that tax differentials are of no importance for state economic development policy. However, he goes on to recommend a package of conventional tax policy changes, some of which make sense if indeed tax differentials have no locational effects, but others of which are based explicitly on the proposition that the tax feature in question does have a significant locational effect.

11   This is the report whose simulation analysis was mentioned in note 9, above. The report, described as a staff working paper and dated December 31, 1984, is characterized as "Preliminary Analysis, Not for Quotation or Reproduction," but it has been widely circulated in New York and received media attention.

12   "The most recent studies" examined at length include Schmenner (1982), Kieschnick (1981), and Carlton (1979), with briefer references to ACIR (1981) which was a literature review itself, Wasylenko (TRED, 1982, location within metropolitan areas), Birch (1979) Simon (1980, Cleveland area), among others. The review of "earlier literature" is rather uniformly negative, but it does not note some studies that show opposing results (see below).

13   Levin (1966). Levin modeled retail sales of house furnishings and apparel (about two–thirds of the consumption expenditure base of the sales tax) over time to estimate the extent to which the sales tax reduced sales in New York City of those items. His results were very strong: each one percentage point of the tax reduced sales by about 6 percent, for a reduction of nearly 25 percent by 1964 when the sales tax rate differential was 4 percentage points (4 percent in the city; zero outside).

14   Grieson, Hamovitch, Levenson and Morgenstern (1977). In this study, the observations are provided by differential changes in tax burdens among industries in New York that resulted from the switch from a gross receipts to a net profits tax (for most industries). Manufacturing employment was significantly related (negatively) to the tax, which was not the case for other industries. The estimated elasticity for manufacturing was a very high

−0.35, and the authors concluded that the rates on manufacturing were higher than optimal from a revenue standpoint, that is, the rates put the city on right-hand, declining portion of the Laffer curve.

15 Grieson (1980). Using time-series data for the 1965–75 period, the study examined the employment effects of increases in the Philadelphia city income tax by major industry groups and concluded that there were very large negative effects: an elasticity of −0.31 for manufacturing and even larger ones for the nonmanufacturing sectors, with net revenue losses attributable to excessively high tax rates.

16 White (1985).

17 He studied employment growth between 1973 and 1980 in six major industrial groups and for "administrative and auxiliary" for Minnesota, five Midwest states, the three biggest Sunbelt states, New York and the US, as a function of market accessibility, labor force characteristics, energy prices, climate and a group of business climate variables. The econometric model tested for the effects of both nominal and effective tax rates. Only a few of the tax variable coefficients are statistically significant, and some of those are hard to explain, but that is not the case for the personal income tax.

18 For example, see the New York State Legislative Tax Study Commission staff working paper on the investment tax credit (1985). It appears that, even at the national level, investment tax credits have unattainable break-even points, and this must be even more true at the state level.

19 The Federally-defined metropolitan areas include a larger number that appear to be interstate. However, in some cases (for example, Minneapolis-St. Paul) the interstate spillover is trivial in numbers and is really an artifact of the criteria used in the definition, rather than a bona fide economic phenomenon.

20 In the Wasylenko study for Minnesota discussed above, for example.

21 Take for example the six states with the highest state personal income taxes, as measured by revenue from the tax as a percentage of personal income in fiscal 1983: (in descending order) Delaware, Minnesota, Oregon, New York, Massachusetts and Wisconsin. In these states, the personal income tax provides 40 percent or more of total state tax revenue (66 percent in Oregon). Thus, if they were to reduce their state income taxes to the level of the median state (by this measure – 2.0 percent of personal income), they would suffer revenue losses ranging from 17 percent of total state tax revenue in Wisconsin to 35 percent in Oregon. Data from US Census Bureau, *State Government Finances in 1983* (1984).

22 This conclusion is almost identical with that of the New York State Legislative Tax Study Commission staff working paper (1984) cited at two points above. I disagree with some of the body of that report, but the conclusion is sound.

23 In theory, properly designed user charges will not distort private economic decisions and, therefore, tax instruments that really work like user charges should not impose efficiency losses. The trouble is that there simply are no tax instruments that do work like efficient user charges. Also, in theory, taxes on land value (that is, the value of sites apart from any improvements

on those sites) should be – as Henry George claimed a century ago – entirely neutral with regard to private economic decisions; for the most part they are, but not entirely so, for a variety of reasons.

24 There is another dimension of inefficiency for all real-world taxes, and they differ in this respect: collection costs. The greater the collection costs (including the taxpayers' compliance costs), the wider the spread between the amounts that taxpayers must give up and the amounts that governments have to spend on the provision of useful services.

25 The excessive taxation of interstate transportation companies soon will be a thing of the past. Federal legislation in 1976 (the so-called "4-R Act") outlawed the practice, and the states are gradually complying, not without a lot of litigation in Federal courts. Subsequent Federal legislation extended the protection to motor carriers and airlines.

26 Some people even today believe that consumption taxes are evil; that ideology might lead to the support of extending the sales tax to cover a wide range of services that one business purchases from others. That, for example, is the position of the New York Public Interest Research Group.

27 See McLure (1980).

28 For example, the "employment incentive credit" in New York, which is a proportional supplement to the state's investment tax credit, and which appears totally unrelated to employment. See New York State Legislative Tax Study Commission (1985).

References

Birch, David, *The Job Generation Process*, MIT Program on Neighborhood and Regional Change, 1979.

Brazer, Harvey E., "The Value of Industrial Property as a Subject of Taxation," *Canadian Public Administration*, Vol. 55 (June 1961).

Carlton, D., "Why New Firms Locate Where They Do: An Econometric Model," in *Interregional Movements and Regional Growth*, William Wheaton, editor, The Urban Institute, 1979.

Due, John F., "Studies of State-Local Tax Influences on Location of Industry," *National Tax Journal*, Vol. 14 (June 1961).

Gayer, David, with Joseph Miller, "Effects of Changes in Non-Residential Property Tax Assessments," in *Real Property Tax Policy for New York City*, Graduate School of Public Administration, New York University, 1980.

Grieson, Ronald E., Hamovitch, William, Levenson, Albert M. and Morgenstern, Richard D., "The Effect of Business Taxation on the Location on Industry," *Journal of Urban Economics*, Vol. 4, April 1977.

Grieson, Ronald E., "Theoretical Analysis and Empirical Measurement of the Effects of the Philadelphia Income Tax," *Journal of Urban Economics*, Vol. 8, July 1980.

Kieschnick, Michael, *Taxes and Growth: Business Incentives and Economic Development*, Council of State Planning Agencies, 1981.

Levin, Henry M., "An Analysis of the Economic Effects of the New York City

Sales Tax," in Graduate School of Public Administration, New York University, *Financing Government in New York City*, 1966.

Long, Sharon K., Witte, Ann D., Tauchen, Helen and Archer, Wayne. The Location of Office Firms, draft paper, October 1984.

McLure, Charles E., Jr., "The State Corporate Income Tax: Lambs in Wolves' Clothing," in Henry J. Aaron and Michael J. Boskin. editors, *The Economics of Taxation*, The Brookings Institution, 1980.

Netzer, Dick, Gayer, David and Miller, Joseph, "Taxation of Telephone Service in New York State," a report prepared for New York Telephone Company, 1981.

New York State Legislative Tax Study Commission Staff, "Interstate Business Locational Decisions and the Effect of the State's Tax Structure on After-Tax Rates of Return of Manufacturing Firms." Staff working paper, December 31, 1984.

New York State Legislative Tax Study Commission Staff. "The New York State Investment Tax Credit." Staff working paper, February 20, 1985.

Papke, James A., "The Taxation of the Saturn Corporation: Interstate Microanalytic Simulations," Purdue University Center for Tax Policy Studies, March 1985.

Papke, James A. and Papke, Leslie E., "State Tax Incentives and Investment Location Decisions: Microanalytic Simulations," in James A. Papke, editor, *Indiana's Revenue Structure: Major Components and Issues, Part II*, Purdue University Center for Tax Policy Studies, March 1984.

Schmenner, Roger W., *Making Business Locations Decisions*, Prentice Hall, 1982.

Simon, Carol J., "Analysis of Manufacturer Location and Relocation in the Cleveland Metropolitan Area: 1966–71," *American Economist*, Vol. 24 (Fall, 1980).

Stolper, Wolfgang F., "Economic Development, Taxation, and Industrial Location in Michigan," in *Michigan Tax Study Staff Papers*, Harvey E. Brazer, editor, Lansing, 1958.

US Advisory Commission on Intergovernmental Relations, *Regional Growth: Interstate Tax Competition*, Report A-76, March 1981.

Vaughan, Roger J., *State Taxation and Economic Development*, Council of State Planning Agencies, 1979.

Wasylenko, Michael, Impacts of the New Federalism on the Intra-Metropolitan Location of Households and Firms: A Review of the Evidence on Intra-Metropolitan Location, paper presented at a conference of the Committee on Taxation, Resources and Economic Development, Cambridge, MA, September 1982.

Wasylenko, Michael, "The Effect of Business Climate on Employment Growth." A report to the Minnesota Tax Study Commission, June 28, 1984.

White, Michelle J., Property Taxes and Firm Location: Evidence from Proposition 13, paper published in 1986 in a National Bureau of Economic Research conference volume.

Part III

Applications: The Fiscal Conditions of Cities

Introduction to Part III

Principles of taxation and tax incidence do not fascinate the public. But the fiscal crises of big local governments – Orange County, New York City – are front page news. This final part covers the fiscal situation of cities. There are two broad themes which run through the eight pieces included in this part. The first is the city as victim; the victim of powerful forces – economic, demographic, political – beyond its ability to control. The second is the city as the creator of its fiscal difficulties, able but unwilling to do the right thing. Those views are not contradictory. They may both be correct, even for the same city at the same moment in time.

The first piece by William Baumol lays out inexorable economic forces which, he argued almost 30 years ago, would force cities to either raise the real burden of taxes or cut services. So that article sets the stage for the city as victim theme. The second article by Wilbur Thompson lays out sins of omission and commission by municipal governments whereby they give away or wrongly price resources controlled by the municipality. So that article sets the stage for the city as fiscal bungler theme.

The Drennan piece is about the 1990s fiscal problems of New York City and State, illustrating that much has remained the same since the dramatic New York City fiscal crisis of 1975. Which is all to the bad for New York City's fiscal condition.

The final five articles view the fiscal condition of all cities in light of a dramatically altered fiscal landscape and economic trends which are more negative than positive. The altered fiscal landscape includes the sharp decline of federal aid to cities from its peak in the late 1970s, federal tax reform of 1986, and a conservative consensus for disengagement of the federal government from urban issues. The economic trends are stagnant real wages and strong divergence in the economic fortunes of regions within the United States.

Introduction to Chapter 19

This article by Baumol has become a classic and has been reprinted many times, but this is probably the first time it has been included in a collection of public finance readings. It is in this article that Baumol first presented his famous "cost disease" hypothesis. Although the title and the article itself relate the cost disease to the fiscal problems of cities, in following work, his own and many others, the cost disease hypothesis is applied to understanding productivity growth and sectoral shifts in employment over the long run and across nations. He has also used it in his analysis of the economics of the performing arts. The upshot of the cost disease hypothesis for cities is that if municipal services are part of the "non-progressive" sector of the economy, i.e., the sector with little or no opportunities for productivity improvement, while municipal wages grow in line with all wages, then the relative costs of providing a fixed level of municipal services will rise perpetually. This reasoning leads Baumol to expect that cities will inexorably face mounting fiscal pressures, an expectation which has been borne out. Baumol may have been too pessimistic on the opportunities for productivity improvement in delivering municipal services, and indeed for delivering other services as well. Nonetheless, his analysis serves as a sound conceptual backdrop for viewing the fiscal condition of cities, the topic of this last set of articles.

19

Macroeconomics of Unbalanced Growth: The Anatomy of Urban Crisis*

William J. Baumol

There are some economic forces so powerful that they constantly break through all barriers erected for their suppression. Such, for example, are the forces of supply and demand which have resisted alike medieval efforts to abolish usury and contemporary attempts to control prices. In this paper I discuss what I believe to be another such mechanism which has colored the past and seems likely to stamp its character on the future. It helps us to understand the prospective roles of a wide variety of economic services: municipal government, education, the performing arts, restaurants, and leisure time activity. I will argue that inherent in the technological structure of each of these activities are forces working almost unavoidably for progressive and cumulative increases in the real costs incurred in supplying them. As a consequence, efforts to offset these cost increases, while they may succeed temporarily, in the long run are merely palliatives which can have no significant effect on the underlying trends.

The justification of a macroeconomic model should reside primarily in its ability to provide insights into the working of observed phenomena. Its aggregation of diverse variables usually deny it the elegance and the rigor that are provided by microeconomic analysis at its best. Yet macro models have succeeded in explaining the structure of practical problems and in offering guidance for policy to a degree that has so far eluded the more painstaking modes of economic analysis. This article hopes to

* The author is professor of economics, Princeton University. He wishes to thank the Ford Foundation and the National Science Foundation whose grants greatly facilitated completion of this paper. The basic hypothesis was originally developed jointly with William G. Bowen in the study of the performing arts conducted for the Twentieth Century Fund. In this paper there is no attempt to document the illustrative empirical observations though in every case the data have been examined and appear to support the assertions.

follow in the tradition – the structure of its basic model is rudimentary. Yet it can perhaps shed some light on a variety of economic problems of our generation.

19.1 Premises

Our model will proceed on several assumptions, only one of which is really essential. This basic premise asserts that economic activities can, not entirely arbitrarily, be grouped into two types: technologically progressive activities in which innovations, capital accumulation, and economies of large scale all make for a cumulative rise in output per man hour and activities which, by their very nature, permit only sporadic increases in productivity.

Of course, one would expect that productivity would not grow at a uniform rate throughout the economy so it is hardly surprising that, given any arbitrarily chosen dividing line, one can fit all goods and services into one or the other of two such categories in whatever way the dividing line is drawn. I am, however, making a much stronger assertion: that the place of any particular activity in this classification is not primarily a fortuitous matter determined by the particulars of its history, but rather that it is a manifestation of the activity's technological structure, which determines quite definitely whether the productivity of its labor inputs will grow slowly or rapidly.

The basic source of differentiation resides in the role played by labor in the activity. In some cases labor is primarily an instrument – an incidental requisite for the attainment of the final product, while in other fields of endeavor, for all practical purposes the labor is itself the end product. Manufacturing encompassess the most obvious examples of the former type of activity. When someone purchases an air conditioner he neither knows nor cares how much labor went into it. He is not concerned one way or the other with an innovation that reduces the manpower requirements for the production of his purchase by 10 per cent if the price and the quality of the product are unaffected. Thus it has been possible, as it were, behind the scenes, to effect successive and cumulative decreases in the labor input coefficient for most manufactured goods, often along with some degree of improvement in the quality of the product.

On the other hand there are a number of services in which the labor is an end in itself, in which quality is judged directly in terms of amount of labor. Teaching is a clear-cut example, where class size (number of teaching hours expended per student) is often taken as a critical index of quality. Here, despite the invention of teaching machines and the use of closed circuit television and a variety of other innovations, there still seem to be fairly firm limits to class size. We are deeply concerned when elementary school classes grow to 50 pupils and are disquieted by the idea of college lectures attended by 2,000 underclassmen. Without a complete revolution in our approach to teaching there is no prospect that we can ever go beyond these levels (or even up to them) with any degree of equanimity. An even more extreme example is one I have offered in another context: live performance. A half hour horn quintet calls for the expenditure of $2\frac{1}{2}$ man hours in its performance, and any attempt to increase productivity here is likely to be viewed with concern by critics and audience alike.

The difference between the two types of activity in the flexibility of their productivity levels should not be exaggerated. It is a matter of degree rather than an absolute dichotomy. The jet airplane has increased the productivity per man hour of a faculty member who is going from New York to California to give a lecture. Certainly the mass media have created what may be considered a new set of products that are close substitutes for live performance and by which productivity was increased spectacularly. In addition, there are, as the reader will recognize, all sorts of intermediate activities which fall between the two more extreme varieties. Yet, the distinction between the relatively constant productivity industries and those in which productivity can and does rise is a very real one, and one which, we shall see, is of considerable practical importance.

In addition to the separability of activities into our two basic categories I shall utilize three other assumptions, two of them primarily for ease of exposition. The reader will recognize, as we proceed, that neither is essential to the argument. The first of the incidental premises consists simply in the assertion that all outlays other than labor costs can be ignored. This assertion is patently unrealistic but it simplifies greatly our mathematical model. A second, far more important, and more realistic assumption is that wages in the two sectors of the economy go up and down together. In the long run there is some degree of mobility in all labor markets and consequently, while wages in one activity can lag behind those in another, unless the former is in process of disappearing altogether we cannot expect the disparity to continue indefinitely. For simplicity I will in the next section take hourly wages to be precisely the same in both sectors, but the model is easily complicated to allow for some diversity in wage levels and their movements.

A final inessential assumption which is, however, not altogether unrealistic, asserts that money wages will rise as rapidly as output per man hour in the sector where productivity is increasing. Since organized labor is not slow to learn of increases in its productivity it is likely to adjust its wage demands accordingly. This assumption affects only the magnitude of the absolute price level in our model, and does not influence the relative costs and prices that are the critical elements in the analysis.

19.2   A Model of Unbalanced Expansion

Assume that the economy is divided into two sectors, sector one, in which the productivity of labor is constant, while in sector two output per man hour grows cumulatively at a constant compounded rate, r. Thus we have for the respective values of outputs Y_{1t} and Y_{2t} in the two sectors at time t:

$$Y_{1t} = aL_{1t} \tag{19.1}$$

$$Y_{2t} = bL_{2t}\,e^{rt} \tag{19.2}$$

where L_{1t} and L_{2t} are the quantities of labor employed in the two sectors and a and b are constants.

We suppose wages are equal in the two sectors and are fixed at W_t dollars per unit of labor, where W_t itself grows in accord with the productivity of sector 2, our "progressive" sector, so that

$$W_t = We^{rt}. \quad \left(W = \text{some constant}\right) \tag{19.3}$$

We may now derive several properties of such a system. First and most fundamental is *Proposition 1*: The cost per unit of output of sector 1, C_1, will rise without limit while C_2, the unit cost of sector 2, will remain constant.
proof:

$$C_1 = W_t L_{1t} / Y_{1t} = We^{rt} L_{1t} / aL_{1t} = We^{rt} / a$$
$$C_2 = W_t L_{2t} / Y_{2t} = We^{rt} L_{2t} / bL_{2t}e^{rt} = W/b.$$

Note that the relative costs will behave in this manner whether or not wages increase in accord with (3) for we have

$$C_1 / C_2 = \left(L_{1t} / Y_{1t}\right) / \left(L_{2t} / Y_{2t}\right) = be^{rt} / a.$$

In practice, we would expect in these circumstances that market demand for the output of sector 1 would decline. Suppose, for example, the elasticity of demand for the two outputs were unity in terms of prices which were proportionate to costs. Then relative outlays on the two commodities would remain constant, i.e., we would have

$$\frac{C_1 Y_1}{C_2 Y_2} = \frac{We^{rt}L_{1t}}{We^{rt}L_{2t}} = \frac{L_{1t}}{L_{2t}} = A \text{ (constant).}$$

Hence the output ratio of the two sectors would be given by

$$Y_1/Y_2 = aL_{1t}/bL_{2t}e^{rt} = aA/be^{rt}$$

which declines toward zero with the passage of time. Thus we have *Proposition 2*: In the model of unbalanced productivity there is a tendency for the outputs of the "nonprogressive" sector whose demands are not highly inelastic to decline and perhaps, ultimately, to vanish.

We may inquire, however, what would happen if despite the change in their relative costs and prices the magnitude of the relative outputs of the two sectors were maintained, perhaps with the aid of government subsidy, or if demand for the product in question were sufficiently price inelastic or income elastic. Then we would have

$$(b/a)Y_1/Y_2 = L_1/L_2 e^{rt} = K.$$

Let $L = L_1 + L_2$ be the total labor supply. It follows that

$$L_1 = (L - L_1)Ke^{rt} \quad \text{or} \quad L_1 = LKe^{rt}/(1 + Ke^{rt}) \qquad (19.4)$$

and

$$L_2 = L - L_1 = L/(1 + Ke^{rt}). \qquad (19.5)$$

Hence, as t approaches infinity, L_1 will approach L and L_2 will approach zero. Thus we have *Proposition 3*: In the unbalanced productivity model, if the ratio of the outputs of the two sectors is held constant, more and more of the total labor force must be transferred to the non-progressive sector and the amount of labor in the other sector will tend to approach zero.

Finally, we may note what happens to the overall rate of growth of output in the economy if the output ratio for the two sectors is not permitted to change. We may take as an index of output a weighted average of the outputs of the two sectors:

$$I = B_1Y_1 + B_2Y_2 = B_1aL_1 + B_2bL_2e^{rt}$$

so that by (19.4) and (19.5)

$$I = L(KB_1a + B_2b)e^{rt}/(1 + Ke^{rt}) = Re^{rt}/(1 + Ke^{rt})$$

where

$$R = L(KB_1a + B_2b).$$

Therefore

$$dI/dt = R[re^{rt}(1 + Ke^{rt}) - Kre^{2rt}]/(1 + Ke^{rt})^2$$
$$= rRe^{rt}/(1 + Ke^{rt})^2.$$

As a result, the percentage rate of growth of output will be

$$(dI/dt)I = r/(1 + Ke^{rt})$$

which declines asymptotically toward zero as t increases. We have, then, arrived at *Proposition 4*: An attempt to achieve balanced growth in a world of unbalanced productivity must lead to a declining rate of growth relative to the rate of growth of the labor force. In particular, if productivity in one sector and the total labor force remain constant the growth rate of the economy will asymptotically approach zero.

19.3   Discussion of the Propositions

The logic of the entire analysis can be restated rather simply in intuitive terms. If productivity per man hour rises cumulatively in one sector relative to its rate of growth elsewhere in the economy, while wages rise commensurately in all areas, then relative costs in the nonprogressive sectors must inevitably rise, *and these costs will rise cumulatively and without limit.* For while in the progressive sector productivity increases will serve as an offset to rising wages, this offset must be smaller in the nonprogressive sectors. For example (ignoring nonwage costs) if wages and productivity in the progressive sector both go up 2 per cent per year, costs there will not rise at all. On the other hand, if in the nonprogressive sector productivity is constant, every rise in wages must yield a corresponding addition to costs – a two per cent cumulative rise in wages means that, year in year out, costs must be two per cent above those of the preceding year. Thus, the very progress of the technologically progressive sectors inevitably adds to the costs of the technologically unchanging sectors of the economy, unless somehow the labor markets in these areas can be scaled off and wages held absolutely constant, a most unlikely possiblity.

We see then that costs in many sectors of the economy will rise relentlessly, and will do so for reasons that are for all practical purposes beyond the control of those involved. The consequence is that the outputs of these sectors may in some cases tend to be driven from the market. If their relative outputs are maintained, an ever increasing proportion of the labor force must be channeled into these activities and the rate of growth of the economy must be slowed correspondingly.

19.4   Some Applications[1]

These observations can be used at once to explain a number of observed phenomena. For example, there is evidence that an ever increasing portion of the nation's labor force has been going into retailing and that a rising portion of the cost of commodities is accounted for by outlays on marketing. Now there have been several pronounced changes in the technology of marketing in recent decades: self service, the supermarket, and prewrapping have all increased the productivity per man hour of the retailing personnel. But ultimately, the activity involved is in the nature of a service and it does not allow for constant and cumulative increases in productivity through capital accumulation, innovation, or economies of large-scale operation. Hence it is neither mismanagement nor lack of ingenuity that accounts for the relatively constant productivity of this sector. Since some sort of marketing effort is an inescapable element in economic activity, demand for this service is quite income elastic. Our model tells us what to expect in this case – cumulatively increasing costs relative to those of other economic activities, and the absorption of an ever growing proportion of society's resources by this sector – precisely what seems to have observed.

Higher education is another activity the demand for whose product seems to be relatively income elastic and price inelastic. Higher tuition charges undoubtedly impose serious hardships on lower-income students. But, because a college degree seems increasingly to be a necessary condition for employment in a variety of attractive occupations, most families have apparently been prepared to pay the ever larger fees instituted in recent years. As a result higher education has been absorbing a constantly increasing proportion of per capita income. And the relatively constant productivity of college teaching leads our model to predict that rising educational costs are no temporary phenomenon – that they are not a resultant of wartime inflation which will vanish once faculty salaries are restored to their prewar levels. Rather, it suggests that, as productivity in the remainder of the economy continues to increase, costs of running the educational organizations will mount correspondingly, so that whatever the magnitude of the funds they need today, we can be reasonably certain that they will require more tomorrow, and even more on the day after that.

But not all services in the relatively constant productivity sector of the economy face inelastic demands. Many of them are more readily dispensable than retailing and education as far as individual consumers are concerned. As their costs increase, their utilization tends therefore to decrease and they retreat into the category of luxury goods with very limited markets or disappear almost completely. Fine pottery and glassware produced by the careful labor of skilled craftsmen sell at astronomical prices, though I am told the firms that produce them earn relatively little profit from these product lines which they turn out primarily for prestige and publicity, obtaining the bulk of their earnings from their mass production activities. Fine restaurants and theaters are forced to keep raising their prices, and at least in the case of the latter we know that volume is dwindling while it becomes ever more difficult for suppliers (the producers) to make ends meet.

An extreme example of an activity that has virtually disappeared is the construction (and, indeed, the utilization) of the large and stately houses whose operation even more than their construction allows for little in the way of enhanced productivity, and whose rising costs of operation have apparently decreased their salability even to the wealthy.

These observations suggest something about the likely shape of our economy in the future. Our model tells us that manufactures are likely to continue to decline in relative cost and, unless the income elasticity of demand for manufactured goods is very large, they may absorb and ever smaller proportion of the labor force, which, if it transpires, may make it more difficult for our economy to maintain its overall rate of output growth.

The analysis also suggests that real cost in the "nonprogressive" sectors of the economy may be expected to go on increasing. Some of the services involved – those whose demands are inelastic – may continue viable on the free market. Some, like the theater, may be forced to leave this market and may have to depend on voluntary public support for their survival. Our hospitals, our institutions of private education and a variety of other nonprofit organizations have already long survived on this basis, and can continue to do so if the magnitude of contributions keeps up with costs. Some activities will either disappear or retreat to a small scale of operation catering primarily to a luxury trade. This fate may be in store for restaurants offering true *haute cuisine* and it is already the case for fine hand-worked furniture and for clothes made to measure. Some activities, perhaps many of the preceding among them, will fall increasingly into the hands of the amateurs who already play a considerable role in theatrical and orchestral performances, in gastronomy, in crafts such as woodworking and pottery. Finally, there is a considerable segment of nonprogressive activity that is dependent on tax support. Some of the problems that go with this position will be considered in the remainder of this paper.

In all the observations of this section there is one implicit underlying danger that should not escape the reader: the inherent threat to quality. Amateur activity has its virtues, as an educational device, as a good use for leisure time and so forth. But in a variety of fields it offers a highly imperfect substitute for the highly polished product that can be supplied by the professional. Unbalanced productivity growth, then, threatens to destroy many of the activities that do so much to enrich our existence, and to give others over into the hands of the amateurs. These are dangers which many of us may feel should not be ignored or taken lightly.

19.5 On the Financial Problem of the Cities

One of the major economic problems of our times is the crisis of the larger cities. Together with their suburban periphery the cities are attracting ever greater segments of our population. Yet at least the core of the metropolis is plagued by a variety of ills including spreading blight as entire neighborhoods deteriorate, increasing pollution of its atmosphere, worsening traffic, critical educational problems, and, above all, mounting fiscal pressures. The financial troubles are perhaps central to the entire issue because without adequate funds one cannot hope to mount an effective attack on the other difficulties. More than one reform mayor has taken office determined to undertake a radical program to deal with the city's difficulties and found himself baffled and stymied by the monstrous deficit which he discovered to be hanging over him, a deficit whose source appeared to have no reasonable explanation. There seems in these cases to be no way to account for the growth in the city's financial needs – for the fact that a municipal budget far above that which was roughly adequate a decade earlier threatens to disrupt seriously the city's most vital services today. Where the political process is involved it is easy to blame growing costs on inefficiency and corruption but when they take office, reform administrations seem consistently puzzled by their inability to wring out the funds they require through the elimination of these abuses.

A critical element in the explanation becomes clear when we recognize how large a proportion of the services provided by the city are activities falling in the relatively nonprogressive sector of the economy. The bulk of our municipal expenditures is devoted to education which, as we have already seen, offers very limited scope for cumulative increases in productivity. The same is true of police, of hospitals, of social services, and of a variety of inspection services. Despite the use of the computer in medicine and in traffic planning, despite the use of closed circuit television and a variety of other devices, there is no substitute for the personal attention of a physician or the presence of a police patrol in a crime-ridden neighborhood. The bulk of municipal services is, in fact, of this general stamp and our model tells us clearly what can be expected as a result. Since there is no reason to anticipate a cessation of capital accumulation or innovation in the progressive sectors of the economy, the upward trend in the real costs of municipal services cannot be expected to halt; inexorably and cumulatively, whether or not there is inflation, administrative mismanagement or malfeasance, municipal budgets will almost certainly continue to mount in the future, just as they have been doing in the past. This is a trend for which no man and no group should be blamed, for there is nothing that can be done to stop it.

19.6　The Role of Static Externalities

Though these may be troubles enough for the municipal administrator, there are other compelling forces that plague him simultaneously. Among them are the general class of externality problems which have so long been the welfare economist's stock in trade.

Since the appearance of Marshall's and Pigou's basic writing in the area a most significant development has been the growing impact of external costs on urban living. No longer are road crowding and smoke nuisance only quaint cases serving primarily as textbook illustrations. Rather, they have become pressing issues of public concern – matters discussed heatedly in the daily press and accorded serious attention by practical politicians. Newspapers devote headlines to an engineer's prediction that the human race is more likely to succumb to its own pollutants than through a nuclear holocaust, and report with glee the quip that Los Angeles is the city in which one is wakened by the sound of birds coughing.

Now there are undoubtedly many reasons for the explosion in external costs but there is a pertinent observation about the relationship between population size in a given area and the cost of externalities that seems not to be obvious. It is easy to assume that these costs will rise roughly in proportion with population but I shall argue now that a much more natural premise is that they will rise more rapidly – perhaps roughly as the square of the number of inhabitants. For example, consider the amount of dirt that falls into the house of a typical urban resident as a result of air pollution, and suppose that this is equal to kn where n is the number of residents in the area. Since the number of homes in the area, an, is also roughly proportionate to population size, total domestic sootfall will be equal to soot per home times number of homes $= kn \cdot an = akn^2$. Similarly, if delays on a crowded road are roughly proportionate to n, the number of vehicles traversing it, the total number of man hours lost thereby will increase roughly as n^2, since the number of passengers also grows roughly as the number of cars. The logic of the argument is simple and perhaps rather general: if each inhabitant in an area imposes external costs on every other, and if the magnitude of the costs borne by each individual is roughly proportionate to population size (density) then since these costs are borne by each of the n persons involved, the total external costs will vary not in proportion with n but with n^2. Of course I do not maintain that such a relationship is universal or even that it is ever satisfied more than approximately. Rather I am suggesting that, typically, increases in population size may plausibly be expected to produce disproportionate increases is external costs – thus pressures on the municipality to do something about these costs may then grow correspondingly.

19.7 Cumulative Decay and Dynamic Pareto Optimality

Economic theory indicates yet another source of mounting urban problems. These are the processes of cumulative urban decay which once set in motion induce matters to go from bad to worse. Since I have discussed these elsewhere I can illustrate the central proposition rather briefly. Public transportation is an important example. In many urban areas with declining utilization, frequency of service has been sharply reduced and fares have been increased. But these price rises have only served to produce a further decline in traffic, leading in turn to yet another deterioration in schedules and another fare increase and so on, apparently *ad infinitum*. More important, perhaps, is the logic of the continued flight to the suburbs in which many persons who apparently would otherwise wish to remain in the city are driven out by growing urban deterioration – rising crime rates, a growing number of blighted neighborhoods, etc. Once again, the individuals' remedy intensifies the community's problems and each feeds upon the other. Those who leave the city are usually the very persons who care and can afford to care – the ones who maintain their houses, who do not commit crimes, and who are most capable of providing the taxes needed to arrest the process of urban decay. Their exodus therefore leads to further deterioration in urban conditions and so induces yet another wave of emigration, and so on.[2]

It is clear that these cumulative processes can greatly increase the financial pressures besetting a municipality and can do so in a variety of ways: they can increase directly municipal costs by adding to the real quantities of inputs required for the upkeep of buildings, to maintain levels of urban sanitation, to preserve the level of education attained by an average resident, etc.; they can reduce the tax base – the exodus of more affluent urban inhabitants causes a decline in the financial resources available to the city; and with the passage of time the magnitude of the resources necessary to arrest and reverse the cumulative processes itself is likely to grow so that the city may find it increasingly difficult to go beyond programs that slow the processes slightly.[3]

19.8 Conclusion – The Financial Problems of the Large City

The story is perhaps completed if we add to the preceding observations the fact that each city is in competition with others and with its own surrounding areas for industry and for people with the wherewithal to pay taxes. No city government acting alone can afford to raise its tax rates indefinitely. Even if they were politically feasible, mounting tax rates must eventually produce diminishing and perhaps even negative returns as they depress the tax base further.

We can now quickly pull the pieces of our story together. We have just seen that our municipalities are perhaps unavoidably subject to a variety of growing financial pressures: the limited sources of tax funds, the pressures imposed by several processes of cumulative decay, the costs of externalities which seem to have a built-in tendency to rise more rapidly than the population. These phenomena imply that the activities of the municipality will have to be expanded if standards of city life are to be maintained. But the funds available for the purpose are extremely limited. And over all this hangs the shadow cast by our model of unbalanced growth which has shown that the costs of even a constant level of activity on the part of a municipal government can be expected to grow constantly higher.

The picture that has been painted is bleak. It suggests strongly that self-help offers no way out for our cities. All of this would then appear to offer stronger theoretical support for the Heller-Pechman proposal that the federal government can provide the resources necessary to prevent the serious crisis that threatens our larger urban communities and whose effects on the quality of life in our society may become one of the nation's most serious economic problems.

Notes

1   Some of the ideas in this section arose out of discussions with Eugene Beem of Sperry and Hutchinson.
2   As is to be expected, such dynamic processes may be monotonic or oscillatory, stable or unstable. As examples we might expect the public transportation scheduling problem to grow monotonically while automotive road crowding may be inherently oscillatory. More specifically, let f represent frequency of public bus departure and p be the number of bus passengers. We would expect the relevant relationship to be something such as

$$p_t = a + bf_t \ \text{(demand for public transport)} \ \text{and}$$

$$f_{t+1} = w + vp_t \ \text{(lagged public transport supply response)}$$

so that

$$f_{t+1} = w + av + vbf_t$$

in which the coefficient vb is presumably positive. On the other hand, if D represents average delay on some road and A is the volume of automotive traffic, the corresponding relationships would be

$$D_t = a' + b'A_t \ \text{(delay grows with traffic volume)} \ \text{and}$$

$$A_{t+1} = w' - v'D_t \ \text{(delays today lead to lower traffic tomorrow)}$$

so that we have a negative coefficient $-b'v'$ in the difference equation

$$A_{t+1} = w' - a'v' - b'v'A_t.$$

Since monotonic and oscillatory time paths correspond respectively to positive and negative variable coefficients in a first-order difference equation, our result follows. An intuitive explanation is fairly simple in each case: increased automotive traffic today causes delays and so may reduce traffic tomorrow. But a decline in number of passengers which causes a deterioration in service leads to still another fall in volume.

    As stated, the time path in each case may be stable. But in the latter case, even though the declines will not be unbounded, the limit toward which they tend may be very low and totally unacceptable as a matter of public policy.

3   I have argued that the cumulative processes involve what may be considered dynamic externalities. Each passenger who uses public transportation less frequently imposes the increased likelihood of poorer schedules not only on himself but on others as well. As a result these processes will yield results that do not maximize social welfare. For the private and social marginal rates of transformation between present and future will then differ from one another. The individual will tend to cut down on his use of public transportation by an amount greater than that which is optimal because he himself does not bear all of the costs of his action. There is a marginal rate of transformation between the utility derived from public transportation today and that obtainable from transportation tomorrow. If relative prices do not equal that marginal rate of transformation a misallocation of resources is likely to result. The consequences may even be what might be called Pareto-nonoptimal. That is, everyone may be harmed. For example, when automobile traffic becomes sufficiently bad it may become clear that everyone will be better off if passenger cars are banned completely from the downtown area in order to make possible a faster, more efficient public transportation system.

References

1. W. J. Baumol and W. G. Bowen, *Performing Arts: The Economic Dilemma.* New York, 1966.
2. Jean Fourastié, *The Causes of Wealth.* Glencoe, Ill., 1960.
3. Tibor and Anne Scitovsky, "What Price Economic Progress?" *Yale Review,* Autumn 1959, *49*, 95–110.

Introduction to Chapter 20

This piece is a breezy *tour de force* through the often brainless use or non-use of the price system by municipal governments. Thompson wrote one of the first and long-used textbooks in urban economics. In this article he argues that too many local public resouces which are in fact scarce are made available "free" of charge, such as use of expressways at rush hour, curb parking, and bridge crossings. Others which have low prices and a large subsidy component tend to redistribute income upward given their usual clientele, such as municipal golf courses, tennis courts, boat marinas and museums. He correctly excludes from his criticism local public goods such as street lighting and police protection, merit goods such as education, and income redistribution programs. That leaves much else, traditionally provided by municipal governments, where prices can be effectively employed in the allocation of scarce resources. He attributes some of the cause of urban sprawl to the failure of municipal governments to charge full prices for costs of incremental infrastructure such as new streets, water lines, and sewer lines required for residential development on vacant land. He attributes some of the cause of bad educational outcomes at inner city schools to the bureaucracy's and teachers' insistence on equal pay at all schools, which perversely channels the most experienced teachers to preferred schools and the new least experienced teachers to the most difficult schools. The passage of time since Thompson wrote this piece has seen a more rational application of user fees in many American cities. But there are new more egregious examples of redistribution of income upward in municipal subsidies to professional sports, and in legal bribes paid to large firms to not move away in the form of tax abatements. The euphemism invented for labeling such giveaways is "economic development."

20

The City as a Distorted Price System

Wilbur Thompson

Wilbur Thompson, a pioneer in the field of urban economics, is Professor of Economics at Wayne State University. He is the author of A Preface to Urban Economics, *a well-known textbook in its area. This widely acclaimed essay, which first appeared in* Psychology Today *in August 1968, contains a perceptive critique of the system of prices implicit in the provision of urban facilities and urban public services.*

The failure to use price – as an *explicit* system – in the public sector of the metropolis is at the root of many, if not most, of our urban problems. Price, serving its historic functions, might be used to ration the use of existing facilities, to signal the desired directions of new public investment, to guide the distribution of income, to enlarge the range of public choice and to change tastes and behavior. Price performs such functions in the private market place, but it has been virtually eliminated from the public sector. We say "virtually eliminated" because it does exist but in an implicit, subtle, distorted sense that is rarely seen or acknowledged by even close students of the city, much less by public managers. Not surprisingly, this implicit price system results in bad economics.

We think of the property tax as a source of public revenue, but it can be reinterpreted as a price. Most often, the property tax is rationalized on "ability-to-pay" grounds with real property serving as a proxy for income. When the correlation between income and real property is challenged, the apologist for the property tax shifts ground and rationalizes it as a "benefit" tax. The tax then becomes a "price" which the property owner pays for the benefits received – fire protection, for example. But this implicit "price" for fire services is hardly a model of either efficiency or equity. Put in a new furnace and fireproof your building (reduce the likelihood of having a fire) and your property tax (fire service premium) goes up, let your property deteriorate and become a firetrap and your fire protection premium goes down! One bright note is New York City's one-year tax abatement on new pollution-control equipment; a timid step but in the right direction.

Often "urban sprawl" is little more than a color word which reflects (betrays?) the speaker's bias in favor of high population density and heavy interpersonal interaction – his "urbanity." Still, typically, the price of using urban fringe space has been set too low – well below the full costs of running pipes, wires, police cars and fire engines farther than would be necessary if building lots were smaller. Residential developers are, moreover, seldom discouraged (penalized by price) from "leap frogging" over the contiguous, expensive vacant land to build on the remote, cheaper parcels. Ordinarily, a flat price is charged for extending water or sewers to a new household regardless of whether the house is placed near to or far from existing pumping stations.

Again, the motorist is subject to the same license fees and tolls, if any, for the extremely expensive system of streets, bridges, tunnels, and traffic controls he enjoys, regardless of whether he chooses to drive downtown at the rush hour and thereby pushes against peak capacity or at off-peak times when it costs little or nothing to serve him. To compound this distortion of prices, we usually set the toll at zero. And when we do charge tolls, we quite perversely cut the commuter (rush-hour) rate below the off-peak rate.

It is not enough to point out that the motorist supports roadbuilding through the gasoline tax. The social costs of noise, air pollution, traffic control and general loss of urban amenities are borne by the general taxpayer. In addition, drivers during off-peak hours overpay and subsidize rush-hour drivers. Four lanes of expressway or bridge capacity are needed in the morning and evening rush hours where two lanes would have served if movements had been random in time and direction: that is, near constant in average volume. The peak-hour motorists probably should share the cost of the first two lanes and bear the full cost of the other two that they alone require. It is best to begin by carefully distinguishing where market tests are possible and where they are not. Otherwise, the case for applying the principles of price is misunderstood; either the too-ardent advocate overstates his case or the potential convert projects too much. In either case, a "disenchantment" sets in that is hard to reverse.

Much of the economics of the city is "public economies," and the pricing of urban public services poses some very difficult and even insurmountable problems. Economists have, in fact, erected a very elegant rationalization of the public economy almost wholly on the nonmarketability of public goods and services. While economists have perhaps oversold the inapplicability of price in the public sector, let us begin with what we are not talking about.

The public economy supplies "collectively consumed" goods, those produced and consumed in one big indivisible lump. Everyone has to be counted in the system, there is no choice of *in* or *out*. We cannot identify individual benefits, therefore we cannot exact a *quid pro quo*. We cannot exclude those who would not pay voluntarily; therefore we must turn to compulsory payments: taxes. Justice and air-pollution control are good examples of collectively consumed public services.

A second function of the public economy is to supply "merit goods." Sometimes the majority of us become a little paternalistie and decide that we know what is best for all of us. We believe some goods are especially meritorious, like education, and we fear that others might not fully appreciate this truth. Therefore, we produce these merit goods, at considerable cost, but offer them at a zero price. Unlike the first case of collectively consumed goods, we could sell these merit goods. A schoolroom's doors can be closed to those who do not pay, *quite unlike justice*. But we choose to open the doors wide to ensure that no one will turn away from the service because of its cost, and then we finance the service with compulsory payments. Merit goods are a case of the majority playing God, and "coercing" the minority by the use of bribes to change their behavior.

A third classic function of government is the redistribution of income. Here we wish to perform a service for one group and charge another group the cost of that service. Welfare payments are a clear case. Again, any kind of a private market or pricing mechanism is totally inappropriate; we obviously do not expect welfare recipients to return their payments. Again, we turn to compulsory payments: taxes. In sum, the private market may not be able to process certain goods and services (pure "public goods"), or it may give the "wrong" prices ("merit goods"), or we simply do not want the consumer to pay (income-redistributive services).

But the virtual elimination of price from the public sector is an extreme and highly simplistic response to the special requirements of the public sector. Merit goods may be subsidized without going all the way to zero prices. Few would argue for full-cost admission prices to museums, but a good case can be made for moderate prices that cover, say, their daily operating costs, (e.g., salaries of guards and janitors, heat and light).

Unfortunately, as we have given local government more to do, we have almost unthinkingly extended the tradition of "free" public services to every new undertaking, despite the clear trend in local government toward the assumption of more and more functions that do not fit the neat schema above. The provision of free public facilities for automobile movement in the crowded cores of our urban areas can hardly be defended on the grounds that: (a) motorists could not be excluded from the expressways if they refused to pay the toll, or (b) the privately operated motor vehicle is an especially meritorious way to move through densely populated areas, or (c) the motorists cannot afford to pay their own way and that the general (property) taxpayers should subsidize them. And all this applies with a vengeance to municipal marinas and golf courses.

Prices to Ration the Use of Existing Facilities

We need to understand better the rationing function of price as it manifests itself in the urban public sector: how the demand for a temporarily (or permanently) fixed stock of a public good or service can be adjusted to the supply. At any given time the supply of street, bridge, and parking space is fixed; "congestion" on the streets and a "shortage" of parking space express demand greater than supply at a zero price, a not too surprising phenomenon. Applying the market solution, the shortage of street space at peak hours ("congestion") could have been temporarily relieved (rationalized) by introducing a short-run rationing price to divert some motorists to other hours of movement, some to other modes of transportation, and some to other activities.

Public goods last a long time and therefore current additions to the stock are too small to relieve shortages quickly and easily. *The rationing function of price is probably more important in the public sector where it is customarily ignored than in the private sector where it is faithfully expressed.*

Rationing need not always be achieved with money, as when a motorist circles the block over and over looking for a place to park. The motorist who is not willing to "spend time" waiting and drives away forfeits the scarce space to one who will spend time (luck averaging out). The parking "problem" may be reinterpreted as an implicit decision to keep the money price artificially low (zero or a nickel an hour in a meter) and supplement it with a waiting cost or time price. The problem is that we did not clearly understand and explicitly agree to do just that.

The central role of price is to allocate – across the board – scarce resources among competing ends to the point where the value of another unit of any good or service is equal to the incremental cost of producing that unit. Expressed loosely, in the long run we turn from using prices to dampen demand to fit a fixed supply to adjusting the supply to fit the quantity demanded, at a price which reflect the production costs.

Prices which ration also serve to signal desired new directions in which to reallocate resources. If the rationing price exceeds those costs of production which the user is expected to bear directly, more resources should ordinarily be allocated to that activity. And symmetrically a rationing price below the relevant costs indicates an uneconomic provision of that service in the current amounts. Rationing prices reveal the intensity of the users' demands. How much is it really worth to drive into the heart of town at rush hour or launch a boat? In the long run, motorists and boaters should be free to choose, in rough measure, the amount of street and dock space they want and for which they are willing to pay. But, as in the private sector of our economy, free choice would carry with it full (financial) responsibility for that choice.

We need also to extend our price strategy to "factor prices"; we need a sophisticated wage policy for local public employees. Perhaps the key decision in urban development pertains to the recruiting and assignment of elementary- and secondary-school teachers. The more able and experienced teachers have the greater range of choice in post and quite naturally they choose the newer schools in the better neighborhoods, after serving the required apprenticeship in the older schools in the poorer neighborhoods. Such a pattern of migration certainly cannot implement a policy of equality of opportunity.

This author argued six years ago that

> Egalitarianism in the public school system has been overdone; even the army recognizes the role of price when it awards extra "jump pay" to paratroopers, only a slightly more hazardous occupation than teaching behind the lines. Besides, it is male teachers whom we need to attract to slum schools, both to serve as father figures where there are few males at home and to serve quite literally as disciplinarians. It is bad economics to insist on equal pay for teachers everywhere throughout the urban area when males have a higher productivity in some areas and when males have better employment opportunities outside teaching – higher "opportunity costs" that raise their supply price. It is downright silly to argue that "equal pay for equal work" is achieved by paying the same money wage in the slums as in the suburbs.

About a year ago, on being offered premium salaries for service in ghetto schools, the teachers rejected, by name and with obvious distaste, any form of "jump pay." One facile argument offered was that they must protect the slum child from the stigma of being harder to teach, a nicety surely lost on the parents and outside observers. One suspects that the real reason for avoiding salary differentials between the "slums and suburbs" is that the teachers seek to escape the hard choice between the higher pay and the better working conditions. *But that is precisely what the price system is supposed to do: equalize sacrifice.*

Prices to Guide the Distribution of Income

A much wider application of tolls, fees, fines, and other "prices" would also confer greater control over the distribution of income for two distinct reasons. First, the taxes currently used to finance a given public service create *implicit* and *unplanned* redistribution of income. Second, this drain on our limited supply of tax money prevents local government from undertaking other programs with more *explicit* and *planned* redistributional effects.

More specifically, if upper-middle- and upper-income motorists, golfers, and boaters use subsidized public streets, golf links, and marinas more than in proportion to their share of local tax payments from which the subsidy is paid, then these public activities redistribute income toward greater inequality. Even if these "semiproprietary" public activities were found to be neutral with respect to the distribution of income, public provision of these discretionary services comes at the expense of a roughly equivalent expenditure on the more classic public services: protection, education, public health, and welfare.

Self-supporting public golf courses are so common and marinas are such an easy extension of the same principle that it is much more instructive to test the faith by considering the much harder case of the public museum: "culture." Again, we must recall that it is the middle- and upper-income classes who typically visit museums, so that free admission becomes, in effect, redistribution toward greater inequality, to the extent that the lower-income nonusers pay local taxes (e.g., property taxes directly or indirectly through rent, local sales taxes). The low prices contemplated are not, moreover, likely to discourage attendance significantly and the resolution of special cases (e.g., student passes) seems well within our competence.

Unfortunately, it is not obvious that "free" public marinas as tennis courts pose foregone alternatives – "opportunity costs." If we had to discharge a teacher or policeman every time we built another boat dock or tennis court, we would see the real cost of these public services. But in a growing economy, we need only not hire another teacher or policeman and that is not so obvious. In general, then, given a binding local budget constraint – scarce tax money – to undertake a local public service that is unequalizing or even neutral in income redistribution is to deny funds to programs that have the desired distributional effect, and is to lose control over equity.

Typically, in oral presentations at question time, it is necessary to reinforce this point by rejoining, "No, I would not put turnstiles in the playgrounds in poor neighborhoods, rather it is only because we do put turnstiles at the entrance to the playgrounds for the middle- and upper-income-groups that we will be able to 'afford' playgrounds for the poor."

Prices to Enlarge the Range of Choice

But there is more at stake in the contemporary chaos of hidden and unplanned prices than "merely" efficiency and equity. *There is no urban goal on which consensus is more easily gained than the pursuit of great variety and choice – "pluralism."* The great rural to urban migration was prompted as much by the search for variety as by the decline of agriculture and rise of manufacturing. Wide choice is seen as the saving grace of bigness by even the sharpest critics of the metropolis. Why, then, do we tolerate far less variety in our big cities than we could have? We have lapsed into a state of tyranny by the majority, in matters of both taste and choice.

In urban transportation the issue is not, in the final analysis, whether users of core-area street space at peak hours should or should not be required to pay their own way in full. The problem is, rather, that by not forcing a direct *quid pro quo* in money, we implicitly substitute a new means of payment – time in the transportation services "market." The peak-hour motorist does pay in full, through congestion and time delay. But *implicit choices* blur issues and confuse decision making.

Say we were carefully to establish how many more dollars would have to be paid in for the additional capacity needed to save a given number of hours spent commuting. The *majority* of urban motorists perhaps would still choose the present combination of "underinvestment" in highway, bridge and parking facilities, with a compensatory heavy investment of time in slow movement over these crowded facilities. Even so, a substantial minority of motorists do prefer a different combination of money and time cost. A more affluent, long-distance commuter could well see the current level of traffic congestion as a real problem and much prefer to spend more money to save time. If economies of scale are so substantial that only one motorway to town can be supported, or if some naturally scarce factor (e.g., bridge or tunnel sites) prevents parallel transportation facilities of different quality and price, then the preferences of the minority must be sacrificed to the majority interest and we do have a real "problem." But, ordinarily, in large urban areas there are a number of near-parallel routes to town, and an unsatisfied minority group large enough to justify significant differentiation of one or more of these streets and its diversion to their use. Greater choice through greater scale is, in fact, what bigness is all about.

The simple act of imposing a toll, at peak hours, on one of these routes would reduce its use, assuming that nearby routes are still available without user charges, thereby speeding movement of the motorists who remain and pay. The toll could be raised only to the point where some combination of moderately rapid movement and high physical output were jointly optimized. Otherwise the outcry might be raised that the public transportation authority was so elitist as to gratify the desire of a few very wealthy motorists for very rapid movement, heavily overloading the "free" routes. It is, moreover, quite possible, even probable, that the newly converted, rapid-flow, toll-route would handle as many vehicles as it did previously as a congested street and not therefore spin off any extra load on the free routes.

Our cities cater, at best, to the taste patterns of the middle-income class, as well they should, *but not so exclusively*. This group has chosen, indirectly through clumsy and insensitive tax-and-expenditure decisions and ambiguous political processes, to move about town flexibly and cheaply, but slowly, in private vehicles. Often, and almost invariably in the larger urban areas, we would not have to encroach much on this choice to accommodate also those who would prefer to spend more money and less time, in urban movement. In general, we should permit urban residents to pay in their most readily available "currency" – time or money.

Majority rule by the middle class in urban transportation has not only disenfranchised the affluent commuter, but more seriously it has debilitated the low-fare, mass transit system on which the poor depend. The effect of widespread automobile ownership and use on the mass transportation system is an oft-told tale: falling bus and rail patronage leads to less frequent service and higher overhead costs per trip and often higher fares which further reduce demand and service schedules. Perhaps two-thirds or more of the urban residents will tolerate and may even prefer slow, cheap automobile movement. But the poor are left without access to many places of work – the suburbanizing factories in particular – and they face much reduced opportunities for comparative shopping, and highly constrained participation in the community life in general. A truly wide range of choice in urban transportation would allow the rich to pay for fast movement with money, the middle-income class to pay for the privacy and convenience of the automobile with time, and the poor to economize by giving up (paying with) privacy.

A more sophisticated price policy would expand choice in other directions. Opinions differ as to the gravity of the water-pollution problem near large urban areas. The minimum level of dissolved oxygen in the water that is needed to meet the standards of different users differs greatly, as does the incremental cost that must be incurred to bring the dissolved oxygen levels up to successively higher standards. The boater accepts a relatively low level of "cleanliness" acquired at relatively little cost. Swimmers have higher standards attained only at much higher cost. Fish and fisherman can thrive only with very high levels of dissolved oxygen acquired only at the highest cost. Finally, one can imagine an elderly convalescent or an impoverished slum dweller or a confirmed landlubber who is not at all interested in the nearby river. What, then, constitutes "clean"?

A majority rule decision, whether borne by the citizen directly in higher taxes or levied on the industrial polluters and then shifted on to the consumer in higher produce prices, is sure to create a "problem." If the pollution program is a compromise – a halfway measure – the fisherman will be disappointed because the river is still not clean enough for his purposes and the landlubbers will be disgruntled because the program is for "special interests" and he can think of better uses for his limited income. Surely, we can assemble the managerial skills in the local public sector needed to devise and administer a structure of user charges that would extend choice in outdoor recreation, consistent with financial responsibility, with lower charges for boat licenses and higher charges for fishing licenses.

Perhaps the most fundamental error we have committed in the development of our large cities is that we have too often subjected the more affluent residents to petty irritations which serve no great social purpose, then turned right around and permitted this same group to avoid responsibilities which have the most critical and pervasive social ramifications. It is a travesty and a social tragedy that we have prevented the rich from buying their way out of annoying traffic congestion – or at least not helped those who are long on money and short on time arrange such an accommodation. Rather, we have permitted them, through political fragmentation and flight to tax havens, to evade their financial and leadership responsibilities for the poor of the central cities. That easily struck goal, "pluralism and choice," will require much more managerial sophistication in the local public sector than we have shown to date.

Pricing to Change Tastes and Behavior

Urban managerial economies will probably also come to deal especially with "developmental pricing" analogous to "promotional pricing" in business. Prices below cost may be used for a limited period to create a market for a presumed "merit good." The hope would be that the artificially low price would stimulate consumption and that an altered *expenditure pattern* (practice) would lead in time to an altered *taste pattern* (preference), as experience with the new service led to a fuller appreciation of it. Ultimately, the subsidy would be withdrawn, whether or not tastes changed sufficiently to make the new service self-supporting – provided, of course, that no permanent redistribution of income was intended.

For example, our national parks had to be subsidized in the beginning and this subsidy could be continued indefinitely on the grounds that these are "merit goods" that serve a broad social interest. But long experience with outdoor recreation has so shifted tastes that a large part of the costs of these parks could now be paid for by a much higher set of park fees.

It is difficult, moreover, to argue that poor people show up at the gates of Yellowstone Park, or even the much nearer metropolitan area regional parks, in significant number, so that a subsidy is needed to continue provision of this service for the poor. A careful study of the users and the incidence of the taxes raised to finance our parks may even show a slight redistribution of income toward greater inequality.

Clearly, this is not the place for an economist to pontificate on the psychology of prices but a number of very interesting phenomena that seem to fall under this general heading deserve brief mention. A few simple examples of how charging a price changes behavior are offered, but left for others to classify.

In a recent study of depressed areas, the case was cited of a community-industrial-development commission that extended its fund-raising efforts from large business contributors to the general public in a supplementary "nickel and dime" campaign. They hoped to enlist the active support of the community at large, more for reasons of public policy than for finance. But even a trivial financial stake was seen as a means to create broad and strong public identification with the local industrial development programs and to gain their political support.

Again, social-work agencies have found that even a nominal charge for what was previously a free service enhances both the self-respect of the recipient and his respect for the usefulness of the service. Paradoxically, we might experiment with higher public assistance payments coupled to *nominal* prices for selected public health and family services, personal counseling, and surplus foods.

To bring a lot of this together now in a programmatic way, we can imagine a very sophisticated urban public management beginning with below-cost prices on, say, the new rapid mass transit facility during the promotional period of luring motorists from their automobiles and of "educating" them on the advantages of a carefree journey to work. Later, if and when the new facility becomes crowded during rush hours and after a taste of this new transportation mode has become well established, the "city economist'" might devise a three-price structure of fares: the lowest fare for regular off-peak use, the middle fare for regular peak use (tickets for commuters), and the highest fare for the occasional peak-time user. Such a schedule would reflect each class's contribution to the cost of having to carry standby capacity.

If the venture more than covered its costs of operation, the construction of additional facilities would begin. Added social benefits in the form of a cleaner, quieter city or reduced social costs of traffic control and accidents could be included in the cost accounting ("cost-benefit analysis") underlying the fare structure. But below-cost fares, taking care to count social as well as private costs, would not be continued indefinitely except for merit goods or when a clear income-redistribution end is in mind. And, even then, not without careful comparison of the relative efficiency of using the subsidy money in alternative redistributive programs. We need, it would seem, not only a knowledge of the economy of the city, but some very knowledgeable city economists as well.

Introduction to Chapter 21

In the aftermath of the national recession of 1989–90, the fiscal condition of both New York State and New York City became perilous. In that regard they were not unusual. The states of the Northeast and Far West had more severe economic declines than other regions of the United States in that recession and so the fiscal condition of their state and local governments suffered more strain. In this article, Drennan attempts to sort out three broad causes for rising expenditure by function: increases in demand, inflation, and improvements in quality or reductions in productivity. His empirical findings for New York State and New York City indicate that in some major functions either productivity is falling or quality is rising because neither inflation nor increases in demand for the service can account for the large expenditure increases. Although he does not refer to Baumol's theoretical analysis of stagnant productivity in labor-intensive government services (chapter 19), the implication is that the reality for those two governments is worse than the theory would predict.

A regression analysis originally performed by Gramlich twenty years ago in his study of the 1975 fiscal crisis of New York City is repeated by Drennan with data for 1989. Some of the results are quite similar to what Gramlich found, some are quite different. The upshot of Drennan's article is that the recent fiscal difficulties of New York State and City are mostly of their own making. They are not hapless victims of economic changes.

21

The Present and Future Fiscal Problems of the Two New Yorks: What Happened This Time

Matthew P. Drennan

The state and city of New York have chronic fiscal difficulties, namely, expenditures that tend to exceed revenues by significant amounts. The deficits were moderate in the 1980s but have become large and acute in the 1990s as the state and city economies have been in a prolonged recession. Deficits are expected to continue well into the future. Supply side factors, particularly high wage levels, are the main causes of the state's deficits. For the city, supply side factors, particularly high employment, and demand side factors are main causes. Federal aid reduction is a minor cause. The city's fiscal condition is compared with that of the thirty other largest US cities in a regression analysis which updates Gramlich's analysis of the period immediately before the famous New York City fiscal crisis of 1975.

In state and local fiscal analysis, state governments are compared with each other and municipal governments are compared with each other. What is unusual is to compare the fiscal condition of a large city with the state in which the city is located. Here I analyze and compare the fiscal problems of New York City and New York State because their problems are linked through their shared economic base, their shared tax base, and their division of expenditure responsibilities. Certainly their fiscal conditions are linked by the financial markets, which historically act as if all debt instruments with "New York" in the name are the same. But there are two New Yorks, and this article is about the fiscal problems of both.

The city and state of New York each have chronic fiscal difficulties which have been exacerbated by the economic decline of the 1990s.

Expenditures tend to exceed revenues, requiring eleventh-hour revenue enhancements or expenditure cuts. Although both governments have been able to avoid end-of-year deficits (in the context of the accounting methods that they use), they have both experienced persistent *ex ante* deficits.

The first part of this article shows the size and duration of the past deficits as well as the projected deficits for coming years. Past deficits are analyzed over two time periods. The first, 1982–9, was a period of strong economic growth for the state and city and deficits were smaller. The second, the early 1990s, has been a period of severe economic decline which has made the deficits much larger. The magnitude of future deficits projected by the state and city suggests that economic recovery, incremental expenditure cuts and tax increases, and "one-shot" revenue enhancements will not eliminate the projected deficits. Structural reform is required for long-term budget balance.

The second part explores different hypotheses about causes of the deficits – sluggish revenue growth, federal aid reductions, demand-side factors, and supply-side factors. The analysis indicates that supply-side factors, particularly high wage levels, are the main causes of the state's structural deficit. For the city, supply-side factors, particularly high employment levels, and demand-side factors are about equal in importance. Federal aid reduction plays a minor, but significant, role in creating chronic deficits.

The third part compares the New York City fiscal situation to that of other large US cities, replicating an analysis done by Gramlich in the wake of the 1975 New York City fiscal crisis. The conclusion identifies some major steps, indicated by the prior analysis, which the two New Yorks might take to eliminate their deficits.

Deficits: How Big? How Long?

The federal deficit is not elusive. It is estimated before the fact and calculated after the fact, when the actual revenue and expenditure data are available. In fiscal years when expenditures exceed revenues (each of the last twenty-three years),[1] the difference is the federal deficit. The New York State (NYS) and New York City (NYC) deficits are more elusive. Unlike the federal government, NYS and NYC are required by law to "balance" their annual budgets. In the case of NYS, the books are kept on a cash basis. This means balance may be achieved by borrowing, by postponing payment of liabilities incurred, by transferring money from special funds into the general fund, and by non-recurring transactions.

When the NYS data are presented under generally accepted accounting principles (GAAP), the annual deficits and the accumulated deficit become visible (see table 21.1). The accumulated deficit at the end of any fiscal year is simply the sum of past deficits and surpluses in the operating budget. For example, table 21.1 shows an accumulated deficit for fiscal year (FY) 1982 of $2,903 million. In the next fiscal year, FY 1983, there is a deficit of $1,083 million. So the accumulated deficit for

Table 21.1 Surplus/(deficit) position of New York State & New York City, FY 1982–97 (millions of $)

| Fiscal year | New York State | | New York City | |
	Surplus/ (deficit)	Year-end accumulated deficit	Ex ante surplus/ (deficit)	Ex post surplus/ (deficit)
1982	$(552)	$(2,903)	$(421)	$41
1983	(1,083)	(3,986)	(854)	34
1984	(345)	(4,331)	(580)	23
1985	(106)	(4,437)	(484)	12
1986	156	(4,281)	(302)	7
1987	1,001	(3,280)	(577)	8
1988	(141)	(3,421)	(413)	10
1989	(1,136)	(4,557)	(758)	7
1990	(673)	(5,230)	(495)	5
1991	(1,835)	(7,065)(a)	(1,018)	6
1992	67	(6,998)(a)	(1,900)	4
1993	(16)	(7,014)(a)	(1,507)	NA
1994	51		(2,135)	
1995	(1,300)		(3,129)	
1996	(1,800)		(3,844)	
1997	NA		(4,212)	

(a) Some short-term debt was converted to long-term debt by the state. Because it all arose from operating deficits, it is treated here as part of the accumulated deficit. The accumulated deficit estimated by the state for FY 1993 is $4,168 million.

Note: All of the NYS and NYC data from FY1982–FY1997 are on a GAAP basis. As explained in the text, the NYC *ex ante* deficits are the projected deficits for the next fiscal year as reported in each January *Financial Plan*. The 1994–7 NYC *ex ante* deficits shown are all from the January, 1993 *Financial Plan*. The *ex post* surplus or deficit for NYC are as reported at the end of the fiscal year in the Comptroller's Report.

Source: New York State data. FY1982–FY1992, from the Office of the Comptroller, and *Annual Report of the Comptroller* various years. City data, FY1982–FY1997, from City of New York, *Financial Plan*, January 1981 to January 1993. New York State projected data, FY1984–FY1996, from State Division of the Budget. New York City projected data from *Financial Plan*, City of New York, January, 1993.

FY 1983 is $3,986 million, i.e., $2,903 + $1,083. In the twelve fiscal years from 1982 through 1993, NYS had nine annual operating deficits. At the end of FY 1982, in a severe national recession, the state's accumulated deficit was $2.9 billion (about 15 percent of operating revenues). Thereafter, the state's economy expanded strongly through 1989, but the accumulated deficit was not reduced. It increased to $4.6 billion at the end of FY 1989, still 15 percent of operating revenues. Only two of the seven years of good economic growth, 1983–1989, were in surplus.

Then the state's economy went into a sharp economic decline which persisted through 1993. Large deficits were recorded in two of the four years, 1990–3, raising the accumulated deficit to $7.0 billion at the end of FY 1993, or 20 percent of operating revenues. To cope with the budget crunch of the 1990s, NYS increased taxes $1.8 billion in FY 1991, $0.9 billion more in FY 1992, and another $0.6 billion in FY 1993.[2] Relating those total increases to FY 1990 state tax revenues, that represents a 12 percent increase.

Although the large state deficits in FY 1990 and FY 1991 in part reflect the severe and protracted economic decline, in the state and the entire northeast, what explains the chronic deficits and rising accumulated deficit over the 1980s? The explanation is not a weak economy. From 1982 through 1989, private sector employment in NYS increased 1.9 percent per year, not much below the strong national employment growth of 2.3 percent annually. Per capita personal income growth in NYS over that period averaged a full percentage point higher than in the nation – 7.4 percent versus 6.4 percent annually. And in every single year, 1982 through 1989, the state's unemployment rate was lower than the national rate.[3]

The nature of NYC deficits is conceptually more complex than that of NYS because the city's books are kept in accord with GAAP. In fact, as a result of the reforms imposed on NYC during the 1975 fiscal crisis, it is on a short financial leash compared with NYS. It is illegal for NYC to have a deficit. There are virtually no *ex post* NYC deficits on a GAAP basis as there are for NYS, as shown in the last column of table 21.1. There are *ex ante* deficits which are estimated for the next four years in the annual Financial Plan of NYC. The Financial Plan, prepared by the Mayor's Office of Management and Budget (OMB), projects revenues and expenditures assuming no changes which have not already been legislated in tax rates, tax bases, aid formulas, or expenditure mandates. If there are any years with a projected deficit, then OMB must present as part of the Financial Plan a "gap closing" program.

In each of the eight fiscal years between 1982–9, the period of strong economic expansion, the city's budget was projected to be in deficit in the Financial Plan immediately preceding that year. The projected budget gaps, averaging $0.5 billion FY 1982–1989, were closed, however, without major tax increases.

But beginning in FY 1991, the projected deficits became much larger – $1.0 billion in FY 1991, $1.9 billion in FY 1992, and $1.5 billion in FY 1993. To close these projected gaps, the city increased taxes $873 million in FY 1991 and added additional tax increases of $752 million in FY 1992.[4] Relating those total increases to FY 1990 tax revenues, that represents an 11 percent increase.

Although the city's large projected deficits in the 1990s may be understood in part as a consequence of the severe and protracted economic decline, why did NYC have chronic, albeit manageable, projected deficits in the 1980s? As with NYS, the answer is not a weak economy. Private sector employment in the city rose 0.9 percent per year from 1982–1989, and per capita personal income expanded 7.3 percent per year in that period, much better than the national growth of 6.4 percent annually.[5]

The budget offices of the state and the city have made forecasts of their respective revenues and expenditures for the coming fiscal years. The results of those forecasts are summarized in table 21.1. Although economic recovery is expected to occur in 1994 and beyond, the state's budget office projects deficits of $1.3 billion in FY 1995 and $1.8 billion in FY 1996, about 4 percent of expenditures. If roughly correct, those forecasts would boost the accumulated deficit to $10 billion at the end of FY 1996.

New York City's Office of Management and Budget (OMB) projects deficits rising from $2.1 billion to $4.2 billion for fiscal years 1994 through 1997, or 7–12 percent of projected expenditures.

Those grim forecasts do not assume deepening recession, nationally or regionally. The city's OMB made its projections under the assumptions that US real GDP would grow about 3 percent per year. Total employment in New York City is projected to rise in those four years, and the city's personal income is expected to grow faster than inflation.[6] The state's Division of Budget (DOB) does not provide the economic forecast it used in developing revenue and expenditure projections. However, DOB does use a national economic forecasting service; none of these are currently anticipating four more years of recession. The persistence and the magnitude of state and city projected deficits over four presumably expansionary years suggests that the deficits are structural and worsening.

Reasons for the Deficits

Sluggish revenue growth

Governments with revenue structures insensitive to economic growth and inflation would have repeated budget deficits; revenues would grow more slowly than the economy, inflation, and expenditures. That was not the case for NYS or NYC in the 1980s.

Tax revenues of NYS expanded 8.0 percent per year in the 1980s, faster than growth in the state's nominal personal income of 7.5 percent annually over that period. More than half of the state's tax revenue is from the personal income tax, and that revenue source accounted for most of the rapid rise in NYS tax revenues from 1981 through 1990 (see table 21.2).

Tax revenues of NYC also increased faster than nominal personal income in the city from 1981 to 1990 (table 21.2). There were few tax increases and no new revenue sources for the city in that period. Unlike the state, the NYC strong growth in tax revenues in the 1980s is not attributable to any single tax. Four of the seven major groupings of taxes imposed by NYC increased faster than personal income over the 1981 to 1990 period. Even the property tax increased faster than nominal personal income over the decade as large gains in market value of commercial property in NYC carried through (with a lag) to large gains in assessed value. The fastest growing revenue source for NYC was the commercial occupancy tax, a tax on the rent paid for commercial space. The boom of the 1980s raised commercial office rents substantially and added roughly 70 million square feet to the stock, accounting for the 12.3 percent per year growth in commercial occupancy tax revenues.

The estimated elasticity of NYC personal income tax revenues with respect to NYC personal income is +1.3,[7] but, like the state, the city made the income tax less progressive in response to federal tax reform in 1986. Consequently, the NYC income tax elasticity is likely to be lower in the future. Economic recovery over the next few years will not generate such strong income tax revenue growth as in the past.

In sum, during the 1980s, tax revenues grew rapidly in both NYS and NYC so that their chronic, albeit smaller, deficits during that decade cannot be attributed to sluggish revenue growth. However, the down side of rapid revenue growth during economic expansions can be severe revenue growth contraction in recessions. Thus, the state's total tax revenues increased only 0.9 percent annually from 1990 to 1993, much more slowly than the sluggish growth in state personal income over that

Table 21.2 Tax revenues, income, population, & inflation: New York State & New York City, FY 1981–93 (millions of $)

	1981	1990	1993	Avg. ann. % change 1981–90	Avg. ann. % change 1990–93
New York State					
Tax revenues					
Personal income tax	6,747	14,978	15,060	9.3%	0.2%
Consumption & use taxes	4,191	7,549	6,361	6.8	−5.5
General business taxes	2,391	3,340	5,346	3.8	17.0
Other taxes	269	1,287	1,090	19.0	−5.4
Total tax revenues	13,598	27,154	27,857	8.0	0.9
Personal income	208,172	398,366	436,200	7.5	3.1
Population (thousands)	17,567	18,002	18,166	0.3	0.3
US consumer price index (1982–4 = 100)	90.9	130.7	144.6	4.1	3.4
New York City					
Tax revenues					
Property tax	3,298	6,543	7,929	7.9	6.6
Personal income tax	1,019	2,538	3,292	10.7	9.1
Sales tax	1,311	2,431	2,338	7.1	−1.3
General corporation tax	637	1,123	1,154	6.5	0.9
Commercial occupancy tax	241	685	696	12.3	0.5
Other taxes	1,141	1,697	1,808	4.5	2.1
Total tax revenues	7,647	15,017	17,217	7.8	4.7
Personal income	88,659	164,965	180,101	7.1	3.0
Population (thousands)	7,077	7,329	7,339	0.4	0.1

Source: State tax revenue from state of New York, *Comprehensive Annual Financial Report of the Comptroller*, fiscal years 1981 to 1991. City tax revenue from city of New York, *Comprehensive Annual Report of the Comptroller*, fiscal year 1991. Personal income and population from US Dept. of Commerce, Bureau of Economic Analysis. *Survey of Current Business*, April 1992 and unpublished tables, April 1992. CPI from *Economic Report of the President*, 1992.

period of 3.1 percent annually. NYC tax revenue growth slowed to 4.7 percent annually from 1990 to 1993, compared with slower personal income growth in the city of 3.0 percent per year. The marked slowdown in state and city revenue growth in the 1990s occurred despite significant increases in taxes by both governments.

Federal aid reductions

Has real per capita federal aid to the state and city increased or decreased since fiscal year 1982? Real per capita federal aid to New York State increased 2.3 percent annually over the 1982–90 period. In the economic decline of the 1990s, real per capita federal aid expanded 14.5 percent per year (see table 21.3).

The picture for New York City is different. Real per capita federal aid to New York City fell from $361 in 1982 to $290 in 1990 (1982 dollars). It then rose slightly to $304 by 1993. If federal aid to the city had been maintained at the real per capita 1982 level, the city would have received $780 million more in 1990 and $605 million more in 1993 in nominal dollars. Those additional funds would have wiped out the *ex ante* deficit in fiscal year 1990 of ($495) million and would have significantly reduced the *ex ante* deficit in fiscal year 1993 of ($1,507).

However, most federal aid to the city is categorical aid for AFDC which is tied to the size of the client population, aid formulas (which did not change much in the 1980s), and federal and state rules on eligibility. The latter have been tightened by the federal government, but it is not possible to estimate the dollar impact. Whatever the impact, every additional dollar of federal categorical aid in New York City's revenues would be partly offset by $0.50 more in city expenditures on those categorical programs because the aid formula for welfare is roughly 50 percent federal money, 25 percent state, and 25 percent city.

The conclusion, then, is that the relative reduction in federal aid to New York City (the nominal dollars received have increased) bears some of the responsibility for the city's current fiscal problems.

Demand side and supply side factors

One possible explanation for the chronic deficits of NYS and NYC is that expenditure growth is driven by rapidly rising demand for public services. That could occur in a state or city with strong population growth or expansion in particular client populations such as school age children, welfare recipients, or prisoners. Table 21.4 shows the size and

Table 21.3 Federal aid to New York State & New York City: FY 1982–93 (millions of $)

	1982	1990	1992	Avg. ann. % change	
				1982–90	1990–2
New York State					
Federal grants	6,955	11,535	15,743	6.5%	16.8%
NYS population (thousand)	17,590	18,002	18,112	0.3	0.3
US CPI (1982 = 100)	100.0	135.4	140.3	3.9	1.8
Real federal grants per capita (1982 $)	395	473	620	2.3	14.5
	1982	*1990*	*1993*	*1982–90*	*1990–3*
New York City					
Federal grants	2,563	2,874	3,226	1.4%	3.9%
NYC population (thousand)	7,100	7,329	7,339	0.4	0.0
US CPI (1982 = 100)	100.0	135.4	144.6	3.9	2.2
Real federal grants per capita (1982 $)	361	290	304	-2.7	1.6

Source: State of New York, *Annual Report of the Comptroller*, fiscal years 1982, 1990, and 1992. City of New York, *Comprehensive Annual Report of the Comptroller*, fiscal years 1982 and 1992; 1993 from Citizens Budget Commission. See table 21.2 for source of CPI and population data.

Table 21.4 Demand indicators for public services: New York State & New York City, 1982–1992 (thousands of $)

	FY1982	FY1990	FY1992	Avg. ann. % change 1982–90	1990–2
New York State					
Population	17,590	18,002	18,112	0.3%	0.3%
Public school enrollment (a)	2,661	2,569	2,614	−0.6	1.8
Higher education enrollment					
Full-time	347	347	NA	0.0	NA
Part-time	208	256	NA	2.6	NA
Full-time equivalent	451	475	NA	0.7	NA
Prison population (a)	31.0	54.9	57.9	10.0	5.5
Public assistance caseload	1,296	1,323	1,510	0.3	6.8
Medicaid caseload	1,916	2,360	2,750	2.6	7.9
New York City					
Population	7,100	7,329	7,355	0.4	0.2
Public school enrollment	924	939	972	0.2	1.7
Higher education enrollment					
Full-time	31.6	33.5	38.2	0.7	6.8
Part-time	16.7	27.6	28.2	6.5	1.1
Full-time equivalent	40.0	47.3	52.3	2.1	5.2
Prison population	9.3	19.6	21.4	9.8	4.5
Public assistance caseload	864	886	1,008	0.3	6.7
Medicaid caseload	1,221	1,496	1,724	2.6	7.4
Felony complaints	624	570	529	−1.1	−3.7
Felony arrests	87	137	122	5.8	−5.6
Fire department emergency response	342	355	382	0.5	3.7
Garbage collectors (thousand tons)	3,217	3,421	3,411	0.8	−0.1

(a) Earliest available year shown is 1984, and latest year shown is 1991.
Source: NYC data from City of New York, *Annual Financial Report of the Comptroller*, fiscal year 1992. NYS data from NYS Department of Education, NYS Department of Correctional Services, and NYS Department of Social Services.

growth of the germane populations in NYS and NYC over the good years, the 1980s, and the bad years, the 1990s.

In the 1980s, the total population of NYS rose a slight 0.3 percent per year. Public school enrollment declined and the public assistance population barely changed. Full-time enrollment in the State University and City University (both funded by NYS) was flat over the decade but part-time enrollment rose rapidly (2.6 percent per year). In terms of full-time equivalent students, higher education enrollment rose 0.7 percent per year. The Medicaid population grew 2.6 percent per year. By far the most rapid rise in client population was in the state's prisons, which expanded at 10.0 percent per year.

In the period of economic decline, 1990–2, the state's client volume in public assistance and Medicaid rose sharply – 6.8 percent and 7.9 percent per year, respectively. The prison population growth slowed but was nonetheless high – 5.5 percent annually. So except for the prison population, there was no substantial rise in client populations for NYS in the 1980s, but that situation was reversed in the early 1990s.

For NYC the pattern is similar. In the 1980s, total population increased 0.4 percent per year while public school enrollment and the public assistance population increase was less. Higher education enrollment (community colleges funded by the city) grew significantly, particularly among part-time students (6.5 percent per year), pushing full-time equivalent enrollment up 2.1 percent per year. The Medicaid population increased 2.6 percent per year. As with the state, the area of phenomenal growth was public safety. The prison population of NYC expanded almost 10 percent per year and felony arrests rose 5.8 percent per year.

In the period of economic decline, five of the nine categories of city services (schools, higher education, prisons, public assistance, Medicaid, felony complaints, felony arrests, fire department, and garbage collection) shown in table 21.4 had sharply higher increases in volume, particularly the costly categories of education, public assistance, and Medicaid. So one could argue, for both the city and the state, that much more rapid increases in client volume in the 1990s translated into expenditure rises which worsened their fiscal plight. Sudden and sharp rises in populations requiring costly public services can result in budget shortfalls, especially if revenue growth slows, as it did in the 1990s (see table 21.2). That is not a notable finding. What is notable is that in the good years of the 1980s, both the state and the city laid the groundwork for their severe fiscal strain in the 1990s by *substantially raising real expenditures per client.*

Growth in expenditures by service category may be partitioned into three components: growth attributable to inflation, to change in client volume, and to growth in real expenditure per client. The first two are primarily demand factors beyond the control of state and city governments.[8] But growth in real expenditure per client is a supply side factor which reflects public policy choices about the quality or efficiency, or both, of services delivered.

Table 21.5 presents the 1980s growth in expenditures by service category partitioned into the three components. For New York State, growth in volume and inflation account for all the growth in higher education and prison expenditures; real expenditures per client declined over the period for these two services. In the case of elementary and secondary education, the state expenditure growth of 8.0 percent per

Table 21.5 Growth in Expenditures Partitioned Into Components: New York State and City, FY 1982–90

	Average annual growth, FY1982–90				Drop in '90 expenditure if . . . (a)	
	Expenditures	Client volume	CPI	Real exp/ client	No rise in real exp/cl.	No rise in client volume
New York State						
Higher education	5.4%	0.7%	4.8%	-0.1%	NA	(53)
Medicaid	14.7	2.6	7.3	4.1	(1,164)	(799)
Prisons	13.1	8.5	4.8	-0.5	NA	(455)
Grants, local education	8.0	-0.5	4.8	3.6	(1,710)	NA
Public assistance	5.4	0.3	4.8	0.3	(23)	(23)
New York City						
Higher education	9.5	2.0	4.8	2.4	(51)	(43)
Medicaid	9.0	2.6	7.3	-1.0	NA	(329)
Prisons	19.0	10.5	4.8	2.8	(187)	(415)
Elementary & secondary education	8.9	0.2	4.8	3.8	(687)	(28)
Police & judicial	9.9	5.8	4.8	-0.9	NA	(739)
Sanitation	8.6	0.8	4.8	2.9	(204)	(60)
Public assistance	5.6	0.3	4.8	0.4	(22)	(17)

(a) These hypothetical dollar amounts are calculated as follows.

No rise in real expenditures per client: $(EXP_o)[(1 + CV)(1 + CPI)]^n - EXP_t$

No rise in client volume: $(EXP_o)[(1 + CPI)(1 + REC)]^n - EXP_t$

Where EXP_o is total expenditures in the first year, EXP_t is total expenditures in the last year, CV is average annual growth in client volume. CPI is average annual growth in consumer price index. REC is average annual growth in real expenditures per client, and n is the number of years, either 8 or 7.

Source: Calculated from dollar amounts shown in Appendix Table A.

year is attributable to real expenditure per pupil growth of 3.6 percent per year plus inflation of 4.8 percent per year. State public school enrollment actually declined 0.5 percent. If there had been no growth in real expenditures per pupil over the period, New York State expenditures for elementary and secondary education in fiscal year 1990 would have been $1,710 million less than the actual amount of $7,861 million. In other words, expenditures would have grown 4.3 percent instead of 8.0 percent annually.

State Medicaid expenditures increased most rapidly (14.7 percent per annum), reflecting increases in volume, real expenditures per patient, and very strong increases in inflation. If there had been no growth in real expenditures per patient over the period, the state's Medicaid expenditures in fiscal year 1990 would have been $1,164 million lower than the actual amount of $4,155 million.

For New York City, changes in volume and inflation account for all of the increase in Medicaid, in police and judicial expenditures, and for most of the increase in prisons. But in the other five categories shown, real expenditures per client increased at annual rates ranging from 0.4 percent to 3.8 percent. If there had been no growth in city expenditures per pupil, expenditures for elementary and secondary education in fiscal year 1990 would have been $687 million less than the actual expenditure of $2,692 million. If there had been no growth in real expenditure per prisoner or per ton of garbage collected, then expenditures in fiscal year 1990 would have been roughly $200 million less in each of those categories.

The net effect of real expenditure per client growth and volume growth, state and city, are summarized below.

	Decrease in Fiscal Year '90 Expenditures		Fiscal Year '90 Deficit
if . . .			
	No volume rise	*No real exp/client rise*	
NYS	−$1,330	−$2,897	−$673
NYC	−$1,626	−$1,111	−$495

For New York State, the adverse fiscal impact of increasing real expenditure per client (all in education and Medicaid) was two times larger than the adverse impact of increasing volume. For New York City, the adverse impact of increasing real expenditure per client was smaller by one third than the adverse impact of increasing volume.

These forces highlight two points. First, expenditure increases attributable to changes in volume (a largely uncontrollable demand factor) are more than two times larger than the state's FY 1990 deficit and three times larger than the city's *ex ante* FY 1990 deficit. Second, expenditure increases attributable to increases in real expenditure per client (a more controllable supply factor) are roughly four times larger than the state's deficit in FY 1990 and roughly two times higher than the city's *ex ante* deficit in FY 1990. The state's expenditures were almost $3 billion higher than they would have been if real expenditure per client had not been increased, while for the city the comparable amount was $1 billion. The conclusion then is that despite the increases in demand, both the state and the city could have avoided deficits, *ceteris paribus*, by capping real expenditures per client at the 1982 levels.

Employment and wages

Personal service items (wages, salaries, fringes, and pensions) comprise over one-half of the city's expenditures and one-fifth of the state's. Consequently, staffing and pay levels are important factors in understanding the fiscal problems of the two New Yorks.

In the strong economic expansion of the 1980s, New York City local government employment rose 2.7 percent annually in fiscal years 1982 through 1990. That was much higher growth than city population (0.4 percent per year) or private sector employment (0.7 percent). The total gain in city government jobs was almost 47,000 in eight years. Compensation per city government employee, including fringes and pensions, did *not* rise faster than private sector compensation per employee in New York City: 6.2 percent versus 6.9 percent annually (see table 21.6).

New York State government employment growth was slower, 1.3 percent per year from 1983 (earliest available) to 1990, or over 22,000 jobs in seven years. Almost all of that gain, 21,000 jobs, occurred in two areas with significant expansion in client volume, corrections and higher education. Including these areas of growing client volume, state government employment growth of 1.3 percent annually was well under private sector employment growth in the state of 1.8 percent annually. However, the state was far above the private sector in compensation per employee growth: 10.4 percent per year compared with 5.5 percent per year.

In sum, the city had very high employment growth and the state had very high compensation per employee growth relative to the private sector in the economic boom period of the 1980s. If the state had limited compensation per employee growth to the private sector rate, then the actual rise in total compensation of $5.3 billion would have been cut in half and the state would have spent $2.6 billion less in 1990. The state's deficit in fiscal year 1990 was about $0.7 billion. Similarly, if the city had limited employment growth (even excluding the four areas with

Table 21.6 Government employment and earnings: New York State & New York City FY1982/83–FY1992/93

New York State (a)	FY1983	FY1990	FY1992	Absolute change		Avg. ann. % change	
				1983–90	1990–2	1983–90	1990–2
Employment							
Mental health & retardation	67,198	64,125	54,900	(3,073)	(9,225)	−0.7%	−7.5%
Higher education	50,770	57,298	54,231	6,528	(3,067)	1.7	−2.7
Correction & parole	17,910	32,613	30,845	14,703	(1,768)	8.9	−2.7
Police & judicial	15,780	18,491	18,428	2,711	(63)	2.3	−0.2
Transportation	12,021	13,096	11,824	1,075	(1,272)	1.2	−5.0
Health & social service	10,985	11,107	10,418	122	(689)	0.2	−3.2
All other	60,024	60,405	58,663	381	(1,742)	0.1	−1.5
Total employment	234,688	257,135	239,309	22,447	(17,826)	1.3	−3.5
Compensation (mil. $)							
Wages & salaries	2,958	7,816	NA			14.9	NA
Fringes	808	1,638	NA			10.6	NA
Pensions	712	362	NA			−9.2	NA
Total compensation	4,478	9,816	NA			11.9	NA
Compensation per employee	19,081	38,174	NA			10.4	NA
Private sector							
Employment (thou.) (b)	7,233	8,213	7,679			1.8	−3.3
Compensation (mil. $)	151,046	250,249	NA			7.5	NA
Compensation/employee	20,883	30,470	NA			5.5	NA

Table 21.6 *Continued*

New York State (a)	FY1983	FY1990	FY1992	Absolute change 1983–90	Absolute change 1990–2	Avg. ann. % change 1983–90	Avg. ann. % change 1990–2
Employment							
Education	70,891	86,224	84,713	15,333	(1,511)	2.5%	-0.6%
Police	29,583	32,976	36,362	3,393	3,386	1.4	3.3
Social services	22,190	31,491	29,098	9,301	(2,393)	4.5	-2.6
Environment	16,259	18,300	17,911	2,041	(389)	1.5	-0.7
Correction	5,589	12,987	13,716	7,398	729	11.1	1.8
Fire	13,025	12,769	12,512	(256)	(257)	-0.2	-0.7
Higher education	3,598	3,843	3,761	245	(82)	0.8	-0.7
All other	35,016	44,500	39,844	9,484	(4,656)	3.0	-3.6
Total employment	196,151	243,090	237,917	46,939	(5,173)	2.7	-0.7
Compensation (mil. $)							
Wages & salaries	4,888	10,494	10,758			10.0	0.8
Fringes	769	1,954	2,003			12.4	0.8
Pensions	1,464	1,806	1,851			2.7	0.8
Total compensation	7,121	14,254	14,613			9.1	0.8
Compensation per employee	36,304	58,637	61,421			6.2	1.6
Private sector							
Employment (thou.) (b)	3,285	3,480	3,149			0.7	-3.3
Compensation (mil. $)	73,754	133,037	NA			7.7	NA
Compensation/employee	22,452	38,229	NA			6.9	NA

(a) Earliest year shown for NYS is 1983, not 1982, because it is the earliest year for which the data is available.
(b) Private sector employment data, 1992 & 1993, partly estimated.

Source: New York State government employment data from Office of State Comptroller payroll records. Compensation data from the *Comprehensive Annual Financial Report of the Comptroller*, State of New York, FY1983 to FY1991. NYS and NYC private sector data from United States Department of Commerce, Bureau of Economic Analysis, *Personal Income and Employment, Counties*, unpublished tables, April, 1992. New York City government data from the *Report of the Comptroller for Fiscal 1991*, City of New York, and Citizens Budget Commission.

significant rise in client volume) to the private sector rate of 0.7 percent annually, then the actual rise in compensation of $5.1 billion would have been cut 30 percent and the city would have spent $1.5 billion less in 1990. The city's *ex ante* deficit in fiscal year 1990 was $0.5 billion.

In the economic contraction of the 1990s, New York State cut its public employment by almost 18,000, wiping out most of the rise of the prior period. That reduction translates to −3.5 percent annually, about the same as the reduction in private sector employment in the state in the 1990s. Compensation data is not available for the state for those years.

In contrast, New York City reduced its public employment by only 5,000 from 1990 to 1993 after the large increase of 47,000 from 1982 to 1990. The city job reduction amounted to only −0.7 percent annually from 1990–3, compared with the private sector sharp employment contraction of −3.3 percent per year. Compensation per employee growth for city government jobs was scaled back to 1.6 percent annually in the 1990s compared with 6.2 percent annually in the 1980s.

Thus, it appears that New York State sharply reduced its public employment in line with the contraction in the private sector. On the other hand, New York City government did not retrench in its employment, which accounted for half of its expenditures. Having expanded its employment four times faster than the city's private sector in the economic boom of the 1980s and then failing to cut back jobs significantly in the 1990s, it is not surprising that the city has a severe fiscal problem.

A Comparison: New York City and Other Large Cities' Fiscal Condition

A different and fruitful approach for understanding the underlying causes of the New York *City* deficits is to re-examine the hypotheses about causes of the city's deficits, which Gramlich explored in the previous and famous fiscal crisis of 1975–6.[9] Those hypotheses were: (1) the city's deficits were the result of taking on spending functions either not taken on by other cities or taken on at a less ambitious scale, and (2) the city's deficits were a result of overspending in pay and benefits for city employees. As Gramlich notes, "These competing hypotheses can be tested very loosely by examining the city's budget in more detail."[10] Table 21.7 splits city expenditures into three categories: marginal functions, i.e., functions usually not financed by municipal governments, education expenditures, and normal functions. Intergovernmental aid for these functions is subtracted to yield net expenditures in each category. It is net in the sense that it represents expenditures from the city's own-source revenues. Data are shown for fiscal years 1982, 1990, and 1992.

Table 21.7 NYC own source revenues & net expenditures, FY1982, FY1990, & FY1992 (millions of $)

	FY1982	FY1990	FY1992	Avg. ann. % change 1982–90	1990–2
Own source revenues	9,349	17,265	19,316	8.0%	5.8%
Net expenditures					
Marginal functions					
Social services	1,155	2,575	3,031	10.5	8.5
Health	488	1,095	993	10.6	−4.8
Higher education	167	182	333	1.1	35.3
Housing	312	484	456	5.6	−2.9
Pension contributions	1,418	1,693	1,371	2.2	−10.0
Total marginal functions	3,540	6,029	6,184	6.9	1.3
Education	1,357	2,686	2,788	8.9	1.9
Normal expenditures	4,410	8,453	10,264	8.5	10.2
Personal income (mil. $)	91,702	164,965	174,242	7.6	2.8
Population (thousands)	7,100	7,329	7,355	0.4	0.1
CPI, NYC (1982–4 = 100)	95.3	138.5	150.0	4.8	4.1

Note: Net expenditures are defined as total expenditures in each category minus earmarked grants from higher levels of government in the respective category. Although it can be argued that pension contributions are part of normal expenditures, they are put in marginal functions to be consistent with Gramlich.

Source: NYC revenue and expenditure data from *Report of the Comptroller For Fiscal 1991 & 1992*, City of New York. Income, population, and CPI data from source cited in table 21.2.

The city's net expenditure for marginal functions, those Gramlich called the "marginal function deficit," grew 6.9 percent per year over the 1982–90 period. This was slightly higher than inflation (4.8 percent per year), but well under growth in own-source revenues (taxes plus charges) of 8.0 percent per year. The marginal function deficit fell from 38 percent of the city's own-source revenues in fiscal year 1982 to 35 percent in fiscal year 1990. Thus, the relative burden of the marginal function deficit was diminishing over the 1980s.

In the early 1990s, the marginal function deficit hardly increased at all, and as a share of own-source revenues it dropped to 32 percent. So despite the deteriorated economy, in the 1990s, the relative burden of the marginal function deficit was cut.

Net expenditure growth in the other two categories was higher than in marginal functions in both periods. The city's net expenditures for education rose 8.9 percent per year, and net expenditures for normal functions rose 8.5 percent per year from 1982–90. Those two categories also grew faster than the city's own-source revenues over that period.

From 1990 to 1992, however, net expenditures for education growth slowed markedly – to only 1.9 percent annually – while net normal expenditures growth was somewhat higher than in the 1980s.

Gramlich noted a very different pattern over the 1960s and early 1970s leading up to the New York City fiscal crisis. In FY 1974, the marginal function deficit was 40 percent of the city's own-source revenues. And unlike the 1980s, Gramlich found that growth in the marginal function deficit outstripped growth in net education expenditures and net normal expenditures in the years before the 1975–6 fiscal crisis. Gramlich tentatively concluded that "as on overall impression it does appear that the city's problems stem more from the fact that it subsidizes a broad array of functions than from the fact that the employees are gaining very high wages for performing normal public services."[11] Gramlich did not look at wages per se. His unstated inference is that if normal expenditures and education expenditures are not out of line, then presumably wages are not out of line.

To continue the parallel analysis with the Gramlich article of sixteen years ago, I have compared the New York City budget, on a per capita basis, with the twenty-nine other largest US cities. Unlike New York City, most large cities have independent school districts and their education expenditures are not part of the municipal budget. But school expenditures are certainly financed by the taxpayers of those large cities, however, since they are included in this analysis.

Table 21.8 presents normal revenues (excluding any education grants), net normal expenditures, net school expenditures, the marginal function deficit, and the current account surplus,[12] on a per capita basis for fiscal year 1989, for the thirty largest US cities. The cities are in rank order based upon their 1990 population.

For four of the five measures shown in table 21.8, Washington, D.C., is an extremely high outlier because of its unique status. Excluding Washington, New York City ranks first in per capita normal revenues ($2,582), with Boston ($1,865) and San Francisco ($1,844) in rather distant second and third place. Only six additional cities had per capita normal revenues above $1,000 in FY 1989. Again excluding Washington, San Francisco, not New York, ranks first in per capita normal expenditures ($1,336) followed closely by New York ($1,207), Philadelphia ($1,120), and Detroit ($1,051). On per capita net education expenditures, excluding Washington again, Portland is first at $534, followed by four cities in the $400 to $500 range. New York City, at $384, is not at the top. On the per capita marginal function deficit, if Washington ($2,462) is excluded. New York ranks first ($956) with Boston ($467) and Detroit ($356) in very distant second and third place. On the

Table 21.8 Budget data, thirty largest US cities, FY 1989 ($ per capita)

	Normal rev. excl. schl. grnt.	Normal expend.	Educ. expend. excl. grnts.	Marginal function deficit	Current account surplus
New York City	$2,582	$1,207	$384	$956	$78
Los Angeles	820	611	137	207	(1)
Chicago	797	655	218	161	(28)
Houston	636	568	209	49	19
Philadelphia	1,252	1,120	199	222	(89)
San Diego	585	513	187	115	(43)
Detroit	1,338	1,051	238	356	(72)
Dallas	685	578	375	88	20
Phoenix	842	615	99	68	156
San Antonio	406	453	64	30	(83)
San Jose	612	406	54	163	44
Baltimore	1,567	935	178	110	321
Indianapolis	875	512	65	194	168
San Francisco	1,844	1,336	51	241	263
Jacksonville	702	615	448	152	(65)
Columbus	718	649	314	4	64
Milwaukee	779	690	295	127	(38)
Memphis	767	411	237	102	4
Washington	5,770	2,598	759	2,462	(182)
Boston	1,865	891	418	467	38
Seattle	1,007	953	90	161	(108)
El Paso	321	298	114	23	(1)
Cleveland	830	717	351	85	28
New Orleans	950	783	147	165	2
Nashville-DVD	1,267	752	331	128	(4)
Denver	1,162	1,006	423	94	62
Austin	748	662	403	78	7
Fort Worth	672	580	285	51	40
Oklahoma City	560	519	114	48	(8)
Portland	757	613	534	143	1

Source: US Bureau of the Census, *City Government Finances 1989*, and *Government Finances–Individual School Systems*, 1989.

per capita current account surplus measure, thirteen of the thirty cities had deficits in FY 1989 and New York City was not among them.

The per capita budget values for New York City are in no way typical of large US cities. The means for twenty-eight cities (excluding New York and Washington, D.C.) are compared with the New York City amounts in table 21.9. New York City per capita normal revenues are almost three times larger than the mean for twenty-eight cities and normal expenditures are almost two times larger. Education expenditures per capita are two-thirds larger than the twenty-eight city mean. The city's marginal function deficit per capita ($956) is about seven times larger than the twenty-eight city mean ($137). Those extreme variations in FY 1989 are quite similar to what Gramlich found in FY 1974.[13] The extreme variations above the means may be due to special characteristics of New York City, what Ladd and Yinger would call a "harsh environment" for providing public services.[14] Following Gramlich, I regressed the per capita budget variables on population, density, per capita income, percent minority, per capita grants, percent of persons below poverty level, and dummy variables for region and city-county structure. The sample for FY 1989 excluded New York City and Washington. Then the New York City values of the independent variables in FY 1989 were plugged into the regression equations in order to estimate the per capita dependent variables for New York City. The regression estimates are compared with the actual values for New York City in table 21.9. The estimated regression equations are in Appendix table 21.B.

Table 21.9 NYC compared with 28 city means & regression estimates ($ per capita)

	Normal rev. excl. schl. grnt.	Normal expend.	Educ. expend.	Marginal function deficit	Current account surplus
			Fiscal year 1989		
NYC	$2,582	$1,207	$384	$956	$78
Mean 28	906	696	235	137	25
NYC-Mean	1,676	510	149	819	53
NYC	2,582	1,207	384	956	78
NYC Est Y	1,837	1,251	207	481	(43)
NYC-Est Y	745	(44)	177	475	121
Est Y/Actual Y	71%	104%	54%	50%	−54%
			Fiscal year 1974		
NYC	$962	$493	$207	$326	$(64)
NYC Est Y	758	362	226	99	72
Est Y/Actual Y	79%	73%	109%	30%	−113%

Source: Actual NYC values and means computed from Table 21.8. Estimated NYC values from regression equations.

For normal revenues, normal expenditures, and the marginal deficit, the regression estimates are much closer to the actual New York City values than are the means of the twenty-eight large cities, as one would expect because the regression equations take New York's characteristics into account. Nonetheless, for two of those three per capita budget variables, the actual city values are far higher than the values predicted by the equations. Predicted normal revenues per capita are only 71 percent of the actual New York City value, even though the regression prediction is about double the mean for twenty-eight cities. It is the marginal function deficit, however, that shows the largest relative discrepancy. The predicted per capita marginal function deficit for New York City is $481, well above the twenty-eight city mean ($137) but only 50 percent of the actual value ($956). Normal expenditures per capita predicted by regression is $1,251, which is slightly higher than the actual value of $1,207.

On the other hand, for education expenditures and the current account surplus, the regression estimates are further from the actual New York City values than are the means of the twenty-eight cities. Per capita education expenditures in New York City predicted by the regression equation are only $207 compared with the twenty-eight city mean of $235 and compared with the actual New York City value of $384. The current account surplus predicted by regression is −$43, not as favorable as the actual surplus of +$78.

So New York City does slightly better than expected on normal expenditures, worse than expected on education expenditures, a great deal worse than expected on the marginal function deficit, and better than expected on the current account surplus. That is somewhat different from what Gramlich found for FY 1974: "New York runs a substantially greater current account deficit than is predicted on the basis of other cities, has somewhat greater expenditures on normal functions, virtually no greater expenditures on schools, and much greater deficits for marginal functions."[15]

The comparison, then and now, is made more precise in table 21.9. Back in FY 1974, predicted normal expenditures were 73 percent of actual normal expenditures. In FY 1989, predicted normal expenditures were 104 percent of actual. So normal expenditures per capita are no longer higher than would be expected given New York's characteristics. Now in the more recent period, predicted education expenditures per capita are only 54 percent of actual education expenditures per capita, whereas in 1974, the predicted value was 109 percent of the actual. In FY 1974, the predicted marginal function deficit was only 30 percent of the actual marginal function deficit. But in FY 1989, the predicted marginal function deficit was 50 percent of actual. The tentative conclusion, then, is that New York City is no longer out of line or worse than other large cities in normal expenditures per capita and in current account surplus per capita. But the city has become out of line in education expenditures per capita compared with the large cities. The city continues to be way out of line or worse than other large cities in the marginal function deficit per capita, but it is nonetheless much closer to the predicted value than it was in FY 1974.

The evidence on growth in city spending in the 1980s pointed to high growth in normal expenditures and school expenditures rather than marginal functions as contributing to the city's current fiscal problem (see table 21.7). The comparison with other large cities, however, indicates that the New York City marginal function deficit is far above the predicted value based upon the city's characteristics. These are not contradictory findings. Although the marginal function deficit per capita is far above the predicted value, it is less out of line than when Gramlich analyzed the city's fiscal situation. The marginal function deficit did not grow faster than other expenditure categories and faster than revenues from 1982–1990, which it had been doing, as Gramlich pointed out, in the years immediately preceding the New York City fiscal crisis of 1975–6. Indeed, in real per capita terms from FY 1982 to FY 1990, the marginal function deficit increased at almost the same rate as real per capita income for New York City and its growth was sharply curtailed in the 1990–1992 period of economic decline. The fact that Gramlich found, and I reconfirmed, that the marginal function deficit of New York City is far above what would be expected given the city's quantifiable characteristics does not establish that as the major cause of the city's current fiscal problem. Recall that the city's per capita revenues are also far above what would be expected given the city's characteristics. Real per capita own-source revenues of the city grew 2.6 percent per year from 1982–90 compared with 1.6 percent per year for the real per capita marginal function deficit. So the real burden of the marginal function deficit was diminishing, not increasing, in the 1980s and diminished further from 1990–92.

The static comparison with other large cities confirms what the expenditure growth data suggests, namely that net education expenditures per capita are out of line on the high side based upon the city's characteristics. That was not the case on the eve of the 1975 fiscal crisis. However, in the recent economic decline, the city has sharply curbed the growth in education expenditures (see table 21.7). Indeed, in real per capita terms, net education expenditures have declined from 1990–92.

Conclusion

The evidence on expenditure growth related to client volume indicates that the two major and roughly equal sources of the city's fiscal problem are on the demand side (rising client volume) and on the supply side (rising expenditures per client). And part of the supply side problem lies in the fact that city employment growth was high in functions which did *not* experience rising client volume from 1982–1990. Further, in the severe economic decline since 1990, the city has not substantially cut its employment (see table 21.6). The comparison of New York City with other large cities indicates two facts. First, the city is far above other cities in the marginal function deficit, which is not new. Second, in net education, the city is now above other cities and above what would be expected given its characteristics, and that is a new development. For the state, the major source by far of its fiscal problem is on the supply side, and part of that problem lies in high increases in the compensation of state employees.

The analysis above points to some areas on the expenditure side where the city and state governments could act decisively to reduce or eliminate their fiscal problems while maintaining service delivery at the average of the early 1980s. For New York State, the obvious choice is to cut grants for local education without cutting real aid per student below some recent standard. New York City could also cut education expenditures without reducing real expenditure per pupil below some recent standard, say 1985. Based on preliminary data for FY 1993, New York State has halted the growth in grants for local education, but whether the lid will be kept on those grants beyond 1993 is an open question. New York State has taken additional steps in the 1990s to cut its deficit. The state government employment rise of 22,000 from 1983–90 was mostly wiped out by a drop of 18,000 between 1990 and 1992. In contrast, the city government employment rise of 47,000 from 1982 to 1990 has been only very slightly offset by a 5,000-job cut between 1990 to 1993 (see table 21.6).

Notes

1 Council of Economic Advisors, *Economic Report of the President, 1992*, US Government Printing Office, Washington, D.C.: 1992, p. 385.
2 Citizen's Budget Commission, "Political Leadership in the Two New Yorks: Fiscal Policy in the 1990's." Table 8, page 18, June 1993.
3 Per capita personal income, US and NYS, from US Department of Commerce, Bureau of Economic Analysis, *Survey of Current Business*, April 1992

and earlier years. US unemployment rate from *Economic Report of the President*, Feb. 1992. New York State unemployment rate from *Employment Review*, NYS Department of Labor, Dec. 1991.

4 Citizens Budget Commission, *op. cit.*, table 7, p. 16.

5 NYC employment from NYS Department of Labor; personal income from US Department of Commerce, Bureau of Economic Analysis, unpublished tables, May 1993.

6 City of New York, *Financial Plan*, January 1993.

7 From the equation, LDPYTX = −8.8196 + 1.286LCALLY + 88.91RATE; period 1970–87, n = 18; R2 = .996. The dependent variable is the natural log of real personal income tax revenues, New York City. The independent variables are the natural log of real value added, New York City (CALLY), and the top rate of the City's personal income tax (RATE).

8 Of course, client volume − unlike inflation − is not completely in the hands of the gods. It can be manipulated through changing accessibility and administrative rules. For example, stiff state or federal penalties for ineligible welfare clients found in audits motivate city government to screen welfare applicants more carefully, probably resulting in the rejection of many eligible applicants.

9 Edw. M. Gramlich, "The New York City Fiscal Crisis: What Happened and What is to be Done?", *American Economic Review*, 66 (May 1976): 415–29.

10 *Op. cit.*, 418–19.

11 *Op. cit.*, 420.

12 The current account surplus as defined by Gramlich is: (normal revenue plus school grants) − (normal expenditures + school expenditures + marginal function deficit) = current account surplus. See Gramlich, table 3, p. 419.

13 Gramlich, 420.

14 Helen F. Ladd and John Yinger, *America's Ailing Cities* (Baltimore: Johns Hopkins University Press, 1989), 78.

15 Gramlich, 421.

Appendix

Appendix table 21.A Clients & expenditures, city & state services, fiscal years 1982 & 1990

	Clients (thou.)		Expend. (mil. $)		Real expend. per client	
	1982	*1990*	*1982*	*1990*	*1982*	*1990*
New York State						
Higher educ. (a)	451	475	763	1,105	1,695	1,680
Medicaid	1,916	2,360	1,385	4,155	781	1,081
Prisons (a)	31	55	442	1,048	14,287	13,756
Grants local govt. education (a)	2,661	2,569	4,581	7,861	1,725	2,209
Public assistance	1,296	1,323	718	1,092	581	596
New York City						
Education (net of grants)	924	939	1,357	2,692	1,541	2,070
Higher education	40	47	141	291	3,699	4,442
Medicaid	1,221	1,496	884	1,759	763	722
Prisons	9	20	188	755	21,919	27,256
Police & jud. (b)	87	137	963	2,047	11,615	10,788
Sanitation (c)	3,217	3,421	518	1,005	169	212
Public assistance	864	886	412	635	500	517

CPI, all items, NYC (1982–4 = 100)		CPI, medical care, US (1982–4 = 100)	
1982	95.3	1982	92.5
1983	99.8	1983	100.6
1990	138.5	1990	162.8

(a) Earliest year shown for NYS is 1983, not 1982, because it is the earliest year for which the data are available.
(b) Volume measured by felony arrests.
(c) Volume measured by thousands of tons of garbage.
Source: Expenditure data from Comptroller reports of NYS and NYC. NYC client data from NYC Comptroller reports. NYS client data from Department of Education, Correctional Services, and Social Services.

Appendix table 21.B

Regression output: Y = norm. rev. ex. schl. grant (excludes NYC & Wash.)

Constant	1210.312								
Std err of Y est	216.1668								
R squared	0.790744								
No. of observations	28								
Degrees of freedom	18								
	POP	DENS	MD HH INC.	GRT N FN	MINOR %	CNTY DUM	MIDWEST	SOUTH	POVERTY
X coefficient(s)	-50.8329	0.048019	-0.01441	1.072937	-267.181	215.7128	-135.782	65.97547	-14.5012
Sid err of coef.	88.12363	0.024135	0.019666	0.329376	844.9534	265.4100	133.6205	151.8817	31.65698

Regression output: Y = normal expend. (excludes NYC & Wash.)

Constant	1214.509								
Std err of Y est	160.0555								
R squared	0.700801								
No. of observations	28								
Degrees of freedom	18								
	POP	DENS	MD HH INC.	GRT N FN	MINOR %	CNTY DUM	MIDWEST	SOUTH	POVERTY
X coefficient(s)	-46.0492	0.032006	-0.01824	0.200555	-191.255	263.4784	-84.4491	-18.5625	-5.42656
Std err of coef.	65.24902	0.017870	0.014561	0.243879	625.6255	196.5164	98.93609	112.4572	23.43965

Regression output: Y = cur acct surp (excludes NYC & Wash.)

Constant	224.3301	
Std err of Y est	101.8658	
R squared	0.286086	
No. of observations	28	
Degrees of freedom	18	

Appendix table 21.B *Continued*

	POP	DENS	MD HH INC.	GRT N FN	MINOR %	CNTY DUM	MIDWEST	SOUTH	POVERTY
X coeffient(s)	-34.8284	0.006715	-0.00272	0.131856	304.6490	17.97650	37.32049	29.05244	-15.8599
Std err of coef.	41.52710	0.011373	0.009267	0.155214	398.1732	125.0709	62.96691	71.57229	14.91793

Regression output: Y = marginal function deficit (excludes NYC & Wash.)

Constant	-268.045
Std err of Y est	71.28133
R squared	0.660117
No. of observations	28
Degrees of freedom	18

	POP	DENS	MD HH INC.	GRT N FN	MINOR %	CNTY DUM	MIDWEST	SOUTH	POVERTY
X coefficient(s)	26.96988	0.001055	0.007564	0.345013	-209.366	54.26385	-31.9718	-19.1010	9.732677
Std err of coef.	29.05889	0.007958	0.006485	0.108612	278.6246	87.51933	44.06155	50.08323	10.43893

Regression output: Y = educ expend ex grants (excludes NYC & Wash.)

Constant	512.6328
Std err of Y est	134.9721
R squared	0.351078
No. of observations	28
Degrees of freedom	18

	POP	DENS	MD HH INC.	GRT N FN	MINOR %	POVERTY	MIDWEST	SOUTH	CTY CNTY
X coefficient(s)	8.635415	0.009345	-0.00906	0.062134	-716.583	7.895244	-8.35214	100.7476	-170.066
Std err of coef.	55.02341	0.015070	0.012279	0.205659	527.5795	19.76626	83.43115	94.83328	165.7190

Acknowledgments

Much of the data for tables 21.1 through 21.7 and Appendix table 21.A were generously provided by Charles Brecher, research director, and Raymond D. Horton, president, of the Citizens Budget Commission. I am indebted to Charles Brecher for careful reading of earlier versions of this paper and to two anonymous referees. Remaining errors and omissions are my own.

Introduction to Chapter 22

This article summarizes the findings in the most sophisticated and comprehensive analysis of municipal fiscal condition, *America's Ailing Cities* by Ladd and Yinger (1989). Ladd identifies four factors which hampered the revenue raising capacity of big cities from the late 1970s to the 1980s. She then considers evidence which sheds light on the question of whether fiscal condition in large cities improved or deteriorated in the 1980s. In the large study referred to above, Ladd and Yinger concluded that the fiscal condition of US cities, particularly large cities, deteriorated substantially between 1972 and 1982. Although their conclusions have not been challenged, some have argued that in the post 1982 period the fiscal condition of cities has improved. Ladd argues otherwise in this article, contending that city averages of broad indicators such as poverty rates and per capita income suggest further deterioration in the fiscal condition of large cities.

22

Big City Finances in the New Era of Fiscal Federalism

Helen F. Ladd

New York City's financial crisis in 1975 focused national and worldwide attention on the fiscal problems of US cities. Like many other older cities, New York suffered from the failure of its tax base to grow in line with the revenue needs of an increasingly dependent population and from the adverse effects on its budget of inflation and recession. Also like many other older cities, its heavy reliance on intergovernmental assistance made it vulnerable to reductions in external aid. Poor fiscal health turned to financial crisis, and ultimately to the need for an emergency federal loan, when city officials responded to the 1974–5 recession and a slowdown in intergovernmental assistance largely by borrowing rather than by raising taxes or decreasing spending. With much of this additional borrowing in the form of short-term debt, the crisis was triggered when investors lost confidence in the city's ability to repay its loans.

For the first few years after New York's financial crisis, big cities throughout the country benefited from the expansion of the national economy and the injection of new countercyclical aid. However, federal aid to state and local governments peaked in 1978 and two years later the economy slid into recession. After a brief recovery, the economy deteriorated again and the country entered its worst recession since the Depression. Simultaneously, cities experienced significant new cutbacks in

This paper was completed while the author was a Visiting Scholar at the Federal Reserve Bank of Boston. It draws heavily on the material in Helen F. Ladd, "Big City Finances" to be published under the auspices of the Taubman Center for State and Local Governments, Kennedy School of Government, Harvard University. The author thanks the Ford Foundation for financial assistance for the larger project. This paper also draws on Helen F. Ladd and John Yinger. *America's Ailing Cities* (Baltimore: Johns Hopkins University Press, 1989).

federal aid at the hands of the Reagan administration and faced local voters who were reluctant to pay higher taxes. By the end of 1982, the economy began to recover, but federal assistance to cities continued to fall. The recession, high interest rates, a nationwide tax revolt, and loss of federal aid presented major new challenges for city governments in the early 1980s and raised the specter of financial crises in other big cities. But, in fact, America's big cities muddle through the fiscal challenges of the early 1980s with no serious financial crises.

However, the absence of financial crises does not mean that big cities are in strong fiscal health. Indeed, a main theme of this paper is that the capacity of cities to provide adequate public services to their residents at reasonable tax rates has been declining over time. After a brief summary of the recent changes in cities' fiscal environment, the paper first examines changes in the financial or budgetary condition of big cities, then turns to changes in city tax burdens and service levels, and, finally, analyzes changes in their underlying fiscal health. The paper shows that the fiscal health of many big cities has been deteriorating over time and concludes that many cities will need additional state or federal assistance to provide adequate public services at reasonable tax rates.

Impediments to Raising Revenue

In his excellent 1976 comprehensive study of big city finances, George Peterson of the Urban Institute asserted that 1975 would be remembered "for its rediscovery of the budget constraint."[1] During the 1960s and early 1970s, cities had behaved as if they were not constrained. Spending by big city governments had grown dramatically, fueled largely by the growth of federal assistance. Between 1962 and 1972, spending by the twenty-eight largest cities (including that of their overlying school districts) nearly tripled and grew about 20 percent faster than the state and local public sector at the time when that sector was increasing its share of Gross National Product by 40 percent.[2]

During the following decade, spending by big cities slowed down both absolutely and relative to that of all state and local governments as cities faced new impediments to financing public services. These impediments took the form of cutbacks in federal aid and the demise of the federal-local partnership, the vigorous opposition of taxpayers throughout the country to increased state and local taxes, and the increased difficulty of raising funds through the municipal bond market. In 1986, cities were faced with another change in federal policy that is likely to exacerbate their future fiscal problems, namely, the Tax Reform Act of that year.

The end of the federal-local partnership

During the 1960s and early 1970s, two different philosophies had motivated the growth of direct federal assistance to cities. First, federal policy makers believed that cities needed narrowly defined categorical aid to meet the needs of their impoverished residents.

Recognizing a collection of unmet needs in urban areas, such as inadequate housing and transportation, deteriorating neighborhoods, high crime, failing schools, and limited job opportunities, especially for minorities, and believing that cities had neither the financial nor the political capacity to deal with these needs, federal policymakers provided categorical aid for an assortment of new programs, such as neighborhood health care, legal aid, and manpower training. In contrast, the 1972 introduction of general revenue sharing was motivated by the view that the superior revenue-raising capacity of the federal government should be harnessed to provide no-strings-attached aid to state and local governments to use as they pleased. The categorical programs together with revenue sharing resulted in a dramatic upsurge in direct federal assistance to cities.

Neither philosophy survived into the 1980s. During the Reagan years, cities were no longer viewed as the deserving level of government, and huge federal deficits left no surplus revenues for state and local governments.[3] As early as 1974, federal assistance to cities had begun to level off. But the underlying trend in federal assistance was not fully perceived because of a temporary surge in the late 1970s in federal jobs programs and countercyclical assistance provided through the Comprehensive Employment and Training Act (CETA), Anti-Recession Fiscal Assistance (ARFA), and Emergency Local Public Works. Federal aid to cities, and also to all state and local governments, peaked in 1978. The elimination of the countercyclical programs and the leveling of other programs halted the twelve-year growth in federal aid to cities even before the 1980 election of President Reagan. President Reagan's budget cutting agenda greatly accelerated the decline as various categorical programs for cities were consolidated into block grants to states, programs of special importance to urban governments were slashed, and revenue sharing was eliminated in 1986. The fall from grace of the cities during the Reagan years is demonstrated by the fact that aid programs for urban areas declined by 47 percent between 1980 and 1987 at the same time that all other federal grant programs (including Aid for Dependent Children – AFDC – and Medicaid) experienced a 47 percent increase.[4]

By 1982, federal aid to all cities had declined to 18.4 percent of own-source revenue, its level in the early 1970s, and by 1986 it had declined further to under 12 percent. Moreover huge federal budget deficits, combined with the 1985 Gramm-Rudman mechanism to reduce them, portend no turnaround in the downward trend. Thus, the 1977–86 decade witnessed a major change in federal-city relations. During this period, the federal government made it clear that it would no longer serve as the funding source for increased city spending and that it would no longer provide aid to alleviate the fiscal stress of cities during recessions. Instead the cities were left to fend for themselves or to rely on assistance from their states.

The tax revolt

But the late 1970s and early 1980s was not a good time for cities to rely more heavily on their own revenue or that of their states. Spurred on by the success at the polls of California's Proposition 13, taxpayer voters across the country joined the tax revolt bandwagon and passed referenda to limit state or local taxes or both in many states and made elected public officials more reluctant to vote for tax increases. This national tax revolt lowered total state and local taxes from 11.5 percent of personal income in 1977 to 10.3 percent in 1982.

Cutbacks in federal aid and the tax revolt also affected state governments and thereby diminished their ability to assist big cities. Consequently, the average big city adjusted to the decline in federal aid on the revenue side almost entirely by increasing the share of revenues from its own sources (see table 22.1). The percentage of general city revenues from the federal government in the average big city declined from 20 percent in 1977 to 10 percent in 1986 while the share from own sources increased from 61 to 71 percent. During this same time period, the share of city revenue from state governments decreased from 16.6 to 16.1 percent. Only in thirteen big cities did the share of revenue from the state government increase during this period and in most of them the increase was not sufficient to offset the decline in federal aid. One exception was Boston where additional state aid partially compensated the city for its loss of property tax revenues under Massachusetts's stringent tax limitation measure.

Turbulence in the municipal bond market

Historically, cities raised about 50 percent of their funds for capital projects by issuing bonds in the municipal – or tax-exempt – bond market. During the 1970s, this proportion declined with the increased

Table 22.1 Mix of revenues – 1977, 1982, 1986
(thirty-three big cities)

	1977	1982	1986
Percentage of general revenues from			
Federal government	20.2	16.4	10.1
State government	16.6	16.6	16.1
Other local governments	2.3	2.2	3.3
Own sources	60.8	64.8	70.5
Percentage of own-source revenues from			
Taxes	68.4	61.2	59.4
Charges	20.2	20.9	20.7
Miscellaneous (not interest)	5.5	6.5	9.4
Interest	5.4	11.4	10.5
Percentage of taxes from			
Property	55.2	48.0	47.5
General sales	11.8	13.7	13.0
Selected sales	11.5	14.4	14.5
Income	13.8	15.6	16.2
Other	7.7	8.4	8.7

Note: Simple unweighted averages for thirty-three big cities.
For list of cities, see note 8.
Source: US Department of Commerce, Bureau of the Census,
City Government Finances, 1977, 1982, and *1986* (Washington,
D.C.: US Government Printing Office).

availability of intergovernmental aid, primarily from the federal government, for capital projects. With the fall in federal aid, cities were expected to increase their reliance on the municipal bond market.

However, the early 1980s witnessed turbulence in the municipal bond market as interest rates on tax-exempt bonds escalated, both absolutely and relative to comparable taxable bonds. In 1982, for example, interest rates on high grade municipal bonds rose to 11.57 percent, only 11 percent below the rate of return on taxable US Treasury securities. The combined effects of record interest rates on long term bonds and the tax revolt made it increasingly difficult for city officials to garner support for general obligation bonds to finance capital projects. Instead they turned increasingly to various forms of creative financing, including sale leasebacks, to revenue bonds which do not require a public vote, and to special authorities that could issue revenue bonds financed by user charges. Between 1977 and 1986, the typical big city decreased the share of its general purpose debt backed by the full faith and credit of the city from 69 percent of all new general purpose debt to 44 percent. Only by shifting to nonguaranteed bonds were cities able to raise much money through the municipal bond market.

Federal tax reform

In 1986, big cities were faced with another major change in federal policy, in the form of the Tax Reform Act, that could adversely affect their future ability to raise revenue. This landmark legislation reduced individual tax rates, eliminated the deductibility of state and local sales taxes, and placed new restrictions on borrowing through the tax-exempt bond market. The fact that sales taxes alone are no longer deductible may encourage cities that use sales taxes to alter the mix of their taxes somewhat in favor of other deductible local taxes. In addition, the restrictions on tax-exempt borrowing and the fall in the value of tax exemption because of the lower federal tax rates are likely to encourage some cities to reduce their debt issues, to increase the use of current revenues to finance capital projects, to require developers to underwrite more of the costs of infrastructure, and to make more use of (the more expensive) taxable bond market.[5]

Two indirect effects are likely to be important for those cities, such as many in the Northeast and Midwest, that are located in jurisdictionally fragmented metropolitan areas. By returning a portion of their tax payments in the form of lower federal taxes, deductibility of state and local taxes serves as a bribe to keep high-income households in high tax rate, low-income jurisdictions. The tax reform act reduces the value of this bribe and may reduce city tax bases by encouraging middle and high income households to move out of central cities. In addition, cities will be hurt if state governments respond to federal tax reform either by curtailing the total amount of aid to local governments or by redirecting state aid away from central cities toward suburban areas. This latter outcome would occur if state policymakers respond to political pressures from high income suburban itemizers who face the largest increases in the net burden of state taxes as a result of federal tax reform.[6]

Cause for Concern

The combination of cutbacks in federal aid, recession, high interest rates, and the tax revolt raised serious concerns in the early 1980s about the ability of cities to cope. However, some observers have concluded that cities survived these pressures surprisingly well and were in remarkably strong fiscal condition in the early 1980s. In a recent study for the Committee on National Urban Policy of the National Research Council, Philip Dearborn concluded that as of 1984 [the major cities] were in perhaps the best financial condition they had been in since 1971, as judged by their success in balancing budgets and maintaining balance-sheet surpluses and liquidity. This favorable condition can be expected to continue for most major cities, as least as long as the national economy remains healthy.[7]

But this conclusion was overly sanguine and, more importantly, was based on cities' short run budgetary or financial condition, with little attention to what was happening to city service levels and tax rates. In the following sections, we look first at changes over time in cities' short run financial condition, then turn to tax rates and service levels, and finally to longer run trends in their underlying ability to provide adequate services at reasonable tax rates.

Financial Management

A city has a weak financial condition if its current expenditures continually exceed its current revenues, it relies excessively on short-term debt, or it has difficulty meeting its cash needs. This budgetary or financial perspective, which is the focus of this section, is important because it is the context within which most local goverment spending and financing decisions are made in the short run. However, one should be careful not to interpret an improvement in a city's budgetary condition as an improvement in the city's fiscal health, that is, in the underlying tradeoff the city faces between lower taxes and more publicly provided goods and services.

Putting aside the specific pressures associated with recession, the budgetary or financial condition of big cities has apparently strengthened over time, but only modestly and not for all cities. This conclusion is based on a comparison of various financial measures for thirty-three big cities during two comparable three-year periods.[8] The periods 1977–9 and 1984–6 are similar in terms of how they relate to the economic cycle. Both periods begin two years after a recession (the 1974–5 recession in the former case and the 1981–2 recession in the latter case) and encompass years of economic expansion. Thus the data should be free of the effects of recession, and, because they cover three years, make it possible to distinguish long-term trends from short-term aberrations.

More conservative financial management

Average budgetary surpluses in the thirty-three big cities were slightly higher in the later three-year period than in the earlier period. Specifically, the average general purpose surplus for these cities rose from about 13.5 percent of expenditures in the 1977–9 period to over 14.5 percent in the 1984–6 period.[9] Although not large, the fact that this increase occurred when federal aid was falling is noteworthy. Despite such cutbacks, or perhaps because of them, cities appear to be managing their budgets more conservatively. Cities also appear to be managing their pension plans for city employees more responsibly. Historically, many city pension plans were operated on a pay-as-you-go basis, but recently cities have been putting more money aside annually in a fund to meet future liabilities. Boston changed its behavior the most during the period, increasing its contributions from 6 percent of wages and salaries in 1977 to 23 percent in 1986. Other cities such as Cincinnati, Memphis, Miami, Milwaukee, Jacksonville, and Chicago also significantly increased their contributions.

It addition, cities seem to have learned from New York City's 1975 financial crisis of the potential dangers of extensive use of short-term debt. Although the average amount of short-term debt outstanding at the end of the fiscal year has remained relatively constant as a share of general revenue over time, the number of big cities with such debt declined from 24 cities in 1977 to 17 in 1986. Several cities such as Detroit, New York, Pittsburgh, and Seattle that made significant use of short-term debt in 1977 apparently changed their ways and reduced their reliance on such debt to more manageable levels in many of the other five years. Although extensive use of short-term debt continues to be common practice in many big cities, cities in the aggregate appear to have become somewhat more conservative about their use of such debt.

Continuing budgetary pressure

However, improvement over time in the financial condition of big cities should not be overstated. Many cities that faced budgetary pressure in the earlier period also faced such pressure in the later period. Table 22.2 lists the cities that had low general purpose surpluses in each period. Based on a cutoff of 10 percent, twelve of the thirty-three cities had low or negative surpluses during at least two years in both periods. Thus, budgetary problems in many cities have persisted over time. Three cities that had low surpluses in the 1970s, Columbus, Memphis, and St Louis, showed some improvement according to this measure over time.In contrast, three Western cities, Portland, Seattle, and San Francisco, experienced more severe budgetary pressures in the 1980s than in the 1970s. Thus, we find a stubborn persistence of budgetary pressures in more

Table 22.2 Budget balances over time

Big cities with low budget surplus in at least two of three years

A. In both early period (1977–9) and late period (1984–6)

Boston	Minneapolis
Chicago	New York
Cleveland	Philadelphia
Detroit	Pittsburgh
Miami	San Antonio
Milwaukee	Washington, D.C.

B. In early period (1977–9) only
Columbus
Memphis
St. Louis

C. In late period (1984–6) only
San Francisco
Seattle
Portland

Notes: The budget surplus is calculated as total general purpose revenues minus general purpose current account expenditures divided by expenditures. Total revenue includes both own source and intergovernmental revenue. Total expenditures are general expenditures minus capital outlays plus long-term debt retired (adjusted for refunding) plus contributions to city retirement systems. A low budget surplus is less than 10 percent of expenditures.

Source: US Department of Commerce, Bureau of the Census, *City Government Finances*, various years (Washington, D.C.: US Government Printing Office).

than a third of America's big cities and emerging budgetary problems in a few Western cities.

Capital spending and bond ratings as indicators of budgetary pressure

Changes over time in capital spending as a percent of general purpose spending also indicate a somewhat bleaker picture. Cities that are facing budgetary pressure are more likely than those without such pressure to reduce their spending on capital projects such as roads, bridges, and buildings, because the short run effects of such cuts are less visible than are cuts in services such as public safety. Between 1977 and 1986, the typical big city decreased its capital spending from 20 to 16 percent of its general purpose spending. This decline is consistent with the view that cities faced significant budgetary pressure during the period.

A final indicator of changes in the financial condition of big cities is changes in their bond ratings over time. Moody's Investors Service grounds its rating on a city's economic base, measures of indebtedness, administration factors, and financial factors. Hence, a city's rating reflects more than just current financial condition. Nonetheless, bond ratings partially reflect such conditions. Moreover, they directly affect those conditions; by raising the cost of current borrowing, a downgrading of a city's general obligation bond rating increases the pressure on a city's current budget.

Table 22.3 lists the eleven cities whose ratings were lower in 1987 than in 1977 and the four cities whose ratings improved during the same

Table 22.3 Changes In Bond Ratings

	Bond ratings	
	1977	*1987*
Cities with downgrade		
Houston	Aaa	Aa
Milwaukee	Aaa	Aa
San Francisco	Aaa	Aa1
Chicago	A1	Baa1
New Orleans	A	Baa
Boston	A	Baa1
Cleveland	A	Baa
Philadelphia	A	Baa
Pittsburgh	A	Baa1
St. Louis	A	Baa
Buffalo	Baa1	Baa
Cities with upgrade		
Phoenix	Aa	Aa1
San Diego	Aa	Aaa
Baltimore	A	A1
New York	Ba	Baa1

Key to ratings: Aaa, best quality; Aa, high quality; A, upper-medium grade; Baa, medium grade; Ba, speculative; B, lacks characteristics of desirable investment; A1 and Baa1, strongest investment characteristics within the category.
Source: Moody's Investors Services as reported in the International City Management Association, *Municipal Year Book* (Washington, D.C.: ICMA, 1987 and 1988).

period. Significantly, more ratings were lowered than were raised. The seventeen big cities not shown in the table (excluding Washington, D.C., which does not issue bonds) experienced no change in their bond ratings. Among the cities with declining ratios are three – Houston, Milwaukee, and San Francisco – that began the period with the highest rating and many cities that were listed in table 22.2 as having budgetary problems. Notwithstanding the fact that bond ratings measure more than just financial condition, the large number of downgrades suggests a deterioration in the average financial condition of big cities.

Summary

The evidence on city financial condition is mixed. Although the average budgetary surplus of thirty-three big cities was slightly higher in the 1980s than in the 1970s, evidence of persistent skimpy surpluses suggests little improvement in the budgetary condition of many big cities. Moreover, the fall in capital spending and the fact that more cities experienced downgrades than upgrades in bond ratings suggests that, contrary to the view of other observers, budgetary pressures persisted into the 1980s.

Tax Rates and Service Levels

Cities' more conservative financial management during the 1980s helped them cope with the fiscal pressures of the period and to avoid the severe financial crisis that New York City had faced in 1975, when it nearly defaulted on its loans. But their larger budgetary surpluses do not mean that big cities were more successfully meeting the public service needs of their residents. To the extent that balanced budgets were achieved by shifting to less desirable revenue sources, boosting tax rates, or cutting the quality of public services, city residents were worse off in the 1980s than in the 1970s. Hence, in this section, we look at the choices cities made during this period about taxes and service levels.

Revenue mix

As was noted earlier, reductions in intergovernmental aid forced cities to rely more heavily on their own revenue sources. In addition, voter resistance to property taxes led many cities to increase their revenue from a variety of narrowly defined taxes and user fees. In 1977, the typical big city obtained 55 percent of its tax revenue from property taxes. By 1986, this share had fallen to 47.6 percent. Cities partially made up the slack by increased reliance on general sales, selective sales, and income taxes, and also a variety of narrowly defined taxes (see table 22.1).

California cities, for example, maintained expenditures on basic services in the face of declining intergovernmental aid and property taxes by increasing utility users' taxes, transient lodging taxes, franchise fees and also by turning to nontax revenues from user charges.[10] Between 1977 and 1986, San Francisco increased the share of its own source revenues from user charges from 18 to 29 percent and Los Angeles increased its user charge share from 18 to 25 percent. However, not all big cities expanded reliance on user fees. Overall, eighteen of the thirty-three cities reported on did so while the other fifteen decreased their relative reliance on fees, perhaps because the fee schedules they had at the beginning of the period were not increased in line with the price level.[11] The shift to user charge financing in many cities may have provided incentives for more efficient spending decisions, but the general pattern of moving away from broad based taxes to narrowly defined taxes and fees probably increased the distortions of the tax system and certainly raised questions of tax fairness.

New nontax funds for cities also came from increased interest earnings and miscellaneous sources such as special assessments and sales of property. Thanks to high interest rates and more aggressive management of city assets, interest income increased from about $5\frac{1}{2}$ percent to $10\frac{1}{2}$ percent of own source revenues in the average big city during the period. Other miscellaneous revenues also increased by almost as much. To the extent that these miscellaneous funds come from sales of property, they are not revenue in the standard sense; instead they represent sales of assets and hence a diminution in the wealth of the government.

Tax burdens

Tax burdens on city residents in the thirty-three big cities declined between 1977 and 1982, but then increased sufficiently after 1982 to produce a higher tax burden on city residents in 1986 than in 1977.[12] The decline in tax burdens in the early period largely reflects the effects of the tax revolt. Even though few big cities experienced the property tax rollbacks forced on California and Massachusetts cities, less-stringent tax limitations plus fear of taxpayer revolts apparently made city councils less willing to raise taxes than they might have been in a different tax environment.

After 1982, city officials became more willing to increase taxes. This increased willingness was partially a response to large cutbacks in federal aid under the Reagan administration, but may also reflect an attempt to maintain the quality of public services in the face of rising costs. Between 1982 and 1986, city tax burdens in the average big city rose by 19 percent for three broad based taxes and by 21 percent for all city taxes. Unless these tax increases were offset by comparable increases in local public services, they imply that city residents were worse off on average in 1986 than in 1982 or 1977.

Quality of public services

Because few good output measures are available, determining how the quality of public services provided to city residents has changed over time is a difficult task. Nonetheless, various pieces of evidence suggest that the quality of services received by city residents deteriorated between 1977 and 1986.

Consider, for example, safety from crime. Despite the measurement problems associated with the crime rates reported in the FBI's Uniform Crime Reports, changes in such rates undoubtedly provide useful information about changes over time in the safety of individual cities.[13] Between 1977 and 1982, the crime rate in the thirty-three big cities increased on average by 18 percent, with high increases in Miami, Philadelphia, Seattle, and Washington, D.C. During this five-year period, the reported crime rate fell in only four of the thirty-three. After 1982, the situation apparently improved with sixteen of the cities experiencing falling crime rates. Nonetheless, even in this more recent period, the average crime rate across all the cities in the study increased another 4.3 percent, yielding an average increase over the 1977–86 period of over 20 percent. This increase provides support for the view that residents of big cities experienced a lower level of public safety in the mid-1980s than in the mid-1970s.

The situation in urban schools has also become increasingly bleak over time. Cities have become the home for growing numbers of minority households who experience poverty at much higher rates than white households, and for large numbers of families headed by single parents with school-age children, who also are disproportionately poor. In addition, cities are increasingly bearing the burden of concentrations of extreme poverty. Thus, urban school systems have to cope not only with the learning handicaps associated with the poverty found in individual households, but also with the problems such as drug use, teenage parenting, violence, and unemployment associated with concentrations of extreme poverty. As a result, achievement levels are low and dropout rates high throughout urban school districts, but especially so in predominantly minority schools.[14]

Changes in city spending provide some indirect, but hard to interpret, information on city service levels. Table 22.4 summarizes average changes in per capita spending on all functions, on a set of functions that are common across most cities, and on public safety, with all numbers deflated by the national deflator for state and local government purchases. The table shows that per capita spending declined between 1977 and 1982 and then rebounded sharply after 1982. Over the entire period, real per capita spending increased by about 6 percent.

However, this 6 percent increase in real spending does not translate into a comparable increase in the quality of services. The main reason is that the state and local deflator does not include the effects on the cost of providing public services of changes in the environmental characteristics of the city. A city that has a harsher environment for providing public services, perhaps because a greater number of its residents are poor or because it has more commuters to serve, encounters higher costs of providing services than a city with a less harsh environment. Similarly, deterioration over time in the conditions under which cities provide services, caused, for example, by an increase in the incidence of poverty, boosts the cost of providing a given quality of public services. Ladd and Yinger have estimated that between 1977 and 1982 changes in city characteristics such as the poverty rate, per resident private employment in the city, and the composition of city economic activity boosted the costs of providing public safety in the average big city by over 35 percent and of other services by about 6 percent.[15] Even if we assume unrealistically that costs remained constant after 1982, the spending rebound in the recent period falls far short of what would have been needed to offset the service declines of the previous five years. Hence, despite the small increase in real spending between 1977 and 1986,

Table 22.4 Per capita expenditures, 1977–86 (averages, thirty-two big cities)

	1986 (dollars)	Percent change		
		1977–82	1982–6	1977–86
All functions (current account)	735	−1.8	9.7	5.6
Common functions	446	−2.9	9.6	6.3
Public safety	222	−5.0	12.7	6.6

Notes: See note 8 for list of cities. Washington, D.C., is excluded. Expenditures were deflated by the national deflator for state and local government purchases.
Source: US Department of Commerce, Bureau of the Census, *City Government Finances*, various years (Washington, D.C.: US Government Printing Office).

service levels in big cities appear to be lower in 1986 than they were in the mid-1970s.

Fiscal Health

The rise in tax burdens and the fall in service quality reflect a basic deterioration over time in the ability of big cities to provide adequate public services at reasonable tax rates, that is, in their fiscal health. A city has poor fiscal health if its capacity to generate revenue is small relative to its expenditure needs.

The concept of expenditure need recognizes that some cities face higher costs of providing a given package of public services than others because of city characteristics such as population density or the incidence of poverty that are outside the control of city of officials. Revenue-raising capacity represents the revenue a city could generate by imposing a standard tax burden expressed as a percentage of income on its residents augmented by its ability to export tax burdens to nonresidents. A city in poor fiscal health would have to impose above-average tax rates to provide a standard package of services or must accept below-average service levels if it chooses to impose average tax rates. A city in strong fiscal health, in contrast, has substantial capacity to generate revenue relative to its expenditure need and can achieve standard service levels at below-average tax rates.

Over time two sets of factors affect the fiscal health of cities. The first set includes economic and social factors, such as the income of city residents, the poverty rate, and the suburbanization of employment that affect either a city's ability to raise revenue or its cost of providing a given quality of public services or both. The second set includes the fiscal institutions within which the city operates. For example a city that has access to broad taxes other than the property tax, receives a lot of state aid, or provides a limited array of public services will have stronger fiscal health, all other factors held constant, than will a city whose power to tax is restricted to the property tax, that receives minimal state aid, and that has extensive service responsibilities.

Standardized fiscal health

In their comprehensive study of seventy major central cities, Ladd and Yinger document a significant deterioration between 1972 and 1982 in the fiscal health of US central cities, and more specifically America's biggest cities.[16] Table 22.5 summarizes their results for their concept of standardized fiscal health, the calculation of which is based on the

Table 22.5 Standardized fiscal health in 1982 (seventy central cities)

	Number of cities	Revenue-raising capacity	Standardized expenditure need	Capacity minus need	Fiscal health index
Illustrative cities					
Atlanta	1	$505	$640	$(136)	−26.9%
Baltimore	1	331	483	152	−45.7
Boston	1	501	561	59	−11.9
Detroit	1	341	654	(313)	−91.9
Denver	1	532	505	27	5.0
Washington, D.C.	1	624	535	89	14.3
All cities in sample					
Average	70	$425	$458	$(33)	−10.9%
Standard deviation	70	80	109	128	32.2
Maximum	70	649	737	290	47.2
Minimum	70	286	243	(386)	−109.7
Cities grouped by population (in thousands)					
Less than 100	6	$457	$384	$74	16.4%
100–250	19	473	421	52	9.1
250–500	26	420	473	(53)	−13.5
500–1,000	14	385	466	(80)	−22.9
Greater than 1,000	5	341	586	(245)	−72.8

Note: See note 16 for description of the seventy cities.
Source: Helen F. Ladd and John Yinger, *America's Ailing Cities: Fiscal Health and the Design of Urban Policy* (Baltimore, MD: Johns Hopkins University Press, 1989), tables 5.1 and 5.2.

assumption that each city operates within the same standardized set of fiscal institutions. *Revenue-raising capacity* indicates the amount of revenue that a city could generate from three broad-based taxes – property, general sales, and earnings – at a standard tax burden on its residents. *Standardized expenditure need* indicates the amount the city would have to spend to provide a standard set of public services, given the effects of its socioeconomic characteristics, such as its poverty rate, on the costs of providing those services. *Standardized fiscal health* is defined as each city's revenue-raising capacity minus its expenditure need expressed as a percentage of capacity. Because of the assumption of uniform fiscal institutions, differences across cities and over time in standardized fiscal health reflect economic and social factors alone.

The top panel of the table reports indexes of standardized fiscal health in 1982 and its components for six illustrative big cities and averages for seventy central cities grouped by size of city. The indexes are constructed using a 1972 baseline service level, defined as the quality of services that the average city could provide at a standard tax burden on city residents in 1972. A positive fiscal health index, such as those for Denver or Washington, implies that the city's revenue-raising capacity was greater than its expenditure need and indicates that the city's fiscal health in 1982 exceeded that of the average major central in 1972. The specific value (5 percent for Denver and 14 percent for Washington) indicates the percentage of its revenue the city would have had left over for increases in service quality or for tax cuts in 1982 after it had provided the 1972 average service quality at the standard tax burden.

A negative fiscal health index, such as those for Atlanta, Baltimore, Boston, and Detroit, implies that a city's 1982 capacity was less than its expenditure need and indicates that the city's fiscal health was weaker in 1982 than that of the average major central city in 1972. For example, Detroit's fiscal health index of −92 indicates that it had a standardized expenditure need that was almost twice as high as its standardized revenue-raising capacity. Detroit would have had to receive a 92 percent boost in its revenue-raising capacity from outside sources to be able to provide services of the quality that the average city could provide out of its own broad-based revenue sources in 1972.

The average standardized fiscal health of the cities in the Ladd-Yinger study was −11 percent in 1982. This figure means that the typical central city would have needed a boost in revenues of 11 percent from outside sources in 1982 to provide the 1972 baseline service level at the standard tax burden. In other words, economic and social forces significantly weakened the fiscal health of the typical city during the period.

Cities with population over 250,000 fared the worse. The negative average index in the three largest size categories of cities indicates that the standardized fiscal health of America's biggest cities was significantly poorer than that of smaller cities. In contrast to the −11 percent index for all seventy cities, cities in the three largest size categories had average indexes of −14, −23, and −73 percent.

Actual fiscal health

Dropping the assumption that cities operate within a uniform set of fiscal institutions leads, in the Ladd-Yinger terminology, to a city's actual fiscal health. Actual fiscal health measures the balance between a city's actual expenditure need (its need adjusted for its service responsibilities) and its restricted revenue-raising capacity (its capacity restricted by the taxes it is empowered to use, adjusted for capacity used up by overlying jurisdictions, and augmented by state aid). Standardized to a 1972 average service level, actual fiscal health measures a city's ability to provide the 1972 baseline service level at a standard tax burden on city residents, given the fiscal institutions within which the city operates.

Table 22.6 provides information on 1982 levels and 1972–82 changes in actual fiscal health for cities grouped by population.[17] The measures of actual fiscal health are interpreted analogously to those of standardized

Table 22.6 Actual fiscal health (averages by category of city, seventy central cities)

	Number of cities	Actual fiscal health	Change in actual fiscal health (percentage point)
Average[a]	70	−4.9	−4.9
Cities grouped by population (in thousands)			
Less than 100	6	14.6	7.0
100–250	19	6.4	−9.2
250–500	26	−9.0	−4.4
500–1,000	14	−5.5	−4.6[b]
Greater than 1,000	5	−48.1	−20.8

[a] See note 16 for description of the sample of cities.
[b] Figure excludes Cincinnati because of a possible data problem with the 1972 figure for that city.
Sources: Helen F. Ladd and John M. Yinger, *America's Ailing Cities: Fiscal Health and the Design of Urban Policy* (Baltimore, MD: Johns Hopkins University Press, 1989), tables 9.2 and 9.3.

fiscal health. In particular, the −4.9 percent in the first cell of column 2 means that the average city in 1982 would need additional resources equal to almost 5 percent of its revenue-raising capacity to provide the 1972 baseline service level at the standard tax burden on city residents. This negative number implies that the typical city was worse off in 1982 than in 1972. However, comparing the 4.9 percent decline in average actual health with the 10.9 percent average decline in standardized health from table 22.5 indicates that changes in fiscal institutions have helped offset some of the adverse effects of economic and social factors; in other words, state actions such as authorizing use of additional taxes, taking over welfare services, or giving more aid mitigated some, but not all, of the adverse fiscal effects of economic and social trends that buffeted American cities during the 1970s.

Even after accounting for the beneficial effects of state fiscal institutions, the 1982 average fiscal health of cities in the three largest size categories was negative. The largest cities, for example, would have needed additional revenues equal to 48 percent of their revenue-raising capacity to provide the 1972 baseline service level at the standard tax burden on city residents. This finding contrasts with a positive average fiscal health of 14.6 percent for cities with less than 100,000 people. In contrast to the larger cities, these smaller cities not only could raise sufficient revenues at the standard tax burden to provide the 1972 baseline service level, but they would also have had revenues left over to improve services or to reduce tax burdens.

By construction, the average 1972–82 change for all seventy cities is the same as the average index for 1982. Column 3 shows that the largest cities experienced the greatest decline in capacity relative to needs; on average their actual fiscal health declined by almost twenty-one percentage points during the decade. In general, no clear pattern of decline emerges across cities grouped by population size. The main point is simply that, on average, cities in all the size categories over 100,000 experienced declining actual fiscal health during the 1972–82 decade.

Recent trends

Because 1982 was a recession year, one might wonder whether the cities' poor fiscal health in that year reflects a short term cyclical downturn rather than the effects of longer term trends. However, this cyclical interpretation of the 1982 figures is not consistent with the trends since 1982 in three key contributors to city fiscal health: the income of city residents, central city poverty rates, and support from state governments.

With respect to the major determinant of the revenue-raising capacity of a city, namely the income of city residents, cities fared less well during the 1981–5 period than during the 1977–81 period.[18] During the four years ending in 1985, real resident income declined in fifteen of the thirty-three big cities listed in note 8, while the average big city experienced only a 0.6 percent increase. During the previous four-year period, resident income declined in ten cities and the average city experienced a 1.7 percent increase. Over the entire period, real income declined in two out of five of the thirty-three big cities. To be sure, the income situation brightened in some cities. Notable examples are Boston, where real income grew by 21 percent during the eight-year period, Atlanta, where income grew by 7.5 percent in the recent period, after declining in the earlier period, and Portland, Oregon, where resident income partially recovered in the recent period from its dramatic decline in the earlier period. Nonetheless, many US cities experienced declining real income during the 1980s and this trend is likely to continue into the future.

The aggregate incidence of poverty in all central cities was substantially higher in 1986 than in 1970. Although the 1986 rate of 18 percent fell below the 1982 peak of 19.9 percent, the trends provide little reason for optimism; the poverty rate in US central cities has exceeded the US average by about a third for each of the past several years. With no national leadership to reduce poverty, the rate of poverty in the nation's big cities and the costs associated with that poverty of providing public services are likely to remain high. Cities will continue to be called upon to provide social services for the poor, shelters for the homeless, and additional police services to deal with the social problems that arise when there are concentrations of extreme poverty.

Moreover, fiscal pressures at the state level have kept the states from doing much to help their cities in the mid-1980s. How much the states have assisted their cities since 1982 is difficult to determine because, as discussed above, state assistance encompasses more than just the provision of state aid; it also includes state assumption of city expenditure responsibilities and authorization to use additional broad-based taxes. If we focus just on state aid, however, the one component of the assistance package for which recent information is available, we find no evidence of increased state support for big central cities in recent years. Indeed, between 1982 and 1986, average state aid to thirty-two of the big cities (excluding Washington, D.C.) remained constant at 19 percent of city general expenditures; aid as a percent of spending went down in seventeen cities and up in fifteen cities. Moreover, no clear pattern emerges across cities grouped by their 1982 fiscal health. This trend since 1982 contrasts with the trend before 1982 when state aid increased from under 16 percent to 19 percent of city spending.

Summary and Conclusion

The Ladd-Yinger measures of the underlying or structural fiscal health of US cities indicate a significant deterioration over time. They imply that social and economic trends made it more difficult for many big cities in 1982 than in 1972 to provide a standard package of public services at reasonable tax burdens on their residents. Although state governments offset some of the adverse effects of these trends, state assistance was not large enough to keep the fiscal health of the big cities from deteriorating. Moreover, recent trends in the income of city residents, poverty rates, and state aid suggest that the trends identified by Ladd and Yinger have continued into more recent years.

Overall, the fiscal outlook for many of America's big cities is not rosy. Although more conservative financial management has helped them to avoid the financial problems faced by New York City in 1975, the new 1980s brand of federalism has not been kind to them. Through no fault of their own, many big cities are experiencing declining fiscal health. This trend is likely to continue and may be exacerbated by the effects of the Tax Reform Act of 1986. During the 1970s, federal aid to cities played an important role in helping cities provide adequate public services at reasonable tax rates. But much of that assistance is no longer forthcoming. Without additional injections of either federal aid or state assistance to their cities, residents in many big cities will continue to experience significant deterioration in the quality of public services or higher tax burdens or both.

Notes

1   George E. Peterson, "Finance," in W. Gorham and N. Glazer, eds., 35, *The Urban Predicament* (Washington, D.C.: Urban Institute Press, 1976).
2   Ibid. Table 2, p. 41.
3   For an insightful discussion of the forces that led to the rise and fall of federal aid to urban areas, see Robert Reischauer, "The Rise and Fall of National Urban Policy: The Fiscal Dimension," in Marshall Kaplan and Franklin James, eds., *The Future of National Urban Policy* (Durham, NC: Duke University Press, forthcoming).
4   The federal programs of importance to urban local governments and the percentage change in their budget authority between 1980 and 1987 include Wastewater Treatment Construction (−32.2), Urban Mass Transportation (−27.4), Urban and Secondary Roads (−22.5), Community Development Block Grants (−20.0), Urban Development Action Grants (−66.7), Housing Subsidy Programs (−56.7), Training and Employment (−46.0), Compensatory Education (−10.3), and General Revenue Sharing

(−100). Together the budget authority for these programs declined from $45.3 billion in 1980 to $24.1 billion in 1987. During this same period budget authority for all other grants increased from $59.7 billion to $87.6 billion. Excluding AFDC and Medicaid, budget authority for all other grants increased from $37.6 billion to $49.5 billion or by 31.8 percent. Source: Peggy L. Cuciti, "A Non-Urban Policy: Recent Policy Shifts Affecting Cities," in Marshall Kaplan and Franklin James, eds., *The Future of National Urban Policy* (Durham, NC: Duke University Press, forthcoming), Table 3.

5   For a discussion of the impacts of the TRA on the municipal bond market, see John Peterson, "Examining the Impacts of the 1986 Tax Reform Act on the Municipal Securities Market," *National Tax Journal* 40, 3 (September 1987), 393–402 and for its initial impacts on city finances, see Michael A. Pagano, "The Effects of the 1986 Tax Reform Act on City Finances: An Appraisal of Year One" (research report of the National League of Cities, Washington, D.C., 1987).

6   See Edward M. Gramlich, "The Deductibility of State and Local Taxes," *National Tax Journal* 38, 4 (December 1985), 447–65; Roy Bahl, "Urban Government Finance and Federal Income Tax Reform," *National Tax Journal* 40 (March 1987), 1–18; Paul Courant and Daniel Rubinfeld, "Tax Reform: Implications for the State-Local Public Sector," *Journal of Economic Perspectives* (Summer 1987), 87–100; and Howard Chernick and Andrew Reschovsky, "The Effect of Federal Tax Reform on State Fiscal Systems: Some Preliminary Evidence," paper prepared for the session on Federal, State, and Local Relations of the American Economic Association, December 1988.

7   Philip M. Dearborn, "Fiscal Conditions in Large American Cities, 1971–84," in Michael M.G. McGeary and Lawrence Lynn, eds., 281, *Urban Change and Poverty* (Washington, D.C.: National Academy Press, 1988).

8   The data for these comparisons come primarily from US Department of Commerce, Bureau of the Census, *City Government Finances* (Washington, D.C.: USGPO, various years). The thirty-three cities are Atlanta, Baltimore, Boston, Buffalo, Chicago, Cincinnati, Cleveland, Columbus, Dallas, Denver, Detroit, Houston, Indianapolis, Jacksonville, Kansas City, Los Angeles, Memphis, Miami, Milwaukee, Minneapolis, New Orleans, New York, Philadelphia, Phoenix, Pittsburgh, Portland, St. Louis, San Antonio, San Diego, San Francisco, San Jose, Seattle, and Washington, D.C.

9   For each city, surpluses (or deficits) are measured as the difference between annual current account expenditures (which include debt service and contributions to city retirement systems, but exclude capital outlays) and revenues expressed as a percentage of expenditures. Revenues exclude the primary source of financing for capital projects, namely bond proceeds. However, because the revenue measure includes some intergovernmental aid for capital projects and possibly some own-source revenues used for capital projects, it represents more than revenue for current expenditure.

This fact should lead to larger measured surpluses (or smaller deficits) than would occur if current account revenues were correctly measured.

10   For a detailed analysis, see Gary Reid, "How Cities in California Have Responded to Fiscal Pressures Since Proposition 13," *Public Budgeting and Finance* 8, 1 (Spring 1988), 20–37.

11   Another possible explanation is that some cities may have set up special authorities, such as the water and sewer commission in Boston, to provide services financed more heavily by user charges. The resulting increased reliance on user charges would not show up in the city's general purpose revenues.

12   Measuring tax burdens on city residents is complicated because some of a city's taxes are exported to nonresidents, and cities differ in the range of public services for which they are responsible and hence in the taxes required to meet those responsibilities. To make them comparable across cities with different economic and fiscal structures, the tax burdens referred to in the text were calculated as a city's tax revenues divided by its restricted revenue-raising capacity. See below for further discussion of restricted capacity, and for more detail on the calculation and interpretation of big city tax burdens see Helen F. Ladd, "Big City Finances" (paper to be published under the auspices of the Taubman Center for State and Local Government, Kennedy School of Government, Harvard University).

13   Criticisms of the *Uniform Crime Reports* include the fact that the crime index includes only those crimes known to the police, that guidelines for reporting crimes may vary from one police department to another, that police officers exercise some discretion in what they report, that the index weights different crimes equally, and that rates are not expressed relative to the populations that could be exposed to that crime. See, for example, Albert J. Reiss, Jr., "Assessing the Current Crime Wave," in Barbara McLennan, ed., 23–44, *Crime in Urban Society* (New York: Dunellen, 1970).

14   For a detailed discussion of the problems of urban education, see Frank Newman, Robert Palaich, and Rona Wilensky, "Re-engaging State and Federal Policymakers in the Problems of Urban Education," in Marshall Kaplan and Franklin Jones, eds., *The Future of National Urban Policy* (Durham, NC: Duke University Press, forthcoming).

15   These estimates of cost indexes are based on a regression model of city expenditures that isolates the impact on city expenditures of city characteristics that are outside the control of local officials. For a full discussion of the underlying theory and measurement of these cost indexes, see Helen F. Ladd and John Yinger, *America's Ailing Cities: Fiscal Health and the Design of Urban Policy* (Baltimore: Johns Hopkins University press, 1989), chapter 4.

16   The sample of seventy cities is a subset of the eighty-six major American central cities where major central cities are defined as cities with population over 300,000 in either 1970 or 1980 or smaller cities that served as central cities in one of the nation's fifty largest metropolitan areas in either 1970 or 1980. The sample of seventy cities represents all cities other than

Washington, D.C., for which complete data were available. For the list of cities, see Helen F. Ladd and John Yinger, *America's Ailing Cities*, table 1.1, p. 11.

17 Breakdowns by revenue-raising capacity and expenditure need are not presented because the components of fiscal institutions are too intertwined to permit a meaningful interpretation of the capacity and need sides of actual fiscal health. For example, a city that has low service responsibilities is likely to have more of its local revenue-raising capacity used up by overlying jurisdictions and consequently to have a smaller revenue-raising capacity than a city with a larger, wider range of responsibilities. In addition, the city may well receive less state aid. Hence, the observation that a city has low actual expenditure needs is not meaningful without reference to its revenue-raising capacity; what matters is the balance between the two, as measured by actual fiscal health.

18 The dividing year is 1981 because the Ladd-Yinger capacity measures for 1982 are based on 1981 income; the income of city residents is not available for even years.

Introduction to Chapter 23

In this speculative essay the author considers whether municipal fiscal crises are looming for large US cities in the 1990s. He presents reasons why their finances have become more difficult since the 1980s. Market values of real property have fallen sharply since the real estate boom of the 1980s ended, reducing or at least curtailing the growth in property tax revenues. The continuing retreat of the federal government from funding urban programs has put fiscal pressure on city governments, which has been worsened by the 1990s trend of reduced or curbed aid from state governments to municipalities. On the expenditure side, the urban scourges of crack addiction, homelessness, and AIDS have put increased pressure on city budgets. Resistance to tax increases, particularly property taxes, has become stronger. Reschovsky considers various routes to expenditure reduction but sees little hope there. The curious fact is that he concludes on an upbeat note.

23

Are City Fiscal Crises on the Horizon?

Andrew Reschovsky

Introduction

In many parts of the country the beginning of the 1990s has been a period of often dramatic declines in the value of real estate. For example:

- In Boston, condominiums that were worth $250,000 in 1988 were selling for under $150,000 in early 1992.

- Again in Boston, office towers have fallen dramatically in value. Between 1988 and 1991 per-square-foot rents in some office buildings have fallen by as much as 50 percent. In 1992 the downtown office vacancy rate probably reached 20 percent, with a 50 percent vacancy rate in many new buildings.

- In New York City the market value of total taxable property fell by nearly 10 percent in 1990 and 1991.

- In Dallas, property values in 1992 were about 15 percent lower than they were in 1986.

- The market value of high-valued single-family homes in Los Angeles fell by over 11 percent in 1991.

These examples hide the fact that some property owners have been facing much larger than average declines in the value of their property. The savings and loan crisis has highlighted the fact that as the real estate market fell sharply in some areas, the owners of a substantial number of properties, especially commercial developments, defaulted on their mortgages, which in too many cases were held by (now-defunct) S&Ls. In addition, many homeowners are suffering from the decline in market values away from the glare of television cameras and out of sight of newspaper reporters. For example, in Boston, the value of many houses purchased in the late 1980s (1986–9) was 25 to 30 percent less in 1992 than the purchase price. The current value of many houses is below the amount of the outstanding mortgage. As a consequence, homeowners are, at best, locked into their current houses. Many of those who have lost their jobs will lose their homes and forfeit their downpayments.[1]

Although falling property values have a direct impact on individuals, the purpose of this chapter is to explore the impact of the decline in property values on big-city finances. Many big cities are in financial trouble; many face the near-term prospect of large budget deficits. Discussions of large service cuts, increases in city taxes and fees, and in a few cases the possibility of bankruptcy are regularly reported in the press. Crystal-ball gazing is a risky business, and I don't claim any special proficiency. In fact, I must admit, that as I have been thinking about this question, my crystal ball has become cloudier. Nevertheless, I would like to speculate about whether the ongoing decline in property tax bases will lead to a rash of city fiscal crises, with city governments unable to function in an ordinary manner.

A second purpose of this chapter is to explore the options available to city governments facing serious fiscal problems induced by falling property values or other factors.

I have found it useful to address the question of whether declines in market value will result in fiscal crisis in large American cities by asking five specific questions:

- *How important is the property tax in the financing of city services?* As the most direct link between market values and the fiscal health of cities is the property tax, we must begin by asking what role the property tax plays in financing city governments.

- *Are the current declines in market values an ordinary cyclical occurrence?* Are declines in property values common events in large cities, occurring with some regularity during recessions? Are property values naturally cyclical, and are we now observing the down side of a boom-and-bust pattern that has been repeated often in history? Or are there indications that the pattern we are currently observing is somehow unique?

- *Can we expect market values to rebound quickly and to continue growing at a reasonable rate?* Even if market values are depressed now, can we expect them to rebound quickly?

- *Have falling property values been reflected in shrinking city tax bases?* As the property tax is levied on the assessed value of properties, we must ask how well changes in the real estate market are reflected in city tax bases, namely, the assessed value of property. This is a question about both the efficiency of tax administration and about fiscal institutions put in place explicitly to loosen the link between the real estate market and a city's property tax base.

• *How do we recognize a city fiscal crisis?* What questions should we ask? Will shrinking property tax bases lead to municipal bankruptcies? What difficulties will cities face in providing "reasonable" levels of public services at affordable rates of taxation?

Measuring changes in the market of real property in American cities is not an easy task. There exist no comprehensive national data on trends in the market value of property. The most recent data for a broad sample of US cities date from 1981.[2] The only way to compile current data on market values is to collect them on a city-by-city basis; I have, therefore, chosen to concentrate my attention on the experiences of a handful of large cities that have experienced large recent reductions in property values. Although these cities do not constitute in any way a random sample of all large cities, I believe their experiences in the last few years are indicative of broader trends as well as being of interest in their own right.[3]

How Important is the Property Tax in the Financing of City Services?

As documented by Dick Netzer, over the course of this century the property tax has been slowly declining as a source of municipal finance. Nevertheless, in many large cities, it sill accounts for an important portion of locally raised revenues. The property tax accounted for nearly 29 percent of own-source general revenue and 42.5 percent of own-source tax revenue in FY 1989 in the nation's fifty-three largest cities. This percentage understates the impact of the property tax on residents of big cities because forty-five of the largest fifty-three cities have independent school districts that rely on it heavily.

The importance of the property tax varies substantially among cities currently experiencing declining property values. On one extreme, Boston gets about 64 percent of its total locally raised revenue from the property tax. On the other extreme, Philadelphia relies on the property tax for less than 15 percent of its total own-source revenue. In between are Los Angeles (20 percent), New York City (32 percent), Dallas (37 percent), and Baltimore (52 percent).

To the extent that weak real estate markets do in fact translate into reductions in property tax revenues, nearly all cities will be affected, but clearly the potential impact of falling property values will be greater in cities like Boston that rely heavily on the property tax.

Are the Current Declines in Market Values an Ordinary Cyclical Occurrence?

Data series on changes in the market value of property in the nation's largest cities are simply not available. Thus, it is not possible to provide a definitive answer to a question about the cyclical nature of property values. Although the current recession has almost certainly had a negative impact on property values, it appears that those cities where property values have fallen the most are those cities that experienced the largest increases in property values during the 1980s. Based on limited data, it also appears that while during recent recessions market values may have stagnated, actual declines in value were relatively rare. In California, for example, housing prices rose rapidly from the mid-1970s through 1981; despite the severe recession during the early 1980s, housing prices in California stopped increasing but did not decline. As the housing market softens, homeowners tend to respond by staying put or by leaving homes on the market for a long period, until they get an offer at or near the asking price. In a recent paper, Karl Case and Robert Shiller (1988) drew on a survey of recent homebuyers to explore the reasons that residential real estate prices tend to be sticky downward. Among the reasons they suggest for observed price rigidity are the high transactions cost involved in selling a house, a psychological disposition to hold on to losing investments so as "to avoid the pain of regret," and a widely held belief that waiting may in fact pay off.

Although the statistical evidence is limited, it appears that the current decline in market values, especially in the residential real estate market, is a relatively rare phenomenon, one that is not automatically associated with economic downturns.

Can We Expect Market Values to Rebound Quickly and to Continue Growing at a Reasonable Rate?

There is no easy answer to this question. As James Follain indicates, there is considerable debate over the future of housing prices. In a study that has received a great deal of attention, Mankiw and Weil (1989) predicted a fall in the real price of housing of nearly 50 percent over the next twenty years. Follain, on the other hand, argues that the real value of housing will increase modestly during the 1990s. If a city's underlying economy remains strong, there are good reasons to believe market values will rebound. One hypothesis is that in cities such as Houston and Dallas, which had market values that were near the national average before values started to decline, we can expect a complete and relatively rapid rebound of prices. In the Northeast and in California, it is reasonable to assume that speculative pressures pushed housing values much higher than the national average and that now that the speculative bubble has burst, real estate prices will take many years to return to their previous (nominal) highs. Karl Case (1991) suggests that in Boston, following a tremendous boom and a precipitous decline, the real estate market has returned to about where it was in 1984. He points out, however, that in 1984 the Massachusetts economy was much stronger than it is now. In 1984 the state unemployment rate was 4.8 percent, while in early 1992 it was over 9.1 percent. This suggests, that at least in Boston, recovery of the real estate market will take a long time.

It is also likely that the market value of central city office buildings will experience limited growth well into the 1990s. Vacancy rates in major downtown office buildings have been increasing over the past several years (CB Commercial 1991). Although in many of the nation's largest cities on the east and west coasts, vacancy rates are still below the national average (as of December 1991), several factors suggest that rates may rise in 1993 and beyond, continuing to put downward pressure on the market values of commercial property. In a number of cities, large office building projects that were begun in 1988 and 1989 are just now coming onto the market, further increasing the excess supply of office space. In addition, mortgages on a number of downtown commercial buildings (especially second tier, class B property) were held by now bankrupt savings and loans. Many of these properties are now held by the Federal Deposit Insurance Company or the Resolution Trust Corporation. Both of these organizations have strong incentives to sell these properties as quickly as possible, further depressing the commercial real estate market.

Have Falling Property Values Been Reflected in Shrinking City Tax Bases?

A weak real estate market will have a direct impact on a city's property tax base only if the *assessed value* of property is reduced to reflect falling market values. Until quite recently, in most cities changes in assessments were made infrequently. In some cases, decades passed between reassessments (Oldman and Aaron 1965). As long as reassessments were conducted infrequently, taxpayers were unaffected by either increases or decreases in the market value of their property. However, a direct consequence of infrequent assessments was a high degree of assessment inequity between and within neighborhoods.

Two things happened about fifteen years ago that led to substantial improvements in the quality of assessments in many parts of the country. First was the widespread adoption of Computer Assisted Mass Assessment (CAMA) techniques. CAMA relies on the development of a hedonic index based on data on the physical and locational characteristics of a sample of recently sold properties. Assessed values for properties that have not sold are determined by values attributed to each characteristic from the hedonic regression. The major impact of CAMA is that it allows local governments to completely reassess all property on an annual or biannual basis.

A series of state court decisions, for the most part in the late 1970s, also led to greatly improved assessment quality. In a number of states, including New York, Texas, and Massachusetts, the courts ruled that assessments had to be conducted in a timely fashion and had to reflect the true market value of property.

As a result of these two factors, falling market values in a number of states are probably for the first time being quite accurately reflected in assessed values. Let me provide two examples: In Boston, the assessed value of property mirrored the rapid rise in market values during most of the 1980s and the steep decline during the beginning of the 1990s. Because by statute assessed values in any given fiscal year reflect the market values six months before the start of the fiscal year, the downturn in assessments lags the downturn in the real estate market. Thus, the assessed value of all taxable property reached a peak of $36.4 billion in FY 1991 and then fell by 18 percent to $29.8 billion in FY 1992 (City of Boston 1991). Although the housing market bottomed out by the third quarter of 1991, it appears that the value of commercial property, especially in the Boston Central Business District, is continuing to fall (during the first half of 1992). Thus, it is extremely likely that the value of Boston's tax base will be lower in FY 1993 than in FY 1992.

Texas has experienced a severe and more protracted decline in property values than most of the rest of the country. The precipitous drop in petroleum prices in the mid-1980s led to a decline in the value of property starting in 1985. In Houston, the market hit bottom in FY 1989, while in Dallas prices were falling through FY 1991. In both cities the assessed value of property has followed the decline of market values quite closely (State of Texas 1992).

Another important reason that assessed values tend to reflect falling market values is that owners of property, especially commercial property, are highly motivated to appeal their assessments (apply for an abatement). In recent years there has been a growth of firms, sometimes franchised, that will file commercial appeals on a contingency basis. The major bond-rating agencies have recently paid increased attention to the magnitude of cities' "abatement liabilities." City governments must convince the rating agencies that they are not going to have to abate large amounts of property tax revenue as a result of successful appeals of assessments. This implicit pressure from the bond-rating agencies is likely to lead to relatively conservative assessments of commercial property.

In a falling real estate market, homeowners, especially those anxious to sell, are more likely to appeal their assessments because they are too low rather than too high. Especially in cities with large amounts of nonresidential property, these appeals by homeowners are likely to be unsuccessful because the consequence of overassessing residential property is that city residents will collectively have to bear a larger share of the city's property tax levy relative to the owners of business property.

Prior to the series of court cases mandating full market value assessments, residential property tended to be assessed at a much lower proportion of market value than commercial and industrial property. The process of bringing all property up to its market value would have resulted in a substantial shift in the total property tax levy from business to residential taxpayers. The potential political consequences of increased property taxes on residents, with no corresponding increase in public services, led a number of states to search for ways to prevent this shift. Several states, including Massachusetts, adopted a system of property tax classification that allowed local governments to tax residential property at a lower rate than nonresidential property. In California in 1978, the voters approved Proposition 13, which not only placed a 1 percent ceiling on effective property tax rates but limited increases in the assessed value of individual properties to 2 percent per annum, unless the property was sold, in which case its assessment would be increased to reflect its current market value.

An important (perhaps unintended) consequence of Proposition 13 is that local governments are partially sheltered from the consequences of declining market values. For example, in San Francisco, where market values grew rapidly in the late 1980s, property tax revenues actually increased by an annual rate of about 10 percent even though the property tax rate was slightly reduced. The rapid growth in property taxes occurred because of a quite active real estate market, allowing in many cases dramatic increases in the assessed value of the properties being sold. Since 1990 although property values in San Francisco have been falling, total assessed value continues to rise, albeit at a much slower annual rate (about 5 percent). To see how rising assessed values can occur as market values fall, consider a house, assessed at $75,000, that has been lived in by the same owner since the early 1970s. In 1990 assume that this house had a market value of $400,000. Since then, its value has fallen by 12.5 percent to $350,000, at which price it is sold. Although its value has fallen in recent years, its assessed value suddenly climbs by $275,000.

New York State responded to a court case (*Hellerstein v. Assessor, Town of Islip*) that would have resulted in a substantial shift of property tax liabilities from commercial-industrial to residential taxpayers, by allowing local governments to tax residential property at a different rate from nonresidential property. In addition, the state passed a law requiring that any assessment increases on most types of property had to be phased in over a period of several years. Thus, for example, for one-, two-, or three-family houses, assessment increases cannot exceed 6 percent in any given year or 20 percent over a five-year period. Annual assessment increases on large apartment buildings (over ten units) and on commercial-industrial property are not limited but must be phased in over five years. The consequence of these assessment limits is that while market values in New York City have fallen by about 10 percent over the past three years, total assessed value has continued to climb – by about 9 percent per year between 1989 and 1991 and by 3 percent from 1991 to 1992 (City of New York 1992).

New York's assessment restrictions shelter taxpayers from rapid increases in assessed value. As a consequence, the city's tax base only partially reflected the explosive growth in market values that occurred during the 1980s. The flip side of this is that when property values began to fall, the city's tax base continued to rise. New York City is currently projecting rates of growth in its tax base of about 1 percent per year for FY 1993 and FY 1994 (New York State Financial Control Board 1991). As New York City currently is facing a deficit, the fact that its property tax base is stable in light of a declining real estate market is a big plus.

Despite the fact that the quality of assessments is quite high in many cities, assessors, who tend to be conservative, often set assessed values a little below market values. This means that we should not expect modest declines in market value to be reflected in falling assessed values. As noted above, a number of states have taken steps to insulate taxpayers from the impact of increasing assessments. From the standpoint of municipal finance, these actions reduce the ability of local governments to tap the expansion in the real wealth of its citizens. At the same time

these provisions tend to protect governments from one direct consequence of economic downturns, namely, a reduction in the size of the
property tax base.

How Do We Recognize a City Fiscal Crisis?

In order to predict the likely impact of declining property values on the
fiscal health of big cities, it is important to start with a clear picture of
cities' current fiscal health. If one relies on reports in the press, it is clear
that big cities are in very bad fiscal condition. Let's review some of the
recent reports: In the spring of 1991 Philadelphia was on the verge of
bankruptcy, facing a FY 1992 deficit of $230 million and the adamant
refusal of the banking community to lend it any more money. Only by
agreeing to accept the control of a fiscal watchdog agency appointed by
the state, did Philadelphia regain limited access to the credit markets. In
1991 New York City faced the prospect of a $3.3 billion deficit for FY
1992. Only by raising property tax rates and instituting major spending
cuts will the city be able to balance its budget. San Francisco is also in
the throes of a fiscal crisis: Current projections indicate a FY 1993
general fund deficit of $120 million (out of a $1.5 billion budget). The
city's new mayor campaigned on a pledge not to raise taxes, a pledge he
continues to support. At the same time he continues to promise that
there will be no service cuts. The outcome is unclear.

Despite the dramatic nature of these stories, they fail to provide an
accurate picture of the fiscal position of city governments. They reflect
budgetary practices and the consequences of short-term events. To get a
good sense of the "structural" fiscal health of a city government requires
knowledge of how well the city government performs its basic function,
the provision of public services to city residents, *relative* to the burden it
places on its residents. Thus a city that always balances its budget and
provides a minimum level of public services may be in very weak fiscal
health if it must tax residents at extraordinarily high rates. Alternatively,
a city that manages to maintain both balanced budgets and moderate tax
rates may nevertheless be fiscally stressed if its level of service provision
is very low, with, for example, trash infrequently collected, police not
available, and large classes in its schools. The fact that a city goes
bankrupt or doesn't go bankrupt is not necessarily a good indicator of its
fiscal health.[4]

I want to argue that it is most useful to focus on the *structural*
components of a city's fiscal health, rather than on its short-run budgetary situation. Following Bradbury et al. (1984), let me define a city's
fiscal condition as a gap, expressed in dollars per capita, between a city's

expenditure need and *revenue-raising capacity*. A city's expenditure need indicates the amount that it must spend per resident to provide an average level of public services given its service responsibilities and the harshness of its environment for providing services. A harsh environment increases the costs of providing services, where costs reflect the effects of city characteristics that are outside the control of city officials. A city's revenue-raising capacity indicates the amount of revenue per resident it has available if residents of all cities face the same tax burden.

If this gap, called the *need-capacity gap* is large, a city government will be forced to provide less-than-average-quality public services and/or burden its residents with higher-than-average taxes. Cities in weak fiscal condition by this measure will find it particularly hard to compete with surrounding suburban communities for middle- and high-income residents and for jobs for its residents.

In their book *America's Ailing Cities*, Helen Ladd and John Yinger (1991) provide a measure of the fiscal health of the nation's largest cities using a variant of the need-capacity gap. They find that many of the nation's largest central cities are in very weak fiscal health, with expenditure need substantially greater than revenue-raising capacity. Based on data for 1982, they conclude that the fourteen central cities in the weakest fiscal health would on average have to raise their revenue-raising capacity by 13 percent in order to provide their residents with an average quality of public services while imposing an average tax burden on them. Among the cities in the weakest fiscal position are New York City, New Orleans, and Detroit. Cities in weak fiscal health generally face a number of structural fiscal problems: first, they operate in a harsh fiscal environment, where the costs of providing services are high; second, they often have a wide range of service responsibilities mandated by higher levels of government or by the courts; and third, they face substantial loss in their economic base, as measured in part by falling city employment, especially in the high-wage manufacturing sector.

Ladd and Yinger (1991) demonstrate that the growth in the economy during the 1980s increased the revenue-raising capacity of many large cities. However, the resulting improvements in the fiscal conditions of city governments were offset by two important trends. First, in almost all cities a series of developments over the past decade, most notably the crack-cocaine epidemic, the spread of AIDS, and the explosion of homelessness, have made the fiscal environment much harsher. Although no precise data are available, these factors have undoubtedly raised the costs of public services and increased the expenditure need of many, if not all, large cities. Second, during the past decade cities have had to become steadily more self reliant. During this period the amount of federal aid received by city governments has been dramatically reduced. In Boston, the proportion of general revenue coming from federal grants fell by more than half between 1979 and 1989, from 9 percent to under 4 percent. In San Francisco, the federal share of general revenue fell from 14 to 5 percent during the same ten-year period (US Bureau of the Census 1991). Similar reductions occurred in most large cities.

City governments have been further buffeted by state cuts in grants-in-aid. Gold (1992) reports that in 1991 fourteen states reduced their general assistance to local governments. In some states aid cuts have been substantial. For example, state general-purpose aid to Boston has been cut by about $80 million between FY 1989 and FY 1992 and will be level funded in FY 1993. This amounts to a constant-dollar reduction in aid of 32 percent.

To date no data are available to indicate whether recent state aid cutbacks have favored suburban and rural communities at the expense of large urban communities. However, it appears that a politically popular way of cutting aid is to reduce each community's aid by an equal percentage. When the initial distribution of aid favors big cities, the result of equal percentage cuts is a large reduction in aid relative to total spending in big cities than in smaller places.[5]

The fiscal health of city governments may also be hurt by state government cuts in social service expenditures. A growing number of states are substantially reducing welfare programs, in particular general assistance. Cuts in Medicaid coverage are also widespread. As many of the beneficiaries of these programs are big-city residents, it is at least possible, and I suspect probable, that an unintended effect of these state budget cuts will be increased costs for city governments. This shifting of costs from state to local governments may occur if people whose state-funded benefits are cut end up in cities' homeless shelters, in the emergency rooms of city hospitals, or in cities' criminal justice systems.

At the beginning of this chapter I posed the following question: Will the decline in property values in many of the nation's large cities lead to a new round of fiscal crises? The answer, I believe is that although a shrinking tax base will complicate the fiscal problems faced by city governments, its impact on the structural fiscal problems of cities will be relatively minor. The combination of rising costs, declining federal, and in some cases state, fiscal assistance, and deteriorating economic conditions in many of the nation's largest cities suggests that the fiscal condition of these cities is deteriorating. A temporary fall in market values will certainly exacerbate the fiscal situation, but by itself will not create a new wave of budgetary crises.

Most of the cities experiencing the largest reductions in property values also benefited from the largest increases in values during the late 1980s. I would contend that for many of these cities, the rapid run-up in prices had the effect of delaying the most visible signs of the underlying fiscal crisis. The current fall in market values works in the other direction.

How Can Cities Respond to Falling Market Values?

In the rest of the chapter I turn to the question of how cities can respond to falling market values. My primary focus will be on the option of increasing property tax rates. I will also briefly consider two other options: cutting public spending and adopting alternative revenue sources.

Increasing property tax rates

Raising nominal property tax rates seems like the obvious response to reduced assessed values. Unless rates are raised, nominal property tax liabilities will actually decline for property owners whose property has lost value. Since property taxes are paid out of current income and even during a recession income remains constant or increases for most tax-payers, increases in rates won't increase burdens as long as total property tax liabilities increase less rapidly than incomes.

The argument for raising nominal property tax rates is strengthened by the fact that in a substantial number of large cities, property tax burdens declined during much of the 1980s.[6] For examples, consider the recent fiscal history in Boston, New York, and San Francisco:

Boston In 1980 Massachusetts adopted a property tax classification system that allowed local governments to tax residential property at a substantially lower rate than commercial-industrial property. In 1981, with the passage of Proposition $2\frac{1}{2}$, effective property tax rates were limited to $2\frac{1}{2}$ percent, and annual property tax increases were limited to $2\frac{1}{2}$ percent of the current levy, plus the tax levied on new construction. As a consequence of classification and Proposition $2\frac{1}{2}$, and a very strong construction boom during the mid-1980s, Boston was able to reduce residential property taxes over the past decade. In current dollars, the average tax on single-family homes and condominiums declined from $1,732 in FY 1981 to $1,211 in FY 1992 (City of Boston 1991). In constant dollars this represents a tax reduction of 60 percent. Measured relative to income, the average residential property tax burden declined from 4.1 percent in FY 1981 to 1.9 percent in FY 1992.

New York City   Owners of single and duplex houses are favored by the property tax system in New York. During the 1980s, the tax burden shifted increasingly away from those residents and toward owners of apartment buildings and commercial property. Although tax levies on one- and two-family houses rose in nominal terms during the 1980s, the rate of increase was below the rate of inflation. In the ten years since 1979 the market value of residential property increased dramatically. As a result, the effective residential property tax rate fell by more than half, from 2.15 percent in 1979 to 0.85 percent in 1989 (Chernick 1992).

San Francisco   Because of Proposition 13, effective property tax rates depend primarily on the length of time since properties were last sold. In the active and rapidly rising San Francisco real estate market during the latter half of the 1980s, there was a sharp drop in the effective tax rates faced by property owners who chose not to move. Between 1981 and 1989 the nominal tax rate also fell, from 1.20 to 1.09 percent (City of San Francisco 1991).

Despite the fact that property tax burdens have declined in a number of cities during the 1980s, there is at least limited evidence that city governments are unwilling to raise rates even in the face of a shrinking tax base.

In California, where Proposition 13 has capped rates, raising rates is not an option, as cities already tax at the maximum 1 percent. In New York City, where property tax rates were raised in 1992, Mayor Dinkins promised not to raise rates for the next four years. In Boston, property tax rates have increased during the past three years from approximately $8 per thousand to $11 per thousand; however, the current rate is still only about half of the 1983 rate, and further rate increases are likely to be prevented by the $2\frac{1}{2}$ percent levy limit mandated by Proposition $2\frac{1}{2}$. Although Boston residents can vote to override the levy limit, the prospects of a successful override are small. Through FY 1990 none of the state's twenty-one city governments with populations over 50,000 had even attempted an override. In FY 1991, facing a falling real estate market and substantial cuts in state aid, five cities attempted an override, and only two were successful (Bradbury 1991).[7]

Why property tax rates won't rise

Resistance to property tax rate increases is likely to continue not only in cities where property tax burdens have been rising, but also in cities like Boston and New York, where property tax burdens have been declining in recent years.

I believe there are two important reasons why city government officials are likely to oppose property tax rate increases. First is their desire to remain fiscally competitive with surrounding suburban communities. There is considerable evidence that tax rates and the quality of public services, especially schools, play a role in determining metropolitan area locational choices of both firms and individuals (Reschovsky 1979, Wasylenko 1980, McGuire 1985, Luce and Summers 1987). City officials recognize that regardless of whether their property tax rates are higher or lower than rates in surrounding communities, increases in city rates relative to suburban rates will lead to outmigration by middle- and high-income residents and by business enterprises.[8]

Although comprehensive data are not available, it appears that in a number of metropolitan areas property values have fallen more in the central city than in many of the surrounding suburbs. For example, in Boston the average assessed value of existing property has fallen by about twice as much as property in the adjacent suburban communities. This pattern of changes in values obviously weakens the relative fiscal position of cities and implies that tax rate increases sufficient to maintain current property tax levies will result in an increase in the ratio of city to suburban tax rates. This puts cities in a difficult position. If they choose to maintain their relative tax rate vis-à-vis their suburbs, they will have to operate with reduced property tax revenues. On the other hand, if they raise their rates in order to increase or maintain property tax revenues, their competitive position is weakened.

A second, more speculative, reason city officials may resist any property tax rate increases involves the rising political costs of raising taxes. The newspapers are full of examples of voter anger at politicians who raise taxes or, in some cases, even propose to raise taxes. A prime example is New Jersey, where voters responded to a tax increase approved by a Democratic governor and legislature by providing the Republicans with a veto-proof majority in both houses of the legislature.

One explanation for this (presumed) rise in opposition to both increased public spending and taxes is that *distributional politics* has changed in the last decade or so. As demonstrated by the data in table 23.1, cities have become more ethnically and racially heterogeneous. I hypothesize that as heterogeneity has increased, people have become much more conscious of the distribution of taxes and services among groups of city residents. I suspect that many people, especially in big cities, no longer assume that in return for paying their taxes, they get a bundle of services, such as police and fire protection, sanitation, and public education. Now the question that is asked is, "Will I benefit from a tax increase, or will it all go to 'them' [meaning peoples of other economic, social, or ethnic

Table 23.1 Change in minority population between 1980 and 1990 in thirty largest American cities

| City | 1990 population (in percent) | | | Percentage change from 1980* | | |
	Black	Asian	Hispanic	Black	Asian	Hispanic
New York	28.6	7.0	24.4	13.9	114.2	22.6
Los Angeles	14.0	9.8	39.9	−17.6	48.7	45.1
Chicago	39.1	3.7	19.6	−1.8	61.1	40.0
Houston	28.1	4.1	27.6	1.8	99.7	56.8
Philadelphia	39.9	2.7	5.6	5.6	157.5	47.4
San Diego	9.4	11.8	20.7	5.6	81.0	38.9
Detroit	75.7	0.8	2.8	20.0	49.0	16.7
Dallas	29.5	2.2	20.9	0.3	192.8	69.9
Phoenix	5.2	1.7	20.0	8.3	89.2	35.1
San Antonio	7.0	1.1	55.6	−4.1	74.7	3.5
San Jose	4.7	19.5	26.6	2.2	140.0	19.3
Baltimore	59.2	1.1	1.0	8.0	9.4	0.0
Indianapolis	22.6	0.9	1.1	3.7	67.8	22.2
San Francisco	10.9	29.1	13.9	−14.2	32.0	13.0
Jacksonville	25.2	1.9	2.6	−0.8	98.1	44.4
Columbus	22.6	2.4	1.1	2.3	188.5	37.5
Milwaukee	30.5	1.9	6.3	32.0	245.3	53.7
Memphis	54.8	0.8	0.7	15.1	92.8	−12.5
Washington, D.C.	65.8	1.8	5.4	−6.4	75.1	92.9
Boston	25.6	5.3	10.8	14.3	97.5	68.8
Seattle	10.1	11.8	3.6	6.3	59.5	38.5
El Paso	3.4	1.2	69.0	6.2	47.0	10.4
Cleveland	46.6	1.0	4.6	6.4	69.3	48.4
New Orleans	61.9	1.9	3.5	11.9	44.0	2.9
Nashville-Davidson	24.3	1.4	0.9	4.3	190.2	12.5
Denver	12.8	2.4	23.0	6.7	67.8	22.3
Austin	12.4	3.0	23.0	1.6	188.3	23.0
Fort Worth	22.0	2.0	19.5	−3.5	227.7	54.8
Oklahoma City	16.0	2.4	5.0	9.6	130.9	78.6
Portland, OR	7.7	5.3	3.2	1.3	86.3	52.4
Kansas City	29.6	1.2	3.9	8.0	60.0	18.2
Long Beach	13.7	13.6	23.6	21.2	154.9	68.6
St. Louis	47.5	0.9	1.3	4.2	148.6	8.3
Atlanta	67.1	0.9	1.9	0.8	80.0	35.7
Pittsburgh	25.8	1.6	0.9	7.5	161.9	12.5

* Minus signs indicate the decrease in minority population from 1980 to 1990.
Source: 1980 and 1990 US Census, United States Summary, General Population Characteristic, Tables: Persons by race and sex for areas and places.

backgrounds]?. If this question is in fact being asked, it means that, at least in the minds of many city residents, the link between taxes and benefits has been severed, or at best, weakened.

Those taxpayers for whom the link between changes in taxes and changes in benefits is broken may be much less willing to pay increased taxes to finance increased public spending. It is important to emphasize that changing attitudes and perceptions about public services do not necessarily tell us anything about the preferences for public services of the median voter, only that politically important subgroups of the population may have strongly divergent views.

In order to understand the impacts of these changing perceptions on governmental action it is important to have an underlying model of city government decision making. The conventional model focuses on the median or the "decisive" voter. It is assumed that in order to get elected or reelected, politicians will support policies that reflect the preferences of the decisive voter. Building on the work of Inman (1989) and Chernick (1990), I would like to suggest a model of city government decision making that in contrast to the decisive-voter model, focuses on the impact of various *groups* of citizens within a city on the *political costs* of public decisions. Let us assume that politicians attempt to minimize a political cost function that includes a number of variables that reflect the distribution of public sector benefits and taxes within the city. From the perspective of the politician who must decide whether to propose increased taxes and spending, the political costs are likely to be lowest when politically powerful groups of voters perceive that they will receive net benefits from the proposed increases. On the other hand, political costs are likely to be highest when influential groups of voters believe that in relative terms, other groups of voters will receive the largest benefits. For example, a resident of a middle-class bedroom suburb is likely to believe that his children will benefit directly from a proposed increase in taxes used for public education, while a middle-class resident of a city may believe that extra tax revenue for education will primarily benefit other groups of children, such as those requiring special or remedial education. This implies that the political costs of proposing tax and spending increases may depend critically on the *distribution* of tax burdens and public spending benefits within a community.

The factors that affect the distribution of public service benefits within a community are thus likely to influence the political costs of decision making. For example, communities with a relatively large group of elderly residents may oppose tax increases, especially those for schools. The political costs of increasing taxes and spending may also be higher in places with relatively large poor or minority populations.

This model suggests that if larger communities are characterized by greater population heterogeneity, the political costs of raising taxes may be high if enough groups fear that too much of the additional spending will go to other groups. Political costs may also be high if officials in larger communities have greater uncertainty about voter preferences. Given risk aversion, they will then be less likely to propose tax and spending increases.

One possible consequence of falling property values may be to increase the political cost of raising taxes. I hypothesize that political costs will rise if falling property values are associated with shifts in the *share* of taxes paid by various groups of city residents. Any shifting of taxes among taxpayers implies that there are winners and losers. The losers pay higher taxes but receive no extra benefits, while the winners get a windfall. If the losers are more numerous or more politically powerful than the winners, the result of a shift in the tax base is likely to be heightened opposition to increased spending. In a number of cities the value of commercial property fell much more than the value of residential property, implying a shift in taxes from businesses to residents. There has also been a tendency in some cities for high-valued houses to decline at a much greater rate than low-valued houses. As a result of this pattern, property tax liabilities are shifted from business and high-income families to homeowners of relatively modestly valued houses, a group that in many cities is quite politically active.

Let me provide examples from three cities where declining property values appear to be associated with a shift in the share of property tax liabilities being levied on low- and moderate-income homeowners.

- In Boston, commercial property, primarily downtown office buildings, and high-value houses and condominiums fell in value much more than low-value residential property. While many commercial and high-value residential properties lost about a quarter of their value, low-value houses lost very little value.

- Using data on repeat sales in Los Angeles, Karl Case and Robert Shiller have calculated that in 1991 residential values for the one-third of houses with the highest prices dropped by 11 percent, while the values of the cheapest one-third of houses declined by 1 percent.

- Between 1987 and 1991 the assessed value of single-family houses in Dallas fell by 14 percent, while during the same period the assessed value of industrial property declined by 33 percent (State of Texas 1992).

Voter resistance to higher taxes may also be increasing for several reasons not directly related to falling property values. Budgetary pressure in a number of states has led state governments to cut the amount of fiscal assistance going to city governments. For example, in Boston, state general-purpose aid in FY 1992 is 22 percent below its FY 1989 level. Substantial cuts in state aid have also occurred in a number of other states, including New York, Ohio, Minnesota, Maryland, and Michigan. As a consequence of these aid cuts, local revenue must be used to replace state revenue. As a result, city residents see their taxes going up but do not benefit from any corresponding increase in public services.[9] Again, the link between taxes and service provision has been weakened.

During the past ten years cities have had to respond to a number of new problems, such as homelessness, the AIDs epidemic, and the spread of crack-cocaine. Although it is likely that the majority of city residents believe that government has a responsibility to respond to these problems, the fact remains that much of the cost of the response must be borne by city residents. Cities respond directly to problems by adding newly targeted services – for example, the construction of shelters for the homeless. However, the growth of these new problems also tends to increase the costs to city governments of providing core city services such as police and fire protection, sanitation, and public health. The consequence of the city spending money in response to these problems is that city residents see their taxes increasing at the same time that the quality of the core city services declines or, in the best case, remains unchanged. Again, added taxes are not associated with added public services.

A rational response to these higher costs of providing city services may be to demand fewer services. In a study of local governments in Massachusetts, using 1980 data, Bradbury et al. (1984) statistically identified a set of community characteristics that are beyond control of local officials yet lead to higher spending. Among the "cost factors" they identified were the population density, the crime rate, and the fraction of housing units built before 1940. In a recent study, again using Massachusetts data, Reschovsky and Schwartz (1992a) found that when 1991 data were analyzed most of the cost factors identified in the Bradbury et al. study were not statistically significant determinants of local government spending. One explanation of their inability to identify cost factors is that voters have responded to the higher costs of public services by opposing spending increases. If this is in fact the case, then high values of the cost factors will no longer be associated with higher levels of city government spending.

A further reason why resistance to higher property taxes may be increasing is that the cost of the property tax has risen for many homeowners as a direct result of the Tax Reform Act of 1986 (TRA). As the property tax is deductible, itemizers are able to reduce their total tax burden by an amount equal to their property tax liability times their federal marginal tax rate. TRA reduced marginal tax rates and, by increasing the standard deduction and limiting some deductible items, substantially reduced the number of itemizers. On the margin these provisions raised the tax price of an additional dollar of property taxes. Reschovsky and Chernick (1989) have estimated that as a result of TRA the demand for public services in central cities in New York State and Massachusetts declined by a small amount, probably no more than 1 percent.

The property tax creates a substantial burden on low-income residents. In a recent paper Chernick and Reschovsky (1990) calculated that in 1988 the average property tax burden (measured as taxes relative to income) for families below the poverty line was 7 percent in Massachusetts and 8.8 percent in New York. Families with incomes between 100 and 150 percent of the poverty line had burdens of 4.2 and 5.3 percent in the two states. (These calculations assume that landlords are able to shift 75 percent of the property tax to their tenants.) These are heavy burdens for people with extremely low incomes. It would not be surprising if many of the growing number of low-income residents of our large cities would thus be opposed to all tax increases, even if they know that they will suffer from public service cutbacks.

It is interesting to note that even though residential real estate values have fallen dramatically in a number of cities, the value of most homes is considerably higher in real terms than it was ten years ago. I would like to suggest that this gain in wealth has not resulted, as we might expect, in an increase in demand for public services by homeowners. In fact, I think the argument can be made that many homeowners completely capitalized their unrealized gain. In other words, they assumed that market values couldn't decline, and they adjusted their consumption stream to reflect their new level of wealth. Thus, when values declined, they tended to react with anger. They felt "entitled" to the high values and believed they had suffered a real loss when property values dropped. One outlet for their frustration and anger has been city government. Hence, for all the reasons outlined, I conclude that the prospects for increasing property tax rates are extremely small.

Cutting spending

There are four major strategies that city governments could follow to reduce total spending:

(1)   Cities could take steps to increase the efficiency or productivity of public good provision. In many cases substantial cost savings can be

realized by instituting relatively simple changes in procedures. However, the ability of public officials to realize even modest increases in productivity is often stymied by civil service regulations or union work rules. A recent example illustrates both the promise of productivity increases and the difficulty in achieving them. In New York City, recent recycling efforts have substantially reduced the volume of ordinary trash that must be collected. As a consequence, on many routes sanitation workers are finishing their routes several hours early. Under current union work rules, the Sanitation Department is unable to reassign workers who finish routes early to other tasks, or to lengthen established trash collection routes. Sanitation workers must be paid for a full day's work even though they finish their routes several hours early. Although this situation has received extensive press coverage, negotiations to change these work rules have so far proved unsuccessful.

(2)   The wages and benefits of city employees could be either cut or frozen. As wages comprise the largest single component of city government expenditures, this strategy has the potential to reduce substantially city spending. A number of cities, including Houston and Boston, have recently resorted to wage freezes. Very little is known about the consequences of cutting wages for municipal employees. There are indications that at least in some cities, public employee compensation is substantially more generous than private sector compensation for comparable positions.[10] In cases in which a city government pays a compensation premium over competitive private sector wage levels, it is likely that wage freezes will not jeopardize a city's ability to attract high-quality workers. The question arises, however, of what happens if public sector wages fall below private sector wages for comparable jobs. We know very little about public sector labor markets. In particular, we need to answer the following questions:

- How hard will it be to find qualified public employees if wages fall below wage levels in equivalent private sector jobs?

- Will wage and benefit reductions reduce the morale of public employees so that productivity will fall?

- Will all the young and well-educated workers depart, leaving a less efficient workforce?

(3)   Public spending can clearly be reduced by eliminating some public services. In some cities there are few services that could be cut without placing substantial hardships on certain residents. In other cities, selective service reductions could probably be accomplished without causing

significant hardship. For example, Milwaukee still has behind-the-house trash collection; although its elimination may be politically difficult, it would create few real hardships. City officials face difficult decisions. On the one hand, opposition to tax increases may leave them with few options other than cutting public services. On the other hand, service cuts can be self-defeating if: (a) they lead a substantial number of people (presumably with middle- and upper-class incomes) to leave the city, or (b) they lead people to develop the attitude, "As the government isn't doing anything for me, why should I support higher taxes?"

(4)   A number of authors have recently argued that substantial public sector resources can be saved through *privatization* (Savas 1987, Donahue 1989).[11] City governments could, and perhaps should, get out of the business of providing goods and services that are essentially private in nature. I am skeptical, however, that the use of private firms to provide the core services, those characterized by substantial externalities, will both maintain broad access to the services and result in substantial cost saving. It is particularly unlikely that efforts at privatization will reduce costs if privatization merely replaces a single public sector supplier with a single private sector supplier. There is more promise of achieving cost reductions if a competitive situation, with multiple providers, can be set up within a city.

Although in most large cities there exist real possibilities for reducing costs, it is important to realize that a number of factors in the urban environment are likely to result in rising costs over the next few years. The following list is not meant to be comprehensive, but it includes a number of developments that will probably affect a large number of cities:

- A number of cities have large amounts of unfunded pension liabilities. An aging workforce in some cities means that over the next decade, as public employees retire in growing numbers, a growing fraction of current revenue will have to be allocated to pension payments. As an example of the magnitude of this problem, in Philadelphia 55 percent of all firefighters will reach retirement age within the next five years (City of Philadelphia 1992).

- The recent flooding of the Chicago Loop has only served to highlight the fact that a number of large cities, especially in the Northeast and Midwest, will have to invest substantial resources in repairing and modernizing their public infrastructure. Although deferred maintenance is a common way of dealing with short-run fiscal crises, eventually resources must be spent in order to maintain the viability of public facilities.

- A growing problem in a number of cities is the presence of toxic wastes on a large number of city-owned properties. For example, over the years the city of Milwaukee has acquired through tax fore-closures a number of properties that at some point housed dry cleaners. Unfortunately, many of those properties are badly contaminated with highly toxic dry-cleaning chemicals. The city is left with the responsibility for the cleanup and with little chance of financial reimbursement from the long-departed former owners.

- Despite the rhetoric to the contrary, over the past decade the federal government has passed legislation that will impose a number of costly mandates on city governments. In particular, legislation regulating air and water pollution and providing rights for disabled persons will place substantial liabilities on many city governments during the 1990s.

Increasing the Use of Nonproperty Taxes and User Fees

Aside from the political difficulties associated with raising taxes, the potential for increasing nonproperty taxes and user fees varies across cities. Cities such as Boston and Milwaukee get almost all their locally raised revenue from the property tax. They would benefit from expanded revenue options but are restricted from using alternative taxes by state law. On the other hand, the potential for revenue diversification is limited in San Francisco and New York because those two cities already levy a wide range of local taxes and hence have limited room for expansion to alternative tax instruments.

Conclusion

The fiscal prospects for most large American cities are not good. Although the recent declines in the market value of real estate in many of the nation's large cities will not by themselves lead to devastating fiscal crises, the long-run fiscal prospects are poor because the gap between the costs of providing an adequate level of public services and the revenue-raising capacity of cities is likely to increase over time. I believe that cities will find it increasingly harder to raise taxes from their citizens. Despite the recent attention paid to the plight of cities as a result of the

Los Angeles riots, the prospects of a substantial infusion of new state or federal money into cities are small.

Although it is hard to be optimistic about the long-run fiscal health of big cities, let me conclude by mentioning a few factors that may provide cities with needed rays of hope. First, demographic changes may favor cities. In particular, the number of young workers will decline over the next decade. This will probably lead to labor shortages that will drive up wages in relatively low-skill jobs, providing a mechanism for city residents, especially those now on welfare, to get into the labor force and out of poverty. Second, the growing congestion in the suburbs and the lack of infrastructure to deal with it may allow cities, with their existing public transit networks and infrastructure (like sidewalks), to regain appeal for both individuals and businesses. Third, it is possible that the growing momentum toward restructuring the American health-care system will result in shifting the burden of paying for the health-care needs of the poor completely away from state and local governments to the federal government. Finally, although falling housing prices worsen the fiscal condition of cities in the short run, lower prices may serve to reinvigorate city economies in the long run if they attract a new generation of people into central cities.

Notes

1 While some people suffer from the decline in real estate values, others benefit. The combination of lower mortgage interest rates and lower prices is enabling people to become homeowners who were previously excluded from the housing market.

2 The most recent data on the market value of real property in city governments come from the *1982 Census of Governments*. Collection of these data was discontinued in the 1987 census.

3 I should point out that market values are not declining everywhere. For the most part, property values rose slightly in the Midwest during the 1980s and have continued to rise during the early 1990s. One indication of the regional variation in real estate markets is provided by data from the American Housing Survey, which indicate that while median gross rents increased between 1985 and 1989 at an annual rate of 2.4 percent in the Northeast and 1.2 percent in the West, they decreased at an annual rate of 0.6 percent in the Midwest and 1.3 percent in the South (Apghar 1991).

4 A good example is Philadelphia, one of the few large eastern cities where property values have not fallen. I don't pretend to be an expert on that city, but I think it is clear that while Philadelphia has severe fiscal problems, there are other cities in worse fiscal health. Philadelphia's fiscal problems have a

lot to do with a recent history of weak and fragmented political leadership and hostile relationships between the city and the state government.

5   For a full discussion of consequences of alternative state-aid cutback strategies, see Reschovsky and Schwartz (1992b).

6   According to data compiled by the District of Columbia Department of Finance and Revenue, the effective residential property tax rate in the largest city in about half the states, was lower in 1990 than it was in 1981 (Government of the District of Columbia 1991).

7   Another example of the difficulty of obtaining voter approval to raise property taxes comes from Ohio, where increases in public school budgets cannot be adopted without explicit voter approval in a referendum. In Cleveland, despite repeated efforts to increase school spending, a school budget referendum has not been approved since the mid-1980s.

8   Although a reasonable model of intrametropolitan locational choices suggests that mobility is sensitive to the relative fiscal condition of the city rather than to tax rates alone, the visibility of the tax rates may lead city officials to overemphasize their importance. For example, in Milwaukee under Mayor John Norquist the central focus of the city's fiscal policy has been to reduce the city's mill rate each year. It should also be noted that in some metropolitan areas market values have declined more in the suburbs than in the central city, placing pressure on suburban communities to raise their tax rates.

9   Alternatively, city governments may choose not to replace state assistance. In that case, property taxes remain unchanged, but service levels are cut.

10 For example, in Philadelphia a recent study by the city controller and the Pennsylvania Economy League found that clerks and typists working for the city earned a premium over private sector compensation levels of 50 to 70 percent, janitors and cleaners a premium of nearly 50 percent, and security guards a premium of almost 85 percent (City of Philadelphia 1992).

11 For a well-balanced treatment of the privatization issue, see Gormley (1991).

References

Apgher, William C., Jr. 1991. "Housing the Nation's Poor." Paper prepared for presentation at the La Follette Institute Housing Conference. Madison: La Follette Institute of Public Affairs.

Bradbury, Katharine L. 1991. "Can Local Governments Give Citizens What The Want? Referendum Outcomes in Massachusetts." *New England Economic Review*, Federal Reserve Bank of Boston, May/June.

Bradbury, Katharine L. et al. 1984. "State Aid to Offset Fiscal Disparities Across Communities." *National Tax Journal* 37: 2 (June).

Case, Karl E. 1991. "The Real Estate Cycle and the Economy: Consequences of the Massachusetts Boom of 1984–7." *New England Economic Review*, Federal Reserve Bank of Boston, September/October.

Case, Karl E. and Shiller, Robert J. 1988. "The Behavior of Home Buyers in Boom and Post-Boom Markets." *New England Economic Review*, Federal Reserve Bank of Boston, November/December.

CB Commercial. 1991. "Office Vacancy Index of the United States, December 31, 1991." Los Angeles: CB Commercial Real Estate Group.

Chernick Howard. 1990. "Distributional Constraints on State Decisions to Tax." Paper presented at the 1990 National Bureau of Economic Research Summer Institute on State and Local Finance, Cambridge, Massachusetts.

Chernick, Howard. 1992. "Real Property Taxation in New York City: The Need for Immediate Reform." A report prepared by the City Project, New York, February.

Chernick, Howard and Reschovsky, Andrew. 1990. "The Taxation of the Poor." *Journal of Human Resources* 25: 712–35.

City of Boston. 1991. *Property Tax Facts and Figures; Fiscal Year 1992 Revaluation*. Boston: Assessing Department, fall.

City of New York. 1992. "Press Release on 1992 Assessments, January 15, 1992." New York: Finance Department.

City of Philadelphia. 1992. *Five-Year Financial Plan, Fiscal Year 1992–Fiscal Year 1996*. Philadelphia: Office of the Mayor.

City of San Francisco. 1991. *Comprehensive Annual Financial Report, Fiscal Year 1990–1*. San Francisco: Controllers' Office.

Donahue, John D. 1989. *The Privatizational Decision: Public Ends, Private Means*. New York: Basic Books.

Gold, Steven D. 1992. "State Policies Affecting Cities and Counties in 1991: Shift and Shaft Federalism?" *Public Budgeting & Finance* 12 (Spring): 23–46.

Gormley, William T. Jr., ed. 1991. *Privatization and Its Alternatives*. Madison: University of Wisconsin Press.

Government of the District of Columbia. 1991. *Tax Rates and Tax Burdens in the District of Columbia: A Nationwide Comparison*. Washington, D.C.: Department of Finance and Revenue.

Inman, Robert P. 1989. "The Local Decision to Tax: Evidence from Large US Cities." *Regional Science and Urban Economics* 19 (August): 455–91.

Ladd, Helen F., and Yinger, John. 1989. *America's Ailing Cities: Fiscal Health and the Design of Urban Policy*. Baltimore: Johns Hopkins University Press.

Ladd, Helen F. and Yinger, John. 1991. *America's Ailing Cities: Fiscal Health and the Design of Urban Policy*, Updated Edition. Baltimore: Johns Hopkins University Press.

Luce, Thomas F. and Summers, Anita A. 1987. *Local Fiscal Issues in the Philadelphia Metropolitan Area*. Philadelphia: University of Pennsylvania Press.

Mankiw, Gregory N. and Weil, David N. 1989. "The Baby Boom, the Baby Bust, and the Housing Market." *Regional Science and Urban Economics* 19: 235–58.

McGuire, Therese J. 1985. "Are Local Property Taxes Important in the Intrametropolitan Location Decisions of Firms? An Empirical Analysis of the Minneapolis–St. Paul Metropolitan Area." *Journal of Urban Economics* 18: 226–34.

New York State Financial Control Board. 1991. *Staff Report: New York City Financial Plan FY 1992–5*, August.

Oldman, Oliver, and Aaron, Henry. 1965. "Assessment-Sales Ratios Under the Boston Property Tax." *National Tax Journal* 18: 36–49.

Reschovsky, Andrew. 1979. "Residential Choice and the Local Public Sector: An Alternative Test of the Tiebout Hypothesis." *Journal of Urban Economics* 6: 501–20.

Reschovsky, Andrew and Chernick, Howard. 1989. "Federal Tax Reform and the Taxation of Urban Residents." *Public Finance Quarterly* 17: 123–57.

Reschovsky, Andrew and Schwartz, Amy Ellen. 1992a. "Evaluating the Success of Need-Based Aid in the Presence of Property Tax Limitations." *Public Finance Quarterly* 20: 489–506.

Reschovsky, Andrew and Schwartz, Amy Ellen. 1992b. "The Impacts of Grant-in-Aid Cutbacks on Fiscal Disparities among Recipient Governments." In *Public Finance with Several Levels of Government*, Proceedings of the 46th Congress of the International Institute of Public Finance, Brussels 1990, ed. Rémy Prud'homme. The Hague: Foundation Journal Public Finance.

Savas, E.S. 1987. *Privatization: The Key to Better Government*. Chatham, NJ: Chatham House.

State of Texas, Office of the Comptroller. 1992. "1991 Property Value Study." Austin: Property Tax Division, Comptroller of Public Accounts.

US Bureau of the Census. 1991. *City Government Finance*, Series GF. Washington, D.C.: Government Printing Office.

Wasylenko, Michael J. 1980. "Evidence of Fiscal Differentials and Intrametropolitan Firm Relocation." *Land Economics* 56: 337–49.

Introduction to Chapter 24

This article provides a succinct analysis of the strong expansion of federal aid to cities from 1960 to 1978 and the contraction of such aid from 1978 forward. Political and economic reasons are presented for both the expansion and the contraction. The author persuasively argues that the expansion of federal urban aid carried the seeds of its later contraction. Reischauer notes the hubris of the public policy establishment in the 1960s which assumed that urban problems, such as chronic unemployment, failing schools, and deteriorating neighborhoods, would be solved by programs designed by them and funded by the federal government. Indeed, he argues that the absence of conspicuous successes has contributed to public disfavor for urban interventions by the federal government. Reischauer realistically concludes that the likelihood of a resurgence of federal aid to large cities in the future is zero.

24

The Rise and Fall of National Urban Policy: The Fiscal Dimension

Robert D. Reischauer

Before the Great Depression the federal government provided little in the way of financial assistance to local governments either directly or through the states. Then in the mid- and late 1930s Washington responded to the erosion of urban tax bases and the widespread hardship of the era with a surge of support for local public works, unemployment relief, and public housing programs. Federal aid to local governments rose from $10 million in 1932 to $278 million in 1940. World War II brought a sharp reduction in this aid, but after the war a modest level of federal assistance was reestablished as the federal government acted to support airport construction (1946), urban renewal (1949), urban planning (1954), and education in areas affected by military installations (1950). From 1960 to 1978 a veritable explosion occurred in federal urban policy. The number of federal grants directed at cities and their problems increased dramatically, and, as a result, federal aid became an important source of money for many urban budgets for the first time. The period since 1978 has been characterized by a steady retrenchment, which, if continued, could return federal-local fiscal relations to the levels existing before the Great Society buildup.

This essay reviews the dynamics of the 1960–78 expansion in federal urban aid and its subsequent contraction. The objective of this review is to determine whether national urban policy is currently experiencing a temporary setback that, like the World War II contraction, will be followed by a renewed expansion, or whether the 1960 to 1978 period was an historical aberration that will not be repeated.

The views in this chapter are those of the author and should not be attributed to the staff, trustees, or supporters of the Brookings Institution.

Some Magnitudes

It is impossible to measure precisely the amount of federal aid received by urban areas or how this aid has changed over time. One reason for this is that few federal grant programs are directed exclusively at local governments. In 1987, only fifteen of the federal government's 422 grants were reserved solely for localities; the remaining 407 were available only to states or to combinations of states, localities, and nonprofit organizations (see table 24.1). Of the money directed at local governments, only a small portion is received by large cities and could, therefore, properly be classified as part of the nation's urban policy. Suburban and rural counties, school districts, and municipalities all obtain a share. A second reason why estimates of federal aid to urban areas are imprecise is that much of federal urban aid money is received initially by state governments which then pass it through to local governments. But in such cases the aid may lose its federal identity because it is mixed with state funds. Similar difficulties arise with grants provided to nonprofit organizations that may provide services and programs in urban areas. These difficulties should be kept in mind when interpreting table 24.2, which provides a picture of the recent pattern of direct federal aid to cities.

Through the mid-1960s direct federal aid for cities was relatively inconsequential, especially when compared to the own-source revenues of these governments. But this began to change when the number of grant instruments through which cities could receive direct or indirect federal assistance expanded tremendously during the mid- and late 1960s. New initiatives were begun in many areas, including community action programs (1964), mass transportation (1964), manpower development and training (1964), neighborhood youth programs (1964), elementary and secondary education assistance (1965), basic water and sewer facilities (1965), community health services (1965), and law

Table 24.1 Total number of federal grants and grants available to local governments

	1960	1967	1975	1981	1987
Total	132	379	448	539	422
Localities only	n.a.	n.a.	20	23	15
Localities and other recipients	n.a.	n.a.	260	317	243

Source: US Advisory Commission on Intergovernmental Relations (unpublished tabulations).

Table 24.2 Federal intergovernmental aid to municipalities, 1950–1986

Fiscal year	Federal aid		
	Millions of dollars	Millions of 1984 dollars[a]	As a percentage of own-source revenue
1955	121	760	1.9
1960	256	1,138	2.8
1965	557	2,149	4.5
1970	1,337	3,748	7.1
1975	5,844	11,066	19.3
1978	10,234	15,654	25.8
1980	10,872	13,778	22.8
1982	10,990	12,210	18.4
1984	10,440	10,440	14.5
1986	9,813	9,039	11.6

[a] Deflated by the implicit GNP price deflator for state and local purchases of goods and services.

Source: ACIR, *Significant Features of Fiscal Federalism, 1985–6 Edition* (February 1986). M-146, and US Bureau of the Census, *Governmental Finance in 1986*, November 1987.

enforcement assistance (1968). However, the funding for these efforts remained relatively constrained during the 1960s.

It was not until the 1970s that the budgetary impact of these programs and other new initiatives became significant. Between 1970 and 1978 there was a fourfold real increase in direct federal aid. Such aid peaked in importance at over one-quarter of the own-source resources of city governments in 1978. For some large distressed cities, which Richard Nathan once characterized as "federal aid junkies," dependence on Washington reached much higher levels. For example, federal aid to Phoenix, Cleveland, and Detroit amounted to over half of their local tax revenues in 1978.

The explosion of federal aid not only reflected increased funding for categorical programs but also for two new federal policy thrusts. The first was general revenue sharing which was an intergovernmental income redistribution scheme. The second was the effort made by the Carter administration to enlist states and localities as agents of federal stabilization policy. The countercyclical revenue-sharing program (the Anti Recession Fiscal Assistance Act of 1977), the local public works program (the Public Works Employment Act of 1976), and the expansion of Titles II and VI of CETA (the Comprehensive Employment and Training Act) all poured money into local government budgets in an effort to reduce unemployment and maintain basic public services in areas hit hard by the recession.

While the number of grant instruments available to local governments continued to expand at a healthy clip between 1978 and 1981, federal aid did not keep pace with inflation. The major reason for this was the phase-down of the antirecession effort. A second, less important reason was that most (thirty-nine of forty-two) of the new programs enacted during this period were project grants with fixed budgets rather than formula programs and entitlements with their open-ended funding.

The 1981 initiatives of the Reagan administration reduced the number of grant programs by one quarter. A few small programs were terminated, and many more were consolidated into a dozen block grants. Funding levels for both the consolidated grants and many of the remaining categorical grants were cut sharply, leading to the first nominal dollar reduction in federal aid in decades. Since 1981 the specter of the federal budget deficit has precluded any expansion of aid to cities.

The Forces Behind the Expansion

The reasons why federal aid to urban areas soared from 1960 to 1978 are no mystery. First, federal policymakers thought that they had the financial resources to take on a number of long-neglected domestic problems. These resources were to come from the "fiscal dividend" that would be generated by the interaction of a growing economy and a progressive federal tax system. At that time the federal budget was not dominated by mandatory programs or entitlements, the spending for which increases automatically. Medicare, Medicaid, Supplemental Security Income (SSI), food stamps, Guaranteed Student Loans (GSLS), and the Earned Income Tax Credit (EITC) did not exist in the early 1960s.

Second, federal policymakers felt that they had the intellectual ability and political will to take on the complex set of problems facing America's cities. This spark was embodied in the social scientists and policy activists who were drawn to Washington by Presidents Kennedy and Johnson. This cadre was anxious to test out the theories and proposals they had developed during the 1950s.

Third, federal aid to cities expanded over this period because the American people and their representatives in Congress were willing to accept the propositions that there were serious unmet needs in the cities and that these problems could be effectively addressed through public sector actions.

The fourth reason why urban aid exploded was that these domestic problems became identified with the geographic areas in which they were most apparent. Inadequate housing, poor public transportation, deteriorating neighborhoods, crime, failing schools, and limited job opportunities became identified as big-city problems, not as general domestic problems or as problems of the low-income population. The riots of the mid-1960s only reinforced the view that a preponderance of the nation's unmet needs were located in cities.

A fifth factor underlying the surge of federal assistance to cities was the feeling in Washington that the solutions to these problems were city, not state, responsibilities. Cities were portrayed as a worthy or deserving level of government. States were held in relatively low esteem. They were viewed as backward and uninterested in the plight of the underprivileged. Many states, it was felt, had systematically shortchanged their large urban areas while benefiting rural, and, to a lesser extent, suburban jurisdictions. States could not be trusted to do what was right for their big cities even if they were given federal resources. Therefore, direct federal intervention offered the best hope for addressing urban problems.

A contradictory subcurrent of thinking, one critical of cities, also existed. This view held that political and business forces within the large cities had not come to grips with core urban problems. Sometimes jurisdictions lacked the capacity or resources, but more often indifference, incompetence, or even corruption were to blame. Rather than leading to a policy of federal restraint, this line of reasoning convinced some Washington activists that more radical change was necessary, that improvements would occur only if the federal government intervened to change existing power structures in cities. In other words, some federal officials saw themselves compelled to reform local institutions and political structures if they were to successfully tackle the most pressing domestic problems of the day.

Finally, federal assistance to cities grew because it was good politics. Direct aid to cities and indirect assistance through states provided congressmen with tangible benefits. There was the opening of the health clinic to attend, the new city buses to deliver, and ribbons to cut at the economic development project. It is doubtful that a federal strategy of providing aid directly to individuals or to states in the form of true block grants could have provided as much political payoff.

In addition, the proliferation of grants generated a system of support that kept the grants strategy alive and well long after serious questions had risen concerning its ability to deal with the underlying causes of urban problems. New congressional subcommittees were created to oversee some grants, and the importance of many existing subcommittees was enhanced. New agencies and offices were created both in the federal government and in individual city governments to administer the new programs. And special interest lobbies developed to defend and expand each new grant program.

The Seeds of Destruction

The expansion of federal assistance to local jurisdictions carried within it the seeds of its own destruction. By choosing to deal directly with localities, the federal government became entangled in the complexity that characterizes local government in America. Different governments have different functional responsibilities and different taxing authority. Problems which might be dealt with effectively by the municipal government in New York might require a coordinated response from the county, the municipality, and several independent school districts in Dallas. In some areas the urban problems that concerned federal policymakers were exacerbated, if not caused, by various restraints state laws placed on cities. Examples of this include the limited annexation authority that most large cities had and their inability to tax workers in the city who commuted from the suburbs. In addition, few urban problems respected local jurisdictional boundaries. Thus, the recipient of a federal grant often had only a piece of the problem within its area of responsibility.

By choosing to deal with hundreds of localities, the federal government was confronted with jurisdictions of vastly different capacities, internal structures, and politics. Faced with this complexity, Washington had two options. One was to admit that no central government had the capacity to design and monitor programs that could accommodate even a majority of the different circumstances which would arise. Such an admission would have led to a block grant strategy. Under such a strategy, resources would have been given to jurisdictions for use in solving certain basic types of problems. But the recipient jurisdictions would have been allowed to choose which specific approaches would best address the problem in their particular area.

The second option, which was the one taken, was to design programs in excruciating detail to try to anticipate every circumstance that might arise. This created a system characterized by red tape and regulation under which recipients were forced to submit plans, pre-proposals, proposals, and progress reports. Federal bureaucrats were charged with reviewing these submissions at every stage, thus maximizing the opportunity for conflict and contention. This approach reflected not only the confidence Washington's politicians and policy planners had in their own abilities, but also a political imperative. Loosely directed federal funds were more likely to end up misdirected, sometimes in scandalous ways. This might come back to visit political damage on the sponsoring agency, committee, or individual congressman.

The chosen strategy produced a reaction from both the grant givers and the recipients. The latter chafed under the red tape, excessive regulations, and delays imposed by Washington. The former were overwhelmed by the work load and stung by the criticism they received from what were supposed to be grateful beneficiaries.

The congestion created by the proliferation of grants spawned an intellectual backlash as well. Soon policy analysts were arguing that the intergovernmental fiscal system needed to be rationalized. Many experts came to question whether the needs being addressed by federal-local grants were truly of national importance. Calls for simplification and a sorting out of functions became more frequent.

The inherent inability of Congress to target local grants represented another destructive seed. Severe urban problems were not present in every, or even most, large cities. And yet, for a new grant program to be enacted or an existing one to receive a larger appropriation, the program had to spread its largess widely across as many congressional districts as possible. The incongruity between concentrated needs and dispersed federal aid helped to generate perceptions of inefficiency and waste.

The growing importance of federal-local fiscal relations caused strains with the state governments. Some cities were accused of being more attuned to the wishes and priorities of Washington than to those of the state capital. Some states, witnessing Washington's active interest in urban problems, slacked off their own efforts to deal with the problems of their large urban centers.

The Era of Retrenchment

In the past decade the conditions that contributed to the 1960–78 expansion of federal aid to cities disappeared and a new era of retrenchment began. The retrenchment drew strength from the turbulence that afflicted the economy in the late 1970s and early 1980s and from the growing perception that federal domestic programs were not working. The Reagan administration forcefully articulated these perceptions.

The most significant factor contributing to this retrenchment was the budgetary squeeze that the federal government found itself in starting in the late 1970s. With the tax cuts of 1981, the Reagan administration's defense buildup, and the 1981–2 recession, the squeeze was transformed into the crushing force of $200 billion annual deficits. The battle to reduce these deficits revealed that discretionary domestic spending, of which nonentitlement grants to state and local governments make up a significant portion, was not high on the nation's list of budgetary priorities. Over the 1978–88 decade nonentitlement federal grants were cut by 41 percent in real terms. General revenue sharing and Urban Development Action Grants were eliminated entirely. CETA was replaced by the Jobs Training Partnership Act at one-half the CETA funding level. On an inflation-adjusted basis grants for community and regional development were cut by two-thirds, and those for education, training, and social services fell by 45 percent. Under the strictures of the Gramm-Rudman-Hollings deficit reduction targets, continued pressure to reduce aid to cities should be expected.

While the extreme fiscal restraint of the current period should ease somewhat if the Bush administration deals effectively with the deficit, the longrun outlook for increased urban aid does not look bright. Relative to a decade or two ago, a much larger fraction of the federal budget is now devoted to relatively uncontrollable commitments such as Social Security, Medicare, debt service, farm price supports, veteran's benefits, and military and civilian pay. With the income tax indexed and reformed, there is no possibility that bracket creep or economic growth will generate a significant "fiscal dividend" that could be devoted to expanded domestic programs. Therefore, any significant expansion of domestic programs will require a tax increase, something that is not likely after the deficit issue is resolved.

In addition, the optimism about the effectiveness of government programs that existed in the 1960s has given way to an equally exaggerated feeling that little that the federal government tries works very well. As a mechanism for achieving federal objectives, categorical grants have fallen out of favor. Many programs are regarded as ineffectual; a few are accused of being positively harmful. For example, many analysts argue that federal mass transit aid has built uneconomical subway systems, led to excessive pay for transit workers, and distorted local transportation decisions. Others think that federal economic development efforts have heavily subsidized downtown development that would have occurred without this assistance. Even advocates of federal intervention are hard-pressed to document the programs that have generated dramatic, measurable results. The best they can do is to point to such programs as Job Corps, Chapter 1 (Compensatory Education for the Disadvantaged). Head Start, and WIC (the Supplemental Food Program for Women, Infants and Children), for which there is some evidence of modest positive impacts.

Unlike during the earlier period, cities are no longer perceived as the most worthy or deserving level of government. Their relative status began to fade with the New York City fiscal crisis in the mid-1970s. The wave of municipal corruption, which was covered by the media in excruciating detail, accelerated this fall from grace. States have emerged as the new darlings of Washington policymakers. In large measure the rising status of state government reflects the genuine strengthening of this level of government since the early 1960s. State revenue structures have been strengthened considerably, and there has been a significant improvement in the quality of elected and appointed state officials as well as their staffs. Moreover, when the federal government began to relinquish its role as a policy innovator during the Reagan administration, the states stepped in. In the areas of health cost containment, education, work-welfare, the environment, economic development, housing, and tax reform, states have exhibited a good deal of leadership and innovation.

But Washington's renewed fascination with states also has a practical dimension. As long as retrenchment is required, the federal government will want to distance itself from the ultimate beneficiary of the programs it is cutting back. By channeling grants through the states and by transforming categorical programs into block grants, the political repercussions of federal cutbacks can be diffused. States may compensate for federal cuts by allocating more of their own money to the affected programs. If states choose to validate the federal cuts, some of the criticisms of the cutbacks may be directed at them rather than at Washington. But this is only the case when the aid is channeled through the state.

Not only have states replaced local governments as the focus of federal intergovernmental attention, but "people" have replaced "place" as the primary locus of policy concern in the 1980s. The limited success of the place-oriented strategies of the past and the mobility of the population have led policymakers to look more toward people-oriented approaches to solving the nation's domestic problems. New initiatives are more frequently shaped around individual entitlements, vouchers, or tax expenditures to individuals and businesses than around grants to governments. Housing vouchers, training and retraining payments, tuition tax credits, and tax incentives for economic development and historic preservation are some examples of this trend.

In addition, new actors have appeared on the local scene, actors that compete with and complement local governments. There are the nonprofit organizations and quasi-governmental organizations that often serve as the delivery agents of federal policy. Twenty years ago there were fewer such organizations, and cities had this niche almost entirely to themselves. Furthermore, public-private partnerships, a form of policy intervention which is not conducive to an active federal role, are playing an ever greater part at the local level.

Finally, demographic and economic trends are working against a resurgence of federal fiscal assistance to large cities. The fraction of the population living in large cities continues to decline. Congressional redistricting has taken seats away from the areas of the country which contain the most distressed urban environments. A further reduction, based on the results of the 1990 census, will occur for the 1992 congressional elections. The relative economic position of the large urban centers also has continued to slip. As a result of these trends, the political clout of urban areas has eroded considerably since the mid-1960s, leaving them without the capacity to mount a successful legislative effort to expand federal aid to cities.

Conclusion

The conclusion that arises from this brief review of the past twenty-five years of fiscal federalism is that the 1960 to 1978 era was an aberration, one that is not likely to be repeated. There never existed a neatly defined or coherent national urban policy – a clear notion of what the federal government was attempting to achieve through its interventions to local governments. At first, federal involvement was portrayed as an effort to redevelop blighted neighborhoods. This was replaced by an emphasis on empowering underprivileged city residents and providing them with opportunities to better themselves. The next focus of federal policy was on ensuring that poor urban residents were provided with essential city services. Federal programs then focused on enhancing the fiscal health of cities and on the pursuit of federal antirecession objectives. The final federal thrust emphasized city economic development in partnership with the private sector. The inability to sustain a coherent focus for federal urban policy has not been the fault of the nation's policymakers but rather was inevitable given the inherent complexity and diversity of the federal system and the economic turmoil that characterized the past fifteen years.

Considering the resurgent role of the states, the long-term fiscal constraints that face the federal government, and the diminished political clout of the big cities, renewed efforts to establish a national urban policy that channels significant federal resources to the nation's distressed cities are likely to be futile.

Introduction to Chapter 25

The concepts of standardized fiscal health and actual fiscal health which Ladd and Yinger develop in their book, *America's Ailing Cities* (1989), are here used in investigating the determinants of state aid to cities. In the theoretical part of their paper, the authors present a formal model for determining two variables: state grants to a city, and state institutional aid to a city. The latter is a novel concept which embraces taxing power and expenditure responsibilities of a city, both of which are granted or imposed by the state government. The theoretical model yields two structural equations in which the two key variables are simultaneously determined. And so in the empirical part of the paper the equations actually estimated by regression take that simultaneity into account. The hypotheses which are tested here are: do state governments give more assistance, grant money and institutional help, to cities in poorer fiscal condition?; are these two forms of aid substitutes for one another?; and finally is federal grant aid to cities a substitute for state aid?

This paper is more sophisticated than the usual analysis of state aid to cities. The approach used enables the authors to draw conclusions about separate and combined effects of different types of state assistance. One of the explicit assumptions in their model is that makers of state policy ". . . care about the actual fiscal condition of each city in their state . . ." (p. 481). Before public choice theory influenced state and local public finance, such an assumption would have been implicit.

25

The Determinants of State Assistance to Central Cities***

John Yinger and Helen F. Ladd***

Abstract

This paper examines the determinants of state assistance to 70 major central cities in 1982. State assistance is broadly defined to include both intergovernmental grants and institutional assistance, such as granting a city access to a tax with export potential or state takeover of city service responsibilities. Two key hypotheses are derived: states direct assistance to cities that need help the most, and states regard grants and institutional assistance as substitutes. Both hypotheses are strongly supported by the data. A third hypothesis, that high federal aid to a city is offset by low state assistance, receives no support.

The past ten years have witnessed a lively debate on the nature of the US federal system. Many policymakers want to shift fiscal responsibilities away from the federal government toward the states; other policymakers want to maintain or even strengthen the role of the federal government.

Unfortunately, however, this debate has been hampered by a lack of information about the behavior of key participants in the federal system, particularly state governments. In this paper we address one aspect of this problem by examining the determinants of state assitance to central cities. Do states provide more assistance to cities with greater needs? What are the forms of state assistance to cities? What is the impact of federal assistance to cities on state assistance to cities?

This analysis is made possible by a data set we created for a study of the fiscal health of major US central cities (Ladd and Yinger, 1989).

* Syracuse University, Syracuse, NY 13244.
** Duke University, Durham, NC 27706.
*** The authors are grateful to Jan Ondrich and Gary Solon for econometric advice and to Roy Bahl, Stephen D. Mullin, and two anonymous referees for helpful comments.

This data set contains a comprehensive measure of each city government's fiscal condition, as well as measures of state assistance to cities through both intergovernmental grants and fiscal institutions. The concept of assistance through fiscal institutions is crucial for understanding state assistance to cities. A state obviously can help its cities by giving them intergovernmental grants, but it also can assist cities by allowing them to use taxes, such as commuter taxes, that shift some of the city tax burden to nonresidents or by taking over public services previously provided by cities. Our data set provides a unique opportunity to examine the determinants of state assistance through both grants and institutions and to ask whether state policymakers regard these two types of assistance as substitutes.

We begin by explaining the measures of city fiscal condition and of state and federal assistance to cities that we develop in Ladd and Yinger. In the following two sections, we present our model of state assistance to cities and test it using data for 70 major central cities in 1982. In the final section, we discuss the policy implications of our results.

Measuring State Assistance and City Fiscal Condition

Our analysis is built on the distinction, clearly made by Bradbury (1982, 1983), between a city's budgetary condition and its underlying or structural fiscal condition. A city's budgetary condition reflects the current state of its financial affairs and is heavily influenced by the political and management decisions of city officials. In contrast, a city's structural fiscal condition is its ability to provide public services at reasonable tax rates, as determined by economic and social factors that are outside city officials' control. This paper is concerned with structural fiscal condition, or fiscal condition for short.

A city's fiscal condition reflects the balance between its revenue-raising capacity and its expenditure need. Revenue-raising capacity is defined to be the amount of money a city could raise (per capita) at a given tax burden on its residents. Expenditure need is the amount a city must spend (per capita) to provide public services of a given quality. For the purposes of this paper, we measure a city's overall fiscal condition by its need-capacity gap, which is the difference between expenditure need and revenue-raising capacity.[1]

Both revenue-raising capacity and expenditure need are influenced by a city's economic and social structure and by its fiscal institutions. Economic and social factors determine the potential taxable resources in the city and the cost of providing city services, whereas state-determined fiscal institutions determine which taxes a city is allowed to employ and the extent of a city's responsibilities for providing public services. Our approach is to separate these two types of factors. First, we define a standard set of fiscal institutions and calculate the need-capacity gap each city would have if these institutions were in place. This gap measures the impact of economic and social factors on a city's fiscal condition. Second, we calculate an alternative need-capacity gap that incorporates each city's actual fiscal institutions. The difference between the need-capacity gaps with standard and actual institutions is our measure of the assistance each city receives from the fiscal institutions created by its state.

A city's need-capacity gap with a standard set of fiscal institutions, which we call its *standardized need-capacity gap*, is the difference between the expenditure need the city would have with national average service responsibilities, which we call its standardized expenditure need, and the revenue-raising capacity it would have with three broad-based taxes (property, earnings, and sales), which we call its full revenue-raising capacity.

A city's standardized expenditure need is determined by its costs of providing public services. As first explained by Bradford, Malt, and Oates (1969), public service costs vary from one jurisdiction to another because of variation in both input prices and environmental factors. For example, a city with a relatively high poverty rate or with other environmental characteristics associated with criminal behavior, must spend more than other cities to obtain a given level of protection against crime. Building on the work of Bradbury et al. (1984), we develop (in Ladd and Yinger, 1989) indexes of public service costs and standardized expenditure need for each major central city.

Full revenue-raising capacity is the amount a city could raise from three broad-based taxes at a standard tax burden on its residents. In a closed city economy, this capacity is determined entirely by resident income; the higher is resident income, the greater is the revenue the city could raise at the standard tax burden. With economic flows in and out of the city, however, revenue-raising capacity also is influenced by the city's ability to export its tax burden to nonresidents.[2] This ability to export depends on tax incidence. In the case of the property tax, for example, exporting depends on the shares of the tax that fall on workers, consumers, and property owners – and on the residential locations of these three groups. We calculate each city's ability to export taxes on the basis of a detailed analysis of the incidence of city property, income, and sales taxes (see Bradbury and Ladd, 1985).

A state influences its cities' expenditure needs through its assignment of public service responsibilities. All else equal, for example, a city government must spend more to meet its service responsibilities at a given quality level if the city itself, instead of an independent school district, is responsible for local education, or if the city operates a hospital. In Ladd and Yinger we develop a service responsibility index for each major city. Combining this index with our index for public service costs yields each city's actual expenditure need, which is the amount it would have to spend to meet its actual service responsibilities at an average quality level.

Several state-determined fiscal institutions also directly influence a city's revenue-raising capacity. The state decides which taxes the city can levy and may place restrictions on city tax base definitions and tax rates. These rules are key determinants of tax exporting. In most cases, for example, an earnings tax that applies to commuters into the city allows the city to export a large share of its tax burden; by prohibiting such a tax, therefore, a state may be severely restricting a city's actual revenue-raising capacity. A state also gives taxing authority to other local jurisdictions, such as counties, whose boundaries overlap with a city's. These overlying jurisdictions also draw on the taxpaying ability of city residents; the greater is the taxing authority of overlying jurisdictions, the lower is the capacity left over for the city government to draw on. A city's restricted revenue-raising capacity (before grants) is its capacity after these fiscal institutions have been accounted for.

A city's actual need-capacity gap (before grants) is the difference between its actual expenditure need and its restricted revenue-raising capacity (before grants). Because this actual gap accounts for a city's fiscal institutions whereas the standardized gap assumes uniform fiscal institutions, we interpret the difference between these two gaps as a measure of the impact of fiscal institutions on a city's fiscal condition. If a state assigns heavy service responsibilities to a city but does not provide it with access to taxes with export potential, for example, then the state's fiscal rules may add more to the city's expenditure need than to its revenue-raising capacity. In this case, state institutional "assistance" actually makes things worse; that is, it adds to the city's need-capacity gap. Other cities' fiscal conditions are improved because their states allow them to use a tax with high export potential while assigning them limited service responsibilities. Note that state institutional assistance varies both within and across states. San Francisco, for example, is the only city in California with access to a tax on commuter earnings, and Albany, unlike the other major cities in New York, does not have responsibility for schools.

States (and the federal government) also assist their cities by giving them intergovernmental grants. These grants do not raise such complex conceptual issues and data on grants can be obtained from published sources.[3]

In summary, data taken from Ladd and Yinger (1989) can be used to calculate a city's standardized need-capacity gap, state assistance to a city through institutions and through grants, and federal grants to cities. All of these variables are expressed in dollars per capita. An algebraic description of our calculations and some illustrations are in the appendix.

A Model of State Assistance to Cities

Our model of state behavior focuses on the trade-off between assistance to cities and other state objectives, including political ones. It builds on the observation that many state aid programs include equalizing provisions that direct more aid to local governments in poorer fiscal condition, as indicated by their tax bases or public service costs (see Bradbury et al., 1984).

Key assumptions

The model is based on three key assumptions. First, we assume that state policymakers care about the actual fiscal condition of each city in their state, as they perceive it. In particular, we assume that one of their objectives is to lessen differences across cities in actual fiscal condition by providing more assistance to cities whose fiscal condition before state assistance is relatively poor.

Second, we assume that the standardized need-capacity gap summarizes state policymakers' perceptions about city fiscal condition before state and federal assistance. State policymakers obviously do not carry out the same calculations that we do, but the basic elements of our calculations have been widely discussed and some of them have been incorporated into existing state grant formulas.

Third, we assume that state policymakers recognize that state and federal grants and state assistance through institutions all can contribute to a city's fiscal health, although they may not believe that $1 of state grants makes the same contribution as $1 of state institutional assistance or $1 of federal aid. State grants may be perceived to make a relatively high contribution to a city's fiscal condition, for example, because they can be directed toward types of city spending that state policymakers believe are particularly important for a city's fiscal health. In contrast, state institutional assistance, which is less focused and more difficult to measure, may be perceived to make only a modest contribution to a city's fiscal condition, and some federal grants may be tied to city programs that state policymakers do not value – or at least do not value as must as the programs supported by state aid.

These assumptions lead to the concept of a city's perceived need-capacity gap after state and federal assistance. This gap equals a city's standardized need-capacity gap minus the perceived contributions to city fiscal condition of state and federal grants and of state institutional assistance. Let us define

SGAP = A city's standardized need-capacity gap;
 GAP = A city's need-capacity gap after state and federal
        assistance, as perceived by the state;
    G = State assistance to a city in the form of grants;
    I = State institutional assistance to a city;
    F = Federal grants to a city;

where all of these variables are measured in dollars per city resident. Moreover, suppose that state policymakers believe that \$1 of assistance of type a contributes θ_a dollars to a city's fiscal condition. Then we can write

$$GAP = SGAP - \theta_G G - \theta_I I - \theta_F F. \tag{25.1}$$

A formal model

According to our first assumption, lowering the post-assistance need-capacity gap is a key objective of state policymakers. A simple way to express this objective algebraically is to say that state policymakers want to increase the difference between the maximum observed pre-assistance gap, MAX, and each individual city's post-assistance gap, GAP. (MAX need not be an observed gap. It can be interpreted as a reference gap used by state policymakers – as long as it is greater than or equal to the highest actual post-assistance gap.)

State policymakers can achieve the objective of lowering a city's GAP by raising grants, G, or by raising institutional assistance, I. In deciding how to use these policy tools, however, they must trade off this objective against other state objectives. We summarize these other objectives by assuming that type a assistance to cities must compete with the amount spent (per city resident) on another set of state activities, Z_a. In addition, we assume that B_a is the state budget (per city resident) allocated for Z_a

and city assistance of type a. The notion of a budget for assistance through institutions is somewhat abstract. No such budget literally exists, but all forms of institutional assistance involve some shifting of the burden of city services onto noncity residents. An abstract budget is a convenient way to express the trade-off between institutional assistance and alternative uses of limited resources that is implicit in this type of shifting.

To capture the trade-off between assistance to cities and other state objectives, we assume that state policymakers' preferences are defined by a Cobb-Douglas welfare function with Z_G, Z_I, and $(MAX - GAP)$ as arguments. They maximize this welfare function subject to their perceptions about the contributions of various forms of assistance to a city's fiscal condition and to their budget constraints for grants and for institutional aid.

Thus, the state policymaker's problem is to select Z_G, Z_I, G, and I to:

$$\text{Maximize} \quad W = \left(Z_G^{\alpha G}\right)\left(Z_I^{\alpha I}\right)\left(MAX - GAP\right)^{\beta} \tag{25.2}$$

$$\text{Subject to} \quad GAP = SGAP - \theta_G G - \theta_I I - \theta_F F$$
$$B_G = Z_G + G$$
$$B_I = Z_I + I$$

The first-order conditions of this problem yield the following two structural equations, which indicate how G and I are determined:

$$G = b_{0G} + b_{1G}B_G + b_{2G}SGAP + b_{3G}I + b_{4G}F \tag{25.3}$$

$$I = b_{0I} + b_{1I}B_I + b_{2I}SGAP + b_{3I}I + b_{4I}F, \tag{25.4}$$

where for $a = G, I$ (and $a' = I, G$)

$$b_{0a} = -\alpha_a MAX / \left[\theta_a\left(\beta + \alpha_a\right)\right]$$
$$b_{1a} = \beta / \left(\beta + \alpha_a\right)$$
$$b_{2a} = \alpha_a / \left[\theta_a\left(\beta + \alpha_a\right)\right]$$
$$b_{3a} = -\theta_{a'} \cdot b_{2a}$$
$$b_{4a} = -\theta_F b_{2a}$$

These two equations contain three principal hypotheses about the way states design grants and institutional assistance to cities. The equations indicate that a city with a higher SGAP receives more G and more I. The first hypothesis, therefore, is that states give more grants and more institutional assistance to cities with higher standardized need-capacity gaps. Moreover, a higher level of G leads to a lower level of I (and vice versa). Thus the second hypothesis is that states view grants and assistance through institutions as substitutes for each other. Finally, both G and I are negative functions of federal grants, as long as those grants are perceived to improve a city's fiscal condition. Consequently, the third hypothesis is that relatively high federal grants may lead to relatively low state assistance – of both types.

Equations (25.3) and (25.4) can be estimated with linear regression techniques for a sample of cities. Our measures of SGAP, G, I, and F can be introduced into equation (25.3) or (25.4) in exactly the form derived from our model, and their coefficients can be interpreted as the indicated functions of the model parameters. Because the reference gap, MAX, is constant, it is estimated as part of the constant term. Although B_G and B_I cannot be observed directly, we identify and measure a variety of factors, both economic and political, that influence these "budgets."

The coefficients of SGAP test the hypothesis that state officials attempt to direct each form of assistance toward cities in poor fiscal condition, as measured by their standardized need-capacity gap. To be specific, these coefficients measure the dollar increase in assistance that accompanies a dollar increase in this gap. The coefficient of I in the regression to explain G and the coefficient of G in the regression to explain I test the hypothesis that the two forms of state assistance are substitutes for each other. The perceived contributions of each form of state aid toward city fiscal health, θ_G and θ_I, also can be calculated from these coefficients.[4]

In this model, G and I are jointly determined. Equations (25.3) and (25.4) therefore must be estimated with a simultaneous equations procedure. As reported below, we estimate the model with both two- and three-stage least squares. The factors that influence B_I but do not influence B_G are excluded instruments in the regression to explain G; factors that influence B_G but not B_I are the excluded instruments in the regression for I.

Implementation of the model

To implement our model, we divide federal aid into two types: categorical aid and general revenue sharing. The coefficients of these aid variables can be interpreted like those of the state assistance variables; the absolute value of each coefficient, divided by the coefficient of SGAP, is the perceived contribution of that form of aid toward city fiscal health.[5]

Federal aid to central cities might be influenced by state aid to central cities. For example, the federal government might give more categorical grants to cities that are in poor fiscal health as a result of low assistance from their state.[6] In our judgment, however, state assistance is unlikely to have a significant impact on federal grants. Our strategy, therefore, is to assume that both types of federal grants are exogenous in our basic models and to examine this assumption with the appropriate specification tests.

State grants to cities are the product of the state's budgetary process, so the exogenous factors that influence B_G reflect voter demand and politics. To account for the two key demand factors, namely income and price, we include state per capita income and the share of state population that is in central cities (all central cities – not just those in our sample). The higher is the per capita income in the state, the higher is the demand for state services, including services supported by grants to cities; and the higher is the central city share of state population, the higher is the cost per state resident of providing a certain level of per capita grants to central cities.[7]

We also include state population as a type of price variable, although we cannot determine its sign *a priori*. To the extent that state-provided public services are public goods, larger states can provide the same service quality at a lower cost per capita. A likely response to this lower cost is an increase in the quality of state services, including those supported by grants to cities. To the extent that state-provided public services face diseconomies to scale (from congestion or administrative costs), larger states will have higher per-capita costs and lower service quality.

Several political factors also might influence the outcome of a state's budgetary process. Because they are elected officials, city mayors may have more leverage in obtaining grants than do city managers. Cities with a large share of a state's population have more representation in a state legislature and may have more influence on state budgetary decisions. Moreover, the competition for state funds may be particularly severe in states with many local governments. To control for these three possibilities, our grant regression includes the city's share of state population, the number of local governments with taxing authority relative to state population, and a dummy variable for cities with mayors.

Finally, several city characteristics might influence state grants. City/counties are much more likely than separate cities to have responsibility for welfare and schools. State legislatures may have a particular interest in supporting these two services and may therefore give more grants to city/counties than to other cities with the same standardized need-capacity gap.[8] In addition, cities in which many state government employees work may be treated differently than other cities. This effect could work in either direction. Cities with many state government employees per capita might have extra influence in a state legislature and therefore receive more grants, or locating state employees in a city may be seen as a form of assistance to that city and may therefore be regarded as a substitute for state grants. (The latter possibility implies that the number of state employees per capita is an endogenous variable; we examine this possibility with a specification test.) State capitals also may receive more grants, in part because they have many state government employees and in part because they are the city in which the legislators work and perhaps live. Thus, the control variables in the state-grants regression include the number of state government employees per capita and dummy variables for city/counties and for state capitals.

The exogenous factors that affect B_I reflect state officials' long-run decisions about the nature of their state/local fiscal system. States with higher incomes are likely to be more generous in providing institutional assistance to cities. All forms of institutional assistance shift some of the burden of providing city services onto noncity residents; the higher are state incomes, the higher is the burden that noncity residents will accept.

In addition, we hypothesize that states will take advantage of existing opportunities to provide institutional assistance to cities. First, if a city is small relative to its metropolitan area, then the burden of institutional assistance to a city can be spread out over the relatively large number of noncity residents. In this case, giving a city access to taxes with high export ratios or shifting service responsibility to counties that encompass several cities will not place a large burden on individual suburbanites. Second, a state that does not rely heavily on an income tax itself may find that the additional burden of a city's earnings tax is acceptable and may therefore allow its cities to levy such a tax and hence to boost their tax exporting. To control for these factors, we include the city's share of metropolitan population and the share of state tax revenue from an income tax.

Finally, state decisions about assistance through institutions are likely to be influenced by several characteristics of the institutional setting. As in the case of state grants, state assistance through institutions may favor city/counties, which tend to have high service responsibilities, even controlling for city fiscal condition. A dummy variable for city/counties is included to account for this possibility. Moreover, states with complex

Table 25.1 Variable definitions and hypothesized signs

Variable	Definition	Mean	Hypothesized sign	
			GRANTS	INSTIT
	1. Endogenous variables			
GRANTS	State grants per capita	$81.94	n.a.	–
INSTIT	State assistance through institutions per capita	$10.85	–	n.a.
	2. Exogenous variables			
SGAP	Standardized need-capacity gap per capita	$32.94	+	+
FCAT	Federal categorical grants per capita	$44.75	?	?
FGRS	Federal general revenue sharing per capita	$9.60	–	–
SEMP	State government employment in the city per capita	0.025	?	excl.
SPCY	State per capita income (thousands)	$11.147	+	+
COUNTY	Dummy for city/counties	0.286	+	+
SCCTOS	Share of state population in central cities	0.302	+	excl.
SPOP	State population (millions)	10.167	?	excl.
MAYOR	Dummy for cities with mayors	0.471	+	excl.
RELPOP	City share of state population (percent)	8.480	+	excl.
CAPIT	Dummy for state capitals	0.229	?	excl.
SLOCAL	Local governments per 1,000 people in the state	0.241	–	excl.
METPOP	City share of metropolitan population (percent)	30.700	excl.	–
SRELY	State's reliance on an income tax	0.218	excl.	–
MIXED	Dummy for states with mixed fiscal system	0.457	excl.	–

Notes: The entry "excl." indicates that a variable is excluded from the final or second-stage regression for the indicated dependent variable. However, all exogenous variables, including those marked "excl.", are used as instruments in the simultaneous equations procedure.

fiscal arrangements may find it more difficult to design and obtain agreement on effective institutional assistance. We measure the complexity of a state's fiscal arrangements with a dummy variable for states in which some central cities are city/counties and others separate cities with overlying counties.

Our model is summarized in table 25.1. This table lists the explanatory variables (including endogenous ones) in the regressions for state assistance through both grants and institutions, gives the sample mean for each variable, and states the hypothesized sign of each coefficient in each regression.

Empirical Results

We estimate our model using data for 70 major central cities in 1982. This sample consists of the subset of the 86 major central cities in the US for which we could find complete data. A major central city is defined as a city with a population above 300,000 or the central city of one of the 50 largest metropolitan areas in 1970 or 1980. After presenting our regression results, we explore the implications of the simultaneity between the two types of state assistance, and test several of the hypotheses that are built into our econometric specification.

Regression results

Our regression results are presented in table 25.2. We estimate our model with 2-stage least squares. For comparison, 3-stage least squares results are also presented.[9]

Table 25.2 provides strong support for our two key hypotheses. First, states direct both grants and institutional assistance toward cities in poor fiscal health. If city A's standardized need-capacity gap is $1 higher than city B's, then, all else equal, city A can expect to receive $0.22 more in state grants and $0.42 more in state assistance through institutions. Both of these estimates are significant at the 1 percent level or above. These results indicate that, to some degree, states give more assistance through both grants and institutions to cities with larger standardized need-capacity gaps. Moreover, assistance through institutions is more equalizing than assistance through grants. Indeed, state assistance through institutions offsets, on average, almost twice as much of a city's need-capacity gap as do state grants. One clear illustration of this role for state institutional assistance is given by Ladd and Yinger (1989): 5 of the 6 cities with the poorest standardized fiscal health (and 11 of the 20 least healthy cities) are allowed to tax the earnings of nonresident commuters.

Table 25.2 Estimation results for 1982

Variable	Dependent variable			
	Two-stage least squares		Three-stage least squares	
	GRANTS	INSTIT	GRANTS	INSTIT
GRANTS	–	−0.877	–	−0.858
		(2.80)		(2.97)
INSTIT	−0.403	–	−0.389	–
	(4.88)		(5.32)	
SGAP	0.221	0.421	0.208	0.433
	(3.81)	(3.41)	(4.08)	(3.84)
FCAT	0.430	−0.253	0.491	−0.246
	(2.20)	(0.57)	(2.87)	(0.60)
FGRS	0.414	−0.575	−0.130	0.089
	(0.20)	(0.13)	(0.07)	(0.02)
SEMP	213.529	–	192.407	–
	(1.13)		(1.30)	
SPCY	27.677	11.988	26.526	10.743
	(5.45)	(1.18)	(5.99)	(1.15)
COUNTY	47.658	66.273	46.853	65.193
	(3.46)	(1.83)	(3.88)	(1.97)
SCCTOS	−47.778	–	−88.843	–
	(0.68)		(1.58)	
SPOP	−5.553	–	−5.089	–
	(5.08)		(5.56)	
MAYOR	4.254	–	7.002	–
	(0.38)		(0.78)	
RELPOP	−1.788	–	−1.322	–
	(2.76)		(2.52)	
CAPIT	−17.710	–	−17.825	–
	(1.19)		(1.53)	
SLOCAL	−38.096	–	45.951	–
	(2.04)		(3.03)	
METPOP	–	−1.538	–	−1.730
		(2.59)		(3.40)
SRELYY	–	−457.679	–	−500.847
		(3.35)		(4.20)
MIXED	–	−86.984	–	−74.274
		(3.74)		(3.66)
Constant	−174.326	119.926	−153.638	136.783
	(3.11)	(0.99)	(3.17)	(1.24)
R-squared	0.845	0.625	0.845	0.618
Number of Observations	70	70	70	70

Notes: Absolute values of asymptotic t-statistics are in parentheses. The 2-tailed (1-tailed) 95 percent critical value is 2.00 (1.67). A 2-tailed test is appropriate unless the coefficient has the sign predicted in table 25.1.

Second, states regard assistance through grants and assistance through institutions as substitutes for each other. In the grants regression, the coefficient of assistance through institutions is −0.40; if, because of exogenous factors, city A receives $1 more than city B in state assistance through institutions, it will also receive, on average, $0.40 less in state grants. In the institutions regression, the coefficient of grants is −0.88; differences across cities in grants caused by exogenous factors are almost fully offset by differences in assistance through institutions. Both of these coefficients are statistically significant at the 1 percent level.

Remember from our discussion of equations (25.3) and (25.4) that we can solve for the weight, θ, that state policymakers place on each form of assistance to cities. We find that state policymakers perceive that $1 of assistance through grants lowers a city's actual need-capacity gap, as perceived by state policymakers, by $(0.877/0.421) = \$2.08$, whereas $1 of assistance through institutions, as we measure it, lowers this gap by $(0.403/0.221) = \$1.82$. Apparently, state policymakers value those aspects of city finances that are supported by state assistance, through grants or institutions, more highly than city fiscal condition in general. Moreover, despite the complexity of fiscal institutions, state policymakers perceive that $1 of assistance through institutions contributes almost as much to a city's fiscal condition as $1 of state grants.

Federal general revenue sharing to cities does not have a statistically significant impact on either form of state assistance. According to our conceptual model, this result implies that state policymakers do not believe that general revenue sharing improves a city's fiscal condition. Federal categorical grants to cities also do not have a statistically significant impact on state assistance through institutions, but they do have a significant impact on state grants. In particular, we find that a $1 increase in federal categorical grants leads to a $0.43 increase in state grants. This positive effect contradicts our conceptual model, and we do not have a compelling interpretation of it. Perhaps programs supported by federal grants sometimes attract state funds.

Most of the control variables in the state grants regression perform well. State income, the dummy for city/counties, and the number of local governments per capita are significant at the 5 percent level or above with the expected signs. State population, the sign of which is indeterminate on conceptual grounds, is negative and significant. This result indicates diseconomies of population scale in the delivery of state grants. The share of state population in central cities and the dummy for cities with mayors have the predicted signs but are not significant. The only variable that is significant with the wrong sign is the city's share of state population.

In the assistance-through-institutions regression, all of the control variables have the expected signs, and all except for state per capita income are statistically significant. Of particular interest are the coefficients of the state's reliance on the income tax and the city's share of metropolitan population. The former coefficient suggests that states relying heavily on an income tax are indeed reluctant to allow a city to levy an earnings tax as a way to boost its revenue-raising capacity; the latter coefficient suggests that states are more likely to assist cities through institutions if the burden of that assistance can be spread out over a relatively large number of suburbanites.

The simultaneity between the two types of state assistance

The results in table 25.2 describe the way state officials design each form of assistance to cities. Because the two forms of assistance are simultaneously determined, however, these results do not fully describe the variation in assistance received by cities in different circumstances. To obtain a complete answer, we must solve equations (25.3) and (25.4) for the two unknowns, G and I.[10]

Consider, for example, the exogenous factors that are unique to each equation. Suppose that because of a difference in one of the exogenous factors that is unique to our grants regression, City A receives $1 more in state grants than does City B. As shown in the first row of table 25.3, this positive $1 difference in grants will lead to a negative $1.36 difference in institutional assistance, which will add, in turn, $0.55 to the original difference in grants. The ultimate impact of the original $1 difference in grants, therefore, is only a $0.19 net advantage for City A in total state assistance; in other words, the feedback effects eliminate most of City A's original advantage.

Similarly, a $1 advantage in state assistance through institutions for a city that is caused by one of the exogenous factors unique to our institutions regression will lead to a $0.62 disadvantage in state grants, which will add, in turn, $0.55 to the original advantage in assistance through institutions. In this case, the feedback effects roughly cancel out, and City A's original $1 advantage in institutional assistance becomes a net advantage of $0.92.

We can also determine the impact on total assistance to a city of differences across cities in exogenous factors that appear in both regressions, such as the standardized need-capacity gap (or gap for short). If City A has a gap that is $1 higher than City B's, then the results in table 25.2 indicate that city A will receive $0.22 more in state grants and $0.42 more in institutional assistance than will City B. But these results overstate the link between a city's need-capacity gap and its state assistance

Table 25.3 Net impacts of exogenous factors on state assistance

One-dollar exogenous difference in:	Net impact on:		
	GRANTS	INSTIT	Total Assistance
GRANTS	1.55	−1.36	0.19
INSTIT	−0.62	1.55	0.92
SGAP	0.08	0.35	0.43
SPCY/10	0.35	−0.19	0.16

because they do not consider the fact that the differences in state grants will lead to differences in institutional assistance – and vice versa. After accounting for these feedback effects, we find that City A will receive $0.08 more in state grants and $0.35 more assistance through institutions than will City B, which implies a net advantage in state assistance of $0.43 (see the third row of table 25.3). In other words, state assistance eliminates over two-fifths of the differences in need-capacity gaps across cities.[11] Although most of the public debate has focused on the equalizing role of grants, we find that state assistance through institutions, not state grants, does most of the equalizing.

State income is another key exogenous factor in both equations .The results in table 25.2, which ignore feedback effects, indicate that if per capita income is $10 higher in State A than in State B, cities in State A will receive $0.28 more in grants and $0.12 more in assistance through institutions than the cities in State B. After accounting for feedback, we find that cities in State A will receive $0.35 more in grants and $0.19 less in institutional assistance, for a difference in total state assistance of only $0.16.

Specification tests

To shed further light on our results, we also test two types of hypotheses about our specification: Are any variables that are assumed to be exogenous really endogenous? Are the excluded exogenous variables in each regression (which are the variables that identify the simultaneous equations system) appropriate instruments, that is, are they truly exogenous?

As noted earlier, three of the variables we assumed to be exogenous might be endogenous. Federal aid to a city might be influenced by state assistance to that city, and state decisions about the location of state government employment and about state assistance to cities may be made simultaneously. We examined the endogeneity of these three variables using the chi-squared test developed by Hausman (1978). As explained by Bowden and Turkington (1984), this test can be applied to right-side variables or to excluded instruments.[12] Thus, we also apply the test to each of the instruments identified as "excluded" in table 25.1.

On the basis of our test results, we cannot reject the hypotheses that both forms of federal aid and state government employment are indeed exogenous and that all of our instruments are appropriate.[13] In other words, our results in table 25.2 do not appear to be based on inappropriate assumptions about endogeneity.

Conclusions and Policy Implications

In this paper we present two key hypotheses about the behavior of state policymakers. First, state policymakers want to improve the fiscal condition of their cities and therefore give more assistance, through both grants and institutions, to cities in poorer fiscal condition. Second, state policymakers regard state grants and state assistance through institutions as substitutes for each other; that is, both types of state assistance are believed to improve a city's fiscal condition. Both of these hypotheses are strongly supported by our results.

We also find that, on average, state assistance makes a major contribution toward eliminating differences in fiscal condition across cities. If the standardized need-capacity gap is $1 higher in City A than in City B, City A can expect to receive $0.08 more in state grants and $0.35 more in state institutional assistance than City B – after accounting for the feedback effects between the two types of state assistance. Overall, therefore, state assistance offsets over 40 percent of the differences in fiscal condition across cities. This important equalizing role of overall state assistance has not been observed in previous studies, which do not consider state institutional assistance.

In addition, our results indicate that in the view of state policymakers either $1 of state grants or $1 of institutional assistance contributes more to a city's fiscal condition than a $1 decline in the standardized need-capacity gap, as we measure it. The large perceived impact of institutional assistance is particularly surprising, given the complexity of state institutional assistance. However, $1 of state grants is perceived to contribute more to a city's fiscal condition than $1 of assistance through insitutions.

We find no evidence that state policymakers consider federal aid to cities to be a substitute for state assistance to cities. Cities with higher federal categorical grants and cities with higher general revenue sharing do not receive less state assistance (through grants or institutions) than others.

These results have several implications for the design of our federal system and in particular for federal policy toward cities.

Although states give more assistance to cities with larger standardized need-capacity gaps, 60 percent of the differences in these gaps remains, on average, after state assistance. Moreover, some cities in relatively poor fiscal condition receive relatively little help from – and may even be harmed by – state actions. Ladd and Yinger (1989) find, for example, that very large cities and cities with relatively poor residents are in much poorer fiscal health than other cities even after state grants and state institutional assistance. Thus, federal grants or other federal policies may be required to bring the fiscal condition of some cities up to an acceptable level.

We also discover that state assistance to cities depends on state characteristics, and in particular on state income. Every $1,000 increase in state per capita income is associated with a $16 increase in net state assistance to cities (per city resident), after accounting for the feedback between the two types of state assistance. Otherwise identical cities may receive different levels of assistance because of differences in their states' per capita incomes. To the extent that federal policymakers want to insure that all cities are able to provide some minimum level of public services, they may want to provide additional assistance to cities in low-income states, all else equal.

Our regressions examine state assistance to a cross-section of major central cities in 1982 – not changes in state assistance over time. To the extent that the 1982 situation is an equilibrium, however, our results also provide some insight into the possible effects on cities of various changes in federal urban policies. For example, differences in federal categorical and in general revenue sharing do not appear to cause differences in state assistance to cities – either through grants or institutions. This finding implies that state actions are unlikely to offset the impact on cities of the recent cuts in federal categorical aid or the recent elimination of general revenue sharing.[14]

Overall, our results suggest federal grants still have an important role to play in our federal system.[15] Even after state grants and institutional assistance, many cities are in poor fiscal condition and federal policymakers may want to help the neediest cities. Although we find no evidence that state assistance to cities changes in response to changes in federal assistance to cities, the federal government may want to minimize the possibility of such offsetting behavior by employing grant provisions, such as state matching requirements, that discourage a state from reducing assistance to cities.[16] We also believe that the federal government should not reward states that are miserly toward their cities. To avoid such rewards, federal grants should be directed toward cities with high standardized need-capacity gaps – not high post-assistance gaps.

Notes

1   In Ladd and Yinger (1989), we use a related measure of city fiscal health, namely (capacity-need)/capacity, which is standardized to be zero in the average city in 1972.
2   Revenue-raising capacity also is influenced by tax importing, that is, by taxes residents pay to other jurisdictions. We account for taxes residents pay to overlying jurisdictions, but not for the few taxes they pay to nonoverlying jurisdictions. See Ladd and Yinger (1989).
3   One relatively minor adjustment is necessary, however. Our two measures of need-capacity gap, and hence our measure of state assistance through institutions, are comparable across cities because they are based on a standard state and local tax burden. To make state grants comparable in the same sense, we multiply each city's grants by the ratio of the standard tax burden to the state and local tax burden in that city's state. Our adjusted grants are higher for cities in states that spend a large share of their budget on grants or that tilt their grants more heavily toward large cities, but unlike actual grants they are not higher in cities that receive more grants simply because state taxes (and the programs they support, including grants) are high. See Ladd and Yinger (1989).
4   In each regression, the absolute value of the coefficient of the other form of aid divided by the coefficient of SGAP can be interpreted as θ_a.
5   The division between state and federal assistance is not always clear. Some federal grants are given to the states and then passed through to cities. The Census treats these grants as state aid to cities. The two principal examples of this form of "pass-through" aid are education and welfare programs. In the case of education, the state's only role is administrative; the federal government determines the size of each city's grant and the state simply acts as an intermediary. As a result, we subtracted education pass-through aid from state grants to cities and added it to federal categorical grants to cities. In the case of Aid to Families with Dependent Children, the guidelines are determined by the federal government, but the amount of welfare assistance a city receives is determined largely by state decisions. A state's decisions about eligibility criteria and benefit levels (along with the state's demographic characteristics) determine the amount of federal welfare aid flowing into the state, and the state's decisions about the assignment of welfare responsibilities determine whether that aid flows to cities or counties or remains with the state itself. During the last twenty-five years, for example, most states have taken over responsibility for welfare programs; by 1982, only 9 of the 70 central cities in our sample retained major welfare respon-

sibilities. Moreover, federal matching provisions imply that the state's decisions about welfare affect its budget. Because a state plays a crucial role in determining the federal welfare aid received by its cities and because this aid affects the state budget, we followed the Census procedure of treating welfare pass-through aid as state aid.

6 Programs supported by state grants also might attract federal aid. In addition, the general revenue sharing formula gives more aid to cities with relatively high tax effort; higher state assistance enables a city to lower its tax effort and might lead therefore to a lower revenue sharing grant for that city.

7 In a standard model of local voting, a voter's tax price equals her property tax share multiplied by the marginal cost of public services (see Ladd and Yinger, 1989). We have not included tax shares in our analysis because they are poorly defined at the state level (shares of which tax?) and because they seem unlikely to affect state officials' decisions about aid to cities.

8 Another possibility is that because a city's fiscal condition is difficult to measure, state legislatures give assistance on the basis of easily obtained indicators that are perceived to be correlated with fiscal condition. Thus, because city/counties tend to have higher responsibilities, they may be given relatively high state assistance, even when their fiscal condition, as measured by their need-capacity gap, is relatively good.

9 If our specification is correct, 3-stage least squares will yield asymptotically more efficient parameter estimates than will 2-stage least squares, but 2-stage least squares appears to be less sensitive to specification error than is 3-stage least squares (see Hausman (1978, p. 1265) or Fomby, Hill, and Johnson (1984, p. 507)). Because this type of state behavior has not been widely studied, we are not confident that our specification is correct (and we will examine it with specification tests), so we believe that results obtained using 2-stage least squares should be given more weight. In fact, however, the two methods yield very similar results.

10 The simplest way to solve equations (25.3) and (25.4) is to collapse all the exogenous factors (including their coefficients) in Equation i into X_i, define the matrix transposes $A' = [G, I]$ and $X' = [X_3, X_4]$, and define the coefficient matrix

$$B = \begin{bmatrix} 1 & -b_{3G} \\ -b_{3I} & 1 \end{bmatrix}.$$

Then these equations can be written $BA = X$, and their solution is $A = B^{-1}X$. The impact of a change in any exogenous factor on A is B^{-1} multiplied by the derivative of X with respect to that factor. With the 2-stage least squares estimates in table 25.2,

$$B^{-1} = \begin{bmatrix} 1.547 & -0.624 \\ -1.356 & 1.547 \end{bmatrix}.$$

Thus, as shown in table 25.3, a one unit exogenous change in G – that is, in X_3 – would ultimately raise G by \$1.55 and would lower I by \$1.36.

11   Ladd and Yinger (1989) report, based on a preliminary version of this paper, that state assistance offsets almost two-thirds of the differences in need-capacity gaps across cities. Since that version of the paper was written, we have revised the calculations for state assistance through institutions and now find a somewhat smaller offset.

12   The form of the test is as follows: We run two regressions, one with the variable in question treated as endogenous and one with it treated as exogenous. We then subtract the coefficient vector of the second regression from that of the first regression and the variance-covariance vector of the second regression from that of the first regression. The test statistic is a quadratic form calculated using the differenced coefficient vector and the inverse of the differenced variance-covariance matrix. This statistic has a chi-squared distribution with degrees of freedom equal to the number of coefficients. A high value of the statistic implies rejection of the null hypothesis of no endogeneity. See Hausman (1978) and Bowden and Turkington (1984).

13   In fact, no test comes close to rejecting the null hypothesis of exogeneity. The 95 percent critical value for the chi-squared test with 12 degrees of freedom (about the number of coefficients in each regression) is 21, whereas all the text statistics are below 2.5, except that of the excluded instrument RELPOP, which is 8.7.

14   We ran supplementary regressions to investigate another possibility, namely that federal aid directly to the state government leads to higher assistance from that state to its cities. These regressions included an additional exogenous right-side variable, namely federal aid to the state (which, as defined by the Census, includes pass-through aid) adjusted for the state's share of state-local spending .The coefficient of this variable is negative and insignificant in both the grants and institutional assistance regressions. Thus, the federal government should not count on state governments to act as its agents.

15   For a more detailed discussion of the role of federal grants, see Ladd and Yinger (1989).

16   A more speculative possibility is for the federal government to design grants that, unlike current grants, encourage states to provide institutional assistance. For example, federal grants could be designed to reward states for taking over welfare or other services from cities or for allowing their cities to use earnings taxes that apply to commuters. Because institutional assistance is regarded by state policymakers as less powerful than grants, increases in it are not likely to induce large decreases in state grants.

References

Bradbury, Katharine L. 1982 "Fiscal Distress in Large US Cities." *New England Economic Review* (November/December): 33–44.

Bradbury, Katharine L. 1983 "Structural Fiscal Distress in Cities: Causes and Consequences." *New England Economic Review* (January/February): 32–43.

Bradbury, Katharine L. and Helen F. Ladd. 1985. "Changes in the Revenue-Raising Capacity of US Cities, 1970–82." *New England Economic Review* (March/April).

Bradbury, Katharine L., Helen F. Ladd, Mark Perrault, Andrew Reschovsky, and John Yinger. 1984. "State Aid to Offset Fiscal Disparities Across Cities." *National Tax Journal* 37 (June): 151–170.

Bradford, D. F., R. A. Malt and W. E. Oates. 1969. "The Rising Cost of Local Public Services: Some Evidence and Reflections." *National Tax Journal* 22 (June): 185–202.

Bowden, Roger J, and Darrell A. Turkington. 1984. *Instrumental Variables*. Cambridge, England: Cambridge University Press.

Fomby, Thomas B., R. Carter Hill and Stanley R. Johnson. 1984. *Advanced Econometric Methods*. New York: Springer-Verlag.

Hausman, J. A. 1978. "Specification Tests in Econometrics." *Econometrica* 46 (November): 1251–71.

Ladd, Helen F. and John Yinger. 1989. *America's Ailing Cities: Fiscal Health and the Design of Urban Policy*. Baltimore: The Johns Hopkins University Press.

Appendix

This appendix describes our calculations of the standardized need-capacity gap and of state assistance through institutions. We begin with five variables from Ladd and Yinger (1989), all expressed in dollars per capita:

RRC = Full revenue-raising capacity (with three broad-based taxes and no overlying jurisdictions)

RRRC = Restricted revenue-raising capacity (with actual taxes, actual overlying jurisdictions, and adjusted state aid)

SAID = Adjusted state aid (with no education pass-through aid and an adjustment for overall state tax effort)

SEN = Standardized expenditure need (based on actual public service costs and average service responsibilities)

AEN = Actual expenditure need (based on actual public service costs and actual service responsibilities)

The standardized need-capacity gap, SGAP, equals $[Q(SEN) - RRC]$, where Q is a service quality level that is held constant across cities. We use the value of Q derived in Ladd and Yinger, which insures that SGAP, expressed as a percentage of RRC, equals zero in the average city in 1972. Thus, a positive (negative) SGAP indicates fiscal health below (above) the 1972 average.

The actual need-capacity gap without grants, AGAPNG, equals $[Q'(AEN) - (RRRC - SAID)]$. This gap is affected by actual service responsibilities, actual access to taxes, and actual overlying jurisdictions, but it is not affected by state aid. The value of Q' is selected so that AGAPNG, expressed as a percentage of (RRRC - SAID), equals zero in the average city in 1972.

State assistance through institutions, SINST, is the improvement (or deterioration) in the need-capacity gap due to actual service responsibilities, access to taxes, and overlying jurisdictions. It equals (SGAP − AGAPNG).

The fiscal health measures in Ladd and Yinger equal these gap measures multiplied by minus one and divided by the appropriate capacity measure. In a few cities, AGAPNG is less than SGAP, which implies that state assistance through institutions is negative, whereas AGAPNG/(RRRC − SAID) is greater than SGAP/RRRC, which implies that state assistance through institutions is positive. These results are perfectly consistent. Fiscal institutions can increase the need-capacity gap in absolute terms while increasing capacity so much that they decrease the need-capacity gap in percentage terms.

A city's actual need-capacity gap, AGAP, which is not explicitly considered in this paper, equals [Q*(AEN) − RRRC]. As before, Q* is set so that AGAP as a percentage of RRC equals zero in the average city in 1972. Because Q* is greater than Q′, AGAP does not equal (AGAPNG + SAID).

The values of variables for selected cities are presented in table 25.A.

Table 25.A Need-capacity gaps and state assistance in selected cities, 1982

City	SGAP	AGAPNG	AGAP	SINST	SAID
Buffalo	187.02	314.65	193.13	−127.63	420.88
Cleveland	243.64	30.18	125.51	213.46	83.21
Ft. Lauderdale	−289.75	−209.56	−196.39	−80.19	65.80
Oakland	7.94	33.16	103.44	−25.22	63.26
Providence	44.56	−182.69	−115.83	227.25	224.68
70 Major US Cities					
Average	32.94	22.09	23.33	10.85	182.65
Maximum	385.53	754.24	871.54	245.41	895.03
Minimum	−289.75	−308.82	−282.34	−426.45	9.63

Note: All entries are expressed in 1982 dollars per capita.

Introduction to Chapter 26

This article begins with a review of federal aid to cities from the 1960s through the 1980s, the period of precipitous rise and then precipitous decline. Netzer then considers how cities differ in the extent of federal aid received. Both the redistribution aspect and the economic development aspect of federal aid to cities is addressed, and broad policy proposals are made aimed at improving efficiency and equity. A novel argument presented by Netzer is that the widely noted divergence of economic performance among regions of the United States since the mid-1970s provides a compelling reason for federal aid to economically distressed cities. Such aid he believes should be highly targeted.

The placement of Netzer's article at the end of this collection is not accidental. The last one-third of his piece addresses issues of fiscal federalism that have arisen in the state and local public finance literature since Musgrave wrote his terse analysis of multi-government finance back in 1959 (chapter 3). Both events (huge and chronic federal deficits, relentless economic decline in many urban areas, stagnant real wages, divergence in the economic fortunes of regions) and ideas (the end of liberalism, public choice theory) have colored that literature. The result is that the unanimity of acceptance in the field of Musgrave's sorting out of functions is absent. That is not to say that state and local public finance has become balkanized on that major issue but rather that events and ideas have produced a more subtle, a more nuanced range of views.

26

National Assistance to Urban Areas in the United States

Dick Netzer

The case for central government action directly to assist households and firms located in central cities and to provide financial aid to the subnational governmental entities that serve central cities is a familiar one to public finance economists, rooted in the conceptual framework developed by Richard Musgrave (1959) more than 30 years ago.[1] According to this framework, the central government ought to be (and is, in most countries of the Organization for Economic Cooperation and Development [OECD]) responsible for the alleviation of poverty and related economic distress (Musgrave's redistribution branch); the central government has primary responsibility for stabilization of the economy and therefore should intervene to offset the localized effects of regionally differentiated recessions, as well as dealing with the cycle on a geographically macro basis; and, in Musgrave's allocation branch, the central government ought to be active in the provision of those few public goods whose spatial reach is national, whether the public services in question are produced by the central government itself or by the subnational units. This chapter adheres to that conventional approach. In the next two sections, the actual extent of US federal government assistance to cities and recent trends in that assistance are described. Subsequent sections discuss the appropriateness of present arrangements, in the conventional Musgrave scheme.

Federal Assistance to US Cities: Where We Are Now

National assistance to cities takes three forms. The first is assistance to households and firms and the direct provision of federal services in cities, rather than assistance to the governmental entities that provide public services within cities. The second type of assistance is federal financial aid to the state governments, some of which is expended directly by state government agencies for programs within cities and some of which is paid to local authorities that serve cities.[2] The third type of assistance is direct aid to the urban local authorities themselves: the municipal governments that are normally referred to as "city governments," the autonomous special-purpose authorities (most notably, school districts) that exist in nearly all large urban areas, and, often, county governments that overlay the central cities but include suburban territory as well.

The US federal government has never been important, relatively, as a direct provider of public services. In 1989, state and local government purchases of goods and services were more than seven times as great as federal government nondefense purchases of goods and services.[3] Prior to the Great Depression, the federal government was unimportant in other respects as well, but since then has assumed a major role in making transfer payments to persons – primarily for income support and social security programs – and in making grants to state and local governments.

Table 26.1 describes the character of federal spending in calendar 1989, in terms of both the economic classification of the expenditures and whether or not the expenditures are especially relevant to cities. Because more than 60 percent of federal spending (defense and interest payments aside) is for transfers for income support, social security, and welfare – and such transfers clearly are important components of the incomes of central city residents (many of whom are elderly) – most federal spending does appear to be city-related. But all other federal expenditures for transfers to persons, subsidies, and purchases of goods and services that have much relevance to the populations of central cities as such are less than 0.5 percent of the gross national product (GNP).[4]

Thus, social security aside, the first form of federal assistance to cities – direct provision of services and subsidies to city-resident households and firms – is not, and never has been, important. As table 26.1 suggests, most federal grants-in-aid to state and local governments are for purposes that are highly relevant to cities; in some cases, the specific program definition leads to a concentration of the spending of the grant funds in cities, because the program focus is on the low-income population. However, in 1988–9, only 16 percent of all federal grants to subnational governments went to local authorities. So, the predominant form of federal assistance to cities is the second one, grants to state governments that either provide services in cities directly or that pass-through the federal funds to local authorities.

Unlike the federal government, the state governments are major direct service providers in the American governmental system, and also are

Table 26.1 Character of US federal government expenditures, calendar year 1989 (in millions of current dollars)

	National totals ($)	Expenditures of relevance to cities ($)[a]	Other ($)[b]
Total	1,187,150		
Less: national defense, space, and international affairs	328,861		
Less: net interest paid	172,019		
Equals: civilian expenditure for transfers to persons, subsidies, purchases of goods and services, and grants to state and local governments	686,270	560,809	125,461
Transfers to persons	460,362		
Income support, social security, and welfare		430,833	
Housing and community services		182	
Recreational and cultural activities		404	
Labor training and services		473	
Other (mainly veterans' benefits and higher education grants and loans)			28,470
Subsidies	25,415		
Housing		13,005	
Urban mass transportation		892	
Other (mainly to agriculture)			11,518

Table 26.1 *Continued*

Purchases of goods and services	84,660	
Administration of city-relevant programs listed above		12,018
Water transportation ("rivers and harbors")		4,340
Air transportation (mainly air navigation aids)		4,884
Other (mainly central administration, federal policing and corrections, and veterans' services)		63,418
Grants to state and local governments	118,196	
Elementary and secondary education		7,592
Health and hospitals		4,441
Income support and welfare		68,249
Housing and community services		6,165
Recreational and cultural activities		95
Airports		1,134
Urban mass transportation		2,664
Economic development assistance		414
Labor training and services		3,024
Other (mainly highway grants)		22,055

[a] Attributions of relevance are by the author. Some entries shown here are programs or activities for which central cities account for major shares of the expenditure, like urban mass transportation, cultural programs, air transportation and, most important, federal grants for income support and welfare programs. Other entries are listed here even though most of the expenditure is made outside central cities, because of the great importance of the programs or activities to cities as places – notably, social security payments and federal expenditures for housing programs.
[b] There are expenditures that benefit cities within these categories, but the main focus and rationales for the expenditure are not urban.
Source: US Department of Commerce, 1990, *Survey of Current Business*, table 3.15 (Washington, D.C.: US Government Printing Office). The definitions and concepts are those of the National Income and Product Accounts, which differ in some respects from the US Bureau of the Census reporting on governmental finances, which is the basis for other data in this chapter.

much more important than the federal government as providers of fiscal assistance to local authorities. The state governments are the most important level of government – in terms of direct expenditure – with regard to higher education, courts, prisons, mental health institutional care, highways, medical care for the indigent (Medicaid), and cash public assistance payments (generally known as "welfare" in political and journalistic usage).[5] There is relatively little federal aid to the states for the first four of the seven functions on this list; federal aid amounts to about one-third of state expenditure for highways and about one-half of state expenditure for the last two items on the list, Medicaid and "welfare."

The state governments pass through some of the federal aid they receive in the form of direct services to city residents, notably for explicitly redistributive programs and (to a lesser extent) for highways. In some of the states, where local governments participate in the administration of Medicaid and "welfare," the state passes on to local authorities federal aid received for this purpose. In nearly all of the states, the state governments also pass on to local authorities the relatively small amounts of federal aid they receive for elementary and secondary education and some parts of the federal highway aid they receive.[6]

The modest direct federal fiscal assistance to local authorities – only about 5 percent of their own-source revenue in 1988–9 – consists mainly of grants for housing purposes, for urban mass transportation capital and operating subsidies, as well as a small amount of school aid. Both the housing grants and the school aid are, in the main, explicitly redistributive (a substantial portion of the housing grants are for continuing subsidies to low-income public housing built mostly between 1955 and 1975; much of the rest of the housing grants are for housing voucher programs of the 1980s). Moreover, unlike most past and present federal programs, the surviving direct federal grants to local authorities have a high degree of targeting on the central cities – where the public housing and urban mass transportation are.

The term surviving is used advisedly here. Direct federal aid to city governments (including cities of all sizes and functional description, but excluding aid to special districts and counties that overlie the cities) was the most spectacular fiscal manifestation of the era of federal government social activism from the mid-1960s to the late 1970s. In the mid-1960s, federal direct aid to city governments was trivial, mainly for schools in cities like Norfolk, Va., where there was a major federal presence, as well as for airports, and amounted to only about 3 percent of cities' own-source revenues. Thereafter, the amounts, and the percentage, climbed steeply, reaching a peak of just under 19 percent in 1977–8. After fiscal

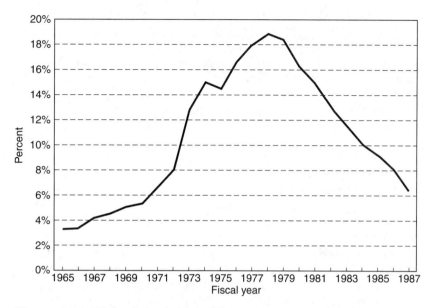

Figure 26.1 Direct federal aid to cities as percentage of city own-source revenue.

Source: US Bureau of the Census. *City Government Finances*, various years, 1964–1987. (Washington, D.C.: US Government Printing Office.)

year (FY) 1978, the absolute amount of federal aid remained almost constant for seven years; it has fallen considerably since then, and in FY 1988 was far below the 1978 level in real terms. As figure 26.1 shows, the percentage of own-source revenue has fallen back to the levels of the late 1960s. The reduction includes major cutbacks in some programs that continue to exist (some housing programs), complete elimination of some manpower and social service programs, termination of the so-called Anti-Recession Fiscal Package, adopted in 1977 as a belated response to the 1974–5 recession, and elimination of general revenue sharing.

Differences Among Cities in the Extent of Federal Aid

Ladd and Yinger in chapter 11 of their painstaking 1989 analysis of the fiscal health of the universe of American central cities, provided a thorough treatment of the differential incidence of federal aid to central city governments in 1982, and of the changes between 1972 and 1982. They found a wide range in the ratio of federal aid to the cities' revenue-raising capacity for the 71 cities in this part of their analysis: federal grants in 1982 did more for the fiscal health of the largest cities than the small ones; they made a large difference in the fiscal health of the cities with the poorest residents; and they were inversely, but weakly, related to the strength of the city's economy.[7] Federal grants were strongly related to their overall measure of fiscal health, a standardized gap between expenditure need and fiscal capacity.

However, it is not self-evident that this generally encouraging set of relationships continues to apply, since federal aid to cities, relative to their own-source revenues, has declined so sharply since 1982, as figure 26.1 shows. To reproduce the Ladd-Yinger (1989) analysis for a more recent fiscal year would be a massive undertaking. Instead, an admittedly simplistic effort to explain differences in federal aid as a percentage of own-source revenue in 1986–87 is made here, using obvious independent variables. The cities are the 57 central cities in the Frostbelt states (that is, those in the Northwest and Midwest) with populations of more than 100,000. Although 49 of the 57 had smaller populations in 1986 than in 1970, they differ considerably in their characteristics, including rate of population decline.

Federal aid for the 57 cities amounted to 9.4 percent of own-source revenues in 1986–87, as both the numerator and denominator are defined here.[8] The percentage is somewhat higher if New York City, which has a disproportionate influence on aggregate city finance data, is excluded – 12.5 percent.[9] The range was from 1.5 percent to 31.7 percent, with a standard deviation of 7.2 percent. Unlike the Ladd-Yinger (1989) findings, there seems to be no relationship between federal aid and city size (but that may be because the Ladd-Yinger denominator is a sophisticated measure of fiscal health), but there is a strong relationship between federal aid and the percentage of the population below the poverty line (in 1979): a 1 percentage point increase in the incidence of poverty is associated with an increase in the federal aid ratio of 0.7–0.8 percentage points, in the different models. Thus, the surviving federal assistance programs do seem, appropriately, redistributive. The only other independent variable with any explanatory power (among numerous ones that were tested) is own-source revenue per capita, where the relationship is, weakly, inverse. Own-source revenue per capita appears to be a measure that mainly reflects differences in the extent of governmental responsibilities assigned to central-city municipal governments (rather than to state governments or overlying local authorities), so the inverse relationship between revenue per capita and the federal aid percentage is not easy to explain. One would anticipate that a wider range of responsibilities – for example, for housing programs and transit system operations – would attract more federal aid.

Federal Assistance to Cities as Redistribution

To the extent that federal fiscal aid to city governments is designed to be a form of income redistribution, it is, of course, redistribution in kind, rather than in money, so far as low-income residents of cities are concerned. There are worthy and venerable arguments in favor of helping the poor by giving money to people rather than places, even if a "places aid" policy can be designed to make it truly redistributive.[10] First, aid to people facilitates geographic mobility, whereas aid to places does the opposite; geographic mobility is a good thing in general and can be especially important for economically active people who have been displaced by economic change. However, the economic incentives for migration, apart from the federal grant system, are now so strong that it seems likely that many of the poor in central cities are in effect stranded there by assorted disabilities, with the grant system of little consequence.

A more persuasive argument for national government assistance to people rather than places is that assistance in the form of public services rather than money is clearly not preferred by the poor.[11] Most of the goods and services that the nonpoor majority would like to see increased for the poor appear to have very low income elasticities among the poor and may even be good examples of the economists' artifact, the inferior good, at least in the bottom quintile or quartile of the income distribution.

Very low income elasticity is certainly true of housing, as shown in both the large-scale social experiments and in careful analyses of housing microdata sets. It seems true of health care – there is virtually zero private spending among nonaged near-poor for health care. It may be true of education: the low take-up rates for the lowest-tuition sectors of public higher education are suggestive. From the standpoint of the overwhelming majority of the nonpoor, the ultimate merit good that we think the poor should consume more of is surely labor force participation. The income maintenance experiments afford good evidence that labor force participation declines with higher cash assistance payments.

So, perhaps, this is true of local government services in general. However, there are two arguments on the other side, in favor of transfers in kind, that are apposite in this discussion. First, the superiority of cash transfers is lessened when the markets for the services proposed to be provided in kind work poorly, because of highly imperfect information on the part of poor consumers, noncompetitive aspects, discontinuities, and economies of scale. Those properties describe the major services provided by city governments. Second, there is the question of the preferences of the donors with respect to income redistribution: it is entirely reasonable for taxpayers to specify in-kind aid in the form of ordinary local government services as an additional element of the income redistribution that they, the taxpayers, prefer. Both donors and recipients are likely to feel themselves better off when a considerable amount is spent for redistribution but some of it is noncash, than when a much lower amount is provided, but entirely in cash.

Oakland (1979) proposed that ordinary local government services, like public safety and the provision of infrastructure, should be seen as elements of the standard of living of the immobile urban poor.[12] That formulation fits well with the Ladd-Yinger scheme mentioned earlier, in which federal aid is allocated to the cities on the basis of their measured fiscal health. Relatively healthy cities – because of a strong local economy, the ability to export city tax burdens, and/or limited fiscal responsibilities for some costly services – can finance a decent package or ordinary city services even if they have many poor residents. Less-healthy cities cannot. In the absence of federal assistance, this means that the overall fiscal system treats equally poor people unequally, the treatment depending upon the city in which the poor live (see Buchanan 1950, for the classic discussion of this).

The appropriate form of federal aid would seem to be unconditional grants tied to measures of fiscal health. If that makes no sense in American politics (which may be the case – see the section following), then the appropriate form is the matching categorical grant, for those city services deemed most important to the poor, with the matching percentage tied to a measure of fiscal health.

National Assistance to Foster Local Economic Development

Federal aid to local governments to foster local economic development can be viewed as income redistribution – bringing jobs to relatively immobile poor, or less directly, increasing the fiscal health of the city so that local authorities can afford to provide better public services to the poor. This is not a wholly unreasonable idea, in light of the large adverse economic changes many central cities have suffered, originating in broad technological, economic, and social trends far beyond the capacity of local governments to affect. In concept, federal aid to promote local economic development could take two forms: the financing of explicit subsidies to private investors undertaking specific economic development projects, or aid to improve the scope and quality of local public services in the expectation that such improvements would attract private business investment and increase the residential attractiveness of communities.

Although federal expenditure to promote local and regional economic development through both direct subsidies and infrastructure has a long history, making such expenditure via local authorities is of more recent vintage. It dates back to the 1960s and the Appalachia and Economic Development Administration legislation.

First, consider federal aid to improve the quality of public services. This strategy differs from the one discussed in the previous section, in that the services to be improved are not likely to be those of special value to the poor, but, rather, the services that are intermediate business inputs (transport services, water supply, etc.) and amenities that are attractive to both businesses and affluent potential residents. The poor benefit by the economic improvement that is fostered by the service improvements (and, at least marginally, from the service improvements themselves). The real issue is the efficacy of such service improvements in developing the local economy.

In the past few years, a considerable amount of literature has been published relevant to this issue. It began at the national level, with the observation that the post-1973 reduction in productivity gains coincided with a large reduction in investment in public capital in real terms, and an actual decline in the net stock of reproducible public capital (overwhelmingly owned by state and local governments). Subsequent econometric investigation suggested that the trends were in fact linked, and that reductions in the public capital stock do restrain increases in total factor productivity (see Munnell 1990, for a summary of the argument). The inquiry continued in the subnational sphere, with comparisons of public capital stock levels and changes and economic growth rates of US metropolitan areas and states. The most recent work suggests that local public investment and private capital are complementary, that the relationship is stronger in distressed cities than in growth cities, and that in older cities public investment tends to be an initiating, rather than a passive, factor in the development process (Eberts 1990). The elasticity coefficients look small, but can be interpreted in ways that make the elasticities seem impressive.

Nonetheless, it is not clear that federal fiscal assistance in conceivable amounts can result in service improvements sufficient to stimulate economic development that, in turn, will lead to better lives for some of the urban poor. This is not to say that the recent literature is wrong, but only that the many links in the chain make this type of income redistribution policy very roundabout – and therefore uncertain.

In contrast, there is some certainty regarding the other form of federal fiscal aid designed to promote local economic development – federal assistance to local governments explicitly tied to specific economic development projects. By and large, these programs have had little or no net multiplier effect: in most cases, the private economic activity induced by the subsidy soon vanished, or there was no real inducement but a superfluous subsidy paid for a location decision that would have occurred in any case.[13] Nor is it obvious that low-income people gain much from successful subsidized economic development efforts. Indeed, it may be that most such efforts have distributional effects much like municipal promotion of commercial sports: enriching the impresarios and the owners of adjacent sites, period.

There is an efficiency argument, in addition to the equity one, for federal intervention to foster local economic development, and therefore for federal grants to local authorities to this end. The argument is that the declining cities contain spatially immobile resources with substantial remaining useful lives that are essential to location decision makers, notably, the public and quasi-public infrastructure. The infrastructure cannot be moved, but would have to be replaced in new areas (suburbs or other regions) to accommodate relocators. Since the location decisions do not confront explicit prices for the services of the infrastructure that are based on the marginal costs of the services they consume, they ignore resource cost considerations that should be factors in determining optimality in location of economic activity.[14]

This, then, is obvious market failure. One difficulty with the argument is that the remaining value of the existing infrastructure in the worst-off cities may be trivial, because the quality of the services the capital produces is so poor. But, in any case, intervention with economic development subsidies seems the wrong way to deal with the obvious problem, the absence of appropriate price signals. Federal policy might contribute efficiently by encouraging, rather than discouraging, marginal cost pricing of local utility and public infrastructure services, by example and by precept.[15]

Increasing Regional Economic Differentiation and the Federal Role

The income-redistribution case for federal aid that is founded on the obligation to help people stranded in cities that have been afflicted by major economic transformations has been strengthened in recent years by what appears to be increasing regional economic differentiation in the United States – local and regional cycles that are quite large in amplitude but vary considerably in timing. This is not just a redistribution argument; in the Musgrave (1959) scheme it also has a stabilization aspect. The more decentralized the public finance system, and the greater the regional economic differentiation, the greater the chances that retrenchment by subnational governments in severe regional recessions will increase the severity and perhaps widen the geographic scope of those recessions.[16]

It seems obvious that a relatively modest fiscal role for the central government will be more efficient and equitable, the less the regional variations in the local fiscal resource base. For decades in the United States, regional disparities were declining, but in the past 15 years or so, the movement has seemed to reverse itself. As the OECD 1989 *Economic Outlook* makes clear,[17] this was the usual case in OECD countries during the 1980s, when the measure of regional differentiation was the rate of unemployment. In 1987, the regional variation in unemployment rates in the United States was less than that in any OECD country except Japan,[18] but the increase in variation since 1975 was one of the sharpest of any country.

This is true of other measures of the level of economic activity.[19] A measure that is highly relevant to the question of fiscal federalism is the size of a standardized tax base, that is, what has been called "taxable capacity." There is evidence that the interstate disparities in taxable capacity have been widening, not narrowing, in part because of the uneven distribution of taxable mineral production. The Advisory Commission on Intergovernmental Relations measures relative taxable capacity by the per capita yield of a "representative tax system," that is, the revenue generated in each state if it imposed all the major state and local taxes at the national average rate for each tax. The standard deviation, for the 50 states and the District of Columbia, from the US average in 1986 was 21.1 percent of that average, compared to 15.7 percent in 1980 and 10.4 percent in 1975 (see Lucke 1982 and Advisory Commission on Intergovernmental Relations 1989).

Although, in theory, fiscal decentralization is inconsistent with large regional economic differentials, whether fiscal decentralization actually makes things worse at a given time is an empirical question. In the United States, federal grants to state and local governments historically have not been at all equalizing. For example, in 1980, the standard deviation of state-local tax capacity plus all federal grants was 14.2 percent, compared to 15.7 percent for tax capacity exclusive of federal grants. Indeed, if all existing federal grants in 1980 had been distributed on a per capita basis, the equalizing effect would be substantially greater: the standard deviation would have been 11.1 percent. This suggests that the substantial reduction in federal grants that occurred during the Reagan years must have been a good thing, from the standpoint of equalization. However, this was not the case. In 1986, the standard deviation of state-local tax capacity plus all federal grants was 24.8 percent, compared to 21.1 percent for tax capacity exclusive of federal grants, so the federal grants programs that had survived the Reagan retrenchment increased inequality. In 1986, if all existing federal grants had been distributed on a per capita basis, there would have been a significant equalizing effect: the standard deviation would have been 16.2 percent.

There is another aspect to American regional economic differentiation that may be even more important for policy with regard to fiscal federalism. Unlike other OECD countries, in which the regions tend to maintain their relative positions over time, in the United States over the past 20 years there have been sharp shifts in relative economic status. That is, regions have experienced cycles that are not coincident with national cycles, as well as divergent secular trends. For example, the OECD study showed that there was a fairly high positive correlation between the regional pattern of unemployment in 1975 and in 1987 – 0.4 to 0.9 – in all the larger OECD countries, but a negative correlation in the United States.

The data in table 26.2, on growth rates in gross regional product in real terms for 10 US regions, show these discontinuities.[20] New England, New York State, the rest of the Mideast, and even California were relatively depressed in the 1967–73 period, but all showed strong growth in the 1982–6 period; the Southwest, the Mountain states, and the Plains states showed the opposite time path. Except for the Southeast region, which had above-average growth rates in all the periods, each region moved from one to another side of the national average at least once during this 23-year period.[21] The standard deviation in regional growth trends for these periods was much larger in the 1970s and 1980s than it had been in the 1960s.[22]

This form of regional differentiation has been in evidence for individual urban economies. A number of the largest ones have experienced sharp, relatively short-term economic cycles that are related to events in the world and national economies, but are magnified in those cities and different in timing from the national and international economic cycles. There are obvious examples in the economic histories, over the past three decades, of Boston, New York, Chicago, and the oil- and natural-resource-dependent cities of the West. During the 1950s and early

Table 26.2 Regional differences in growth in gross product in the United States, selected years, 1963–86 (percentage change in gross state product from previous period, in 1982 dollars)

	1963–7 ($)	1967–73 ($)	1973–5 ($)	1975–9 ($)	1979–82 ($)	1982–6 ($)
US average[a]	24.7	32.3	0.7	22.7	-0.5	17.3
New England	26.4	24.1	-4.0	19.2	2.4	29.8
New York State	22.0	20.9	-4.3	7.6	1.2	23.3
Midwest region, excluding New York[b]	25.2	27.3	-1.4	13.8	-2.0	19.7
Great Lakes	23.1	23.6	-4.1	19.3	-11.4	15.7
Plains	22.3	37.2	-1.7	21.7	-4.6	11.7
Southeast	29.4	44.9	1.8	26.3	2.8	19.0
Southwest	24.9	47.9	11.6	37.7	13.1	4.7
Mountain	15.7	51.0	7.8	34.4	5.5	6.9
California	24.9	31.0	5.5	28.0	-0.0	24.5
Far West region, excluding California[c]	24.0	35.2	5.1	37.1	-7.8	18.2
Standard deviation	3.4	10.2	5.3	9.5	6.6	7.4

Notes: Data on gross state product in current dollars were published in *Survey of Current Business*, May 1988, and were converted to constant 1982 dollars using the price index for the entire gross national product. Gross state product data are on an annual basis only in the years beginning in 1972; the only earlier data are for the years 1963 and 1967. The years 1963 and 1967 are not cyclical turning points, but the subsequent years were peaks and troughs for GNP.

[a] Includes Alaska and Hawaii, not included in the rest of the table's data.

[b] New York is part of the Mideast region, and accounted (in 1986) for about 44 percent of total regional product.

[c] California is part of the Far West region, and accounted (in 1986) for about 79 percent of total regional product.

Source: Renshaw, Vernon, Edward A. Trott, Jr. and Howard L. Friedenberg. "Gross State Product by Industry, 1963–86." *Survey of Current Business* 68(5): 30–46 (May 1988).

1960s, while the national economy was growing – with only minor cyclical downturns – and most urban economies were also doing well, the Boston economy was doing quite badly, in both secondary and tertiary industries. From the late 1960s until quite recently, however, the Boston economy has done extremely well in its service-producing sectors (especially financial services, education, and health) and in high-technology manufacturing, even in periods of national recession. Similarly, the New York economy declined sharply from 1969 to 1977, in periods of national economic strength like 1972 and 1973 as well as in periods of national recession like 1969–70 and 1974–5. However, between 1977 and 1987, the New York economy had strong growth and was barely affected by the recessions of the early 1980s. In contrast, the Chicago economy was prosperous almost continuously from the end of World War II until the late 1970s, and was highly resistant to national recessions during that 30-year period, but had serious economic difficulties in the first half of the 1980s.

Implications for Fiscal Federalism

Despite the failure of the US grant system to be geographically equalizing in effect, it is not difficult to design measures of fiscal federalism that address the two traditional problems of regional economic weakness: long-term economic decline because the main industries of a region are in decline, and the differential vulnerability of regional economies to national economic recessions. It is considerably more difficult to design grant programs that address the more erratic type of regional economic differentiation that has occurred in recent years. The sharp local economic recessions can produce fiscal crises, and have done so on a number of occasions since 1969, not only in the well-known case of New York City. If the local recessions do not coincide with national ones, it is not plausible that a central government would intervene systematically to prevent fiscal crises in individual states or cities.

That is exactly what happened: when most states and cities were in difficulty because of the 1974–5 recession, Congress enacted an Anti-Recession Fiscal Package to help all local governments, but New York was the only city with an individual fiscal crisis to receive federal government aid, and then only because of the fear that if New York City defaulted on its debt obligations, the nation's banking system would be threatened, given the size of the city's debt and the distribution of the holdings of that debt among banks. The Anti-Recession Fiscal Package ended with national economic recovery, and the cities with subsequent fiscal crises, like Cleveland and Chicago, did not receive any federal help.

One reason why the emergence of a pattern of divergent regional and local cycles should lead to more, rather than less, central government intervention is that, in the absence of such intervention, there will be stabilization-branch actions at the regional and local levels. State and local governments will engage in policies to counter the local effects of the cycles, because they must do so. Economic theory tells us that subnational stabilization policies will be at best ineffectual, because of the "leakages" to other regions. More likely, they will be inefficient in a microeconomic sense, increasing locational distortion. At worst, they will add up to a national macroeconomic policy that is cyclically perverse, as state and local governments in combination increase taxes and reduce spending in recession and do the opposite in periods of inflationary expansion.[23]

Data for the period since 1982 show that subnational governments, as expected, do not respond coherently to variations in their economic fortunes. Differences in regional economic growth rates (measured by gross product) explain less than half the variation in revenue growth rates; there is no relationship between economic growth rates and the change in the ratio of revenue to gross product; there is little relationship between differences in the tax burden at the beginning of the period and changes in the tax burden during the period. Some, but not all, states responded to slow growth with increases in the average effective rate of taxation. Some states with relatively fast growth rates actually increased effective tax rates (like New York), while others used their prosperity to reduce tax burdens. Subnational stabilization policy was even more incoherent in earlier years when the regional economic differentials were larger, like the mid-1970s and the 1979–82 period.

No doubt, few people other than economists are concerned about whether regional fiscal actions add up to a coherent macroeconomic policy. Decision makers, as well as the general public, are concerned with the effects of sharply different regional economic trends – in a fiscal regime with a small federal government role – on the provision of public services. From the political perspective, the issue is this: if relatively short, but very sharp, economic cycles are to be the normal experience for regions and even more for individual large cities, especially cycles that are not coincident with the national cycles, then we need new financing institutions and methods for providing services continuously and as a basis for making rational, long-term plans.

It is both inefficient and inequitable for publicly financed services to undergo sharp contractions and expansions along with the local economy, which is what happened in the large-city fiscal crises of the 1970s and early 1980s in the United States, and when fiscal crises affected state governments in the Midwest and Southwest in the 1980s. Moreover, such fluctuations discourage serious long-term planning. It is noteworthy that few large American cities have been doing long-term planning since the mid-1970s. One reason for the decline in interest in long-term planning is the fact that many such plans had serious technical problems, in the design of the forecasting models and in the form of gross overestimates of population and related growth rates. But the sharp cyclical fluctuations are an equally important reason: long-term planning seems futile, if the policies and projects in the plan must be discarded almost as soon as the plan is published.

Conclusion: Policy Choices

As noted earlier, Oakland more than a decade ago and Ladd and Yinger recently have advanced ideas for a new type of federal aid to city governments, one whose major objective may be characterized as ensuring "adequate levels of important public services, including education and police and fire protection, for poor and disadvantaged city residents" (Ladd and Yinger 1989: 306). The logic would extend, presumably, to other local public services that can be construed as elements of a decent minimum standard of living. The longer the list of services provided by city governments that are deemed deserving of federal grants, the more the resulting package will look like unconditional grants and, to some extent, will work like unconditional grants, as the recipient local authorities adjust their use of own-source revenue to the availability of grants for the different functions.[24]

However, I am not advocating reviving unconditional grants to local governments, replacing the old general revenue-sharing program. First, the literature documents that, in theory and practice, unconditional grants have far less effect in stimulating expenditure than matching categorical grants.[25] The Ladd and Yinger (1989) findings show this for large cities in the 1972–82 period, which is consistent with the earlier literature. If the main objective is to improve the standard of living of the poor in cities, it makes little sense to adopt a federal grant program whose main effects are to facilitate reductions in local taxes not paid by the poor or to encourage local authority capital spending for facilities that are only remotely related to the needs of the poor, both of which general revenue sharing did.

Second, although most federal grant programs are designed to diffuse the funds widely in a geographic sense, the experience with general revenue sharing was perhaps worse in this respect than was the case in any other federal aid program. The complex distribution formulas assured that even the least active and most affluent local authority received nontrivial amounts of money. The politics of state government school aid in some states suggest that categorical grants can be vulnerable to the same antitargeting pressures, but there does seem to be a large difference in degree at the federal level, with the categorical grants likely to have at least some element of targeting.[26]

Assume, then, that these grants should be categorical matching grants, rather than a variant of general revenue sharing for cities with poor fiscal health. It is fairly easy, technically if not politically, to target unconditional grants, by making both eligibility for the grants and the amount distributed to each city functions of the city's fiscal health. But the amount of a matching categorical grant received by any given city should be based on its own decision, confronted by an open-ended grant with a specified matching percentage. One device for targeting such grants to poor cities would be a binary eligibility rule: the grant is fully open-ended but available only to cities in poor fiscal health (using appropriate measures to avoid creating perverse incentives with regard to state government assistance), with zero aid to all other cities. That is unlikely in American politics. Perhaps the best device is a variable matching percentage, with a very low federal share for healthy cities and up to more than 50 percent for the poorest cities.

This bears a resemblance to a proposal by Gramlich (1985c: 58) for "categorical-equity grants to poorer communities for merit public services such as education, health, and housing." However, certain aspects of the American experience with federal categorical grants during the 1965–80 period make one hesitant about this genre of proposals. A large number of new federal categorical grants were advocated, and sold, as programs to help poor people in inner cities via their local and, sometimes, state governments. Many such programs failed two crucial tests. First, the expenditure was often for services that are not conspicuously directed at the poor – if at all. Massive capital grants to build new rail metro systems provided the most spectacular example of this type of dissembling. Second, the local public services that were aided often were ones whose benefits are entirely internal to the local jurisdiction – for example, federal grants to acquire land for small local parks. American federal-level decision makers – and the media, with the avid assistance of academic "pop" writers – tend to interpret the fact that many cities confront similar demands for public services as proof that the "problems" are nationwide in incidence.

Therefore, there is the hazard that a new federal interest in "categorical-equity" grants to cities would replicate the earlier experience of highly inefficient and not especially equitable grants made in the name of equity. Presumably, the inefficiency could be minimized if, as a general rule, the federal matching percentages for most categorical grants were low, rather than high, as they have been in the recent past: by 1980, the federal matching percentage for most categorical grants was 80.[27] One element of Gramlich's program for reforming fiscal federalism in the United States is to lower the federal matching share on all existing categorical grant programs to 20 percent, and make them truly open-ended, so that the grant appropriately lowers the taxprice of marginal dollars of spending by local authorities. Criticism of the implicit exaggeration of the external benefits of many of the spending programs of state and local governments, in the form of excessive federal shares and federal aid for expenditure with virtually no external benefits, dates back to at least 1967 (Break 1967); Gramlich has been one of the most persistent critics, and by now there is wide agreement among American public finance economists on this proposition.

Another major element of Gramlich's plan for reform of American fiscal federalism is nationalization of the present federal/state income support system, that is, replacing federal grants to the states that result in highly nonuniform benefits by direct federal income-support programs with minimal supplementation by the states. This enjoyed widespread support among academic policy analysts in the 1960s and 1970s, but that support has diminished with the rise of the revisionist (revision of Musgrave, that is) view that income redistribution is a legitimate function of subnational governments. Many analysts, myself included, have not been persuaded by the revisionists and, with Gramlich, favor nationalization of public assistance. Few cities spend much, if any, of their own funds for public assistance (New York State is the main exception to the rule that the nonfederal share of the funds must come from the state government), but the cities have two interests in nationalization. First, more uniformity in assistance payments levels would be good for cities. Increases in the level of assistance payments in the states where payments are now relatively low, which would occur with nationalization, would directly aid poor people in cities in those states, and more uniformity would decrease the incentives for poor people to concentrate in the cities of the states with relatively high assistance payments levels. Second, the budgetary relief to state governments that nationalization would provide, especially in states with poor fiscal health themselves, should make it feasible for them to do more for their ailing cities.

Gramlich's plan pays for the "equity-categorical" grants and the nationalization of public assistance, first, by the reduced federal matching share for categorical grants and, second – this is also in concert with most public finance economists – by eliminating the federal income tax deduction for state and local tax payments.[28] The argument is that, like all other tax preferences, deductibility is distorting and generates horizontal inequity in order to provide a highly inefficient subsidy to state and local governments. The inefficiency is in lowering the tax price of expenditure with little, if any, relevant geographic externalities. Indeed, the critics generally take the position that a large share of all expenditure by American state and local governments comprises local private goods, including local public goods converted into "club" goods by exclusionary land-use controls exercised by small suburban local authorities.[29] Thus, no federal aid in support of this expenditure, of any kind, is warranted, even aid in the efficient form of optimizing categorical matching grants.

I and a few other academics have dissented from this dominant position on federal deductibility (e.g., Chernick and Reschovsky 1987; Musgrave 1985; Netzer 1985; Oakland 1986). The dissenters have explicitly noted that much public expenditure in large central cities is for public goods, in that the expenditure is occasioned by the presence of poor people combined with a weak revenue base.[30] Deductibility may be a very inept form of federal aid to cities, but it is better than nothing, if other forms of federal assistance are unavailable.

The final element of the Gramlich plan reflects a view not widely shared: activist stabilization policies by state governments. I argue the opposite, as the preceding discussion of increasing regional economic differentiation should suggest. Under conditions of increased regional economic differentiation, state government action is less appropriate than ever. The leakages are at least as great as they always have been, and the vulnerability to adverse locational shifts in response to increased state government tax burdens is greater than ever.

A conceivable case for a role for subnational governments in the stabilization branch might be based on the hypothesis that the critical factor driving long-term regional economic growth is the supply side, the relative quality of local inputs. To the extent that this is true, it is an argument for discretionary action by regional and local authorities to improve the quality of inputs, making strategic choices that central governments do not make wisely (at least in a large country like the United States, where the design, if not the actual effect, of federal policy tends to be as uniform as possible over the regions). But regional and local authorities will not be able to implement sustained policies to improve the quality of inputs if they experience sharp, even violent, fluctuations in their fiscal conditions.

Even if the federal budget deficit were small or nonexistent, it would be difficult to design politically acceptable, and durable, grant mechanisms to ensure against serious impairment of services in particular regions and cities, when those regions and cities suffer from sharp cyclical fluctuations with severe effects on their revenues, and when the cycles do not coincide with national cycles. The Anti-Recession Fiscal Package of the late 1970s was momentarily acceptable because of the national recession of mid-decade, but it was not durable, in large part because it had one highly desirable feature: a high degree of targeting. There were two "triggers," national economic conditions and local economic conditions. The worse were the national economic conditions, the larger was aggregate size of the national program, but how much (if anything) of the national total any city received was a function of its own circumstances.

That program affords a precedent for a new countercyclical federal assistance program, although the design of the earlier program was not ideal. If the goal is to counter the effect of local and regional cycles on the finances of cities (and states), whether or not those cycles coincide in timing with the national cycles, then the only "trigger" that is appropriate is a measure of local conditions. The measure used as the trigger in the earlier program was the unemployment rate, which is not an accurate mirror of variations in local fiscal circumstances. However, the unemployment rate may be the only rapidly available measure of short-term changes in local economic circumstances. Also, the federal countercyclical grants should be explicitly unconditional, rather than nominally conditional, as in the earlier program; the purpose of the grants is not necessarily to stimulate more local spending by lowering the tax prices of merit goods, but to offset declines in the own-source revenue of local authorities, to permit them to maintain total spending at pre-recession levels.[31] With a high degree of targeting, the federal countercyclical grant program would cost little in the aggregate in years in which the national economy was in good shape, while providing substantial assistance to the few cities that were at the bottom of their own cycles.

In an era of national government budgetary stringency, what about priorities among the three forms of federal assistance to cities proposed earlier? Nationalization of public assistance is third on my list, because its effects on the cities would be so indirect in most cases (and because it is surely the least attractive in the context of American politics). An expanded and well-designed program of "equity-categorical" grants is strongly grounded in the theory of fiscal federalism and in the empirical work of Ladd and Yinger, but I place countercyclical grants highest on my list, principally because of the experience of the 1980s. The sharp decline in federal assistance to cities was not a serious problem in the booming regions, but was in the ailing ones. If the divergence in regional economic conditions that has characterized the 1970s and 1980s continues, the local cycles will have much worse effects on the afflicted cities and on the poor people within those cities than will a continued low level of federal categorical grants.

Notes

1   In the Musgrave (1959) formulation, government activity is divided into three "budget branches": the stabilization branch, concerned with affecting the overall level of economic activity; the redistribution branch, concerned with altering the distribution of real incomes among households; and the allocation branch, concerned with altering the composition of the output of goods and services. The roles of the different levels of government in the Musgrave scheme are determined by their capacities to achieve the respective goals.

2   Of course, much of the federal aid to state governments is spent, directly or in grants, outside central cities of metropolitan areas.

3   "Nondefense" also excludes federal spending for international affairs and for space programs (data from *Survey of Current Business*, July 1990, tables 3.15 and 3.16, 63–6).

4   In 1989, direct federal nondefense expenditure other than social security that actually took place within central cities (other than Washington, D.C.) probably amounted to no more than $10 billion.

5   The functions listed accounted for 65 percent of state government direct expenditure (excluding interest and employee retirement payments) in 1988–9.

6   In Hawaii, the schools are operated by the state government, and in Alaska schools in remote areas are state-operated. Otherwise, schools are operated by local authorities, with (on average) just over half the funds provided by state governments.

7   Because of commuting to and from work across municipal boundaries, the relative strength of the city's economy and the relative incidence of poverty in its resident population do not necessarily coincide.

8   To reduce the extent of noncomparability attributable to the wide variation in the roles of the municipal governments (specifically, the extent to which the data reflect assignment of major functions to other governmental entities), own-source revenues of independent school districts are added to those of the municipal governments, and federal aid for schools (includes aid that passed through the state governments) is added to the numerator.

9   New York City's influence is disproportionate because the role of local governments vis-à-vis the state government is unusually large in New York State. Also, New York City does assume responsibility for functions not

done generally by local governments anywhere else in the United States, and the role of separate, overlying local authorities is trivial in New York City.

10   The usual obstacles to a truly redistributive aid program in the United States are: (a) it is politically difficult to keep the allocation formula targeted on places with poor residents, so the aid is often spread widely and thinly, as was the case with general revenue sharing in its 15-year history; (b) the rhetoric notwithstanding, some categorical grant programs support services that are not especially oriented toward the poor, such as grants for mass transportation; and (c) federal grants programs frequently require state and local governments to devote a substantial portion of the grant funds to administration, rather than service provision, which means that the program is income redistributive only if it is staffed by people who otherwise would have been unemployed and poor.

11   Any transfer in kind must be worth somewhat less to the recipient than a transfer in money. The issue here is: Are these transfers in kind worth a great deal less than the same amounts provided in cash?

12   Oakland (1979: 351) justified this proposal primarily on efficiency grounds: it would deal with the locational distortions caused by the excessive tax burden on central-city nonpoor residents and firms to finance the local public service consumption of the poor. But, as Oakland also stated, such a grant program would put the "responsibility for providing the public needs of the poor" on the same footing as "is currently the case for the private needs of the poor," that is, the federal/state income-maintenance program.

13   See Netzer (1991) for a summary account.

14   Much of the governmentally provided infrastructure is financed from general taxes. Where there are user charges, they are, at best, based on average rather than marginal costs; at worst, they are wholly unrelated to unit costs of any kind. In most cases, utility services provided by "investor-owned" firms are priced above marginal costs to business users in old cities and below marginal costs in newer places.

15   The federal government has explicit prices for few of its services, even in cases where state and local governments often have explicit pricing (for example, none of the federal museums – even the heavily congested Air and Space Museum – charge admission fees), and marginal-cost-based pricing in no cases. Moreover, federal law forbids explicit marginal-cost-based pricing by state and local governments in several important cases – for airport use and on most of the Interstate Highway System. Local authorities widely believe that federal approval is required for any major innovation in pricing of facilities built with federal aid or of services subject to federal nonprice regulation (notably, waste management).

16   Most of this section is adapted from Netzer (1990). That paper addresses the somewhat different question of the appropriateness of the fiscal decentralization that occurred in the United States during the 1980s, in light of what I have called increasing regional economic differentiation. The extent of fiscal decentralization has been very large, for so short a period. In 1965,

the federal government financed one-third of all civilian public expenditure other than health and retirement benefits for the elderly. In 1980, the federal share had risen to 44 percent. By 1987, the federal share was back at the 1965 level, and declining.

17 This account is based on the summary of the OECD study that appeared in *The Economist* of July 29, 1989, p. 55.

18 Even so, the unemployment rate for the regions that contain the quartile of the labor force with the highest rate was twice that of the regions with the quartile of the labor force with the lowest unemployment.

19 The change from economic convergence among regions to economic divergence extends even to wage rates (see Eberts 1989).

20 There are eight regions in the standard statistical series; I have broken out California and New York from their respective regions because they are large and have had trends that occasionally diverge from the rest of their regions. Texas is also very large relative to its region, but the trends for Texas and the rest of the Southwest region have coincided.

21 Although some states diverge from the trends in their regions, most do not: the picture for the individual states in much like that in table 26.2.

22 As the gross product data imply, for 18 of the states, the relative positions of states and regions changed considerably between 1975 and 1986 with regard to the "representative tax system" measure of tax capacity. Five of these states were high in the distribution in 1975, but low in 1980 and 1986; eight were relatively low in 1975, but high thereafter; four were low in 1975 and 1986, but high in 1980; and one was low only in 1980.

23 Older readers will recognize this as the "fiscal perversity" hypothesis first proposed by Hansen and Perloff in 1944 to characterize the behavior of American state and local governments during the Great Depression. Subsequent writers have challenged the empirical validity of the proposition in those years. The controversy is reviewed and the evidence for the 1945–64 period examined in Rafuse (1965).

24 This will not be true if the categorical grants are efficiently designed "optimizing grants" – that is, open-ended matching grants with matching percentages that, for each function, closely correspond with the ratio of benefits realized outside the local jurisdiction to the benefits realized internally. This is discussed later in the text.

25 It is true that unconditional grants in practice seem more stimulative than theory would predict – that is, theory predicts minimal effects – because of the celebrated "flypaper effect": the tendency, at least in the United States, for the recipient subnational governments to spend a substantial portion of unconditional grants, rather than reduce local taxes to an extent consistent with our estimates of the elasticity of voters' demand for local public goods. But the stimulative effects of unconditional grants are relatively small, nonetheless.

26 State school aid often takes the form of lump-sum, rather than matching, grants. If the local tax price for the grant is zero, legislators should be expected to insist on their bits of pork.

27   A number of the supposedly categorical grant programs required no local matching of the federal funds. The local authorities in such cases were acting as administering agents of the federal government, rather than as autonomous decision makers confronting a set of tax prices. Usually, that real relationship was not explicit, leading to substantial and recurring misunderstandings.

28   See Gramlich (1985a, b) and Kenyon (1986) for statements of this position.

29   The extreme case for this has been advanced by Sparrow (1986). The implication is that the deductibility of the local property tax should be eliminated even if that of state income taxes is continued.

30   Gramlich (1985a), in a paper that uses empirical evidence for Michigan, did recognize this point. He concluded that deductibility is of little use in lowering the tax price of local public expenditure in the city of Detroit, because incomes are so low that the median voter is almost certainly not affected by deductibility. However, he conceded that the elimination of deductibility is likely to speed the emigration of the relatively few remaining well-off residents of the city.

31   Two of the three components of the 1970s "package" nominally had restrictions on the use to which the grants could be put, they appeared to require some forms of matching, and they had "maintenance of effort" requirements designed to ensure that the grants were stimulative, rather than substitutes for spending from local funds. All these provisions were easily overcome, so that the conditions amounted to no more than a minor increase in the local administrative costs of complying with the federal rules.

References

Advisory Commission on Intergovernmental Relations. 1989. *1986 State Fiscal Capacity and Effort*, Information Report M-165. Washington, D.C.: Author.

Break, George F. 1967. *Intergovernmental Fiscal Relations in the United States.* Washington, D.C.: Brookings Institution.

Buchanan, James M. 1950. "Federalism and Fiscal Equity." *American Economic Review* 40: 583–99.

Chernick, Howard and Andrew Reschovsky. 1987. "The Deductibility of State and Local Taxes." *National Tax Journal* 40: 95–102.

Eberts, Randall W. 1989. "Accounting for the Recent Divergence in Regional Wage Differentials." *Economic Review* (Federal Reserve Bank of Cleveland) 25(3): 14–26.

——. 1990. "Public Infrastructure and Regional Economic Development." *Economic Review* (Federal Reserve Bank of Cleveland) 26(1): 15–27.

Economist, The. July 29, 1989: 55.

Gramlich, Edward N. 1985a. "The Deductibility of State and Local Taxes." *National Tax Journal* 38: 447–66.

——. 1985b. *Economic Consequences of Tax Simplification.* (Discussion of Netzer paper.) Proceedings of a Conference Sponsored by the Federal Reserve Bank of Boston.

——. 1985c. "Reforming US Federal Fiscal Arrangements." In *American Domestic Priorities: An Economic Appraisal,* edited by J.M. Quigley and Daniel L. Rubinfeld. Berkeley and Los Angeles: University of California Press.

Hansen, Alvin H. and Harvey S. Perloff. 1944. *State and Local Governments in the National Economy.* New York: W.W. Norton.

Kenyon, Daphne A. 1986. "Federal Tax Deductibility of State and Local Taxes." *Federal-State-Local Fiscal Relations, Technical Papers.* US Treasury Department, Office of State and Local Finance. Washington, D.C.: US Government Printing Office.

Ladd, Helen F. and John Yinger. 1989. *America's Ailing Cities: Fiscal Health and the Design of Urban Policy.* Baltimore: Johns Hopkins University Press.

Lucke, Robert M. 1982. "Rich States – Poor States: Inequalities in Our Federal Systems." Advisory Commission on Intergovernmental Relations. *Intergovernmental Perspective* 8(2): 22–8.

Munnell, Alicia H. 1990. "Why Has Productivity Growth Declined? Productivity and Public Investment." *New England Economic Review* (Federal Reserve Bank of Boston) (Jan./Feb.): 3–22.

Musgrave, Richard A. 1959. *The Theory of Public Finance.* New York: McGraw-Hill.

——. 1985. "An Overall Assessment – Is it Worth It?" In *Economic Consequences of Tax Simplification.* Proceedings of a Conference Sponsored by the Federal Reserve Bank of Boston.

Netzer, Dick. 1985. "The Effect of Tax Simplification on State and Local Government." In *Economic Consequences of Tax Simplification.* Proceedings of a Conference Sponsored by the Federal Reserve Bank of Boston.

——. 1990. "Fiscal Federalism and Regional Economic Differentiation in the United States." Paper presented at the 19th annual meeting of the Western Regional Science Association, February.

——. 1991. "An Evaluation of Interjurisdictional Competition through Economic Development Incentives." In *Competition among States and Local Government: Efficiency and Equity in American Federalism,* edited by Daphne A. Kenyon and John Kincaid. Washington, D.C.: Urban Institute Press.

Oakland, William H. 1979. "Central Cities: Fiscal Plight and Prospects for Reform." In *Current Issues in Urban Economics,* edited by Peter Mieszkowski and Mahlon Straszheim. Baltimore: Johns Hopkins University Press.

——. 1986. "Consequences of the Repeal of State and Local Tax Deductibility under the US Personal Income Tax." In *Federal-State-Local Fiscal Relations, Technical Papers.* US Treasury Department, Office of State and Local Finance. Washington, D.C.: US Government Printing Office.

Rafuse, Robert W., Jr. 1965. "Cyclical Behavior of State-Local Finances." In *Essays in Fiscal Federalism,* edited by Richard A. Musgrave. Washington, D.C.: Brookings Institution.

Sparrow, F. T. 1986. "The Subsidy Value and Incidence of Tax Expenditures which Benefit State and Local Government – The Case of the Property Tax." In *Federal-State-Local Fiscal Relations, Technical Papers.* US Treasury

Department, Office of State and Local Finance. Washington, D.C.: US Government Printing Office.

US Department of Commerce. 1990. "National Income and Product Accounts." *Survey of Current Business* 70(7): 8–125.

Index